$ 40.00 NEW

A PRACTICAL APPROACH TO
OPERATING SYSTEMS

Programming books from boyd & fraser

Structuring Programs in Microsoft BASIC
BASIC Fundamentals and Style
Applesoft BASIC Fundamentals and Style
Complete BASIC: For the Short Course
Fundamentals of Structured COBOL
Advanced Structured COBOL: Batch and Interactive
Comprehensive Structured COBOL
Pascal
WATFIV-S Fundamentals and Style
VAX Fortran
Fortran 77 Fundamentals and Style
Learning Computer Programming: Structured Logic, Algorithms, and Flowcharting
Structured BASIC Fundamentals and Style for the IBM® PC and Compatibles
C Programming
dBASE III PLUS® Programming

Also available from boyd & fraser

Database Systems: Management and Design
Using Pascal: An Introduction to Computer Science I
Using Modula-2: An Introduction to Computer Science I
Data Abstraction and Structures: An Introduction to Computer Science II
Fundamentals of Systems Analysis with Application Design
Data Communications for Business
Data Communications Software Design
Microcomputer Applications: Using Small Systems Software
The Art of Using Computers
Using Microcomputers: A Hands-On Introduction
A Practical Approach to Operating Systems
Microcomputer Database Management Using dBASE III PLUS®
Microcomputer Database Management Using R:BASE System V®
Office Automation: An Information Systems Approach
Microcomputer Applications: Using Small Systems Software, Second Edition
Mastering Lotus 1-2-3®
Using Enable™: An Introduction to Integrated Software
PC-DOS®/MS-DOS® Simplified

Shelly, Cashman, and Forsythe books from boyd & fraser

Computer Fundamentals with Application Software
Workbook and Study Guide to accompany Computer Fundamentals with Application Software
Learning to Use SUPERCALC®3, dBASE III®, and WORDSTAR® 3.3: An Introduction
Learning to Use SUPERCALC®3: An Introduction
Learning to Use dBASE III®: An Introduction
Learning to Use WORDSTAR® 3.3: An Introduction
BASIC Programming for the IBM® Personal Computer
Workbook and Study Guide to accompany BASIC Programming for the IBM® Personal Computer
Structured COBOL — Flowchart Edition
Structured COBOL — Pseudocode Edition
Turbo Pascal Programming

A PRACTICAL APPROACH TO
OPERATING SYSTEMS

Malcolm G. Lane
James D. Mooney

West Virginia University

COMPUTER SCIENCE SERIES

COPYRIGHT 1988
BOYD & FRASER PUBLISHING COMPANY
BOSTON

CREDITS:

Publisher: Tom Walker
Editor: Marjorie Schlaikjer
Production Coordinator: Donna Villanucci
Director of Production: Becky Herrington
Director of Manufacturing: Erek Smith

Cover Design: Michael Broussard
Cover Photo: © Michael Rochipp/The Image Bank
Chapter Design: Julia Schenden

Manufactured in the United States of America

Library of Congress Cataloging-in-Publication Data

Lane, Malcolm G., 1943–
    A practical approach to operating systems / Malcolm G. Lane, James
D. Mooney.
        p.   cm.
    Bibliography: p.
    Includes index.
    ISBN 0-87835-300-3
    1. Operating systems (Computers)   I. Mooney, James D., 1946–
II. Title.
QA76.76.063L36 1988
005.4'3--dc19   87-31960
                                                                     CIP
10 9 8 7 6 5 4 3 2 1

To Mother
and
James and Mildred Moran
and in memory of
My Father

M.G.L.

To my wife Joan, whom I love
and to our daughters
Tara, Tressa, Alishia, and Asonda

J.D.M.

Table of Contents

Chapter 5: PROCESS MANAGEMENT

Chapter 6: PROCESS SCHEDULING

Chapter 7: INTERACTION OF CONCURRENT PROCESSES

Chapter 8: INTERRUPTS, I/O, AND TIMER MANAGEMENT

Chapter 9: DEVICE MANAGEMENT

Chapter 10: MEMORY MANAGEMENT

Chapter 11: VIRTUAL MEMORY MANAGEMENT

Chapter 12: FILE MANAGEMENT

Chapter 13: A SIMPLE MULTIPROGRAMMING EXECUTIVE (MPX)

Chapter 14: ERROR MANAGEMENT

Chapter 15: RELIABILITY

Chapter 16: SECURITY

Chapter 17: SYSTEM MANAGEMENT AND ACCOUNTING

Chapter 18: PERFORMANCE ANALYSIS

Chapter 19: IMPLEMENTATION AND MAINTENANCE

Chapter 20: PORTABILITY AND STANDARDS

Chapter 21: VIRTUAL MACHINES

Chapter 22: REAL-TIME SYSTEMS

Appendix C: A CATALOG OF OPERATING SYSTEMS

Preface

In our present world of rapidly expanding computer use, few computers perform their duties without some type of operating system. This control software plays an essential role in turning a collection of raw hardware components into a useful system of computing resources. Its role becomes even more important when a single computing system is to be shared by many different users.

The study of operating systems is of fundamental importance to the computer science student. Even those who will never participate in the design of an operating system must learn to interact with such systems in various ways. Manipulation of files and input and output devices, and access to many important services, can only be accomplished by negotiation with the operating system. The perceptions developed by most users of a computing system, including software developers and researchers, are largely shaped by the operating system's user interface.

The opinion has sometimes been promoted that we are on the verge of an era of standard operating systems, in which only a few such systems will survive. Yet the truth is that new operating systems appear as rapidly as new computer types. Dozens, if not hundreds, are in common use; many address needs that cannot be met by the few most dominant systems. Each problem faced by an operating system has many possible solutions. The best approach may depend on many factors and circumstances. So, the universal operating system remains as elusive as the universal programming language.

ABOUT THIS BOOK

This book is designed to support a variety of operating systems courses at the junior or senior undergraduate level. It is based on material that has evolved in a two-semester sequence at West Virginia University over more than fifteen years. The first course in this sequence presents basic concepts of system software and features a series of small-computer team programming projects, culminating in the development of an integrated multiprogramming executive.   The second course studies a broad range of operating system concepts and their implementation in a variety of real operating systems. This course includes a term paper assignment in which students study, describe, and analyze a real operating system of their choice.

The material in the book can be fully covered in two semesters, along with the associated projects. Much of the later material is optional, however, and by judicious choice of topics a variety of shorter courses can be constructed.

As noted above, the text is designed to support the implementation of a series of projects, of which the primary one is the Multiprogramming Executive (MPX) described in Chapter 13.   However, it is not necessary to implement these projects in order to use the book effectively.   If it is not implemented, MPX can still serve as a useful model of a simple multiprogramming executive. In this case, Chapter 13 can be used to bring many of the ideas from earlier chapters together using this MPX model. If no projects are implemented, the basic concepts in Chapters 1 through 12 could be dealt with in as little as a single quarter.

This book is suitable for operating systems courses included in curriculum recommendations put forth by ACM and the IEEE Computer Society.   It also takes note of more recent recommendations that greater attention should be paid to the rapid evolution of hardware architectures and the increasing importance of proper service to human users of computing systems.   The treatment is practical rather than theoretical, and requires little mathematical background. We do not include mathematical analyses of algorithms or formal studies of techniques. These methods are most appropriate to the graduate course. (References to more theoretical treatments are provided in many cases.) The practical material in the text, however, is comprehensive enough to serve as a useful reference for the practicing professional.

The background expected of the student consists primarily of an elementary knowledge of programming, algorithms, and data structures, as provided by most introductory courses. Some additional exposure to assembly language programming and computer organization is desirable but not required. All essential concepts in this area are covered by the review material in Appendix A.

The hallmarks of this textbook include especially the following points:

1. A coordinated sequence of "hands-on" project assignments, allowing students to develop or modify selected components of an actual multiprogrammed operating system.

2. Illustration of concepts by many examples from real operating systems, ranging from the newest systems to those of historical interest.

3. Consideration throughout of the relationship and synergy that

exists between an operating system and computer hardware, and the impact on operating system design caused by the presence or absence of various architectural features.

4. Coverage of a broad range of topics relating to operating systems design, including some not commonly treated in comparable texts.

Project assignments are included at the end of Chapters 4 through 12, and described in more detail in a separate project manual. These assignments allow students or teams to develop working components of a multiprogrammed OS in a controlled environment. The first project manual is designed for use with an IBM PC and the C language. Manuals for other environments are under development.

As an adjunct to the project manual, classes can be supplied with diskettes containing support software and example components for the complete system. Students have the option of developing some components from scratch, modifying existing ones, or using still other components as supplied to produce a complete working system.

Examples from a wide variety of real operating systems illustrate many concepts and techniques. Rather than being isolated in a limited number of case studies, these examples are presented along with the topics throughout the text. The examples are diverse, to prevent the student from too readily confusing examples with basic principles.

Architectural principles are fundamental to an understanding of operating systems, which play a primary role in "bridging the gap" between hardware and software. Issues range from the use of certain CPU instructions and registers, through management of input and output, to the use of optional subsystems designed especially to support OS needs such as paging and segmentation, capabilities, or context switching mechanisms. Hardware issues are considered throughout the text. Some of this treatment is drawn from various courses in computer architecture that have been taught at WVU by one of the authors.

The breadth of coverage in this book is shown by its treatment of a number of topics not commonly found in operating system texts. This practice begins with an extended survey of the historical evolution of operating systems. This study is intended to provide some appreciation of the origin and reasons for many techniques and philosophies in common use today. Although there are many presentations of topics in the history of computing, the evolution of operating systems is not often described in current works.

An essential concern of any operating system is its interface with the outside world. A major design issue is the structure to be chosen for the user interface, the primary vehicle for communication between users and the operating system. Many texts give scant treatment to this topic. Perhaps as a partial result, many operating systems continue to be equipped with user interfaces that are far less well designed than they might be. Although an exhaustive analysis of user interfaces would easily fill a separate text, at least an introductory treatment seems essential for the student of operating systems.

Another important issue is the management of I/O devices, which come in a great variety of types and vary with each installation. We provide a chapter on aspects of device management, including the important practical issues of developing customized device drivers. We include also as an appendix an overview of the physical characteristics of many common I/O devices.

In a similar way, practical issues faced by operating system designers, such as development and testing, error handling, and performance analysis, are each given attention. Operating system design can lead to unique problems in each of these areas. System management issues, such as accounting, user management, customizing and tuning, are all considered as well.

Three special categories of operating systems are each treated in a separate chapter: virtual machines, real-time systems, and distributed systems. Virtual machines can provide an effective solution for some special problems, including system simulation, total isolation of processes, and running multiple operating systems on a single machine. Although the dominant virtual machine system is IBM's VM/370, we provide a more general view that includes virtual machines on other types of hardware.

Operating systems providing support for real-time activities (those with critical timing requirements) are of increasing importance as computers are called upon to control factories, aircraft, military systems, laboratory experiments, and a host of physical activities. Although many of these environments have unique requirements, some general principles are found in the many real-time operating systems in existence today. These principles are very different from those of conventional operating systems, and are rarely treated in texts.

A type of operating system growing rapidly in importance is the distributed system, which seeks to impose a common control mechanism on a network of distinct computers. The majority of current operating system research is devoted to distributed systems, and these systems are emerging from the research laboratories into commercial use. An especially important category of distributed operating system is one which strives for network transparency in a local area network environment. We examine some of the unique problems presented by this type of operating system.

An important practical issue for today's operating systems is the role they play in allowing applications to be transported from one computer system to another. This objective raises problems that are not easy to solve, but can be addressed by techniques such as portable operating systems and industry standard program interfaces. A chapter is devoted to these issues.

ORGANIZATION

The chapters in the book may be logically grouped into several major parts. Chapters 1 through 3 contain introductory material that will be applied throughout the rest of the text. These chapters should be covered by all students. Since many concepts are introduced here in a systematic way, they should be read in the order in which they appear.

Chapters 4 through 12 include one or more chapters on each of the principal resource management responsibilities of a modern conventional operating system. The topics in these chapters are necessarily related, and some cross-referencing cannot be avoided. However, as far as possible each chapter stands by itself. These chapters can be covered in any desired sequence.

Chapter 13 is devoted to a description of the MPX project, which brings together the separate projects from previous chapters into a complete system. It may be omitted from courses in which the projects are not used, but as mentioned previously, the chapter can provide the students with a simple model of a multiprogramming executive. Chapters 14 through 23 consider a variety of advanced topics that may be selected for a longer course or course sequence. Emerging techniques for attaining greater reliability and security are considered, along with practical issues of system management, performance analysis, system implementation, and portability. The specialized OS types, virtual machines, real-time executives, and distributed systems are also treated in these chapters. Each of these chapters stands alone insofar as possible.

Chapters 1 through 13 form an appropriate core of material for a one-semester introductory course. Selected material from later chapters may be included as desired. Some chapters include coverage in their later sections of more advanced or specialized material which may be considered optional. If time is limited due to project assignments, this material can be omitted.

For a longer course, additional topics from the later chapters can be selected in any desired order. These chapters also include optional, specialized material, so a choice can be made between covering selected chapters in depth or surveying a wider range of chapters. The complete text can be covered comfortably in a two-semester sequence.

Throughout the text, references are cited frequently to provide proper attribution for various statements and to suggest sources for further information. A comprehensive bibliography is included as an appendix. An attempt has been made throughout to identify useful references that are readily available, rather than manuals or reports that may be difficult to obtain.

An attempt is also made to present terminology that is most widely used throughout the industry rather than that peculiar to a single system or supplier. Alternate terminology is also mentioned when it seems significant.

In a few cases, more descriptive terms have been substituted for popular ones that are obscure or misleading. In each chapter, new terms that are considered important are printed in **boldface** when they first appear. These terms are summarized at the end of each chapter; they are then defined in a comprehensive dictionary at the end of the book.

A final unique aspect of this book is an appendix cataloging over 500 actual operating systems, with capsule descriptions and references in most cases. We believe that for learning the practical details of OS implementation, there is no substitute for study of real systems. Very often, the best source of descriptions for these systems is found in original publications by their designers, which may provide far more thorough coverage than is possible through case studies in an introductory text. Because of this catalog, references for specific system examples are given less frequently in the body of the text.

MALCOLM G. LANE
JAMES D. MOONEY
Morgantown, WV
January 1988

reface to the Student

As its title suggests, this book presents a *practical* approach to the study of operating systems. Our intention in this study is to prepare you to understand the operating systems you may be using in order to get the greatest benefits from their use; to participate in the selection of operating systems; and to contribute effectively to the design of new operating systems if you have an opportunity. All of these skills are valuable for the computing professional.

The practical approach is maintained by three important elements throughout the text. First, a firm grounding in operating system *principles* is provided, to help you learn the purpose and expected effects of each design decision. Second, a variety of real *examples* are studied, showing the many different ways that systems can be constructed for specific purposes. Third, a series of optional *projects* is included, making it possible for you to acquire direct experience in the design and construction of operating system components.

Projects are described at the end of Chapters 4 through 12. Most of these may be considered components of a large project, the MultiProgramming eXecutive (MPX), described in Chapter 13. If your course is using these projects, you should make use of the accompanying project manual, which describes many of the required details about the projects and the support software provided for implementing them. The projects are based on ones that have been used for many years at West Virginia University. Implementation of such projects has proved to be an effective way to grasp and thoroughly understand the concepts and principles of operating systems presented in this book.

The book is organized so that it is easy to review each chapter's material. A concise summary is given at the end of each chapter. Review questions are provided to test your retention of important concepts. Assignments for each chapter provide the opportunity to explore selected concepts in greater depth. Important terms in each chapter appear in **boldface** and are listed at the end of each chapter. Every term is also defined in the Dictionary at the end of the book, which provides additional study help and an excellent reference for the operating system environment.

The For Further Reading sections in each chapter provide you with sources for more information on topics covered within that chapter. The comprehensive bibliography provides, in a convenient alphabetical form, full references for all the readings that are cited. The great majority of these references should be available at most college and university libraries.

The catalog of operating systems found in Appendix C should make it possible for you to locate more information on any specific operating system that you may be interested in, as well as providing a general appreciation of the wide range of operating systems that exist or have existed.

We encourage you to read the Preface to learn still more about the organization and goals of this book.

Acknowledgments

A project as extensive as the writing of this text requires help from many people. We are grateful to the many students who used the preliminary versions of this book for the two-semester undergraduate courses on operating systems in the Department of Statistics and Computer Science at West Virginia University. Literally hundreds of students have had an impact on the development of the Multiprogramming Executive project described in Chapter 13 and in the project manual. Their hard work and contributions are acknowledged and greatly appreciated.

Three individuals—James F. Williams, Timothy Sesow, and Mary Swim—developed much of the MPX support software for the PDP-11. It is the PDP-11 MPX project that served as the model for the MPX project for IBM PC compatibles described in the first project manual. Digital Equipment Corporation and HRB Singer, Inc. also supported the development of this PDP-11 MPX project with equipment grants and donations for the laboratory that supports the first course in operating systems at West Virginia University. The PC version of the MPX project was developed, in part, by James Knudson, James Patnesky, Cynthia Jarrett, and Anjan Ghosal, each of whom were computer science graduate students at West Virginia University.

Many students in our second operating systems course contributed to the development of the manuscript, especially through their many term reports that provided insights into a great variety of operating systems, identified numerous references, and stimulated development of the catalog found in Appendix C. The reports of Jeff Devine, David Dymm, Dana Falkenstine, Randy Hefner, and Karen Logar were particularly helpful. David Butcher, Susan McCann, Steve Mikes, and Mike Packer all helped to locate errors in the final draft.

Without the support of the Department of Statistics and Computer Science at West Virginia University for the operating systems course development, the systems programming laboratory, and the writing of this book, this book would never have been possible. The encouragement and support of the Chairman of this department, Donald F. Butcher, is especially appreciated.

This support included the use of department computing and printing resources at every stage of development, including production of the final camera-ready pages. The staff of the department—Louise Tudor, Bonnie Kasten, Marlene Farley, Felicia Kelley, and Ann George, were all helpful in many ways. Alan Butcher contributed the example in Figure 4-13, and was a facilitator in many ways. Thanks also to Jim Harner and Mike Cremer for Macintosh expertise and for aiding in the production of Figure 4-6. A very special thanks goes to our overworked system manager, Jim Foltz, who kept all of the equipment working properly when we needed it.

The Department of Information Science at the University of Pittsburgh also was supportive in the final stages of this text, while Malcolm Lane served as AT&T Visiting Professor of Telecommunications in this department for the 1987-1988 academic year. Robert Korfhage, Department Chairman, was very supportive of the time and effort required to complete the text during the fall semester of 1987. The department's students, who used a draft of this book, provided many helpful suggestions. In particular, the example in Figure 11–2 was suggested by Raymond Markiewiez.

We also want to thank the reviewers who provided us with critical comments on various drafts of the manuscript. Helpful reviews were provided by Don Chiarulli, University of Pittsburgh; Roland J. Couture, Southern Connecticut State University; Ralph E. Johnson, University of Illinois; Joseph Kasprzyk, Salem State College; Marguerite Murphy, San Francisco State University; Gary Nutt, University of Colorado; and Satish K. Tripathi, University of Maryland.   Special appreciation goes to Neta Amit of the University of Minnesota for his thorough reviews and helpful suggestions, which improved both the preliminary and final drafts of the book.

Camera-ready pages for this text were produced by the authors using Digital Equipment VAX computers and LN03 laser printers, Apple Macintosh personal computers, the UNIX operating system (Berkeley 4.3 version), and the TEX document formatting system.   We acknowledge the equipment contributions of Digital Equipment and Apple Corporation to our department. Thanks to Dennis Ritchie and Ken Thompson for developing UNIX, and to Don Knuth for producing TEX. Thanks also to Pierre MacKay and his staff at the University of Washington for maintaining the UNIX version of TEX and providing updates in a hurry when required.   The book was set using the Computer Modern typefaces provided with TEX, modified by John Sauter and adapted for the LN03 by Stan Osborne. Final output was printed on an LN03-Plus.

The staff of Boyd & Fraser Publishing Company has been outstanding during the writing and production of this text book. A very special thanks to our editor, Marjorie Schlaikjer, for her constant help and support and for her patience in trying (vainly) to keep us on schedule. We are grateful also to Tom Walker, Editor-in-Chief, for his continuing support, and to Donna Villanucci, Production Coordinator, for all of her contributions. Thanks too to Becky Herrington and her staff at the Boyd & Fraser production facility in Brea, California, for their fine and rapid artwork, production of display pages and assembly of the final text. Effective copyediting under pressure was performed by Darlene Bordwell, while Charley McWha provided final editing of the corrected manuscripts.

We acknowledge the never-ending support of our families: Maureen, Melanie, and Maura Lane, and Joan, Tara, Tressa, Alishia, and Asonda Mooney. Without their love, patience, and understanding, this book could never have been completed. Last but by no means least, we are thankful to God for the talents and abilities we were given that made it possible for us to develop courses in computer science and ultimately to write this book.

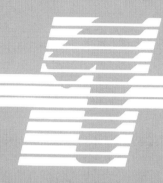

Overview

Overview

1.1 INTRODUCTION

The basic elements necessary to store and process information are contained in any computer. However, these elements are usually provided in a very primitive form that is quite difficult to use directly. Because of this problem, the **hardware** (physical components) of a computer is almost always supplemented by some type of standard **software** (programs and data). Together these elements work to form a more usable **computing system.**

The software portion of a computing system consists mainly of a collection of special programs called **system programs,** which differ from **application programs** that perform the specialized processing required by each user of the system. One type of system program very familiar to programmers is a compiler or language translator, which makes it possible to write programs in high-level languages like Pascal, C or Ada. Another system program is generally responsible for the overall control of the computing system, including communicating with users and directing the execution of their programs. This program is known as the **operating system** (abbreviated **OS).** Except for very early computers or a few special-purpose categories, almost every computer is provided with some type of operating system. This text is devoted to the study of those systems.

1.2 THE ROLE OF AN OPERATING SYSTEM

As we have noted, a computing system consists of both hardware and software. The simplest view, which we will continue to follow unless stated otherwise, is that the computer is hardware and the operating system is software. To be precise, however, the exact boundary between hardware and software varies with each computer. Simple computers have been constructed in which many capabilities usually expected from the hardware, such as multiplication, had to be provided by software instead. On the other hand, driven by the decreasing cost of hardware and the increasing cost of software, many newer computers include hardware functions once expected only from software, such as memory management, direct operations on various data structures, or even direct interpretation of high-level languages. Many common parts of operating systems may fall in this category.

Each hardware or software component of a computing system that is potentially useful to system users or their programs is called a **resource.** Some important resources include memory, files, disks, and printers. An operating system's primary purpose is to *manage the resources* of a computing system. Although most computer professionals will not be called upon to design new operating systems, most will work daily with computing systems whose behavior is greatly influenced by the type of OS provided. Many professionals will also have opportunities to influence their organization's choice of operating systems, to maintain an existing OS, or to adapt an operating system to the specific needs of a particular environment. For these reasons, a clear understanding of how operating systems work is important to the education of all computer scientists.

A computer without an operating system may be compared to a bus without a driver, a situation illustrated in Figure 1–1. Such a bus will still run; but passengers wanting to use the bus are faced with a complicated driving process rather than a comfortable ride. Mistakes are easily made, and may have serious consequences. If several passengers wish to use the same bus, they might fight over who will drive and where the bus should go.

Much the same situation arises in a computing system when a group of users want to perform work on the computer. Without an operating system, each user must take control of the computer and create programs to handle all the messy details of each resource. It will be difficult to share the resources effectively, and users may fight over the right to use them.

With a driver on board the bus, however, someone is in control. This improved situation is depicted in Figure 1–2. Passengers may provide the driver with high-level instructions ("Take me to Main and Walnut") without the need to worry constantly about steering, gearshifts, brakes, or which route to follow. Most of these details are taken care of by the driver, and the bus is much more convenient to use. Even though passengers cannot drive the bus directly to their destination, but must be content with the driver's schedule, they will not usually complain (unless the bus is unduly late).

Similarly, if an operating system is present in a computer system, it can control the resources in detail and provide more effective sharing. Although users must defer to the decisions of the OS in some cases, everyone's work may be completed more quickly and more easily.

Figure 1–1 The Computer as a Driverless Bus

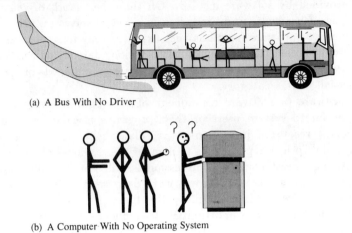

(a) A Bus With No Driver

(b) A Computer With No Operating System

Figure 1–2 The Operating System as a Bus Driver

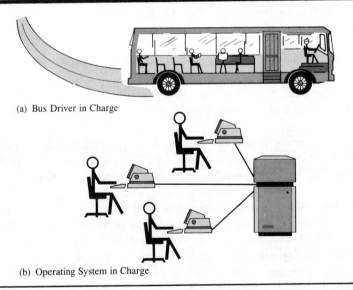

(a) Bus Driver in Charge

(b) Operating System in Charge

1.3 OPERATING SYSTEMS AS RESOURCE MANAGERS

We have said that an operating system is a manager of resources. This leads to some obvious questions:

1. What are the resources managed by the operating system?
2. What is the purpose of resource management?

The resources provided by a computing system may be considered in two broad categories: **physical resources,** also called *hardware resources,* and **logical resources,** also known as *software resources.* As the name implies, physical resources are the permanent physical components of the computer system. The principal physical resources are:

- A central processing unit (CPU)
- Main memory
- Input and output (I/O) devices such as terminals and printers
- Secondary storage devices such as disks and tapes
- Internal devices such as clocks and timers.

Each of these physical resources is discussed more fully in the Appendices.

Logical resources are collections of information, such as data or programs. Logical resources must be stored within physical resources—for instance, within main or secondary memory. Resources of interest in this category may include:

- Units of work, such as jobs or interactive sessions
- Processes (programs in execution)
- Files (named sets of information)
- Shared programs and data
- Procedures that perform a variety of useful services.

The resources that must be managed by a typical general-purpose operating system are summarized in Figure 1–3.

The resource management provided by an OS has two principal objectives. The first objective is to support **convenient use.** In the early days of computing, each user had to provide his or her own programs to manage each detail in the control and use of I/O devices and other common resources. Today's users of computers, by and large, are not programmers. They view the computer as a tool for saving their own valuable time, and they rightly expect such tools to be easy to use. They should not have to worry about

Figure 1–3 Resources Managed by an Operating System

PHYSICAL RESOURCES	LOGICAL RESOURCES
CPU	Jobs and Sessions
Main Memory	Processes
I/O Devices and Controllers	Files
Secondary Storage	System Service Procedures
Timers & Clocks	

complex details involved in resource management. The services provided to the users of today's computing systems must be easy to use, yet provide sufficient power and flexibility to meet each user's needs.

The second objective of resource management by an operating system is to support and enforce **controlled sharing.** When computer systems are shared by more than one user, programs must be prevented from interfering with each other in any way. Especially in a general–purpose computing environment, programs of any type may be run, including many which contain errors or try to do improper things. Allowing a program to have direct control of common resources without the supervision of an OS would place other programs at risk of interference or damage to their code or resources.

Controlled sharing of resources is a complex problem. Besides being properly controlled, the sharing must be *efficient* and *fair*. Resources should seldom have to wait unused when there are programs that need them. When a resource is needed by several programs, each one should get a fair turn.

1.4 EXTENSIONS OF THE HARDWARE

An operating system refines and adds to the capabilities of the computer it controls. The operating system also serves as an **interface,** or communication link, to the users of the computing system. Most users deal with the computer only with the help of, and subject to the control of, the operating system. Thus it is natural to think of an OS as an extension of the computing hardware. This view is illustrated in Figure 1–4. The OS may be thought of as a layer on top of or surrounding the computer, a layer which separates and insulates the users and the computer from one another.

Although personal computer users may be somewhat aware of the

Figure 1–4   The OS as an Extension of a Computer

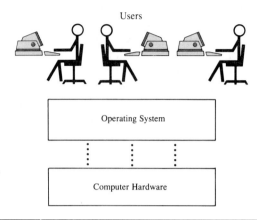

differences between hardware and software, most users of larger computer systems think of their system as a single entity, and rarely distinguish the operating system from the computer hardware. If the computing system fails due to some problem, users observe only that the system is "down." They do not often care whether the problem involves hardware or software (unless it becomes necessary for them to help solve it).

Another natural reason for considering the OS to be an extension of the hardware in some systems is that part or all of the OS may actually be implemented in hardware, or at least stored permanently in a read–only memory. In such systems the OS cannot be removed from memory, and takes control whenever power is turned on. Since the OS is always available, it appears to most users that it is indeed part of the hardware.

The idea of the operating system forming one or more layers of software above the computer is sometimes used systematically to design the structure of the OS. This approach to OS structure, along with several others, is examined in Chapter 3.

1.5 OPERATING SYSTEMS IN PERSPECTIVE

To begin a study of operating systems, we must define the limits of system software responsibilities that we consider to fall under the proper definition of an OS. One possible view is to identify the OS with the *complete computing environment*. We would then consider the entire body of software supplied with a computing system, including editors, compilers, and other software tools, as parts of the OS itself. This view is often held by users, especially when most system software is supplied as a package from a single source. This is the case, for example, with the popular operating systems VMS (for Digital Equipment VAX computers) and UNIX (which runs on a variety of large and small computers, including the VAX). These OSs are frequently praised or condemned for the quality of their editors and compilers, although these tools are quite distinct from the operating system itself.

There is clearly some justification for this unified view. Not only are software tools often supplied together, but they are expected to work well together. Each computing system may have a philosophy, largely determined by the operating system, to which good system software should adhere. An excellent compiler for a UNIX environment may seem badly out of place on an Apple Macintosh. However, since it would clearly be impossible to study such a broad range of tools in a single text, we opt for a much narrower view of the operating system.

A different extreme taken by some texts is to view the OS as a very limited collection of essential resource management procedures, typically those that remain in main memory at all times and are entrusted with all of the privileges that the hardware can provide. These procedures are often referred to as the **kernel** of the operating system.

This text's viewpoint is close, but not identical, to this second extreme. It is suggested by the discussion of the OS as extended machine, forming a layer between the computer and its users. An expanded view of this layer is shown in Figure 1–5. At each side of this layer the OS meets an interface. The interface to the computer hardware provides the OS with access to the physical resources, which form a **hardware environment** with which the OS must work. On the other side of this layer, the OS presents the system users with a **user interface,** which establishes a **user environment** that greatly determines how users perceive the system and how effectively it can meet their needs. Note that users interact with the OS both directly and through their application programs. The commands available for system communication and control, the services available to running programs, the form of terminal displays, and the philosophy established for use by software tools are all parts of this user environment.

Our view of the OS will extend to all functions normally associated with this layer between the user environment and the hardware environment. The software in this layer extends and completes the capabilities of the computer and manages its physical resources. This management, ideally, is designed to provide the necessary control and convenience while remaining as flexible as possible. Its role is to provide a **mechanism** which can effectively manage each resource in accordance with a **policy** selected by those in charge of the specific computer system. This distinction between mechanism, which is a proper responsibility for operating systems, and policy, which generally is

Figure 1–5 Interfaces and Environments

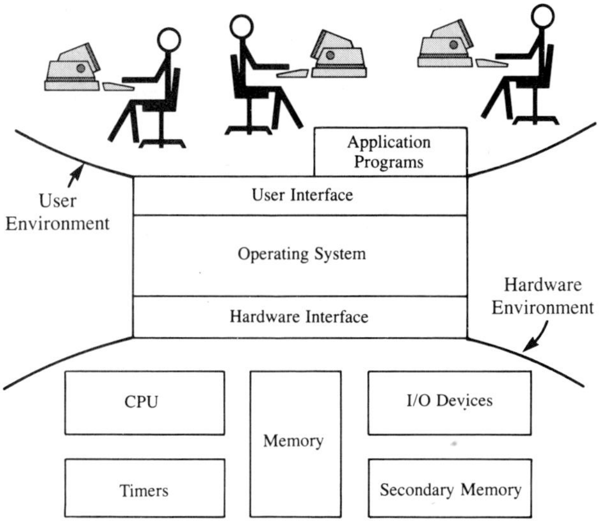

not, is an important distinction for effective OS design.

Although much of the OS software in this view may be part of the permanent, privileged kernel as described above, it can also include resource management programs and procedures which are loaded into memory as needed, or which operate with fewer privileges than the kernel itself.

In general, we restrict our view of the role of the OS to direct management of resources which *must* be controlled by a central authority for the benefit of all users. We deviate from this narrow view, however, in including treatment of two subjects which could arguably be excluded: file systems and the user interface.

We consider **file systems** to be an operating system responsibility. Although files are not pure physical resources, they comprise an important category of shareable logical resources formed from physical storage devices, such as magnetic disks. The design of a file system imposes on all users the same high–level view of these storage devices. In some current operating systems, especially those designed to control multiple computers connected by a network, a file system is treated as a separate and independent component. However, files are an important system resource expected by most computer users, and we follow widely accepted practice in studying them together with operating systems.

The ultimate purpose of a computing system is to provide services to users. The operating system layer in Figure 1–5 would serve little purpose without the user interface at its top. Every OS must communicate with its users, and most have not done this job well. It is surprising that this subject is neglected in a large number of operating system texts. We consider the user interface to include both the command language provided for direct communication from terminals or batch jobs and the system services provided for use by running programs. This interface is an important OS responsibility.

1.6 ORGANIZATION OF THE TEXT

This text is devoted to a study of operating systems. We attempt to develop an understanding of both the important theoretical concepts on which effective operating systems must be based and the many ways these concepts have been applied in actual OS examples. Implementation projects are also included, allowing you to design and experiment with components of an OS that your instructor may select. These projects may be joined with other prototypes supplied by the authors to construct a complete experimental operating system called the Multiprogramming Executive (MPX).

This chapter establishes a framework for the course by surveying the topics to be studied and explaining the organization of the text. In conjunction with the two chapters that follow, it serves as an introductory unit. Chapter 2 examines the history and evolution of operating systems somewhat more extensively than most texts, and introduces some important OSs used as examples throughout the text. We believe that an appreciation of this history is important for understanding why many operating systems have the form they do today, for realizing why a few systems have attained especially great importance and wide acceptance, and for distinguishing OS features that clearly reflect good design from others that are primarily historical accidents. Chapter 3 surveys the great range of considerations that influence the structure of operating systems as software systems, and the many structures that have evolved in response to these considerations.

Some important background material on computer organization and system software is reviewed in Appendix A. Although many students will have covered this material in earlier courses, we recommend at least a brief reading of this appendix. In addition to reviewing important preliminary topics, it also establishes some consistent terminology and perspectives used throughout the text. Descriptions of some important input, output and storage device types are also provided in Appendix B.

The remainder of the text examines in detail a broad range of operating system topics. A number of chapters are concerned with specific responsibilities that most OSs have in the management of various categories of resources. Additional chapters consider practical aspects of operating system implementation, management, and maintenance. Finally, several important special categories of operating systems are examined in the final chapters of the book. The principal topics to be addressed are introduced in the remaining sections of this chapter.

1.7 RESPONSIBILITIES OF AN OPERATING SYSTEM

To fulfill the role outlined in the previous section, an operating system must meet many responsibilities. Some of these, such as file management, are concerned with managing particular categories of resources or interfaces. Others are concerned with services that span a range of resources, such as error handling or security control. Figure 1–6 summarizes the major responsibilities that most operating systems must meet.

Figure 1–6 Responsibilities of an Operating System

User Interface	Error Handling
Process Management	Reliability
Job & Session Management	Security
Device Management	Monitoring
Timer Management	Accounting
Memory Management	System Management
File Management	

The User Interface

Operating systems must be able to communicate with users and their programs. This communication is managed by the user interface, examined in more detail in Chapter 4.

Two components make up the user interface in our view of the operating system. One is the **command interface** provided for the user to enter commands to direct the computer (e.g., via terminals or other input media). The second is the **program interface,** which provides services upon request to programs during execution. These services, requested by a mechanism similar to procedure calls, include such things as input and output, file access, and program termination requests.

The command interface establishes the "user friendliness" of the system. Commands that are consistent and easy to use will result in a user's more rapid acceptance of a computer system. Command structures that are difficult to learn or understand quickly frustrate users and often result in their moving to other computer systems that are easier to use, whenever such systems are available. Although in some environments the command interface may be viewed as a separate, replaceable program, it is a critical element of a complete computing system.

The program interface defines the procedures and conventions programs must follow to request operating system services. Such things as the parameters required and the means of invoking the services of the operating system are defined by the program interface.

Process Management

The term **process** is used to describe a program in execution under the control of an operating system. Another widely used term for process is **task.** We will use the term process consistently throughout this text. Perhaps the most fundamental responsibility of any operating system is **process management.** When there is only one CPU, processes must either run one at a time to completion, or take turns using the CPU for a short period. Allowing processes to take turns in this manner is called **interleaved execution;** processes that share the CPU in this way are called **concurrent processes.** An OS which allows application programs to concurrently share the CPU is called a **multiprogramming system.**

Controlling this interleaved execution so that work proceeds in a fair and effective way is the problem to be solved by **process scheduling.** This scheduling must be considered at several levels, from overall admission of new jobs into a system down to moment-by-moment allocation of the use of the CPU.

For various reasons, concurrent processes may interact with one another. One form of interaction occurs because resources are shared, and some resources required by one process may be in use by another. A second form of interaction occurs when processes deliberately seek to exchange information. Controlling the interaction that may occur among concurrent processes is an important responsibility for a multiprogramming OS.

Because of its central importance, three chapters of this text are devoted to process management. Basic process concepts are developed in Chapter 5. Chapter 6 addresses the issues of scheduling, especially as they concern the assignment of CPU and memory resources to each process. Important issues arising from the interaction of concurrent processes are examined in Chapter 7.

Device Management

All computers have a variety of input, output and storage devices that must be controlled by the operating system. Printers, terminals, plotters, hard disks, floppy disks, magnetic tapes, and communication devices are among the most common devices found in such systems today. In the past, additional devices such as punched card readers and paper tape readers were also prevalent.

In addition, many computers include internal devices that may be accessed to perform special functions. An important example is clocks or timers, which may be used to measure the timing relationships among various events. **Device management** encompasses all aspects of controlling these devices: starting operation, requesting and waiting for data transfers, responding to errors that may occur, and so on.

As might be suspected, the variety of devices that can be attached to a computer use many different commands and controls. The user cannot be expected to write the software to directly control such a wide range of devices. Furthermore, multiprogramming operating systems that support the sharing of a computer system by two or more processes cannot allow an application program to access these devices without going through the operating system program interface. Otherwise, the integrity of other users' and programs' data might be sacrificed (e.g., by a direct write request to a disk that intentionally or erroneously writes over another user's data). Device management, therefore, is a very important function of the operating system. Device support can be quite complex, and implementing such support consumes much of the time and effort in the implementation of any operating system.

Despite its central role in controlling the physical resources of any OS, many texts devote little attention to the details of device management. We address this subject in Chapters 8 and 9. A discussion of the characteristics and requirements of various types of I/O devices is also presented in Appendix B.

In many cases, data transfers that have been started may continue while the CPU is performing other work. Completion of the transfer is then signaled by **interrupts,** events that literally "interrupt" the running program, requiring it to take time out to handle the event before resuming the interrupted work it was doing. This subject is also studied in Chapters 8 and 9.

Memory Management

Memory management is the responsibility of controlling the use of main memory, a critical resource in any computer system. Since secondary storage devices, such as disks and tapes, are used in various ways to extend the storage available in main memory, the subject of memory management must deal with these devices as well. The performance of operating systems can be greatly affected by the way the memory is managed.

Early operating systems allowed only one program to be in progress at a time, so memory management was relatively simple. The operating system used what it needed of main memory to store its own information, and the program could have the rest. Responsibility for managing the available memory rested solely with the application program. Often the OS had no means of protecting even its own memory. If a program interfered with OS memory, it could do harm only to itself, since a failure of the operating system would harm only that single program.

The introduction of multiprogramming systems changed all that, because main memory had to be shared among several processes. In such systems the OS must be responsible for allocating memory and for protecting processes from one another.

Early forms of memory management were concerned primarily with allocating portions of main memory to each process when the process started. Newer strategies allow additional areas of memory to be allocated and removed as desired, and provide for temporary **swapping** of programs and their data from main memory to a disk when not immediately needed. This strategy makes the memory space available for more immediate needs.

As an evolution of swapping techniques, **virtual memory** systems have now become common. These systems can automate the swapping process by a combination of hardware and software techniques, providing powerful solutions to a full range of memory management problems.

Although basic memory management techniques are often covered in data structure courses, they play a critical role in the operation of many OSs. These basic techniques are examined in Chapter 10; virtual memory management is considered in Chapter 11.

File Management

Information stored by a computer system is usually organized into files. **File management** is concerned with all aspects of reading, writing, organizing, and controlling the access to information stored in files. Another major function of such management is to provide security—that is, protection of information from improper access. Security has been one of the weakest aspects of file management in many operating systems. We study file management in Chapter 12; security is addressed in Chapter 16.

Job and Session Management

A complete unit of work performed or submitted by a user may include a series of programs, carried out by a set of processes that may proceed one at a time, or concurrently in some cases. Such a unit is called a **job** when submitted to the OS all at once, as was common in early "batch" systems. When a set of work is specified by a series of commands typed by a user at a terminal, it may more aptly be called a **session.** For various reasons, it is sometimes desirable to manage jobs and sessions as complete units. For example, the OS may need to decide when a new job or session can be started, and it may need to associate the complete job or session with a particular user for authorization or accounting purposes. Aspects of job and session management are discussed in several chapters of this book which include Chapters 7, 16, and 17.

Error Handling

Operating systems must deal with a variety of errors that can occur in a computer system. Such errors include hardware errors in devices, memory, and channels, and software errors in application and system programs. Software errors can be a result of such things as arithmetic overflow, invalid instructions, or references to invalid memory.

Error handling, the process of detecting and recovering from such errors, is considered in Chapter 14. Effective error handling must try to detect as many types of errors as possible. When errors are detected, reasonable attempts should be made to recover and continue, without such drastic actions as terminating the offending process or stopping the entire system. Whenever possible, failures in hardware components should result in the isolation of the faulty component without affecting the rest of the system operation. Software errors should be recognized, corrected if possible, and prevented from causing damage to other programs and resources. In many cases, error detection and recovery should be as invisible as possible to the user. However, some types of errors should be reported to the application program so that appropriate action can be taken.

Reliability and Security

An operating system may have partial responsibility for ensuring that computer systems continue to operate correctly and data and programs are protected from damage or improper access. These goals may need to be met even when errors or failures exist in hardware or software, or unauthorized persons deliberately seek to corrupt or gain access to the system. These system responsibilities are known as **reliability** and **security.** Their importance can vary greatly from one system to another. Providing extremely good reliability and security can be very costly.

The importance of reliability—keeping a computer system running correctly—is evident. The importance of ensuring the security of information stored in files has already been mentioned. In addition to this critical aspect of security, the operating system must protect one process from another, the operating system from a process, a process from the operating system, and the operating system from itself. The most obvious way an OS does this is to isolate memory areas for processes and for itself; another is to protect against the use of privileged instructions and system resources by unauthorized processes. Access to OS services must also be controlled by the OS. Other areas of security include those of session and job management, which require the appropriate identifications, passwords and other mechanisms before use of the system is granted. Reliability and security are studied, respectively, in Chapters 15 and 16.

Monitoring and Accounting

Most sophisticated operating systems, especially in environments where computing is considered to have significant costs, include some facilities for monitoring the behavior of the system as it proceeds and for keeping records of that behavior for various purposes. One important purpose of this monitoring is **accounting,** keeping track of resource use by each user so that users can be billed for the services of the computing system. Another important purpose of monitoring is to measure the **performance** of the system—that is, the effectiveness with which it completes its work within the limitations of available resources. Such monitoring may identify adjustments that should be made to keep that performance as good as possible.

Still another purpose for monitoring may be to detect improper behavior by users and processes, especially in systems highly concerned with security. These issues are addressed in Chapters 16, 17, and 18.

1.8 SYSTEM MANAGEMENT

In addition to examining the principal responsibilities which an OS must meet continuously during normal execution, we will study a number of issues concerned with the management, implementation and maintenance of operating systems. Several of these issues fall under the heading of **system management,** the subject of Chapter 17. Included in this discussion are methods for initial installation of operating systems, adjusting their characteristics to each particular environment; beginning normal operation after a shutdown or serious error; accounting techniques to keep track of the usage of the system by each job or user; maintaining user information and other sensitive records; and providing appropriate responses to any unusual situations that may occur.

An important consideration in real operating systems, especially those that provide sharing of relatively expensive resources by a large number of users, is to maintain the best possible performance. Chapter 18 discusses how the performance of an OS may be measured or predicted, and how adjustments may be made to tune the system to provide improved performance.

As a class of software development projects, the implementation and maintenance of operating systems raises issues not encountered in many other system types. Many concurrent activities must be managed, making testing extremely difficult. Errors are often unrepeatable. While testing or maintaining an OS, there is no reliable OS to help, and the entire system is often unavailable to other (possibly impatient) users. The unusual problems of OS implementation and maintenance, along with possible solution strategies, are examined in Chapter 19.

Finally, as both computing systems and computer applications continue to mushroom, a need is rapidly increasing to move applications among different systems over the course of their lifetime. The operating system can be a significant help—or a major obstacle—to this process. This goal of portability can be supported by various standards that have been established to provide a more common structure at the interfaces of operating systems, even though the systems themselves may differ. Issues of portability and standards are examined in Chapter 20.

1.9 SPECIAL TYPES OF OPERATING SYSTEMS

A number of special categories of operating systems have evolved to meet specialized needs found in a wide class of applications. Although not representative of most OSs in common use today, it is likely that issues addressed by each of these system types will become increasingly important in the near future. Three important system types described in the text are introduced in this section.

Virtual Machines

An unusual type of multiprogramming system called a **virtual machine monitor** can be implemented on suitable types of computers. A virtual machine monitor provides the ability to run multiple operating systems rather than multiple application programs. Each interleaved process is presented with a **virtual machine** which resembles a real hardware machine with no OS. The virtual machine provides apparent access to all hardware resources, including those normally hidden from application programs. The virtual machine approach provides the ability to run different OS types or versions on the same hardware, or to develop OS improvements while a system is also being used for normal applications. Virtual machine monitors are examined in Chapter 21.

Real-Time Executives

An important class of operating systems called **real-time executives** has evolved to support applications in which timing of real events is critical. The control of aircraft, laboratories, manufacturing, and rapid transit require the measurement of events and/or quantities representing events that require response from a computer system. The failure of the computer to respond in less than a specific maximum amount of time would generally result in a failure in the system being controlled.

Operating systems supporting such time-critical real-time systems must follow certain rules in the implementation of device drivers and programs. Such rules place additional constraints on the designers of real-time operating systems. Real-time systems are examined in Chapter 22.

Distributed Systems

Up to this point, our discussions have focused on systems with one CPU. There are also systems that include two or more CPUs. Some systems in this class share a common memory; these systems, referred to as **multiprocessors,** support multiprogramming in which processes reside in the common memory and may be selected for execution using either CPU.

An operating system that is able to control a group of computers connected by a network is called a **distributed operating system.** These systems must use a variety of complex techniques to share resources among users. Distributed operating systems are a category of rapidly increasing importance. We consider some issues related to these systems in Chapter 23.

1.10 SUMMARY

Operating systems are an integral and necessary part of most computer systems. A computer without an OS is like a bus without a driver.

An operating system is a manager of resources. Resources to be managed include physical resources such as a CPU, memory, and I/O devices, and logical resources such as jobs, processes, files, and service procedures. There are two principal purposes for this resource management: convenient use and controlled sharing.

The OS may also be considered as an extension of the computer hardware, forming a layer between the computer and its users. Users interact with the OS both directly and through their application programs. For the purpose of this text, we define the OS to include any functions that rightly belong to this layer.

While some responsibilities vary from one OS to another, there are certain responsibilities that must be provided by almost all operating systems. These include a user interface, process management, device management, storage management, file systems, job management, error handling, reliability, security, monitoring, and accounting. Each of these responsibilities will be studied in this text.

Some additional issues we need to consider in a study of operating systems include system management, performance, implementation and maintenance, and portability. A number of special types of operating systems are important in some applications, including real-time executives, virtual machines, and distributed systems. These subjects will be considered in later chapters as well.

FOR FURTHER READING

A very large body of literature addresses operating system topics. We will cite references to work that focuses on specific issues in the appropriate chapters of this text. Here we list some books which offer a fairly broad coverage.

Introductory coverage of operating system concepts, especially related to small computers, is given by a number of authors. Examples include Zarella [1979] and Dahmke [1982].

A number of texts provide good descriptive coverage of selected topics in operating systems. Shaw [1974] is an older but classic introduction to many important concepts; an updated version is Bic and Shaw [1988]. Another classic work is Madnick and Donovan [1974], which includes especially good treatment of memory management. Deitel [1984] covers a broad range of topics and includes some useful case studies. Effective presentations of selected topics are given by Finkel [1986], Turner [1986], and Janson [1985]. Broad up-to-date coverage is offered by Tanenbaum [1987] and Milenković [1987].

Several texts emphasize the study of example code and algorithms, including detailed study of specific operating systems. Tanenbaum [1987] and Milenković [1987] both include detailed code for pedagogical operating systems. Another text in this category is Comer [1984]. A good general reference for algorithms suitable for small-computer operating systems is

Kaisler [1983]. Peterson and Silberschatz [1985] gives a comparative study of many useful algorithms. A particularly good study of a specific real operating system, UNIX, is found in Bach [1986].

More rigorous studies of theoretical aspects of OS design, including comparative studies of algorithms, are given in a number of advanced texts. Classics in this category include Coffman and Denning [1973], Brinch Hansen [1973], and Habermann [1976]. A newer entry at this level is Maekawa et al. [1987]. These texts focus on theoretical treatments of concurrent programming, scheduling, virtual memory management, performance analysis, and other selected topics.

IMPORTANT TERMS

accounting
application program
command interface
computing system
concurrent process
controlled sharing
convenient use
device management
distributed operating system
error handling
file management
file system
hardware
hardware environment
interface
interleaved execution
interrupt
job
kernel
logical resource
mechanism
memory management
multiprocessor
multiprogramming system

operating system (OS)
performance
physical resource
policy
process
process management
process scheduling
program interface
real-time executive
reliability
resource
security
session
software
swapping
system management
system program
task
user environment
user interface
virtual machine
virtual machine monitor
virtual memory

REVIEW QUESTIONS

1. Why is an operating system such an important part of most computing systems?

2. In a single sentence, state the principal purpose of an operating system.

3. Give the two principal objectives of resource management by operating systems.

4. List and briefly explain five categories of resources that are managed by a typical general-purpose OS.

5. Identify four types of OS responsibilities other than management of specific resources.

6. List several problems associated with the management of operating systems.

7. Explain two reasons why implementation and maintenance of operating systems may raise difficulties not found in most other software systems.

ASSIGNMENTS

1. Are there any computing environments in which operating systems might *not* be necessary or even appropriate? Explain your answer.

2. Analogies are always imperfect. Discuss the limitations of the bus driver analogy given in this chapter. Propose a different analogy that might overcome some of these limitations.

3. According to the view of the OS boundaries taken by this text, which of the following would be considered part of the OS, and which would not? Justify your answers.

   a. A scheduler that chooses which process to run next.
   b. A program for opening files that is loaded only when needed.
   c. A loader for application programs.
   d. A Pascal compiler.
   e. A translator for a "job control language" that describes jobs to the operating system.
   f. An interpreter for commands typed at a terminal.
   g. A text editor.
   h. A database management system.

      i. A login program that checks the authorization of those attempting to use the computer.

      j. A mathematical subroutine library.

4. In your experience with computer use, under what circumstances have you found it necessary or helpful to think of the operating system as a separate part of the total computer system? Explain.

5. For each of the following types of OS, identify some responsibilities that would probably not be important, and some that would be especially important:

      a. A small personal computer that runs only one program at a time.

      b. A computer embedded within an aircraft.

      c. A large, expensive computer that accepts work only in batches and returns results at a later time.

      d. A virtual machine monitor.

History of Operating Systems

History of Operating Systems

2.1 INTRODUCTION

To gain an effective understanding of the concepts and structures of today's operating systems, it is important to review the lessons we have learned through operating systems of the past. However, describing the complete history of operating systems would be lengthy and difficult. We will focus on the origins of concepts that have had a significant influence on the systems that followed. Many of these concepts were introduced in Chapter 1; most of them will be examined in detail in the remainder of this book.

A number of specific operating systems of historical or current importance are introduced in this chapter. Many of these are used for specific examples throughout the text. To provide a perspective on the evolution of these systems and concepts, a brief chronology is presented in Figure 2–1. This chart shows the dates of first appearance for most of the systems and concepts we will discuss.

The first step in understanding the role of operating systems is to recognize the problems that existed in computer use before operating systems were developed. In this chapter, we will explore the computing process in such an environment. The remaining chapters explain the development of important categories of operating systems, in roughly chronological order beginning with the earliest I/O supervisors, proceeding through complex OSs for large and small computers, and concluding with operating systems for personal computers and those serving specialized needs and applications, including distributed environments that are of increasing importance today.

The evolution of operating systems has proceeded in cycles. Three cycles are especially evident, corresponding to the three main categories of computers that have evolved: large **mainframe** computers, smaller and less expensive **minicomputers,** and the newest and smallest **microcomputers,** which provide a complete CPU on a few low-cost integrated circuits.

To some degree, operating systems have evolved independently for each of these categories. The earliest machines had no operating systems and had to be programmed manually. The first OSs for each category served a single user, provided limited services, had little or no file storage, and were equipped with slow and unreliable I/O devices. Later operating systems have become much more sophisticated, managing large memory spaces, supporting a full range of I/O devices, and providing service for large numbers of interactive users. This evolutionary cycle, which has repeated three times, is illustrated in Figure 2–2. Each cycle has proceeded markedly faster than the last, and operating systems for the smallest computers now often seem to outperform many of their larger but older siblings.

The cycle of evolution is predominantly market-driven; computer users always want more for less. The result has been continuing pressure to develop ever more powerful operating systems for similar cost, or to greatly reduce the cost, which may be the beginning of a new evolutionary cycle.

Throughout your study, observe the problems that existed to motivate each new OS concept, and note how newer operating systems have been influenced, for better or worse, by those that have gone before.

2.2 LIVING WITHOUT AN OPERATING SYSTEM

Programming with Lights and Switches

Many of today's young computer users find it difficult to imagine how early computers were programmed with no operating system. Others—more seasoned by experience, to whom the term "young" no longer applies (like the authors of this book)—remember how it used to be. Our memories are of hours spent entering programs in binary form, word by word, using switches on the computer's front panel.

In this type of programming environment, we first entered the starting address for a sequence of data by setting a row of switches and pressing a button. After that, we had to enter each data word in the sequence in the same way. We checked the data by again setting a starting address and reading a sequence of words in binary form from a row of lights. If errors were made, we had to repeat the same procedure for corrections. If a single instruction had to be added to an existing sequence, we sometimes needed to enter dozens of instructions again. This cumbersome method of programming is illustrated in Figure 2–3.

Debugging of such programs was done without any operating systems or software tools. If necessary, programs could be made to execute one

Figure 2-1 Evolution of Operating Systems and Concepts

DATE	SYSTEMS	CONCEPTS
1950	IOS for 701 GM/NAA system for 704	First operating systems I/O supervision Job sequencing
1955	SHARE OS	Assembly language support User-driven design
	FORTRAN Monitor System	High-level language support
	SAGE	Real-time response
	SABRE	Transaction processing
1960	TOS	Tape I/O & storage
	IBSYS	Disk OS
	DOS	System files Improved I/O control Job control Serial batch processing
	ATLAS	Interrupts System calls Virtual memory
1965	MCP/5000	Batch multiprogramming
	OS/MFT OS/MVT	Spooling
	CTSS TOPS-10	Timesharing
	DTSS	Computing for the masses
	DDP-116 IOS OS/8 for PDP-8	First minicomputer OSs
	MULTICS	Segmented virtual memory Dynamic linking Hierarchical file system I/O redirection Device independence Protection rings OS written in high-level language
	T.H.E.	Hierarchical structure Semaphores Deadlock avoidance

Figure 2–1 Evolution of Operating Systems and Concepts (Continued)

DATE	SYSTEMS	CONCEPTS
1970	TENEX	Abstract machines Improved file systems Improved user interfaces
	TSS/8	Timesharing for minis
	RSX/15	Real-time laboratory control
	CP/CMS VM/370	Virtual machines
	RT-11 RSTS RSX-11	OS family for PDP-11
	UNIX	Designed by and for researchers Cheap processes Filters and pipes Replaceable shell New user interface ideas New file system ideas Portability
1975	CP/M	First microcomputer OS
	MVS	Virtual memory for IBM 370
	VMS	Multiple-use support for VAX
	MS-DOS	Improved OS for micros
	Xerox ALTO & STAR	Professional workstations Icons and mouse
1980	PC-DOS	MS-DOS for IBM micros
	Concurrent DOS	Multiuser OS for micros
	NSW & RSEXEC	Network operating systems
	CPM/NET & others	Networking for micros
	Macintosh	Affordable graphics workstation
	PICK	Integral database system
	VRTX	Portable real-time OS
	S1	Building block OS
1985	SUN NFS	Network File sharing
	LOCUS	Distributed transparent OS
	OS/2	Concurrency and extended features for micros

Figure 2-2 Repeated Cycles in Operating System Evolution

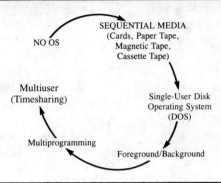

Figure 2-3 Binary Entry of Programs

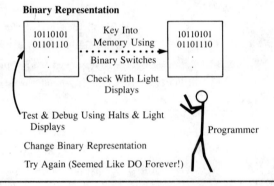

instruction at a time by repeatedly pressing a button. Lights on the front panel displayed the contents of selected registers or memory locations while the program was halted. These displays were studied to discover errors in the program.

While such tedious input and debugging was going on, each programmer necessarily had complete control of the computer. The term "programmer" is appropriate here; no one but trained programmers could possibly use a computer directly. Time was allocated by an **open shop** approach. Programmers signed up for a period of time, and had exclusive use of the computer for that period. Even if the programmer spent much of the time thinking about what to do next, no other programmer could use the computer in the meantime.

Use of Punched Cards

Gradually the use of lights and switches was supplemented by simple input/output devices. Typewriters were attached to the computer, allowing typing of certain input data and printing of output. **Punched cards** provided a medium in which large quantities of information could be prepared in advance and stored for later use. These cards, used with business equipment long before the first electronic computers appeared, were made of stiff paper with information encoded in the form of punched holes. As shown in Figure 2–4, a large deck of punched cards could be loaded into a card reader, which would automatically read, at high speed, the information they contained. Data and instructions for a large program could be encoded into a deck of cards using a separate, typewriter-like "keypunch" device. This information could then be loaded into successive memory locations by pushing a single button. In addition, programs already loaded and running could read data from additional cards.

Figure 2–4 Programming with Punched Cards

Punch

Reader

Early computer systems based on punched cards were further assisted by the development of assembler programs. With assemblers available, other programs could be written in a readable assembly language instead of octal or binary machine language, then translated to machine language by the assembler. Because of the assembly process, though, operation became more complex. First, the assembler itself had to be loaded from cards. The assembler would then run, reading the programmer's **source deck** of cards as its data and producing a translated **object deck** as output. The object deck was then loaded into the computer, and the program could finally be executed.

In some cases, object decks had to be combined with support subroutines before execution. These decks were merged in an additional step by a **linker** program. Assemblers and linkers were the first system programs.

To assist in the management of this process, cards containing system programs were color-coded. The assembler might be pink, the linker yellow, and so on. A special loader card was placed between decks to prepare the system to accept the next program.

A typical sequence of steps involved in processing a program using a card-based system is listed in Figure 2–5. This process appears cumbersome to a modern observer, but it represented a great advancement over entering programs manually in machine language.

Figure 2–5 Sequence of Operation for a Card-based System

LOAD THE LOADER (white deck)

LOAD ASSEMBLER (red deck)

READ PROGRAM (your choice of color)

READ PROGRAM AGAIN (pass two)

PUNCH OBJECT DECK (how about pink?)

LOAD LOADER (white deck again)

LOAD LINKER (green deck)

READ OBJECT DECK (pink deck)

READ LIBRARY ROUTINES (mixed colors)

PUNCH LOADABLE PROGRAM (blue if you like)

LOAD LOADER (white deck, one more time)

LOAD EXECUTABLE PROGRAM DECK (blue deck)

RUN PROGRAM (finally!)

Tapes and Operators

Although the use of punched cards improved the effectiveness of the programming process, computer use continued to be scheduled on an open shop basis. Clearly, these early computers were not being used efficiently; this was a serious problem. Computers were very expensive in the 1950s, and there were very few available. To make more effective use of a very valuable resource, better solutions had to be found.

One improvement became available with the advent of magnetic tape storage. Using machines separate from the computer, programs and data could be transferred from cards to tape. The tapes were then mounted on the computer itself to supply input and receive output. One tape could hold the same amount of data as thousands of cards, and could be processed much faster. This card-to-tape transfer process eventually led to the idea of using separate, simpler computers attached directly to the main computer to manage I/O devices.

A second improvement was to hire trained operators to interact directly with the computer. These operators were supplied in advance with the cards or tapes to be used by a series of programmers. They became adept at loading cards, mounting tapes, and starting the execution of programs. When a program completed, they could rapidly collect its output and start the next one. If anything unusual had to be done, though, the operator required instructions. Frequently it was necessary for the operator to call the programmer when his job was ready to be run, so the programmer could be present to deal with special situations [Auslander et al. 1981].

The use of operators sped things up, but not enough. There was still plenty of idle time, and system managers began to think about automating the operator. If the cards required for a series of jobs could be "stacked" in the card reader or on a tape, as was becoming common, perhaps a "supervisory program" could be devised that would wait in a corner of the memory while one job ran, and then proceed to load the next one. Such a method should improve efficiency, at least as long as programs behaved properly and no special problems arose. This was the principle on which the earliest operating systems were based.

2.3 SUPERVISORS AND I/O SYSTEMS

First Ideas

During the early 1950s, dozens of computers were delivered to the offices of major corporations. Chief among these systems were the UNIVAC I and II and the IBM 701 and 704. Although large and very expensive, these computers were becoming cost-effective for the largest organizations.

As the number of computer users grew, it became clear that they could benefit by joining together and sharing their experiences. User groups were organized, and conferences were held to discuss issues of concern to programmers and system managers. High on the list of topics for discussion by these groups was the problem of idle time between jobs. Another problem of concern was the repetitive, difficult work every programmer had to do to write routines that effectively controlled I/O devices.

According to tradition [Steel 1964], the first serious discussion of the idea of writing an operating system, or supervisory program, to address such problems took place in the hotel room of computer pioneer Herb Grosch at the 1953 Eastern Joint Computer Conference. Present at this informal discussion were programmers from major companies that used IBM computers; one company represented was General Motors.

Shortly after this time, what we consider to be the first actual operating system was designed by General Motors for the IBM 701. Called the **Input/Output System,** this small set of code lived in a corner of the 701's memory, providing a common set of procedures to be used for access to input/output devices. In addition, each program (if properly written) branched to this code when finished, and it accepted and loaded the next program [Ryckman 1983].

Spurred by the GM effort, a number of supervisors were developed by users of the 701's successor, the 704. In fact, GM combined with another user, North American Aviation, to produce one of the first 704 systems.

A Common Supervisor

These early individual efforts led to interest in an improved common supervisory system that would enable easier sharing of programs. An IBM user's group, **SHARE,** had already been formed to promote such sharing. In an unusual cooperative effort, members of SHARE developed specifications for a new operating system, and IBM implemented it. The **SHARE Operating System (SOS)** [Shell et al. 1959] provided supervisory control and buffered I/O management for IBM's next computer, the 709. It also provided support for programming in symbolic assembly language.

While the SHARE effort progressed, a separate group of users developed a different supervisor for the 709, based on the GM/NAA OS for the 704. This effort incorporated a translator for IBM's new FORTRAN language. The result was the **FORTRAN Monitor System (FMS),** the first operating system to support programming in a high-level language.

The new supervisory software improved operating speed and automated much of the operators job, but did not make the operator obsolete. Cards and tapes had to be loaded and unloaded frequently. Moreover, operating systems included little or no ability to recover from program errors or other unexpected situations so the operator acted as system monitor.

Real-Time and Transaction Processing

Two additional events during this period initiated the development of classes of special-purpose operating systems, which have since gained major importance. The **SAGE** software system, developed by IBM for the AN/FSQ7 military computer, was used for direct monitoring of military equipment

[Everett et al. 1957]. This was the first **real-time control system,** in which the computer was required to respond to time constraints imposed by external events. A few years later, IBM developed the **SABRE** airline reservation system for American Airlines, the earliest **transaction processing system,** which allowed processing of simple jobs from a large number of remote stations [Jarema & Sussenguth 1981].

2.4 TAPE AND DISK OPERATING SYSTEMS

The introduction of punched cards made the first operating systems possible. The appearance of magnetic tape increased the efficiency of such systems by allowing card input and output to be temporarily stored on tape. Gradually, tapes began to be used for more permanent storage of commonly-used data, such as compilers and other system programs. Important tapes were kept mounted at all times, while others could be changed according to the needs of the program. This strategy provided a rudimentary file storage, and led to a series of **tape operating systems.** Typical examples included TOS/360 for the first S/360 computers, and TOS for the RCA Spectra 70.

The potential for permanent data storage mushroomed with the development of magnetic disks. For the first time, it was possible to keep large amounts of data and programs in permanent storage, and to access this data in any desired order. Tape operating systems gave way to **disk operating systems,** widely known as **DOS.** Management of this data became an important new challenge for the operating system.

The first disk operating systems treated disk files as substitute tapes. For example, files commonly had to be "rewound" before use, even though this was physically meaningless. Eventually, the greater power of disk systems for random access to data was exploited more effectively.

Many new computer manufacturers entered the field during this period with computers featuring larger memories, more instructions, and faster execution. Most of these computers were equipped with disk operating systems. Unlike their predecessors, these newer and much more complex operating systems were developed and distributed by the manufacturers themselves. Significant operating systems that had their birth during this period included ADMIRAL for the Honeywell 1800, EXEC I for the UNIVAC 1107, SCOPE for the Control Data 6000, and the first Master Control Program for the Burroughs 5000. The direct successor to the earlier IBM systems was IBSYS, developed by IBM for the 709 and its much-improved but program-compatible descendant, the 7090.

Early DOS greatly reduced the effort involved in operating and using a computer. Although the disks used by these systems had relatively small capacities by today's standards, the speed of loading both system programs and user programs, and the ease of use, were significant improvements over the earlier card and tape systems. However, cards and tapes were still needed on these systems as a means of original input of information.

An important part of the early disk systems was a **resident loader,** which would load system and user programs into memory, prepare them for execution, and pass control to them. Upon termination, a properly behaved program would pass control to another routine within the operating system, which would prepare to accept the next program.

Each new job was expected to begin with a set of instructions to advise the operating system on the task to be done and tapes or other resources that would be needed. These instructions were written in a special language which came to be known as a **job control language (JCL).** When preparing to accept a new job, the OS would first load a special system routine to read and interpret this JCL and take the necessary actions.

Also included in these DOS systems was an improved **input/output control system (IOCS),** which provided support for the devices attached to each computer. Device support generally took the form of a set of subroutines. For some critical devices such as the disk or typewriter console, the necessary support routines remained in memory at all times. For other devices, the necessary routines could be merged with application programs as needed by the system linker, or loaded directly by the loader.

Figure 2–6 illustrates the sequence of steps for preparing and executing a program using a simple disk operating system. Compare this sequence to that of card-based systems (Figure 2–5). The first step in execution of a new program is reading and analyzing the instructions given in the job control language. Guided by these instructions, the OS next loads and executes the assembler, which reads the input program and produces an object program that is temporarily stored on the disk. Again following instructions from the JCL, the linker is invoked to combine the object program with appropriate library subroutines and produce a load module ready for execution. Finally, the load module is loaded into the main memory, and the application program is executed.

2.5 ATLAS IS BORN

Most of the computers that supported the early DOS systems had very similar traditional designs (a notable exception was the stack-oriented architecture of the Burroughs computers). At Manchester University in England, a very different type of computer was being developed that would have a profound effect on the evolution of operating systems. The **Atlas,** developed jointly

Figure 2-6 Operation of a Disk Operating System

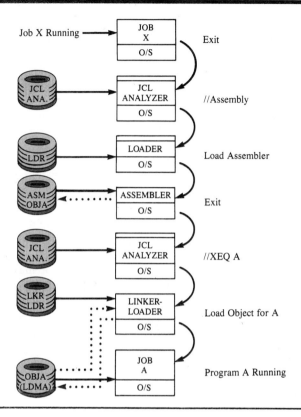

by Manchester University and Ferranti Ltd., became operational around 1961 [Howarth et al. 1961].

Atlas was not a large or fast computer compared to its contemporaries, but its architectural innovations were far ahead of its time. Atlas was the first computer *designed* to support an operating system. This viewpoint led to significant innovations. Atlas introduced the concept of **interrupts,** making it possible for a program in normal operation to be interrupted by an external event, such as completion of an I/O activity. This concept greatly aided the efficient management of I/O concurrent with normal processing. In addition, Atlas provided a special instruction called an **extracode,** which caused a trap to invoke special routines written in software. Although used originally for simple library functions such as math procedures, extracode was the forerunner of the system call instruction used by later computers to request services from the operating system—an instruction which plays a critical role in making multiuser systems possible.

The innovation for which Atlas is best known, however, is its **one-level store.** This novel hardware/software system included all the basic elements of what is now known as virtual memory. By this technique, a large disk or drum storage could be used as an automatic backup for the main memory, allowing programs to effectively make use of a much larger memory than would otherwise be possible.

2.6 BATCH MULTIPROGRAMMING

Early disk operating systems continued the trend of placing direct control of the computer in the hands of operators and system programs, not the individual programmer. Each job was submitted as a whole in the form of a "batch" of cards; for this reason such systems are known as **batch processing systems.** Jobs were processed one at a time, each one finishing completely before a new one was accepted. The operating systems were thus said to use a **batch serial** method of operation.

As the speed of computers increased, the need for maximizing the use of the central processing unit (CPU) became greater. The relative speed of the I/O devices was slow compared to the increased speed of the CPU. Because of this mismatch, there were often periods of time when I/O devices were operating, the program was waiting for the I/O to complete, and the CPU had nothing useful to do. Once again, expensive equipment was being used inefficiently. This problem could be solved only if there were other programs available for running during this idle time.

These observations became the motivation for **batch multiprogramming,** the shared use of the CPU, memory, I/O devices, and other resources of a computer system by more than one program executing in an interleaved manner. With this technique, several user programs were loaded into memory at the same time, if sufficient memory was available. When a running program had to wait for I/O completion or some other event, the CPU could work on one of the other programs.

A pioneer multiprogramming operating system was the **Master Control Program (MCP)** for the Burroughs 5000 [Oliphint 1964]. Building on the Atlas experience, this system used virtual memory techniques to provide sufficient storage for several programs, which could be chosen alternately for execution. Programs were assigned **priorities**—that is, numerical values representing the relative urgency of each program. These priorities influenced the choice of programs to be run. The Burroughs system was unique in many other respects. In particular, both hardware and software were designed to support programs written in high-level languages; *all* user's programs were expected to be written in either ALGOL or COBOL, and translated by special system compilers.

The most significant development in the evolution of batch multi-programming, however, was the announcement of the IBM System/360 family of computers in 1964. Although the 360 itself was not as powerful as some of its contemporaries (including the B5000), IBM's massive commitment to its computers and customers included a large support staff and a family of computer models capable of executing the same programs. This approach enabled customers to start with a small system and expand as needed over a long period of time. It became an important key to IBM's dominance in the large computer industry.

The extensive 360 family of computers was supplied with an equally extensive operating system, **OS/360,** by far the largest software development project ever undertaken at that time. Because of the scope of the project, the operating system was very late in delivery and early versions included hundreds of errors [Brooks 1975]. However, OS/360 and its descendants have survived, along with the S/360 architecture, to become one of the most widely used operating systems of all time [Mealy et al. 1966; Auslander et al. 1981].

One reason for the longevity of this series has been IBM's continuing commitment to compatibility. The 360 series was very different from the earlier 7090 and other models, and many customers were unhappy at the prospect of having to change procedures and rewrite existing software. Since the 360 appeared, all new versions have been designed so that most programs written for older versions could be used unchanged on the newer ones.

The earliest 360s, awaiting completion of a full-featured OS, were supplied with an interim disk operating system, DOS/360, and an early version of OS/360 called PCP. Both of these systems used a batch serial mode of operation.

By 1965, the first of two batch multiprogramming versions of OS/360 appeared. **OS/MFT,** for smaller S/360 models, and the more powerful **OS/MVT** became the dominant operating systems for the 360 architecture.

One feature of the OS/360 series was the introduction of a large and powerful job-control language, known simply as **JCL.** Much could be done with IBM's JCL; however, its use was complex even for simple jobs, and many installations had to employ full-time JCL experts to aid in writing and debugging the JCL for each application.

In order to reduce delays caused by slow input and output devices, batch multiprogramming systems introduced the concept of **spooling.** The term was both a description and an acronym; it stood for Simultaneous Peripheral Operation On-Line. One special program was given the responsibility of reading input jobs from cards or tapes and storing complete copies of them on a disk. This program tried to read jobs as fast as they became available. The operating system then obtained its input rapidly from the fast disk instead of the slower cards and tapes. A similar technique was introduced for output. Information to be printed was initially placed on disk; a spooling program then copied data from the disk to printers or other output devices.

Figure 2–7 presents an overview of the flow of activity for a typical job using a batch multiprogramming OS (in this case, OS/MVT). A job for this system was made up of a series of job steps. Each step specified the program to be run and the data files and/or devices to be used for the job step. Cards were read and temporarily stored in a job queue, where they remained until selected for execution by the job management portion of MVT. Hence, batch processing was central to the operation of these early 360 systems.

Figure 2–7 Overview of a Multiprogramming Batch System

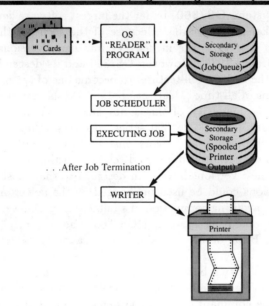

2.7 TIMESHARING SYSTEMS

Although powerful batch operating systems had greatly improved the rate at which work could be done by each computer, users of the new computer systems were not always pleased. In the early days of computing, each programmer had direct control of the computer while his program was running. He was able to observe the progress of the job in detail. If things went wrong, bugs could be located immediately. In many cases, the program could be fixed and allowed to continue its run. With batch processing, this type of interaction was no longer possible.

A more severe problem was the long period of time that elapsed between submission of a job to the operator and results returned to the computer user. This delay was often due to both administrative and technical problems; it was typically several hours and could be as long as several days. Since most jobs had to be run several times before all the errors were corrected, these delays quickly multiplied. The situation was frustrating both to experienced programmers and to new users who wanted to take advantage of the computer for data processing or scientific applications.

Dissatisfaction with the problems of batch computing led many system designers to search for new modes of operation that would restore the advantages of direct interaction with the computer and provide much more immediate results.

The development of disk file systems often made it possible to reduce drastically the amount of direct input needed for a typical job. Large programs and sets of data could initially be prepared and stored in disk files, which could then be edited if necessary by special programs. All system programs now were stored in disk files. Often the information that a programmer had to provide to carry out a job consisted mainly of a few lines of JCL. In such cases, it seemed possible that programmers could type this information on a typewriter attached directly to the computer, and receive at least limited results on the same typewriter. This could relieve many of the frustrations of batch operation, replacing it with a new kind of **interactive computing.**

This attractive idea, however, was not without problems. If interactive computing was carried out by assigning the computer to one user at a time, the computer would be used as inefficiently as in the old open shop arrangements. However, early experience with batch multiprogramming showed that computers could hold several jobs in memory, and divide their time among the various jobs. If the multiprogramming concept could be used to serve a number of programmers at typewriters at the same time, the computer could still be kept busy. In addition, many more programmers might be able to use the computer in a given period of time.

The remaining difficulty was the rate at which the computer would have to switch from job to job. In batch multiprogramming, a switch was made only when the current job reached a stopping point. Often a single job would run for minutes or hours. To support multiple interactive users in a reasonable way, the computer had to be forced to switch from job to job at a much higher rate, a task accomplished by assigning a short time limit, typically one or two seconds, to each job. This limit was called a **time slice** or **time quantum.** A timer was set to interrupt the job automatically when the time was up. Once interrupted, each job had to wait for the others to have a turn before finally receiving more service.

This type of multiuser interactive computing system became known as a **timesharing system** (see Figure 2–8). Timesharing operation was the focus of much of the operating system development in the 1960s and 1970s.

Figure 2–8 Organization of a Timesharing System

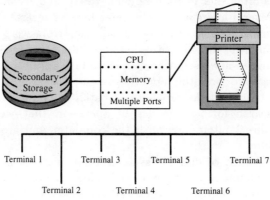

A great many timesharing systems were developed in the early and mid-1960s. Perhaps the first such system was designed by Bolt, Beranek and Newman for the Digital Equipment PDP-1 computer. Another early system that had a significant influence was the **Compatible Timesharing System (CTSS)** developed on a modified IBM 7094 at the Massachusetts Institute of Technology [Crisman et al. 1964]. Originally completed in 1961, CTSS established the effectiveness of the timesharing concept, and also exposed some of its potential problems. CTSS was heavily favored by a large community of users until the mid-1970s.

A noteworthy timesharing system of the mid-1960s was developed by Kemeny and Kurtz [1968] in cooperation with General Electric at Dartmouth, a small liberal arts college in Hanover, New Hampshire. The **Dartmouth Timesharing System (DTSS)** was born of its authors' conviction that computer use should form a part of the education of all liberal arts students. As a further step in making the computer easier to use for nonprofessionals, Kemeny and Kurtz developed the BASIC programming language for use on DTSS. The history of BASIC and DTSS is recounted by the creators in an interesting book [Kemeny & Kurtz 1985]. (They report that DTSS was originally called "Phase II," but that name was discarded because it sounded too much like a bath soap.)

In short order, experimental timesharing systems began appearing for a variety of computer systems. Manufacturers were a little slow to enter the field, but some pursued it vigorously. Digital Equipment Corporation introduced the TOPS-10 timesharing system for its medium-sized PDP-10 computer. IBM produced a virtual memory version of the 360—the 360/67—and began development of TSS/360. Although tremendous effort was expended on this system, which was planned as a likely successor to OS/360, it was never very popular.

Experience with CTSS and similar systems soon showed that timesharing was workable but could lead to serious difficulties. A great deal more time was spent by the operating system in switching between programs. With a large number of users, this switching overhead could leave little time for useful work. Computers with better performance, and carefully designed supervisors, were needed. In addition, the simultaneous use of files and other resources created a need to protect users from each other. An error in one program could damage data of many users and bring the system to a halt. The dangers of deliberate misuse of one user's programs and data by other users was also beginning to be realized.

These problems were studied closely by the members of the computer research group at MIT, Project MAC. They determined that both a new operating system design and an improved computer design were required. In 1964 a project was launched jointly by MIT, AT&T/Bell Laboratories, and General Electric to develop a next-generation successor to CTSS. The new system was envisioned as a "computing utility," which would make the power of computers as accessible to a large community as other utilities, such as electric power or telephone service. The result of this effort was the **MULTICS** operating system.

MULTICS was one of the largest and most ambitious operating systems ever attempted. It explored a wide range of new concepts, including segmented virtual memory, linking and loading segments on demand, a novel method of resource protection, a hierarchical file system, device independence, I/O redirection, and a powerful user interface [Brown et al. 1984]. Along with the software development for MULTICS, extensive hardware development was carried out in the form of modifications to the GE 635 computer. These modifications were designed to support new ideas in virtual memory management and in protecting access to resources. The resulting computer was called the GE 645. MULTICS became operational as the 1960s drew to a close.

MULTICS is known especially for its "rings of protection" scheme, its segmentation system that treated files and main memory uniformly, and for being the first major operating system written almost entirely in a high-level language (PL/I). MULTICS is described in detail in a book by Organick [1972]. Although it did not fully meet its original goals, the system made significant contributions to computer and operating system technology. MULTICS was later acquired by Honeywell, along with GE's line of computers, and is still in use in a number of sites.

2.8 ABSTRACT AND VIRTUAL MACHINES

In the late 1960s, an operating system was developed as a research project by a team led by Edsgar Dijkstra at the Technische Hoogeschool (Technological University) in Eindhoven, Holland. The operating system was named **T.H.E.** [Dijkstra 1968; McKeag et al. 1976] for the Dutch initials of the University. It was a modest batch multiprogramming OS with no user file storage, and requiring all programs to be processed by the system's ALGOL compiler. T.H.E. would have a profound effect on the structure of all operating systems to follow.

The principal contributions of T.H.E. lay in its treatment of interacting processes and in its hierarchical structure. Because it causes competition for the use of resources, the presence of multiple processes in simultaneous execution in a multiprogrammed system can lead to a variety of problems. T.H.E. built the foundation for solving these problems, and introduced a number of ideas that are still widely used today. Among them are some effective approaches to the problem of deadlock and the synchronization mechanism of semaphores.

An equally important contribution was made by T.H.E. in the form of a method for structuring the OS itself. The operating system had a hierarchical structure. Its components formed a series of layers, each one interacting only with the layers above and below. The first layer, for example, managed timers, interrupts, and process scheduling, while the second layer provided virtual memory. Each layer could be said to form an **abstract machine**—that is, an apparent extension of the real machine. All components of the OS above the second layer, as well as application programs, could treat process management and virtual memory as "built-in" features of the machine itself. Moreover, once the lowest layers were correctly implemented, they could be relied on in developing and testing higher layers. Problems at these outer layers could not affect the lower-level software.

A number of hierarchically structured operating systems followed soon after T.H.E. One that made a number of important contributions was **TENEX,** developed in the early 1970s at Bolt, Beranek and Newman for the PDP-10 [Bobrow et al. 1972]. Following the tradition of earlier BBN systems, TENEX was a timesharing OS, supporting a well-designed user interface and file system. Its ideas in these two areas have directly influenced later Digital Equipment operating systems for the PDP-10 and PDP-11.

TENEX provided an abstract machine structure including the file system, extended machine instructions, multiple processes for each user, and virtual memory (although the PDP-10 required hardware extensions to support this feature). It called this structure, with some justification, a "virtual machine," but that term has now been focused more narrowly on a special type of abstract machine that was being quietly developed in the laboratories of IBM.

Beginning in the mid-1960s, a series of experimental systems were developed at IBM's research center in Cambridge, Massachusetts. These systems drew on the experience of CTSS at nearby MIT to create a timesharing system most useful for internal development work by IBM engineers. Researchers were beginning to explore virtual memory concepts, and IBM had produced an experimental virtual memory system, the M44/44X, at another research center in New York. The new system was designed to incorporate both timesharing and virtual memory.

The OS developed at Cambridge was called **CP/CMS** to reflect its two parts. CP stood for Control Program, while CMS could be interpreted as either Cambridge Monitor System or Conversational Monitor System. Its objective was to support all of the research and development activities of IBM engineers at Cambridge; one of these activities was operating systems research. To allow OS work to be timeshared with other activities required a radical view of the services provided by the "abstract machine" to each user. It would have to be a **virtual machine** in the truest sense, providing apparent access to all of the machine features required by an operating system. Just as virtual memory could provide each user with the illusion of a complete private virtual address space, a virtual machine must extend this illusion to a private CPU and possibly I/O devices as well.

The first CP/CMS system at Cambridge ran on a modified S/360 model 40, and was designated CP/40. Shortly afterwards, IBM developed the model 67 with virtual memory support, and CP/40 was succeeded by CP/67. When the System 370, successor to the 360 family, was introduced in the early 1970s, the experimental OS at Cambridge was transferred to the new environment and christened VM/370, or Virtual Machine for the 370. At this time it became an official product of IBM.

2.9 MINICOMPUTER OPERATING SYSTEMS

Ever since the early IBM and UNIVAC systems entered the commercial world in the 1950s, interest blossomed in developing computers that were smaller and cheaper, and thus more accessible to many potential users. As early as 1955 several "small-scale" computers were on the market, moderately priced at under $50,000 [Koudela 1973]. These computers, which included the Burroughs E-101, Bendix G-15, and Librascope LGP-30, were large machines using bulky, unreliable vacuum tubes. They were extremely slow, with several milliseconds required for an arithmetic operation. Their memories were limited to a few thousand words at most, and they had very limited instruction sets. They were programmed in machine language, with no operating systems of any type. Still, some useful software libraries were developed for the small-scale machines, and the LGP-30 was useful enough to support early work leading to the development of BASIC and DTSS at Dartmouth.

The early 1960s saw an expansion of the small-computer field to include machines like the CDC-160 and the IBM-1620. These were the first small computers that took advantage of the new solid-state technology to greatly reduce their size and increase reliability. Both data and instructions on the CDC-160 were limited to 12 bits in length. To address a reasonable amount of memory with such small instructions, relative and indirect addressing were introduced. A rich set of addressing modes has been a characteristic of minicomputers since this time.

Digital Equipment Corporation (DEC), a new player in the field in the early 1970s, introduced the PDP-1, followed in short order by several more models in the PDP series. The 12-bit PDP-8, priced under $18,000, opened up the minicomputer field in earnest and became one of the best-selling computers of all time. The PDP-8 introduced a number of features important for real-time applications, including interrupts, a clock, and direct memory access for high-speed I/O devices. These features gave it the ability to successfully control real-time devices. Laboratory and process control became an important application area for this and many later minicomputers.

Early minicomputers were supplied with limited system software, and there was at first little concept of an operating system. Programming style followed an evolution quite similar to that of the larger computers, with early interaction performed using front panel switches and display lights. Again, the most common medium that emerged for program and data storage was punched paper, but the minicomputer environment favored long rolls of punched-paper tape. Although less convenient and harder to handle than cards, paper tape could be read and punched with much less expensive equipment.

Soon after the appearance of the PDP-8, a new round of minicomputer systems was introduced including the DDP-116 from Computer Control Company (later Honeywell), The DATA-620 from Data Machines, Inc. (later Varian), and the IBM 1800 and 1130. These were 16-bit architectures featuring such innovations as multiple accumulators, vectored priority interrupts, and index registers. Some of these machines were outfitted with magnetic tapes and disks.

The beginnings of a minicomputer operating system appeared with the DDP-116 "Input/Output Selector," paralleling the early Input/Output System for the IBM 701. Soon after, IBM introduced a disk operating system for the 1800. Many of these early minicomputer systems had names like "keyboard monitor" and "real-time monitor." They provided an interactive user interface for a single user, and ran one program at a time. Their principal roles were seen as accepting simple commands from a teletype console, loading and running programs from a disk or tape file system, and perhaps monitoring the operation of real-time laboratory devices.

The popular PDP-8 minicomputer was originally supplied only with paper tape-based software. However, the development by DEC of a low-cost, bidirectional tape system (DECtape) made limited monitors and operating systems possible. Several OSs then appeared for the PDP-8, including OS/8, a single-user monitor, and TSS/8, which provided a limited form of timesharing. Digital's large-scale PDP-10 had its TOPS-10 OS, and the medium-sized PDP-9 and PDP-15 were provided with both single-user monitors and an experimental real-time OS, RSX-15 [Krejci 1971].

In 1970 DEC introduced the PDP-11 minicomputer series. Adopting the strategy that IBM found so successful for its 360, DEC planned the PDP-11 as a family of compatible models with varying size and performance. This strategy was equally successful for the PDP-11 series. By the early 1970s, no fewer than three important operating systems were available for the PDP-11: a clean and simple single-user OS (RT-11), a timesharing system (RSTS), and a real-time executive (RSX-11).

RT-11 was based primarily on OS-8 but used important ideas from TOPS-10 and TENEX, especially in its command interface and file system. Designed to serve a single user, RT-11 normally executed only one program at a time. However, a limited form of multiprogramming was available in the **foreground/background** version of RT-11. This OS allowed one process currently not communicating with the terminal, such as a long compilation, to continue in the "background" while the user interacted with a different "foreground" program.

Although the "RT" in RT-11 stands for "real time," the true real-time executive for the PDP-11 was **RSX-11,** derived from RSX-15. RSX-11 was the most advanced of the PDP-11 operating systems, supporting a powerful command language and file system, memory management, and multiprogramming of a number of distinct programs, which RSX-11 calls "tasks." RSX-11 became the principal ancestor of the powerful operating system that would appear with the next generation of DEC computers.

2.10 THE ORIGINS OF UNIX

Around 1970, Bell Labs began to wind down its involvement in the MULTICS project. Two researchers who had been active on that project, Ken Thompson and Dennis Ritchie were ready to move on to other projects in their software research group. However, they were becoming very dissatisfied with the capabilities of the operating systems available for the minicomputers in their lab. Convinced that there was a better way, Thompson set about to design a new single-user OS more suited to his own research needs. Ritchie soon joined him in this effort. Their design drew upon concepts from their MULTICS experience. The result was an operating system for the DEC PDP-7, which the designers christened **UNIX** [Ritchie & Thompson 1974; Ritchie 1980].

The environment in which UNIX was developed was unique. The Bell engineers were a research group, with wide freedom to pursue projects of their own choosing. UNIX was not an official company project, and Thompson and Ritchie had no requirements to adhere to except their own needs.

The operating system that emerged from this effort was quite different from most that preceded it. Running on the limited PDP-7 hardware, UNIX provided its creators with the effective working environment that MULTICS had so far failed to deliver. It became widely used within Bell Laboratories, and was reimplemented on the PDP-11 when that newer system became available.

Key aspects of the UNIX environment were a simple yet powerful file system with a hierarchical system of directories, and a novel command interface called the shell. The file system treated I/O devices as special cases of files, and the shell made it possible to direct the output produced by any command to any selected file or device. Similarly, input could be taken from any source in response to a shell command.

Although the earliest UNIX systems supported only a single user, the work of one user could be carried out by multiple concurrent processes. The system and the shell supported an effective mechanism for communication between processes, in which an output stream produced by one process could become the input stream of another.

These features made possible some new styles of operation. For example, one process might manage an interactive editing session while another process printed a file and yet another carried out a time-consuming sort or compilation. A selective directory listing might become input to a separate command, identifying files to be printed or processed in some particular way. Although many of the UNIX concepts had been present in predecessors such as MULTICS, CTSS and DTSS, UNIX was an improvement on the previous ideas and tied them together in simple and effective ways.

The first versions of UNIX were written in assembly language. The designers were accustomed to the more sophisticated PL/I language used to implement MULTICS. However, PL/I was unavailable on the PDP computers, and the available languages were unsatisfactory for system programming. Ritchie addressed this problem by creating a new language, simply called "C." C was based on an earlier experimental language "B," which in turn was derived from BCPL. A C compiler for the PDP-11 was developed, and eventually almost all of UNIX was rewritten in C.

UNIX was widely used inside Bell Laboratories, but it did not become an official product for many years. As the parent company of Bell, AT&T was prevented by antitrust regulations from selling software. Instead, UNIX became available for a nominal cost to universities, and eventually to independent developers who were able to convert it to a commercial product. During this period the UNIX system, *complete with source code,* became familiar to a large community of students and researchers. Several enhanced versions were developed, especially at the University of California at Berkeley. The widespread use of UNIX at universities created a demand for commercial versions. UNIX was one of the first operating systems to be distributed separately from the computer system on which it ran; it was eventually implemented on many different computers, becoming one of the first portable operating systems.

2.11 OPERATING SYSTEMS FOR MICROS

Solid-state electronics was the technology that drove the steady improvement and miniaturization of computer components. Starting with the invention of transistors to replace bulky and unreliable vacuum tubes, solid-state advances allowed increasingly complex circuits to be created on small, inexpensive integrated circuit microprocessors, or "chips." The economics of this technology were remarkable: although steady improvements allowed more and more complexity on each chip, the cost of producing the chip did not substantially increase.

This evolution was spurred in the late 1960s by the rise of the pocket calculator. These small devices had many of the elements of complete computers. They could perform many complex calculations, store data, and even execute simple programs. With price tags of a few hundred dollars, they were enormously popular, and there was great competition to further increase their capabilities and decrease their costs by refining integrated circuit technology.

As calculators became increasingly sophisticated, the complexity of the special-purpose chips used to implement them was becoming unmanageable. The first developer to see the possible advantages of developing a more systematic, general-purpose chip for calculators was Intel Corporation. In 1971 Intel announced the 4004, implementing a complete 4-bit CPU on a few circuit chips. Although this first CPU had very limited capabilities, it was adequate for use in calculators; researchers envisioned a few other applications as well. The 4004 was followed shortly by a more powerful 8-bit version, the 8008 [Noyce & Hoff 1981].

After two years of experience with the 8008, Intel released the much-improved 8080. This chip became very widely adopted as the potential of microprocessors became apparent to more and more users. Aided by the heavy demand, the cost of the 8080 dropped to a few dollars per chip. Its architecture has been a major influence on later Intel CPUs.

Other manufacturers soon followed with devices such as Zilog's Z-80, Motorola's 6800, and MOS Technology's 6502. The age of the **microprocessor,** or "CPU-on-a-chip," had arrived.

Intel and other microprocessor developers had little experience with actual computers, and did not consider themselves in the computer business. Others, though, were quick to see the potential of developing complete small-computer systems based on microprocessor chips. If the great cost reductions in CPUs could be matched by similar reductions for memories and other system components, it would be possible to develop **microcomputers** so small and inexpensive that they could be used and afforded by individuals.

As recounted by Freiberger and Swaine [1984], the earliest microcomputers were built by hobbyists. Their experiments led to commercial. ventures by pioneer companies like MITS and Imsai. Although many of the early microcomputer companies did not survive, a few found the right combination of good design and sound business decisions. One well-known survivor was Apple, a company originating from the work of two unconventional young computer hobbyists. Apple made use of 6502 CPUs in novel, self-contained personal computers featuring effective color graphics, sound, and game-playing capabilities. The Apple II became extremely popular.

Computer development had also been undertaken by a few more established companies, notably Tandy (Radio Shack) and Heath. These companies had the advantage of being secure enough to deal with occasional setbacks. As the field began to mature, the future of the microcomputer was assured by the announcement of a personal computer by the biggest survivor of all: IBM.

Like the mainframes and minicomputers before them, the very early microcomputers were programmed with front-panel lights and switches. These computers were equipped with a few thousand bytes of memory and primitive forms of input and output. However, the widespread acceptance of micros created a high demand for better memories and improved, low-cost I/O devices. To a large degree, this demand was fulfilled as the 1970s progressed. Main memories of 64K bytes or more became available at costs of a few cents a bit. The cost of video terminals and printers steadily declined, and their capabilities improved. Printers also decreased greatly in size and became easier to maintain. Affordable storage devices were developed, based first on simple audio cassette tapes and then on the very popular floppy disks.

The new microcomputers thus formed the center of the third evolutionary spiral, following mainframes and minicomputers. Each evolution followed a somewhat similar path, and each moved much more rapidly than the one before. The characteristics of typical systems in each of these families (at similar stages in their evolution) are compared in Figure 2–9.

In spite of the rapid advance in microcomputer hardware, system software was somewhat slow to develop. Simple loaders were sometimes provided in read-only memory, capable of reading data from cassette tapes. Implementations of Dartmouth's already popular BASIC language became common. Microcomputers were seen largely as toys, however, and true large-computer

Figure 2–9 Mainframes, Minicomputers, and Microcomputers

	MAINFRAMES	MINIS	MICROS
cost (thousands of dollars)	500 to 5000	5 to 25	1 to 5
memory size (K bytes)	1000 to 10000	50 to 500	50 to 200
instructions per second (thousands)	1000	250	100 to 250
number of simultaneous users	10 to 200	1 to 20	1 to 4
storage devices	large disks and tapes	small disks and tapes	tape cassettes, floppy disks
I/O devices	card readers and punches, magnetic tape, high-speed printers	paper tape readers and punches, small terminals and printers, laboratory sensors and controllers	cassette tapes and floppy disks, small terminals and printers, embedded sensors and controllers

ideas like operating systems seemed beyond the scope of their tiny CPUs.

This situation began to change with the work of Gary Kildall at Intel. Working as a consultant to develop software for the 8008 microprocessor (predecessor to the 8080), Kildall developed a compiler for a simplified version of the programming language PL/I. The new language was called PL/M, or Programming Language for Microprocessors. It was designed for writing microprocessor system software. To assist in this development he also created a rudimentary operating system, called Control Program for Microprocessors, or **CP/M**. This single-user operating system for the 8080 included a simple interactive command interface, basic I/O device management, and a floppy disk-based file system. Intel was not interested in CP/M, and Kildall obtained the rights to distribute it himself. With his wife he formed a company called Digital Research, and CP/M became its first and most successful product [Freiberger & Swaine 1984].

CP/M was the first microprocessor operating system and remained the dominant one for a number of years. Although some microcomputer companies, such as Apple and Tandy, developed their own proprietary operating systems, most offered versions of CP/M as well.

2.12 LARGE SYSTEMS CARRY ON

The microprocessor began a revolution, but during the 1970s larger computer systems continued to fill an important role in supplying high-performance batch and timesharing services to a wide community of users. The future of minicomputers, though, was somewhat open to question. The DEC PDP-11 had been widely accepted when it first appeared; but its limitations were becoming increasingly evident, especially its 64K byte address space. Digital had been able to dominate its competitors in the minicomputer field, but new microprocessors appearing with 16-bit addresses and data paths competed strongly with the PDP-11's capabilities. DEC responded with the introduction of a "superminicomputer" as successor to the PDP-11, which was called the VAX. The VAX architecture included a very large and powerful set of instructions and the ability to address over four billion bytes. Closely tuned to the VAX design was the **VAX/VMS** operating system. A number of VAX CPU instructions, such as some that directly manage queues, were designed especially to support the needs of VMS. VMS provided an extensive assortment of system services, file management techniques, and associated system programs that placed it second perhaps only to OS/360 in its size, scope and complexity [Kenah & Bate 1984].

The VAX architecture became very widely used, but acceptance of VMS as the VAX operating system was not universal. UNIX and its users were rapidly outgrowing the PDP-11, and the VAX was seen as a natural new host for this OS as well. By 1978 UNIX had been implemented on the VAX and greatly enhanced by researchers at the University of California at Berkeley.

In the meantime, IBM remained dominant in mainframe computers, although alternative systems from Burroughs, Control Data, and a few other companies maintained a limited following. With superminis like VAX challenging the low-performance systems in its series, IBM placed emphasis on its high-performance systems. The S/370 series had added virtual memory capability to the aging 360 architecture. VM/370 offered a novel mechanism for exploiting the 370, but VM served a specialized purpose and was not a complete operating system for general use. The mainstream operating systems for IBM hardware evolved instead from OS/MFT and OS/MVT. The most important successor to these popular systems became known as **OS/MVS** (Multiple Virtual Spaces).

OS/MVS supported an address space of up to 16 million bytes for each process in the system, and was a thorough redesign and updating of MVT for timesharing, based on the earlier timesharing option (TSO) developed for MVT. It continued to support most MVT files and programs. MVS offered effective control for the newer and larger 370 successors [Auslander et al. 1981].

2.13 PERSONAL COMPUTERS AND WORKSTATIONS

In 1970 Xerox Corporation, which had already purchased a small mini-computer company, opened a research facility in California called the Palo Alto Research Center (PARC). Its charter was to carry on pure research at the frontiers of technology; the results of this research had a profound effect on computer hardware and software design.

One of the more striking products of the PARC research was a small computer called the Alto. Designed for personal use by professionals, the Alto introduced a new style of communication between the computer and its user. As an alternative to typing commands at a keyboard and receiving results as text displayed on a screen, Alto users could instruct their system by selecting phrases or graphical symbols displayed on the screen by moving a small device called a "mouse." The Alto provided very high performance for its size and sophisticated graphics.

The Alto was expensive, and it was not a microcomputer. Intel's 8008 was still a novelty as the Alto was being developed. Instead, Alto was described as a professional **workstation** that became a model for many microcomputers that followed.

Alto was not a commercial product, but it was sold to a number of government agencies and inspired other Xerox products that appeared during the late 1970s, including the Star. The Star featured a large display with an Alto-style graphical user interface. It was designed for information-handling tasks in business offices, and was intended to be easy to use by office workers who might be uncomfortable with other types of computers. The Star, an office automation system, was the heart of Xerox's planned "office of the future."

The Xerox Star was expensive and not very successful. But system developers began thinking about this new style of user interaction. Similar products soon appeared, aiming for similar or enhanced capabilities at lower costs. One developer aiming for high-performance was Sun, which produced a series of expensive, sophisticated workstations aimed at professional users, such as scientists and engineers. Apple was also paying attention to the Alto and Star, and this led to the introduction of Apple's Lisa computer in the early 1980s. The world was not quite ready for Lisa, but it was more than ready for Apple's next version, the Macintosh, released in 1984. Taking advantage of the newest microprocessor technology, the Macintosh was by far the lowest-cost computer to follow in the Alto tradition. It provided a complete, self-contained workstation with impressive capabilities for about $2,000. The Apple Macintosh became a great success.

The model of a single-user workstation, responsive to the directions of its user, led to a different conception of operating system design. The OS was long considered the master of the computer system; now it needed to become the servant of its users. This led to the concept of an **open operating system,** one which does not place barriers between application programs and the OS itself. The focus of this type of operating system is on convenience, not control. The OS provides services as desired, but does not interfere with a program. The OS may be viewed as little more than a collection of subprograms. An open operating system does not get in the way of its users, but it may make programs more vulnerable if errors occur.

2.14 NETWORKS AND DISTRIBUTED SYSTEMS

The idea of direct communication among computers was an attractive goal of researchers for many years. Such communication could make information from one system available quickly to another, without manual transfer or transcription. Various types of data communication equipment had been developed by the 1960s, allowing information to be transmitted long distances in digital form between computers connected by wires, or even temporarily linked by telephone lines.

Long-distance data transmission, though, is very prone to errors, and sophisticated techniques were needed to cope with these problems and provide reliable communication in spite of them. In the early 1970s the Defense Department, through its Advanced Research Projects Agency (DARPA), provided an important stimulus to solving these problems by setting up a dedicated computer network, the ARPANET, to connect computers throughout the country that were performing DARPA research. The ARPANET used a combination of hardware and software techniques to provide reliable and efficient data transfer among its attached computers.

Each computer linked on the ARPANET had its own operating system. Communication was viewed as a special I/O activity. A user wanting to transfer data to or from a remote computer had to understand the names and formats required by that computer, as well as have the proper authorization for the transfer. ARPANET allowed for direct interactive use of remote computers as well, but accounts, log-in procedures, and other activities were the responsibility of individual users.

In an effort to allow users to treat the network more as a unified set of resources, several experimental **network operating systems** were developed. One example was known as the National Software Works [Millstein 1977], a project based on a central database of user information maintained at a master site on the network. Users were able to work through this site to gain access to any other resource participating in the system. Although the goals of these network operating systems were important ones, the procedures were still cumbersome, and the systems themselves were not widely accepted.

The work at Xerox PARC had also laid the groundwork for a different type of network. With the rise in popularity of personal computers and workstations, many small computers were appearing within a single company or university campus. The new type of network was designed to provide more effective connection of a group of computers and related devices located within a limited area. Because the distance was not great, data transfer could be supported at a much higher rate than with conventional networks. These networks were called Local Area Networks, or LANs, and the specific network strategy developed at PARC was called Ethernet. A new computing environment was emerging, as shown in Figure 2–10. It consisted of many small computers, and a few large computers, together with terminals, printers, and other devices, all connected by a high performance network. Communication devices could also link this network to other long-distance networks and telephone lines.

Figure 2–10 A Network of Computing Resources

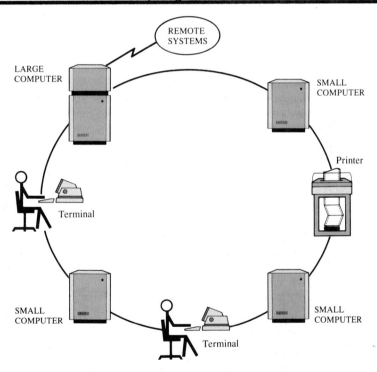

The environment of a high-capacity network within a single organization, linking a number of usually similar computers with common objectives, gave a new interpretation to the idea of a network operating system. The goal of such an OS within a local area network was to provide a common control system for all of the resources on the network, making remote resources as easy to use as local ones. In the extreme case, users and programs would be unable to tell, and would not be expected to care, where the resources they were using were located. An operating system with these objectives was called a **distributed operating system.**

As the 1980s progressed, operating system research focused intensively on distributed operating systems. Dozens of experimental systems were developed, and the majority of them were based on UNIX. One example is LOCUS, described in a book by Popek and Walker [1985]. LOCUS was one of the first distributed operating systems to be transformed into a commercial product.

2.15 THE MICROCOMPUTER MATURES

Although CP/M was widely adopted when it first appeared, it had many weaknesses in its user interface and file and device management, and it completely lacked other OS features, such as memory management and multiprogramming. More elaborate operating systems would strain the capacity of the 8080, but more powerful microprocessors were appearing which could handle greater demands from their software.

Improvements were slow to emerge from Digital Research, and a few companies began to develop alternative operating systems. These OSs added capabilities not present in CP/M, although they tried to remain compatible with the CP/M program interface and file system.

One improved OS was developed by Seattle Computer Products. Called SCP-DOS, this system was designed for Intel's new 16-bit microprocessor, the 8086. SCP-DOS was quite similar to CP/M, but added such features as memory and timer management, interrupt support, and a more sophisticated file system. SCP-DOS was acquired by Microsoft Corporation, renamed **MS-DOS,** and implemented on a variety of computer systems. When the IBM Personal Computer (PC) was introduced in the early 1980s, a version of MS-DOS, called PC-DOS, was chosen as its operating system.

As the power of microprocessors grew to compare with the CPUs of many minicomputers, users who had spent time at universities began to envision UNIX implementations in microcomputer environments. Ironically, UNIX was no longer the lean and simple system that Thompson and Ritchie created for the PDP-7. If it had been, a moderately powerful microcomputer could have handled it well. But later versions of UNIX had grown huge in their VAX environments. A typical Berkeley version occupied several hundred thousand bytes of main memory, and required tens of megabytes of file storage for all the associated system programs.

However, if UNIX itself was out of reach, it was still possible for existing microprocessor OSs to adopt some of the features that made UNIX seem attractive. As a response to this need, Microsoft released version 2.0 of MS-DOS, which included a command interface with features from the UNIX shell, a UNIX-like program interface coexisting with the CP/M-style system calls, and a hierarchical file system. MS-DOS (and PC-DOS) became a bridge between the CP/M model and the UNIX model for microcomputer operating systems.

MS-DOS version 2 included some important features of UNIX, but lacked any support for concurrent processes. As microprocessor power has continued to grow, further enhancements have been added to both MS-DOS and CP/M. These enhanced versions are able to support several users and in some cases several processes for each user, each communicating through a separate window on the terminal screen.

Despite improvements in MS-DOS and CP/M, the development of UNIX versions for microcomputers was inevitable. Advances in processing power, memory capacity, and affordable high-capacity disks all made the larger microcomputer environments ready to handle even Berkeley-style UNIX. When AT&T was divested in 1983, it was also freed from restrictions on development and sale of computer products. UNIX quickly became an official AT&T product. Their System V UNIX formed a major alternative to Berkeley UNIX, and it was promoted actively. Although its resource demands were still substantial, one version or another of UNIX was implemented in dozens of different microcomputer environments.

2.16 RECENT HISTORY

In recent years, large scale computing has continued to be dominated by IBM MVS-based systems. Even the 16-megabyte address space of the S/360 and 370 have become limiting, but IBM has responded with new architectures that are modest extensions of the previous ones. Operating system evolution has been equally slow.

Medium-scale computing has been dominated by the VAX, and both VMS and UNIX are widely used on this architecture. Neither operating system has changed dramatically. The newest VAX architectures provide improved facilities for communication and resource sharing among multiple processors.

Small-computing environments come in many sizes and shapes, and although many are similar to the IBM-PC, no single architecture dominates completely. One common alternative is the Macintosh. Small computers by Apple, Tandy, Commodore and Atari are all widely used, as are workstations from DEC, Sun, and many others. There are also "micro" versions of the VAX and the S/370.

Small-computer operating systems are dominated by MS-DOS and assorted versions of UNIX, with CP/M becoming less popular. Many widely used systems from Apple, Commodore, Atari and others use unique, proprietary operating systems. A new competitor in this category is OS/2, the operating system for IBM's PS/2 series of microcomputers.

Enabled by the vast reduction in the costs of developing and producing new hardware, many experimental architectures have been developed in the 1970s and 1980s, and new categories have begun to emerge. Some important categories seek to gain the highest possible performance by use of multiple CPUs and other system components, or multiple computing elements within a single CPU. These architectures are classified as parallel processors, or "supercomputers." Examples range from the CRAY series of high-speed supercomputers to experimental "multiprocessors" like Cm* or the Connection Machine. Architectures of this sort are usually unique, and thus require unique operating systems for their effective control.

Other operating systems have continued to develop to meet new categories of needs. Much of the new OS development has focused on improving security and reliability. Advances in this area run the gamut from secure versions of the basically insecure UNIX [Popek et al. 1979] to operating systems for secure object-oriented computer architectures, such as CAP [Wilkes & Needham 1979], or highly reliable architectures like those developed by Tandem [Serlin 1984]. Other systems have focused on improving their information handling capabilities, raising the file system to the level of a database manager. The PICK system [Sisk & VanArsdale 1985] is a small computer OS illustrating this approach.

Operating systems for real-time applications have also developed steadily. Although many such applications require special-purpose system software for the highest possible speed, others benefit from the use of general-purpose real-time operating systems. OSs of increasing sophistication have been supplied with control-oriented minicomputers like IBM's System/34 and Series/1 and similar systems from DEC and other manufacturers. Many control-oriented microcomputers have likewise been supplied with real-time operating systems. A few general-purpose real-time OSs have also been developed independently and implemented on several different computer types. VRTX [Ready 1986] is a prominent example.

2.17 SUMMARY

Computers and their operating systems evolved in cycles. In each of the three main categories—mainframes, minicomputers, and microcomputers—operating systems have had similar progressions from primitive, single-user monitors to sophisticated multiprogramming systems. Each cycle has been faster than the one before.

The earliest computers had no operating systems. The need for common procedures to load successive programs and access I/O devices led to the first OSs for IBM computers. These systems accepted simple commands from their users via typewriters or punched cards, and could be used by only one person at a time. Most early computers followed a traditional architecture, but a few, such as Atlas, made innovations that were important to later operating systems.

As magnetic tapes and disks were developed, the need for effective management of information led to systems with more extensive capabilities. To get the most work out of expensive computers, most operating systems processed jobs in batch mode. When memories grew large enough to hold several jobs, these batch systems were multiprogrammed for greater efficiency. An important example is IBM's OS/MVT for the S/360 computers.

To meet the demands of programmers for better response time and effective interaction, timesharing systems were developed that used multiprogramming techniques, allowing many users to work at terminals at the same time. Significant systems in this class include CTSS and MULTICS.

Operating systems were becoming complex, and problems were caused by the interaction of multiple processes. Dijkstra's T.H.E. introduced the abstract machine organization to help control this complexity, and offered solutions to process interaction problems as well. The abstract machine concept led to IBM's development of virtual machine systems.

Smaller computers, which came to be called minicomputers, were also being developed. Their small address spaces and other limitations required new design strategies, such as multiple addressing modes. Simple operating systems developed for these minicomputers, eventually becoming more sophisticated like their mainframe predecessors. The most widely used minicomputers were produced by Digital Equipment Corporation, who provided them with several OSs, such as RT-11 and RSX-11. Minicomputers were used by researchers at Bell Labs to develop an OS called UNIX, based loosely on MULTICS and other timesharing systems, but with many innovations. UNIX was very widely adopted and became a major influence on most later systems.

The microprocessor was developed in the early 1970s, and its capabilities advanced rapidly. It provided compact chips with great computing power for very low costs. The first microprocessor operating system was CP/M.

Although primitive, it filled an important need and was widely used. MS-DOS was an improved version of CP/M for more powerful microprocessors, and was adopted for the IBM PC. UNIX also came to be an important OS for larger microcomputer systems, and influenced the evolution of MS-DOS and CP/M.

As the 1970s came to a close, DEC developed the VAX architecture and the VMS operating system as successors to PDP-11 systems, while IBM developed VM/370 and MVS for its virtual memory 370 family. Xerox PARC developed the Alto, the forerunner of a new breed of professional workstations.

Recent years have seen the rise of networks and distributed systems, the increasing dominance of UNIX, and the development of operating systems to meet special categories of needs, such as security and reliability, database handling, and real-time applications, or serve special types of architectures, such as parallel processors and supercomputers.

≡ FOR FURTHER READING ≡

A number of surveys and more extensive treatments of aspects of operating system history have been published. Surveys of operating systems in the early period were published by Rosen [1967, 1969, 1972], Rosin [1969], and Weizer [1981]. Steel [1964] provides a good snapshot of the industry in this early period. For an in-depth treatment of one very early system, the series of papers on SOS [Shell et al. 1959] are worthwhile. A good discussion of early IBM systems is also contained in the extensive history by Bashe et al. [1986].

Various papers have presented the evolution of operating systems for specific computers or classes of computers. These include the IBM S/360 and S/370 [Auslander et al. 1981], DEC PDP-10 [Bell et al. 1978], Univac 1100 series [Borgerson et al. 1978], IBM real-time computers [Harrison et al. 1981], and minicomputers [Koudela 1973].

The subject of virtual machine operating systems is covered in surveys by Buzen and Gagliardi [1973] and Goldberg [1974]. The evolution of VM/370 is presented by Creasy [1981].

The early evolution of UNIX is described by Ritchie [1980]. Quaterman et al. [1985] discuss later UNIX history, covering VAX versions. The early history of microprocessors at Intel is reviewed by Noyce and Hoff [1981]. A detailed and interesting book by Freiberger and Swaine [1984] describes the evolution of microcomputers, from their earliest versions up to the appearance of personal workstations, including coverage of CP/M and MS-DOS.

Among more specialized topics, Barron et al. [1972] discuss the evolution of job-control languages, and Fosdick [1979] surveys the use of high-level languages for writing operating systems.

IMPORTANT TERMS

abstract machine
Atlas
batch multiprogramming
batch processing
batch serial
Compatible Timesharing System
  (CTSS)
CP/CMS
CP/M
Dartmouth Timesharing System
  (DTSS)
disk operating system
distributed operating system
DOS
extracode
foreground/background
FORTRAN Monitor System (FMS)
input-output control system (IOCS)
Input Output System
interactive computing
interrupt
job control language (JCL)
linker
mainframe
Master Control Program (MCP)
microcomputer
microprocessor
minicomputer
MS-DOS
MULTICS
network operating system

object deck
one-level store
open operating system
open shop
OS/360
OS/MFT
OS/MVS
OS/MVT
priorities
punched cards
real-time control system
resident loader
RSX-11
RT-11
SABRE
SAGE
SHARE
SHARE Operating System (SOS)
source deck
spooling
tape operating systems
TENEX
T.H.E.
time quantum
time slice
timesharing system
transaction processing system
UNIX
VAX/VMS
virtual machine
workstation

REVIEW QUESTIONS

1. Name two important OS ideas first explored by the T.H.E. operating system.

2. Name two OS features pioneered by the ATLAS system.

3. Name two unusual characteristics of the MULTICS system.

4. Explain at least three developments in system hardware and software that had occurred by the late 1960s that made timesharing more feasible than it could have been ten years earlier.

5. What was the greatest problem in designing a timesharing system that was not faced by batch systems?

6. Name an operating system that meets each of the descriptions in the following list:

   a. A very early OS developed by an IBM users group
   b. A large OS written almost entirely in PL/I
   c. Introduced the concept of interrupts
   d. Popular OS originally created by programmers for their own use
   e. Introduced the idea of layered system organization
   f. The largest and most complex OS ever developed
   g. First operating system for microcomputers
   h. A transparent distributed OS based on UNIX
   i. A pioneer OS for personal workstations

7. Explain briefly why the objectives of a batch operating system conflict with those of an interactive system.

8. What is unusual about the manner in which the UNIX operating system was developed?

9. Give a principal reason why the VAX was developed.

10. Why were the goals of operating systems for local area networks different than those for long-distance networks?

≡ ASSIGNMENTS ≡

1. Draw a graph based on Figure 2–1, showing which early operating systems were a significant influence on each later one. Identify some of the distinct separate lines of development.

2. Discuss the reasons for the widespread popularity of each of the following: MVS, VMS, UNIX, PC-DOS.

3. Support or refute the following claim: In general, operating systems developed by computer manufacturers have been less influential than those developed independently.

4. Trace the genealogy of a current OS of your choice. Identify several features of this OS that are design innovations, and several others that are included primarily for historical reasons.

Operating System Structure

Introduction • Components of an Operating System • Source Code Organization • Storage Organization • Execution Structures • Component Interaction • Hardware Control • Adaptability

Operating System Structure

3.1 INTRODUCTION

The capabilities and performance of an operating system are strongly affected by the structure and organization of the component parts that comprise it. This chapter examines the ways in which operating systems are divided into parts and how those parts interact.

Some of the issues to be considered in this study include:

- How are the responsibilities of the OS divided among various modules?
- When and where are various parts of the OS loaded in memory?
- When and how are specific components executed?
- How do distinct components interact and affect each other?
- How can partitioning of the OS make it easier to adapt to new requirements?
- How does the computer hardware organization influence the OS organization?
- What models does the OS present to the application programs?

3.2 COMPONENTS OF AN OPERATING SYSTEM

An operating system is a software system, or collection of programs. It has similarities to many other types of software systems, yet it must meet unique requirements as well. Because of the critical role of the OS in the operation of a computer, it is especially important to ensure that the OS is as reliable and as efficient as possible. One step in achieving these goals is to organize the system carefully, using the principles of software engineering.

Many operating systems are very large. The MVS operating system for the IBM S/370, with all its support programs, fills 17 large magnetic tapes and includes over half a billion bytes of information [Auslander et al. 1981]. The central components of a much earlier version of OS/360 included over 125,000 assembler statements [Buxton et al. 1976, p. 41]. A typical UNIX system kernel includes tens of thousands of lines in the C language.

One essential step in managing the complexity of a large software system is to divide the system into parts. It is then possible to discuss separately the structure and characteristics of each part, and the way all the parts fit together.

Each distinct operating system has a different set of objectives. The intended applications, hardware environment, number of users, type of input and output required, and many other factors result in unique combinations of requirements. Because of this diversity the organizations of OSs vary greatly; no single organization is best. However, a set of common issues influence the organization of most systems, although their relative importance may vary.

The responsibilities of an operating system divide logically into a number of categories, as discussed in Chapter 1. These functional divisions motivate various types of structural divisions into distinct components. We must consider a variety of factors in choosing the appropriate divisions. Moreover, the organization of the OS may be quite different when examined from differing viewpoints. Some of the viewpoints that should be considered include:

- SOURCE CODE ORGANIZATION. The source program code for an operating system is composed of procedures and data that are normally grouped into a number of distinct modules. These modules should be defined so that related elements are grouped together as much as possible. For example, the principal data structures used for process management, together with the procedures that operate on processes, may form a module.

- STORAGE ORGANIZATION. A running OS is divided into components that may occupy storage in various locations and for different periods of time. Some components may remain in memory at all times, while others are loaded when required. Some components may always be placed in the same storage area. A related but distinct issue is the form and location of master copies of each component, usually on secondary storage.

- EXECUTION CONDITIONS. The OS is partitioned into executable program units, each of which must run at appropriate times and under appropriate conditions. The units may be organized as procedures, processes, or other types of units. Each may require specific hardware states, memory access privileges, and the like. We must also consider the relation of these units to those of the application programs.

- COMPONENT INTERACTION. Each executable unit of an OS may be restricted to making use of other program and data units only in limited ways. Access to other units may be prohibited. This technique often results in a structure based on levels, in which a few components control critical hardware resources and provide essential services. Other components access the first group rather than accessing resources directly. Additional levels may also exist.

- HARDWARE CONTROL. Components may be identified that control and interact with various subsystems of the computer hardware, especially specific types of I/O devices. These subsystems may differ among system installations. The components of each system must match the actual hardware available.

- ADAPTABILITY. An operating system must be modified from time to time to match the needs and resources of a new installation, or changing conditions at an existing installation. In addition, improvements and corrections may become available and need to be installed. Components may be identified that can be modified in controlled ways to meet these requirements. Some components may be replaceable as a whole, or their use may be optional.

Each of these viewpoints provides useful insights into the ways that operating systems may be partitioned and organized. We will further explore these methods of organization in the following sections.

3.3 SOURCE CODE ORGANIZATION

Division into Modules

The program code comprising a complex operating system is normally organized into small program units, such as procedures, to make it possible to design, develop and maintain the system without being overwhelmed by its complexity. Usually, groups of related procedures are also organized into larger units, which may be stored in separate files and independently maintained. Related data structures are grouped in a similar way. The units into which the source code is divided do not necessarily correspond to distinct units of the executable code. For example, the source code for the early version of OS/360 mentioned above was divided into almost 500 modules.

The typical procedure for assembling an operating system from its source code is similar to that of many large software systems. Initially, groups of source modules are compiled or translated into object modules. This process may make use of additional source modules, such as those containing needed definitions, which have been stored in libraries. Collections of object modules can then be linked or combined into load modules. This process also may include additional modules from object libraries. A typical OS consists of a number of distinct load modules. These modules are stored on secondary storage in a suitable form, and may be loaded when the system is initialized, or as needed during the course of its operation. Figure 3–1 illustrates the relationships among these various types of modules during the process of constructing software systems.

Figure 3–1 The Software System Construction Process

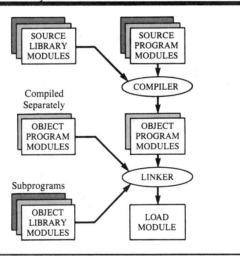

Many books have been written on how to choose the most appropriate division of a software system into source modules and procedures (see, for example, Myers [1975], Gillett and Pollack [1982], and Sommerville [1982]). One often-recommended principle is that each procedure or set of data should be no longer than about two pages when listed, so it can be easily understood. Other principles include:

- All the code and data used for one distinct job should be placed together.

- Each module should only have access to information it really needs.
- Each module should interact with only a small number of others.
- Interaction between modules should use simple, well-defined interfaces.
- Most anticipated design changes should affect only a small number of modules.

These rules apply quite generally to many types of software systems, and are all particularly applicable to operating system organization. In the OS context, however, we must balance them against the OS's exceptional need for compact code and high performance. Some of the requirements often conflict, so choices must be made.

The earliest operating systems were often written as huge nests of assembly language, divided into units based on arbitrary considerations such as the number of punched cards that would fit in a box. This approach contributed to numerous errors and problems, especially in large systems like the OS/360. Developers of recent systems have the benefit of more experience, so generally use a more careful, modular approach.

Small operating systems may be divided into only a few modules. These modules may be chosen primarily to correspond to parts of the OS that will be stored or executed as distinct units. By contrast, larger systems contain many interrelated modules. They may divide one internal unit into many source modules, or occasionally include several internal units in one source module (see Figure 3–2).

Implementation Languages

Operating systems play a critical role in the activities of a typical computing system, so it is important that they perform their duties as efficiently as possible. It is widely believed that programs written in assembly language can be made much more efficient than any produced by a high-level language compiler. In addition, an operating system must directly control the physical resources of a computer, such as registers, I/O ports, and specific memory locations, that are normally hidden by high-level languages. For these reasons, the majority of operating systems, until quite recently, have been written primarily in assembly language.

This situation is changing for several reasons. Modern OSs are growing so complex that they are extremely difficult to manage without the more powerful control structures and data structures of high-level languages. Although a good assembly language programmer may produce highly efficient code for simple procedures, manual achievement of the highest performance

Figure 3-2 Source Structure of Small and Large Operating Systems

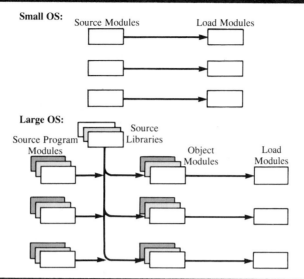

over large and complex systems is much more difficult. This problem was particularly evident in the long and difficult development of the OS/360 operating systems.

Even as operating systems are becoming more complex, we are relying on computers for increasingly more critical work. Reliability of many systems has become extremely important. Great care must be taken to be sure that the components of these operating systems work correctly, even at the cost of some performance. The required reliability may be difficult or impossible to achieve without the aid of well-structured high-level languages and error-checking compilers.

Finally, several good languages have been developed recently that can be classified as **system implementation languages (SILs).** These languages are designed to generate highly efficient code and provide direct control of hardware elements, even though other traditional high-level features may be compromised.

The idea of writing operating systems in a high-level language is not new. In the 1960s, the MULTICS operating system was produced almost entirely in a version of PL/I. However, MULTICS remained fairly unique in this respect until the appearance of UNIX in the early 1970s. Initial versions of UNIX were written in assembly language. However, the C language was simultaneously being developed, and eventually most of the UNIX kernel—together with its vast assortment of support programs—was written or rewritten in C. At about the same time, Digital Equipment Corporation began to make extensive use of the BLISS language, and later versions of OS software for the PDP-11 and the VAX have been coded in BLISS. The first microcomputer operating system, CP/M, was written with a low-level version of PL/I called PL/M.

With the emergence of Ada as a general-purpose language with many of the characteristics of a SIL (including the potential for highly efficient code generation) the choice of future implementation languages continues to increase.

A further potential advantage of OS implementation in a higher-level language is portability, an approach that may make it possible to use the same operating system on several different types of computers. This potential has been exploited in particular by UNIX and by the UCSD p-system.

Currently, the major category of operating systems still programmed in assembly language are those designed for real-time control purposes, where performance is extremely critical. However, even in these cases, initial versions of the system are best programmed in a high-level language for all the reasons cited above. Once this is done, those few code units primarily responsible for performance problems can be identified, and the necessary code can be rewritten in assembly language for the fastest possible execution or the most compact size.

System Examples

The source structure of a small operating system for a personal computer can be illustrated by CP/M. This OS includes three distinct parts that reflect its principal resource management functions: The BDOS (Basic Disk Operating System) for overall control and file management, The BIOS (Basic I/O system) for device management, and the CCP (Console Command Processor) for the user interface. Each part is maintained in a separate storage area and used in a slightly different way.

The source organization of these systems reflects this internal structure. The BDOS is a single source module of about 1,000 lines in the PL/M language. The CCP is another module half that size. The BIOS must be modified for each installation, since it contains the low-level code for device management. It is distributed as a separate module, typically including 2,000 to 3,000 lines of assembler code.

The UNIX operating system provides a good example of a large structure because its source code is widely available to students at licensed sites, especially at universities. The source code for most other operating systems is seldom available. Ironically, UNIX was first designed as a small and simple OS, but it has grown tremendously as its popularity has increased.

A typical set of source modules for the widely-used version 4.2 of Berkeley UNIX for the VAX is summarized in Figure 3–3. The main body of the source code for the UNIX operating system consists of almost 100 files, totaling about 35,000 lines of C code. As shown in the figure, these modules are distributed over the various operating system responsibilities which we have discussed. A typical file is a few hundred lines long and contains several related procedures. Many procedures directly implement the services requested by the many UNIX system calls. Others provide support for these primary procedures; still others provide procedures to be executed when various interrupts occur.

Figure 3–3 Source Modules for Berkeley 4.2 UNIX

CLASS	# of MODULES	# of LINES
C SOURCE FILES:		
Initialization	2	548
Main kernel	15	4683
Terminal handler	7	2959
File System	12	5573
Memory Management	12	4582
Process Communication	8	3110
Quota Management	4	1391
System Call Table	1	162
Miscellaneous	8	2237
VAX-specific	18	4905
TOTAL	87	30150
C HEADER FILES:		
Machine Independent	61	4150
VAX-specific	20	1275
TOTAL	81	5425
ASSEMBLER FILES		
VAX-specific	1	1231
GRAND TOTAL	169	36806

This table summarizes the source module organization for a particular version of Berkeley BSD 4.2 Unix, installed on VAX 11/750 processors at West Virginia University.

The UNIX source modules make use of about 100 definition, or header, files totaling an additional 5,500 lines. A typical header file defines a system data structure and some related information.

A single assembly language module of about 1,000 lines specifies some highly machine-dependent code and data, such as interrupt traps and I/O register usage. This is the only portion of the OS not written in C.

3.4 STORAGE ORGANIZATION

Resident and Transient Components

During normal system operation, some portions of an operating system remain loaded in main memory. These portions are referred to as **resident components.** Generally, resident components are responsible for critical services that must be available no matter what programs are running. These services include process dispatching, timing, error handling, access control, and initial handling of resource requests. Other components, which are needed less frequently and may be loaded from files or special storage areas as required, are called **transient components.** Some components that may be handled in this way include the command interface and various specialized elements of the file management system.

The resident components of an OS always include those procedures that carry out the most critical and constantly needed control functions, such as scheduling of processes and other activities, enforcement of security, or management of critical resources. The limited portion of the OS that performs these functions is sometimes called the **nucleus.** The term *kernel* is also used, but this term is more often given a restricted meaning, as discussed in Section 4.6. The nucleus of an OS *must* remain resident. In some systems, much more of the OS remains resident as well.

Since the continued operation of a computer system depends on the integrity of the resident components of the OS, destruction of these components must be avoided. In some computers the resident components are stored in read-only memory, ensuring that the OS remains permanently resident and cannot be destroyed. However, such an OS can be modified or upgraded only by physically replacing the read-only memory. This technique is most appropriate for very small home computers or dedicated controllers, where modification is not anticipated and reloading the OS would be difficult. In most other computers, the resident OS resides in ordinary memory. If it is damaged, it can be reloaded from secondary storage, which usually requires a complete initialization of the operating system.

Component Location

Resident components of the OS usually remain in a fixed area of the physical memory. This area includes the region with the lowest addresses, since many low addresses have special functions assigned by hardware that the OS must control. In particular, these include the addresses to which control is transferred after various interrupts, and the destination address for system calls. In some systems, portions of this storage are implemented as read-only memory.

Additional resident components may be loaded into other fixed areas of memory. Often it is convenient to load all application programs starting at a fixed low address just beyond the region with hardware-determined special functions. The remaining resident portions of the OS are then loaded at the highest possible addresses, leaving the largest possible region in between for the application program. Note that, since memory size may vary from computer to computer, the highest addresses are not always the same. The OS must determine the memory size when it is installed or initialized.

In some computer architectures, a portion of the address space is reserved for memory-mapped I/O. Addresses in this portion refer directly to input and output devices rather than true memory. Although these addresses do not contain executable code, access to memory-mapped locations is usually reserved for the OS.

Transient components are loaded into available space as needed. They may share a reserved area of memory, or they may compete for memory space with application programs. On many computers, these portions of the OS must be **relocated**, a process consisting of adjusting branch addresses and data references to the correct values for the specific memory locations to be used. Relocation may be performed by software, hardware, or combined techniques, depending on the hardware support available.

In systems employing memory protection or mapping hardware, portions of the OS may not be accessible to application programs, or may be accessible for read access only. Simple protection hardware is sufficient to prevent or limit access to specific memory locations. More sophisticated memory-mapping hardware can be used to provide the user with an address space that includes only a portion of the physical memory. In this case, the operating system may be kept inaccessible outside this address space. When this mechanism is used, selected portions of the OS may still be made accessible to support communication or simplify storage management.

System Examples

This section presents some **memory maps** illustrating the use of storage by some typical operating systems. A memory map is a snapshot illustrating the contents of a region of virtual or physical memory at a particular moment in time. In general, we should consider three distinct views: the content of the virtual address space when an application program is executing; the content of the virtual address space when the OS is executing; and the content of the physical memory. Not all of these views are distinct or interesting for every system. Because of the variation that can exist in OS storage organizations, we present a number of examples. For consistency, all addresses shown on the maps and referred to in the text are decimal addresses.

CP/M. Figure 3–4 illustrates the structure used by CP/M. Since CP/M uses no memory mapping, all virtual and physical views are identical. The maximum memory for a CP/M system is 64K bytes.

Figure 3–4 CP/M Memory Map

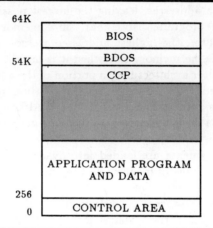

Two resident components are assigned to upper memory. The BIOS system occupies the highest locations, and the BDOS is stored just below the BIOS. The BIOS size may vary, but typically these two components occupy about 10K bytes. Included in this region is a small, fixed area for the stack. This stack area is used by the operating system and some programs. If a program requires a larger stack, it must create space for it within its own data area. In addition, the lowest 256 bytes are reserved for system data and buffers, including the current command line, and branch instructions at predetermined transfer points, which are executed, for example, when the computer is first started, or after a system call.

The CCP is loaded when needed into the region between location 100 and the BDOS, which CP/M calls the "transient area." The CCP is about 2K bytes in size and occupies the highest part of the transient area. Most application programs are loaded into the lower part of the transient area, beginning at address 256. The entire transient area above the program is available for data storage.

If a large application program needs the space occupied by the CCP, it can be used. The CCP is destroyed and must be reloaded when the program completes. It is a responsibility of the program to request that the CCP be reloaded. If the CCP is not destroyed by the program, it may be reused without reloading. Both the CCP and the application programs are always loaded into the same position and do not need to be relocatable.

PC-DOS and MS-DOS. A typical storage structure for PC-DOS, the IBM version of MS-DOS, is shown in Figure 3–5. The 8086 architecture on which this system runs does include memory mapping, and provides each program with separate 64K byte address spaces for program, data, and stack. The maximum physical memory is 1 megabyte. On the IBM PC, much of the highest range of this address space is reserved for video memory and for programs stored in read-only memory. Other MS-DOS systems differ principally in the use of this upper memory. Many systems have less than a full megabyte of memory installed, but a reasonable MS-DOS or PC-DOS installation will have at least several hundred kilobytes.

Figure 3–5 PC-DOS Memory Maps

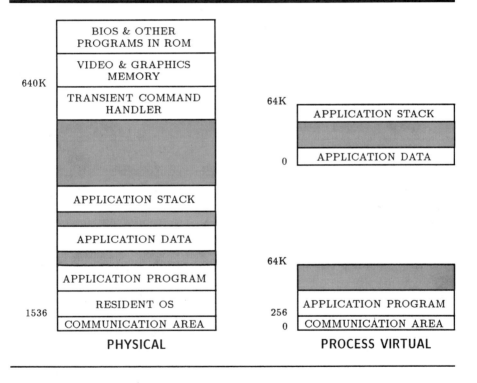

The operating system, including parts of the command interpreter, remains in memory at all times unless damaged. A second part of the command handler is loaded into the highest available memory, and will remain unless the space is needed. Up to about 600K bytes are available for application programs. At any moment, however, due to limitations of the 8086 architecture, a program's address space is limited to 64K each for program, data, and stack. In practice, the data and stack usually share the same address space.

The first 256 bytes of the program's address space are reserved for a communication area identical to that used by CP/M. Programs begin at location 256. Thus, programs developed for CP/M in many cases can be easily transported to an MS-DOS environment.

UNIX. Some memory maps for a typical UNIX system are shown in Figure 3–6. UNIX has been implemented on a variety of computer architectures, on which the size of the address space varies greatly.

Figure 3–6 UNIX Memory Maps

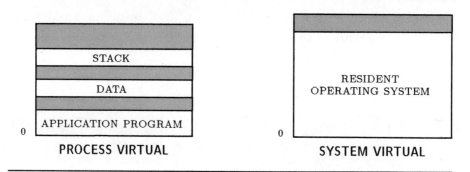

The virtual address space seen by a UNIX process contains regions for program, data, and stack. No part of the operating system is visible, nor are any data structures maintained by the OS to manage this process. Although UNIX supports multiple processes, in most versions no portion of the address space can be shared among different processes. UNIX isolates each process from the OS and other processes, and does not allow shared memory as a method of communication (for efficiency, processes sometimes share the program code when more than one program is executing, but this fact is unknown to the processes themselves). The command handler, along with other system components such as printer control, run as ordinary processes in UNIX and share the same view described above.

The virtual address space seen by the operating system nucleus consists simply of the nucleus itself. All of the many source modules for the UNIX kernel are compiled and linked into a single monolithic load module. This entire nucleus, over a quarter of a million bytes, is resident in virtual memory at all times. Its procedures are executed on demand when programs invoke system calls, or when interrupts occur.

The physical memory map is not shown. All UNIX systems use memory mapping, combined with either swapping or virtual memory techniques. These techniques try to maintain currently needed information in the physical memory while keeping copies of other information on disk storage. In such environments the content of physical memory is complex and changes frequently, and is not relevant to our current discussion.

The meaning of resident and transient components is also blurred in a swapping or virtual memory environment. All components of UNIX remain resident in virtual memory; a true resident component is one that is exempt from swapping.

VAX/VMS. Figure 3-7 presents the memory maps for the VAX/VMS system. The VAX architecture provides a huge address space of 4 billion bytes, divided into four portions that are managed independently. Under VAX/VMS, one portion is assigned to the program and data for the current process; one portion is assigned to the control structures maintained for that process; and one portion is assigned to the operating system. The fourth portion is not used. Normally a user's process can access only its program and data. The entire address space is visible to the operating system.

VAX/VMS makes use of virtual memory techniques to manage the more modest physical memory. Critical parts of the OS are exempt from swapping.

Figure 3-7 VAX/VMS Memory Maps

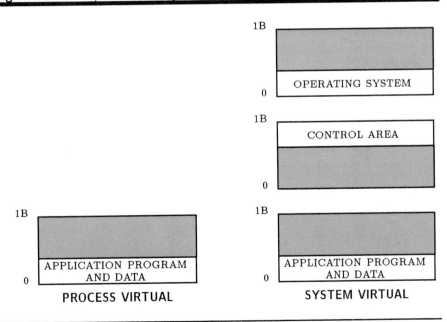

OS/MVT. The memory map for the OS/MVT operating system is shown in Figure 3–8. MVT runs on the IBM S/360 architecture, which does not support memory mapping. Thus all address spaces are identical. The maximum address space in a 360 is 16 megabytes, but a typical installation includes about 2 megabytes of physical memory. The OS is confined to the physical memory available.

Figure 3–8 OS/MVT Memory Map

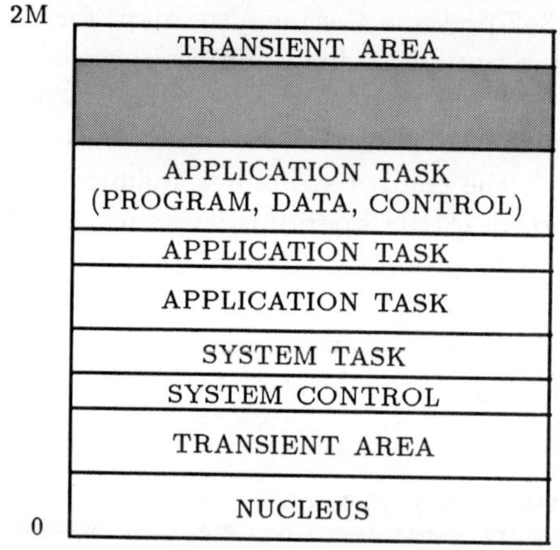

OS/MVT is a multiprogrammed OS, supporting a number of simultaneous processes or tasks. The lowest and highest portions of the memory are reserved for the operating system, including its resident nucleus, transient areas, and control area. Each task, whether running an application program or a system component, is assigned a contiguous region from the remaining area. The region assigned to a task includes program code, data, and most of the control structures associated with that task (the S/360 does not use stacks).

The entire memory map is in the address space visible to each process. A simple memory protection scheme is available to prevent processes from accessing locations outside of their own region.

The MVT layout is similar to that used by other versions of OS/360. OS/MFT is identical to OS/MVT, except that the size and location of the partitions cannot vary. OS/SVS for the S/370 transforms the map into a single virtual address space of 16 megabytes, and manages the physical memory by virtual memory techniques.

OS/MVS. The last example we will consider is OS/MVS, the advanced virtual memory version of MVT for the IBM S/370. Its memory map (Figure 3–9) shows a typical virtual address space as seen by either a user's process or the system. The operating system occupies the low and high portions of this space, much as in MVT. This part of the address space is shared by all processes. The remaining portion is private to each process, and includes space for program, data, and control structures.

Figure 3–9 OS/MVS Memory Map

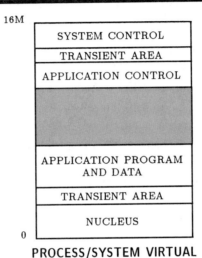

16M

SYSTEM CONTROL

TRANSIENT AREA

APPLICATION CONTROL

APPLICATION PROGRAM
AND DATA

TRANSIENT AREA

NUCLEUS

0

PROCESS/SYSTEM VIRTUAL

A portion of the common area is reserved as a communication area, which can be used for shared memory communication between processes.

3.5 EXECUTION STRUCTURES

The program code of an operating system is divided into executable units. Specific events cause execution of each unit. Many portions of the OS are executed by specific request of a program, as by a call instruction, or in response to interrupts or other separate events. These portions may complete their work before returning to the program, or they may schedule work for completion later. Once begun, they may be subject to interruption by more urgent units.

Many units of the operating system may execute with privileges, enforced by hardware, which are not available to application programs. They may be permitted to execute privileged instructions that affect system control registers, and they may be able to access memory that most other programs cannot use. Recently, there has been a greater tendency to limit these privileges to those really needed, even for operating system components.

Traditional Organization

The traditional organization of an OS views the system as essentially a collection of subroutines that can be executed upon request to manipulate system resources. These routines are invoked by a system call or in response to a specific event. A system call differs from a normal subroutine call, and generally increases the privilege level of the computer. At the same time, it transfers to a standard predetermined location always controlled by the operating system.

The increased privilege level allows the routines of the OS to use all instructions and access all registers. Any locations in memory can be accessed as well. All components of the OS operate in the same totally privileged state.

Most of the OS routines execute code that is in a permanently resident part of the OS. Some routines may cause additional transient components to be loaded and executed. The routines in these components execute with the same privileges as the rest of the OS.

Most of the OS routines complete their work before returning to the calling program. Some of these routines, however, may start an input/output activity or other chain of events which will continue at the same time that programs are running. Often the program that called the OS is suspended from further execution at this time, but other programs may still run.

When these events complete, an interrupt may occur. The CPU stops what it is doing and executes a program to handle the interrupt. The interrupt handler may modify various data structures, and may enable suspended programs to continue execution.

The great majority of operating systems use some variation on this basic form. A few very simple systems, such as CP/M, do not make use of interrupts. In this case all system services, including those that perform I/O, must complete their work entirely before the application program is resumed. This is a conceptually simple approach, but leads to difficulties in managing concurrent events, even for the simplest systems.

System Processes

In a number of operating systems, OS activities that must continue over a period of time while user processes are running may be viewed as processes themselves. Examples of such activities include managing the sending of output to a printer, monitoring a communication line and periodic housekeeping tasks. Many of these activities do not require special hardware privileges, and may be managed by techniques similar to those used for application programs.

To take advantage of these observations, the concept of **system processes** has been introduced. A system process performs services for the OS, but is logically managed and scheduled by techniques similar to those used for application processes. Substantial parts of an OS may be organized as system processes. A limited portion always remains, including critical functions, such as the process scheduler itself. This portion may be only a small fraction of the total operating system.

A few differences often occur between system processes and normal application processes. System processes may have higher scheduling priorities, may be protected from swapping out of main memory, and may be managed with a simplified, efficient structure that recognizes their special status.

The use of system processes wherever possible can reduce errors in an operating system design by providing more systematic management of many OS activities. In addition, the use of system processes can increase reliability. These processes are not given unnecessary privileges, and errors that may occur in them are not able to do as much damage to the rest of the system. UNIX and VMS are examples of operating systems that use some system processes effectively, although each has a very large portion that is not organized into processes.

Open Environments

Most operating systems are designed to provide a clear and rigid distinction between application software—even procedures from a common library—and the operating system itself. Although system services can be thought of, to some degree, as procedures they are structured and accessed in a very different way, and their use is strictly controlled.

This division is maintained in various ways. Operating system components may execute with privileges not available to application programs. The storage used by the OS may be outside the application program's address space. The system call instruction, which enables appropriate changes of hardware state, is used as a gateway to access system services.

The separation of the OS from the user is a necessity in a multiuser environment. Without such separation, mistakes or misbehavior by one user's program could disrupt the OS, causing serious problems for all other users. In a single-user system, however, this separation is less necessary, and there may be advantages in treating the OS and application programs in a more uniform way.

An alternate model that is sometimes used in single-user computer systems treats the operating system literally as a collection of procedures and nothing more. This approach has been called an **open system** [Lampson 1974] or an **open environment**. It has been used by simple minicomputer OSs, and more recently by a number of workstation environments, such as MeDos on the Lilith, or the operating systems of the Xerox Alto and Apple Macintosh. In an open environment, no distinction is made between OS services and other procedures. All procedures operate with full privileges, and share the same address space.

An operating system treated in this way is easily extendable. Users may freely add to or subtract from the set of procedures that they think of as "the operating system." The basic concept of an open environment is that the boundary between the OS and the application is almost nonexistent.

3.6 COMPONENT INTERACTION

Controlled Interaction

Like most software systems, an operating system is largely a collection of many procedures and data structures. In an uncontrolled organization, any procedure could be called by any other, and any data could be referenced by any procedure. For all but the smallest systems, such an unstructured approach leads to a highly unreliable system. It is difficult or impossible to predict the effects of any changes because we cannot determine which parts of the system rely on the procedures or data that were changed.

Because of this problem, it is necessary to restrict the set of procedures and data that a given procedure can access. Questions arise: How can this restriction be accomplished? What types of interaction should be allowed?

Restrictions on component interaction can be enforced in a number of ways during the development or execution of an operating system. During system development, restrictions can be imposed by programming and documentation rules, or enforced by compilers. Reliance on voluntary rules alone is rarely satisfactory, because mistakes are too easily made. Compiler enforcement can be more helpful, if the OS is written in a high-level language that supports information hiding, and if the system is divided into source modules that properly reflect the restrictions to be imposed. This is the most common method of controlling interaction in present-day systems.

During operation, interaction can be restricted by limiting the visible address space and privilege level of most procedures so that only appropriate information can be accessed. This type of restriction requires a high level of hardware assistance and may not be feasible on most architectures. Although hardware techniques are effectively used to isolate user processes from the OS and each other, in practice compiler enforcement is the most effective way to control interaction among elements of the OS itself.

The question of what type of interaction should be allowed leads to a variety of possibilities. Some of these are considered in the following subsections.

Unstructured Interaction

In most early operating systems, no attempt was made to control or restrict interaction between separate modules. In many cases the programs were written in assembler language, and the appropriate structures were not yet well understood. This type of organization has been used without too much difficulty in small systems; full interaction does not lead to serious difficulties in CP/M, which has only three modules. However, this approach quickly becomes unmanageable in larger environments, and has led to serious difficulties in the development of complex systems such as OS/360.

Isolation of Modules

The concept of limiting interaction with the aid of compilers or hardware has been an important tool in the organization of many OSs written in high-level languages. Examples range from MULTICS to VAX/VMS. In most cases, modules are grouped according to the major function they support, such as memory management. Common data structures that support each function can be accessed only by the relevant modules. Other modules are permitted to interact with the memory management group only in limited ways.

Levels and Abstract Machines

A structuring concept pioneered by Dijkstra's T.H.E. operating system has become the foundation for a variety of more recent systems. This technique organizes the major portions of the operating system into a series of levels, beginning with the computer itself as the lowest level. Each level uses the resources of the level below it to implement an increasingly powerful **abstract machine.** Each abstract machine adds new capabilities to the total system, but prohibits direct access from higher levels to some or all of the facilities of the lower levels. This prohibition is most commonly enforced by compilers. The concept is often illustrated by an "onion-skin" diagram, in which modules are shown as partial layers surrounding a central portion known as the **kernel.** A typical diagram appears in Figure 3–10.

Figure 3–10 A Level-Structured Operating System

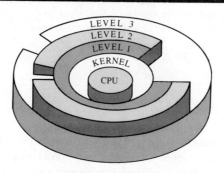

The level structure has some profound advantages for construction of reliable operating systems. Each layer can be developed and tested separately, starting with the lowest. Once each level has been validated, its facilities can be relied on and used in the construction of higher levels. For example, if the lowest levels implement multiple processes and memory management, these tools may be freely used to construct the remaining parts of the system.

A second advantage of the level structure is the opportunity to isolate the most critical portions of the OS in the lowest levels. These portions of the system require the most careful construction and testing, since an error here could cause disaster. If the lowest levels are as small as possible, they can be verified much more effectively; Dijkstra claimed to have demonstrated the correctness of the T.H.E. system "with a rigor and explicitness that is unusual for the great majority of mathematical proofs" [Dijkstra 1968].

The kernel of a level-structured OS contains only its most critical functions. Highly reliable and secure operating systems have been constructed by focusing attention on verifying the correctness of this kernel. Examples in this category include Data Secure UNIX at UCLA [Popek et al. 1979] and the Provably Secure Operating System (PSOS) [DeLashmutt 1979].

The choice of functions to assign to each level, of course, is a critical step in designing a satisfactory system. There is no common agreement on details, but it is clear that critical tasks, such as process scheduling, memory management, and enforcement of protection, should come below higher-level tasks like file management and the user interface. T.H.E. included four levels for the OS itself, plus two for the application program and the operator. A recent hypothetical structure presented by Brown et al. [1984] includes eleven levels between the hardware and the application. These structures are shown in Figure 3–11.

Figure 3–11 Level Structure for two Example Systems

a. Levels defined in T.H.E. [Dijkstra 1968]:

Level 0: Process scheduling, interrupt handling
Level 1: Virtual memory management
Level 2: User's console handling
Level 3: Input & output buffering

Level 4: Application programs
Level 5: The operator

b. Levels proposed by Brown et al. [1984]:

Level 1: Electronic circuits
Level 2: CPU instruction set
Level 3: Procedure mechanisms

Level 4: Interrupt handling
Level 5: Primitive Process management
Level 6: Local secondary storage management
Level 7: Virtual memory management
Level 8: Capabilities (Security)
Level 9: Interprocess communication
Level 10: File management
Level 11: Device management
Level 12: Stream I/O
Level 13: User process management
Level 14: Directory management
Level 15: Command interface

Virtual Machines

A special type of abstract machine can be constructed on some computer architectures, in which the facilities available from the abstract machine are a copy of the bare computer hardware. This copy, however, is made available through timesharing techniques to a number of users at the same time. When these conditions are met, the abstract machine is known as a **virtual machine.**

In a virtual machine environment, each user starts with a bare computer on which a private operating system can be installed. Several different operating systems can be run at the same time (see Figure 3–12). This approach can be valuable if different operating systems are needed, or if operating system modifications need to be tested while normal work continues on the same equipment. A disadvantage to the virtual machine structure is that users are highly isolated from one another, making communication and sharing difficult.

Figure 3–12 A Virtual Machine System

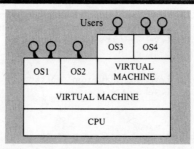

Virtual machines have been implemented on a variety of computers, but by far the most widely used example is the VM/370 system for the IBM S/370.

3.7 HARDWARE CONTROL

Another important consideration in organizing the components of an operating system is the close dependency between some OS functions and portions of the computer hardware. This problem does not arise in most other types of software systems. In many cases, the choice of algorithms or design concepts must be partly determined by the hardware. In addition, some hardware systems may vary in structure or be omitted in different installations of the same operating system.

It is clear that an operating system that effectively controls an unusual computer system must be designed from the start to match the requirements of the system architecture. Examples include parallel processors, multiprocessors, and architectures specialized to support high-level languages or applications. Most systems in this category are outside the scope of this text.

Even when running on conventional hardware, the structure of some subsystems is likely to vary and must be considered carefully in organizing the OS. This variability arises in two ways:

1. PORTABILITY REQUIREMENTS. An operating system may be designed to be adaptable to a number of distinctly different computer types. Even computers within the same family may be quite different from an OS viewpoint.

2. VARYING CONFIGURATIONS. Each installation of a computer system, although of the same type, may vary in well-defined ways. Important examples include differing amounts of physical memory and differing numbers and types of I/O devices. In addition, some CPU subsystems, such as floating-point arithmetic processors, are often optional.

Adapting to a new architecture obviously requires some rewriting, but you should control the number of modules that must change. In some cases, differences in configuration require only adjustment of parameters when the OS is initialized. For example, the size of physical memory can be determined in this way.

However, when subsystems may be completely absent or vary in type, substantially different software is needed for each case. This concern is greatest for the highly variable set of I/O devices. Each device type requires a specific control module, called an **I/O driver.** All knowledge of the details of each device type should be confined to the driver, so that no other modules need to change if a new type of printer or terminal is acquired.

A few simple operating systems include all possible device drivers as part of the resident nucleus. In most cases, the configuration for a specific installation is specified when the OS is assembled or initialized, and the appropriate drivers are included. The most flexible structure allows I/O drivers to be loaded when the OS is running. Once loaded, they become part of the resident nucleus as long as they are needed.

3.8 ADAPTABILITY

A final concern in partitioning an operating system is the expectation of the need for future change. Changes related to hardware were discussed in the preceding section. The physical configuration may change periodically even at the same site.

Periodically, you may plan improvements to the operating system. It should be possible to update subsystems, such as memory management or file management, without the need to change other portions of the OS. It is critical that a new version of an OS be installable with minimal disruption to its users. It would be unacceptable if a new OS version required all software to be recompiled because addresses within the OS had changed. The system call instruction plays an important role here; it provides a means for accessing the OS that will not change unnecessarily when new versions are developed.

Requirements and applications may also change or vary at different installations, leading in some cases to the need for distinct differences in OS structure. A few operating systems address this problem by a "building block" approach, in which each user can configure an operating system by selecting specific components. The configuration may vary because of hardware differences, because some OS functions are not needed or wanted, or because different strategies are preferred in areas such as memory management or process scheduling. This may be especially important in real-time systems, where unnecessary parts of the operating system should not be included.

One OS that uses a building-block structure is VRTX [Ready 1986]. Designed for real-time applications, this system makes many functions optional, such as file management, and provides for user-supplied extensions or substitutions of most of its modules.

Another OS that uses the building-block approach is S1 [Little 1984]. This system allows a user to select from a menu of components to configure a total operating system. Different installations of S1 may thus have extremely different properties. A list of modules included in S1, based on [Little 1984], is shown in Figure 3–13.

Figure 3–13   Modules which can be included in an S1 System

multiuser support	program management	command processor
groups	absolute	menu
privilege classes	relocating	conventional
network	linking	prompting
	overlay	
networking		command lists
	file processing	
tasking	stream	resident commands
multitasking	record	
gates	indexed	terminal support
events		line
	file allocation	full screen
messages	linked	windowing
intertask	mapped	bit-mapped
general	contiguous	vector graphic
queues		
	file directories	character conversion
scheduler	hierarchical	
voluntary dispatch	flat	device management
round-robin		
priority	arithmetic	time management
dynamic		

3.9 SUMMARY

An operating system is typically a large software system. General software engineering principles apply to OS design, but there are special considerations as well. An important question is how the OS should be divided into parts, and issues to consider include source code organization, storage organization, execution conditions, component interaction, hardware control, and adaptability.

Standard software engineering techniques address the question of source code organization. Reasonable high-level languages are becoming available for OS implementation. A more unusual consideration is the location of some components in main memory, and the time when they must be present. Some components are permanently resident and must be located in specific areas. Others may be loaded only as needed.

Another consideration in identifying modules of an OS is the way in which each procedure is executed. Traditionally, OS procedures are either invoked directly by system calls, triggered by events such as interrupts, or called by other OS procedures. These procedures run in fully privileged mode. Other organizations may implement some OS activities as system processes, often with lesser privileges, or may treat the entire OS as an ordinary library of procedures.

It is important to limit the direct interactions between modules. An effective way to do this is a layered organization, which views the OS as a series of abstract machines, or extensions of the hardware machine. One way in which this approach may be developed leads to the virtual machine concept.

Modules in an OS may also be identified based on the hardware units with which they interact, since some hardware, especially I/O devices, may be changeable. Finally, the OS structure must support the need to adapt the OS to the different and changing requirements of each installation. The building-block approach, exemplified by S1, offers an effective way to address this problem.

≡ FOR FURTHER READING ≡

A vast number of publications on general software engineering principles are available. Many of the fundamental ideas are presented in papers reprinted in the collection by Yourdon [1979]. A few of the many useful texts include McGowan and Kelly [1975], Myers [1975], Gillett and Pollack [1982], and Sommerville [1982].

Descriptions of system implementation languages include Wulf et al. [1971] for BLISS, Kernighan and Ritchie [1978] for C, and the Ada Reference Manual [ANSI 1983]. McGowan and Kelly [1975] discuss macro extensions to assembly languages for structured programming.

A few operating system texts give special emphasis to issues of OS structure. A good treatment is found in Janson [1985]. Detailed case studies of real systems provide an effective way to appreciate realistic OS structure design issues. A good overview of the relatively simple structure of PC-DOS is given by King [1983]. Many other microcomputer OSs are described in the books by Zarella [1981, 1982, 1984]. Bach [1986] provides an excellent study of UNIX System V. Other good studies include Kenah and Bate [1984] (VAX/VMS) and Organick [1972] (MULTICS). The Kenah and Bate study is encyclopedic, while Organick writes in a popular style that may seem tedious to the computer science student.

Good case studies are also available of operating systems developed for teaching purposes. Examples include MINIX [Tanenbaum 1987], KMOS [Milenković 1987], XINU [Comer 1984], and the structured operating system of Welsh and McKeag [1980]. Many additional case studies for all types of operating systems may be found in the references cited throughout the catalog in Appendix C of this book.

A number of topics mentioned briefly in this chapter are also covered in more detail in later chapters of this text. Secure OS kernels are discussed in Chapter 16. Virtual machines are treated in Chapter 21. I/O drivers receive detailed attention in Chapter 9, and real-time systems like VRTX are examined in Chapter 22. Chapter 17 includes a look at system initialization, and Chapter 20 treats portability issues. The hardware overview in Appendix A is also useful for background reading.

≡ IMPORTANT TERMS ≡

abstract machine
I/O driver
kernel
memory map
nucleus
open environment
open system

relocation
resident component
SILs
system implementation language (SIL)
system process
transient component
virtual machine

≡ REVIEW QUESTIONS ≡

1. State and briefly explain five issues or viewpoints to be considered when deciding how to organize the modules of an operating system.

2. A large present-day OS is considered to be composed of a number of distinct interacting components. Like any large software system, the source modules of an OS are partitioned according to good software engineering principles. List and describe two additional viewpoints that you should consider in selecting the components of an operating system.

3. Explain briefly the purpose of the three major parts of the CP/M operating system.

4. What are transient routines, and why do they exist in an operating system?

5. Why is it desirable that system processes have lesser privileges than other parts of the operating system?

6. Why is the concept of an open system not feasible for a system serving multiple users?

7. Explain the difference between an abstract machine and a virtual machine.

8. List several types of hardware components that may vary between different installations of the same computer type.

9. Identify three ways in which an OS may need to adapt to changing requirements.

ASSIGNMENTS

1. List several features that would be important in a systems implementation language. Name a language you are familiar with that would *not* be suitable as a SIL, and explain why.

2. Using the memory maps presented in Figures 3-4 through 3-9, identify the main differences and similarities in the mapping of memory by these operating systems.

3. In an operating system without memory management, the OS is often split between the lowest and highest memory addresses. Why isn't the entire system placed in low memory?

4. Some operating systems keep data structures that are managed by the OS but control a particular process, in the address space of that process. Give an advantage and a disadvantage for this approach.

5. In VAX/VMS and MVS, the program code and data for the current process are within the address space of the operating system. This is not the case in UNIX. Explain the advantage of having this information visible to the operating system. Why do you think UNIX uses a different approach?

6. Comment on the following statement: With the large address spaces supported by today's computers, it is a good idea to keep the entire operating system resident at all times.

7. Suppose an operating system consists of five program modules, and there is a possibility of interaction between any two modules. How many potential interfaces exist (one for every possible pair of modules that can interact)? Repeat the question if there are 50 modules.

8. Now suppose that an operating system has 50 modules organized in ten layers, with five modules per layer. Modules in any layer can interact with any in the layer above or below, but no others. How many interfaces exist?

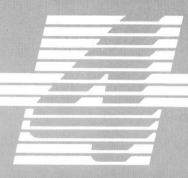

The User Interface

The User Interface

4.1 INTRODUCTION

If a computing system is to perform useful services, it must support communication with the system's users—the people who use it to support their application programs. This communication involves a two-way transfer of information: a user informs the system when specific services are required, and the system provides the user with the results of those services. The communication may be direct, such as through a typed dialog at an interactive terminal, or indirect, through jobs or programs submitted for batch execution. The operating system component responsible for managing this communication is the **user interface.**

The user interface is the gateway for interaction and communication between a computing system and its users. To many users, the acceptability of an entire computing system is largely determined by its user interface. Yet many operating systems seem to do a poor job of user-interface design, and many OS texts do not consider the subject. Although there is no widespread agreement on the form an ideal interface should take, some common ideas have taken shape that could improve the quality of many existing user interfaces and help in designing better ones in the future. These ideas are the motivation for this chapter.

The user interface includes two major parts. The **command interface** directs the processing of a set of programs by providing high-level communication between the user and the operating system. This interface is so named because users normally type or submit a series of **commands** to tell the OS what actions to perform. The command interface is discussed in Sections 4.2 through 4.8.

The **program interface** manages running programs and provides interaction between these programs and system-controlled resources and services. This interface is discussed in Sections 4.9 and 4.10.

The program and command interfaces are usually related, as shown in Figure 4–1. The command interface is implemented by a program unit, often a system process. Like other programs, the command interface uses the program interface to access system services. Moreover, in some operating systems the program interface includes a method to invoke the command interface, a feature that allows programs to construct commands and pass them to the command interface for execution.

Figure 4–1 The User Interface

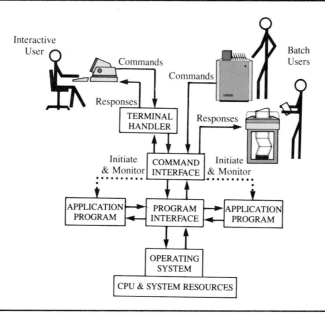

4.2 THE COMMAND INTERFACE

The command interface provides the mechanism for humanly understandable, two-way communication between an operating system and computer users. Whatever its actual form, this communication can make use of one or more languages. A language by which a user conveys instructions to the operating system is called an **Operating System Command Language (OSCL).** A language by which the OS returns information to the user is called an **Operating System Response Language (OSRL).** Languages that integrate both these functions may be referred to as **Operating System Command and Response Languages (OSCRLs)** [Beech 1980].

A command interface has two fundamental tasks:

1. Interpret commands in the OSCL and convey instructions to the rest of the operating system to carry out those commands.

2. Accept messages for the user from the operating system and present them using the OSRL.

In some systems, the command interface is an integral part of the operating system, while in others it may be implemented as a separate program. All operating systems provide some type of command interface, except, perhaps, those dedicated to permanent device control applications.

The purpose of the command interface is to enable users to execute programs or procedures by specifying **commands.** A typical command requests the system to locate a file, containing either a system program or an application program, and to load and execute that program with appropriate parameters.

Note that the term "command" is properly used to describe the instructions that are typed in order to invoke a program, not the program itself. Sometimes there is a confusing tendency to refer to editors, compilers, and other system programs that may available by the name "command."

Types of Command Interfaces

The command interface may take a variety of forms. For the batch user, it is implemented primarily as a **job-control language** through which the user specifies a sequence of program steps to be executed in the course of a complete job. The statements in a job-control language are often focused primarily on describing the characteristics of a job step, such as the specific files and other resources to be used.

An example of a job control sequence for ATLAS is shown in Figure 4–2. This example is based on Barron and Jackson [1972, p. 146]. The statements in this figure specify characteristics of a job to be run on the ATLAS system.

The most widely known job-control language is that used on IBM's OS/360 series systems. Figure 4–3 shows an example of IBM JCL for a simple FORTRAN program based on Barron and Jackson [1972, p. 149]. The statements in this figure instruct an IBM system to compile, link, and run a FORTRAN program. The first card identifies the user and specifies job attributes. The next group runs the compiler (most cards are concerned with defining data files). The next group runs the link program. The final group runs the compiled program itself.

Interactive users have a similar facility, commonly called the **command language.** However, in the interactive environment the interface is often

Figure 4–2 Example of ATLAS JCL

```
JOB

U123456 JAMES MOONEY

INPUT

1  SPECIAL  DATA

OUTPUT

0  LINEPRINTER  5000 LINES

3  CARDS  250  LINES

7  FIVEHOLE  TAPE  2  BLOCKS

TAPE

1  MALCOLM  LANE

TAPE  COMMON

3

COMPUTING  10  MINUTES

EXECUTION  15  MINUTES

STORE  71  BLOCKS

COMPILER  FORTRAN

***T
```

much more complex. The language itself may have an elaborate structure. Various types of prompting and typing assistance commands may be available. The interface may include conventions for returning system messages to the user. Other features might include intelligent **terminal handling, immediate commands, help facilities, command logs,** and packaging of commands into **command files.** These features are made available when a user communicates with the operating system itself. In some cases they are supported for communication with other programs as well.

A basic interactive command language provides stream-oriented communication, in which commands and messages are processed as lines of text. This

Figure 4–3 Example of IBM JCL

```
//MOONEY    JOB    (1023,20,47),LANE,MSGLEVEL=2,PRTY=6,CLASS=B


//COMP      EXEC   PGM=IEYFORT,PARM='SOURCE'
//SYSPRINT  DD     SYSOUT=A
//SYSLIN    DD     DSNAME=SYSL.UT4,DISP=OLD,
//                 DCB=(RECFM=FB,LRECL=80,BLKSIZE=800)
//SYSIN     DD     *
                          ...
                   (Source Program Cards)
                          ...



//GO        EXEC   PGM=FORTLINK,COND=(4,LT,C)
//SYSPRINT  DD     SYSOUT=A
//SYSLIN    DD     DSNAME=*.COMP.SYSLIN,DISP=OLD
//SYSLIB    DD     DSNAME=SYSL.FORTLIB,DISP=OLD
//FT03F001  DD     SYSOUT=A,DCB=(RECFM=FA,BLKSIZE=133)
//FT05F001  DD     DDNAME=SYSIN
//FT06F001  DD     SYSOUT=A,DCB=(RECFM=FA,BLKSIZE=133)
//FT07F001  DD     UNIT-SYSCP



//GO.SYSIN  DD     *
                          ...
                   (Program Data Cards)
                          ...


/*
```

type of powerful, concise language, generally most suitable for an experienced user, is illustrated in Figure 4–4.

Screen-oriented command interfaces, such as **menu systems,** provide an alternative approach in which the user chooses from a set of options offered by the system. This method, which can be helpful to novice users because they need remember no commands, is especially appropriate in certain applications, such as text editing. However, because menu systems restrict the user to a limited number of options at any time and require time for the display of menus, they are not usually favored by experienced users. A menu system is illustrated in Figure 4–5.

Another communication mode that is becoming popular on workstations with high-resolution graphic capabilities is based on **icons.** An icon is a picture that symbolizes an object or activity, such as a file folder to represent a file or a trash can to represent disposal. The user of such a system requests deletion of a file by moving the *file* icon to the *trash can* icon using a pointing

Figure 4–4 A Stream-oriented Command System

```
>dir
      MYPROG1.PAS
      MYPROG2.PAS
      YOURPROG.FOR

>delete MYPROG2.PAS

>pascal MYPROG1

>link MYPROG1 SYSLIB

>run MYPROG1

      This is a test

>
```

Figure 4–5 A Typical Menu System

```
      AVAILABLE OPTIONS

   1. Compile FORTRAN program
   2. Compile Pascal program
   3. File services
   4. Print services
   5. Terminal emulation
   6. Run an application program
   7. View additional options

   Select number (? for help):
```

device, usually a mouse. This type of operation was introduced by the Xerox Alto, and has been made especially popular by the Apple Macintosh.

An example of icon-based communication, taken from the Macintosh, is given in Figure 4–6. The figure shows a typical screen presented by an icon interface. Each small "document" in the top window is an icon representing a file. File folders represent directories, and the trash can represents the place where files are put when deleted. A basic menu of commands appears on the top line, with submenus available for each menu item. In the example, the shaded document has been selected by moving the arrow (using a mouse) and pressing a button. A listing of the file appears in a separate window.

Figure 4–6 Communication by Icons

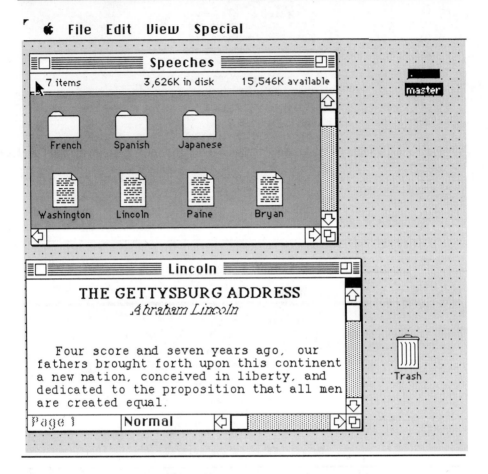

Other communication modes, including speech, pictures, and touch, are occasionally used in icon interfaces. These techniques are sure to become more common in the future.

Command Interface Structure

The remainder of this chapter concentrates on stream-oriented interactive command languages. We make this choice because this type of communication is the most common, offers the greatest power and flexibility to the user, and is convenient and efficient for frequent and experienced users.

The command interface is implemented by a program module called a **command handler** or **shell** (a term denoting the way in which this interface encloses the rest of the OS from the viewpoint of a user). The term "shell" was introduced by MULTICS and has become widely known through its use on UNIX systems.

The command handler or shell may be implemented in a variety of ways. For example, it may be:

- an integral part of the OS, as in OS/MVT or VAX/VMS.

- a distinct module of the OS that can be modified or replaced, as in RT-11 or CP/M.

- an ordinary program that may be easily replaced, as in UNIX.

These structures are contrasted in Figure 4–7. In some of these cases it is possible to substitute a customized command interface for the standard one. In a multiuser UNIX system, each user may even have a different interface at the same time.

Figure 4–7 Structuring Techniques for the User Interface

```
        OS
     INCLUDING
        C.I.
```

(a) Command Interface as an Integral Part of OS

```
        OS
       C.I.
   . . . . . . . . . . .
   . . . . . . . . . . .
   . . . .  . . . . . . .
```

(b) Command Interface as a Distinct Module

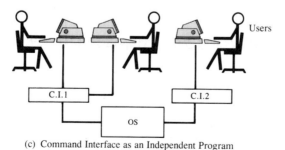

(c) Command Interface as an Independent Program

4.3 THE TERMINAL HANDLER

The user of an interactive command interface communicates with the OS through an I/O device. Most often this device is a video display terminal (VDT). Input is transmitted to the system primarily by means of a keyboard. In some cases, a pointing device such as a **mouse** may also be present. Output is presented on a screen that is able to display a number of lines of text, and in some cases also offers graphic capabilities. The terminal device is managed by a software component known as the **terminal handler.**

Although the terminal is managed by techniques similar, in part, to those used for other devices, its central role in the user interface gives it a special status. This role is evident from the terminal handler's position in Figure 4–1. Decisions made by the terminal handler can have a substantial effect on the overall command interface presented to the user, and can determine the form of communication available between users and application programs as well. For this reason, the terminal handler must be considered an integral component of the user interface.

Some issues that directly affect the command interface must be resolved by the terminal handler. They include:

- ECHOING. The terminal handler normally sends each character to the screen as it is received from the keyboard. This process is called **echoing.** Occasionally the user may want to display a different character or no character. Echoing may need to be disabled entirely for terminals accessed through remote communication lines. In this case, echoing is left to the remote terminal to avoid communication delays.

- TYPEAHEAD. If input characters are typed before a program is ready to process them, they may be saved in a buffer or thrown away—a process called **typeahead.** If saved, the buffer may be of limited capacity. When it is full, either further input may be ignored, or old contents may be destroyed. If typeahead (buffering) is permitted, echoing may occur when the characters are typed (as in most UNIX shells), when they are requested by the program (as in VAX/VMS or CP/M.), or both (as in at least one version of the UNIX shell).

- CHARACTER CONVERSION. The code representing some input characters may need to be translated when they are typed. This **character conversion** may convert lowercase letters to uppercase, or vice versa, or switch to a whole new coding system. Conversion may also be required before echoing, such as converting tab characters to a suitable number of spaces.

- LINE BUFFERING. The terminal interface may hold input until a full line is typed before sending it to the program. This **line buffering** technique offers users a valuable opportunity to check, edit, or even cancel a line, as long as the end-of-line key has not been pressed. However, some programs are designed to take immediate action when individual characters are typed, and must receive their input characters one by one.

- BREAK CHARACTERS. Most interactive command interfaces reserve a few special characters, called **break characters,** to cause immediate action. On many systems, for example, typing CTRL-C aborts the current program and reinitializes the command handler. Break characters must be recognized and acted on immediately, even if other input typed before them is still in a buffer.

- COMMAND HERALDS. The terminal interface forms a constant layer between the user and *all* programs that communicate through the terminal, including editors and other interactive programs as well as the command interface. A **command herald** [Rayner 1980] is a special character or sequence, recognized universally when typed as a prefix for a special command sequence. The terminal handler can recognize such a command herald and convey the following command to the command interface, without special arrangements required in the running program. A command herald may be used, for example, to allow selective logging of any interactive dialog, regardless of what program is running. This technique is discussed further in Section 4.6.

4.4 COMMAND LANGUAGES

Command Language Structure

The purpose of a command language (or job control language) is to specify a sequence of actions to be performed by the OS. In the most common type of stream-oriented command language, the user specifies each action by typing a line of instructions called a **command line.** Each command line begins with a single-word command that identifies the action to be performed. Most commands cause a program to be run that carries out the requested action.

For many commands, you may need to specify additional details, such as the names of files to be used for this particular run. You can make this specification through **command arguments,** which are typed on the command line following the command itself. You can compare a sequence of commands to a computer program in which each statement is a procedure call with appropriate arguments. Figure 4–8 details some typical commands for several command interfaces.

A typical command language defines a set of commands to specify the desired actions, together with the arguments required for each command. The simplest possible command language would include a single command:

```
RUN progname (arguments)
```

This command causes the execution of a specified program. The program name forms the first argument for the command RUN. (The general form of arguments will be discussed later.) This is analogous to a programming language providing only a call statement. Since any possible action desired can be embodied in a program, this language has the necessary power; however, it has many practical weaknesses, and no real OS uses such a language.

An extreme alternative is to eliminate the RUN command and make the name of every program a separate command. This approach, which would correspond to procedure calls in a language with no explicit CALL keyword (such as Pascal), may require searching many large file directories for each command. This approach is used in the standard UNIX command interfaces.

A compromise between these methods is to provide a limited set of standard commands, plus a RUN command to invoke additional programs from files. The standard commands cause execution of a system-controlled set of programs, which may be parts of the OS itself or may be programs stored and maintained in a special way. This approach, used in a great many systems, provides a fixed and visible distinction between system programs and user programs.

In still other cases the OS maintains a basic set of commands, but the user can install additional commands. Thus, some user programs can be accessed using their own name as a command, while others are executed using a RUN command. This technique is used by RSX-11 and VAX/VMS. Unfortunately, the installation process is complex.

Common Commands

Command languages that provide a fixed or initial set of commands normally include commands to access the programs considered most important in the total computing environment. These programs vary widely. In a typical general-purpose computing environment, commands will probably exist for at least the following activities:

- Display a list of the files in a directory

Figure 4–8 Some Typical Commands

UNIX:

```
ls                          list current directory
who                         show who is logged on
grep "ABC" file1            list lines containing "ABC"
                              from file1
pr *.txt |lpr               print all files whose names
                              end with ".txt"
sh proc1 3  7  "Hi there"   execute a command file named
                              "proc1"
```

MS-DOS:

```
copy file1 file2            copy file1 to file2
dir c:                      list directory of disk drive c
erase filea                 delete a file
edlin fileb                 edit a file
proc1                       run a command file named
                              "proc1.bat"
```

VAX/VMS:

```
pli myprog /list=listfile /optimize
                            compile pli program with selected
                              options
run myprog                  run user program (after compiling
                              and linking)
define filename $logname    define an alternate name for a
                              file
set default [newdir.proj1]  select a new default directory
type file1.pas;3            display a file on terminal
@proc1                      run a command file named
                              "proc1.com"
```

RT-11:

```
         ):*.mac            delete all files on disk 0 whose
                              names end with ".mac"
com      ortran /list:lfile myprog
                            compile FORTRAN program and
                              produce list file
run myprog                  run user program
load mt:                    install a device handler
@proc1                      run a command file named
                              "proc.com"
```

- Copy, rename, or delete files
- Run editing programs to create and edit text files
- Compile and link programs in various languages
- Display information about the system or the user's environment

A particular system may support many additional commands. Although common operations occur in most systems, there is little similarity between the names or argument formats used. For example, a command to change the name of a file would take the following form on several common systems:

```
CP/M:    REN newname oldname
PC/DOS:  RENAME oldname newname
UNIX:    mv oldname newname
```

```
VMS:     RENAME /OLDNAME=oldname /NEWNAME=newname
         CMS:    rename oldname * * newname = *
```

or, in IBM JCL:

```
//RENAME   EXEC  PGM=IEHPROGM
//SYSPRINT DD    SYSOUT=A
//SYS1     DD    UNIT=3330, VOL=SER=SYS001
//VOL1     DD    DISP=OLD, UNIT=3330, VOL=SER=ABC123
//SYSIN    DD    *
```

```
RENAME   DSNAME=oldname,VOL=3330=ABC123,NEWNAME=newname
         /*
```

Ongoing attempts to establish standard commands and command languages, especially by international researchers, are described in Unger [1975], Beech [1980], and Hopper and Newman [1986]. So far, these efforts have met with limited acceptance.

Command Arguments

To provide the necessary information for each specific use, commands may be augmented by arguments. The alternative is a separate command for each possible variation, a highly impractical approach. However, a tradeoff is possible between having many separate commands with few arguments, or a few commands with many arguments. The first method offers concise commands but allows fewer variations, and a large command set is difficult to remember. The second technique is most flexible but may require more typing for each command.

There are two common approaches to the syntax of arguments:

- POSITIONAL ARGUMENTS. **Positional arguments** are a sequence of strings separated by blanks or commas. Their meaning is determined by position, as in subroutines in most programming languages. This method is concise and simple, but the user must remember the rules for each command. It is difficult to leave arguments out. Giving arguments in the wrong order can lead to unexpected—possibly disastrous—results.

- KEYWORD ARGUMENTS. Each **keyword argument** is identified by a specific name and may or may not also have a data string. More typing is required, but more variations are possible; and each command, if recorded in a log or command file, is better documented.

An example of a command using positional arguments to invoke a Pascal compiler is:

```
PASCAL  prog1.pas prog1.obj
```

In this example, the first argument is expected to specify the file containing the source program, while the second argument names the file to receive the object code. If the arguments are accidentally reversed, the source program may be destroyed.

A similar example using keyword arguments is:

```
PASCAL  /SRC=prog1.pas  /OBJ=prog1.obj /NOLIST
```

Operating systems emphasizing simplicity, such as CP/M and UNIX, often use positional arguments. Those favoring a more powerful command structure support the keyword approach. Many larger systems, such as VAX/VMS, combine elements of both approaches.

If the program knows what types of arguments to expect, another method of obtaining them is to interactively ask the user for the necessary information. If information about expected arguments is stored with each program, the OS can automatically query for missing arguments. Relying exclusively on the dialog approach, however, can slow down system use, and makes it difficult to run programs in non-interactive environments.

Command Abbreviation and Completion

If commands are designed to be descriptive, they can be fairly long. It is tedious for experienced users to type frequently used commands in their entirety. Because of this, many command interfaces provide for **command**

abbreviation. With this technique, certain abbreviations are recognized to represent complete commands. The OS may define specific abbreviations that will be accepted for selected commands, such as e for `edit`, `dir` for `directory`, and so on. Alternatively, the command handler may be designed to accept *any* abbreviation, provided that it forms a unique prefix for exactly one recognized command. This approach is used by VAX/VMS; `dir`, `dire`, **and** `direct` are all acceptable abbreviations for the `directory` command. However, `di` is ambiguous, since several commands start with these two letters. As a further refinement, in some cases users or the OS can specify which choice should be used for ambiguous abbreviations, such as e for `edit`.

Command abbreviation requires that the user know the full set of potential commands, and may require a lot of searching when this set is large. For this reason it is not used by some standard UNIX shells. Another technique, however, called **command completion,** *is* used by certain UNIX shells. Introduced by TENEX, the command completion method allows a user to type an abbreviation for a command, followed immediately by a special control character, such as ESC. If the control character is typed, the command handler will determine if the characters typed so far form a valid, unambiguous abbreviation. If so, it will accept the command and *display the rest of its name on the terminal.* The screen will appear just as though the user had typed the entire command. If the abbreviation matches no command or more than one command, the interface will ring a bell. In this case the user is free to back up or to type additional letters.

A few interfaces have used a variation of command completion in which the interface watches each character typed and *automatically* completes the command as soon as the user provides a unique abbreviation. However, this technique is usually undesirable because of its high **astonishment factor**—in other words, users will be surprised by sudden and unexpected output while typing a word.

Command Recall and Editing

A few command interfaces retain a record of some number of recently used commands. If desired, users can recall commands from this record, edit them, and use them again. The UNIX C-shell is an example of an interface that supports this mechanism. If a complicated command or short series of commands is to be repeated, the recall mechanism allows the original commands to be reentered, avoiding retyping and the likelihood of error. This facility is especially useful when a long command has been typed with a slight error. Usually, the error is not detected until the entire line has been typed, and it is necessary to start over to correct it. With a recall feature, the almost-correct command can be corrected and reused.

Wild Cards

A different type of abbreviation often assists users in abbreviating file names. This technique, known as "wild cards," also allows identification of a whole set of files with similar names by a single character string. In a typical wild card mechanism, a special character such as "*" may be typed to represent any string of characters, including none. Thus the string j*.obj may stand for any (and all) file names which start with j and end with .obj, including jim.obj, joe.obj, j.obj, and so on. Usually a second special character is defined, such as "?," which may be used to stand for exactly one unspecified character.

Wild cards are a powerful and desirable mechanism for users, but they present problems for a command interface. If the command handler interprets the abbreviations, it must search for all possible matches and then present this information to programs in a reasonable form. This can be difficult and time-consuming if there are many matches. Alternatively, each program can interpret wild cards in its own arguments, and perhaps handle them more intelligently using standard subroutines. However, wildcards will then be available only when invoking programs that choose to deal with them.

Quality in Command Languages

Evaluation of the good and bad features of a specific command language is a subjective judgment that can lead to heated arguments among users. However, Schneider et al. [1980] have identified some characteristics which seem desirable in almost any good command interface. These include:

- CONSISTENCY. **Consistency** becomes an issue when we ask questions such as: Do the same terms and structures always mean the same thing? Is the same activity usually specified in the same way? Some common commands, such as COPY or LIST, mean very different things in different systems or environments. LIST may mean display a directory on the terminal, display a file on the terminal, print a file on a printer, and so on. Often compilers for various languages are invoked in very different ways, or similar command arguments are handled inconsistently by different commands.

- NATURALNESS. Do the terms and structures used seem "right" to each user? Does the system behave as expected, that is, have a low astonishment factor? Since all users will not agree on **naturalness,** this goal may be attainable only by systems that allow users to customize their own command interface.

- REASONABLENESS. Examples illustrating **reasonableness**

are shown in Figure 4–9. Does the system seem cooperative, impose no rules that seem unnecessary, and provide help and alternative actions? An interface that requires commands to be uppercase only, or in fixed column positions on a line, is not reasonable. A system that demands input the user may not understand, with no obvious means of help or escape, is unreasonable; so is one whose responses are rude or witty rather than helpful and polite.

- COMPLETENESS. The concept of **completeness** requires mechanisms available in one context to be usable in other appropriate contexts. Can the user do everything that "seems like it should work"? For example, if wild cards are sometimes allowed in file names, this facility should be available for all commands.

- SOUNDNESS. The **soundness** concept imposes a burden on an interface that strives for completeness. It requires that all commands that are syntactically correct will cause predictable and reasonable behavior.

Several additional factors contributing to a good command language are also discussed by Schneider et al. [1980]. One factor is the need to adapt the interface to the level of sophistication of each user. Novice or occasional users may require detailed prompts or menus and extensive help messages. Experienced users prefer brief prompts, concise messages, and the ability to abbreviate commands. The CMS command handler, for example, can be switched between **verbose mode,** which provides detailed messages and prompts, and **brief mode,** in which displayed information is kept short.

One other important concept is the principle of **force,** which says that the effort required to specify a command should be appropriate to the effect of that command. In most cases, commands should require little force. Abbreviations should be accepted, defaults provided for missing arguments, and so on. However, on a CP/M system it is too easy to type

ERA *.*

which results in deletion of all files. Such a drastic result should require more force. One solution is used by VAX/VMS, which requires file deletion commands to include the entire filename. For example:

delete myprog.pas;7

is the form necessary to delete even a single file, and

delete *.*;*

makes it slightly harder to delete all of them.

Figure 4–9 Some Examples of Unreasonableness

a. User cannot get further information or escape:

```
DO YOU WANT THE MASTER FILE INVERTED?
>?
INVALID RESPONSE
>no
INVALID RESPONSE
>quit
INVALID RESPONSE
>help
INVALID RESPONSE
      ...
```

b. System requires excessive confirmation:

```
>delete myfile
DO YOU REALLY WANT TO DELETE MYFILE?
>yes
ARE YOU SURE?
>yes
IF I PROCEED, THE INFORMATION IN MYFILE WILL BE
DESTROYED.  SHALL I PROCEED ANYWAY?
>yes
```

c. Rude and unhelpful responses:

```
>print file1 on lpr2
THERE'S NO SUCH PRINTER, YOU DUMMY!
```

d. Error detected, no further explanation:

```
>run prog1
ERROR
```

In many environments, a drastic request like "delete all files" will also result in a request for confirmation from the OS. These confirmation messages, however, should not be too extreme (see Figure 4–9).

To be fair, we should observe that some of the quality measures we have discussed conflict with each other. Moreover, real consistency is possible only if all parts of the user environment, including all compilers, editors, and other programs invoked by commands, are designed to conform to a common user interface philosophy. The operating system cannot meet this requirement alone. However, the command interface is the most central component. It must establish a standard of consistency and quality to make these attributes a possibility for the total environment.

4.5 RESPONSE LANGUAGES

As mentioned earlier, an operating system response language is a language by which an OS communicates information back to the user. This information comprises various messages, either in response to a user's direct request, or to provide the user with information about the current conditions and activities within the system. The types of responses that need to be considered by an OSRL are discussed here.

Messages

A command interface is a two-way street. Besides listening to the user, the system must return messages for various reasons. The interface may assist in the processing of messages from other interactive programs as well, helping to assure a consistent treatment.

Messages from the system serve a number of purposes. The following are the most frequent types:

- PROMPT MESSAGES. **Prompt messages** let the user know the OS is waiting for instructions or information. If they are not provided, the user may be unsure if the system is ready for input, or what type of input is expected.

- HELP MESSAGES. **Help messages** provide the user with information to help decide what to do next.

- PROGRESS MESSAGES. **Progress messages** tell the user that a long activity is still progressing, and possibly how much has been done. Relatively long activities, such as compiling, can benefit the user with periodic progress messages. They provide reassurance that the work is progressing and may aid in estimating how much longer it will continue.

- TERMINATION MESSAGES. **Termination messages** tell the user that the current activity has finished. This category includes error messages.

Each of these categories plays an important role in an effective command interface. Help facilities, which are especially valuable and require careful consideration, are discussed in the next section.

Help Messages

Help messages provide information on request about what can be done and how to do it. Help information is vital to the confused user who needs guidance. However, it can be verbose and should not be imposed on the user who doesn't need it. Some guidelines that may apply to a good help system are:

- Most help should be available on request, and successive requests should lead to more details.

- Some help should always be available when input is requested, ideally in any environment, and should correctly explain the current options to the user.

- The "standard" amount of help should be adjustable to give more to the inexperienced user and less to the experienced user.

A good example of a help facility that supports these principles is the hierarchical help system of VAX/VMS. In this system, typing the command HELP with no arguments causes a list of available commands to be displayed, as shown in Figure 4–10. This list is generally adapted to the user's current environment; for example, a list of editing commands may appear if help is requested while the editor is in use.

If the user then types HELP followed by a specific command name as an argument, an explanation of that command is displayed, in addition to a list of possible arguments, variations, or related topics. The user may obtain more information on these topics by typing HELP with additional arguments.

Help systems can often make effective use of a menu style, especially in environments that support rapid screen updating. An example is the version of PC-DOS supported on NCR computers (see Figure 4–11.) In this facility, a request for help (by pressing a special HELP key) from the normal command level results in a display list of all available commands. Users can select a specific command by moving the cursor to its name. A summary of the meaning of each selected command appears immediately at the bottom of the screen. If the user types another special key, more detailed help is displayed for the selected command.

A straightforward approach taken by UNIX systems is to provide help by displaying pages from the system reference manual directly on the screen. This idea is conceptually simple and attractive, but results in compromises in the manual structure that make it of limited usefulness in either displayed or printed form. The problem of designing help facilities that are equally effective whether displayed on-line or printed as manuals is a difficult but important design problem.

Figure 4-10 HELP on the VAX/VMS System

```
DIRECTORY

    Provides a list of files or information about a  file  or  group  of
    files.

    Format:

      DIRECTORY  [file-spec[,...]]

    Additional information available:

    Parameters Command_Qualifiers
    /ACL      /BACKUP    /BEFORE   /BRIEF    /BY_OWNER /COLUMNS    /CREATED
    /DATE     /EXCLUDE   /EXPIRED  /FILE_ID  /FULL     /GRAND_TOTAL
    /HEADING  /MODIFIED  /OUTPUT   /OWNER    /PRINTER  /PROTECTION
    /SECURITY /SELECT    /SINCE    /SIZE     /TOTAL    /TRAILING  /VERSIONS
    /WIDTH
    Examples

DIRECTORY Subtopic?
```

Figure 4-11 HELP on the NCR-DOS System

```
                    NCR On-Line Help Menu
                       Version 1.30

        _ ANSI       _ DEL        _ GOTO       _ RENAME
        _ ASSIGN     _ DEVICE     _ GRAFTABL   _ RESTORE
        _ BACKUP     _ DIR        _ GRAPHICS   _ RMDIR

                         . . .


        _ CTTY       _ FOR IN DO  _ RECOVER    _ VOL
        _ DATE       _ FORMAT     _ REM
     Press the Arrow Keys (↓↑→←) to select, the press    for HELP.
     Press the End Key to exit On-Line Help.
     Description: DIR [d:] [pathname] [filename [.ext]] [/P] [/W]
                  Lists files in a directory. Displays name, size, date.
```

4.6 COMMAND FILES

Many command interfaces allow commands to be written in advance and
stored in a file. The commands can then be executed by invoking the file by a
special shorthand. Such a file has many names, such as RT-11's indirect files,

CP/M's submit files, and CMS's exec files. We will refer to them generically as **command files.**

A command file mechanism provides a way of packaging sets of commands into named files. The file name may then be used as a command or command argument to invoke the entire set of commands at once. Command files are often thought of as batch files, but in a well-designed interface they can be much more powerful: command files can be a *tool for constructing programs,* and these programs, quite unlike batch jobs, can *interact* with the user as they progress. The commands in a command file, as well as the programs invoked by those commands, can receive input from *either* the terminal or the command file itself, and can have their output directed either to the terminal or to another destination.

A powerful command file facility can offer many desirable features. The following list gives some possibilities:

- accept arguments like standard commands, to be substituted in their text like macro arguments.

- allow command files to invoke other command files in a nested structure.

- allow input to come from either the terminal or the command file.

- allow optional display of the commands executed on the terminal, and optional logging to a file or printer.

- allow comments in command files for documentation purposes.

- allow the user to intervene when an error is detected, and then resume the command file at a suitable point.

The ability of command files to pass input to programs makes them a powerful mediator of prepackaged communication between users and all programs. Use of a command herald can play the same role here as in the terminal handler. Features such as those listed above can be made available to all programs. This mechanism is illustrated by the version of the DOS-99 operating system discussed by Mooney [1979]. A list of capabilities available through the command herald structure on this system (called **immediate commands**) is shown in Figure 4–12. In the system outlined by the figure, the ampersand (&) serves as a command herald. It is recognized in *any* interactive context, and the characters immediately following are given special meaning. The system uses three modes. In addition to normal (interactive) and command file modes, escape mode allowed temporary interactive input while command files were being processed. This was especially useful for error correction.

These facilities were put to good use in a software production environment, in which large command files were used as scripts to assemble selected modules into customized software systems.

Figure 4-12 Immediate Commands in DOS-99

(Command herald: "&")

COMMANDS USEFUL IN BOTH COMMAND FILES AND INTERACTIVE MODE:

&;	Begins a comment line (note that the comment will be inserted in any active log file).
&⤵	Continues to a new line on the terminal or command file without passing it to the program.
&S	Suppress logging, if a log file is open.
&L	Resume logging, if previously suppressed.
&&	Insert a single ampersand.

COMMANDS USEFUL IN COMMAND FILE AND ESCAPE MODES ONLY:

&n	Substitute the nth parameter that was passed to the command file, where n is a digit 1-8.
&\⤵	Toggle between command file mode and escape mode.
&\n⤵	If in command file mode, switch to escape mode, resume command file mode but skip n lines of the command file.
&*	If in escape mode, resume command file mode.
&#	Terminate the current command file. If nested files are active, terminate only the current one.
&!	Terminate all current command files.
&I	Ignore errors in future processing.
&E	Switch to escape mode if errors occur in future processing.

Figure 4-13 A UNIX Shell Program

```
#! /bin/csh -f
set file=/tmp/med.$$
cat <<'fin' >$file
g/Good morning!/d
g/Good afternoon!/d
g/Good evening!/d
g/What are you doing on at this time of night?/d
$-1a
'fin'
set time='date | awk 'printf $4' | awk -F: 'print $1''
if ($time < 6) then
        echo 'What are you doing on at this time of night?' >>$file
else if ($time < 12) then
        echo 'Good morning\!' >>$file
else if ($time < 18) then
        echo 'Good afternoon\!' >>$file
else
        echo 'Good evening\!' >>$file
endif
cat <<'fin' >>$file
```

4.7 COMMAND VS. PROGRAMMING LANGUAGES

The notion of a command file makes possible the use of control flow statements, such as branches, conditionals, and loops, in a sequence of commands, allowing command languages to take on many of the aspects of a programming language. In many cases, such command languages can be used to write useful programs without using a programming language at all. A major example of such programs "interpreted" by the command processor is the UNIX Shell. Figure 4–13 contains an example of a program written for the Shell. This program generates an appropriate greeting depending on the current time of day. The date command is first executed, which determines the current date and time. This information is filtered by a command called awk to extract the hour. A suitable phrase is selected depending on the hour, and a simple editor is used to place this phrase at the end of a file containing the "message of the day," a message which is displayed for all users when they log on. Similar facilities are provided in the EXEC processor of CMS, and in VAX/VMS DCL.

Programmability is also a feature of some older command languages, such as those of KRONOS and MULTICS. Colijn [1976, 1981] has demonstrated the use of these languages to solve the Tower of Hanoi problem and compute Ackermann's Function. Colijn's MULTICS programs for these applications are shown in Figure 4–14.

In applications where one programming language is used exclusively, if the language is suitable for interpretive use, it is sometimes possible to make it serve as the command language as well. This has been done, for example, with versions of LISP and BASIC.

4.8 OTHER COMMAND INTERFACE ISSUES

User Environments

In the course of interacting with a computing system, a user is presented with a **user environment** that establishes the type of commands or other input that may be meaningful at any given moment. The user environment is frequently changing. At any moment, the user environment is determined by the operating system, the program being executed, and the current conditions within that program.

An important element of the user environment is the **name space,** which is available to the user at any time. It defines the names that will be recognized

Figure 4–14 MULTICS Command Language Programs

```
&         Hanoi.ec - solve the Tower of Hanoi Puzzle
&
&         Calling sequence:  ec Hanoi n "s" "i" "d"
&
&         where n=no. of discs, and s,i, and d are the
&         names to be printed for the three stacks.
&
&command_line off
&if [greater &1 1] &then ec Hanoi [minus &1 1] &2 &4 &3
&print move disc &1 from &2 to &4
&if [greater &1 1] &then ec Hanoi [minus &1 1] &3 &2 &4
```

(a) This procedure prints the transfer sequence for the Tower
of Hanoi, calling itself recursively as required.

```
&         Ackermann.ec - compute Ackermann's function
&
&         calling sequence:  ec Ackermann m n
&
&                   n+1         if m = 0
&         A(m,n) =  A(m-1,1)    if m>0,n=0
&                   A(m-1,A(m,n-1)) if m>0,n>0
&
&command_line off
value$set_seg whocares
ec p1 &1 &2
value$dump A
&command_line on

p0.ec:  &command_line off
        value$set A $1

p1.ec:  &command_line off
        &if [nequal &1 0] &then ec p0 [plus &2 1]
        &if [nequal &1 0] &then &quit
        &if [ngreater &2 0]
        &then ec p2 &1 [minus &2 1]
        &else ec p1 [minus &1 1] 1

p2.ec:  &command_line off
        ec p1 &1 &2
        ec p1 [minus &1 1] [value A]
```

(b) This procedure computes and prints Ackermann's function. Three
subordinate procedures are used; the main procedure and p0
are concerned principally with setting up a numerical variable.
p1 and p2 do the actual calculations. The "command_line off"
statements suppress echoing of commands on the terminal.
Both examples are based on [Colijn 1981].

by commands and programs for files and other objects. Some command interfaces provide the user with various capabilities to influence this name space. VMS allows the definition of alternate names called **logical names** for files, which can be reassigned at will to real file names or portions of file names. The UNIX C-Shell provides for the definition of various types of commands as **aliases** for other commands, allowing abbreviations for commonly used commands and arguments.

Another aspect of the user environment may be the establishment of various options that affect how commands are processed or the behavior of certain programs. A wide variety of options may be maintained by various user interfaces. Examples include the extent of the prompt message that may be displayed between commands (CMS EXEC); the number of previous commands to be saved for possible recall (UNIX C-Shell); default format for printer output (DOS-99); treatment of special terminal input and display (many systems).

Any program that conducts a dialog creates a user environment. The command interface provides a command environment in which commands are the expected input. An interactive editor creates an editing environment with different expectations. Other types of environments may be produced by other interactive programs. Often the overall characteristics of the environment for an interactive session or job can be set by a special command file called a **profile,** which is executed automatically when the job or session is started.

The notion of different environments raises several issues:

- Does the command interface behavior, such as prompts or help facilities, suit the current environment?

- Is it possible to easily change between environments?

- How can command structures and names be kept as consistent as possible even in different environments?

- Is it possible or desirable to have only one environment in which system commands, file editing, or other activities are equally possible at any time?

The possibility of a single environment has been explored on systems as diverse as WYLBUR for MVS, Macintosh, and various LISP programming environments.

To some extent these issues transcend the design of an OS command interface alone. They can be resolved only by a unified *philosophy* that establishes a recommended format for all types of user interaction. A system with such a unified philosophy uses a consistent approach in its command interface, standard editor, and other interactive system programs, and recommends the same philosophy to application programs as well. The philosophies of UNIX, VMS, or Macintosh are markedly different. A word processor that fits comfortably into one of these environments would not be well suited for another without significant changes.

Filters

In some operating systems, programs that follow certain conventions may be usable as **filters** (programs that read a data file and produce a modified version, which may be processed in turn by a series of other programs, as in an assembly line). Filters play an important role in the UNIX philosophy. They are well matched to the UNIX communication structure called "pipes," which allow output from one program to be directly routed into the input of another concurrently running program.

Programs intended for use as filters must adhere to a suitable philosophy in their design. They are expected to read data from a single input stream, and produce a single output stream without extraneous information. For example, a filter to list the files in a directory should produce a listing with no headings or extra lines. These characteristics are not as suitable when programs are to be executed alone at a terminal. Because a filter program may also need to be run interactively, it may be designed to determine whether it is being run as a filter or not, and adjust its behavior as appropriate.

4.9 THE PROGRAM INTERFACE

The program interface is the means by which an OS provides services to, and communicates with, a running program. It is used by all user programs and often by components of the operating system as well, in particular the command handler. One responsibility of the program interface is to load and set up a program that is ready to begin. In addition, the interface must offer the proper response to normal or abnormal termination. While a program is in execution, the program interface accepts requests for system services and resources, and communicates them to the resource managers of the OS. This structure consists primarily of system calls by which programs communicate with the operating system.

System calls form a special type of procedure call, usually implemented by a distinct machine instruction. In addition to providing an efficient mechanism for invoking OS subprograms, this instruction performs a switch into privileged mode. (The system call instruction is described in more detail in Appendix A.) System calls are viewed by a program as low-level procedures, directly accessible only from assembly language. Most programs written in high-level languages will access these calls through subprogram libraries, where the subprograms carry out the system calls and may perform other functions as well.

A well-designed OS will provide calls for simple, efficient access to all the services it can perform. In addition, it is desirable that many common services are accessible in a similar way in various systems so that programs can be easily moved from one OS to another—such as agreeing on a standard set of system calls.

Initialization and Termination

Part of the responsibility of the program interface is to load and initialize programs for execution. In a simple, single-user OS, this function might be performed by a loader, always resident in memory, which reads program code from a file, copies it directly into a standard area of memory, and transfers it to a standard starting location. More commonly, the program in the file is not an exact copy of memory, and the storage area is not fixed. The loader may have to perform relocation, initialize data areas and so on. If the loader is complex, it may itself be a transient part of the OS, copied into memory when needed.

The program loader works closely with other components of the OS, such as job management and storage management. These modules identify programs to be started, assign the required memory, and invoke the loader to perform initialization. If the program is moved or suspended in the course of execution, the storage manager is responsible for this activity.

Program termination may be invoked by a system call or may occur automatically at the end of the program. Use of a system call allows the program to return information, such as a status code to another process or to the user through the command interface. The responsibilities of the program interface include managing this returned information and returning the program's resources to the available pool. In particular, this responsibility means properly closing any files left open, and reclaiming all memory used for the program's code and data.

System Services

The purpose of system calls is to request system services. Many of these request direct use of system resources, such as access to files or input or output on various devices. Other calls request permission for future use of a resource, such as opening a file or allocating a region of memory. Additional system services may provide information, such as system load conditions, time of day, or the present status of an I/O activity.

Some of the types of services provided by system calls in typical systems are summarized below. Specific services in each of these areas will be identified in appropriate chapters throughout the text.

- USER INTERFACE. User interface services allow a program to find out information about its environment, such as resource limits, standard I/O channels, or command language variables. They also allow a program to access the command arguments specified when the program was invoked, making it possible for a program to operate in a variety of environments. We consider this category in the next section.

- PROCESS MANAGEMENT. Services in this category support management of multiple processes and communication between processes.

- DEVICE MANAGEMENT. These services manage physical I/O devices in ways appropriate to their structure and purpose. They also include various services for communication with remote systems.

- TIME MANAGEMENT. This group includes services to time events and to determine the actual time of day, and to manage explicit timers and timed events.

- MEMORY MANAGEMENT. These services support dynamic allocation of memory and access to memory status information.

- FILE MANAGEMENT. These services manage file space and file access, and may also provide access to I/O devices treated as special files.

- EXCEPTION HANDLING. These are services that establish procedures for the later handling of errors or exceptional conditions that may arise due to program actions or events external to the program.

- SYSTEM MANAGEMENT. Services in this category provide suitably privileged system managers with overall control of system operation, such as scheduling control, setting clocks, initialization and shutdown, adding and removing resources, performance monitoring, or maintaining user records and system logs.

- OTHER CATEGORIES. Other possible types of system calls include program initialization and termination; control of specific I/O devices and device types, such as terminals and printers; special services to support high reliability, real-time system requirements, and distributed operation.

4.10 USER INTERFACE OPERATIONS

A few system calls provided by various OSs directly access and control the user interface. We consider some examples in this section.

The command and arguments by which the program was invoked may be accessed in several different ways. In UNIX the individual arguments (but not the original line) are available as named variables in the user environment. The original command line may also be available uninterpreted, as in VMS, RT-11, or CP/M.

Some program interfaces allow programs to present lines to the command interpreter to be parsed, or processed, as commands. This facility is provided by RT-11. Although UNIX does not allow a program to call the shell through a system call, any process can create a new process with a private shell that can be used in a similar way. Many OSs, including CP/M, MS-DOS, VMS, and UNIX, provide system calls or other mechanisms to aid in parsing and interpreting file names. A variety of system calls may exist to obtain information about the user environment or the system itself, or to make changes to the environment, such as setting options.

The proposed system calls related to the user interface in IEEE [1985a] provide mechanisms to obtain basic information about the OS; obtain the original command line; obtain arguments one by one from the command line; and determine information about some "standard" input and output channels.

4.11 SUMMARY

The user interface is the gateway between a computer system and its users. It has two parts: the command interface and the program interface.

The command interface supports two-way direct communication between users and the operating system. This communication may take a variety of forms (touch, sound, graphics, menu), but the most prevalent form is an interactive stream command language.

An important element of the command interface is the terminal handler. This module is responsible for managing characters and lines as typed or controlling the screen display. It also manages communication with other programs.

You need to consider many issues in the design of a command language: the set of commands to be included, use of a run command, choice of positional or keyword argument syntax, command abbreviation, and wild cards.

A command language is also a response language. Types of responses in an interactive environment include prompt, help, progress, and termination messages. Help messages are especially important and should be designed to be adaptable to the needs of each situation.

Command files are a useful hybrid between batch and interactive commands. They provide a means for packaging commands into a file that can be invoked by a single command. Unlike batch jobs, the command file can interact with its submitter.

The program interface provides the means by which programs obtain services from the operating system. The primary mechanism is the system call. Important services you can invoke by system calls will be discussed throughout the text.

≡ FOR FURTHER READING ≡

A number of books have given comprehensive treatment to user interface issues, focusing especially on interactive command interfaces of various types. An early broad survey was provided by Martin [1973]. A more recent review of many issues in user interface design is provided by Shneiderman [1987].

The evolution of job control languages is described by Barron and Jackson [1980]. An early icon-based command interface, the Xerox STAR, is described by Smith et al. [1982]. A series of conferences has focused on command language issues and possible standard command languages. Some interesting ideas may be found in the proceedings of these conferences [Unger 1975; Beech 1980; Hopper & Newman 1986].

Quality issues in command languages are considered by Schneider et al. [1980]. Rayner [1980] describes command heralds, and their use in DOS-99 is explained in Mooney [1979]. The use of a command language (the UNIX shell) as a programming language is studied by Dolotta and Mashey [1980]. A user interface structure to support logging and command files is described by Mooney [1982]. Sakamura [1987c] describes the novel "man-machine interface" developed by the BTRON project.

Frank and Theaker [1979b] describe the user interface on the portable MUSS system. A good presentation of the standard UNIX shell is contained in Kernighan and Pike [1984]. Aspects of the KRONOS and MULTICS command languages are discussed by Colijn [1976, 1981].

A good and consistent treatment of the program interface is given by Milenković [1987]. A standard set of system calls suitable for portable applications is proposed in IEEE [1985a]. The UNIX program interface is described by Bach [1986], and a standard form for this interface is proposed in IEEE [1986]. Other useful treatments of specific program interfaces include Kenah and Bate [1984] for VMS, Popek and Walker [1985] for LOCUS, Ready [1986] for VRTX, Ohkubo et al. [1987] for CTRON, Monden [1987] for ITRON, and many of the presentations in Zarella [1981, 1982, 1984].

≡ IMPORTANT TERMS ≡

alias
astonishment factor
break character
brief mode
character conversion
command
command abbreviation
command argument
command completion
command file
command handler
command herald
command interface
command language
command line
command logs
completeness
consistency
echoing
filter
force
help facility
help message
icon
immediate command
job-control language
keyword argument

line buffering
logical name
menu system
mouse
name space
naturalness
operating system command
    and response language (OSCRL)
operating system command
    language (OSCL)
operating system response
    language (OSRL)
positional arguments
profile
program interface
progress message
prompt message
reasonableness
shell
soundness
terminal handler
termination message
typeahead
user environment
user interface
verbose mode

≡ REVIEW QUESTIONS ≡

1. Explain briefly three different measures of the quality of a command language.

2. Explain briefly three features of a command language that are important primarily because of their usefulness in command files.

3. State one advantage to use of a RUN command in a command language.

4. State one advantage to use of keyword arguments rather than positional arguments.

5. Why would it be important for a program to know whether it was invoked by a terminal command or a command file?

6. What is the principal difference between submitting a batch job and running a command file?

7. Describe two desirable qualities of a command interface and illustrate each with a specific example.

8. List and describe briefly five characteristics of a command language that are desirable primarily to support command files.

9. List and briefly describe three possible criteria that you can use to evaluate the quality of a command language.

10. List three examples of common system calls unrelated to file management.

ASSIGNMENTS

1. In an icon-based command interface, such as the Macintosh example of Figure 4–6, commands are formed by using a mouse (or similar pointing device) to select objects from a screen display. For example, you might enter a command to print a copy of a file by selecting the icon for the file and then selecting an icon or menu item representing the print operation. This may cause a new window to appear, allowing further option selections. Discuss the advantages and disadvantages of this approach as compared to stream-oriented command languages. Would the icon method be more attractive to some categories of users than to others? Which ones?

2. Suppose a terminal handler supported none of the capabilities described in Section 4.3. Instead, it passed every typed character directly to the command handler or application program as received, without buffering, interpretation, or echoing. Which of the missing features could be provided by the program? What difficulties would be encountered?

3. Suppose a stream-oriented command interface recognizes commands from a predefined set. The interface is expected to match characters to commands incrementally as typed and signal when an unambiguous prefix has been typed. Design a data structure for representing command names. What steps are required to add new commands to your structure?

4. Consider a command interface as described in Assignment 3, except that any file name may be used as a command. What data structures

could be used in this case? What additional difficulties would be encountered?

5. Suppose that a command interface has no knowledge of the specific arguments expected by each command. How could the arguments, actually received, be organized and made available to the program? Consider both positional syntax and keyword syntax.

6. How could a program supply information to the command handler about the specific arguments expected? Suggest a data structure to represent this information.

7. Outline an algorithm for a procedure that determines if a particular file name matches a wildcard specification. Let the character "?" represent any single character, and let the character "*" represent any number of characters (including zero).

8. Consider any specific command interface with which you are familiar. List five characteristics of this interface which have a high astonishment factor.

9. Collect several examples of unreasonableness, inconsistency, and similar problems found in a command interface of your choice. Suggest design changes to correct these problems.

10. List some important ways in which the requirements of an effective on-line help system differ from those of a printed manual. Discuss how you might organize a set of information intended both for on-line help and for printing of manuals on demand.

11. An example of a command file might allow a user to type

```
pascal  file1, file2, file3
```

to compile a series of any number of programs in Pascal. Suppose that such a command should be translated as

```
pascom  file1.pas
pascom  file2.pas
pascom  file3.pas
link    file1.obj, file2.obj, file3.obj
```

Suppose further that if any file name is invalid or not recognized, the user should have an opportunity to correct the name without restarting the entire procedure.

    a. List the capabilities required in the command file system.

    b. Select a command interface which supports command files. Can the described command file be written on your system? If not, what capabilities are missing?

12. Investigate how the environment created by your favorite command interface can be customized to suit the preferences of each user. Prepare a profile command file for this system, specifying the environment as completely as possible. List some changes a user might want to make that are not possible.

13. As discussed in Section 4.10, it is sometimes useful for an application program to invoke the command interface to parse or execute program-generated commands. Discuss how this might be done with each of the organizations shown in Figure 4–7.

14. Select a command interface that you have used for a computing system. State and explain two strengths and two weaknesses of this interface. Give concrete examples to support your answers. Concentrate on the command interface itself *not* on system tools, such as editors or compilers.

15. Suppose you could design a command interface to your own tastes, with no constraints and with no need to keep it similar to any other interface. Outline the characteristics of this interface. What features discussed in the text would you include? Give reasons for your choices.

≡ PROJECT ≡

This section describes a programming project to construct a command interface for a simple multiprogramming operating system. You should read the general description in this text in conjunction with the more specific descriptions given in your project manual. The interface to be constructed is an important component of the multiprogramming executive (MPX) project described later in the text.

The command interface is called COMHAN (short for command handler). Its role is to *read* a command entered via the system console keyboard, to *analyze* the command, and to *execute* the command. The important characteristics of consistency, naturalness, reasonableness, completeness, and soundness are important considerations in the design of COMHAN.

Commands will be added to COMHAN by other projects in this book so the necessary system commands to control the MPX operating system will be present when needed. The initial set of commands which COMHAN should support is as follows:

1. VERSION: Print the version number (including date) for COMHAN and MPX.

2. DATE: Set the date in COMHAN for use later by MPX. This command is also used to display the current date.

3. DIRECTORY: Print a directory of the programs on disk which are loadable under MPX. (Support software is provided to read the directory entries from disk.)

4. STOP: Stop execution of COMHAN and MPX, and returns to the normal operating system of the computer system on which COMHAN is being run.

5. HELP: Print help information about all commands or a specific command.

The above commands should be supported by COMHAN in a manner consistent with the characteristics desired in a command interface. You must decide what must be entered for a command and what the responses of the commands should be. The following questions should be considered while designing COMHAN:

- Are command abbreviations allowed?

- What wild cards (if any) are allowed?

- How is help information requested? When requested, what is the format of the help output?

- What is the display format of COMHAN going to be (a simple menu, a simple prompt, or a fancy selection screen using the display features available)?

Remember that commands will be added to COMHAN in the future. Hence, such commands must be easy to add. This implies that COMHAN should be table-driven using the appropriate data structures to provide for the easy addition of new commands.

The project manual provides the details of the support environment available to you, and of other specific requirements for completing this project within that environment.

Process
Management

Process Management

5.1 INTRODUCTION

The central purpose of any computer system is to perform useful work for the system's users. This work is carried out through the execution of application programs. Increasingly, the activities performed by these programs have come to be represented in operating systems by a model known as a **process.**

Another name often used for *process* is *task.* This term is widely used in some environments, especially in connection with real-time executives or large IBM systems. Some writers consider a task to be a part of a process, so that a process may consist of multiple tasks. For consistency in this text we will stick with the term *process.*

The precise meaning of the process concept, introduced in Chapter 1, varies with each operating system. Informally, you could think of a process as a *unit of activity* or a *program in execution.* Note that a process is an active concept. A program stored in a file or in memory is not a process. It becomes a process only when it is "in execution." This does not imply that a process is actually running at all times; in fact, partially executed processes often must wait while the computer performs other actions. However, each process is "working on" a program, even if its activity is temporarily stopped.

In most cases a process may be referred to more descriptively as a **sequential process,** to emphasize the fact that each process represents a single sequence of actions that take place one at a time. However, multiprogramming techniques can be used to share a computer's resources among many processes at a time. Using these techniques, a set of processes can all be in progress at the same time, taking turns at execution by the CPU. The execution of these processes is said to be **interleaved.** Interleaved processes provide the illusion of concurrent execution, and form a system of **concurrent sequential processes.**

True simultaneous execution may be possible in a multiprocessor environment, which includes more than one CPU. This type of system introduces some subtle difficulties not found with a single CPU, and its discussion will be deferred to a later chapter. Here we will assume that there is only one CPU, and that concurrent execution means interleaved execution.

To do useful work, a process must execute a program. However, it is not necessary that each program correspond to exactly one process. In some systems (e.g., VMS), a single process may execute a series of different programs. In other environments (such as UNIX), it is common for a program to consist of several distinct processes, each representing a separate sequence of activities that logically continue at the same time.

The process model is a powerful concept that can effectively represent most of the activities that present-day operating systems are expected to support. Most operating systems represent application programs by some type of process. In many cases, major parts of the operating system are represented by processes as well. When it is necessary to distinguish these cases, we will use the terms **application process** or **system process,** respectively. For systems that make full use of the process model, effective management and control of processes becomes a critical responsibility.

To become an effective mechanism for managing a set of activities, a process must be formally defined and represented by an operating system. The basic ideas are handled by different OSs in many different ways. Often the choice of techniques has a major impact on the ways in which processes can be used to support various applications. The remainder of this section will identify the principal issues, and outline their more detailed treatment, which will appear in the rest of the chapter and those that immediately follow.

Although a process is not a data object, the OS must represent each process by a data structure in order to keep track of its status and manage its activities. This data structure, usually called a **process control block (PCB),** is described in Section 5.2. Some systems maintain a large set of descriptive and status information in the PCB of each process, allowing more intelligent operations on processes, but perhaps requiring considerable space and time to maintain the process control blocks.

Throughout its operation, a process must make use of a set of **resources.** The exact resources needed in this set will vary as time goes on. The two resources that are *always* needed by each process for execution are a CPU and memory space. Other resources that may sometimes be required include files, I/O devices, and shared information in main memory. By their nature, many of these resources may be used by only one process at a time. Because of this, processes may be required to wait when needed resources are not available. The interaction of processes and their resources is discussed in Section 5.3.

Processes and resources are complex subjects, raising issues that must be studied with care. Two chapters following this one are devoted to a fuller exploration of these issues. One issue is scheduling the use of certain resources by processes, a problem that we will examine in Chapter 6. A second set of problems is caused by the interaction, intentional or not, of processes that execute concurrently. This interaction forms the subject of Chapter 7.

Because of the need to wait when necessary resources are in use, each process alternates between running and waiting. A waiting process may be waiting for a variety of reasons, and these reasons determine how the process should be treated. To represent these distinctions, a process is considered to move through a series of distinct states. Process states are considered in Section 5.4.

A running process makes use of the registers and other physical elements of a CPU. When that process is required to wait, information in these registers must be saved in some way, so it can be restored intact when the process receives another turn at execution. The information to be saved is called the **context** of the process. This information may also be referred to as the *CPU state.* The act of saving the context of one process and restoring that of another is called **context switching.** If this switch takes too much time, it may limit the frequency with which processes may reasonably be switched. This subject is examined in more detail in Section 5.5.

Some older operating systems that made use of the process concept supported only a small, permanent set of processes with little explicit interaction. Today many systems allow processes to be freely created and destroyed, and to establish various types of relationships. We develop these ideas in Section 5.6.

Although basic process management can proceed without any direct involvement by the processes themselves, many OSs support explicit operations by which processes may access or modify their own attributes, or interact with one another. These operations fall into three categories:

1. process creation and control
2. interprocess communication
3. scheduling control

Operations in the first category are discussed in Section 5.7. Issues and operations for interprocess communication require a more extended discussion, which is deferred to Chapter 7. Explicit operations for scheduling control are found primarily in real-time executives.

5.2 PROCESS REPRESENTATION

The principal data structure used by an OS to represent a process is the process control block. The PCB contains all the information the OS elects to maintain about a process to describe its attributes and keep track of its status.

The size and content of a PCB varies considerably. A real-time executive like VRTX squeezes all necessary information into 80 bytes, while more complex OSs like UNIX or VMS require hundreds of bytes per process.

Despite this wide variation, a fairly standard set of information may be found in most process control blocks. This information includes:

- process name, by which the process may be identified by users or by other processes. Sometimes there is a distinct external name for users (usually a character string) and an internal name (usually an integer).

- process state, a code representing the current state for this process, or a link to a queue that represents that state.

- process context (CPU state), a storage area for register contents and other information that must be saved when the process is not running.

- memory use, information about the memory allocated to this process and the current location of its program code and data.

- resource use, information about resources currently in use by this process, and any restrictions or quotas on future resource use.

- process priority, a value that helps determine the relative priority to be given to this process when scheduling CPU use and allocating resources.

- relationships, information about relationships that may exist between this process and other processes, such as those it has created.

- accounting information, records of time and other resources that have been used by this process, and who owns the process, to be used for billing or analysis.

In addition, a variety of specialized information representing other aspects of the execution of a process may be found in specific PCBs. Most of the information contained in a typical PCB will be described in more detail in later sections of this chapter or in later chapters.

An operating system may be organized with a fixed array of PCBs in a suitable data area, or may allocate PCBs as needed, collecting them on a linked list. A possible declaration for a PCB data type might take the following form:

```
TYPE PCB:

    /* pointer to next PCB */
    next_PCB:       pointer to PCB;

    /* process identifiers */
    external_name:  char[20];
    internal_name:  integer;

    /* scheduling priority */
    priority:       integer;

    /* state and associated queue */
    state:          integer;
    state_queue:    pointer to PCB;

    /* data for CPU state */
    context:        integer[32];

    /* relatives */
    parent:         pointer to PCB;
    children:       pointer to PCB queue;

    /* memory use */
    program_start:  address;
    program_size:   integer;
    data_start:     address;
    data_size:      integer;

    /* resource control block */
    resources:      pointer to RCB;

    /* up to 10 file control blocks */
    files:          FCB[10];

    /* owner's id code */
    owner:          integer;

    /* time spent executing and performing I/O */
    CPU_time:       integer;
    IO_time:        integer;

END PCB;
```

5.3 PROCESSES AND RESOURCES

To make further progress at any moment in carrying out its assigned activities, a process must be able to use certain resources that, in general, must be shared with other processes. One obviously necessary resource is a CPU to execute the instructions of the process. Other important resource categories include main memory space, secondary storage space, and I/O devices. Each of these are **physical resources**—that is, they are permanent components of the computer, and must be controlled by the operating system.

Although files are not physical resources, they are usually treated in this category because of their possibly long lifetimes and ability to be shared. Thus, files are also controlled by the OS.

Another important category of resources is formed by information structures stored within files or main memory. These are **logical resources,** which often have a much shorter lifetime than physical resources. Many logical resources are *not* under the direct control of the operating system. They are considered resources only when a set of processes agrees to share them.

By their nature, physical resources are **reusable.** They are not destroyed when used, so they may be used repeatedly. In most cases, however, such resources may only be used by one process at a time. Two processes cannot use the same memory at once for separate purposes, nor output data at random to the same printer. A reusable resource that can be used by only one process at a time is called **serially reusable.** To maintain the integrity of these resources, the OS must allocate, or assign, each one to a process as it is needed. The OS must keep records showing the current status of each resource (either "available" or "allocated to process P"), and must have a strategy for deciding when to allocate each resource to a particular process—and when to deallocate the resource as well. Finally, for effective control, the OS must be able to prevent use of the resource by processes to which it has not been properly allocated.

Other reusable resources, especially files, may be shared by more than one process under some conditions. However, a similar type of allocation is necessary with these resources as well.

Resources that are not reusable are **consumable;** they can be created by one process and destroyed after use by another, such as blocks of data in a message. There is a similar need for an allocation strategy for these resources, but this strategy must be established by voluntary cooperation among the processes involved. An important goal of the allocation strategy is to ensure **mutual exclusion,** preventing processes from improperly accessing resources while they are in use by other processes. This is an important problem with a number of subtle difficulties. We will defer a detailed examination until Chapter 7.

The way we can solve these allocation problems depends on the nature of the resource. As already suggested, two resource types demand special treatment: CPUs and memory. These resources have two special characteristics:

1. They are accessed *directly,* not through system calls.
2. They are *always* needed by every process.

The first of these observations is true because each process uses the CPU and accesses memory during execution of each machine instruction. The OS cannot monitor and control each use; it must use other means to prevent misuse of these resources. The tools required for effective control include privileged instructions, memory protection mechanisms, and an interrupting timer.

Because of the second observation, the OS must assume that any process that does not currently have its CPU and memory resources allocated is waiting for their use. Thus, there will often be many processes waiting, and a strategy is needed for deciding which waiting process should receive each resource as it becomes available. This leads to the problem of **scheduling.** You need to consider a great many issues in developing a suitable scheduling strategy for CPUs and memory resources; we will explore these issues in Chapter 6.

Other system-controlled resources, including files and I/O devices, do not have the special characteristics listed above. Actual use of these resources, such as reading a file or printing a line on a printer, is accomplished by system calls. The operating system may require that these be preceded by requests to allocate the resources. The OS will reject a request for use if the resource has not been allocated. It will defer a request for allocation, requiring the process to wait, if the resource is not currently available.

Because resources in this category are needed only occasionally, processes are expected to signal their needs by explicitly requesting allocation. There will be few processes waiting for each specific resource, and the scheduling problem is greatly simplified. However, other problems arise in the efficient management of these resource requests, especially the potentially serious problem of **deadlock,** in which resources that some processes are waiting for cannot be made available because they are held by other processes, which in turn are waiting for other unavailable resources. These problems are also discussed in Chapter 7.

The OS must maintain a record of processes waiting for each distinct resource it manages. This record usually takes the form of a queue, whose entries can be added or removed in some systematic order. The queue is an important data structure for process management. In most cases, the most natural form for such a queue is a linked list; but other representations, such as tables or arrays, are also used. The most common order of service for such a queue is first in, first out. In an operating system queue, however, many other orderings are possible. This is especially true for process scheduling queues.

A process is entered into a queue by linking its PCB to the list in some manner. For some queues, especially those used for CPU scheduling, a link field may be reserved in the PCB itself. Each PCB on the queue contains a pointer to the next in this dedicated field. This is an efficient technique for queues on which most processes are frequently entered, but it requires dedicating a special location in every PCB. For other queues that are less frequently used, separate entries may be constructed with pointers to each PCB in the queue. These techniques are illustrated in Figure 5–1.

Figure 5–1 Queue Structures for Process Management

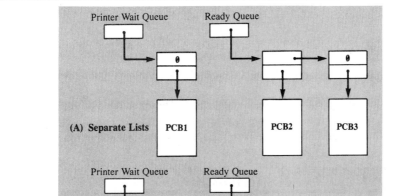

5.4 PROCESS STATES

The concept of **process state** is widely used to keep track of the current status of each process: At each moment, a process is considered to be in one of a small set of states which represent its current activity or resource needs.

An active process is either running or waiting; if not running, it is waiting for some resources (including at least a CPU) required for further progress. In addition, it may be waiting for the occurrence of a specific **event,** such as a signal from another process, or the completion of an I/O operation. The simplest possible model for process states would include two states: **running** and **waiting.**

However, because the CPU is such a critical resource, no process is given the CPU while it is waiting for something else. Thus, processes waiting for the CPU are treated in two distinct categories, depending on whether they are also waiting for something else. A process that is waiting *only* for the CPU is in a **ready state,** while one that is waiting also for other resources, or for the occurrence of specific events, may be said to be in a **blocked state.**

A state diagram illustrating the three principal states for a process is shown in Figure 5–2. The circles in a state diagram represent possible states, and the arrows represent permissible transitions from state to state. In the usual sequence, a process begins in the *ready* state. When its turn comes, the CPU is assigned to it. The process is now in the *running* state. It runs until it requires more resources or needs to wait for some event, when it enters the *blocked* state. When the resource is allocated or the event occurs, the process returns to the *ready* state, awaiting another turn at the CPU.

The dashed arrow in the figure represents a transition directly from the *running* state to the *ready* state. This transition can occur in environments such as timesharing systems. In such systems the execution of a process may be stopped when a time limit has expired, or when a more important process becomes *ready,* even though the running process has no other reason to wait.

Figure 5–2 A Basic Process State Diagram

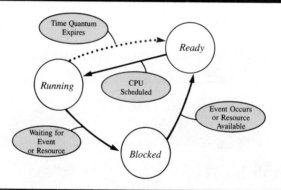

The names we have used for the states of a process are typical ones; the exact names used by each OS vary widely. In addition, the blocked state may be partitioned in various ways, depending on what the process is waiting for. A useful distinction can be made between waiting for events that are expected to occur very soon (e.g., completion of a disk transfer), or for events that may not occur for a long time, if ever (e.g., a signal from another process or terminal user). A process that is waiting for long-term events may be placed in a **suspended** state. Often, the programs and data for a suspended process may be removed from memory and swapped to disk. When the awaited event occurs, the process is no longer blocked by that event but may have to wait further to be restored to memory. This leads to a more complex state diagram such as the one shown in Figure 5–3. Also shown in this figure is an **initial state** for processes that have been created but have not yet begun to execute, and a **terminal state** for processes that have completed execution. The purpose of the terminal state is to allow final status information to be obtained from a process before it is completely destroyed.

Figure 5–3 State Diagram with Additional States

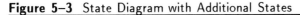
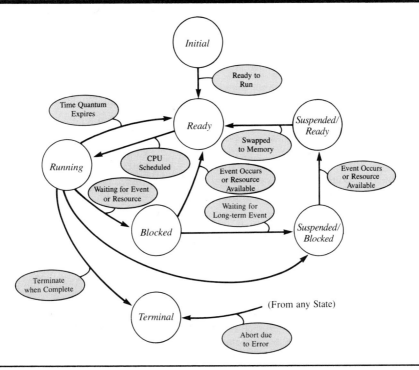

If the computer system has one CPU, only one process can be running at any instant in time. To achieve an illusion of concurrency, processes execute in an interleaved manner. Multiprogramming becomes efficient because this use of the CPU by one process can take place while other processes are waiting for I/O operations to complete, or for other events to occur. Each process then goes through many cycles of alternate running and waiting.

Figure 5–4 illustrates a series of successive phases that might be experienced by a typical set of processes running in a multiprogramming operating system. At any moment, only one process can be in the *running* state. Other processes vary between the *ready* and *blocked* states. However, because a number of processes are available, some process is running at all times.

Figure 5–4 Process States vs. Time (Simplified)

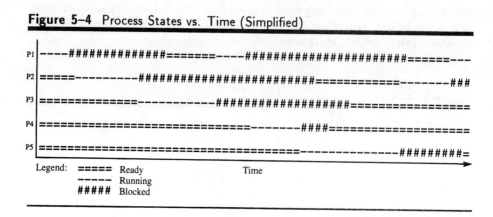

Figure 5–4 is actually unrealistic in two respects. First, even with many processes, there may be times when all of them are simultaneously blocked waiting for external events, residing in time periods called **idle time** during which no process is running. During such times a portion of the operating system is executing, but not necessarily doing any useful work. Sometimes the OS runs a special system process, called an **idle process**, which simplifies the scheduling problem by guaranteeing that some process is always ready to run. On early versions of UNIX, such a process was put to work on problems such as finding prime numbers or computing the constant *e* to a million decimal places.

The second unrealistic aspect of Figure 5–4 is its neglect of the time used between processes. Every time a process stops running, the OS must run for a short period to select and activate a new process and perform a context switch. This extra time is a form of overhead that can be significant if processes are changed too frequently or if the scheduling strategy is too complicated. A more realistic example is presented in Figure 5–5.

Figure 5–5 Process States vs. Time (Realistic)

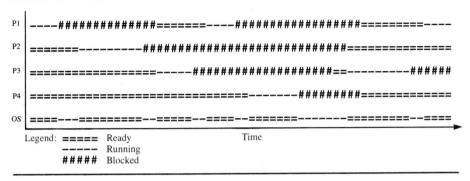

Legend: ===== Ready
         ----- Running
         ##### Blocked

Time

5.5 CONTEXT SWITCHING

Since processes running in a multiprogramming operating system must periodically give up control of the CPU, we must have a way to preserve the information stored in registers, status flags, and the like while the CPU is in use by the OS or by other processes. In switching from one process to another, it is necessary to save all information that the first process maintained in the CPU registers in some convenient way, and to replace it with the corresponding information for the second process. As we noted, this information is known as the **context** of the process, and the activity is called **context switching.** It may occur thousands of times a second in large timesharing systems.

The importance of keeping track of the exact status of a process can be shown by an analogy from human experience. Our minds may be capable of keeping track of a couple of simultaneous activities, but mistakes are likely if the number of activities becomes large, as illustrated in Figure 5–6. If we are using a recipe in baking a cake, we have a series of steps that we must follow. If we are on step three—add the first of the two cups of flour required— and the telephone rings, our activity will temporarily change from baking to speaking on the telephone (in other words, a "human mind context switch" takes place). Upon completing the telephone conversation, hanging up and returning to the activity of baking, we must remember exactly where we were in the recipe. If we remember adding the flour but forget we had only added the first cup of two, the result will not be the cake that the recipe is supposed to produce. Similarly, a failure to save all of a process's registers or status upon a context switch will (usually) cause the process to produce incorrect results.

Figure 5-6 Failure to Remember the Status of an Activity (Process)

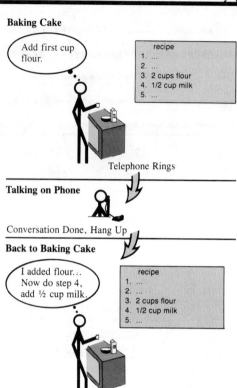

ERROR!! ONE CUP FLOUR SHORT!

In the simplest cases, processes give up control of the CPU voluntarily at convenient points in their program and can prepare by saving the necessary information. In more complex cases, loss of control can occur asynchronously as a result of interrupts at any time; hence, the loss and regaining of CPU control must be transparent to a process. When the process resumes, everything in the execution environment (register contents, status words, address spaces, stacks, current location in the program, and so on) must appear exactly as it was when the process ceased execution.

It is important that a context switch be performed as efficiently as possible. To a large extent, the cost of context switching is determined by the CPU architecture. Generally, when there is more information to save, the cost is greater. Many architectures have special instructions providing rapid saving and restoring of required information to reduce overhead. Some machines provide multiple register sets, so that in some cases information can be left in one set while the next process uses a different one. It is especially helpful to supply the operating system with a private set of registers, so that less switching is needed if short OS procedures must be executed during the operation of a single process.

In some complex architectures, full context switching is necessarily a time-consuming activity. Operating systems in these environments may support a separate category of **lightweight processes** to serve short-term system needs. An example is found in the "fork processes" of VMS. Intended mainly to perform I/O operations and deal with interrupts, these high-priority processes have simplified PCBs and limited context. They are expected to use only a limited set of registers and other CPU resources, and they are efficiently managed with these assumptions in mind.

5.6 PROCESS CREATION AND CONTROL

In early multiprogrammed operating systems, processes were permanent entities. The number of application processes was fixed at one per user. The number of system processes, if any, was fixed as well. CDC SCOPE, for example, provided seven application processes plus one system process, while T.H.E. supported 15 processes—five for users, and the rest primarily for controlling I/O devices. PCBs were permanently allocated in memory, and processes were never created or destroyed. These systems may be said to provide **static process management.** Handling processes in such environments is relatively simple, but the usefulness of the process concept is limited.

By contrast, in an OS that supports **dynamic process management,** processes may be created and destroyed during the operation of the system. In the simplest case, the number of processes changes only as the number of concurrent jobs or users; there is always one process per job. In newer OSs, it is possible for one process to explicitly create another by use of system calls. Thus a user may employ several processes, all running simultaneously, to perform a total job. Processes created by an application may be considered to have equal stature with the main process, or they may be viewed as **subprocesses** with restricted capabilities.

In some operating systems, processes and subprocesses are relatively expensive to create and maintain. Each one may require a large PCB with extensive links to other data structures throughout the system. This is the case with MVT and VMS, which expect processes to only occasionally have subprocesses. Other environments, notably Tenex, MULTICS and UNIX, were designed to encourage the use of multiple processes by each user. These systems treat all processes equally, and require efficient algorithms for process creation and management.

The ability of processes to create new ones gives rise to a **process hierarchy,** as shown in Figure 5–7. A new process is called a *child* of its creator, which is considered the *parent.* Children of the same parent are called *siblings.* Other related terms, such as *grandparent, ancestor,* and *descendant,* may also be used in the obvious way.

Figure 5–7 A Hierarchy of Processes

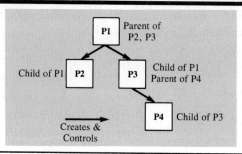

In most cases this hierarchy directly reflects the lines of authority that allow certain processes to control others. A parent may control its children (and indirectly, all its descendants) by examining and changing their properties, starting and stopping them, or even destroying them. Usually, a process can exercise little control over other processes that are not among its descendants.

5.7 PROCESS CONTROL OPERATIONS

Some operating systems that do not provide for process creation or inter-process communication provide few if any system calls for explicit operations on processes. When processes are allowed to create and control other processes and to deliberately interact in various ways, a number of useful operations may be provided. In this section, we discuss operations used by processes to directly control one another. We will consider operations useful for interprocess communication in Chapter 7.

Process Creation

If an OS supports dynamic process creation, new processes may be created upon request by an existing process. Typically the request takes the form of a **create process** system call. The calling process may be running a system program, such as the command interface, or an application program. A hierarchical relationship is established among the processes, as we discussed in the previous section. The newly created process is a child of its creator. A parent process generally has special authority and responsibilities for the children it has created.

Creation of a process that is ready to run requires the following distinct activities:

- Create or allocate a process control block;
- Allocate initial memory space for program and data;
- Load the program to be run;
- Assign initial attributes and resource limits to the process;
- Allocate initial resources to the process, if any;
- Establish the starting state for the process, and setup or complete the PCB.

The method for allocating PCBs varies among different operating systems. Some systems maintain a pool of permanent PCBs. Free PCBs are either linked together in a free PCB list or identified by a status flag in the PCB itself. This method is shown in Figure 5-8.

Figure 5-8 PCB Allocation from a Permanent Pool

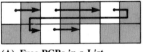
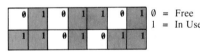

0 = Free
1 = In Use

(A) Free PCBs in a List   **(B) Free PCBs Marked With Flag**

More complex systems use dynamic memory allocation to get memory for a PCB. A specific storage area may be reserved for allocation of PCBs and other system data structures. This area, sometimes called a *system queue area* or *system control block area,* is the strategy used by versions of OS/360, such as MVT.

UNIX employs a mixed approach, as shown in Figure 5-9. The PCB is divided into two parts. Critical portions are collected in a permanent data structure called the *process table*. The process table then includes a pointer to the remainder of the PCB, called the *user area*, which is allocated only when needed.

Figure 5-9 The UNIX Process Table

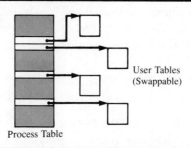

User Tables
(Swappable)

Process Table

In addition to the allocation of memory for a PCB, memory must be allocated for the (first) program to be loaded and executed. The process may not be created unless sufficient memory is available.

The loading of the program is usually done by a relocating loader, a resident component of the operating system. The loader reads programs stored in "executable" form in files, and copies their instructions and initial data into the allocated memory. The loading process may be complicated because the addresses at which the program information will be stored are not known until it is actually loaded. Branch addresses and data references contained in the program may need to be adjusted to reflect the actual locations. As we pointed out in Chapter 3, this **relocation** process may be carried out by a combination of hardware and software techniques depending on the architecture of the addressing mechanisms of the CPU. Systems that support virtual memory, in general, do not require relocation.

When a process is created, its initial attributes and resource limits must be established, and in some cases initial resources besides memory may be assigned to it. We use several strategies to determine the attributes and limits to assign to a newly created process. Some examples include:

- Derive attributes from the known properties of the batch job being run (MVT)
- Provide default attributes based on the characteristics of an interactive user (VMS)
- Allow the creator process to specify, within limits, what the child's attributes should be (VMS)
- Assign the child process attributes derived from or identical to those of its parent (UNIX)

In most cases, a new process is not automatically allocated any resources except memory. Additional resources are assigned only on request. An exception is found in UNIX, in which a child process *inherits* the allocation of resources, such as open files, from its parent. The newly created process shares access to these files with its creator.

Although it seems most natural to provide a newly-created process with a program and place it immediately in a ready state, these steps are separated in some systems. UNIX provides two distinct operations, *fork* and *exec,* a strategy that is illustrated in Figure 5–10. The *fork* operation creates a new process and makes it ready, but instead of loading a new program, the child process initially runs the *same* program (from the same location) as its parent. (All programs under UNIX are reentrant and may be shared by multiple processes.) The data areas used by the two processes are independent. The *fork* procedure returns a result parameter that is different in each process and may be used to distinguish parent from child. Each *fork* call is normally followed by a test so that each process can take the appropriate actions. Usually the child process then performs an *exec* call. This operation loads a new program for the calling process, completely replacing the old one. The process then begins executing at the start of the new program.

Figure 5–10   Process Creation in UNIX

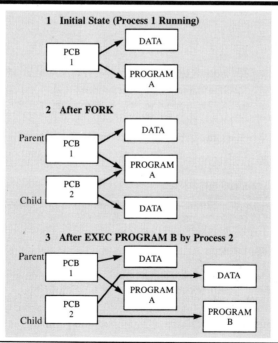

The UNIX strategy does take some getting used to, but it provides flexibility in special cases. A child process may be created to execute a short procedure in the parent program, without the overhead of loading (or finding space for) a separate program. This strategy is followed by standard UNIX shells, which use forking alone to process simple commands whose program code is part of the shell itself. The following algorithm is a typical example:

```
LOOP
    get a command from terminal;

    /* perform fork, return status value
       to both processes */
    status := fork();

    /* signal error if fork failed */
    IF status < 0 THEN      /* fork failed */
      signal error

    /* parent receives child's id and waits */
    ELSE IF status > 0 THEN
      wait for child process

    /* child receives 0, and executes the command */
    ELSE
      IF command is a procedure within shell THEN
        call command procedure;
      ELSE IF command is a program THEN
        exec (command); /* load new program */
        signal error; /* exec failed */
      ELSE          /* command is not recognized */
        signal error;
      END IF;
      terminate;  /* child destroys itself */
    END IF;

END LOOP;
```

Occasionally you will want to create a process and place it in a suspended state to begin running at a later time, an action that is particularly useful in real-time environments. This strategy is often followed by real-time executives that support dynamic process creation, such as RSX-11.

Process Destruction

The removal or destruction of a process can occur for several reasons, such as those in the following list:

- The process itself has requested normal termination
- A nonrecoverable error has occurred in the process execution
- An operator command has terminated the process
- A parent process has terminated either normally or abnormally
- An authorized process has requested termination

Destruction may be invoked by a **destroy process** system call by the process itself or another process, or it may be an automatic consequence of certain events. Destruction of a process involves the following steps:

- Remove PCB from its current state queue, and other queues to which it may be linked
- Destroy or reassign child processes
- Free allocated memory and other resources
- Free the PCB

The destroy process operation may perform these steps immediately; alternately, it may switch the process to a terminal state. In this case, final destruction may be deferred until certain clean-up actions have been performed by the OS or the parent process.

An important question is how to deal with active children of the destroyed process; an obvious answer is to destroy them as well. However, these children may be intended to have longer lifetimes. For example, an interactive user's main process may create other processes to carry out a long compilation, calculation, or printing job. The user may then want to log off the system, terminating the main process, but the child processes should continue. Because of this, child processes are sometimes allowed to survive even though their parent is destroyed. These processes may be *inherited* by a higher-level parent, or they may be considered *orphans* without a parent. The children of a destroyed process in UNIX are inherited by the system process at the very top of the hierarchy.

VMS provides two distinct process categories: *subprocesses* which do not survive when their parents are destroyed, and *detached processes,* which have a lifetime independent of any parent. The concept of detached processes is also used by TOPS-20. This mechanism further allows a user's main process to be suspended rather than destroyed when an interactive session terminates. If the session terminates abnormally, such as due to a communication failure, suspension occurs by default. When the same user begins a new session, it is possible to continue with the same process.

Reading and Changing Attributes

Operations may be provided to allow a process to obtain information from its own PCB or those of certain other processes. Most of the information recorded in the PCB could be useful to a process in some cases, and can be obtained simply.

In many systems ranging from small real-time executives to OS/MVT, the PCB is maintained within the address space of the process it controls. In this case, the process can read the PCB (and possibly modify it) directly. If the PCB is not directly accessible, a **read-PCB** system call may be provided, which reads the entire PCB into a buffer in the address space of the calling process. These methods allow a process to examine all attributes in the PCB, but the process must know how to interpret them.

Alternately, there may be distinct calls to obtain various categories of information, such as current state, priority, resources allocated, or CPU time used. This allows programs to be less dependent on the precise format used for PCBs.

Processes may also have a limited ability to change their attributes or those of other processes, such as their children. Information that might be subject to change includes process names, resource allocations and limits, and (within limits) scheduling priority.

Suspension and Wakeup Operations

The OS may allow a process to put itself, or another process it controls, into a suspended state via a **suspend** or **sleep operation.** The request for suspension may specify an event that the process is waiting for, which may be caused by action of another process, by an interrupt, or by arrival of a specific time. The OS must then watch for this event and associate the process with it in some way (as by a special queue). When the event occurs, the OS will resume or "awaken" the process by restoring it to a ready state. Alternately, the suspend call may not specify any event. In this case the process relies on an explicit **wakeup operation** by another process that specifies that the original process should resume its activity.

Examples

Process management operations available in common versions of UNIX include *fork* to create a child process, *kill* to destroy a process (or, more generally, to send a "signal" to a process), and *exit* by which a process terminates itself. Other system calls allow processes to find out their own internal name, get and set priorities and resource limits, and get statistics about their own behavior or that of their children.

Processes may be delayed until a specific time. A more general suspend-wakeup mechanism is provided by allowing processes to send signals to other processes and to wait until signals are received. Generally, each process may control and access only itself and its descendants.

VMS provides system services to allow processes to create and delete other processes; suspend themselves or others, possibly scheduling a wakeup at a predetermined time; resume a suspended process, obtain information from the PCB, and set process names, priorities, and privileges. The authority of each process to control others in various ways is determined by a complex system of privileges assigned to each process.

The real-time executive VRTX provides system calls to create, delete, suspend and resume processes, to obtain PCB information, and to change priorities. In VRTX, like many real-time executives, any process can control any other one.

A standard set of process management system calls for use in portable applications is defined in the IEEE MOSI standard [IEEE 1985a]. These include *create process, destroy process, suspend, resume, get status,* and *change priority*. This set also defines operations by which a new process can initialize itself and obtain information from its creator.

5.8 SUMMARY

The process model is a central one for most multiprogrammed operating systems. A process is a program in execution. This concept is formalized so that most activities throughout the OS can be viewed as a system of concurrent sequential processes.

Each process is represented concretely by a process control block, a data structure that maintains all necessary information about each process. Processes must make use of various resources that are continuously scheduled or allocated on demand. Most resources managed by an OS are serially reusable, and a process must wait for them when they are being used by another. These waiting processes are entered in various queues, which form another important structure for process management.

A process moves through a variety of states, the most important of which are *running, ready, blocked,* and *suspended.* These states reflect the resources the process currently holds and the ones it is waiting for.

Processes taking turns at the CPU must perform a context switch by saving their registers in memory when their turn is over. Context switching may be slow on some computers, making it undesirable for them to frequently change processes.

Most current OSs allow processes to create other processes, leading to a hierarchy. A process that creates another usually has special authority over the new process. System calls may be provided to create and destroy processes, to examine and change attributes, and to suspend and wakeup processes.

FOR FURTHER READING

Although there are few books or articles devoted to basic process management, the subject is well covered in a variety of general OS texts. Good overviews are given by Deitel [1984] and Milenković [1987]. More theoretical treatments may be found in Coffman and Denning [1973] or Brinch Hansen [1973]. Kaisler [1983] provides a detailed treatment of data structures and algorithms for process management. Detailed implementations for pedagogical operating systems are presented by Tanenbaum [1987] and Milenkovic [1987]. A set of standard system calls for process management is described in the IEEE MOSI standard [IEEE 1985a].

A number of books and articles cover, in detail, process management in specific real operating systems. Important examples include Bach [1986] for UNIX, Kenah and Bate [1984] for VMS, and Organick [1972] for MULTICS. Process management in several older systems, such as SCOPE and T.H.E. is described by McKeag et al. [1976]. Case studies of MVS and VM/370, among others, are provided by Deitel [1984].

Further readings for process management focusing on scheduling or process interaction, respectively, are given in this text at the end of Chapters 6 and 7.

IMPORTANT TERMS

application process
blocked state
concurrent sequential processes
consumable resource
context
context switching
create process
deadlock
destroy process
dynamic process management
event
idle process

idle time
initial state
interleaved execution
lightweight processes
logical resource
mutual exclusion
physical resource
process
process control block (PCB)
process hierarchy
process state
read-PCB

ready state
relocation
resource
reusable resource
running state
scheduling
sequential process
serially reusable resource
sleep

static process management
subprocess
suspend
suspended state
system process
terminal state
waiting state
wakeup

≡ REVIEW QUESTIONS ≡

1. Give examples of some resources that are (a) serially reusable, (b) reusable and shareable, and (c) consumable.

2. How does a typical queue structure as used within an operating system differ from the usual definition of a queue?

3. In the simplified process state diagram of Figure 5–2, explain why there is no transition

   a. from the *ready* state to the *blocked* state.
   b. from the *blocked* state to the *running* state.

4. Identify five explicit operations on processes that an OS might provide in response to system calls.

5. Describe the steps performed by a typical OS during dynamic creation of a new process.

6. Contrast the UNIX *fork* and *exec* mechanism with the more common *create process* operation.

7. Explain why it may not be desirable to destroy all the descendants of a process when the parent process is destroyed.

8. Why does UNIX divide its PCBs into two parts?

≡ ASSIGNMENTS ≡

1. List some additional difficulties a process manager might face if there is more than one CPU (i.e., more than one process may be in the *running* state at the same time).

2. List all the information included in the context (CPU state) that must be saved for each process for three different computer architectures. Determine what instructions are provided by each architecture to save or switch contexts. Estimate the average time required for a context switch using a typical implementation of each architecture.

3. Draw a process state diagram for an OS in which *blocked* states waiting for I/O requests are to be kept separate by device. For example, waiting for terminal input, printer output, or disk transfer are all to be considered separate states. What effect would this more detailed division of *blocked* states have on PCB structure and system mechanisms for state representation? What would be the effect of providing separate states for suspended processes?

4. Using a time chart similar to Figure 5–5, contrast the way in which a set of five programs might execute on a uniprogrammed OS and a multiprogrammed one. Are there cases in which the programs might complete their work as soon or sooner without multiprogramming? Why or why not?

5. List all the information actually contained in a typical PCB for a large operating system, such as VMS or MVS. Classify this information according to the categories of Section 5.2. Are any additional categories needed?

6. Define a data structure PCB_Q for a collection of PCBs using a high-level language such as C, Pascal, Ada, or another language of your choice. What language features are important for defining a data structure of this type? Why?

≡ PROJECT

This section describes a programming project to develop a representation for processes using process control blocks (PCBs), and to implement basic operations on the PCBs. You should read the general description in this text in conjunction with the more specific descriptions given in your project manual. The interface to be constructed is an important component of the multiprogramming executive (MPX) project described later in the text. This project has three parts.

a. Implement a PCB queue using the PCB frame approach (statically allocated). The PCBs should form a singly linked list ordered by process priority. Information required in each PCB includes:

- PCB_Ptr (1 word): pointer to next PCB
- PCB_Pname (8 bytes): process name
- PCB_Type (1 byte): PCB type; possible values are 0 (free), 1 (system process), or 2 (application process)
- PCB_Priority (1 byte): process priority; values may range from −126 to +126 for application processes, and from −128 to +127 for system processes
- PCB_State (1 byte): process state; possible values are 0 (ready), 1 (running), or 2 (blocked)
- PCB_Suspend (1 byte): process suspended flag; possible values are 0 (not suspended), or 1 (suspended)
- PCB_Save (size as needed): process context save area
- PCB_Memory (1 word): pointer to memory for loading process
- PCB_MemSize (1 word): size of memory area
- PCB_LoadA (size as needed): memory area for process

The number of PCBs should be easy to change via recompilation. The minimum number of PCBs to be supported is 10.

b. Implement the following procedures to manipulate the PCB queue you have defined:

1. P=Search_PCB(PCB_Q,pcbname): returns the address of the PCB with the process name pcbname. If the process is not found, the value 0 is returned.
2. P=Get_PCB(PCB_Q): returns the address of a free PCB. A value of 0 is returned if no free PCB is available.

3. `E=Change_PCB(PCB_Q,P,priority)`: changes the priority of the PCB whose address is in P to the priority specified by `priority`. Values to be returned are:

> 1: Priority change successful
> −1: Invalid PCB address in P
> −2: Invalid priority

4. `E=Free_PCB(PCB_Q,P)`: frees the PCB whose address is in P and sets its priority to −128. Values to be returned are:

> 1: PCB freed
> −1: Invalid PCB address
> −2: PCB already free

5. `E=Build_PCB(P,name,status,state)`: Places the specified `name`, `status`, and `state` into the PCB identified by P. Values to be returned are:

> 1: PCB completed
> −1: Invalid PCB address in P
> −2: Invalid Status
> −3: Invalid State

c. Add commands to the project COMHAN of Chapter 4 to display the contents of a PCB or PCBs in the PCB queue. The commands to be added are as follows:

1. SHOW FREE: display all free PCBs.
2. SHOW ALL: display all PCBs allocated to any process.
3. SHOW SYSTEM: display all PCBs allocated to system processes.
4. SHOW APPLICATION: display all PCBs allocated to application processes.
5. SHOW SUSPENDED: display all PCBs allocated to suspended processes.

The format of the display should include:

- PCB address
- process name

- process priority
- process type (system or application process or free PCB)
- process state
- process suspended or not suspended
- next instruction to be executed
- program load address and size
- context save area address

NOTE: You will need a setup routine to call the appropriate procedures described in step **b** above in order to build a PCB queue test environment. This could be done upon the entry of another COMHAN command (e.g., Build PCBs) and could even allow dynamic changing of the PCBs being built. See your project manual for additional details.

Process Scheduling

Introduction • Levels of Scheduling • Process Categories • Scheduling Objectives and Measures • Some Important Concepts • Scheduling Batch Processes • Scheduling Interactive Processes • Scheduling Real-time Processes • Combined Methods • Hardware Assistance

Process Scheduling

6.1 INTRODUCTION

Because a computer system has a limited set of resources that must be shared in a controlled manner among its processes, the operating system is responsible for assigning these resources to programs to meet their needs in a fair and reasonable way. Determining the best sequence for reassigning resources, and choosing from a set of competing requests for use of a resource, are the problems addressed by **scheduling.**

We described the basic characteristics of the process model in Chapter 5. Since most scheduling is performed on behalf of processes, it is natural to refer to the scheduling problem in general as **process scheduling.**

The resources that are most heavily in demand and therefore most in need of scheduling are CPUs and memory. Every process needs a CPU and some memory space in order to execute. Since memory is limited and often only one CPU is available, competition is continuous and inevitable. Processes do not request these resources; they are assumed to require them at all times.

Scheduling the use of CPUs and memory is the subject of this chapter. We assume a computer system with a single CPU; multiple CPUs will be considered later. CPU and memory scheduling proceed continuously at several levels. The highest level concerns the admission of complete jobs to begin competing for resources; the lowest level concerns the selection of processes for the next immediate turn at use of the CPU. Memory use may be scheduled at a level in between these two. Each scheduling level is introduced in the next section.

To achieve satisfactory scheduling, it is necessary to treat all processes fairly, but also to recognize and respond to the unique characteristics and needs of each process. Some basic categories of processes are described in Section 6.3, followed by a discussion of appropriate criteria and objectives for scheduling, means of recognizing the characteristics of each process, and some measures for the effectiveness of a scheduling strategy.

Section 6.5 introduces several new concepts that play an important role in scheduling strategies. Sections 6.6 through 6.8 discuss specific strategies, with examples, that may be used at each level for each principal category of process.

The final two sections of the chapter discuss some combined and special-purpose strategies, and additional issues that may arise in the actual implementation of a practical scheduling mechanism.

6.2 LEVELS OF SCHEDULING

Scheduling of CPU and memory use by processes in an OS proceeds at several distinct levels. Three levels are most commonly identified; each will be described in this section. The terminology we use to describe these levels varies widely. We will choose appropriate names for each level, and also list other names in common use.

We will call the highest level of process scheduling **long-term scheduling** or **job scheduling.** (Other terms used for long-term scheduling include *high-level scheduling* or *admission scheduling.*) The objective of long-term scheduling is to control the order in which new processes are admitted to the system. When a job is admitted, a process is created or assigned to perform its activities and the PCB is initialized. The new process may need to compete for its initial resource needs before actual execution can begin.

The next level of scheduling, **medium-term scheduling,** (also called *intermediate-level scheduling*), is concerned with selecting the set of existing processes that can compete actively for use of the CPU. These processes may be said to form the **active set.** One reason this set must be limited is due to the amount of memory space available for programs and data. To schedule this space effectively, inactive processes may be subject to **swapping**—that is, temporary copying of their programs and data to disk storage to make space available for additional processes. Since the set of active processes is the set of processes that are permitted to occupy main memory, the name **storage scheduling** is also appropriate for this level.

In some cases, processes are assigned memory when they are admitted to the system, and occupy that space continuously until complete. In this case there is no distinct storage scheduling; its effect is performed once only by the job scheduler. In many systems, however, processes that have had a sufficient turn at the CPU, or need to wait a long time for some event, may be declared inactive and subject to swapping.

The lowest level of process scheduling, **short-term scheduling** (also called *low-level scheduling, CPU scheduling,* and *processor scheduling*), is concerned with establishing the order in which ready processes are to be assigned a turn at the CPU, and selecting and preparing each process for actual execution. Often these two steps are considered distinct, and are performed by different modules of the OS. Maintaining the active set of processes and establishing the execution order is the province of a **scheduler** module, while preparing each process for execution is performed by a **dispatcher.** The scheduler, which can run at relatively convenient times, does as much of the decision making and preparation as possible. The dispatcher, which must be ready to go with high efficiency, performs only the simplest tasks.

The progress of a typical process through these various levels of scheduling is diagramed in Figure 6–1. The figure is a time chart in which time flows from top to bottom. The process follows the solid line in moving through various status regions. The boundary between each pair of regions is controlled by a distinct scheduling level.

Figure 6–1   The Life of a Typical Process

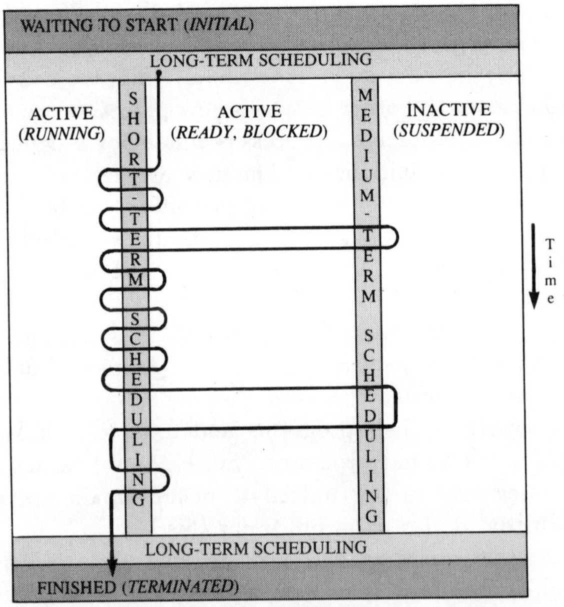

Each region represents one or more process states. Thus, we should examine the progress of the example process with the help of a process state diagram, such as the one in Figure 5–3. A slight variation of that figure appears in Figure 6–2.

Figure 6–2 Typical Process State Diagram

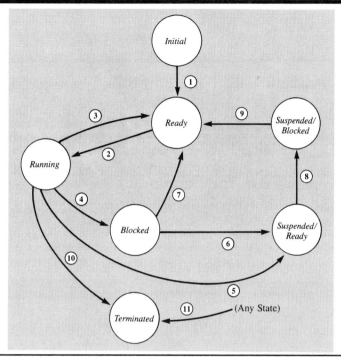

The regions of Figure 6–1 correspond to process states except that, for simplicity, no distinction is shown between *ready* and *blocked* states (or their *suspended* counterparts). The process begins in the *initial* state. When admitted by the long-term scheduler, it is assigned its initial memory needs and placed in the *ready* state. The process remains for a period of time in the active set, alternating between the *running* state and the other active states *(ready* and *blocked)* under control of the short-term scheduler.

When the process needs to wait for a longer time, it may be switched to an inactive state. Even if there is no need to wait, processes may still be rotated out of the active set to provide fair sharing of the available memory. The example process periodically moves in and out of the inactive states *(suspended/blocked* and *suspended/ready)* as directed by the medium-term scheduler.

Finally, when the process chooses to exit, or is aborted due to some abnormal condition, it enters the *terminal* state. It may survive in this state for awhile to make final status information available; it is then destroyed.

Figure 6–2 also shows each of the transitions that may reasonably occur between these states. The transitions actually permitted for a particular process may depend on the process category and the OS. The table in Figure 6-3 lists each allowable transition, the OS module that controls it, and the conditions that cause it to occur.

Figure 6-3   Process State Transitions

TRANSITION	CONTROLLED BY	WHEN PERFORMED
1. INITIAL → READY	LT Scheduler	When the job's turn has arrived and initial resources are available
2. READY → RUNNING	ST Dispatcher	When the process' turn arrives, the CPU is available, and no higher priority processes are ready
3. RUNNING → READY	ST Scheduler	When the CPU time quantum has expired
4. RUNNING → BLOCKED	Process and ST Scheduler	When a resource or service has been requested
5. RUNNING → SUSPENDED/BLOCKED	MT Scheduler	When storage time quantum has expired
6. BLOCKED → SUSPENDED/BLOCKED	MT Scheduler	When the event being awaited is not expected soon
7. BLOCKED → READY	Event Handler or Resource Scheduler	When awaited event occurs or resource is available
8. SUSPENDED/BLOCKED → SUSPENDED/READY	Event Handler or Resource Scheduler	When awaited event occurs or resource is available
9. SUSPENDED/READY → READY	MT Scheduler	When turn arrives and storage is available
10. RUNNING → TERMINATED	Process or Timer Interrupt Handler	On voluntary termination or time limit expiration
11. (non RUNNING) → TERMINATED	Other Process or Condition Handler	When terminated by another controlling process, or due to an extraordinary system condition

6.3 PROCESS CATEGORIES

In most operating systems, each application process may be considered to be in one of the following categories:

- **batch processes,** which perform a job submitted by a user as a whole. Usually a batch process performs a relatively long computation. Batch processes do not interact with users during their execution.
- **interactive processes,** which respond to requests made by a user at an interactive terminal. In general, they are short computations that may interact with the user during execution.

- **real-time processes,** which monitor and control external events and must meet rigid timing constraints. They usually interact with one or more I/O devices.

The roles of each process type are contrasted in Figure 6–4. Each one has a distinct set of characteristics and requirements that should be recognized by an effective scheduling strategy. Batch processes are often submitted with good estimates of their anticipated running time, and their need for memory and other resources. In addition, they may include instructions that explicitly determine the relative importance and scheduling requirements of different processes. The user measures the effectiveness of batch scheduling by the speed with which final results are returned. Since most batch computations have substantial time and resource requirements, equally sizable processing delays may be accepted.

Figure 6–4 Process Categories

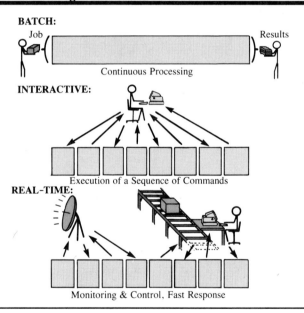

Interactive processes are assumed to perform work on behalf of a user who remains present at an interactive terminal. Many of these processes have very short running times and resource needs. They may display information for the user as they progress, or require terminal input at various points in their processing. Interactive processes are rarely provided with information on resource use or scheduling requirements. The user initiating such a process expects rapid and consistent response throughout its execution, not only when the process is complete.

Real-time processes are designed to interact with external events and objects, such as tracking air traffic or controlling the flow of chemicals in a laboratory experiment. The resource requirements of real-time processes are generally known. They are further characterized by absolute timing requirements, which must be met regardless of other activities in the total system.

Each type of process requires a different approach to scheduling. The importance of each of the scheduling levels also varies depending on the process category. Figure 6–5 summarizes the interaction of scheduling levels and process types. Note that if the OS supports more than one category of process, the dominant category may determine the methods employed. We will consider principles and examples for scheduling each process type in later sections of this chapter.

Figure 6–5   Process Categories and Scheduling Levels

	BATCH	INTERACTIVE	REAL-TIME
LONG-TERM	Job admission, based on characteristics and resource needs	Sessions and processes normally accepted unless capacity reached	Processes either permanent or accepted at once
MEDIUM-TERM	Usually none — jobs remain in storage until done	Processes swapped on rotating basis when necessary, using storage time quantum	Process never swapped or suspended
SHORT-TERM	Processes scheduled by priority. They usually continue until they wait voluntarily, request service, or are terminated	Processes scheduled on rotating basis. They continue until service is requested or CPU time quantum expires. Optional preemption	Scheduling based on strict priority with immediate preemption. Optional time sharing among equal priority

Many operating systems are specialized to recognize only one of these process categories. OS/MVT is batch oriented; UNIX is designed for interactive processes; VRTX supports only real-time processes. A few systems like VMS attempt to support two or more of these process types; however, this approach requires compromises, and usually provides satisfactory support in, at most, one process category. A more complex scheduling strategy is necessary when several categories of processes are to be supported.

6.4 SCHEDULING OBJECTIVES AND MEASURES

Scheduling Objectives

The strategies used for scheduling decisions at each level vary widely. To choose a reasonable strategy, you first need to determine its objectives. The possible objectives of a scheduling strategy are numerous. Some of the most important ones usually include:

- Throughput: Get the most work done in a given (long) time period.
- Turnaround: Complete jobs as soon as possible after they have been submitted.
- Response: Service individual steps within a process, especially those requiring only short processing, as quickly as possible.
- Fairness: Treat each process or job in a way that corresponds "fairly" with its characteristics. Note that when processes differ, there may be disagreement on what the fairest treatment is.
- Consistency: Treat processes with given characteristics in a manner which can be predicted and does not vary greatly from time to time.
- Resource use: Keep each category of resource used as fully as possible, yet avoid excessive waiting for certain resources.

Some of these objectives are inherently conflicting. To achieve short and consistent response times, for example, it is necessary to switch contexts frequently, which reduces throughput. It is not possible to meet all of the requirements in an optimum way at the same time.

Some objectives also face theoretical limitations. Kleinrock [1965] showed that it is not possible to significantly reduce overall turnaround delays by choosing a suitable scheduling algorithm.

Distinguishing Processes

Meeting the desired objectives requires that processes be distinguished based on various characteristics, which the processes may be known or observed to have. Some of the more important characteristics to be considered include:

- Process category, as discussed in the previous section
- Original priority assigned when the process was created
- Anticipated running time and resource needs
- Running time and resource use so far
- Association with an interactive terminal
- Frequency of I/O requests
- Time spent waiting for service

Note that some of these factors are intrinsic properties of each process, while others can change dynamically as the process executes.

Measuring Success

As observed in Chapter 5, processes waiting for a resource are entered in a queue associated with that resource. In the case of processes waiting for service by the CPU, the queue is the ready queue. To evaluate the success of a scheduling algorithm in meeting its goals, the queues of processes waiting for service or resources may be observed over a period of time. Alternately, the behavior of these queues may be simulated in some way or computed by analytical means. Some specific parameters of these queues are often measured. These include:

- **waiting time,** the time a process spends in a queue waiting for service. In general, this time should be as low as possible.
- **queue length,** the size of the queue of waiting requests. Queue length must be kept reasonable to conserve storage.
- **response ratio,** a measure of waiting time balanced against the service time required for each request: $R = W/(W+S)$. A consistent response ratio means that better service is being given to shorter processes, which is usually considered fair.

Each of these parameters varies over time, and each is characterized by a statistical distribution. Properties of this distribution that are interesting and measurable include the **mean,** or average, value; the **variance,** which indicates how widely typical values tend to deviate from the mean; and the **kth percentile value,** which measures the maximum or minimum values encountered for k percent of all observations. Typically, we are interested in values such as k=90 or k=95. Notice that it is not possible to measure true worst case performance (k=100), since in a statistical distribution the worst case is generally unbounded.

6.5 SOME IMPORTANT CONCEPTS

Priorities

We may use many of the characteristics that distinguish one process from another to establish a relative importance among processes. This importance is usually quantified by a number, termed a **priority,** which is assigned to each process. The priority concept allows fast decision making by the various scheduling levels. If two processes with different priorities are candidates for service, or use of a resource, the higher priority is always selected.

The choice of permissible values for the priority is quite variable. MVT allows priorities to range from 0 to 15, with 0 being the highest. VMS provides priorities 0 through 31; in this case higher numbers indicate higher priorities. A priority value in UNIX may be chosen from a wide range of integers, positive or negative. Lower values indicate higher priorities. Negative priorities as a class are higher than positive ones; these are reserved for system processes.

Processes may be assigned a priority when initially submitted to the system. This initial priority may be used unchanged throughout the lifetime of the process. A scheduling strategy in which the priority of a process never changes is said to be based on **static priorities.** More often, the history of a process is also considered in determining its current priority. In this case, the priority can change with time; for example, a process that has waited a long time for service may be given a higher priority. This approach is said to use **dynamic priorities.**

The priority of a process may be stored explicitly as a number in the PCB. Alternately, it may be represented implicitly. Often this is done by maintaining a separate queue for each priority value, and linking each PCB on the appropriate priority queue (see Figure 6–6).

Preemption

An important property of some dispatching and storage scheduling strategies is the possibility of **preemption.** In a non-preemptive strategy, a process is assigned the CPU until it voluntarily gives it up; thus, a single process may continue for a long time (e.g., hours) until it terminates or requests I/O or another type of OS service. Events or requirements associated with other processes cannot cause the CPU to be taken away. In a preemptive strategy, when a high- priority process becomes ready, it may be given the CPU immediately or within a limited period of time, although a lower- or equal-priority process is currently running. Preemption may occur at both the short-term and medium-term scheduling levels.

Figure 6–6 Representation of Process Priorities

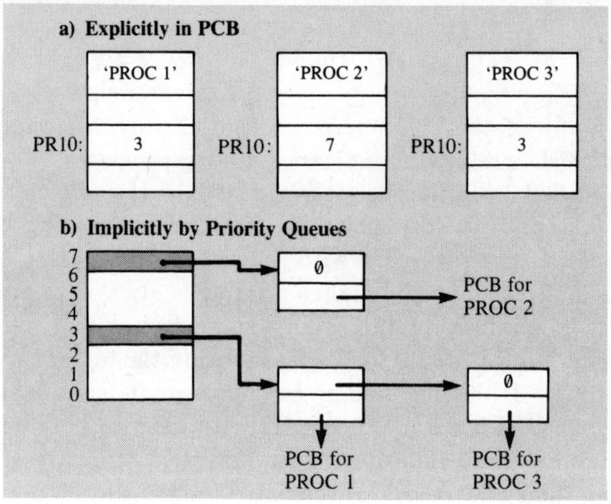

a) Explicitly in PCB

b) Implicitly by Priority Queues

Note that even though a process enters the ready queue with a higher priority than the currently running process, there is no guarantee that the current process will be interrupted immediately. The scheduler or dispatcher are run only when desired by the OS, and no change will take place until these procedures are executed. The OS must decide which events (such as system calls or interrupts) will cause the scheduler to run, leading to a possible change of processes. Because this change must be triggered by selected events, we say that preemptive process switching is **event-driven.**

The presence of preemption has a profound effect on the behavior of a scheduling strategy. For one thing, it tends to favor higher-priority processes more strongly than a non-preemptive method. Some batch-only systems use non-preemptive scheduling. However, preemption is necessary in an interactive environment to maintain reasonable response time for each user. It is even more necessary in a real-time system to meet the absolute timing constraints that are necessary.

Overhead

Often, analyses of dispatching and storage scheduling are simplified by assuming no effort is required to switch between processes. In reality, this context switching will take some time, introducing a performance penalty, called **overhead,** which can have a major effect on total performance.

In short-term scheduling, overhead comes from two sources: the decision making process and the work required to switch contexts. The first of these can be controlled by organizing scheduling queues in such a way that the time required to dispatch the next process is minimal. This work may be done by the scheduler at a reasonably convenient time. The second type of overhead can be reduced by hardware mechanisms that allow a context switch to be completed in a small number of machine instructions.

In medium-term scheduling—although decision making is still involved—the dominant source of overhead (in non-virtual memory systems) comes from swapping memory. The time required to copy the information for one process from memory to disk and load information for another process is a very severe penalty.

In effect, overhead makes it necessary to limit the frequency of context switching, especially when swapping may be required.

6.6 SCHEDULING BATCH PROCESSES

A batch job is submitted by a user complete with all information and instructions required for its execution. This initial information includes all input data, identification of files, or input devices from which the data should be taken. The job usually performs a lengthy sequence of computations or file manipulations. There is no interaction with the user while the job is in progress; the user sees only final results.

Batch jobs normally are provided by the user with estimates of their expected run time and resource needs. The user expects the OS to enforce these estimates as upper limits, but give better service to jobs whose resource estimates are low. Because of this, the resource estimates will tend to be generous but fairly accurate. In many cases, users are permitted to specify a base priority for each job, within allowable limits.

From the user's point of view, the most important objective of a batch scheduling strategy is short and reasonably predictable turnaround time. Usually, however, the delays and variance that may be tolerated are much greater than in an interactive environment. Historically, maximum total throughput of the computing system has also been an important goal.

Long-term Scheduling

The initial priorities and resource usage estimates supplied with a batch job lead to significant choices to be made at the job scheduling level. Batch jobs tend to be large consumers of resources, and relatively few of them can be admitted at one time.

The example of batch job admission and initiation shown in Figure 6–7 is based on the operation of MVT. The programs and data required for each job are submitted in a batch, accompanied by job control statements that specify a *job name*, a *class*, and a *priority*. The job is composed of a series of *job steps*, each of which will run a distinct program. Each job step includes job control statements specifying the resources it will need, including memory, files, and total CPU time.

Figure 6–7 Long–Term Scheduling of Batch Jobs

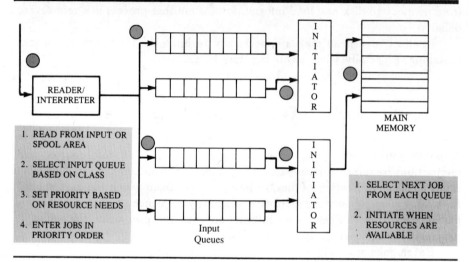

Jobs are read in from various input sources and placed into one of a set of *input job queues*. One such queue exists for each job class. Classes are assigned according to the nature of the job: one class for short student jobs, another for jobs using a certain compiler, and so on. Jobs in each input queue are ordered by priority and by time of arrival within each priority group.

A set of system processes called *initiators* examine the input queues when the system is ready to accept more work. Each initiator controls one or more input queues. The initiator selects the next job in a queue and determines if all resources needed for the first job step are available, including enough memory space. If not, the job must wait while jobs from other queues are serviced. When the needed resources are available, they are all assigned to the job step, and it begins execution.

Each new step for the job is also admitted only when all necessary resources are available. Once a step is begun, it normally holds all its resources until completion. A timer is set while the process is running to ensure that it does not exceed its planned CPU time.

Medium-term Scheduling

In a batch environment, the medium-term scheduling level is usually not distinguished. Jobs are admitted as processes only when sufficient storage is available to meet their announced needs. Thereafter they retain that storage and remain in the active set until they are terminated.

Short-term Scheduling

Short-term scheduling of batch jobs has the following characteristics:

1. When the CPU is available, a ready process is selected according to some type of priority.
2. When a process is running, it continues until one of the following events occurs:

   - The process terminates
   - The process voluntarily suspends itself
   - The process requests an I/O transfer or other service for which it is required to wait
   - The process is stopped by the system because it has exhausted its running time
   - A higher-priority process becomes ready and preempts the running process

Preemption is less important in a batch environment because there is no need for a consistent pattern of response time. Because preemption is more complex to manage, increases overhead, and magnifies the difference between processes having distinct priorities, it is not usually used.

Note that with a preemptive strategy, it is possible for a process that performs no I/O to complete all of its work without interruption. In many pure batch environments, a single job could run continuously for hours.

The choice of a preemptive or non-preemptive strategy and the assignment of priority values lead to many possible variations. Some common ones are discussed below.

First-in, First-out Scheduling

The simplest dispatching method, based on a **first-in, first-out (FIFO)** queue with no preemption, is illustrated in Figure 6–8. All ready jobs are considered to have equal priority, and are serviced in the order in which they arrive in the queue. This would be the fairest method if all jobs deserved equal treatment. In practice, however, we usually want to favor some jobs, especially those with limited resource needs.

Figure 6-8 Short-Term Batch Scheduling: FIFO

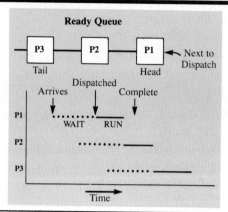

Static Priority Scheduling

Priority dispatching methods select processes according to some priority value. If there is more than one ready process with the highest priority, then the first one in the queue is selected—usually the process that has been waiting the longest. This approach is illustrated in Figure 6-9.

In a static priority method, the priority of a process does not change. The best known example of this class is the **shortest job next (SJN)** algorithm. Here priority is based on the total expected running time of the process, which is known from initial estimates. This expected running time may be adjusted if the process suspends or waits after using part of its time, but it will not change while the process is in the ready queue.

For a given set of processes, the long-term throughput and total waiting time for all non-preemptive scheduling methods is the same. However, SJN can be shown to have the minimum possible *average* waiting time because most of the waiting is concentrated in a few long jobs, and that experienced by the majority of jobs is much shorter.

This method gives very favorable treatment to short jobs, which is usually desirable. However, it can be excessively unfair to large jobs. Any static priority method is subject to the possibility of **starvation;** if there are always high-priority processes waiting in the ready queue, it is possible that low-priority processes will never get service.

Figure 6–9 Short-Term Batch Scheduling with Priorities

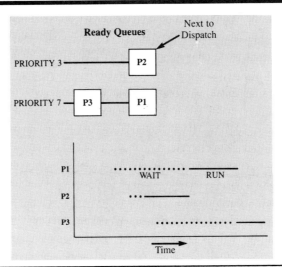

Dynamic Priority Scheduling

Because static methods may be too unfair to low-priority jobs, most actual schedulers use some form of dynamic priority, in which the priority of a process can be increased while the process is waiting for service. With this approach, a low-priority process that is constantly passed over will eventually become a high-priority process, and better treatment is assured.

From a theoretical viewpoint, a good compromise may be to select the process with the highest response ratio. Recall from Section 6.4 that this is a measure of both the expected service time (that is, running time) and the waiting time of a process. It serves as a priority that gradually increases for all processes, but increases more slowly for long ones.

The response ratio is a good measure in theory, but cannot be used in practice because it varies continuously and must be recalculated for each scheduling decision. A compromise technique called **aging** is usually used instead. This method periodically adds a fixed increment to the priority of each waiting process, so processes that have waited a long time will develop higher and higher priorities, eventually exceeding those of processes that arrived more recently. All waiting processes will be served in a reasonable time, even if their initial priority was very low.

Preemptive Scheduling

If preemption is employed, higher-priority processes get immediate service when ready; thus they are even more strongly favored than with non-preemptive methods. A process that is preempted is returned to the ready queue, and its priority may be recalculated. This leads to methods such as **shortest remaining time next,** the analog of shortest job next. Some type of aging method is essential in a preemptive environment.

Examples

Early batch operating systems, such as MCP on the Burroughs B5500, SCOPE on CDC computers, and George 3 on ICL 1900s, generally made use of FIFO dispatching with limited provision for priorities. MCP considered initial priorities in moving processes from *blocked* to *ready* state, but dispatched *ready* processes in a strictly FIFO order. SCOPE provided for priority "sublevels" within a single base priority, to provide limited aging for a waiting process. George 3 computed priorities dynamically in a higher-level scheduler, and passed them as fixed values to the dispatcher.

OS/MFT assigned each process a static priority based on running time and other considerations. Preemption was allowed, and there was no provision for aging. OS/MVT used a similar approach, except that the priorities were computed in a different way. MVT systems were often modified by inclusion of the HASP [IBM 1971] scheduling system. HASP substituted a scheduling method very similar to those discussed below for interactive processes.

6.7 SCHEDULING INTERACTIVE PROCESSES

An interactive process—one associated with a user at an interactive terminal—performs computations in response to requests made by the user. Although some of these computations may be quite long, the great majority are for short bursts of service, such as listing directories of editing lines of text.

Some OSs represent an interactive session by one continuous process, which executes a succession of programs on request. VMS is a system with this viewpoint. Other systems, such as MULTICS or UNIX, create a new process for each distinct service request.

Nothing is normally known about the resource needs of an interactive process when it is first created. All such processes are initially treated equally. Once a process has run for awhile, its pattern of past behavior may be used to infer information about its probable behavior in the future.

The most important objective for most interactive process schedulers is consistent and rapid response. Interactive users expect fast response to each request, especially very short requests; even more important, they expect the response to be consistent and predictable.

Long-term Scheduling

Long-term scheduling of interactive processes involves few decisions. New sessions and newly created processes are normally accepted immediately, unless the system is too heavily loaded. A limit may be established on the number of processes permitted to exist at one time. If a request to create a new process would exceed this limit, the request is rejected. The creating process must try again at a later time.

Time Quanta

To provide adequate response time for a set of interactive processes, the dispatcher must ensure that the CPU is shared at a high frequency so that no process waits too long for a turn at service. If storage scheduling is necessary, the available storage must be shared in a similar way. At both of these scheduling levels, the required sharing is enforced using the concept of a **time quantum,** a time limit assigned to a process each time it is selected for service. If the process uses up its time quantum, it is removed from service to give other processes a turn. Distinct time quanta may be used for each process for short-term and medium-term scheduling. The size of the time quanta assigned to each process can vary based on the known characteristics of that process.

Short-term scheduling makes use of a **CPU time quantum.** A timer is set to this time limit when the process is selected to run. If the time is exhausted before the process voluntarily gives up the CPU, the timer will cause an interrupt, and the CPU will be preempted in favor of another waiting process. Typical values for this quantum may range from about 100 milliseconds to several seconds. Use of time quanta to share the CPU in this manner is also called **time slicing.**

Medium-term scheduling makes use of a **storage time quantum,** a value that may be considerably larger than the CPU time quantum. Each time a process is placed in the active set by the medium-term scheduler, a counter in its PCB is set to the value of its storage time quantum. When the process completes a turn at the CPU, this counter is reduced by the running time the process consumed. A reduction may also be made when the process makes I/O requests. When the storage time quantum expires, the process leaves the active set in favor of other processes. Typical values for the storage time quantum range from a few seconds to several minutes.

Medium-term Scheduling

In some of the earliest timesharing systems, medium-term scheduling was identical to short-term scheduling. There was room in main memory for only one process at a time.

In a typical, current interactive environment, our description of the storage time quantum forms the heart of the medium-term scheduling technique for interactive processes. A process that has used up its storage time quantum is placed in an inactive state; inactive processes are not considered candidates for dispatching. The storage used by such a process is marked as available for swapping; it will actually be copied to the swap device only when the space is needed for another purpose.

Inactive processes are selected for return to the active set based on several factors. The assigned priority of a process, its time in the inactive group, and its storage requirements are some of the factors to be considered in making this decision.

Short-term Scheduling

The short-term scheduler in an interactive environment may select jobs based on priorities, or may consider only their order of entry in the ready queue. Preemption of a low-priority process by a higher-priority one may be allowed, but frequently is not. The most striking difference between interactive dispatching and most batch methods is use of the CPU time quantum in interactive systems to limit the continuous time any one single process is permitted to run.

A running interactive process may be stopped for all of the reasons listed for batch processes, except expiration of its total running time, which is generally not known. To this list we add one more reason: A process is interrupted by the OS if its CPU time quantum has expired.

Round-robin Scheduling

The simplest method for scheduling a set of ready processes in an interactive environment is called **round-robin scheduling.** In this method, illustrated in Figure 6–10, the PCBs of all processes in the ready state are linked on a single queue. Each process is assigned a fixed CPU time quantum. When the CPU is available, the process at the head of the queue is selected to run.

If that process uses up its allotted time, it is interrupted and placed on the back of the queue. Thus, all ready processes continue to be serviced in a circular order. As new processes become ready, they are added to the end of the queue.

Figure 6–10   Round–Robin Scheduling

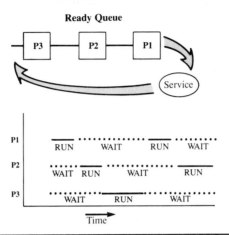

Priority Methods

The round-robin approach can be applied to a set of processes with assigned priorities. In this case, processes are maintained in order by priority; within each priority group round-robin dispatching is used. If there are a limited number of possible priority values, a separate queue may be maintained for each priority. Otherwise, a single queue is used, and processes are inserted into the queue by the scheduler so as to keep the queue ordered by priority.

In any case, the process selected to run is dispatched in round-robin fashion from the highest priority group that has a ready process. This strategy is depicted in Figure 6–11.

When priority methods are used, the priority of each process may be computed from various factors, and usually will change with time. Often a process that has completed its time quantum will be assigned a lower priority when it is returned to the queue. Often, too, a distinct time quantum size is associated with each priority; as a general rule, lower-priority processes, which are expected to run less frequently but require more time, get longer time quanta.

Figure 6–11 Round-robin Scheduling with Priorities

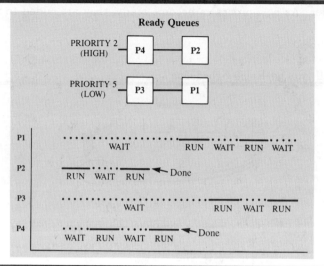

These considerations lead to many variations in specific priority methods. Some common ones are described below.

Aging Methods

An aging technique similar to that described in the previous section may be used to gradually raise the priority of a process that is waiting a long time for service. Periodically, the process queues are examined; all processes that have received no service during the last time interval are raised to the next-higher-priority level. There is usually an upper bound to the priority permitted for any process.

Feedback Queues

A process performing a long computation will use up many time quanta before it terminates or performs I/O. Such a process is said to be **compute-bound.** Conversely, a process performing only one or more short computations will not use up many successive time quanta. A process in this category is called **I/O-bound.**

It is reasonable to give more favorable service to I/O-bound processes by gradually reducing the priority of processes that use up a succession of time quanta without requesting I/O. The method of **feedback queues,** first used in CTSS, accomplishes this effect. With this method, each time a process is stopped because its quantum has expired, it is moved to a lower-priority level. Since such a process is expected to require longer CPU service, the next time it will be given a somewhat longer time quantum. The lowest-priority queue continues to be serviced with round-robin scheduling. Feedback queue scheduling is shown in Figure 6–12.

Figure 6–12 Scheduling with Feedback Queues

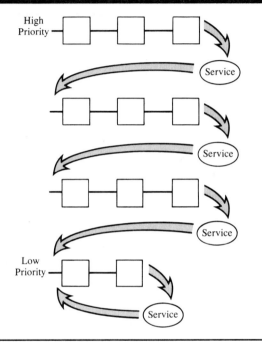

Selfish Scheduling

An interesting variation on basic interactive short-term scheduling methods is **selfish scheduling,** proposed by Kleinrock [1970]. This strategy favors processes that have been "accepted" for processing. New arrivals must wait to be accepted for service. Once processes are accepted, any of the usual scheduling methods may be used.

In selfish scheduling, as shown in Figure 6–13, processes newly arriving in the ready state are placed in a separate queue. All processes are assigned a special priority value, unrelated to the priority used for normal dispatching.

The priority of each new process starts at zero. The priority of both new and accepted processes is increased periodically by an aging technique; however, new processes gain priority at a faster rate. When a new process catches up to the priority value held by the accepted processes (which is identical for all), it is accepted into the main ready queue.

Figure 6–13 Selfish Scheduling

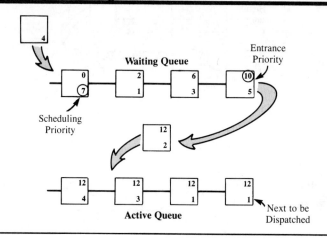

Fair-share Scheduling

Although the scheduling strategies discussed so far generally attempt to be fair, they cannot guarantee a specific level of service for any specific process or group of processes. For various reasons, such as service purchased by customers or real-time response requirements, a guarantee may be necessary. This problem is addressed by the concept of **fair-share scheduling,** depicted in Figure 6–14. A fair-share strategy divides all processes into distinct groups. Although the number of processes in each group may vary, each group is guaranteed an equal share of the available CPU time. This objective is not difficult to meet. It requires keeping track of the total CPU time used by each group, and assigning higher priorities to processes when their group CPU time is low. Fair-share scheduling has been used by VM/370 [Agrawal et al. 1984], and by some variants of UNIX [Henry 1984, Kay & Lauder 1988].

Figure 6–14 Fair-share Scheduling

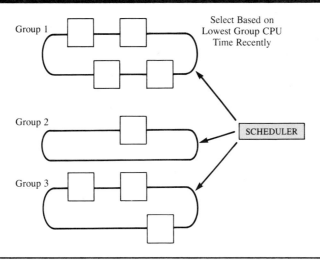

Examples

The UNIX OS makes use of a single dispatching queue due to its many possible priority values. The priority of user processes is adjusted periodically within permissible ranges, based on the amount of CPU time the process used during the most recent real-time interval. This formula favors processes that are not CPU-bound, while providing automatic aging when processes have not received service.

Processes are not formally partitioned into active or inactive sets. However, processes may be swapped out when higher-priority processes that have been swapped are ready to run. Processes are also swapped if they suspend voluntarily, or request resources not currently available. The process that has been in memory the longest may be selected for swapping, provided it has had a certain minimum residence time. This time is thus equivalent to a storage time quantum.

CTSS provided nine priority levels, the highest being level 0. Initially, processes running small programs were assigned to level 2, while larger processes began at level 3. The priority of each process was recomputed if its size changed.

Scheduling proceeded in CTSS with multilevel feedback queues. Each lower level received a time quantum twice as large as the previous one. A process could be preempted when a higher-priority one was ready, in which case the preempted process returned to the head of its previous priority queue.

MULTICS uses an explicit storage quantum as described above to partition processes into two groups, called "eligible" and "ineligible." Only eligible processes may be selected for running. Ineligible processes are subject to gradual swapping through the virtual memory system.

A multilevel feedback queue method is used in MULTICS for short-term scheduling. As in CTSS, each lower-priority queue has an associated time quantum that is double the previous one. The priority of each process can vary within a fixed range. The range allotted to known interactive processes (those connected to terminals) is higher than that for other processes.

6.8 SCHEDULING REAL-TIME PROCESSES

Real-time processes must be scheduled in such a way that absolute timing requirements may be met. This can require very careful scheduling that gives some processes extremely high priority, even higher than parts of the OS itself.

Real-time processes will be examined in detail in a later chapter. Here we will list some of the characteristics often associated with a real-time scheduling system:

- No long-term scheduling. Most processes are permanent. Dynamically created processes are admitted immediately.

- No storage scheduling. All processes remain active and resident in main memory at all times.

- Real-time processes are trusted. They may control each other, and they may influence the overall scheduling algorithm.

- The maximum resource needs of real-time processes are usually known. Other information about their expected behavior may be known and utilized as well.

- Strict priority-based scheduling. Usually high-priority processes can preempt those of lower priority. However, processes can lock themselves to block preemption.

- Optional timesharing within priority groups. This may be enabled or disabled by any process.

- Processes may be scheduled to run periodically at specific intervals, or to be started in response to certain events.

- Processes may be required to complete an activity by a specific deadline.

- Processes may create "microprocesses" and schedule these privately within their allotted time.

6.9 COMBINED METHODS

Some operating systems employ scheduling strategies that attempt to service more than one category of process. VAX/VMS is an example which recognizes all three categories: batch, interactive, and real-time. As shown in Figure 6–15, VMS makes use of 32 priority levels, ranging from 0 (lowest) to 31 (highest). The choice of 32 levels is not arbitrary; it allows extremely efficient priority dispatching in the VAX architecture, since the state of each queue (occupied or empty) can be summarized in a single 32-bit word.

Figure 6–15   Priority Levels in VMS

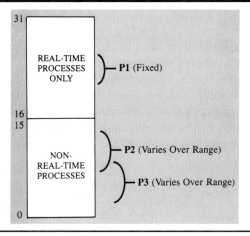

The lower half of the priority range, values 0-15, is used for batch or interactive processes. The upper range, 16-31, is reserved for real-time processes. The scheduling strategy differs for the two priority ranges.

Interactive and batch processes are assigned a base priority and a range above that priority; that range, however, can never exceed level 15. After a process has received service, its priority is set to the lowest value in its range. It is then raised as the process waits. Batch processes in VMS are explicitly identified because they are submitted to special batch queues. However, these processes are scheduled much like interactive ones except that they may receive a lower base priority.

Real-time processes are assigned priorities in the upper range, and their priority never changes. To accommodate these processes, strict preemption is employed. A higher-priority process can always immediately preempt a lower-priority process when it becomes ready. In particular, any real-time process will preempt any non-real-time one.

6.10 HARDWARE ASSISTANCE

Although the scheduling techniques discussed in this chapter can be implemented on computers having no special hardware support, schedulers can take advantage of selected hardware assistance that is sometimes provided. The most important hardware support features include timers and interrupts. Without these, little effective scheduling is possible.

A substantial impact on scheduling performance can be made by architectures that provide effective assistance for context switching. Techniques like multiple register sets and instructions designed for fast swapping of appropriate registers can allow extremely fast context switches, making it feasible to perform them much more often.

Specialized CPU instructions may be provided to speed up several aspects of scheduling algorithms. The VAX architecture provides direct support for insert and remove operations on queues, testing the 32-bit summary word, and other features exploited effectively by VMS.

A few computer types have offered more direct hardware support for scheduling. An example was the Singer Ten minicomputer, which provided ten independent register sets and automatic round-robin time slicing for ten processes. This support could be quite effective if pure round-robin scheduling was desired and ten processes were sufficient, but was less helpful in supporting other requirements.

6.11 SUMMARY

Processes and jobs are subject to several levels of scheduling. Long-term scheduling concerns the initial admission of new jobs into the system. Medium-term scheduling is used to share main memory effectively by periodically swapping processes to secondary storage. Short-term scheduling deals with the frequent reassignment of the CPU among ready processes.

Most processes fall into one of three main categories: batch, interactive, or real-time. Batch processes are submitted as a whole to perform a long computation. Interactive processes perform a series of shorter jobs and communicate with a user at a terminal. Real-time processes control and monitor external events and must meet rigid timing requirements. Scheduling must be performed differently for each category. Most OSs are specialized for a single type.

The objectives of scheduling include high throughput, fast and consistent response and fairness, among others. Processes are distinguished for scheduling by various attributes, including initial priority, predicted resource use, and observed behavior. Scheduling effectiveness may be measured by observing the queues in which processes wait for service.

Batch systems are concerned with long-term job admission and short-term CPU scheduling. Job admission selects a suitable job for admission to service when its resource needs can be met. CPU scheduling runs jobs without preemption, allowing them to complete unless they require service or I/O. Common techniques include FIFO or SJF with aging adjustments.

Interactive processes experience medium-term memory scheduling and short-term CPU scheduling. Both of these basically use rotated (round-robin) methods, switching processes when their time quantum has expired. Priorities are derived by observing the behavior of each process, giving favored treatment to those that seem "more interactive" due to frequent I/O requests and shorter periods of pure computation.

Real-time processes must be treated very differently and carefully, and are usually handled by specialized real-time operating systems. These processes are handled with extreme speed and allowed to make many of their own scheduling decisions. VMS is one of the few systems that attempts to support batch, interactive and real-time processes in a single scheduler.

FOR FURTHER READING

A number of studies and comparisons of scheduling techniques for batch and interactive systems have been published. Coffman and Kleinrock [1968] discuss a variety of scheduling methods and ways in which users might be able to "cheat" to obtain better service. A number of timesharing strategies are examined by McKinney [1969] and Kleinrock [1970]. Bunt [1976] surveys batch and interactive techniques, and their use in MFT, MVT, MULTICS, and UNIX. An early description of interactive process scheduling based on observed behavior is given by Ryder [1970]. Real-time scheduling issues are discussed, for example, by van der Linden and Wilson [1980]. For additional references related to real-time processes, see Chapter 22 of this text.

More theoretical treatments of process scheduling have been given by Coffman and Denning [1973], Brinch Hansen [1973], and Kleinrock [1975]. Brinch Hansen provides a readable analysis of various scheduling algorithms based on queuing theory.

For detailed treatment of process scheduling in specific systems, see Organick [1972] (MULTICS), Kenah and Bate [1984] (VMS), Bach [1986] (UNIX), and McKeag et al. [1976] (MCP, SCOPE, T.H.E., and TITAN).

IMPORTANT TERMS

active set
aging
batch process
compute-bound
CPU time quantum
dispatcher
dynamic priority
event-driven
fair-share scheduling
feedback queues
first-in, first-out (FIFO)
interactive process
I/O-bound
job scheduling
kth percentile value
long-term scheduling
mean
medium-term scheduling
overhead
preemption
priority

process scheduling
queue length
real-time process
response ratio
round-robin scheduling
scheduler
scheduling
selfish scheduling
shortest job next (SJN)
shortest remaining time next
short-term scheduling
starvation
static priority
storage scheduling
storage time quantum
swapping
time quantum
time slicing
variance
waiting time

REVIEW QUESTIONS

1. Identify the three major classes of processes that must be distinguished in a process scheduling strategy. For each class, state two important facts about its properties or requirements that distinguish it from other classes.

2. Explain a possible weakness of each of the following short-term scheduling strategies for batch processes.

    a. First-in, first-out
    b. Shortest job next

3. Explain why the scheduling levels listed below are not normally used for the indicated categories of processes:

    a. Medium-term scheduling for batch processes
    b. Long-term scheduling for interactive processes
    c. Medium-term scheduling for real-time processes

4. Explain how "CPU-bound" processes can be identified in an interactive system, and why these processes should be distinguished.

5. Explain two possible "measures of success" for a scheduling algorithm.

6. State five criteria that can be used to select processes for low-level scheduling. Explain briefly why each is reasonable.

7. Identify the three levels of process and job scheduling, and describe briefly the purpose of each.

8. Name two significant differences between batch processes and interactive processes that affect the low-level scheduling strategy.

9. Which of the following scheduling algorithms may cause some processes to wait indefinitely: FIFO, SJF, HRN, round-robin, LRU.

10. List three types of hardware support for process scheduling provided by some CPU architectures.

11. Why does the VMS operating system provide *exactly* 32 scheduling priority levels?

≡ ASSIGNMENTS ≡

1. Explain why CPUs and memory are the resources normally managed by the scheduling techniques discussed in this chapter. Under what conditions might scheduling techniques be useful for other resources, such as I/O devices or files? Identify some difficulties that might arise in scheduling the use of such resources.

2. Figures 6–2 and 6–3 identify 11 possible transitions between states. List the transitions that you would expect to see included in a system that primarily supports (a) batch processes, (b) interactive processes, or (c) real-time processes. Justify the transitions you did *not* include on each list.

3. It has been suggested that a finer distinction should be made among interactive processes according to their application. For example, a process supporting a graphics terminal might require different treatment than one used for routine data entry. How might an operating system recognize different types of processes? What distinctions would be appropriate in scheduling them?

4. The discussion of feedback queues for interactive processes indicates that some processes will tend to be compute-bound, and others will be I/O-bound. In fact, many processes will move between these categories, alternating "bursts" of I/O activity with longer computations. What difficulties will processes of this type cause with feedback queues, if any? What adjustments could be made to account for their characteristics?

5. List the steps required to swap one process to disk storage and replace it by another process. Suggest some design techniques to limit the overhead caused by swapping.

6. Discuss the approach that should be taken in medium- and short-term scheduling of interactive processes if the main memory can hold only a few of the existing processes at a time. What if it can hold almost all of them?

7. Explain one possible advantage and one disadvantage of providing a large number of distinct priority values.

8. Without looking forward to the chapter on real-time processes, give a possible reason for five of the characteristics of a real-time scheduling algorithm listed in Section 6.8.

≡ PROJECT ≡

This section describes a two part programming project to construct a simple, round-robin short-term scheduler and dispatcher for a simple multiprogramming operating system, and to install commands to control the loading and scheduling of processes. You should read the general description in this text in conjunction with the more specific descriptions given in your project manual. The scheduler/dispatcher is an important component of the multiprogramming executive (MPX) project described later in the text.

a. Implement a simple round-robin scheduler/dispatcher using the PCB structure from Chapter 5 to represent each process. Your instructor will supply program files for five test processes to be dispatched. These processes will be linked with your dispatcher and statically loaded. Each time a test process is dispatched, it will display a message to the screen and give up control to the dispatcher, which must save the context and select the next process to be dispatched. When a process has completed, it will indicate termination as specified in the project manual. When a process terminates, the dispatcher should free its PCB in the PCB queue and dispatch the next process. When all PCBs are free, the dispatcher should terminate.

b. Using the dispatcher developed in the previous step, add the commands listed below to the project COMHAN defined in Chapter 4. Your instructor will provide program files for the test processes to be run. In addition, procedures will be supplied to load a file in a specified area, and to list a directory.

1. LOAD *name:* create a new process called *name,* loading the program contained in the file called *name* into the load area. The process should be initialized to the *suspended/ready* state.

2. RESUME *name:* resume or awaken the application process called *name.* If *name* = *, then all application processes should be resumed.

3. RUN *name:* create a new process called *name,* loading the program from the file called *name* into the load area. The process should be initialized to the *ready* state.

4. SUSPEND *name:* suspend the application process called *name.* If *name* = *, then all application processes should be suspended.

5. TERMINATE *name:* terminate the application process called *name,* and free its PCB. If *name* = *, then all application processes should be terminated.

6. SETPRIORITY *name=nnn:* set the priority of the application process called *name* to *nnn,* where $-127 < nnn < 127$.

7. DIRECTORY: display the names of all programs in your directory that are loadable as processes.

8. DISPATCH: verify that all PCBs are built correctly by dispatching each application process in the PCB queue once in priority order. Each process will display a message to the screen before relinquishing control.

Note that the PCB queue becomes a part of the command handler in this project. The above commands allow PCBs to be built, and processes to be loaded and dispatched in a test environment. This verifies that all process loading is correct before moving to a full interrupt-driven, priority dispatching environment.

Interaction of Concurrent Processes

Interaction
of Concurrent
Processes

7.1 INTRODUCTION

In the previous two chapters we studied basic process concepts and examined the problems of scheduling the use of CPUs and memory. In this chapter we consider the problems raised by the shared use of other resources. We will be concerned with the interaction of processes in **concurrent execution.** Even though they may take turns using a single CPU, concurrent processes are, in a sense, executing at the same time. However, each individual process represents a single, sequential thread of execution. As we stated in Chapter 5, we may emphasize this view by referring to these processes as **concurrent sequential processes.**

A full study of all of the issues arising in the interaction of concurrent processes and the various solutions that have been developed for these problems would require a text in itself. A number of good texts and articles have been written on these topics; some of these are discussed in the For Further Reading section at the end of this chapter. Here we will provide a brief presentation of important issues and problems, and a look at some of the most effective and widely used solutions to those problems.

7.2 PROCESS INTERACTION

If processes had no need to interact, few problems would arise in their management. We could view an ideal environment for a set of processes as one including enough resources (including multiple CPUs) to meet the maximum needs of all processes at the same time. No competition for resources would exist, and each process would remain in the running state at all times.

As we have already learned, however, there is frequently only a single CPU, and we must consider the complex issues of scheduling and context switching to share the CPU in a correct and effective way. In a realistic environment, other resources are also limited; there is only so much memory space or file storage, only so many printers, communication lines, or tape drives. Processes must compete for the use of these resources as well.

Even in the presence of infinite resources, complete independence would hold only as long as processes had no wish to share information. Whenever two processes need to use the same file, inform each other about their progress, or have the power to control one another in any way, other types of interaction cannot be avoided.

There are then two principal reasons why concurrent processes may interact:

- **resource sharing.** Processes interact when they must share limited resources and compete for opportunities to use those resources. Resource sharing is *involuntary* interaction. Processes do not deliberately invoke it, are not normally aware of it, and gain no direct benefit when it occurs.

- **communication.** Processes interact when they choose to share information, to cooperate for a common purpose. This type of interaction is *voluntary*. Processes choose to communicate at specific points in their execution in order to gain some visible benefit.

Each of these categories of interaction leads to certain types of problems. The principal problems arising from interaction due to resource sharing are **deadlock** and **mutual exclusion** (see Chapter 5). Deadlock may occur when a set of processes each hold some resources while requesting others. If each process in the set needs something held by another, no progress can be made. (We discuss this problem in more detail in Section 7.4.) Mutual exclusion refers to the requirement that some resources, by their nature, must be used by only one process at a time. If such a resource is in use by a process, other processes that require that resource must wait. When there are competing requests for use of a resource, the OS is responsible for scheduling its use in a fair and efficient way. (We consider this subject in more depth in Section 7.5.)

Communication can also lead to problems of deadlock and mutual exclusion. The mutual exclusion problem in this context can be especially difficult to solve. In addition, other problems arise from the need to construct correct and efficient mechanisms to support the types of communication that may be desired. (We'll examine these issues in Section 7.6.)

All of the discussions in this chapter assume a centralized operating system with a single CPU. In the context of a distributed OS, process interaction is much more extensive, and the problems may be more difficult to solve effectively. We will consider process interaction in distributed operating systems in a later chapter.

7.3 DETERMINISM

Although some types of interaction among processes can be desirable, it is essential to ensure that, in spite of interaction, the outcome of these processes is not affected in unintended ways. Processes that are not designed to be influenced by external events should have the property of **determinism,** meaning that their outputs should be "determined" only by their inputs. If a process is executed repeatedly with the same inputs, its output should be identical every time, despite the variations it may experience in scheduling and despite the concurrent activities of other processes or the OS itself.

It is a responsibility of the process manager to guarantee determinism for each process that meets the following two conditions:

1. The behavior of the process is not intended to depend on real-time measurements.
2. The outputs of the process are not designed to depend on communication with other processes.

A system that shares resources over time among processes cannot guarantee that a process experiences an identical time interval between each of its steps every time it runs. If a process measures the time between events, or examines the time of day, outputs dependent on these variables will vary between executions.

If processes communicate, then the output of one process may depend by design on the behavior of another. In many cases, however, a group of communicating processes may be viewed as a cooperative set that communicate only among themselves. If this view applies, then the combined output of the set of processes, taken as a whole, should be deterministic.

No single technique or procedure can be used by a process manager to ensure determinism. Instead, it must be viewed as a requirement to be maintained as you consider and solve a variety of problems of process interaction. We consider some of the important problems that may pose a threat to determinism in the following sections.

7.4 DEADLOCK

In a resource-sharing environment, many processes compete for a limited set of resources, most of which can logically be used by only one process at a time. For example, a specific area of memory cannot be used independently by two processes at the same time. Although files that are not subject to change may be read concurrently by many processes, a process that writes to a file usually requires exclusive access to that file.

Efficient sharing of resources requires that they be allocated to each process only when needed. Critical resources like disks or file directories are in heavy demand, and must not be tied up by processes that do not need them immediately. Memory can be shared most effectively if processes are permitted to request space as needed. At the same time, processes must hold some resources for long periods of time. For example, a printer must be dedicated to one job until it is complete, not shared on a line-by-line basis. The memory required to hold the main program for a process must be held as long as that process is active.

These conflicting needs for correct but efficient resource sharing can lead to the possibility of deadlock, when a group of processes are each requesting access to some resources while holding the exclusive right to access others. This type of deadlock occurs due to competition for a specific set of resources. The difficulties and possible solutions for the deadlock problem will vary as each type of resource is considered. Deadlock based on resource competition is sometimes called **resource deadlock** to distinguish it from certain other types of deadlock, which we'll look at later in this section.

Although the deadlock problem has been studied extensively, the solution remains elusive. Few operating systems can guarantee total freedom from deadlock; many do not even try. Reliable solutions may require unacceptable overhead costs. The deadlock problem is especially serious in a distributed environment, in which some types of deadlock may be so likely that methods for dealing with them are essential.

A Familiar Example

A familiar example of deadlock in a context far removed from operating systems is shown by the pattern of automobile traffic in Figure 7-1. In this situation, no cars can make progress; each is blocked by a car in the space ahead, which is also blocked. This situation has frequently been called "gridlock."

The deadlocked cars are competing for specific areas of space within the road. Since each car requires a space currently occupied by another, and no space can be used by two cars at once, no progress can be made.

Figure 7–1 Deadlock in a Traffic Situation

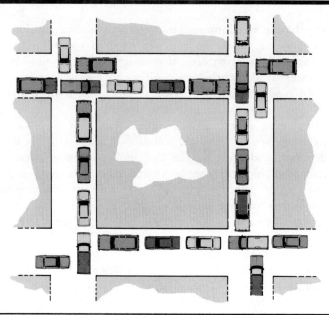

This situation will be corrected only when the problem is recognized and some unusual corrective action is taken. Notice that each driver observes only that the traffic in front is presently stalled. No one is aware of the full extent of the problem. Eventually, a driver must decide to pull out of line voluntarily, or a police officer must arrive and direct some cars to make way for others. Only with this extraordinary action, which disrupts the travel of some of the cars, can the deadlock finally be broken.

In a computer system, similar conflicts arise when processes compete for the use of various resources (see Figure 7–2). As you can see, a strong analogy exists between traffic deadlock and the deadlock in computer systems. We will see a number of conditions that must hold in any system for deadlock to be a possibility, and a number of strategies, some more practical than others, which can be considered to resolve the deadlock problem in specific situations. Each of these can be illustrated with the traffic example as well as examples in resource allocation. The rest of this section examines these necessary conditions and solution strategies.

Figure 7-2 Deadlock in a Computer System

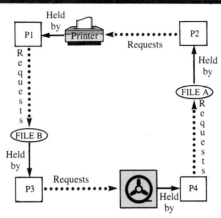

Necessary Conditions for Deadlock

In order for deadlock to be possible for a specific type of resource, four conditions must be true about the way that resource is managed by the system. These conditions, identified by Coffman et al. [1971], are:

- **mutual exclusion.** Processes must be required to use the resource one at a time. If all of the processes that need to use a resource can use it simultaneously, deadlock cannot occur.

- **resource holding.** Processes must engage in resource holding while requesting others. If a process is required to request all of its resources at once, or to give up all its current resources before requesting new ones, deadlock is impossible.

- **no preemption.** It must not be possible for the system to temporarily take away resources from one process and assign them to another; there must be no preemption. If this can occur, even though some processes may be treated unfairly, a deadlock can be broken.

- **circular requests.** The order in which successive requests are permitted from a process must allow a circular pattern to occur. If requests must be presented in a strict order to be honored by the system, then deadlock will be prevented.

The need for all of these conditions gives us hope that deadlock may be less of a problem than we supposed. If we can deny at least one condition for each resource, deadlock will be effectively prevented.

Unfortunately, removal of even one of these necessary conditions is impossible or impractical in many cases. We can see its futility in our gridlock example. Mutual exclusion is unavoidable; two cars cannot occupy the same area of the road. Each car must occupy some space continuously, moving into a new area before it has fully left an old one. No force is available to pluck a car out of the road and suspend it in the air (the police officer may direct cars to the side of the road, but only if that space is free of parked cars). Finally, there is no natural order to the road space resources, which could be used to develop a rule for yielding and prevent deadlock from occurring. A traffic light would impose an ordering on a single intersection, but would be insufficient to resolve the problem in a larger context.

Removing one of the necessary conditions, where possible, is a first line of defense against deadlock. This defense can be successful for some types of resources, but unusable for many others. Let's consider other possible solution strategies.

Deadlock Solution Strategies

Strategies that may help us deal with deadlock fall into three categories:

- deadlock prevention
- deadlock avoidance
- deadlock detection and recovery

Deadlock prevention—the strategy of managing a resource so that at least one of the four necessary conditions does not hold—can be effective for some resource types, but impractical for others. **Deadlock avoidance** is a technique for processing resource requests in a "safe" order so that an immediate danger of deadlock never arises. This technique has been used in some specialized situations but is not practical as a general solution. **Deadlock detection** refers to strategies for detecting the presence of deadlock when it has occurred. As we have seen from the traffic example, the existence of deadlock is not always obvious to the casual observer. If deadlock is detected, a strategy is also needed for **deadlock recovery,** a strategy that must attempt to remove the deadlock while doing the least damage to the work being performed by each process.

Deadlock Prevention

The object of deadlock prevention is to manage resources in such a way that some of the necessary conditions do not hold. It is a *design strategy* for an OS; the system is designed in such a way that some types of deadlock cannot arise. We have already seen the futility of deadlock prevention in the gridlock example. However, the technique may be used to address some types of deadlock in a computer system.

The requirement for mutual exclusion is an intrinsic property of many resources, such as memory and most I/O devices. Although we may identify a few resource types that do not require mutual exclusion, such as read-only files, there is no way to remove this requirement from other types.

Nonetheless, the mutual exclusion condition may in some cases be bypassed for resources whose usage is purely input or purely output and may be processed as a batch. In such cases, pooling techniques may be useful. Printer output is an obvious example. Using spooling, the output from several processes may be gathered concurrently into *separate* spool files; each complete file may then be scheduled for actual printing by a system process when its turn arrives.

The resource holding condition can be removed in some cases by requiring that processes request resources all at once. You could consider this strategy for memory allocation; it would require that each process be given its maximum memory requirement when the process is first created. However, this would prohibit dynamic memory allocation from a global pool, and lead to inefficient use of memory.

The importance of dynamic memory allocation for effective sharing of memory makes it unattractive to exclude this feature for most modern operating systems. However, exactly this solution was used in the design of OS/360. The original plan to allow full dynamic memory allocation in that system was changed to a system of fixed partitions because of the risk of deadlock over memory space [Auslander et al. 1981, p. 476].

Preemption is usually impossible with physical I/O devices, or files opened for writing. Preempting a printer would cause the output of one process to be interleaved with that of another, a seemingly unacceptable prospect. However, T.H.E. did allow this type of preemption [Dijkstra 1968]. Printer output was interleaved by pages, relying on the operator to sort the pages for each process. It was expected that with only a few users, actual conflicts would be rare.

For memory resources, preemption is equivalent to swapping, and is a reasonable solution if sufficient secondary storage is available. If a process requesting additional memory is swapped when the need cannot be met, deadlock over memory can be avoided.

A technique for avoiding circular requests is **hierarchical ordering**, first studied by Havender [1968]. This strategy avoids circular requests by assigning a priority to each category of resources and enforcing this rule:

- A request for resources at a given priority level will be honored only if the process holds no resources at the same or higher levels.

If a suitable set of priorities can be assigned, this rule will not allow a cycle to arise in the resource allocation pattern. The difficulty with this method lies in assigning priorities to some categories of resources, especially memory blocks and files. The number of resources in each of these categories is large and highly variable, and there is no basis for giving some units higher priority than others. However, if they were all assigned the same priority, no file could be opened while another was already open, and dynamic memory allocation would also once again be impossible.

Hierarchical ordering was used systematically for physical devices in Brinch Hansen's RC 4000 OS [Brinch Hansen 1973, Ch. 8], and is used for this category of resources by a number of current OSs, including VMS [Kenah & Bate 1984]. MVS uses this technique to prevent deadlock on an important category of internal resource: lock variables used to enforce mutual exclusion on various sharable system data structures when multiprocessing (multiple CPUs) is used [Scherr 1973].

Deadlock Avoidance

The strategy of deadlock avoidance is a dynamic strategy attempting to ensure that resources are never allocated in such a way as to place the system in an "unsafe" state—that is, one in which there is an imminent danger of deadlock. The best known algorithm for deadlock avoidance is the **banker's algorithm,** first introduced by Habermann [1969] and used by Dijkstra in T.H.E.

We will not present the bankers algorithm here. It is studied in detail in a number of advanced texts; for example, see Brinch Hansen [1973] or Peterson and Silberschatz [1985]. Although this algorithm has been used in T.H.E. and a few other systems to avoid deadlock for a limited set of resources, it is not generally practical for two reasons:

1. Reliable upper bounds are required on the resources to be used by each process. Such bounds are normally unavailable for interactive processes.

2. The algorithm must be executed every time a process requests resources. Its running time increases rapidly as the number of processes and resources grows. So, the overhead required in a practical environment would be severe.

Because of these problems, you can use deadlock avoidance to combat deadlock only in specialized situations.

A certain type of avoidance strategy could be used to address the traffic gridlock problem: Allow no vehicle to enter an intersection unless a clear path exists to the other side. Such a rule would be difficult to enforce by a central authority, but might be usable by a set of cooperative drivers. (No one said this example had to be realistic.) Even with this rule, however, a problem could arise if cars approach an intersection simultaneously from all directions, and no one is willing to enter. This type of "indefinite blocking" is a special kind of deadlock we will consider in a later section.

Deadlock Detection

The process of examining the state of an operating system to determine if deadlock exists is called deadlock detection. Very often, deadlock can arise as a complicated circular linkage of requests and resource holdings involving dozens of processes. At the same time, many other processes not involved in the deadlock may be making progress normally. Even if the OS (or an operator or irate user) notices that certain processes have been waiting a long time without service, it may not be clear that an actual deadlock exists.

A simple automatic procedure for detecting deadlock can be used as long as the OS maintains a central record of the resources being held by each process, the current requests by each process, and the resources presently available. The idea of the detection algorithm is to take a very optimistic view of the future behavior of each process. We assume that any process that can have its current resource requests fulfilled will proceed to completion without requiring any more resources. If there are processes that will be unable to make progress even under these optimistic assumptions, then those processes are deadlocked.

The deadlock detection strategy may be summarized as follows:

1. Find a process for which current requests can be met from the presently available resources. In particular, a process that has no current requests is an obvious candidate.
2. Let all the resources presently held by this process be considered (for purposes of the algorithm) to become available.
3. Repeat from step 1 until no further processes can be served.

If any processes remain that cannot have their requests met, then deadlock exists. Moreover, the remaining processes are exactly the ones that are deadlocked. The outcome does not depend on the order in which processes are selected; the same set of deadlocked processes, if any, will always be found.

This algorithm provides a practical technique for detecting deadlock. Unlike the avoidance algorithm, you need to use it only occasionally. One strategy may be to perform deadlock detection only when the time that any process has been waiting for a resource exceeds a certain threshold. This strategy is applied effectively by VMS [Kenah & Bate 1984, pp. 256-262].

Although deadlock can be detected in a practical manner, many operating systems include no provision for deadlock detection. In these systems, deadlock may be discovered only when operators or users observe a substantial lack of progress throughout the system. In this case, effective recovery may be difficult.

Recovery from Deadlock

If deadlock is discovered (or strongly suspected), either by the detection algorithm or by human observation, recovery steps must be taken by breaking the circle of waiting processes. In the traffic example, we must recover by requiring some cars to pull out of line or back up where possible. The remaining vehicles can then proceed, and the cars that were required to wait may resume their journey.

In an OS context, a reasonable recovery requires first that some corrective actions are possible even in the presence of deadlock. In some early versions of UNIX, deadlock could frequently occur on buffers used throughout the system for file data. No buffers were reserved for use by a recovery process; even highly privileged processes could do little without buffers. This type of deadlock was easily detected, since no processes could make any progress, but the only recovery possible was to reinitialize the entire OS, losing all of the work currently underway by each process.

Assuming an operator or recovery process is able to proceed, the most drastic step would be to terminate all processes involved in the deadlock. However, this technique is much more drastic than needed. Deadlock can usually be broken by removing only some of the processes involved. In some cases, processes may be able to "back up" to a convenient point rather than being completely restarted.

We may consider a variety of issues in removing processes to break a deadlock situation. Among them:

- Which processes are contributing the most to the deadlock? Sometimes a deadlock can be ended by removing one or two processes, if the right ones are chosen.

- Which processes are capable of being restarted? If a process was in the midst of updating a file, it may be impossible to restart the process and produce correct results. In some cases, restartable processes are identified when submitted.

- How much work must be repeated? It is costly to restart a process from the beginning that has already completed many hours of work. Some processes, however, may have saved their state periodically as "checkpoints." In this case, they may restart from the most recent checkpoint.

• What is the priority of each process? For a variety of reasons, some processes may be more important than others. Processes of lower priority should be removed first.

Choosing the right set of processes to remove is an art, often best performed by a human operator. VMS supports the concept of a "deadlock priority" for each process, but the problem of assigning these priorities appropriately has been difficult to solve [Kenah & Bate 1984, p. 262]. As we have seen, the police officer must break the gridlock by removing cars at random, looking only for those that have an available place to go. The choice made by the computer operator or OS must be the best compromise from a variety of considerations.

Other Types of Deadlock

The discussion in this section has concerned the most commonly studied type of deadlock: resource deadlock. In this situation, processes are blocked waiting for resources currently held by other processes.

We will close the discussion by mentioning two other categories of deadlock that are less commonly identified, but of increasing concern in systems with large sets of interacting processes, especially distributed environments. **Communication deadlock** can occur when processes wait for consumable resources, such as messages or signals from other processes. For various reasons, a process may wind up waiting for a message that will never arrive. **Livelock,** or **indefinite blocking,** refers to the case where a process, although not formally deadlocked, cannot be guaranteed progress in any finite amount of time. An example of livelock occurs in static priority short-term scheduling, in which processes with low priority may be blocked indefinitely by those of higher priority. We will encounter other examples in the discussions of mutual exclusion and communication that follow.

Total System Strategies

To banish deadlock as completely as possible from an operating system, suitable solutions must be considered for each category of resource to be managed. It is likely that different resources will require different strategies, so an overall solution must employ a mixture of techniques.

The most suitable techniques for fighting deadlock involving the principal resource types are summarized in Figure 7–3. As shown in the examples throughout this section, most OSs will use a combination of prevention techniques to minimize deadlock at the design stage wherever possible. The deadlock that may slip through is often simply tolerated, relying on limiting the system load or the like, so that deadlock is a rare occurrence. Although deadlock detection algorithms can be quite practical, they are not often used, and automatic recovery from deadlock is even rarer.

Figure 7–3 Deadlock Strategies for Principal Resource Types

RESOURCE TYPE	DEADLOCK STRATEGY
CPU	Prevention; CPU cannot be held
Memory	Fixed initial allocation; swapping (preemption) periodically or when blocked
I/O and storage devices	Hierarchical ordering; bypass mutual exclusion by spooling; avoidance
Files	Sharing where possible; detection and recovery
Locks and other control structures	Hierarchical ordering; detection and recovery
Consumable resources	Detection and recovery

7.5 MUTUAL EXCLUSION

The problem of mutual exclusion arises when it is necessary to ensure that sharable resources are not accessed simultaneously by two or more processes. As we have noted, many resources may be considered to be serially-reusable resources. They may be used repeatedly, but only by one process at a time. Memory and most I/O devices usually fall into this category, as do files that may be modified. However, information within memory or files may be shared in some cases, if processes cooperate in sharing this data in a useful way. This leads to another important category of serially-reusable resources: shared data structures that may be created within shared files or memory.

System-controlled Resources

Many of the resources commonly shared by concurrent processes in a computer system are **system-controlled resources.** Examples include the CPU, memory, I/O devices, and files. For some of these resources, all direct access is actually performed by the operating system. User processes are prevented by hardware methods from executing direct input and output instructions.

Instead, they must use system calls to request the OS to perform I/O on their behalf.

User processes can directly access memory, and execute instructions on the CPU. However, even in this case the OS sets limits. Memory protection hardware can ensure that every memory reference is within proper bounds. The CPU is assigned to processes by the OS, and processes will be interrupted if they run too long or attempt improper actions.

For system-controlled resources, mutual exclusion is easy to enforce. The OS is the sole decision maker. If a process requires exclusive access to a resource for a series of operations, it must first allocate the resource. In the case of files, allocation is performed by an *open* operation. These system calls are *requests for permission* to use a device, memory block, or file. If the resource is currently allocated to someone else, the requesting process will be suspended until it becomes available. When the present user terminates or frees the resource, the OS will wake up the next waiting process. Figure 7–4 illustrates management of system-controlled resources.

Figure 7–4 Mutual Exclusion for System-Controlled Resources

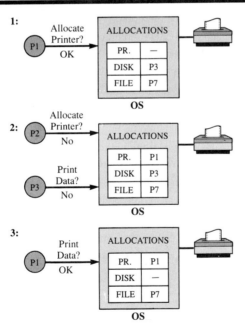

It is crucial to observe that the OS is in full charge of this allocation, and *can prevent interruption* by any processes. Although high-priority events

may be allowed to interrupt some OS activities, they will never lead to the unexpected dispatching of a different process. Processes can neither interfere with the allocation decisions nor bypass them, since direct access is impossible without the OS's consent. Thus mutual exclusion is assured in a simple way if the OS enforces it correctly.

User-controlled Resources

The situation is very different for another category of resources, called **user-controlled resources.** This category generally includes shared data structures; in some systems it may include other resources as well. These resources are *not* under the direct control of the operating system. It is physically possible for any process to access them in a way that violates correct sharing. Mutual exclusion must be maintained by *cooperative* actions by the processes themselves.

Resources in this category are not controlled by the OS because it is neither necessary nor desirable to give the OS that responsibility. It is not necessary, because the resources are temporary and useful only to the processes that have chosen to share them. Improper use would not cause a problem for other processes or the OS itself. It is not desirable, because assigning such low-level resources to the OS would burden the OS with a very large and fast-changing set of resources, and would add overhead to allocation and use that could overwhelm the time required to actually use the resource.

Although the OS does not manage user-controlled resources directly, it is important that OS designers understand the problems raised by these resources and possible solution mechanisms for two principal reasons:

1. The OS may be required to supply support services to assist in managing user-controlled resources.
2. The OS itself may use these mechanisms to control some of its own internal resources.

An example illustrating the mutual exclusion problem for user-controlled resources is shown in Figure 7–5. The figure depicts a portion of a student grade file that may be accessed simultaneously by two processes, ProcessA and ProcessB. Both processes control terminals used to display and enter data. Suppose the user at the terminal controlled by ProcessA (UserA) requests the record for student number 23456, and at more or less the same instant UserB requests the same record. Without mutual exclusion, two copies of the record will be read into main memory, with one being displayed on UserA's terminal and the other being displayed on UserB's terminal.

Now suppose UserA changes a grade in MATH 111 from C to B, and UserB changes a grade in ENGLISH 224 from B to C. Each change would be entered at the appropriate terminal and hence stored in the corresponding copy of the record in each user's address space. Eventually, each user will request that the modified record be updated in the file. Both records cannot be written simultaneously, so one record update is done after another. Suppose that ProcessB's update is done before ProcessA's. The grade change in ENGLISH 224 will then be lost, because the last record written will contain the original record with a change to the MATH 111 grade from C to B. The integrity of the data file has been sacrificed by the failure to prevent two processes from accessing the data at the same time.

Figure 7–5   Mutual Exclusion for User-Controlled Resources

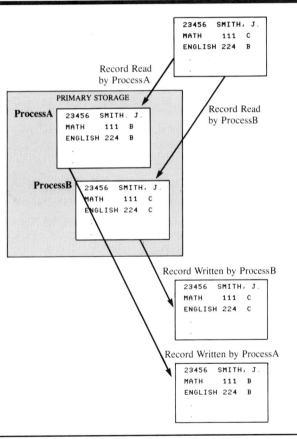

Critical Sections

The problem in the example above arises because the processes did not ensure that mutual exclusion was maintained on the records to be updated. A cooperative solution is needed to ensure the type of mutual exclusion required. To enforce mutual exclusion voluntarily for user-controlled resources, it is first necessary to identify each program sequence in every process that constitutes a series of accesses to a shared resource that should not be interrupted. Such a sequence is called a **critical section.** In the example, the sequence of program steps, during which each process copies a grade record and then updates it, forms a critical section for the grade file.

To prevent this type of interference that leads to a violation of determinism, it is necessary to restrict the activities of some processes while another process is executing code within a critical section. This can be accomplished by preceding each critical section with a sequence of instructions, called an **entry protocol,** and ending each critical section with a similar sequence, called an **exit protocol.** These protocols must provide a means of communication between processes using the resource to ensure that mutual exclusion is enforced.

Specifically, we require the protocols to enforce the following rule:

- If a process is executing within a critical section for a particular resource, no other process may enter a critical section for that same resource.

This rule is sufficient to guarantee mutual exclusion. Note that we do not insist that other processes do nothing during a critical section, only that they do not interfere with the same resource. In practice we will need several other rules to ensure that a set of protocols does not impede overall progress. These rules were first formulated by Dijkstra [1965]:

1. If any processes are waiting to enter a critical section, and no process is currently within one, then some process must be allowed to enter within a finite time.
2. The behavior of a process outside of its critical sections must not influence the treatment of processes waiting to enter their critical sections.
3. There must be a limit on how many times one process can repeatedly enter critical sections while another process is waiting.

We must make one more assumption: no process may fail, or remain indefinitely, within a critical section. These rules will then guarantee progress and fair treatment of all processes. Of course, all processes must use the protocols correctly.

Solution Strategies

Implementing a set of mutual exclusion protocols that meets all the necessary requirements is not easy. The problem lies in the fact that the protocols themselves require communication between processes, and this communication may involve shared variables that have their own requirement for mutual exclusion. Defining an entry and exit protocol does not remove the mutual exclusion requirement; instead, it attempts to isolate it at a lower level, where it can more easily be solved by other means.

At the lowest level, mutual exclusion must be enforced by one of the following mechanisms:

1. By the hardware, which ensures that processes can be interrupted only between machine instructions and that multiple accesses to the same memory location cannot occur at the same time.
2. By the operating system, which can perform critical activities immune from interruption, preventing interference as long as there is only one CPU.

Although the OS can provide fundamental mutual exclusion by providing entry and exit protocols as system services, in many cases the overhead involved in these OS calls will be unacceptable. In other situations, there may be no OS to rely on. In particular, this mechanism is of no help in implementing the operating system itself.

In some cases the CPU can meet this need directly by including in its instruction set an instruction with certain special properties, such as the "test and set" instruction discussed below. However, not all CPU architectures include a suitable instruction.

If a specialized instruction is not available, and calls to an OS cannot be used, then mutual exclusion must be obtained by software algorithms that rely only on standard machine instructions. This may be necessary with some architectures, for example, to provide mutual exclusion within the procedures of the operating system itself.

Software Solutions

A variety of pure software protocols for mutual exclusion have been proposed. These techniques rely on no lower-level mutual exclusion mechanism except the indivisibility of individual reads or writes of memory. Most of these protocols require a number of shared variables per process, and include complex mechanisms to prevent unnecessary blocking and ensure fairness. Nonetheless, many proposed mechanisms have failed to meet progress or fairness criteria, or have failed in some cases to guarantee mutual exclusion.

As an illustration of the subtle problems involved, consider a proposed solution in which a flag is associated with each process, intended to indicate when that process is within its critical section (for some specific resource). Each flag is a shared variable, directly accessible to both processes. In the simple case where there are only two processes, the protocols proposed for each process have the form:

```
ENTRY PROTOCOL:


    WAIT while my neighbor's flag is set
    set my flag to TRUE


EXIT PROTOCOL:


    set my flag to FALSE
```

Although this solution appears simple, it does not actually guarantee mutual exclusion. Suppose that an interrupt occurs at an unfortunate moment during the entry protocol (remember that interrupts can occur after any machine instruction). The process may be interrupted just after discovering that the other flag is no longer set, but *before* setting its own flag. If this interruption leads to a switch to the other process, and that process happens to then perform its entry protocol, it will discover no flag set and proceed to its critical section. When the first process resumes, however, it too will enter its critical section, since it has already finished examining the flags.

An alternate idea is to reverse the two steps in the entry protocol, causing each process to set its own flag before testing the other. The flag now indicates either that a process is in its critical section, or that it is *waiting* to get in. This algorithm does ensure mutual exclusion, but another problem arises. If the first process is interrupted immediately after setting its own flag, we may wind up with both processes examining each other's flags, while both flags are set. Neither process will ever make progress—a subtle form of deadlock.

A few correct solutions have been proposed and presented in a number of advanced texts. They generally suffer from the following weaknesses:

- They are complex and require a large number of variables, which increase with the number of processes.
- They are designed to deal with only two competing processes, and are not easily extended to larger numbers.
- They require processes to consume CPU time, with constant testing of variables when processes are required to wait. This problem is known as **busy waiting.**

Recently, Peterson [1981] presented a correct two-process solution with a much simpler form than those previously known. This solution makes use of a flag for each process as above, plus an additional shared variable indicating who has the "turn"—that is, the right to enter a critical section. Peterson's solution takes the following form:

```
ENTRY PROTOCOL:


    set my flag to TRUE
    give the turn to my neighbor
    WAIT WHILE my neighbor has the turn
        AND his flag is set



EXIT PROTOCOL:


    set my flag to FALSE
```

This algorithm avoids most of the problems of previous proposals. It is analyzed in detail in [Peterson 1981] and several advanced texts.

Even Peterson's method becomes quite complex when extended to more than two processes. Most practical solutions for more than two processes are based on the "bakery algorithm" proposed by Lamport [1974]. This method uses the "take a number" concept, similar to customers waiting their turn in bakeries. Each process waiting to enter a critical section takes a number, and the turn passes to the process holding the lowest number. This approach is of particular interest in distributed environments.

Semaphores

As an alternative to pure software solutions, Dijkstra proposed the mechanism of **semaphores,** which was first used successfully in T.H.E. The semaphore proposal is based on an assumption that a simple sequence of operations can be performed *without interruption,* which must be guaranteed either by the hardware or by the operating system. If this assumption is valid, the semaphore offers an elegant and effective solution to mutual exclusion and to other problems of process interaction as well.

The simplest type of semaphore is a **binary semaphore.** We can view a binary semaphore as an integer or boolean variable with special properties. It is allowed to assume only the values 0 or 1. When used in a mutual exclusion context, it is initialized to 1. Thereafter, it may be accessed *only* by two special operations. These operations are traditionally designated P and V. (The names represent Dutch words, but there is disagreement over their exact meaning [Andrews & Schneider 1983]. They are often given in English as *wait* and *signal.*) A simple form of the P and V operations is:

```
P(S):    WHILE (S=0) do nothing
         S := 0


V(S):    S := 1
```

Each of these operations must be *uninterruptible,* except that the P operation can be interrupted while the process is waiting.

If a semaphore S is associated with each shared resource, then P(S) and V(S) are precisely the required entry protocol and exit protocol, respectively, to be used with each critical section for that resource. As long as the assumption of uninterruptible operations holds, the semaphore mechanism can meet the required conditions for mutual exclusion and progress, regardless of the number of processes competing for the resource.

It is not clear, however, that the semaphore operations as stated above can guarantee fairness. Each process that is "doing nothing" is in fact repeatedly testing the value of S. If several processes are waiting when a V operation is performed, only the first one to make a successful test will be able to proceed. It is possible that one process will wait indefinitely while others proceed.

Another problem is still with us: the problem of busy waiting. The repeated testing of the semaphore consumes CPU time with little chance of success.

The busy waiting problem can be solved if there are system calls available for *sleep* and *wakeup* operations. Although it may be inefficient to give the OS full charge of semaphore operations, the overhead of a *sleep* call can be tolerated when a process must wait. A process which has to wait during a P operation can put itself to sleep, and a V operation can be used to wake up a waiting process.

In order for a process executing V to wake a sleeper, however, it must know what the waiting processes are. This information can be available if a queue or linked list of process identifiers is associated with each semaphore. This leads to a representation such as shown in Figure 7–6. With this approach, each waiting process inserts its own id on the queue before sleeping. The V operation wakes the single process, if any, at the head of the queue. Fairness is also assured, since processes are served in first-in, first-out order. When a process awakens, it can immediately proceed.

Figure 7–6 Semaphores with Associated Queues

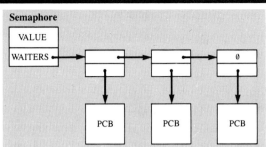

The algorithms now become:

```
P(S):   IF (S=0) THEN
            insert i.d. in queue
            sleep
        END IF
        S := 0


V(S):   IF (queue is empty) THEN
            S := 1
        ELSE
            remove i.d. at head of queue
            wake that process
        END IF
```

Semaphore Implementation

While the semaphore mechanism is attractive, it is only useful if we can implement semaphores effectively. The most efficient implementation will be one on which the necessary indivisibility can be guaranteed by hardware. This requires some type of single instruction in the CPU instruction set that can both test the value of a register or flag, and set it to a new value at the same time.

An example is the "Test and Set" instruction available in the IBM S/360 architecture. This instruction sets the 360 condition codes, depending on whether a selected memory byte has a logical TRUE or FALSE value, and simultaneously sets the byte to TRUE. If the byte is taken to represent a semaphore value, we may implement the P and V operations as follows:

```
P(S):   LOOP
                 test-and-set (S)
        UNTIL (code=FALSE)


V(S):   S := FALSE
```

Here we interpret the TRUE and FALSE values to correspond to 0 and 1, respectively. We can also use other mechanisms to implement semaphore instructions; examples are discussed by Shaw [1974] and Raynal [1986].

If no suitable CPU instruction can be used, P and V may be implemented as OS system calls. In this case, a semaphore may be considered a resource to be allocated and managed by the OS or—as a more efficient alternative—the semaphore operations may be passed a reference to a semaphore variable in the address space of the process. The OS makes use of its ability to control interrupts and process dispatching to ensure that the operations are not interrupted.

Extended Use of Semaphores

The concept of a binary semaphore is often extended to a **general semaphore,** also called a **counting semaphore,** that can assume values greater than one. This type of semaphore can be used to keep track of the available quantity of resources for which a number of units exist.

The power of semaphores is not limited to the mutual exclusion problem; they may also be used to solve many other problems of process synchronization. These additional uses of semaphores are often supported by higher-level mechanisms in the programming language used, as discussed below.

Higher-level Mechanisms

The use of a semaphore to enforce mutual exclusion is a voluntary mechanism. Semaphores are not intrinsically related to resources; rather, the cooperating processes must assign a semaphore to each resource, and use the P and V operations on it consistently and correctly. Without some assistance from compilers or other programming tools, mistakes by the programmer are likely. Such mistakes can introduce subtle errors that may not be detected for a long time and may be very difficult to diagnose.

Because of the likelihood of error in the proper use of semaphores, some programming languages that support concurrent processes include direct support for critical sections. If a region of code is identified as a critical section for a particular resource, the compiler can automatically allocate a semaphore and provide the proper protocols.

Concurrent programming languages may provide support for a number of other synchronization mechanisms that can be built from semaphores. An important example is the **monitor.** Using the concepts of modularity encouraged by software engineering experience, a monitor collects the definition of a resource, and *all* of the critical sections that access that resource, into a single shared module. No process is allowed to enter any of these critical sections while one is currently in use, so the required mutual exclusion is ensured.

Monitors and other high-level mechanisms may be quite useful for operating systems written in concurrent languages that support them. They may be simulated with more difficulty in some languages that do not provide direct support. Although the subject of concurrent programming may be important to OS designers, it is a large subject deserving of a text in itself, and a number of such texts are available. One example is Brinch Hansen [1977]; other examples are given in the readings section at the end of this chapter. Due to its enormity, we will not pursue the subject of concurrent programming languages in this book.

7.6 INTERPROCESS COMMUNICATION

Processes that plan to cooperate on a common task must share information in some way to achieve that cooperation. Developing effective methods for such information sharing is the problem of **interprocess communication,** or **IPC.** As computing systems are increasingly viewed as systems of interacting processes, perhaps distributed over many physical locations, the IPC problem becomes more and more important.

Basic Models for Communication

All methods for information exchange between processes use one of the following basic models:

- **shared memory.** In the shared memory model, shared variables and data structures are directly available in the address space of more than one process. Usually this is accomplished through memory translation arrangements, which map part of the memory of multiple processes to the same physical area. In some cases, shared files can be used as an alternative.

- **message passing.** In the message passing model, one process explicitly sends information and another explicitly receives it.

The operations are viewed as a type of I/O, rather than direct, access to shared information. The unit of information exchanged, however large or small it may be, is called a **message.**

These models are contrasted in Figure 7–7. The shared memory model offers the fastest and simplest communication when overlapping address spaces are possible. To exchange information, one process simply writes to a shared data structure, and another process reads from it. In the case of shared files, the speed is lessened but the process is almost as simple.

Figure 7–7 Shared memory vs. Message Passing

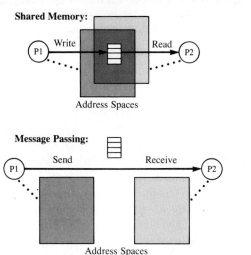

On the other hand, use of shared memory raises problems, such as mutual exclusion, which must be solved by the participating processes. There are further timing concerns as well. A process reading information may need to know when new data has been written. The writer, in turn, may need to know when the written information was accepted, so further information can be supplied. These problems must be solved by the processes themselves. Only the memory sharing mechanism itself is supported by the OS.

Message passing is less efficient in general, but solves a broader range of problems. Many processes can have no common address space. This is clearly true of processes in different physical locations. All processes, however, can exchange messages. The rest of this section focuses principally on the message-passing model.

Exchanging Names

Before two processes can communicate, regardless of the method to be used, a connection must be established between them involving the shared use of some resources. The processes must be able to identify these shared resources (and possibly each other) by use of common names or identifiers. The particular types of names that need to be shared depend on the communication method used. Agreement on these names can be established in several ways:

- External Agreement. Resources may have permanent names known in advance, or processes may select a common name to be used for a resource to be dynamically assigned. The names are supplied to each process externally, usually before they begin running.

- Inheritance. When a process creates children, the children may inherit knowledge of resource and process names from the parent. This method is commonly used in UNIX and other systems.

- Message Passing. Once a method for exchanging messages has been established, further names may be exchanged within messages.

Synchronization

The simplest types of communication mechanisms are those in which only a single bit of information is exchanged. By these mechanisms, processes may inform other processes that a certain event has occurred, or that they have reached a certain point in their own execution. Mechanisms in this category are known as **synchronization** mechanisms.

We have already examined a simple category of synchronization mechanism. A process may go to sleep or suspend itself, possibly specifying the name of a *signal* for which it is waiting. Another process at a future time can produce the specified signal, or can wake the sleeping process by name. If the signal or wake-up request never comes, the process will remain suspended forever. In particular, this can happen if a process tries to wait for an event that, in fact, has already occurred. The past occurrence of the signal is forgotten; this method has no memory.

A variation of this method provides a one-bit buffer for each signal; these buffers are called **event flags**. Once processes agree on the identity of a common event flag, it may be shared by any number of processes. Some processes can wait until the flag is set to a certain value; others can signal by setting or clearing the flag. If a process tries to wait for a signal that has already occurred, the flag will remember and the process will proceed immediately.

This type of synchronization can also be accomplished with binary semaphores. Suppose the value of a semaphore is initialized to zero. Then a process may signal an event by a V operation, while another process may wait using a P operation. If the event has not yet occurred when the P is executed, the semaphore will still be zero and the process will wait. If it has already occurred, the semaphore will be one and the process can proceed immediately. When the waiting process proceeds, the semaphore is set back to zero for future use. This method becomes more complex when more than two processes are involved.

Direct Communication: Send and Receive

The most straightforward method for passing messages between processes is direct communication using **send** and **receive** operations. In this method, the process sending a message issues a *send* system call, passing the message itself and the name of the intended receiver as parameters. If the message is large, the address of a message buffer might be passed rather than the message itself.

The OS is then expected to accept the message, or copy it from the buffer, and supply it to the receiving process. Occasionally, the buffer address rather than the message itself might be supplied to the receiver. This can be a more efficient method, but is only possible if the message buffer is in a shared memory.

The receiver must signal its intention to receive a message. This is done with a *receive* system call. There are two principal forms for this request. In **symmetric message passing,** the receiver names the expected sender. It will then be given only messages from that one sender. In **asymmetric message passing,** the receiver does not name a sender. It will be given the next message sent to it regardless of sender, and told who the sender was.

This type of communication is illustrated in Figure 7–8. Message passing works most effectively if both sender and receiver are ready at the same time. In reality, of course, processes may send messages for which no receiver is ready, or try to receive messages that have not yet been sent. In the worst case, this last situation can lead to communication deadlock if, due to some misunderstanding or error, the expected message never occurs.

Direct Communication using Pipes

A variation on explicit *send* and *receive* operations is to view message passing as a special form of file access. With this view, a link between two processes

Figure 7–8 Direct Communication with Messages

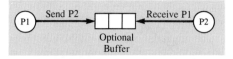

is viewed as a type of file. Messages are sent by *write* operations to this file, and received by *read* operations.

This approach is taken by the **pipe** mechanism of UNIX, illustrated in Figure 7–9. A pipe, a channel established between two processes, is operated on like a file. In UNIX, pipes are always created by a common parent and passed to its children by inheritance. Thus, pipe communication is restricted to processes that have inherited a common pipe. Also, UNIX allows any number of processes to share a pipe, and any of them may read or write at will. However, the mechanism is most useful when there is one sender and one receiver only.

Figure 7–9 Communication by Pipes (UNIX)

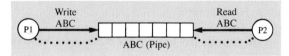

Indirect Communication: Mailboxes

An alternative to direct communication can use a common storage buffer (maintained by the OS in its own address space) to eliminate the need for senders and receivers to identify each other by name. Such a buffer, called a **mailbox,** may be viewed as a queue with a certain capacity for storing messages. When mailboxes are to be used, a sender process uses a *send* operation but specifies the mailbox name rather than a specific process as the destination. The names of mailboxes may be permanently known, or chosen by cooperating processes that create them dynamically. The receiver specifies the mailbox as a message source and receives the next available message, if any, regardless of the sender. This method, illustrated in Figure 7–10, is the principal communication technique in VMS and a number of real-time executives.

Figure 7-10 Communication by Mailboxes

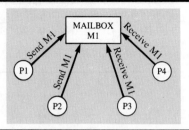

Buffering and Blocking

If the sender and receiver of every message were always ready to process the message at exactly the same moment, message passing would be straightforward. Since senders and receivers are never perfectly synchronized, however, we need to consider several issues. The most important questions are: What space is available for storage of messages in transit? Under what conditions will each process be required to wait? These issues may be resolved in many different ways.

The following issues must be considered in the design of a complete, practical message passing system:

- Does the OS supply any temporary storage for messages sent but not yet received? If so, what is the capacity of this storage?

- What happens to messages when the temporary storage, if any, is full?

- Under what conditions are senders and receivers made to wait?

Clearly these issues are related. For example, one reason for a sender to wait is that there is no place available for a message that needs to be sent.

In the simplest case, no buffer is provided. A process attempting to send a message is therefore made to wait until a receiver is available. The receiver also waits for a sender, so the two processes must be synchronized for a message exchange to occur. This model, called a **rendezvous**, is the principal communication method supported by the Ada programming language.

The mailbox mechanism is an example of an explicit buffer. With direct communication, the OS may provide buffers that are not directly visible to the participating processes. If buffer space is available, its capacity may range from one message to a large number. It is always finite, so it is possible for the buffer to become full.

As a further complication, messages may be of variable size. Large messages may need to be processed in parts, and it is possible that only part of a message may fit into the available buffers.

When there are available buffers, a sender does not have to wait. Usually the OS will make the process wait if the buffers are full. However, in some network communication environments it is possible that senders never wait, and if the buffers are full the message could be lost.

Sometimes processes want assurance that a message has been received. In this case, they may be able to specify that a reply is expected. The sender will then be put to sleep until the reply message arrives. The receiver, of course, must not fail to send a reply, or the sender will wait indefinitely.

Senders may thus have various occasions to wait while an outgoing message is being processed. Receivers always have reason to wait if no message is available. However, sometimes processes prefer to simply be informed if the request has been completed, and to carry on other tasks and check back later. The OS should allow processes to specify whether they prefer to be suspended or not, and to provide additional operations for testing the status of ongoing message requests. As a generalization, a process may have the ability to specify a time limit, and to wait only as long as that time is not exceeded.

A more difficult problem arises in allowing processes to wait for a number of events at once. The process may want to proceed when any of several events occur, or perhaps only on some logical combination of events (e.g., either A or both B and C). Few operating systems provide direct support for this type of waiting, as it is difficult to specify and monitor the desired combinations. Instead, the process usually must resort to busy waiting, checking each condition without blocking until the right combination has occurred.

7.7 SUMMARY

Concurrent processes interact for two reasons: to share resources and to communicate. This interaction leads to a number of potential problems, the most important of which are determinism, deadlock, mutual exclusion, and communication mechanisms.

Determinism imposes the requirement that the results produced by one process must not be affected by unplanned interaction with other processes. Ensuring determinism is a constant requirement for all aspects of concurrent process management.

Deadlock arises when each of a set of processes is waiting for a resource currently held by another. No process will make further progress without intervention by the OS. Several conditions must hold for deadlock to be possible; one strategy for deadlock prevention is to remove one of these conditions, which is possible for some resources but not all. An interesting second strategy is to try to make resource allocations in a safe order so that deadlock will not occur. This is possible in special cases but cannot provide a general solution. If deadlock occurs it may not be obvious, but it can be detected by reasonably straightforward methods. Once deadlock is detected, human intervention is usually required in selecting processes to back up or terminate.

Mutual exclusion is the problem of ensuring that only one process at a time uses a resource that cannot be shared simultaneously. This can be ensured by the OS for system-controlled resources, but is a difficult problem for resources such as shared data structures controlled by users. The processes involved must establish voluntary protocols. Pure software solutions are possible, but are likely to be complex and inefficient. Semaphores provide an effective solution mechanism if modest assistance is available from the hardware or OS to implement them. Semaphores may serve as building blocks for higher-level mechanisms as well.

Deliberate communication between processes may be performed using shared memory or by message passing. The latter strategy is more general and may be used in almost any environment. A special case of communication is synchronization, which exchanges single bits of information by event flags or similar mechanisms.

To begin message exchange, processes must first solve the problem of sharing names for each other or for message buffers. Mechanisms that may then be used include direct communication using send and receive, direct communication by pipes, or indirect communication using mailboxes. Other important issues include the nature of message buffers available, what happens when no buffers are available, and under what conditions senders and receivers may have to wait.

≡ FOR FURTHER READING ≡

Many of the classic ideas in concurrent process management were first introduced by Dijkstra [1965]. The principal issues are well described in texts by Shaw [1974] and Peterson and Silberschatz [1985]. Good theoretical treatments are given by Coffman and Denning [1973] and Maekawa et al. [1987]. Deadlocks were studied by Dijkstra [1965], and solutions for OS/360 discussed by Havender [1968]. Coffman et al. [1971] surveyed many issues and identified the necessary conditions for deadlock. An extensive bibliography is provided by Zobel [1983].

Software solutions for mutual exclusion were first studied by Dijkstra

[1965] and are well presented by Shaw [1974] and Peterson and Silberschatz [1985]. These same sources provide good discussions of semaphores. Peterson's algorithm (not the same Peterson) is presented and proved in a short but remarkable paper [Peterson 1981]. An effective survey of concurrency control mechanisms is given by Andrews and Schneider [1983]. Raynal [1986] offers a comprehensive study of mutual exclusion mechanisms. Issues in the design of concurrent programming languages are discussed in a number of texts, including those by Brinch Hansen [1977], Ben-Ari [1982], and Hoare [1985]. Some interesting but highly theoretical perspectives are contained in Hoare's book.

A good recent treatment of message passing issues is found in Milenković [1987]. Standard system calls for supporting semaphores and messages are proposed by the IEEE MOSI standard [IEEE 1985a].

IMPORTANT TERMS

asymmetric message passing
banker's algorithm
binary semaphore
busy waiting
circular requests
communication
communication deadlock
concurrent execution
concurrent sequential processes
counting semaphore
critical section
deadlock
deadlock avoidance
deadlock detection
deadlock prevention
deadlock recovery
determinism
entry protocol
event flags
exit protocol
general semaphore
hierarchical ordering

indefinite blocking
interprocess communication (IPC)
livelock
mailbox
message
message passing
monitor
mutual exclusion
no preemption
pipe
receive
rendezvous
resource deadlock
resource holding
resource sharing
semaphore
send
shared memory
symmetric message passing
synchronization
system-controlled resource
user-controlled resource

REVIEW QUESTIONS

1. Explain the two principal ways that concurrent processes interact.

2. State the four conditions that must hold for deadlock to be possible.

3. Deadlock can be prevented by hierarchical ordering of resources. Which of the four conditions does this prevent?

4. Name a resource that cannot be handled by hierarchical ordering, and give a reason why.

5. Explain why deadlock detection algorithms may be practical, while deadlock avoidance algorithms usually are not.

6. Give three examples of resources that normally must be managed by the operating system.

7. Give one example of a resource that should be managed by application programs, *not* the operating system, and explain why.

8. Explain why mutual exclusion is not a difficult problem to solve for system-controlled resources.

9. Describe carefully and completely the required characteristics of a binary semaphore data type. Be sure to state any necessary assumptions.

10. Even when semaphores can be implemented directly in hardware, semaphore operations usually make use of system calls. Why?

11. Describe briefly three issues to be considered in designing an interprocess communication facility based on message passing.

12. Explain the difference between binary semaphores and event flags.

13. Before two processes can share a common resource, they must agree on a name or identifier for that resource. Explain two ways that processes can share names.

ASSIGNMENTS

1. Determinism may be violated if two concurrent processes "interfere" with one another. Interference can be prevented if there is no resource required by both processes. Is there a weaker criteria that would be sufficient? If so, can it be used in practical situations?

2. Identify three types of resources for which deadlock prevention may be possible, other than the examples given in the text. State which conditions may be denied for each resource.

3. Assign a hierarchical ordering for the following resources: disks, printers, terminals, communication devices, and files. What limitations would be imposed on programs which follow your ordering?

4. Present an argument to demonstrate that the outcome of the deadlock detection algorithm does not depend on the order in which processes are selected.

5. Suggest some reasons why deadlock detection is not actually practiced by many operating systems.

6. One method for ensuring that a critical sequence of actions in an entry or exit protocol for mutual exclusion is not interrupted would be to disable all interrupts. Why is this not a practical solution in general? Under what conditions would it be acceptable?

7. The text describes two incorrect software solutions to the mutual exclusion problem. Describe a specific sequence of actions that demonstrates the failure of these methods in a system containing two processes.

8. As an alternative to the test-and-set instruction, semaphore operations could be implemented using a *swap* instruction, which exchanges the values stored in two different locations. Show how the P and V operations could be implemented using a swap instruction.

9. Explain the following statement: "Shared memory is a more powerful communication mechanism than message passing, but also a more dangerous one."

10. Give an advantage of symmetric message passing and an advantage of asymmetric message passing. Describe a problem that would be more easily solved by one method than by the other.

11. Suppose that an OS supports only the rendezvous model for message passing, and provides no buffering. Describe how the advantages of buffering could still be made available to application processes.

12. In Ada and other languages that support concurrent processing, a process may specify a list of conditions to wait for simultaneously, such as the arrival of several types of messages or the occurrence of various events. This addresses the problem of waiting for multiple events. What problems arise in providing a general facility of this type as an operating system service? Discuss possible ways of overcoming these problems.

≡ PROJECT ≡

This section describes a two-part programming project to implement a set of binary semaphore operations and a message passing mechanism for a simple multiprogramming operating system. You should read the general description in this text in conjunction with the more specific descriptions given in your project manual. These mechanisms are important components of the multiprogramming executive (MPX) project described later in the text.

a. Define a data structure to represent a set of ten binary semaphores, identified by the numbers 1-10, with associated queues of pointers to PCBs. The value of all semaphores should be initialized to 1. Implement a set of procedures within the scheduler/dispatcher of Chapter 6, which may be called by test processes to perform wait (P) and signal (V) operations on these semaphores. The operation of these procedures is as follows:

1. `Wait_Semaphore(id)`: Test the value of the semaphore whose identifier is `id`. If that value is zero, suspend the current process and place a pointer to its PCB on the semaphore queue. Dispatch the next process. Otherwise, set the value to zero and return to the calling process.

2. `Signal_Semaphore(id)`: If the semaphore queue for semaphore `id` is not empty, awaken the next process and remove its PCB from the semaphore queue. Otherwise, set the semaphore value to 1.

Run a set of processes provided by your instructor to test the correctness of your semaphore implementation.

b. Add additional procedures to the dispatcher to support direct symmetric message passing between processes identified by name. Assume a message is a block of data 256 bytes long. Your message passer should be able to buffer at least two messages. Design problems to be solved include when to require waiting and what to do if the buffers are full.

The procedures to be implemented are:

1. `Send_Message(procname,message)`: Send the block of data identified by `message` to the process called `procname`.

2. `Receive_Message(procname,message)`: Receive a pending message, if any, from the process called `procname` into the location identified by `message`.

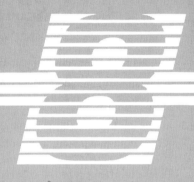

Interrupts, I/O, and Timer Management

Interrupts, I/O, and Timer Management

8.1 INTRODUCTION

Device management is a major responsibility of any operating system. In order to understand device management, it is absolutely necessary that one have a thorough understanding of interrupts, from both the hardware and software viewpoints. This chapter presents interrupts in section 8.2 and introduces hardware input/output control techniques in section 8.3.

Timer management is another important OS responsibility. We cover clocks and clock support in section 8.4 and illustrate the use of interrupts using a simple clock interrupt handler. Section 8.5 presents timer management with a discussion of timer queues and the manipulation of the timer queue.

8.2 INTERRUPTS

An important feature of almost all present-day architectures is the **hardware interrupt** facility, which provides a mechanism to temporarily suspend one program and execute another one when some special event (detected by the hardware) has occurred. An important use of interrupts is to assist in device management by allowing an I/O device to obtain service from the CPU when needed without requiring constant polling of the device by software.

An analogy from the kitchen might aid in understanding interrupts. In cooking a roast, one could place a thermometer in the roast and constantly check it for the correct temperature (a procedure called polling). Some ovens provide for a temperature probe and an automatic reading of the temperature of the meat. The oven shuts off and perhaps generates an audible alarm when the meat has reached the desired temperature. You can go about other chores, knowing that the oven will inform you of the completed event. Another obvious alternative would be to set a timer that will produce an audible alarm at the time the roast should be done. You would then need to check a meat thermometer to be sure the roast is done. Figure 8–1 illustrates the technique of polling and the automatic signaling of event completion.

Figure 8–1 Polling vs. Interrupt Signaling

a) Polling   b) Automatic Signalling

The "interrupts" generated by the oven in this example will likely call you away from another task, such as reading a book or writing a letter. One thing that is very important when leaving an interrupted task is to remember where you were in that task. For example, say you were reading a book and the oven began signaling the completion of the event. If you close the book without marking the place where you were reading, it might be difficult to find your place quickly.

As human beings, we often find it difficult to remember our place in what we were doing when more than one "interrupt" occurs in a short period of time (for instance, if the oven signal, telephone, and doorbell all ring within 15 seconds). This problem is illustrated by Figures 8–2 and 8–3. Computers have hardware interrupts similar to the type of interrupts demonstrated in the oven example. The automatic temperature probe mechanism is like a device interrupt that informs the CPU when a device has completed an operation. Some timer interrupts are also similar to the one demonstrated by the oven timer. In processing any interrupt, a computer that is interrupted must "remember" precisely what was executing and preserve the integrity of its environment.

Unlike human beings, computers can handle thousands of interrupts per second. For every interrupt that occurs, hardware and software must remember what was interrupted and guarantee that nothing is changed in the expected environment of the interrupted process.

With the analogy of everyday interrupts in mind, let us consider how interrupts work in a computer system.

Figure 8-2 Human Interrupt Processing

Figure 8-3 Multiple Interrupt Handling with the Human Mind

Interrupt Processing

Without the presence of interrupts within a computer system, execution proceeds sequentially from one instruction to the next until a branch instruction causes a transfer of control to another memory location. With the introduction of a hardware interrupt facility, transfer of control within a CPU can occur automatically when an interrupt condition is signaled (e.g., by an I/O device). This automatic transfer mechanism, like a call instruction, must provide the capability to save the address that would have been the next instruction executed had the interrupt not occurred. The problem is actually more difficult, because when the interruption is complete, the exact state of every CPU register and status flag must be restored just as if the interrupt had never occurred. While different computer architectures provide different mechanisms for saving this information, the basic concept is the same. After each instruction is executed, the hardware performs the following algorithm or its equivalent:

```
        IF interrupt THEN
                save execution address (PC)
                save status information
                transfer control to interrupt handler
        ENDIF
```

Just what address is branched to is dependent on the computer's architecture. Some systems, such as the PDP-11, are **fully vectored,** which means they provide the capability of storing an interrupt handler address for each device in a special memory location called an **interrupt vector** (see Figure 8–4). The algorithm for a fully vectored system then becomes:

```
        IF interrupt THEN
                save execution address (Program Counter)
                save status (Program Status Word)

                CASE interrupt IS

                    WHEN device1: transfer control to
                            device1 interrupt handler

                    WHEN device2: transfer control to
                            device2 interrupt handler

                    WHEN device3: transfer control to
                            device3 interrupt handler

                    WHEN device4: transfer control to
                            device4 interrupt handler

                ENDCASE
        ENDIF
```

With this method, the cause of the interrupt can be determined without further program execution.

Other systems, such as the IBM S/370, have categories of interrupts. For example, all I/O interrupts cause control to pass to the same **first-level interrupt handler (FLIH)** as shown in Figure 8–5. This handler then tests some type of register to determine which I/O device caused the interrupt. The FLIH then branches to the appropriate **second-level interrupt handler (SLIH)** to process the interrupt. The logic of the FLIH is:

```
FLIH:    save registers
         read interrupt_status_register
         CASE interrupt_status_register IS
           WHEN device1: call device1_SLIH
           WHEN device2: call device2_SLIH
           WHEN device3: call device3_SLIH
         ENDCASE
         restore registers
         RETURN from interrupt
```

Figure 8–4 Single-level Interrupt Handler (PDP-11)

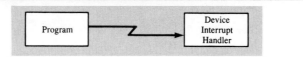

Figure 8–5 Hierarchical Interrupt Handlers (IBM S/370)

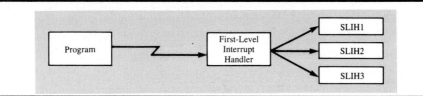

Just how can the execution address and the status be saved? Two basic techniques are prevalent:

1. The information may be saved on a stack.
2. The information may be stored in a special memory location, usually at a low address, reserved for this particular class of interrupts.

Let us consider an example from the PDP-11. Each device on the PDP-11 has assigned to it a unique address (by hardware configuration), in low memory, called an interrupt vector. The assignment of a vector location for a particular device depends on the hardware configuration. Each interrupt vector helps determine where to branch as well as the new status word to use upon the occurrence of an interrupt caused by that device. Each vector consists of two 16-bit words. The first is the address of the interrupt handler. The contents of this word are placed into the PC after the necessary information about the interrupted program has been saved on the stack. The second word is a new status word to be transferred to the PSW before control is given to the interrupt handler. The contents of the previous PC and PSW are saved on a stack. The algorithm for the hardware interrupt facility invoked after each instruction on the PDP-11 is:

```
IF interrupt THEN
        push PS
        push PC
        IF cause=device1 THEN
                PC := vector(device1)
                PS := vector(device1)+2
        ENDIF
        IF cause=device2 THEN
                PC := vector(device2)
                PS := vector(device2)+2
        ENDIF
            .
            .
    ENDIF
```

Categories of Interrupts

Not all interrupts are associated with I/O operations on devices. This section describes a variety of interrupt types. Interrupts can be classified in the following categories: I/O completion, alert, timer, system request, program fault, and machine fault. Not all computer systems have all categories of interrupts. Almost all, however, have I/O completion, timer, and system request interrupts of some form or another.

I/O Completion Interrupts. An **I/O completion interrupt,** generated by a device, indicates that service is needed from a device interrupt handler. Types of service that may be required include transferring another character to or from a character-by-character device, servicing the completion of a total I/O request like a block of data being read or written, or handling an error condition that occurred during the I/O operation.

Alert Interrupts. An **alert interrupt** is a somewhat unexpected interrupt that generally results from conditions outside of the computer system. Some computers provide an **interrupt key,** which an operator can use to activate the command interpreter. This could be considered an alert interrupt.

Another example occurs in a multiprocessor, when one computer signals another to signify some condition or request service from the other CPU.

Timer Interrupts. A **timer interrupt** could be considered a type of I/O completion interrupt, but since no physical I/O occurs, it is best to think of these interrupts in a category of their own. An interrupt generated from an interval timer means that the last unit of time placed into that timer (counter) has expired. An interrupt may also be generated at regular intervals by a hardware clock. Each interrupt means that another fixed fraction of time has expired, and that the software clocks should be updated accordingly.

System Request Interrupts. Processes request service from the operating system by some type of **system request interrupt,** also known as a supervisor request, which is generated deliberately by a machine instruction. The system call instruction is an important example of this category. Other instructions, with names such as TRAP and IOT, may perform a similar action. The principle for handling each of these instructions is the same: An interrupt transfers control to the operating system to indicate that a process desires some type of service. The interrupt vector or a parameter list can implicitly specify the type of service. The operating system will analyze the request and provide the requested service, possibly blocking the process requesting the service until the requested service has been completed (e.g., an I/O operation).

Program Fault Interrupts. Computer users often associate interrupts with programming errors in their programs because many such errors cause what is called a **program fault interrupt.** The occurrence of such an interrupt is often announced by a message displayed on the user's terminal or printed on an output listing. Among the variety of program fault interrupt types, you may find:

- an attempt to divide by zero
- overflow or underflow during an arithmetic operation
- an invalid memory reference
- an invalid or privileged instruction
- an attempt to access a protected resource
- an operation attempted on incorrectly formatted data

Users can specify how such errors are to be handled within their programs by specifying the address of a routine to execute when an error occurs. If they do not specify such an error routine, the operating system will normally terminate the execution of the process.

Machine Fault Interrupts. Depending on the sophistication of the hardware, a variety of interrupts may signal that a hardware error has occurred. This **machine fault interrupt** can indicate a memory fetch error, I/O device error, or the like. Many operating systems simply report such errors and terminate operation. More sophisticated operating systems, with suitable hardware available, might attempt to isolate a failing component, lock it out to prevent further use, and keep running with alternative components.

A simpler way to view interrupts would be to reduce the number of categories to three: process complete interrupt, service request interrupt, or error interrupt. In this view, **process complete interrupt** can be either hardware I/O or timer completion, or software process completion. **Service request interrupt** would include both operator "attention" requests and system request interrupts. **Error interrupt** would include both program faults and machine faults. We can summarize this new classification as follows:

- Process Complete Interrupts

    Timer
    I/O
    Software Service

- Service Request Interrupts

    Operator request
    Program request

- Error Interrupts

    Program Fault
    Machine Fault

Interrupt Ordering and Masking

Systems that generate interrupts have priorities for various interrupt types. This means if two interrupt signals occur simultaneously, one has priority over the other. Once the high-priority interrupt has been serviced, the lower-priority interrupt will be generated. It is possible for interrupt servicing to be nested; in other words, a low-priority interrupt handler's execution can be interrupted by a higher-priority interrupt, thus invoking another interrupt handler. Once the higher-priority interrupt is serviced, a return from interrupt instruction is issued and the lower-priority interrupt handler regains control to complete processing.

Sometimes such interrupting of an interrupt handler is undesirable. You can prevent it in most systems by the use of **interrupt masking.** This technique allows certain interrupts to be blocked, so they will not be accepted by the CPU. Interrupt masking is performed by setting bits in a CPU register, called an **interrupt mask register,** which correspond to specific interrupts or classes of interrupts to be blocked. An alternative method is used by the PDP-11—each interrupt is assigned a priority level, and a priority value in the program status word may be set greater than the priority of certain interrupts. In this case, only interrupts having a priority greater than the priority in the PSW will be accepted. Such blocked interrupts remain pending until the processor priority is reduced to a value less than the signaling priority of the previously blocked interrupt.

It should be obvious that masking or blocking of interrupts in a real-time system must be minimized. Rules for how long interrupt handlers can run with interrupts blocked are established and strictly observed in implementing real-time operating system interrupt handlers.

Timing of Interrupts

Obviously, many types of interrupts can occur in an operating system environment. In most systems, the current instruction is completed before an interrupt is generated, although there are some systems that have interruptible instructions (e.g., the MVCL instruction on the IBM S/370). Certain interrupts are immediate and predictable; they occur as the result of a machine instruction, such as a system call or trap instruction. Such interrupts generally cannot be masked. Program fault interrupts also occur immediately, although they cannot be predicted because they result from the program environment (e.g., dividing by a register whose contents is 0). Similarly, machine fault interrupts occur immediately when the condition is detected.

I/O completion interrupts are known to be pending once the I/O operation is started, but the exact time at which such interrupts occur is unknown (although there are certain maximum limits within which the interrupt will occur). These interrupts are said to be **asynchronous interrupts** because the exact time of the interrupt is not known. The operating system responds to the interrupts when they are generated and should not be affected by variations in timing between successive I/O completion interrupts from the same or different devices. Timer interrupts are similar to I/O completion interrupts, although it is generally known when they should occur. Timer interrupts can also be blocked under some conditions; hence, even they do not occur exactly when predicted.

There are some devices that must be serviced within a certain period of time to avoid a problem called **device read overrun.** A device transferring one character at a time to the CPU requires that the previous character be processed by the device interrupt handler prior to the next character being transferred. If the operating system blocks such interrupts for too long a period (the time between successive characters), then the previous character is lost.

The timing of interrupts does indeed vary. The systems programmer will often be asked to solve a problem that seems to be random, but ultimately is a result of timing differences in the occurrence of interrupts. Only in certain orderings of interrupts do such problems occur, and so these problems can be extremely difficult to solve because the exact ordering of interrupts cannot be easily observed or repeated.

8.3 INPUT AND OUTPUT

As we have noted, an extremely important function of any operating system is the control of input and output devices. The operating system designer must understand each device thoroughly in order to write the software to support these devices. This section introduces some concepts of input and output devices.

I/O Instructions

Every computer must provide instructions to control and access the I/O devices to which it is connected. A few older architectures, such as the PDP-8, offered an independent set of instructions tailored to each type of device that could be used. Today it is clear that the number of potential device types is far too vast to be supported on a case-by-case basis. Instead, generic instructions are provided, the meaning of which can be interpreted differently by each type of device.

With this approach, each distinct device is physically connected to a particular computer by means of a hardware component called an **I/O interface.** This interface allows the device to be accessed through a set of registers, which the CPU views as **device registers.** A simple device like a printer may have only one or two such registers, while a complex disk storage system may have dozens. Each device register is assigned a number to identify it to the system hardware and software and to provide an address for the I/O device. This number, called a **channel number** or **port number,** is established by the way the device is physically installed, and it can then be used by programs to refer to that device.

Because device registers have addresses, they can be considered to occupy an address space, just like memory locations. This address space, called the

Figure 8-6 Separate I/O Space for Device Registers

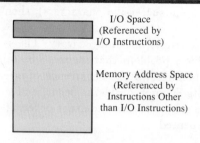

I/O space, is illustrated in Figure 8-6. In the majority of computers, the I/O space is distinct from memory address spaces. It is accessed by a separate, usually small, set of I/O instructions that can read, write, or perform control operations on any specified device. Because these instructions are distinct, they may be designated as privileged instructions. This strategy provides the operating system with exclusive control of most I/O devices.

Figure 8-7 Memory Mapped I/O

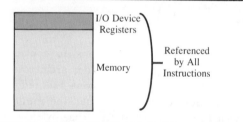

An alternate approach, used especially by PDP-11 and VAX computers, is to consider I/O devices and memory locations as sharing a *single* address space. This strategy, known as **memory-mapped I/O,** is illustrated in Figure 8-7. Because memory and devices are treated uniformly, no distinct I/O instructions are needed. Instead, all instructions that read or write memory locations can perform the same operations on device registers just by using the appropriate addresses. In addition to simple data transfers, arithmetic and other data manipulations may be performed directly on the contents of device registers. A disadvantage of memory-mapped I/O lies in the fact that the devices cannot be protected by the privileged instruction mechanism. Instead, memory protection techniques must be used to limit the accessible regions of the address space.

I/O Device Control

The general strategy for handling a particular device falls into one of three categories, depending on both the device type and the computer architecture:

- Simple I/O. The **simple I/O** strategy, also called **programmed I/O,** is used on small and medium computers to manage character-by-character devices, which can produce or accept data one byte (or word) at a time, at the convenience of the CPU. A distinct I/O instruction is used to transfer every word of data to or from the device.

- Block transfer. The **block transfer** technique is used on small and medium computers for devices like disks and magnetic tapes, which must transfer data in large blocks at a high speed. The devices are attached to a sophisticated type of I/O interface termed an **I/O controller,** which contains sufficient storage and control logic to independently manage the transfer of an entire block. The controller in turn is connected to the memory by a technique called **direct memory access (DMA).** The CPU sends the controller sufficient information to begin the transfer of the block. Then, the CPU can proceed to other work while the controller independently transfers the entire block to or from memory.

- I/O processors. The **I/O processors** technique is used uniformly for control of most I/O devices on some larger computers, such as the IBM S/370 and its successors and the CDC Cyber series. Each device is connected to a special-purpose processor that is capable of fetching and executing instructions to direct an I/O transfer or a series of such transfers. Usually there are a small number of such processors, each in turn handling many devices. These processors may understand only a few special instructions, or they may have most of the features of a general-purpose CPU. Their programs may be stored in a private memory, or they may be obtained from the main memory of the computer system. This strategy allows the initiation of many different I/O requests by the CPU using one machine instruction. The processor then continues the I/O sequence by fetching and interpreting the instructions in the I/O program.

Other Issues

Managing a series of data transfers to or from an I/O device can require careful communication. Before each new transfer, the CPU must somehow determine that the device is ready. Simple I/O devices can be managed by a technique of **device polling,** in which status values are examined periodically or constantly to see if the requested I/O operation has been completed. As we will see in Chapter 9, device polling is not efficient in today's operating systems and is generally not used.

The alternative to polling is the use of an I/O completion interrupt to indicate when a device has completed an operation, or series of operations, and is ready for further instructions. Many devices offer several types of interrupts that may be selectively enabled or disabled by the operating system.

Devices often require an area for intermediate storage of data before they are placed into memory. A good example of this is an asynchronous communication interface that is receiving data. A character is assembled in a receiving buffer and then transferred into a buffer available to the CPU, allowing receipt of data bits to continue without worrying about whether the received character has been fetched by the CPU before the next bit arrives. Of course, the CPU must fetch the character before the next character finishes or an overrun will occur (the previous character will be overlaid by the next character). A **hardware buffer** may exist in a device controller to handle this problem; if not, similar buffering techniques may be needed in software.

8.4 CLOCKS

A **Clock** or **timer** is a hardware or software mechanism for measuring time. Unless stated otherwise, we will use this term to refer to a **hardware clock,** that is, a physical device which measures time. Clocks are essential to almost any operating system. The requirements for time-of-day reporting and timing of resource usage for accounting in large operating systems represent two obvious uses. We will consider many other uses of clocks.

Hardware clocks are unique devices in that they do not transfer any information outside the computer, in either block mode or character mode. Their purpose is to provide a means of measuring time intervals. Because clocks cause periodic interrupts and often must be reset, control of clocks can still be provided by a device driver, even though clocks differ from other devices.

A clock is a relatively simple hardware device that merely generates interrupts upon the expiration of a time interval. The software must do all the work; the software is implemented as the clock driver and as timer management routines.

It is possible to have multiple **virtual clocks** or **software clocks** based on a single hardware clock. Examples include time-of-day clocks and clocks for timing a process's current time quantum. Other such clocks are needed for accounting in large systems so that users can be billed appropriately. Each such clock is represented by a data item in main memory, which is updated in an appropriate way whenever a signal from the hardware clock is received.

Types of Hardware Clocks

Two types of hardware clocks are found in today's computers: line clocks and programmable clocks, illustrated in Figures 8–8 and 8–9. **Line clocks,** the simplest type of clocks, derive their name from the fact that they interrupt at a frequency that is based on that of the electric power line voltage cycle on which the computer is operating. This frequency is usually 60 Hertz (cycles per second) in the U.S., and 50 Hz. in many other countries. Hence, a computer that receives a standard 110 volt A.C. power signal at 60 Hz. would interrupt every 1/60th of a second. A clock driver can use this interrupt to update software clocks appropriately.

Figure 8–8 A Typical Line Clock

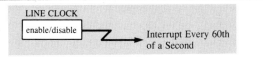

Figure 8–9 A Programmable Clock

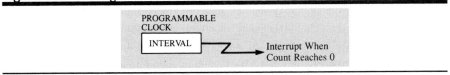

Programmable clocks have a counter register, which is decremented at a fixed periodic rate until its value is 0, when it generates an interrupt. Some programmable clocks can automatically refresh the counter with a holding register, thus avoiding the overhead of interrupt software having to reset the counter. Thus, a programmable clock can have the frequency at which it interrupts the CPU set by the software. Also, a variable interval could be used to signal only specific timed events.

Clock Drivers

Clock drivers deal with interrupts that represent **clock ticks**—either a programmable clock's counter has reached zero or a line clock has interrupted at its fixed interval. A variety of techniques can be used to maintain a time-of-day clock and other software clocks. Almost all of them rely on these clock ticks as units that are updated in the software clocks. One method of maintaining the time of day is to convert it when set to clock ticks past midnight, with the date being advanced and the clock tick counter being set to zero when the number of clock ticks in the counter equals the number of clock ticks in a 24-hour day. In this case, the real time is kept internally in clock ticks past midnight, and requests for the time of day convert this counter to hours, minutes and seconds.

Clock Interrupt Handlers. Interrupt handlers for line clocks are relatively simple and provide an excellent illustration of the format of an interrupt handler. In its simplest form, a clock interrupt handler must adjust a time-of-day clock that is maintained in clock ticks (past midnight) and then check to see if this clock exceeds the 24-hour maximum. In this case, the date must be advanced and the time-of-day clock set back to zero. The logic of this simple clock interrupt handler is shown below:

```
Clock_Interrupt:  save registers
                  increment Time_Of_Day_Clock
                  IF Time_Of_Day_Clock > 24 hours THEN
                         set Time_of_Day_Clock to 0
                         advance date
                  ENDIF

                  restore registers
                  RETURN from interrupt
```

Time-of-Day Reference Points. Rather than keep clock ticks only, it is possible to use the same scheme above with seconds as the unit of time past midnight. This requires two counters: one representing seconds past midnight, and one representing the number of clock ticks in the current second. When the counter that tracks the number of clock ticks equals the number of clock ticks in a second, the clock interrupt handler must increment the second counter and set the clock tick counter to zero. Conversions for time of day will now convert seconds past midnight to hours, minutes, and seconds. When the second counter reaches the number of seconds in a 24-hour day, the date can be advanced and the second counter set back to zero.

There are, of course, other aspects to maintaining the time-of-day clock. The date portion of the support that keeps track of days, months, and years can be complicated by such things as a leap year. Furthermore, most systems provide the facility to determine the day of the week based on the date entered.

Time reference points other than midnight could be used—for example, the system **boot time** (the time when the OS is loaded into the computer memory and initialized) or a fixed known time in the past. For instance, MVS uses midnight of January 1, 1900 Greenwich Mean Time (GMT) as a reference point, so the time-of-day clock contains a count of the total number of microseconds that have elapsed since this reference point. Hence, the specific time of the reference point must be maintained, and the time entered when the clock is set must be converted to intervals, such as microseconds or clock ticks past this fixed time. When the hardware clock interrupts, a clock tick or interval is added to this base time to maintain the time of day. The time-of-day value is converted to the appropriate date and time (hours, minutes, and seconds) when required by a process or the operating system.

8.5 TIMER MANAGEMENT

Timer management includes a broad class of user services, such as:

- maintain the time of day (real time)
- provide "watchdog" or monitoring timers for systems processes and expected events
- provide suspension of a process for a specified interval
- provide suspension of a process until a specific time of day
- provide for the startup of a process at a specific time of day
- provide for timing of expected events and asynchronous execution of procedures upon expiration of the interval (timeouts)
- provide for cancellation of previous timer requests

Many of these timer services go beyond a simple clock device driver, although simple operating systems do not need much more than such a simple driver. Complex multiprogramming operating systems can have hundreds of timer service requests pending at any instant in time. Such systems require the management of a timer queue, just as process management requires the management of process scheduling queues.

Timer Queues

While it is possible to have multiple hardware clocks, it would never be possible to have enough hardware clocks for all clocks and timer requests required by an operating system and the processes in the system. Hence, it is necessary to support multiple virtual clocks; one way to do so would be to keep a linked list of elements containing the time in clock ticks (or perhaps microseconds) representing timer requests. Such a list, ordered by increasing time of request, is called a **timer queue.** Each element of the timer queue is called a **timer queue element** and in this case contains the real time of a timer request. Figure 8–10 illustrates a timer queue with timer queue elements containing these time-of-day values.

Figure 8–10   Timer Queue Elements Using Time-of-day Units

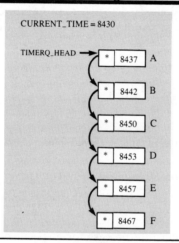

Every time the real time is updated, this list would be checked to see if the time (time of day) in an element or elements has been reached. If so, the appropriate actions specified by the timer queue element would be taken by the operating system. This action includes such things as resuming a suspended process, removing CPU control from a process, or triggering the execution of a timeout routine. A second-level interrupt handler could be scheduled to search the timer queue while still permitting the system time-of-day clock to be updated by the clock interrupt handler. A possible algorithm for checking the timer queue is:

```
Timer_Search:       Set P to Top_TQE
                    DO WHILE Time_Of_Day_Clock
                       > P->TQE_TOD
                             schedule action of P->TQE
                             set P to next TQE
                    ENDWHILE
                    set Top_TQE pointer to
                       TQE pointed to by P
                    RETURN
```

The interrupt handler overhead of processing real-time units in timer queue elements can be reduced by storing clock intervals, or time quanta, between successive timer queue element requests. In this case, a particular timer request represented by a timer queue element is for a total time interval, equal to the sum of the quanta in this element and all elements that precede it in the list. For example, if the current time in clock ticks is 8430, as shown in Figure 8–11, the timer queue element D is for a timer request that will occur after 23 clock ticks (the sum of 7+5+8+3, i.e., clock ticks in elements A through D) or at real-time 8430+23=8453, the same as it was for element D in Figure 8–10. The sum of the interval approach has been used in most IBM mainframe operating systems.

Figure 8–11 Timer Queue Elements Using the Sum of Time Quanta

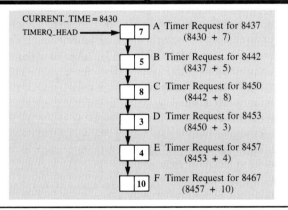

Tracking the Current Timer Interval

There are several possibilities for decrementing the currently active clock interval in the timer queue. One is to have the clock software decrement the time quantum in the top element of the queue on each clock tick interrupt.

When it becomes zero, the appropriate timer request action is taken. Because it is indeed possible to have two or more timer requests for exactly the same time, the next element is checked for zero as the time quantum. Search of the timer queue continues until the next positive time quantum is found. This then becomes the element to be decremented on the next clock tick interrupt. While it might appear that the searching of the timer queue could create high overhead, it is really unlikely that many requests in the timer queue are for *exactly* the same time. A variation of the technique of decrementing the top element would be to have a current element clock tick counter decremented rather than the top element itself. In this case, the time for the top element has occurred when this counter reaches zero.

In some computers, like the IBM S/370, the time quantum in the top element of the timer queue may be placed into a programmable clock. This quantum is automatically decremented by the hardware clock using its **clock resolution.** This minimizes the number of clock interrupts. However, it is possible for a process to make a timer request for a time prior to the time that the current hardware clock interval will expire. In this case, the hardware clock must be modified to a smaller interval than the one remaining in the clock, and a new timer queue element must be placed at the top of the timer queue. The previous top element's time quantum also must be adjusted, as Figure 8–12 demonstrates. Assume the top element has a time quantum of 730 which was placed in the hardware clock. Suppose the hardware clock has been decremented to 685 (no interrupt yet) and a new request for a time quantum of 457 from the current time is being serviced. The hardware clock will have to be updated (reduced from 685) to 457. However, 45 time units have already expired from element A's time quantum, meaning only 685 are left. If the new clock interval is to be 457, the time quantum for element A must be changed to 685-457=228, and a new timer queue element representing the current request must be inserted with a time quantum of 457.

In supporting such a clock manipulation that reduces the interval in a programmable clock, we need a rapid update of the hardware clock. This is done in the S/370 case by a single-move character instruction, which moves the old hardware clock contents into an adjacent work location and sets the hardware clock to the new interval (457). The old hardware interval (685) is then used to compute the time quantum in element A by subtracting the top timer queue element's time quantum of 457 from 685 to produce the value 228 as shown in Figure 8–12. This procedure keeps the hardware clock interval as accurate as possible.

Additions to the Timer Queue

Additions and deletions to the timer queue are necessary as more timer requests are made and as some requests are cancelled. Adding a timer request

Figure 8–12 Managing a Timer Queue with a Programmable Clock

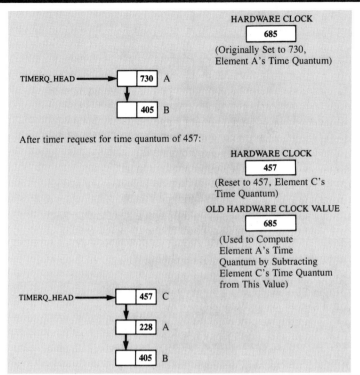

element that represents a time in the middle of some existing timer queue element's time quantum will require changing the existing element's quantum and adding a new element. For example, if the timer queue is as shown in Figure 8–11 and a timer request is made for a time interval of 18 clock ticks from the current time of 8430, the time of this event would be at 8448. Since element B represents a time of 8430+7+5=8442 and element C represents a time of 8430+7+5+8=8450, the requested time is in the middle of the start and finish of element C's time quantum. In this case a new element, G, will be added between elements B and C with a time quantum of 6 (since 8430+7+5+6=8448, the requested time). Element C's time quantum will be set to 2 (8–6, because the requested time of element C is 8450=8430+7+5+6+2), as shown in Figure 8–13.

When a new timer request is for a time that is the next time requested (i.e., the timer queue element will be the top element) manipulation of the timer queue depends on how the clock ticks are being decremented for the old top element. If the top element itself has its time quantum decremented, then

Figure 8–13   Manipulation of a Timer Queue When Adding an Element

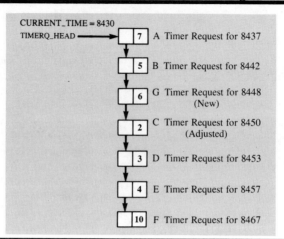

insertion is the same as that just described (i.e., insert new element before top element A and adjust A's remaining time quantum by the time quantum in the new top element). If a separate counter is being used, that counter must be first subtracted from the top element to determine how many clock ticks in the current interval have already occurred. In this case, insertion must subtract the already expired portion of the time quantum from the top element before doing the insertion of the new element.

The amount of time spent processing a clock interrupt is critical to the accuracy of the timing facility within an operating system. Real-time system requirements specify rules and procedures for implementing clocks and device drivers, and for how long interrupts can be disabled in various drivers. One thing is certain: the clock must be the highest priority interrupt if clock ticks are to be counted accurately. The ability to block all but clock interrupts will allow certain critical work to be done without interrupts from devices, but still provide accuracy in the clock.

Contents of a Timer Queue Element.   In addition to pointers to the previous and next timer queue element and the time quantum, contents of a timer queue element include:

- PCB of requesting process
- address of procedure to call
- type of request (user or operating system)

Figure 8–14 illustrates the format of such a timer queue element.

Figure 8–14 Timer Queue Element Structure

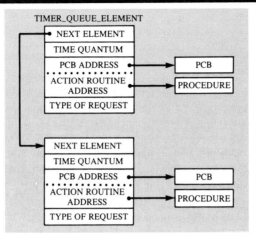

Timer Services

Maintaining the Time of Day. As has been discussed, time-of-day maintenance requires constant update of the time-of-day clock and the ability to convert from clock ticks to hours, minutes and seconds. It also requires that the date be advanced when midnight occurs. This could be done by simply having a system timer request in the timer queue that expires at midnight, invoking a portion of the clock routine that appropriately updates the time-of-day clock and advances the date.

Monitoring Systems Processes. Operating systems often require a timer request to monitor part of their own operation. For example, if an input device is started for a read, and it is possible under certain conditions for there to be no response, it is necessary for the operating system to request a **timeout interval** be set, so that when it expires, the appropriate error action can be invoked in the device driver. If data communications is part of the operating systems software, timeouts for receiving data are another example of the need for alerting the operating system if expected events fail to occur.

Process Suspension for a Specific Time Interval. Suspension of a user or system process for a specific time interval, by means of a *sleep* or *suspend* system call, is often required. This is the type of request that may be used, for example, to process an Ada DELAY statement. To handle such a request, the OS must:

- suspend the process by changing its status in the PCB
- resume the process by changing its status in the PCB upon the expiration of the requested time interval

Process Suspension until a Specific Time of Day. Suspension of a process until a specific time of day is similar to suspension for a specified interval of time, only the user provides the real time as the parameter. The action taken would only differ by how the timer queue element is created.

Startup of a Process at a Specific Time of Day. Many operating systems, particularly real-time systems, provide the facility to start a process in the future at a specific time of day. One possibility for implementation is to create the process when the request is made, but suspend it until the specific time of day; however, this could tie up valuable memory resources, and might not be the most effective method of implementation. Another technique would be to have a small startup process for each process to be started in the future, which is suspended until the startup time. Figure 8–15 illustrates this technique.

Figure 8–15 Starting a Process at a Specific Time of Day

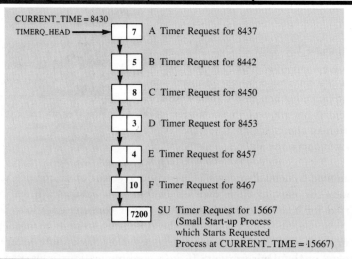

Timing of Events and Invoking Timeout Procedures. User and systems processes often require specific actions to be taken upon the expiration of a timer request. This timer service request would have to specify the timer interval or time of day and the procedure (action routine) to be called upon the signaling of this timeout.

Cancellation of Pending Timer Requests. It is always possible that a particular timer service request will be cancelled. Normally, an application process would only be permitted to cancel a timer service request that it issued. Since each timer queue element will contain a pointer to the PCB of the requesting process, this can be easily verified. The appropriate timer queue element must be removed from the timer queue and the timer queue entry following the one to be removed must be updated by adding the time quantum in the deleted element to the next element.

8.6 SUMMARY

Interrupts are extremely important in the implementation of operating systems. Whether they are process complete interrupts, service request interrupts, or error interrupts, the operating system must handle them efficiently and completely. Interrupts cause a transfer to special locations determined by the hardware, where different types must be distinguished and the interrupt processed. Two common hardware techniques for distinguishing interrupts are the fully vectored approach and the use of first and second level interrupt handlers. Selected interrupts may be blocked or disabled using an interrupt mask register or a system of priority levels.

I/O devices are handled in a consistent manner by most architectures. They are accessed device registers maintained in I/O interfaces. Three basic strategies are commonly used for I/O. In simple I/O, the CPU transfers every word; this is suitable for character devices. Block transfer provides for reading and writing whole blocks between memory and devices once a transfer is initiated by the CPU. The most sophisticated technique makes use of I/O processors, separate special-purpose computers to handle I/O. This technique is used primarily on large mainframe systems.

Clocks, or timers, are essential devices for most operating systems. A single hardware clock may support a variety of software clocks. Timer interrupts form the basis of timer management. Timer queues represent timer requests for both processes and the operating system itself. The structure of the timer queue is an important factor in determining how efficient an operating system is in timer management.

FOR FURTHER READING

Because interrupts are very specific to a computer's architecture, and the handling of interrupts is specific to particular operating systems, various manuals accompanying each OS are the best source for understanding interrupts and interrupt handlers in a particular environment. Discussions about the IBM-compatible microcomputers' interrupts can be found in Norton [1985], while examples of interrupt handlers can be found in various IBM Technical Reference Manuals (Personal Computer XT, IBM, 1984 and Personal Computer AT, IBM, 1984), which describe the PC-DOS operating system's basic input/output system (BIOS). The IBM MVS Supervisor Logic Manual provides an excellent discussion of interrupt handling as well as timer queue management in the MVS environment.

A useful discussion of clock and timer management is contained in Tanenbaum [1987, Sec. 3.7].

IMPORTANT TERMS

alert interrupt
asynchronous interrupts
block transfer
boot time
channel number
clock
clock resolution
clock tick
device polling
device read overrun
device register
direct memory access (DMA)
error interrupt
first-level interrupt handler (FLIH)
fully vectored
hardware buffer
hardware clock
hardware interrupt
interrupt key
interrupt mask register
interrupt masking
interrupt vector
I/O completion interrupt

I/O controller
I/O interface
I/O processor
I/O space
line clock
machine fault interrupt
memory-mapped I/O
port number
process complete interrupt
program fault interrupt
programmable clock
programmed I/O
second-level interrupt handler (SLIH)
service request interrupt
simple I/O
software clocks
system request interrupt
timeout interval
timer
timer interrupt
timer queue
timer queue element
virtual clocks

≡ REVIEW QUESTIONS ≡

1. What is the purpose of an interrupt? What mechanisms exist to transfer control to interrupt handlers?

2. List three broad categories of interrupts and explain the types of interrupts in each category.

3. Contrast the three types of I/O device controls.

4. What is the disadvantage of polling a device to determine when it has completed an I/O operation? How do interrupts solve this problem?

5. Explain the role of each of the following in interrupt processing in a computer system:

   a. program counter

   b. interrupt vector

   c. processor status (word)

   d. second-level interrupt handler

   e. first-level interrupt handler

6. How does an architecture that supports a separate I/O space differ from an architecture that supports memory-mapped I/O?

7. What is the difference between a line clock and a programmable clock?

8. Outline the types of timer services a programmer would expect to find in a multiprogramming operating system.

9. How is a timer queue element used? Illustrate.

10. What effect would the masking of timer interrupts by other interrupt handlers have on device and timer management?

11. If timer management uses a programmable clock, and a timer request for a time prior to the expiration of the current interval in the hardware clock is made by a process, how can it be serviced (since the hardware clock already contains a value greater than the one necessary for this request)?

≡ ASSIGNMENTS ≡

1. From the programmer's point of view, what are the advantages and disadvantages of a computer system containing fully vectored interrupts?

2. From the programmer's point of view, what are the advantages and disadvantages of a computer system that does not have fully vectored interrupts?

3. What is the advantage of having hardware stack support in servicing interrupts? What problems are there in a hardware environment that does not have a hardware stack?

4. Why would a programmer wish to process program fault interrupts? In what circumstances would one choose not to process program fault interrupts and let the operating system perform default servicing on such interrupts?

5. In a system with memory-mapped I/O, how are devices protected from application processes that are not privileged to access these devices?

6. What would happen if an interrupt handler masked all interrupts and never unmasked them prior to returning from servicing the interrupt?

7. Under what conditions would a program cancel a pending timer request to invoke a specific procedure upon the expiration of the requested timer interval?

≡ PROJECT ≡

This section describes a three-part programming project to implement a set of binary semaphore operations and a message passing mechanism for a simple multiprogramming operating system. You should read the general description in this text in conjunction with the more specific descriptions given in your project manual. These mechanisms are important components of the multiprogramming executive (MPX) project described later in the text.

a. Implement a clock interrupt handler that maintains the number of clock ticks since midnight. The time-of-day clock that maintains clock ticks should be called CLOCK.

b. Using the clock interrupt handler developed in Part **a.**, implement a set of procedures within the scheduler/dispatcher of Chapter 6, which may be called by test processes to make use of clock services. The operation of these procedures is as follows:

1. `Start_Clock`: Start the operation of CLOCK, so that subsequent interrupts by the hardware clock will affect its value.

2. `Stop_Clock`: Stop operation of CLOCK, so that further interrupts will have no effect on its value.

3. `Set_Clock(val)`: Set the value of CLOCK to `val`. The value is expressed in clock ticks past midnight. Note that this does not affect whether the clock is started or stopped.

4. `Read_Clock(val)`: Read the value of CLOCK into the variable `val`.

c. An operating system that requires users to think in clock ticks is not particularly user friendly. Refine the clock support to provide additional procedures and data structures which:

1. Set the present date

2. Read the date

3. Set the clock in hours, minutes, seconds

4. Read the clock in hours, minutes, seconds

Details for all parts of this project are contained in the project manual for your environment.

Device
Management

Device Management

9.1 INTRODUCTION

One of the major support services provided by an operating system is the management of I/O devices. Early operating systems provided little, if any, I/O service request capability. In many instances in simple disk operating systems, I/O support was provided by library subroutines written for a specific device, which were loaded into the user memory space. Multiprogramming operating systems that support multiple users and processes, however, cannot allow applications to directly control input/output. Hence, the operating system must provide I/O services to control all devices in the system; for example, to issue read/write commands, process device interrupts, and handle error detection and recovery for devices. The operating system must also keep track of processes waiting for the starting and completion of I/O events in order to schedule subsequent I/O operations, and make appropriate changes in process states that are caused by I/O events.

An OS component that manages a specific I/O device or type of device is called a **device driver.** Because of the wide variety of I/O devices, specialized device drivers are often needed for a particular installation; systems programmers are more likely to be called upon to write device drivers than any other type of OS component. Section 9.2 deals with approaches to implementing device drivers. As an aid in understanding the devices to be controlled, the characteristics of physical devices are briefly discussed in Section 9.3; more detailed descriptions of a number of common devices are contained in Appendix B. Characteristics of the interfaces which connect I/O devices to a computer system must also be understood by the OS designer; these are presented in Section 9.4. Once device and interface characteristics are understood, we can consider specific techniques for I/O programming. This is the subject of Section 9.5; further discussion about device management routines continues in Sections 9.6 through 9.8.

9.2 DEVICE DRIVERS

In the majority of operating systems, all routines which access and control each type of I/O device are collected in a program unit called a device driver. Because of the great variation in the set of I/O devices used at each installation, almost all systems make some provision for adding new device drivers, and for adapting the set of drivers in use to the actual I/O configuration.

In some operating systems, device drivers are an integral part of the nucleus, or kernel, and can be modified only by a complete regeneration of the OS. In such systems, the I/O portion of the kernel is sometimes called the **I/O supervisor.** Adding devices to such an operating system cannot be done dynamically because the entire kernel must be regenerated to support a new device.

In other operating systems, the device drivers are structured as independent modules, stored on disk as files, and can be loaded when required by the operating system. This is especially beneficial for systems with limited main memory, since it allows loading of only the drivers required for devices which are actually in use. In these systems, a device table contains information about each device, including the name of the device driver to load. Adding a new device to such a system can often be done by a dynamic `install` command. This command checks for the presence of the device driver; if it is found, the device is added to the device table, provided that the table has a slot in which to store information about the new device.

Hence, there are generally two models for device support:

- device drivers are a part of the kernel of the operating system
- device drivers are separate modules that are dynamically installable and loadable

The first model is typified by UNIX; the second by RT-11. We shall use the term **I/O subsystem** to describe the I/O management portion of an operating system, regardless of which model of implementation applies. Figures 9–1 and 9–2 illustrate the two possibilities for implementing I/O subsystems.

If reentrant programming techniques are used to implement device drivers in the I/O subsystem, each device type may require only one device driver. This means that all disk drives of the same type may be controlled by one driver, with different **I/O control blocks,** used to represent the individual disk units. Similarly, a single device driver could control all terminals, another all printers, and so on. Of course, an installation may have several types of disk drives, for example, each requiring a separate driver. Generally, though, an operating system will have as few device drivers as necessary in the I/O subsystem to provide support for all devices actually present.

Figure 9–1 Device Drivers as Integral Parts of the OS

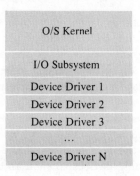

Figure 9–2 Device Drivers as Separate Modules

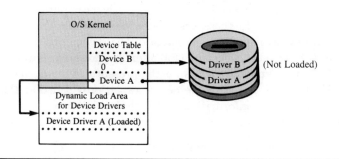

Virtual Devices

Some device drivers manage simulated devices which do not correspond directly or one-to-one to any physical device. These devices are called **virtual devices** or **software devices.** For example, disk units may be simulated by allocating a part of main memory to store data as if they were a disk unit, primarily to improve the performance of application software in small systems with relatively slow disks. These simulated disks are called **RAM disks** (random access memory disks). In other cases a single physical disk, may be divided up into several logical or **virtual disks,** each one viewed by users as an individual device. This type of disk plays an important role in virtual machine systems, to be discussed in a later chapter.

As yet another example, a common device now found even within microcomputer operating systems is a **spool device,** or **spooler,** which captures output intended for a printer or similar device, and stores it in a buffer until the device is ready to accept it. This is another type of virtual device that improves system performance and usability because users do not have to wait for a printer to finish before being able to use the computer for another task.

Device-independent Structure

Since device drivers are frequently written by programmers other than the designers of the operating system, most OSs require device drivers to adhere to certain rules for implementation. Some systems try to maintain the concept of device-independent driver structure by which the structure of device drivers is more or less uniform across device types. Most UNIX device drivers, for example, are designed for two broad classes of devices: character-oriented (such as terminals and printers), and block-oriented (such as disks and tapes). Despite the wide variation in device details, all drivers within a class are expected to have the same overall structure. From a user's point of view, device independence also means that a consistent set of operations, invoked by commands or by system calls, may be applied to most devices which logically could support them (the OS cannot make it meaningful to read from a printer!). The more independence of this type there is, the easier it will be for the user to utilize various devices in the system.

9.3 CHARACTERISTICS OF PHYSICAL DEVICES

Some Basic Issues

Implementation of device drivers for physical devices requires a thorough understanding of the characteristics of the the specific devices being controlled. Detailed descriptions of many common device types are given in Appendix B. In this section we discuss some issues that should be kept in mind when confronting various types of devices. Here are some important considerations:

- devices differ greatly
- programming devices can be quite complex
- dynamic operation of devices is often ambiguously described in hardware documentation
- testing can be difficult, particularly testing of error recovery routines

It is important to understand a specific device thoroughly before attempting to design and implement a device driver for it. The goal of device independence must be balanced against the requirements of specific device types, as discussed below. It is also important to remember that you must know the general requirements for writing device drivers for your specific operating system before implementing such a driver. Examples of these requirements will be considered in a later section.

The Variety of Device Characteristics

In addition to common operations such as *read* and *write,* many devices have unique control operations that must be supported in their device drivers. Printers, for example, may require special operations for selecting character sets, completing pages, and other control functions. Terminals often require operations to clear the screen or move a cursor to a specific position. Magnetic tape units are capable of many control operations like *rewind, backspace record,* and *forward space record.* Disks are capable of direct access to a particular track, and thus *seek* operations must be supported. While often hidden from the user, all these special operations and capabilities must be provided as operating system services that are used by various high-level and access method software. Figure 9–3 outlines I/O data transfer and control operations for a variety of typical devices: a "typical" disk, magnetic tape, two types of terminals, and a line printer.

A special type of device, discussed in detail in the previous chapter, is the clock. Although clocks are not exactly I/O devices, in many cases clock drivers are implemented in the same manner as device drivers. The main difference between a clock and an I/O device is that a clock performs no physical input or output; it only generates a signal to be used internally by programs.

9.4 INTERFACE CHARACTERISTICS

Simple Interfaces

Physical device control mechanisms differ greatly from computer to computer. In all cases, though, some type of **I/O interface** provides the connection between a device and the rest of the system. Most of you will quickly become familiar with the terms **serial interface** and **parallel interface** when

Figure 9–3 I/O Operations for Typical Devices

DEVICE	CONTROL OPERATIONS	DATA TRANSFER OPERATIONS
Disk	Seek to Sector, Track Cylinder Seek Home Position	Read Sector Write Sector
Magnetic Tape	Rewind Rewind/Unload Forward Space File Forward Space Record Backspace Record Backspace File Write Tape Mark	Read Record Write Record Read Backwards
Line Printer	Skip to Channel (Carriage Control)	Print Line* Print Character* Load Font
"Standard" Terminal		Write Character* Read Character
Buffered Terminal		Write Page* Read Page

* Can include special control characters for formatting screens, changing displays, printer character size.
  No special control operations are generally needed.

working with microcomputers. These simple interfaces help transfer data to devices such as printers and terminals, one character at a time. The serial interface transmits the bits in a character on a single wire one bit at a time, while the parallel interface transmits all the bits at once over multiple wires. An example of a simple serial interface connection is shown in Figure 9–4.

Figure 9–4 A Simple Interface for Character-by-character Transfer

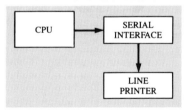

I/O Controllers

More complex I/O interfaces are often called **I/O controllers,** or I/O

control units. Controllers provide features such as:

- **direct memory access (DMA)** data transfer, which allows for transfer of data between memory and a device without program intervention
- support of multiple devices (for example, multiple disk units)
- support of **overlapped control operations,** such as seek operations on disks, which can be initiated on one device while another device is performing another control operation.

Some controllers even provide for reading or writing on one device while one or more other devices are performing a control operation. Using such a controller, only one unit attached to the control unit can be busy transferring data at a given instant in time. In other words, the control unit can only select and control one device at a time for data transfer.

Programming controllers can be more complex than programming simple interfaces, because of the multiple devices that must be supported on one controller. A device driver will support a single controller, but must be able to keep track of the control and status of each device attached to the controller. Figure 9–5 illustrates a controller used to control multiple devices.

Figure 9–5 An I/O Controller Controlling Several Devices

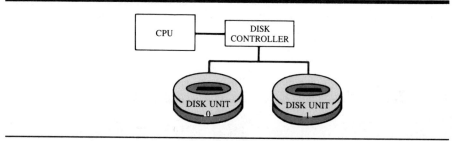

I/O Processors

Another mechanism for device management, common on large mainframes, is the use of I/O processors, introduced in the previous chapter. In the context of IBM mainframes, such a processor is called a **channel.** Multiple I/O controllers can be attached to a single channel. Channels function like special-purpose CPUs, with their own machine language. They can execute a series of I/O commands contained in a **channel program,** which in the 370 architecture resides in main memory. The address of this channel program is sent to the channel by an SIO (start I/O) instruction. The **channel command words (CCWs)** in the channel program are read from memory using DMA techniques; the channel executes these commands using the selected controller. This obviously adds another complexity to the implementation of device drivers in such an environment. Three interacting physical devices must be considered:

- the I/O channel (which executes channel programs and controls data transfer between controllers and main memory)

- the I/O controllers (which control individual devices)

- the I/O devices (which actually perform appropriate input, output, and control operations)

Data Transfer Techniques

The choice of a basic technique for data transfer—direct I/O, block transfers, or channel programs—is a fundamental decision for the designer of device drivers. Normally, the choice is determined by the nature of the interface or controller. Simple interfaces, such as serial and parallel interfaces on microcomputers, require little to start an I/O operation, but the device driver must process *every* character. Direct memory access controllers are designed for block transfer, and require no device driver software intervention during data transfer, but I/O initialization is more complex than with a simple interface. In addition to a command such as *read* or *write* for a device, a device driver for such a controller must also supply other required information to the device so that the I/O operation can proceed without software intervention. For example, a disk read on a single platter disk might require the following control information:

- track address

- sector address

- number of bytes to read

- memory address into which to read data

This information must be provided to start the I/O operation for the device. Exactly how the information is provided to the device is dependent on the architecture of a particular computer and the I/O controller; typically a series of transfers into device registers is required, often in a specific order.

9.5 TECHNIQUES FOR PROGRAMMING DEVICES

A few simple examples will help us understand device control and various techniques that we can use when writing device drivers. We will examine two techniques for monitoring device activity or status: **device polling** (or simply **polling**) and the use of interrupts. As we shall see, polling can work in some simple environments such as those of single user operating systems, but this is not generally acceptable in multiprogramming systems.

Polling

Chapter 8 introduced the concept of polling a device for its status before issuing the next I/O command. After a command is sent to such a device, it must once again be polled to determine when the operation is completed so that the next operation, if any, can be begun. If the device is a character-by-character device, this sequence of I/O and polling must be continued until all characters have been transferred between the device and main memory. A simple polling algorithm for this type of I/O is given in Figure 9–6.

Figure 9–6 A Simple Polling Algorithm for Device Control

```
/* initialize pointer and count */
I:=0
COUNT:=BUFLEN

/* begin polling loop */
WHILE COUNT>0 AND no device error

   /* wait while device is busy */
   WHILE device is busy
   ENDWHILE

   /* process character if no error */
   IF no device error THEN
      WRITE BUFFER(I)      /* write next character */
      COUNT:=COUNT - 1     /* decrement count */
      I:=I + 1             /* increment pointer */
   ENDIF

ENDWHILE
```

In this example, it is assumed that there are methods of testing the status of a device to detect busy and error conditions. In addition, a means of transferring the single character in the BUFFER array must be provided. In simple memory-mapped I/O, as is found in the PDP-11, it could be possible to test the device registers themselves for various status bits (BUSY, ERROR) and to move the character directly into the memory location, which is the data transfer register for the device. The algorithm can then can be modified to that shown in Figure 9–7.

Figure 9–7 Simple Polling with Memory-mapped I/O

```
/* initialize pointer and count */
I:=0
COUNT:=BUFLEN

/* begin polling loop */
WHILE COUNT>0
     AND error_bit of status_register=OFF

  /* wait while device is busy */
  WHILE status_bit of status_register=BUSY
  ENDWHILE

  /* process character if no error */
  IF error_bit of status_register=OFF THEN
    MOVE BUFFER(I) TO DATA_REGISTER
    COUNT:=COUNT - 1     /* decrement count */
    I:=I + 1             /* increment pointer */
  ENDIF

ENDWHILE
```

The algorithms depicted in Figures 9–6 and 9–7 are typical for polling control of a device. No device executes an I/O operation if its status indicates that it is busy or an error condition exists. It is possible to have a polling type of operation on a DMA device as well, although the CPU will not have to be involved in the data transfer itself once the I/O command has been sent to the device or device control unit.

As an illustration, Figure 9–8 shows the use of polling for a simple diskette device on a PDP-11, which requires a sequence of information to be sent to the device before it can respond to the requested command. A read operation on this diskette unit consists of two I/O operations: *read sector* (which transfers data from the diskette to an internal buffer in the control unit) and *empty buffer* (which uses DMA to transfer data from the internal buffer of the control unit to the internal memory of the computer). A protocol consisting of device communication to the CPU, followed by the CPU's response, is required after each operation.

Upon receiving the *read sector* command, the device sends back a transfer request signal to the CPU via the device status register. The CPU responds by sending the sector address to a data register. The device once again responds with a transfer request to the CPU, and the CPU responds with the track address. At this point in time, the *read sector* operation is active. The device status will indicate BUSY, or not DONE, so the program can now poll the status register for the DONE state. Once DONE is indicated, an *empty buffer* command is sent to the control unit, which once again responds with two transfer requests: one for the number of words to transfer, and the other for the address in main memory that will be used to store the data. Once again, the status register is tested for DONE while the data transfer to memory is taking place. Note that polling actually takes place at many points during the operation, both to check for readiness after transfer of each item of control information, and to wait for each of the two operations to be complete.

In all of the previous examples (Figures 9–6 through 9–8), we assumed that no interrupts were generated by the device. Systems capable of such polling in general have a means of disabling any interrupts which might occur. The simplest device driver might be little more than an extension of these simple polling models. This would be a possibility, but the obvious drawback is that the CPU is going to waste much time in polling loops waiting for devices. More importantly, the basic principle of multiprogramming systems, that one program or process may execute while another is blocked waiting for I/O completion, would be violated. Hence, device drivers implemented with polling cannot be used in a multiprogramming environment.

Use of Interrupts

The use of interrupts in device management allows an I/O operation for a device to be started by the device driver, and the device driver to return to the process that made the I/O request (or, as we shall see later, pass control to the operating system to schedule another process if the requesting process is blocked waiting for I/O completion). In this case, a **device interrupt handler** becomes an integral part of the device driver. This interrupt handler receives control when the device (or control unit, or channel) generates the interrupt signal, which causes the CPU to transfer to the handler address. Obviously, how this is done in the hardware is dependent on the architecture of a particular computer system.

In most operating systems some type of data structure, either a simple one-bit flag called an **event flag**, or a more elaborate structure called an **event control block (ECB)**, is used by a process or the operating system to represent events, such as the completion of a particular I/O operation. When simple I/O is performed with interrupts, although characters are actually transferred one at a time, use of event flags or ECBs can make the device

Figure 9–8 Polling A Simple DMA Device

```
MOVE read sector command TO CONTROL_STATUS_REGISTER

WHILE TRANSFER_BIT OF CONTROL_STATUS_REGISTER=OFF
ENDWHILE

MOVE sector address TO DATA_REGISTER

WHILE TRANSFER_BIT OF CONTROL_STATUS_REGISTER=OFF
ENDWHILE

MOVE track address TO DATA_REGISTER

WHILE DONE_BIT OF CONTROL_STATUS_REGISTER=OFF
ENDWHILE

MOVE empty-buffer command
              TO CONTROL_STATUS_REGISTER

WHILE TRANSFER_BIT OF CONTROL_STATUS_REGISTER=OFF
ENDWHILE

MOVE word count TO DATA_REGISTER

WHILE TRANSFER_BIT OF CONTROL_STATUS_REGISTER=OFF
ENDWHILE

MOVE memory buffer address TO DATA_REGISTER

WHILE DONE_BIT OF CONTROL_STATUS_REGISTER=OFF
ENDWHILE
```

appear to operate the same as a DMA device. This is because the signaling of an I/O event's completion is done by this event flag for both types of data transfer.

To illustrate this process, Figure 9–9 presents a modification of the polling algorithm from Figure 9–6. In this case, device initialization involves setting up a count and a buffer pointer, and enabling interrupts for the device, which will be processed by the device interrupt handler when they occur. As each character is transferred, the interrupt handler receives control, processes the character, and—when all characters have been written—sets a device event flag to indicate that the requested operation is complete. Although this event flag is polled by a simple loop in the example, it could be tested at any point in a program without affecting the progress of data transfer to the device.

In a single-process environment, the interrupt handler in Figure 9–9

Figure 9–9   Use of Interrupts and Event Flags for Simple I/O

```
MAIN PROGRAM:

        /* initialize pointer, count, and device flag */
        I:=0
        COUNT:=BUFLEN
        DEV_FLAG:=0

        enable interrupts for device
        .
        .
        /* loop until all characters written */
        WHILE DEV_FLAG=0
        ENDWHILE
        .
        .



INTERRUPT HANDLER:

        save registers

        /* check for errors */
        IF error THEN
            DEV_FLAG:=-1      /* set flag to error code */
            disable interrupts for device
            restore registers
            return from interrupt
        ENDIF

        /* check for completion */
        IF COUNT=0 THEN /* operation completed */
            DEV_FLAG:=1  /* set flag to completion code */
            disable interrupts for device
            restore registers
            return from interrupt
        ENDIF

        /* no error, not complete; process character */
        WRITE BUFFER(I) /* write next character */
        I:=I + 1           /* increment pointer */
        COUNT:=COUNT - 1/* decrement count */
        restore registers
        return from interrupt
```

would simply return to the interrupted program, at the point of interruption, and resume execution. In a multiprogramming system, interrupts provide an opportunity for forcing a context switch when a device completes its requested operation. The device event flag could be a part of the PCB itself, and could be used to determine if a process is to change from a *blocked* state, waiting for device I/O, to the *ready* state. In this case, control may not return to the interrupted program. Instead, control may transfer to the operating system, which ultimately invokes a dispatcher to schedule the next process to use the CPU. This would be a likely outcome when preemptive scheduling is used, whereby low-priority programs lose control of the CPU if a higher-priority process becomes ready. Since the completion of an I/O operation requested by a process may indeed cause a process to become ready, the operating system must be able to get control for a possible context switch.

Buffer Management

The time required for physical I/O on devices is quite long when one considers the number of instructions that a CPU can execute during this time. One goal in an operating system would be to minimize **device idle time,** hence maximizing **device throughput.** We can use a technique called **buffering** to improve device throughput as well as CPU throughput. Buffering, in this context, is the use of temporary storage areas in memory (**buffers**) to store data that is read from an input device before it is needed or can be used by a process, or to store data produced by a process before it can be accepted by an output device.

Character input devices can often have a complete block of data received and stored (buffered) by a device driver before this block is transferred to a process requesting it. (see Figure 9–10). Often, character buffering for input in such a device driver uses a FIFO buffer, called a **ring buffer** because of the way it operates. The buffer is processed in a ring fashion, with an ordering such that the next input data character after the character stored in the last physical location of the buffer is stored back at the beginning of the data area (if it is free); in effect, characters in the buffer form a **circular list.** Two pointers, RING_IN and RING_OUT, manage the buffer. RING_IN keeps track of the next free location into which the interrupt handler will place the next character read. RING_OUT determines the next character to be placed in the process buffer. A ring buffer counter and the ring size are maintained so that we know when the ring buffer is full or empty. The RING_IN and RING_OUT pointers can never "pass each other." RING_IN is manipulated by the device driver interrupt handler, while RING_OUT is manipulated by the device driver read routines, which send data to the process buffer. Figure 9–11 illustrates the ring buffer concept.

Device drivers for DMA devices can also buffer data on block transfers.

Figure 9–10 Buffering for a Character-by-character Device

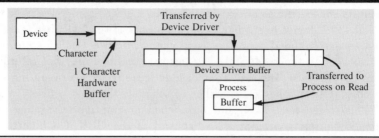

Figure 9–11 Use of a Ring Buffer for Buffering Input

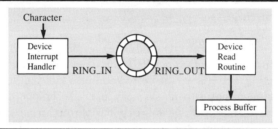

The most typical buffering occurs when data are blocked (multiple logical records in one physical record), and only one logical record is transferred to a buffer of a requesting process each time a read is requested. This buffering is most effective in sequential operation, whereby logical records will be requested in the order in which they appear in the physical block. A physical block with seven logical records would have seven logical records buffered, and would only do a physical read on every seventh read request, as illustrated in Figure 9–12.

Similar buffering to build physical blocks occurs on the output side prior to the writing of data. In the case of output data, it is easy to see why multiple records could be lost if the system fails, requiring a reload of the operating system.

Double Buffering

The device management routines of an operating system should provide features that both maximize the throughput of individual devices, and support the operation of devices simultaneously with other devices or CPU activities.

Figure 9–12 Buffering for a DMA Device

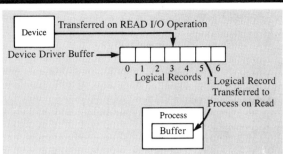

The buffering techniques just described do help, but additional techniques can provide further improvement. **Double buffering** is a technique for gaining speed in a data transfer by the use of two or more buffers by a device driver, or perhaps by a process. While one buffer is being processed by the CPU, another buffer may be read or written by the device. In a device driver supporting a block device with multiple logical records, we can use double buffering to improve performance in at least two ways:

1. Upon request for the last logical record in the internal buffer of a device driver, initiate the read of the next physical record, even though it is not known that this physical record will be required. This allows the device read to proceed while a record is being processed, resulting in overlapped I/O and processing.

2. Provide two buffers for physical records. Upon opening the device, two physical records can be read "immediately," one after another. Then, when records are exhausted in buffer one, a read can be initiated to read more data into buffer one, while records from buffer two are available immediately.

The use of two buffers can be very significant when blocking is small or non-existent because the delays waiting for the next physical read can be greatly reduced.

It is possible to allow an application process to manage buffers of this type, and gain increased throughput, if the operating system supports **asynchronous I/O,** that is, I/O operations such as *read* and *write* which return control to the caller as soon as the operation has been set up, even though the actual transfer has not completed or perhaps has not even begun. This means that I/O system calls do not automatically result in the process being blocked, as illustrated in Figure 9–13. While this capability is of little value in many high-level programs, which typically assume that read or write operations will be completed before any following statements will be executed, it is of great use in other applications, especially real-time processes and many system programs. The requesting process must be provided with an event flag or an additional system call, which can be used to determine if the previous I/O operation has completed.

Figure 9–13 A Process Performing Overlapped I/O on Two Devices

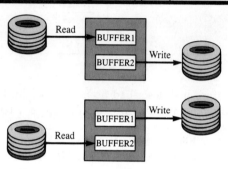

The advantages of double buffering by a process may be illustrated by a simple copy program. Suppose such a program is to copy a file from a tape on tape drive 1 (TAPE1) to tape drive 2 (TAPE2), each tape drive having its own controller so that tape I/O operations can overlap. If we use the typical READ/WAIT, WRITE/WAIT sequence, we might follow this procedure:

```
WHILE NOT END_OF_FILE(TAPE1)
    READ TAPE1,BUFFER1
    WAIT TAPE1
    IF NOT END_OF_FILE(TAPE1)
        WRITE TAPE2,BUFFER2
        WAIT TAPE2
    ENDIF
ENDWHILE
```

The device throughput for both tapes would be approximately fifty percent of their maximum rates because while TAPE1 is busy, TAPE2 is idle, and vice versa.

Now consider the following double buffering algorithm:

```
READ TAPE1,BUFFER1
WHILE NOT END_OF_FILE(TAPE1)
   WAIT TAPE1
   WAIT TAPE2
   IF NOT END_OF_FILE(TAPE1)
      READ  TAPE1,BUFFER2
      WRITE TAPE2,BUFFER1
   ENDIF
   WAIT TAPE1
   WAIT TAPE2
   IF NOT END_OF_FILE(TAPE1)
      READ  TAPE1,BUFFER1
      WRITE TAPE2,BUFFER2
   ENDIF
ENDWHILE
```

Here it is assumed that READ and WRITE pass control back to the program upon initiating the I/O request. The program must check the I/O operation with the WAIT operation. If both tape drives operate at the same speed, near-maximum throughput will be realized (OS overhead or other use of the tape controllers may prevent throughput from reaching 100%). Now, while TAPE1 is reading, TAPE2 is writing, and vice versa. Note the beginning read of TAPE1 was required to get the double buffering scheme "rolling."

If the devices used do not operate at the same speed, double buffering still helps, but improvement is limited to the amount of time required for the faster device's I/O operations, as illustrated in Figure 9–14.

Figure 9–14 Improvement in Device Throughput using Double Buffering

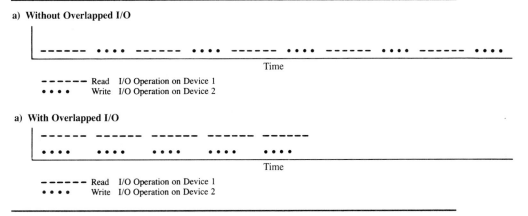

a) Without Overlapped I/O

Time

------ Read   I/O Operation on Device 1
• • • •   Write I/O Operation on Device 2

a) With Overlapped I/O

Time

------ Read   I/O Operation on Device 1
• • • •   Write I/O Operation on Device 2

Software Caching

We can improve device performance by eliminating a certain percentage of reads and writes for a device by a different buffering technique called **software caching,** similar to hardware caching. This approach is now commonly used in disk file servers in local area networks to improve performance.

Let us consider an environment supporting disk caching. A set (cache) of buffers is allocated to hold disk records that have been recently read or written. The size of each buffer is usually a multiple of the sector size on the disk being supported. Consider the situation where five "records" (identified by a number for the sake of this example) have been read in an environment with five disk cache buffers in the computer's memory, as shown in Figure 9–15. Now suppose a write of record 72 is requested by a process. In this environment, no I/O takes place (at least not immediately); rather, the disk caching facility simply updates the record in memory, thus avoiding an I/O operation. If a read of record 104 is requested, the record is provided from the memory-resident disk cache buffer, and no I/O takes place. The assumption is that recently accessed records will tend to be accessed again, and thus should be kept in the cache; a similar assumption underlies the operation of virtual memory systems, to be discussed in a later chapter.

Figure 9–15   Use of Disk Cache Buffers to Improve Performance

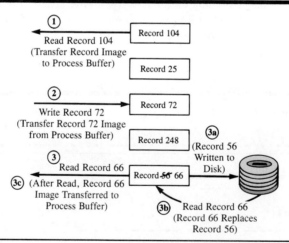

Suppose now that a read request for record 66 occurs. Since this record is not in the cache, a cache buffer must be freed by writing the contents of the buffer to disk (if it is not the same as the record on disk, i.e., it has been changed by a previous write operation). The cache software algorithm selects a buffer to be used for the read and, if necessary, writes its contents to disk before reading record 66 into this cache buffer. The cache buffer chosen usually reflects recent usage of disk cache buffers—for example, it selects the least recently used buffer.

Disk throughput improves in this instance because many disk I/O operations are eliminated for repeatedly used records that remain resident in disk cache buffers.   An environment such as one with a repeatedly used database index would be a likely one in which improvements in disk performance could be easily observed because the index, or portions of the index, would remain resident in the disk cache. Note that records referred to in this example are actually areas of the disk (contiguous sectors) and many logical records might be contained in a single cache buffer.

A disadvantage of software caching is that cache buffers could be lost in a system failure, resulting in a corrupted file system or files.   Systems supporting disk caching usually provide for the automatic, periodic writing of the disk cache buffers at intervals specified by a system operator, and for the writing of disk cache buffers via a system command or on system shutdown. In such environments, one does not simply turn off the computer—it must be shut down in an orderly manner. UNIX provides disk caching, which is the primary reason that orderly system shutdowns are required before powering off the computer system. To minimize the problem, UNIX provides a system call and command *(sync)* to flush all buffers to the disk, and automatically executes this command every few minutes.

Data Structures in Device Management

I/O operations that are in progress or have been requested are represented by some type of data structure in every operating system. The format for such data structures is determined by the rules for device driver implementation. This data structure is called by various names, including **device control block (DCB), I/O block (IOB), I/O control block (IOCB), unit control block (UCB), and channel control block (CCB).** It is a data structure that represents a device, channel or controller to the device driver, and an activity of the device, channel or controller to the operating system and/or a process. Some operating systems have a hierarchy of these control blocks, all requiring access by the device driver. For example, in the VAX/VMS operating system, a channel control block points to a unit control block, which in turn points to other control blocks. Hence, data structures for representing device, controller, and channel activity can become quite complex. In this text, we use the term I/O control block, or IOCB, for a data structure representing I/O activity. Figure 9–16 lists some information that might be found in a "typical" I/O control block.

In addition to IOCBs, device tables representing the various device

Figure 9–16 Information Stored in an I/O Control Block

Channel Number

Controller Address

Device Name

Device Address

Interrupt Vector Address

Address of Interrupt Handler

Device Type

Address of Open Routine

Address of Close Routine

Address of Start I/O Routine

Address of Cancel I/O Routine

Buffer Address

Buffer Length

Current Buffer Pointer

Current Data Count

Current I/O Operation

Address of PCB of process which requested
    current I/O operation

Address of I/O Request Parameters

Address of ECB for current operation

drivers in the operating system must be maintained. Operating systems that allow dynamic installation of device drivers would perform the installation by adding entries to such a device table. The contents of a typical device table entry are shown in Figure 9–17.

Once again the complexity of implementing device drivers increases, since these additional data structures must be used and understood in a given operating system environment.

9.6 DEVICE MANAGEMENT ROUTINES

Every device driver or I/O supervisor must provide mechanisms to support certain basic activities for each device. These activities include:

Figure 9–17 Content of a Typical Device Table Entry

Device Name

Device Status

Device Driver File Name or Disk Address

Entry Point in Main Memory, if loaded
  (otherwise 0)

Device Size

Device Driver Size

Logical Name(s)

- preparing for I/O
- starting I/O
- interrupt servicing
- error detection and recovery
- completion of I/O
- cancellation of I/O

In addition to these activities, an I/O system call interface is needed, including procedures to service common system calls; the operations supported generally must include *open, close, read, write,* and a variety of control operations. These system calls, when directed to a specific device, invoke components of the corresponding device driver in executing each specific operation.

Most device drivers and control routines are divided into two parts: the main driver and the interrupt handler. Figure 9–18 illustrates a common structure along with the functions provided by each component.

Figure 9–18 Structure and Functions of Device Drivers

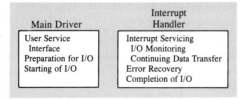

Main Driver	Interrupt Handler
User Service Interface Preparation for I/O Starting of I/O	Interrupt Servicing I/O Monitoring Continuing Data Transfer Error Recovery Completion of I/O

The two-part structure of such a device driver is such that the main driver receives control to check the validity of the I/O request, prepare for that I/O request, and start the I/O. Rather than polling for I/O to complete, the driver then returns control to the caller, and the interrupt handler intermittently receives control until the I/O operation is completed. This process is illustrated in Figure 9–19.

Figure 9–19 Flow of Control in Device Driver

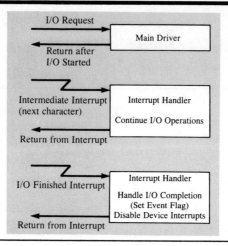

I/O System Call Interface

Operating system standards for system calls and device driver implementation specify how a device driver gets control and how parameters are passed to the device driver. System call standards depend on both the operating system and the architecture of the computer system. In some systems, different instructions can generate a supervisor call or trap; for example, the PDP-11 has TRAP and IOT (I/O trap) instructions. IOT is the "natural" choice for invoking a system call to a device driver.

Once the device driver gets control, what is the format of the parameters? How are they found? Most systems will specify a parameter list with a register pointing to the address of this list—all of this is determined by the I/O system call interface standards.

Preparing for I/O

Preparation for I/O is the first activity of a device driver when invoked via one of the device system calls. Since device drivers must adhere to operating system interface standards, the I/O system call parameters must specify the type of operation requested (read, write, control), the address of the data buffer to be used, the size of the data area, and other relevant information. In addition, device-dependent parameters, such as track and sector numbers for disk operations, may also be required.

Preparation of I/O components of a device driver validates device-specific parameters of an I/O request. Appropriate error return codes must be provided to the user for any errors detected in the service request parameters.

The preparation for I/O might include temporary buffer allocation or initialization, formatting of data, and placing information in the appropriate location(s) in some I/O control block that is accessible to the device interrupt handler and the operating system. Once the I/O request parameters are validated, the device status must be checked. If the device is busy or not ready, the device driver must take appropriate action. This action is dependent, of course, on the operating system. If an error condition or problem such as "device not ready" is detected, the driver might take action causing the application process to terminate, or it might simply provide a return code to be passed back to the process, which then must deal with the problem in a suitable way depending on the application. In a multiprogramming operating system, the response may include queueing the I/O request for a shared device that is presently busy with another operation.

Starting I/O

If the requested device is not busy and no abnormal conditions were detected, the driver starts the actual I/O operation. Once again, the means of doing this is both device-dependent and computer-dependent. In some instances, the driver simply enables interrupts for a device. In that case, all other device service is provided by the interrupt handler.

Some computers have specific I/O machine instructions to begin operations, such as eXecute I/O (XIO) or Start I/O (SIO). Computers using memory-mapped I/O (such as the PDP-11) start I/O by writing to device control registers using addresses in the memory space. Figure 9–20 lists the type of information required to start I/O operations for various devices. This information may be provided via an operand to the I/O instruction or by special operations after the I/O instruction is issued.

Starting I/O can be as simple as enabling interrupts so that the interrupt handler can continue to monitor I/O operations. This is particularly true of character devices. In more complex devices, an I/O command may have to be built and sent to the device with the appropriate I/O instruction. Once I/O is started, control is returned either to the caller or the device driver, which may in fact be a portion of the operating system.

Figure 9–20   Information Required by Devices When Starting I/O

DEVICE	REQUIRED I/O INFORMATION
Disk and Drum	Operation Code Memory Transfer Address Number of Bytes to Transfer Track Address Sector Address
Magnetic Tape	Operation Code Memory Transfer Address Number of Bytes to Transfer
Terminal, serial port, printers	Operation Code (read/write) Character to Transfer (non-DMA) Buffer Address (DMA) Number of Bytes to Transfer (DMA)
Timers	Interval

Interrupt Servicing

The most complicated part of most I/O drivers or I/O supervisor modules is the interrupt handler. Much of the device control is embedded in the interrupt handler, which is given control asynchronously when the device needs service. This could involve processing the next character for a device in the case of a non-DMA device, or starting a second or third phase of an I/O operation for DMA devices (for example, a read after a seek to sector on some disks).

Information needed by the interrupt handler must be provided by the main portion of the device driver. Such information is usually contained in the I/O control blocks that represent the current I/O operation, just as PCBs represent process execution to the dispatcher.

Device interrupt handlers must save all registers and hardware status of the interrupted program. In a stack machine, this merely involves saving information on the stack and restoring it before returning to the interrupted program. Recall that the program counter and program status word are automatically saved by the hardware interrupt.

Certainly the most complex part of interrupt handler service is error recovery (which we'll cover in the next section). Error recovery routines can be either resident or dynamically loaded when needed, depending on operating system design and requirements.

Error Detection and Recovery

Implementation of device drivers would be far simpler if one could assume an error-free environment. The same is true for all programs. Unfortunately this is never the case. Just what types of errors can occur? The answer, of course, depends on the type of device. A summary of some common errors for various device types is presented in Figure 9–21.

Figure 9–21 Possible Errors for Various Devices

DEVICE	POSSIBLE ERRORS
Disk and Drum	Invalid Track, Sector Wrong Density Power Unsafe CRC Error Deleted Sector
Tape	Backwards at Load Point End of Tape (EOT) CRC Error Drop Ready
Printer	Paper Out Ribbon Out Off-line

Just as the types of errors vary, appropriate recovery methods also vary from device to device. Recovery may be as simple as reporting a printer out of paper to the user or, more likely, to the operating system for operator intervention and subsequent continuing of the I/O operation. In other cases, the error recovery may be quite complex. As an example, the algorithm in Figure 9–22 illustrates an error recovery procedure for a magnetic tape drive, which is invoked when the device signals an error during an attempt to read a block of data.

The algorithm shown in the figure retries the tape read nine times by backspacing a record and then rereading. If the error persists, the tape is backspaced ten records, forwardspaced nine, and then reread (to try to "clean off" the tape). This entire procedure is repeated ten times, yielding a total of 100 retries. The actual implementation of this process involves starting I/O operations in the interrupt handler, then servicing the interrupts for these error recovery operations when the interrupts occur. Thus, the interrupt handler must know it is performing error recovery and keep track of where it is in the overall recovery procedure.

This algorithm seems complex enough, but consider the case of an error occurring during the error recovery procedure. Suppose that the record in error is only the fourth record on the tape. Then, when the fifth backspace operation is attempted while trying to backspace ten records, a "backwards at load point" signal will occur, indicating an attempt to backspace past the beginning. While not really an error, this is an unexpected condition and must

Figure 9–22 An Error Recovery Algorithm for a Tape Drive

```
ERROR HANDLER:

        /* initialize counter and flag */
        LOOP:=0
        TAPE_ERROR=TRUE

        /* repeat entire process up to ten times */
        WHILE LOOP < 10 AND TAPE_ERROR

            /* backspace and reread up to nine times */
            COUNT:=0
            WHILE COUNT < 9 AND TAPE_ERROR
              backspace record
              read record again
              IF read is ok THEN TAPE_ERROR:=FALSE
              ELSE COUNT:=COUNT + 1
            ENDWHILE

            /* if error still present, back up further */
            IF TAPE_ERROR THEN

              /* backspace ten records */
              COUNT:=0
              WHILE COUNT < 10
                backspace record
                COUNT:=COUNT+1
              ENDWHILE

              /* skip forward nine records */
              COUNT:=0
              WHILE COUNT < 9
                forward space record
                COUNT:=COUNT+1
              ENDWHILE

              /* try reading again */
              read record
              IF read okay, TAPE_ERROR=FALSE
            ENDIF

            LOOP:=LOOP+1   /* prepare for retry */

        ENDWHILE    /* repeat if necessary */
```

be provided for in the logic of the interrupt error recovery routine. Note that the error recovery algorithm in Figure 9–22 does not handle this unexpected condition.

In spite of the complexity, the device driver must do all that is possible to recover from errors, particularly read or write errors to magnetic media,. If recovery fails, it is important to preserve the integrity of the data as much as possible. Users may wish to operate as best as possible on erroneous data, but the indication of such non-recoverable errors must be provided to the application program so that it may decide how to proceed in light of the error.

I/O Completion Processing

Once the requested I/O operation has finished, certain cleanup functions remain. These include setting the status of the process requesting the operation, clearing the device of busy status, and possibly disabling interrupts. One other function might be to search a device queue for another operation pending for the device that is now free, thus maximizing device throughput. I/O completion processing is usually a subcomponent of the device interrupt handler.

The responsibilities of each component of the device driver are summarized in Figure 9–23.

9.7 I/O SCHEDULING

Scheduling I/O for a device can range from a very simple problem to one that is quite complex. In a single-user operating system, I/O requests can be serviced by suspending the process requesting the I/O and waiting for the I/O to complete. As we discussed previously, I/O requests should allow overlapped I/O and execution of the calling program if the calling program indicates it wants control back prior to the completion of the I/O. In such cases, either a subsequent system call (e.g., *checkio*) or an event flag or ECB (as described previously) can be used to determine the status of the I/O operation.

Multiprogramming Environments

Multiprogramming systems require that device queues be supported. Such device queues are needed to service I/O requests for devices that are not

Figure 9–23 Device Driver Components and Responsibilities

I/O System Call Interface
        Mechanism to invoke device driver
        Format of parameter list
        Locating parameter list

Preparation for I/O
        Validate parameters
        Save parameters in I/O control block
        Pass error codes to process or to OS
        Place in I/O queue or invoke start component

Starting of I/O
        Enable interrupts
        Issue first I/O command to device
        Return to calling process or to OS

Interrupt Servicing
        Save registers
        Determine cause of interrupt
        IF error, invoke error recovery routine
        IF operation not done, issue next I/O command
                        advance pointer(s)
                        decrement count(s)
                        restore registers
                        return from interrupt
        ENDIF

        IF operation complete, set event flag
                        invoke completion routine
        ENDIF

Error Detection and Recovery
        Invoke error recover algorithm
        IF error recovers, resume in interrupt handler
        IF error permanent, set event flag to error code
                        invoke completion routine
        ENDIF

Completion of I/O (Return to Idle)
        Set event flag
        Disable interrupts
        Move process just finished with device to ReadyQ
        Invoke I/O scheduler
        Invoke dispatcher

Cancellation of I/O
        If I/O request in I/O queue, remove it
        Return to caller

ready (tape or disk not mounted or printer out of paper) or that are shared devices or control units busy with another process's I/O request. Support of such queues includes routines to add requests to a device queue and to delete requests (should an I/O request be terminated before it starts). Another requirement in such a system will be to respond to I/O completion of one request with a search of a device queue to start the next request. This requires that the interrupt handler for a device be able to invoke the device scheduler at the completion of I/O for a device.

I/O Queues. The I/O queues that represent pending I/O requests have two possible structures:

1. a single I/O queue for all devices
2. multiple I/O queues (e.g., one for each device and/or controller in the system)

A queue entry in such queues would consist of a PCB address of a process with an I/O request waiting to be started. Figures 9–24 and 9–25 illustrate the two queueing possibilities. There are various ways of representing pending I/O requests and active I/O for a process. We describe here just one possibility, involving two distinct, mutually exclusive *blocked* states, **IO_init** and **IO_active.**

Figure 9–24 A Single I/O Queue

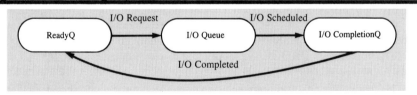

Figure 9–25 Multiple I/O Queues

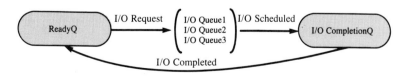

If a valid I/O request is received but the device is not presently available, the requesting process is placed in the blocked state *IO_init,* indicating it is waiting for the initiation of the requested I/O operation. A process in the *IO_init* state is represented by linking its PCB into an **IO_init queue.** If or when the device is ready to start the operation, an IOCB is set up for the requested operation, and the process is placed in the *IO_active* state. This is represented by linking its PCB into an **IO_active queue.** In most operating systems, the default strategy is to *block* processes waiting for I/O initiation or completion. Hence, once the I/O request is queued or started, the dispatcher is invoked to select the next process for execution. Typically the IO_init queue is organized as a linked list of PCBs, whereas the IO_active queue may be a linked list of IOCBs that point to PCBs. Much of I/O scheduling involves the manipulation of the linked list(s) that make up these two queues.

Figure 9–26 illustrates a structure using a single I/O queue for each state, and IOCBs to represent I/O activity on a disk and a printer. The I/O queues are designated IO_initQ and IO_activeQ, and the ready queue is also shown. In this example, PROCESS6, represented by PCB6, is in the *IO_active* state waiting for a disk I/O operation; PROCESS7, represented by PCB7, is in the *IO_active* state for a printer I/O operation. PROCESS1, PROCESS2, PROCESS3, PROCESS4, and PROCESS5, represented by PCB1, PCB2, PCB3, PCB4, and PCB5 respectively, are in the *IO_init* state waiting for initiation of I/O for the devices indicated.

Suppose now that the disk operation requested by PROCESS6 completes. A disk I/O interrupt will be generated and the disk interrupt handler will receive control. This interrupt handler will determine that the operation is complete and invoke an algorithm similar to the one shown in Figure 9–27. This algorithm results in PROCESS0, which was *running,* being returned to the *ready* state, PROCESS6 making a transition from the *IO_active* state to the *ready* state, and PROCESS2 making a transition from the *IO_init* state to the *IO_active* state.

The result prior to the dispatching of the next process is shown in Figure 9–28. The transitions described are depicted in the expanded state diagram in Figure 9–29. We now have two blocked states, *IO_init* and *IO_active,* in place of the single state called *blocked.* Note that there is generally one IOCB for each I/O device (or perhaps controller) in the system. The IOCBs represent I/O in progress and identify the PCB of the process with I/O active.

Device Scheduling Techniques. **Device scheduling** is the process of selecting the next request to be processed by a device from one or more I/O queues. The request to be selected depends on the scheduling techniques being used. Most commonly, the selection is made by a simple first-in, first-out strategy. In other cases the priority of the requesting process might be used to determine which request to select. This method is necessary, for example, in real-time systems.

Figure 9–26 Queue Structures for IO_init and IO_active States

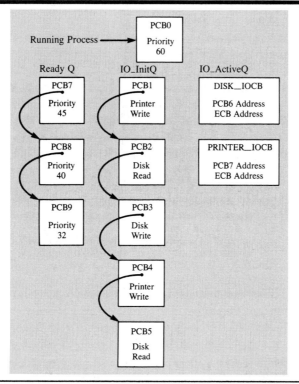

Special problems occur in scheduling the use of disk drives. Not only are there likely to be many requests pending in large systems, but the time required to service a request may depend heavily on the position on the disk to be accessed, especially if moving-head disks are used. The time required to perform a transfer with such disks is dominated by the seek time, which in turn depends on the distance between the track to be accessed and the track at which the disk access arm was previously positioned.

Because of this situation, significant time may be saved by adopting a **shortest-seek-time-first** strategy, always selecting the request that causes the arm to move the shortest distance. However, problems arise similar to those encountered by shortest-job-next strategies for long-term process scheduling. Requests for access to locations close to the lowest or highest numbered tracks will be less likely to be close to the arm, and will tend to be discriminated against. In the extreme case, starvation is possible. What's more, the basis for discrimination, physical position of the data to be transferred, is not under control of processes and is not in any way a fair

Figure 9-27 Handling an I/O Request Complete Interrupt

```
IO_COMPLETE:

          /* Cleanup after disk operation,
             switch waiting process to ready state */
          IF operation complete THEN
            Save context of currently running process
               in PCB, and insert its PCB in ReadyQ
            Set DISK_ECB for disk I/O just completed
            Move PCB address in DISK_IOCB to ReadyQ
            Set DISK_IOCB to represent idle state
          ENDIF

          /* setup next disk operation, if any */
          Search IO_WaitQ for another disk request
          IF disk request found THEN
            Move PCB address of next disk I/O request
               to DISK_IOCB
            Move DISK_ECB address to DISK_IOCB
            Start requested disk I/O operation
          ENDIF

          Invoke dispatcher to dispatch next process
```

basis for assigning priorities.

Because of these problems, compromise methods are needed. The most common alternatives are based on requiring the arm to proceed in one direction until all pending requests are serviced before returning to deal with accesses in the other direction. These methods are further discussed, for example, by Peterson and Silberschatz [1985].

Some disks can sense rotational position, so that optimized scheduling could determine the request to schedule next by determining the sector that will come under the disk head soonest. This is an algorithm that would most likely be added to a fixed-head disk or drum.

I/O scheduling can become quite complex when optimization is added. The net benefit from such optimization is improved performance of the devices; however, it is often found in practice that the amount of improvement over a simple FIFO strategy is not great for the majority of systems.

Figure 9–28 Queues after I/O Completion for PROCESS6

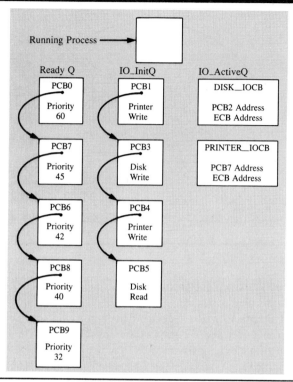

9.8 WRITING DEVICE DRIVERS

Every operating system has specific requirements for supporting I/O devices, whether through dynamically loaded device drivers or by adding support to an existing I/O supervisor. As previously noted, the implementation of device drivers is probably more common for systems programmers, and even application programmers, than the implementation of any other portion of an operating system, particularly in systems with dynamically loaded device drivers, in which *adding* device drivers is relatively straightforward. Because of this, design and programming guides for device drivers spelling out the necessary requirements are often included with the operating system documentation. These requirements must be followed if one expects to be successful in supporting such devices. Requirements or standards for implementing device drivers may include techniques for setting interrupt vectors, interface requirements, position independence, and setting device characteristics.

Figure 9–29 State Transitions with IO_Init and IO_Active States

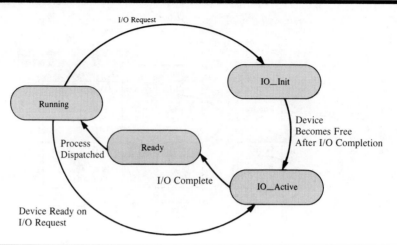

Preparation for Writing a Device Driver

Anyone who attempts to write a device driver must do some careful planning. You must keep in mind several important considerations in undertaking the implementation of a device driver:

- KNOW THE DEVICE. Study the hardware manuals carefully to fully understand the characteristics of the device you are dealing with. Experiments with the hardware may be required to resolve ambiguities in the device manuals.

- KNOW THE STRUCTURE OF A DEVICE DRIVER. For any given operating system, consult the device driver information in the system manuals. Be sure to know every aspect of a device driver's structure.

- STUDY OTHER DEVICE DRIVERS. Many operating systems describe model device drivers in their documentation. Study the example(s) carefully. Use them as a guide for implementing the new device driver. Be sure to find a model that is similar to the device you are to support (e.g., a block device vs. a character-by-character device).

- CONSIDER SPECIAL FEATURES OF THE DEVICE. Most devices have unique features. Determine how these features affect the implementation and how you will support them.

9.9 SUMMARY

Device management is a major responsibility of any operating system. This responsibility is most often met by a collection of device drivers. Usually a device driver is associated with each type of device. Because of the great variety of I/O devices, it is likely that new device drivers will need to be developed for individual installations. Thus developing device drivers is a likely activity for systems programmers.

Device drivers differ depending on the characteristics of individual devices. The structure and programming strategy for the I/O interface must also be considered. Key decisions include the choice of Simple I/O, block transfers using DMA, or I/O programs for I/O processors or channels. Interrupts must normally be used except in single-process environments, and other possible mechanisms include event flags or ECBs and various types of buffering.

Despite the variation, device drivers generally have a consistent structure and set of responsibilities. Most drivers consist of a main body and an interrupt handler. They are responsible for a series of standard activities, such as preparing for I/O, starting I/O, error handling, etc. They also must implement an I/O system call interface, providing support for a common set of I/O system calls.

I/O scheduling can become complex when many requests are pending from multiple processes. A system of queues is needed, and it may be useful to establish new process states depending on the status of pending I/O. Most requests are scheduled by a simple FIFO approach, but special problems arise in disk scheduling, where the time required to service a request may depend on the disk location to be accessed.

FOR FURTHER READING

Device management has sometimes been neglected in OS texts. However, a reasonable treatment is contained in Tanenbaum [1987, Ch. 3]. A good older treatment of many important issues is presented in Chapters 2 and 5 of Madnick and Donovan [1974]. Extensive discussions are given by Finkel [1986. Ch. 5], and Milenković [1987, Ch. 2].

For a thorough understanding of device drivers, there is no substitute for a study of actual implementations and OS guides. Device drivers in UNIX and VMS are fully described by Bach [1986] and Kenah and Bate [1984], respectively. The simple structure of the I/O subsystem in microprocessor OSs such as PC-DOS is reviewed by King [1983], among others. Some effective guides for writing device drivers are those produced by Digital Equipment for RT-11 [Digital 1981a], RSX-11 [Digital 1981b], and VMS [Digital 1984b]. Device drivers for MS-DOS are discussed by Wong [1986].

The topic of disk scheduling is thoroughly discussed in Chapter 7 of Peterson and Silberschatz [1985]. A more theoretical treatment is given in the classic text by Coffman and Denning [1973, Ch. 5].

IMPORTANT TERMS

asynchronous I/O	I/O controller
buffering	I/O interface
buffers	I/O subsystem
channel	I/O supervisor
channel command word (CCW)	IO_active state
channel control block (CCB)	IO_active queue
channel program	IO_init state
circular list	IO_init queue
device control block (DCB)	overlapped control operations
device driver	parallel interface
device idle time	polling
device interrupt handler	RAM disk
device polling	ring buffer
device scheduling	serial interface
device throughput	shortest seek time first
direct memory access (DMA)	software caching
double buffering	software device
event control block (ECB)	spool device
event flag	spooler
I/O block (IOB)	unit control block (UCB)
I/O control block (IOCB)	virtual device
I/O control unit	virtual disk

REVIEW QUESTIONS

1. List the items of information that must be supplied to a disk controller to set up a DMA read operation.

2. Give two reasons why it is especially important in smaller systems to have device drivers that are modular and easy to replace.

3. How does a clock differ from a "typical" device? How is it similar?

4. What are the disadvantages of disk (software) caching?

5. Why is polling of devices generally unacceptable in a multiprogramming operating system?

6. What functions are commonly provided by device drivers? Are there cases in which not all these functions are necessary? Why or why not?

7. What are the possible actions an operating system could take upon the detection of a disk error on a user disk read or write request? When and how would a process be informed of such a severe error?

ASSIGNMENTS

1. How would the use of a channel program change the structure and complexity of a device driver? What would be required of a printer process that sets up pages read from a spool file to be printed by a device driver, which will simply execute a channel program?

2. Using pseudocode, specify the logic of a RAM disk driver that simulates a real disk.

3. Modify the error recovery algorithm in Figure 9–22 to provide for the handling of the unexpected condition "backward at loadpoint" so that error recovery can continue.

4. Define data structures to represent I/O currently in progress on a device.

5. Compare device driver structures in two different operating systems (referring to the appropriate operating system manuals and textbooks). What implementation languages are used? How are interrupts used?

6. In a multiprogramming operating system, what happens when an I/O request is made by a process for a device that is busy with another I/O request?

PROJECT

This section describes a three-part programming project to implement a set of device drivers for a simple multiprogramming operating system. You should read the general description in this text in conjunction with the more specific descriptions given in your project manual. These mechanisms are important components of the multiprogramming executive (MPX) project described later in the text.

a. Design and implement a simple device driver for an RS-232 (asynchronous) serial interface. The driver must provide the following procedures, or services:

1. RC=COM_OPEN(com_flag): Initialize the device for operation, enabling interrupts so that data can be captured in an internal "ring buffer" before it is needed by a process. Set com_flag as the event flag to be used for subsequent operations to determine if a requested operation has completed. RC is a return code with a value of 0 if the requested operation is correct and has been initiated, or a negative value if an error has been detected. No I/O is initiated if RC is negative.

2. RC=COM_READ(buffer,length): Read data from the device. buffer is the data area into which characters are read, and length specifies how many characters are to be read. Upon return, RC should indicate how many characters were read, if no error occurred; otherwise it should contain an error code as described above.

3. RC=COM_WRITE(buffer,length): Write data to the device. buffer is the data area from which characters are written; length specifies how many characters are to be written. If the length parameter is omitted, the entire character string in buffer is written to the device designated COM. Upon return, RC should indicate how many characters were written, if no error occurred; otherwise it should contain an error code.

4. RC=COM_CLOSE: Reset the device, disabling interrupts. Upon return, RC should have the value 0 if no error occurred; otherwise it should contain an error code.

b. Design and implement a simple line printer device driver. The services supported by this device driver are:

1. RC=PRT_OPEN(prt_flag): Initialize the printer for operation. prt_flag is an event flag, and RC is a return code, as described in part **a.**

2. RC=PRT_PRINT(buffer,length): Print data on the printer. buffer is the data area from which characters are written; length specifies how many characters are to be printed. If the length parameter is omitted, the entire character string in buffer is printed.

3. RC=PRT_CLOSE: reset the printer, disabling interrupts.

c. Design and implement a low-level disk device driver. The services to be supported by this device driver are:

1. RC=DISK_OPEN(disk_flag): Initialize the disk for operation. disk_flag is an event flag, and RC is a return code, as described in part a.

2. RC=DISK_READ(track,sector,buffer,length): read a block of data from the disk, beginning at the specified track and sector. The location to copy the data to is given by buffer and the size of the block is specified by length; this must be less than or equal to the sector size. The return code is used as described in Part a.

3. RC=DISK_WRITE(track,sector,buffer,length):   write a block of data to the disk, beginning at the specified track and sector. The location to copy the data from is given by buffer and the size of the block is specified by length; this must be less than or equal to the sector size. The return code is used as described in Part a.

4. RC=DISK_CLOSE: reset the disk to an idle state.

5. RC=DISK_STATUS(status): set the value of status to the current hardware status of the disk.

Memory
Management

Memory Management

10.1 INTRODUCTION

Managing the memory resources of a computing system for most effective use by its application programs is the responsibility of **memory management.** This problem is concerned chiefly with managing the main memory of the system, although it will have some concern with secondary memory as well. The main memory resource is known by many names, including *primary storage, real storage, main storage, internal memory,* and so forth. Old-timers refer to main memory as **core** because, until fairly recently, most main memories were physically constructed from tiny magnetic rings known as cores. In this text we will sometimes use the terms memory and storage interchangeably, but we will usually refer to the principal memory resource as main memory.

The problem of main memory management is composed of three principal subproblems:

- **allocation,** the problem of assigning suitable storage space to processes as required. An efficient memory allocation mechanism may be expected to respond quickly to requests for assorted amounts of memory, to assign memory only when needed, and to reclaim memory promptly when its use is complete.

- **relocation,** the problem of matching programs and data to the memory locations that have been allocated. In some cases, modifications must be made to addresses in machine instructions and data to reflect the addresses actually used.

- **protection,** the problem of restricting a process's access to memory that has actually been allocated to it. This problem cannot be solved by privileged instructions, but must be addressed by other means.

The evolution of memory management techniques was shaped very much by the resource's characteristics in the early days of computing. Memory was expensive and slow, and only very limited amounts were available in most computers. Multiprogramming evolved partly because of the need to share such expensive resources among several concurrent processes. With the tradeoff available between cost, size, and speed, hierarchical memory systems were developed.

Because of the intensity of memory usage by operating systems and application processes, full control of this resource is not possible without assistance from hardware mechanisms. In most computing systems today, the most effective memory management systems make use of advanced hardware translation concepts, including paging, segmentation, and virtual memory. These concepts, and the OS techniques that use them, will be discussed in detail in Chapter 11. This chapter focuses on memory management strategies that require more limited, if any, hardware assistance. These techniques have been widely used in past systems, and are still appropriate in small systems and specialized contexts where hardware translation is not available.

10.2 SIMPLE ALLOCATION

Webster's New Collegiate Dictionary [Webster 1981] provides the following definitions for the term *allocate:*

1. to apportion for a specific purpose or to a particular person or thing
2. to set apart or earmark

Memory allocation refers to the apportioning of particular parts of memory for use by particular processes. Usually memory is allocated in discrete blocks or regions that must be **contiguous**; that is, they must occupy consecutive addresses in the **logical address space** or **virtual address space** of the process (the addresses as seen by the programmer). Since early operating systems allocated space in **physical memory** with little or no hardware assistance, these operating systems were actually concerned with the allocation of contiguous areas of this limited physical memory. In such an environment, operating systems may support a wide variation of memory allocation strategies, from very simple to very complex.

No Allocation

Certainly the simplest allocation strategy is none at all. With this approach, possible only on systems that run a single program at a time, each program has total access to all portions of memory and can manage it and use it in any manner (see Figure 10–1). While this is a simple approach that costs nothing to implement because it entails no operating system service, the disadvantage is precisely that no services are offered from the operating system. Programs can use all memory, including that formerly occupied by the OS. It is the program's responsibility to reload the OS when it completes. This technique, sometimes called the "bare machine" approach, was used heavily in the early days of computing. Today it is restricted primarily to applications that do not require a true OS, especially some real-time applications. In such systems, a specific dedicated program (usually in read-only memory) is the only thing that is ever stored in memory.

Figure 10–1   A Bare Machine with No Memory Allocation

Single-user Operating Systems

The simplest type of operating system is one which serves only a single user and runs only one process at a time. Allocation of memory in this type of OS is usually simple: a program may use whatever memory it needs as long as the required memory exists and is not needed by the OS itself. This approach is shown in Figure 10–2. Memory in such systems is viewed as being divided into two areas, one for the operating system and one for the application program.

As discussed in Chapter 3, the placement of the resident monitor in memory can be in either high or low memory addresses, or both. Many systems use low memory for the resident monitor, at least in part, because this region contains locations with special built-in properties, such as interrupt vectors. This is the view taken in Figure 10–2. Many single-user operating systems use such a placement strategy for the resident monitor.

Figure 10–2 Memory Allocation in a Simple Single-user System

Even though it is necessary for the OS to control special hardware locations in low memory, the OS itself may be located in high memory, as illustrated by RT-11. This OS places the resident monitor in high memory, but reserves the first 512 bytes for interrupt vectors and a user stack area as shown in Figure 10–3. A similar strategy is used by CP/M and MS-DOS.

Figure 10–3 Memory Allocation in the Middle of Memory (RT-11)

Protecting the Nucleus

In a sense, allocation is only meaningful when accompanied by protection. Some mechanism should exist to prevent a process's access to unallocated locations. Such protection is only possible with hardware mechanisms not found on the simplest minicomputers or microprocessors. However, many simple single-user operating systems are implemented on computers without any provision for hardware protection of the nucleus or other unallocated space. Since these are single-user systems, the problem is considered less serious; destruction of the nucleus would only affect the work being done by one person. The single user operating systems RT-11, CP/M, and MS-DOS, as examples, all lack any type of memory protection.

In most newer architectures, protection is obtained as part of a comprehensive memory translation mechanism. However, some older systems provide limited protection using simpler hardware. We discuss these techniques in Section 10.6.

10.3 ALLOCATION FOR MULTIPROGRAMMING

The strategies used in the simplest operating systems are only concerned with a single program that occupies all or part of memory. Multiprogramming operating systems require that memory be shared among two or more processes. Thus, portions of the memory must be chosen for allocation to each process.

Static vs. Dynamic Allocation

A simple approach for allocating memory to processes in a multiprogrammed system is **static allocation**. With this method, when each process is loaded and started, it is assigned all the memory it is expected to require; it cannot be loaded until sufficient memory is available. The process keeps all its memory throughout its lifetime but cannot obtain more. Static allocation is simple to manage but does not allow effective sharing of memory in a multiprogrammed system.

For more efficient memory usage, a **dynamic allocation** strategy is required. With this approach, each process is permitted to request additional memory as needed during execution, and is expected to release memory it no longer needs. The operating system is presented with an unpredictable sequence of **allocate** and **free** requests to assign and release individual blocks of memory. The requested blocks may vary widely in size. Usually, each request must be filled by a single contiguous region to be made available in the virtual address space of the requesting process.

Early Environments

As late as the mid-sixties, the size of the memory to be shared by all users of a system was often only 512K bytes to 1 megabyte, even on large computers. The cost of such amounts of memory was often in the hundreds of thousands of dollars. Management of this resource included allocation to a particular process, placement and loading of programs, protection of memory areas (if possible), and freeing of memory upon termination of a process. Since the resource was so expensive, efficient utilization of memory was extremely important.

Most early multiprogramming operating systems only allowed a process to be allocated one contiguous block in memory. Because of this, we shall assume use of static memory allocation for the remainder of this section, as we present strategies for an OS's definition and tracking of available memory to be allocated for loading a process.

Defining Memory Available for Allocation

Obviously, only a fixed amount of (physical) memory is available for allocation to processes by an operating system. An OS can use two strategies for defining how many and what size memory blocks can be assigned to processes being loaded:

- **static memory area definition,** in which the number of blocks and the size of each block is defined when the operating system is loaded (or perhaps when it was generated). The number of blocks available for loading processes does not change once the OS loads.

- **dynamic memory area definition,** in which the OS determines the number of blocks and the size of blocks upon servicing a request for memory allocation for loading a process. The current state of memory—both allocated and free—determines whether a block can be defined and allocated and where it is located. After the operating system is loaded, free memory is viewed as a "pool" in which memory blocks can be defined for allocation to a process to be loaded.

We shall refer to memory blocks defined and allocated in a static memory area definition environment as **fixed partitions,** or simply **partitions.** We shall refer to memory blocks defined and allocated to processes in a dynamic memory area definition environment as **regions.**

Assuming a multiprogramming operating system uses static allocation and either static or dynamic memory area definition, several possibilities exist for loading programs into memory:

- Several processes with a fixed maximum number of processes can share memory, each being allocated the *same amount of space* using statically-defined *fixed partitions.*

- Several processes with a fixed maximum number of processes can share memory, each being allocated *different amounts of space* using statically-defined *fixed partitions*.

- Several processes with the maximum number of processes being determined by the "state of the system" can share memory, each being allocated *different amounts of space* using a variable number of variable-size *regions*.

Statically Defined Partitions

A fixed memory partition strategy divides all available space into a fixed number of partitions. This strategy is common in real-time systems because a fixed number of real-time processes are usually run in such environments. The partitions do not have to be all the same size, but each has a fixed size established when the OS is first loaded and initialized. In some early systems, each program had to be written to run in a specific partition; it could run in no other. More powerful systems included methods for program relocation (to be discussed below). These methods allowed programs to run in any partition large enough to hold them.

Figure 10–4 illustrates how memory is partitioned in a fixed partition system. In this example, five partitions allow up to five processes to execute concurrently. Memory allocated to a process which is not needed by that process is wasted. Also, if no programs can fit in the smaller partitions, they are not used.

The use of fixed partitions greatly simplifies memory management. The operating system only has to keep track of whether a partition is free or allocated, and update its data structures after allocation to reflect the process using the partition.

Disadvantages of fixed partitions include the fact that the number of processes that can run is fixed, and unused memory at the end of each partition is wasted. Thus, the very strategy used to partition memory actually wastes a good portion of it because not all processes can use all the memory available in the partitions assigned to them.

Dynamically Defined Regions

In a strategy allowing the dynamic definition of a variable number of variable-size memory regions, each region is defined at the size required and allocated by the operating system as needed. The number of concurrent processes becomes variable depending on the number of regions available at a given time. This strategy is illustrated in Figure 10–5. Control blocks are used to

Figure 10–4 A Fixed Partition Environment

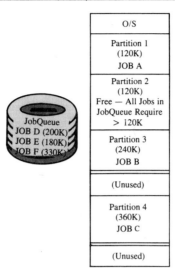

keep track of regions allocated to processes, and of free memory. Unlike the control blocks required for fixed partitions, which remain fixed in number, these control blocks must be created dynamically by the operating system.

Figure 10–5 A Variable Partition Environment

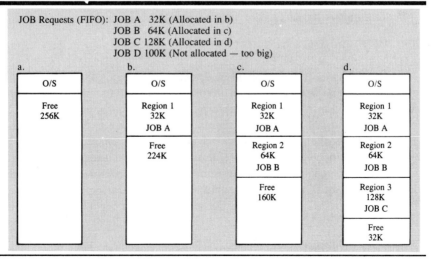

A dynamically defined region strategy is a cross between the static and dynamic methods. From the viewpoint of an individual process, the allocation is static. The space assigned to each process is determined when the process starts, and does not change until the process completes. However, the OS must take a dynamic viewpoint, as it deals with many processes of different sizes that must start and complete at unpredictable times. Thus, this method includes many of the problems of the full dynamic allocation to be discussed in the next section.

Figure 10–6 shows the dynamic allocation of memory regions to different processes over a period of time. Initially there are 360K bytes of memory free. A process P1 requiring 120K is selected for execution, as shown in the figure. Then a process P2 requests a 60K region and begins execution. Process P3, requiring 120K, is loaded and executed, leaving a 60K block remaining. The next process to be executed, P4, requires 120K of memory and must wait. Process P2 terminates and 60K bytes are freed. There are now 120K bytes of free memory, but it is not contiguous, so process P4 still must wait. This illustrates a major problem that can occur in dynamic region definition and subsequent allocation: the problem of **fragmentation,** a term describing the gradual division of free memory into many separate small sections that are not large enough to meet the needs of most processes waiting to be loaded. Fragmentation may also be used to describe the wasted space (that which is allocated to a process, but is never used by the process) within a fixed memory partition.

10.4 DYNAMIC ALLOCATION

Operations and Data Structures

The principal operations involved in dynamic memory allocation are *allocate* and *free*. These operations, each invoked by a system call at the program interface, form the basis of a dynamic memory management strategy called **heap management.** Available memory is viewed as a collection of blocks of random sizes that will be allocated and freed in an unpredictable order. Dynamic heap management is a useful programming strategy that is discussed in many texts on advanced programming and data structures. Here we review some basic concepts and place the subject in an operating system context.

The *allocate* call presents the OS with a request for a specific amount of memory. Usually there is no requirement that the allocated memory be in a specific place, but it *is* necessary that it be contiguous. The OS must locate a suitable region of memory and make it available in the address space of the

Figure 10–6 Fragmentation in Variable Space Allocation

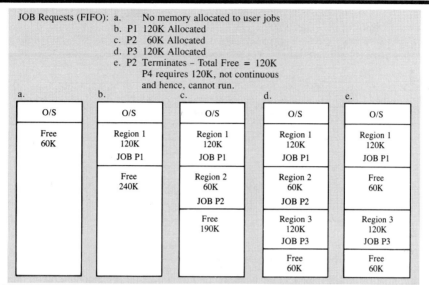

JOB Requests (FIFO): a.   No memory allocated to user jobs
b. P1 120K Allocated
c. P2 60K Allocated
d. P3 120K Allocated
e. P2 Terminates – Total Free = 120K
P4 requires 120K, not continuous
and hence, cannot run.

a.	b.	c.	d.	e.
O/S	O/S	O/S	O/S	O/S
Free 60K	Region 1 120K JOB P1	Region 1 120K JOB P1	Region 1 120K JOB P1	Region 1 120K JOB P1
	Free 240K	Region 2 60K JOB P2	Region 2 60K JOB P2	Free 60K
		Free 190K	Region 3 120K JOB P3	Region 3 120K JOB P3
			Free 60K	Free 60K

requesting process. If no suitable region is available, the process must wait until the request can be fulfilled.

The *free* operation is used by a process to release blocks no longer needed. Usually each allocated block must be freed in its entirety. The operating system must reclaim the freed blocks and make them usable for later allocation requests. Any remaining unfreed space belonging to a process is reclaimed when that process terminates.

Memory Control Blocks. Just as processes are represented by process control blocks, blocks of memory, whether allocated or free, are described by **memory control blocks (MCBs).** Such control blocks are given different names by different operating systems. For the sake of example, we will call control blocks representing free memory **free memory control blocks (FMCBs).** Those representing allocated storage will be called **allocated memory control blocks (AMCBs).** Free memory space is then represented by a linked list of FMCBs usually maintained in one (or both) of two orders: by decreasing size, and/or by increasing memory address.

FMCBs and AMCBs may be stored in a system control block area that is separate and protected, similar to PCBs. Alternately, each may be a part of the corresponding storage block itself, most conveniently placed as a header at the beginning of the block. This approach neatly solves the problem of allocating the control blocks, since space is always available in each distinct storage block. This method of organizing FMCBs and AMCBs is illustrated in Figure 10–7.

Figure 10–7   Memory Control Blocks

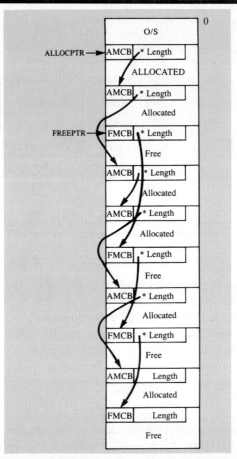

A method devised by Knuth [1973], called the **boundary tag** method, places at the end of each storage block an additional control block that contains the size of the block and an indication of whether the block is free or allocated. A similar indication of whether the block is free or allocated is placed in the beginning of the storage block, along with the size and appropriate pointers to the next and previous FMCBs. This method provides some slight simplifications in combining adjacent blocks as they are freed because adjacent blocks can be easily checked to see if they are allocated or free by simply checking these boundary tags (which are physically located immediately before and after a block of memory being freed).

Bit Maps. Another approach to keeping track of free and allocated memory is the use of **bit maps.** This method is suitable when memory is considered to be partitioned into blocks of equal, fixed size. Each block is represented by a bit, and the value of the bit indicates whether the block is free or allocated (0 means free, 1 means allocated). Allocation of memory is done in multiples of these fixed-size blocks. Figure 10–8 illustrates this representation of free and allocated blocks of memory. The block size is assumed to be 1K bytes. The first three bits in the map indicate that the first 3 blocks are allocated to PROCESS1, while the fourth and fifth bits of the map indicate that the fourth and fifth blocks of memory are free, and so on. Note that the bit map does not identify what process each block is assigned to; it only "knows" the units are allocated. The address and size of the memory allocated must be kept in a PCB so that when a process terminates, the appropriate bits in the bit map can be set back to zero to indicate these memory units are now free.

Figure 10–8   Memory Management Using Bit Maps

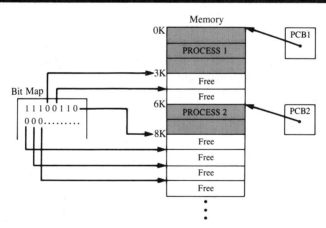

Allocation Strategies

Any memory management system supporting dynamic allocation of variable-size blocks must include a strategy for choosing the locations to be allocated in response to each request. If several distinct free memory blocks are large enough to fulfill the request, which of them should be chosen, and how should memory be divided to perform the allocation? Several strategies can be used to choose a suitable block. Each has certain advantages and disadvantages. We will discuss each of these strategies in the following sections.

First-fit. The first allocation strategy to be considered is called **first-fit.** We have already seen this strategy in the example of Figure 10–6. The first-fit method examines each FMCB starting from the beginning of the list (usually the lowest address), and selects the *first* one large enough to fulfill the request. Generally, the selected block is then divided into two parts. A portion large enough to fulfill the request is allocated; the remainder is returned to the FMCB. The mechanism for dividing blocks is considered in more detail below.

The first-fit strategy is appealing because it is simple and fast. However, it will often fulfill a small request from a large area, leading to the rapid breakdown of large blocks. When a larger area is later required, it may not be available as a contiguous block. Tests by Knuth [1975] indicate that there is a tendency for small, rather useless blocks to collect at the front of the list because all requests begin searching at the front of the list. Larger blocks will generally be found near the end of the list.

Next-fit. A variation of the first-fit strategy is called **next-fit, or first-fit-with-roving-pointer.** This strategy is similar to first-fit except that it begins each search where the previous search ended (that is, the place where the last block was allocated). A "roving pointer" to the list is maintained to remember where to begin the next search. The list is treated as a circular list, so the pointer returns to the beginning after the last FMCB is examined. If the pointer returns to the place where it began, the request cannot be fulfilled. This strategy is illustrated in Figure 10–9.

The next-fit strategy eliminates some of the problems of the first-fit strategy because small blocks do not tend to collect at the beginning of the list. The memory is used more evenly. However, large blocks do not tend to remain at the end of the list, and this strategy may be less likely to keep very large blocks available when needed.

Best-fit. Neither strategy discussed above considers the size of the block selected. The **best-fit** strategy, by contrast, examines *all* free blocks and chooses the one whose size most closely matches the request. This requires a search for the one best-fitting block; this search can be much more efficient if the FMCBs are linked together in order of size.

The best-fit strategy is attractive because it wastes the smallest amount of memory for each allocation. However, the leftover portions from each block tend to be very small and therefore probably useless. The best-fit strategy is illustrated in Figure 10–10.

Figure 10–9 The Next-fit Allocation Strategy

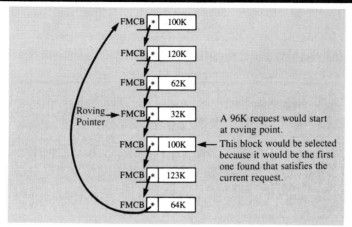

Figure 10–10 The Best-fit Allocation Strategy

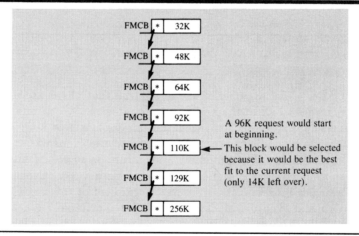

Worst-fit.   A **worst-fit** strategy selects the block that yields the largest remainder after it is divided. In other words, it always allocates from the largest block available. To support this method, the FMCBs should be linked in descending order by size. The worst-fit strategy is depicted in Figure 10–11.

While this strategy may seem foolish, it does have the advantage of producing leftovers that are likely to be large enough to still be useful. However, the largest blocks always get consumed first, and large blocks will probably not be available when required.

Figure 10–11 The Worst-fit Allocation Strategy

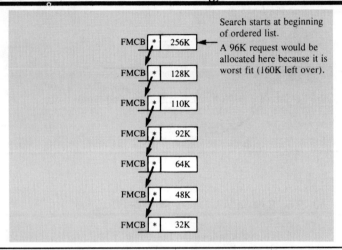

Making a Choice. The arguments above suggest that there are advantages and disadvantages to all of these allocation strategies. Which one should be chosen? A useful measure of an allocation strategy is how long it takes to *block*—that is, to be unable to meet a request because of insufficient memory available in one piece. Unfortunately, the future sequence of allocate and free operations is unknown, and sequences can be devised to make any one of these strategies into winners or losers. Regardless of the strategy chosen, fragmentation and eventual blockage are almost inevitable. When blockage does occur, it must be resolved by some type of drastic action (Two possible solutions, swapping and compaction, are discussed in the last section of this chapter).

The behavior of actual systems has been studied extensively for various allocation strategies. These studies tend to show that the two first-fit strategies, and the best-fit strategy, have about equal track records for postponing blockage in general-purpose applications. Because first-fit is the simplest to implement, it is most often chosen, but next-fit and best-fit are frequently used as well.

Dividing Free Blocks

As previously noted, the free block chosen for an allocation request will usually be larger than required; as a result, the block is normally split into two parts: one to be allocated, and a remainder to be returned to the free list. If the remainder block is very small, however, it may be of little use as an independent free block. Since such a block can be useful only when it is rejoined to a neighbor, the memory manager may choose not to split the block if the remainder is less than some minimum size. Instead, the original block is kept intact, and the extra space is unused temporarily until the block is released. When a *free* operation is performed on the block, the entire block rejoins the free list. This approach may be especially desirable with a best fit strategy, since remainder blocks tend to be very small.

Still another strategy may be to limit the ways in which blocks can be divided. In the well-known **buddy system,** for example, each block must be used intact or divided exactly in half. If a block is divided, the two halves are considered "buddies." A free block may combine only with its buddy to form a larger block.

Recovering Memory Blocks After Use

A heap manager relies on the use of *free* operations by programs to return storage blocks to the system when they are no longer needed. These blocks must then be returned to the free list in a way that makes them as useful as possible for future allocations. Freeing memory could be as simple as removing the block's MCB from the allocated list and adding it to the free list. However, you should take an important additional step to make these blocks as useful as possible. That step is to recognize when blocks of memory in the free list are adjacent to each other, and combine them into a single larger block. Two steps in effectively combining blocks are to:

1. recognize when a newly freed block is adjacent to other free blocks on either side
2. merge the block with either or both adjacent neighbors, forming a single new block with a single FMCB

If the linked list of free memory blocks is ordered by increasing memory address, then it is possible to determine when adjacent blocks are being freed by computing the beginning of the next block from the current FMCB and checking to see if the next FMCB points to that address. The boundary tag method also makes adjacent free blocks easy to detect.

If the FMCBs are organized as a list, it is a simple matter to remove a sequence from the list and replace it with a single new one. The new control block must describe the newly expanded memory block that previously was represented by two or three MCBs.

Performance Considerations

The object of an effective memory manager is to perform allocate and free operations in a manner that is fast and reliable and makes the most effective use of all available storage. The allocation strategies discussed are reasonably fast and economical of storage. Best-fit is slower if a search is required, but can be made quite fast if FMCBs are linked in order by size.

Besides performing both allocate and free operations efficiently, the memory manager must also work to avoid fragmentation and blockage. This art can be accomplished only by a judicious choice of control block forms and linking strategies, allocation strategies, and methods for dividing and combining blocks. Although the problems are old, new strategies are still being devised. For example, a method called "fast fits" is reported by Stephenson [1983]. This method combines FMCBs in a special tree structure rather than linear lists, providing some of the speed advantages of the buddy system without a similar amount of wasted space.

10.5 RELOCATION METHODS

Most multiprogramming operating systems and many single-user operating systems allow programs to be loaded into memory areas that may differ on each execution or may not have been determined at the time the program was written. Because a program contains references to memory locations in both its instructions and its data, correct operation may require that those references be adjusted to reflect the actual locations being used. The process of adjusting a program so it can run at the memory locations in which it is loaded is called **relocation.** If relocation is performed at the time a program is loaded or before, it is called **static relocation.** If it can be achieved after the program has been loaded and begun execution, we call it **dynamic relocation.** Relocation may be achieved by either software or hardware methods.

Relocation by Software

Programs may be relocated by software means if you can determine which references should be changed and in what way when the actual memory addresses are known. In order to identify these references, the object file produced by compilers or assemblers may include a **relocation dictionary** which identifies all instructions and addresses that may need to be modified depending on where the program is loaded. This object file is then converted to an executable file by a **relocating linker,** or processed when loaded into memory by a **relocating loader.** This relocating software makes adjustments to the appropriate memory references as identified by the relocation dictionary so that they correspond to the actual locations in (virtual) memory. The translation is illustrated in Figure 10–12.

Figure 10–12 Program Relocation by a Relocating Loader

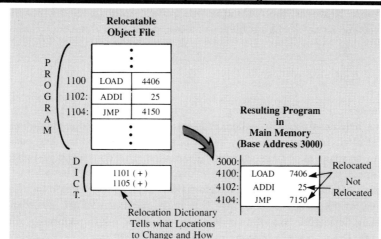

Relocating software can be time consuming to use, requiring significant extra information to be maintained in the object files. Since the relocation information is not loaded into memory with the program, no further relocation is possible once the program has been loaded. Thus, this strategy is able to provide only static, not dynamic, relocation. To achieve dynamic relocation and limit the other problems cited, some type of hardware assistance is required, as described below.

Based Addressing

One type of hardware assistance for relocation, provided by architectures such as the IBM S/360, is **based addressing.** In this method, a **base register** is maintained to represent the first, or base address for the program. For each address reference in the machine instructions of the program which specifies the use of based addressing, the effective address is formed by adding the contents of the specified base register to the value in the address field (the displacement). This mechanism is further explained in Appendix A. Relocation can be achieved with base addressing by loading this base register with the actual starting address of the program. If it is necessary to move the program at a later time, the base register may be changed to reflect the new location.

The effectiveness of base addressing in the S/360 was somewhat reduced because instructions could only reference 4K bytes of memory at one time; thus, each 4K region required a separate base register. Note also that based addressing requires that each instruction specify use of the correct base register, and the technique is of no help in relocating address constants such as pointers. However, the technique was quite helpful in the 360 environment in alleviating some of the problems of both static and dynamic relocation.

Relative Addressing

A variation on based addressing, exemplified by the PDP-11, is the use of **relative addressing,** also called **PC-relative addressing**; this mechanism, also detailed in Appendix A, is essentially based addressing using the program counter as a base register. Displacements contained in instructions which specify relative addressing are displacements from the address of the instruction itself, and dynamic relocation can be performed without the necessity of explicitly modifying the base register. Just as with based addressing, effective use of this strategy requires a programming discipline to specify the correct addressing technique for all memory references; this discipline is referred to as **position-independent coding.**

Relocation Registers

As an improvement upon the base register concept, some computer systems have a **relocation register** that is *always* added to every instruction address or data address before the instruction or data is fetched by the CPU. Unlike the base register, the relocation register is used uniformly for all memory references, and need not be specified by each instruction. Such a register greatly simplifies relocation. In this case, programs that are designed to start at location 0 can be relocated to any address so long as this relocation register contains the address at which the program is loaded. In such systems, the relocation register contents for each process must be saved and restored via the PCB on a context switch. Figure 10–13 illustrates the use of a relocation register.

Figure 10–13 Use of A Relocation Register for Dynamic Relocation

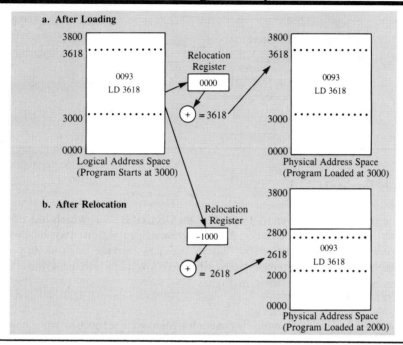

10.6 MEMORY PROTECTION

The object of memory protection is to prevent processes from accessing memory that was not allocated for their use. Effective memory protection is impossible without hardware support.

In the simplest operating systems, as we have seen, memory is divided into two contiguous regions, one for the OS and one for the program. Some computers provide a simple means of checking if a user program reference is in the portion of memory reserved for the OS. This may be done by establishing a **fence address** beyond which any memory references will cause a trap. This fence address could be a fixed value, but it would be difficult to choose the value correctly. If it were too large, unused memory would remain beyond the fence, inaccessible to applications; if too small, not all of the operating system would be protected. An improved solution is a **fence register**, which can be set when the operating system is initialized (that is, when the resident monitor is loaded). The use of a fence register to identify the boundary between the user program and the resident monitor is illustrated in Figure 10–14. A fence may also be called a **boundary,** and a fence register a **boundary register.**

Figure 10–14 Simple Protection using a Fence Register

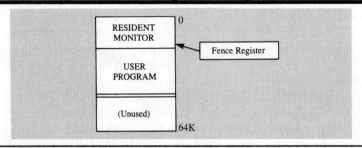

Bounds Registers

A fence register is insufficient to protect an OS like RT-11, which has portions in both high and low memory. A more general protection may be provided by a pair of **bounds registers**. These registers provide both an upper and a lower bound on the memory accessible to an application program. Use of bounds registers is illustrated in Figure 10–15.

Figure 10–15 Use of Bounds Registers for Memory Protection

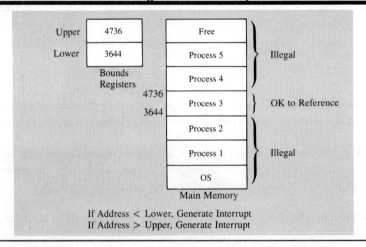

Base and Limit Registers

The use of a **limit register** in conjunction with a base register is another technique for providing memory protection. In this scheme, a variation of based addressing, the limit register represents the largest displacement that can be used. The displacement in each address field is checked to ensure it is within this range. If it is, the value in the base register is added to the displacement to dynamically relocate the reference (see Figure 10–16).

Figure 10–16 Use of Base and Limit Registers for Memory Protection

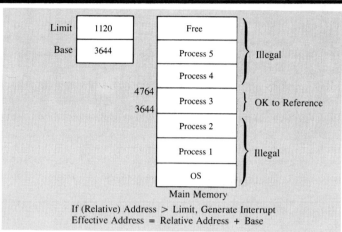

If (Relative) Address > Limit, Generate Interrupt
Effective Address = Relative Address + Base

Protection Keys

The final protection mechanism we will discuss is the use of **protection keys.** With this mechanism, used in the IBM S/360 architecture, each 4K-byte block in memory is assigned a protection key value between 0 and 15. In addition, selected blocks may be marked as "read only." Each process is also assigned a protection key. When a process is selected to run, its key is loaded into a special register. Any attempt to access a block of memory whose protection key does not match the one currently in effect would result in a protection key violation interrupt, and the program would be aborted (see Figure 10–17). Key 0 was assigned to the operating system; if this key was loaded into the register, protection was effectively disabled. Note that this mechanism limited the 360 to 15 different protected regions, and that protection could be specified only in units of 4K bytes.

While many models of the 360 computer supported memory read protection, OS/360 did not make use of this protection. It only guarded against attempts to write to areas of memory not assigned to a process. Hence, processes could read any other area of memory desired, including sections of the operating system and other areas in use by other processes. Obviously, security in these early systems fell short of the type of security needed today.

Figure 10–17 Use of Protection Keys for Memory Protection

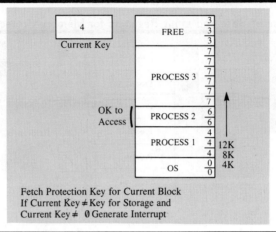

10.7 OTHER ISSUES

Overlays

Early single-user systems had limited memory available, often less than 64K bytes. Execution of larger programs on such systems could be achieved only by dividing the program into a series of **overlays.** Each overlay was a program unit, selected so that not all of them were required to be present in memory at the same time; overlays that did not need to be in memory together were assigned to the same region of memory, termed an **overlay segment.** Any overlay segment to be shared by several programs at different instances in time had to be large enough to hold the largest overlay in the group. Proper assignment of overlays and segments usually required assistance from compilers and linkers.

To manage the loading of overlays, each program using this technique had to include a control routine called an **overlay supervisor** which remained in memory at all times. This supervisor was added to the program by the compiler or linker. When a program attempted to reference procedures or data in an overlay that was not currently loaded, the overlay supervisor was invoked to fetch the required unit and load it into the specified overlay segment. Any previously loaded overlay in that segment was destroyed (overlaid) by the new one. The use of overlays is illustrated in Figure 10–18.

The overhead of loading overlays might seem high, but this technique allowed programs to run in systems with limited memory, which could not have run if all modules had to reside in memory at the same time. Overlay capability is still available in many systems today, in particular on many microcomputers. However, it is no longer commonly used because memory is now relatively inexpensive and not nearly so limited in size.

Figure 10–18   Use of Overlays to Reduce Program Size

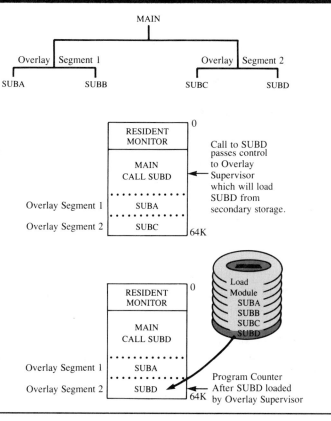

Swapping

For a variety of reasons you may need to remove portions of programs and their data from the main memory before they are complete, with the expectation that they will finish at a later time. The information so removed is placed on secondary storage until the time comes to return it to main memory. This strategy, called **swapping,** was introduced in Chapter 6.

Swapping may be desired for a number of reasons:

- to remove a process that has been suspended by the medium-term scheduler

- to increase free memory if an allocation has been blocked

- to remove a process that is waiting for resources

- to prepare a process for movement to a new location, such as during compaction (see below) or when its size is to be increased

Swapping of programs and data can be an effective management tool. However, each swap must be scheduled and can be time consuming. This strategy adds overhead that can reduce the frequency of process switching allowed.

To provide space for storage of swapped process, an area must be reserved on a fast storage device, such as a disk. You can think of the process of reading and writing swapped data as a special case of file creation and management (discussed in Chapter 12).

Compaction

The collection of free space from multiple non-contiguous blocks into one large free block in a system's memory is called **compaction.** This process is depicted in Figure 10–19. Systems with no relocation register cannot use compaction (even if they support based addressing), because there is no way to ensure dynamic correction of all address constants, including those contained in registers.

Systems with relocation registers, however, merely need to adjust the relocation register contents for each process via the PCB. Storage compaction takes place periodically when used, and can adversely affect performance because all process dispatching must cease while it is taking place. Also, no I/O operations may be underway during compaction, because the data addresses being used for I/O would be changed.

Figure 10–19 Compaction of Storage

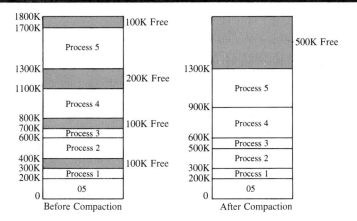

Before Compaction   After Compaction

10.8 SUMMARY

Memory management is the activity of managing the available memory for use by each process. It involves three main problems: allocation, the assignment of memory to processes as needed; relocation, the adjustment of programs and data to work in the assigned locations; and protection, the restriction of access by processes to memory locations which have been allocated to them.

In simple single-user systems, allocation may consist of giving each program free access to all memory, and relocation and protection are usually absent. Simple multiprogramming systems may use static allocation, giving each process all required memory when first loaded. Dynamic allocation uses memory more effectively but requires use of heap management techniques. These include use of memory control blocks or similar data structures, and choice of a basic strategy such as first-fit or best-fit. Methods for dividing and merging blocks are also needed, and mechanisms like boundary tag or buddy systems may be considered. Heap management strategies inevitably lead to fragmentation and eventual blockage; the only solution lies in hardware assisted strategies as discussed in Chapter 11.

Relocation may be performed by software or hardware. Often it is carried out by relocating loaders or linkers, aided by a relocation dictionary in the program's object code. Hardware relocation may be performed by mechanisms such as based addressing, relative addressing, or relocation registers.

Effective memory protection requires hardware mechanisms. Techniques that have been used for this purpose include fence registers, bounds registers, and protection keys.

Other issues of importance in the discussion of memory management include overlays, swapping, and compaction.

FOR FURTHER READING

Memory management is an important concern for many types of software systems, not only operating systems. For this reason many of its issues are dealt with in general programming and data structure texts. Thorough discussion is presented in the classic work by Knuth [1973]. A few other examples include Augenstein and Tenenbaum [1979], Wirth [1976], and Beidler [1982]. An OS text which provides a particularly effective discussion is Madnick and Donovan [1974, Ch. 3].

Some specialized strategies for allocation are presented by Beck [1982], Stephenson [1983], and Oldehoft and Allan [1985].

IMPORTANT TERMS

allocate
allocated memory control
    block (AMCB)
allocation
base register
based addressing
best-fit
bit map
boundary
boundary register
boundary tag
bounds register
buddy system
compaction
contiguous
core
dynamic allocation
dynamic memory area definition
dynamic relocation
fence address
fence register
first-fit
first-fit-with-roving-pointer
fixed partitions
fragmentation
free
free memory control block (FMCB)
heap management

limit register
logical address space
memory control block (MCB)
memory management
next-fit
overlay segment
overlay supervisor
overlay
partition
PC-relative addressing
physical memory
position-independent coding
protection
protection key
region
relative addressing
relocating linker
relocating loader
relocation
relocation dictionary
relocation register
static allocation
static memory area definition
static relocation
swapping
virtual address space
worst-fit

≡ REVIEW QUESTIONS ≡

1. Explain the difference between static and dynamic allocation of memory.

2. What are the advantages of using a bit map instead of memory control blocks to track free memory? The disadvantages?

3. How would a doubly-linked list be used in linking free memory control blocks? Are there any orderings in which the pointer to the previous FMCB might be useful?

4. When are fixed partitions defined for an operating system?

5. How does a relocation register aid in minimizing the impact of memory fragmentation problems?

6. What techniques can we use to simplify combining adjacent free blocks into one single free block when a block of memory is freed?

7. How do memory allocation strategies affect performance?

8. Explain the purpose of a relocating loader. Where is it likely to reside in a multiprogramming operating system? Why?

9. Explain the difference between systems using fixed partitions and (variable) regions.

10. How do overlay supervisors solve problems of limited physical memory size, such as those present in early computer systems?

11. A comprehensive memory management system must include solutions to three major problems.

    a. State and briefly define each problem.

    b. Explain how each problem can be addressed in a system which provides *no* hardware assistance.

12. For each of the four strategies considered for selecting a free block for allocation:

    a. Describe the pattern of free blocks that tends to accumulate in the memory.

    b. Give one argument in favor of that particular strategy.

13. In a variable-space memory management system, free blocks may be kept linked together in two distinct orders at the same time. Identify each order and state its purpose.

ASSIGNMENTS

1. Compare several techniques used for memory protection (without paging or segmentation). Explain their principal advantages and disadvantages.

2. If a process is selected for swapping to disk, can it be reloaded into a different location than that it occupied before it was swapped out? Explain what is necessary to make this possible.

3. What are some disadvantages of allocating AMCBs in the storage block itself?

4. Review the literature and appropriate manuals to determine the format of memory control blocks in an operating system of your choice. Explain the purpose of the information they contain.

5. Identify an operating system that managed memory with little or no assistance from the hardware and describe the techniques used.

PROJECT

This section describes a two-part programming project to implement some dynamic memory allocation mechanisms for a simple multiprogramming operating system. You should read the general description in this text in conjunction with the more specific descriptions given in your project manual. These mechanisms are important components of the multiprogramming executive (MPX) project described later in the text.

a. Add a set of commands to the command handler COMHAN to simulate a first-fit allocation scheme of a simulated area of memory. Use AMCBs and FMCBs to represent memory areas. The required commands are:

1. MEMORY LIST ALL: display a formatted list of all memory areas.

2. MEMORY LIST FREE: display a formatted list of all free memory areas.

3. MEMORY LIST ALLOC: display a formatted list of all allocated memory areas.

4. MEMORY FREE ALL: free all allocated memory.

5. MEMORY FREE *addr*: free the memory represented by the AMCB at the address identified by *addr*.

6. MEMORY ALLOCATE *size*: allocate a memory block of a size specified by *size*, displaying a return code indicating success or failure, and the address of the AMCB for the memory allocated.

b. Implement a set of procedures which provide dynamic memory allocation for loading processes. This support should include identification of a "pool" of free memory from which memory can be allocated for PCBs, regions for loading processes, and dynamic memory requests issued by a process. The following services are to be provided for this dynamic memory allocation:

1. `RC=Allocate(AMCB_address,memory_size)`: allocate a block of the specified size. Return the address of the associated AMCB in the parameter `AMCB_address`. RC is a return code which should receive a value of 0 if the allocation was successful, or -1 if an error occurred.

2. `RC=Free(AMCB_address)`: free the block indicated by `AMCB_address`, and provide an appropriate return code.

The memory management provided in this project is a low-level service that the operating system can use both for allocating memory for itself (for both PCBs and process load areas) and for processes making dynamic memory allocation requests.

Virtual
Memory
Management

Virtual Memory Management

11.1 INTRODUCTION

In our study of memory management in Chapter 10, we considered a number of basic methods for addressing the three primary objectives of allocation, relocation, and protection. Each problem was considered separately, and it was clear that in some cases no solution was possible without the introduction of new hardware mechanisms. Several such mechanisms were examined, especially to deal with problems of relocation and protection.

A more powerful approach to the problems of memory management is possible with the use of some additional hardware support. This hardware provides automatic **memory translation,** which in turn can support the concept known as **virtual memory.** For many years this type of hardware was sufficiently expensive that it was found only on the largest computing systems. Today these techniques are used on a broad range of computers, including many of the newer microprocessors.

Memory translation systems make use of a hardware subsystem that has the ability to translate each **virtual address** specified by a program, at the moment of reference, to a different **physical address** in the actual main memory. The virtual addresses may therefore be chosen for the convenience of the program, while the physical addresses are chosen for the convenience of the operating system. Unlike translation mechanisms, such as base registers and relative addressing, the automatic translation does not depend on information contained in the machine instructions of each program. Applied and enforced on all memory references, it is outside the control of application programs.

Because the virtual and physical addresses can be chosen independently, the problem of allocation can be greatly simplified. Relocation is effectively solved because virtual addresses can remain constant and predictable even if physical addresses must be changed. Finally, the translation mechanism can be combined with a protection mechanism so that illegal references can be detected and rejected while translation is underway.

A memory translation system can also deal with problems that occur when the amount of physical memory provided does not match the size of the virtual address space supported by the computer architecture. If the physical memory is larger, translation provides a way to make use of the full physical memory by sharing it among different processes.

If the physical main memory is smaller than the virtual address space, additional storage space may be available on a disk or other secondary storage device. The virtual memory concept can be used to hide the distinction between these two levels of storage, creating the illusion of a much larger main memory.

Nowhere among the components of an operating system is the close interaction between hardware and software as apparent as it is in memory translation. Because of the high speed and frequency with which translation must occur, parts of the mechanism must be supported by hardware. The OS must work together with this hardware, performing the jobs for which software economy and flexibility are more important. Together the two elements must cooperate to find the best total solution.

11.2 MEMORY TRANSLATION CONCEPTS

The detailed structure of a memory translation system is largely determined by the hardware, and varies significantly among different computer systems. However, most of these structures can be represented by the models discussed in this section.

A Model for Translation Systems

In a computer with memory translation hardware, each effective memory reference address determined by a program—after all visible adjustment such as adding the values of index and base registers—is considered to be a virtual address. This virtual address is subject to an additional automatic translation step before being presented to the main memory.

The model is illustrated in Figure 11–1. Bear in mind that this is a generalized model designed to illustrate the underlying concepts of memory translation; it is not intended to represent a practical implementation. More practical models will be presented later.

The figure shows a mapping between a virtual address space and a physical address space, defined by a **translation table.** This table specifies the physical address associated with each virtual address. The translation table may be located in fast registers or in the main memory itself. Its contents are established and maintained by the operating system.

are established and maintained by the operating system.

Figure 11–1 A Model of Memory Translation

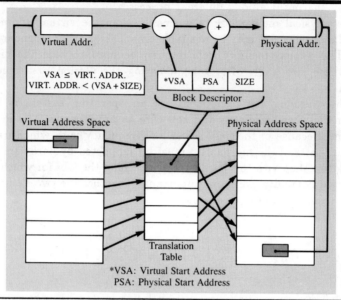

It is neither necessary nor practical to have an independent physical address for each and every virtual address. Instead, translations are specified for blocks of contiguous locations. The virtual address space is divided into a number of blocks, which may be of various sizes. Each block in the virtual space is assigned a block of the same size in the physical space. The positional relation between blocks in the physical memory does not have to match that of blocks in the virtual space.

Each entry in the table is a **block descriptor,** which specifies the location of a virtual block and the corresponding physical block. Each block is described by its **base address** (the first address in the block) and by its size. Since corresponding blocks have the same size, only one size value is needed. Thus each descriptor requires three fields: virtual base address, physical base address, and size.

To perform the translation on a given virtual address, the hardware must first locate the descriptor that describes the virtual block in which the given address is found. The correct descriptor is the one with the highest virtual base address not greater than the address to be translated. However, this base address plus the block size must be greater than the given address, or no translation is possible.

To find its position within the block, the virtual base address is then subtracted from the given virtual address. This value is added to the physical base address to form the final physical address to be presented to the memory.

An example of this translation is shown in Figure 11–2. This figure illustrates the translation of the virtual address 2000. The translation table includes a block descriptor with a virtual start address of 1000 and a size of 2500. This descriptor applies to virtual addresses from 1000 to 3500, which includes the one we are seeking to translate. The translation proceeds by subtracting from the original virtual address (2000) the virtual start address contained in the descriptor (1000), and adding the physical start address (3000). The result of this computation, 4000, is the physical address which corresponds to our original virtual address.

Figure 11–2 An Example of Memory Translation

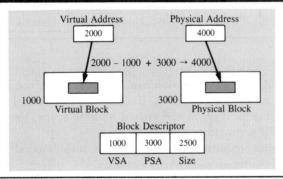

This model is extremely general. In this form it would be difficult to implement effectively in hardware. Because of this, constraints are imposed on the mapping, which make implementation simpler but limit the types of mapping that can be provided. We discuss more practical models in later sections.

Adding Protection to the Model

Since the hardware performs a translation step on every memory reference, it is reasonable for it to deal with the protection problem at the same time by checking each reference for legality. If a reference specifies a prohibited location or a type of access forbidden for that location, an interrupt can be generated to allow the operating system to deal with the violation. Methods for supporting protection during translation are shown in Figure 11–3.

Figure 11-3 A Memory Translation Model with Protection

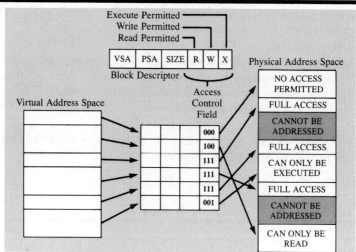

An important type of protection can be obtained by not including some areas of physical memory in the map. If a location in physical memory is not associated with *any* location in the virtual address space, there is no way it can be accessed by a program.

Most processes require far less than the total virtual address space provided by many computers. Virtual locations not currently required do not have to have physical locations assigned; they may simply be omitted from the map. If a program attempts to reference a virtual location not found in the map, an interrupt will result. Thus, the number of physical locations that must be included in the map used by each process is limited to those actually needed.

Limited access to certain blocks, such as allowing reading but not writing, can be controlled by including an **access control field** in each entry in the translation table. This field includes several bits, each representing a type of access. The types normally distinguished are *read, write,* and *execute.* If a bit in the access control field is zero, the corresponding type of access is not allowed for that block.

Segmentation

Memory management in a translation system can often be assisted by using a model, called the **segmentation model,** of the information stored by a process. This model views the information used by a process as divided into

a number of distinct units called **segments** as shown in Figure 11–4. Each
segment contains one or more program or data modules associated with the
process. For example, a main program, assorted procedures, various distinct
data structures, and a stack used by the hardware to manage procedure
calls, could all be treated as distinct segments. In a few systems (notably
MULTICS), files used by the process may be treated as segments as well.

Figure 11–4 Segmentation of Process Memory

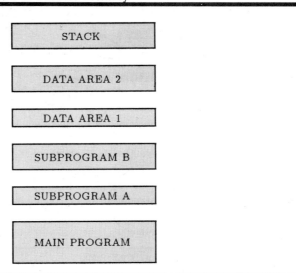

A program normally expects the information within a single segment to
be contiguous in the virtual address space. However, there is no requirement
that any two segments be contiguous. The boundaries of appropriate segments
are usually recorded in the object code files produced by compilers and linkers
so they can be recognized when a program is first loaded.

The segment model makes it possible to view each location as having a
two-part "address" consisting of a segment identifier and a location within
that segment. The segment identifier is usually represented internally as an
integer, giving rise to a two-level address space (see Figure 11–5). The first
level consists of segment identifiers to select a particular segment. The second
level includes a distinct virtual address space for each segment.

The concept of segments assists in memory management by allowing the
total memory for a process to be treated as a set of parts that, to some
degree, can be managed independently. Segmentation is especially useful in
a virtual memory environment because a segment turns out to be a useful
unit to transfer between main and secondary memory as a whole. However,

Figure 11–5   Two-level Addressing in a Segmented Memory

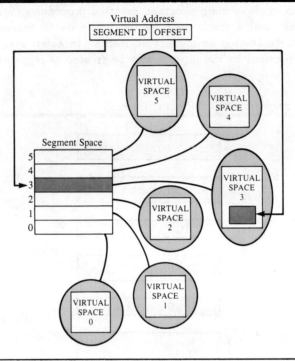

the concept can only be fully exploited if the hardware and operating system support a sufficient number of variable-size segments with a "large enough" maximum size. These conditions are not often fully met by segmentation mechanisms.

11.3 MAPPING REGISTERS

The model presented in the last section is a simple representation of the essential elements required in a translation mechanism. The simplest implementation of this model is based on a set of **mapping registers** within the CPU. Each register contains one entry for the translation table. This technique has been used in various models of the PDP-11 and several other architectures.

Hardware Structure

The translation model with mapping registers takes the form shown in Figure 11–6. The virtual address space is permanently divided into a small number of blocks of equal size. The number of blocks is limited by the number of registers available, since each block descriptor occupies one register. For concreteness, the example shown is drawn from PDP-11 implementations. There are eight registers for a total address space of 64K bytes, so each block is 8K in size.

Figure 11–6 Translation Using Mapping Registers

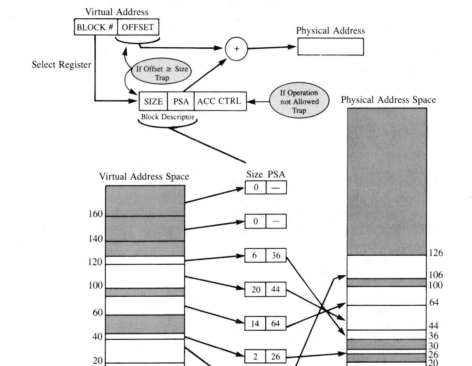

(All Addresses Octal × 1000₈)

Mapping Registers
(Access CTRL not Shown)

Each block is permanently associated with a specific register. Because the base address for each block is fixed, the block and register associated with any specific virtual address can be determined immediately. If the block size is a power of two, a specific set of high-order bits (in this case three) in the binary representation of the address can be interpreted as a block number.

Since the virtual block can be identified implicitly, its base address is not contained in the descriptor. The remaining fields from the model—physical base address, size, and access control—are included. Although the virtual space is partitioned so that one block begins on each 8K boundary, some blocks may be smaller than 8K. The size field allows smaller blocks to be specified when sufficient, allowing more efficient use of the physical memory.

To translate a virtual address, the hardware first separates the address into its block number and offset fields. The block number is used to select the mapping register containing the correct descriptor.

The size field of the descriptor is examined. If the offset of the virtual address is not less than this size, a trap occurs. The access control bits are checked similarly to ensure that the type of reference being attempted is valid.

If each of these tests is passed, the physical block address is added to the offset, producing the complete physical address to be used.

Mapping Registers

A particular set of contents for the mapping registers may be associated with each process in a multiprogramming environment. These values become part of the process context and are stored in its PCB. As each process is dispatched, its mapping table is loaded into the registers. When a process gives up the CPU, it is usually not necessary to save these registers because they will not have been changed.

When a process is admitted to the system or requests memory, the OS selects available physical memory to meet the request and sets up the mapping table. Large requests that span multiple blocks can be allocated in smaller, independent pieces. This breakdown generally makes the allocation job easier and slows down the fragmentation process. Fragmentation and eventual blockage are not eliminated, however; the physical blocks assigned may be of varying size.

In some architectures, such as the PDP-11, physical memory may often be larger than the virtual address space. In this case, mapping registers provide a method for sharing the memory among several distinct virtual spaces. Although each process is limited at any time by the size of the virtual space as determined by the CPU instruction set, a group of processes can effectively share a much larger space.

If a process is considered to be divided into segments, mapping registers can support this concept to some degree. Each segment is assigned to one or more consecutive virtual blocks. The last of these blocks is usually less than full size. Each new segment can begin in a new block. Even though this leaves gaps in the virtual address space, no physical memory is wasted. Because of the limited number of registers, however, only a few segments can be handled in this way.

An example of an OS memory manager designed for use with mapping registers is found in early versions of UNIX (later versions retain the same model but also include virtual memory). As shown earlier in Figure 3-6, each process is assumed to have a private virtual address space that consists of program, data and stack segments. Each segment is mapped by a separate group of mapping registers. If a process needs additional space, the entire process is swapped to the disk, and its space is reassigned with larger segments. The process is then dispatched with a new mapping table. As far as the process observes, more space has simply been added to the end of the appropriate segment.

11.4 PAGING

The mechanism of mapping registers greatly improves the support for the problems of memory management, but some dilemmas remain. The greatest problem is the continued need to partition the physical memory into variable-size blocks. Because of this, isolated regions of free memory can still develop that cannot be used to meet particular requests. This problem can be eliminated only if memory is always allocated in units of the same size.

With mapping registers, hardware limitations allow only a small number of blocks, each fairly large. Because we cannot afford to waste physical memory if only a small part of a block is needed, a variable-size approach is used. If blocks were much smaller, the waste would be acceptable, and every block, physical *and* virtual, could be the same size. A design strategy that uses this approach is called **paging.** In practice, paging is almost always combined with a full virtual memory mechanism, which includes automatic swapping, as we describe in later sections. To focus on the translation process itself, we will first consider a hypothetical *pure paging* system, in which all information is located in main memory. (We will treat more realistic examples later.)

Hardware Structure

Figure 11–7 illustrates memory translation with a paging system. The virtual address space is divided into fixed-size blocks, called **pages.** Each page is assigned a **page number.** Once again we may divide each virtual address into two parts: the page number and the offset within the page.

Figure 11–7 Memory Translation by Paging

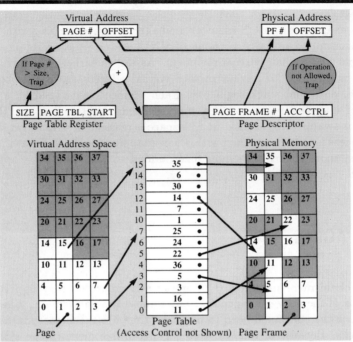

Page Table
(Access Control not Shown)

Typical page sizes may range from 512 bytes to about 4K bytes. The page size is always a power of two, which allows the division of the virtual address into page number and offset. Paged virtual address spaces are often quite large. The 32-bit address space of the VAX, spanning 4 billion bytes, is a good example. Since the VAX uses 512-byte pages, the full address space includes about 8 million pages. Clearly, no CPU can include enough mapping registers for all of these page descriptors.

Fortunately, most processes use only a small part of these vast address spaces, and the required number of pages is more modest. However, it can still be much too large for a mapping register approach, leaving us no choice but to store the mapping table in main memory. In a paging system, memory translation is directed by a table called a **page table,** stored in main memory, and including **page descriptors** for each page actually used in the virtual address space. The size of the page table is a form of overhead that limits how small the pages may reasonably be made.

In place of a collection of mapping registers, a single CPU register with two fields is required. This register, called the **page table register,** gives the start address and size of the current page table.

The physical memory is divided into fixed-size blocks of the same size as the pages. These blocks, called **page frames,** may be thought of as a place to put a page. Each page frame is identified by a **page frame number.**

The required content of a page descriptor is simpler than the block descriptor considered in the previous section. To locate the start of a page frame, only the page frame number is required, not the complete physical address. Because the size of all pages is fixed, the size need not appear in the descriptor. We are left with only two essential fields: page frame number and access control.

To translate a virtual address, the hardware must divide the address into page number and offset. You will find the description of the current page table in the page table register. The page number is first compared with the size field of that register. If it is too large, the reference is out of bounds; an interrupt will occur.

If the page reference is legal, the location of the descriptor is computed from the page number and the page table base. The descriptor is accessed, and the access control field is checked to ensure that the reference being attempted is legal. Finally, the page frame number found in the descriptor is combined with the offset from the virtual address, producing the final physical address.

The Paging Cache

If page tables are stored in main memory, it is clear that a problem of performance can arise. To complete every main memory access, whether reading or writing, a second access is required to read the page descriptor. Even though the exact location of the descriptor can be determined, the number of expected memory accesses is doubled. Since memory transfers often determine overall processing speed, it seems that this speed will be reduced by half.

Cutting computing speed in half is an unacceptable price for the advantages of paging. Fortunately, this speed penalty can be greatly reduced via hardware techniques. The solution strategy is to introduce a small set of registers to serve as a buffer for page descriptors in current use. We will call this buffer a **paging cache** (the name *TLB,* which stands for *Translation Lookaside Buffer,* is often used in IBM systems).

The operation of a paging system with a cache is illustrated in simplified form in Figure 11–8. Instead of reading all page descriptors from memory, the cache is first checked to see if the desired descriptor is in one of its registers. To speed the search process, the cache is organized as a **content-addressable memory.** This structure, also known as **associative memory,** allows simultaneous checking of every register to see if its contents match a certain key. If the cache contains the desired descriptor, memory access is avoided.

Figure 11–8 Use of a Paging Cache

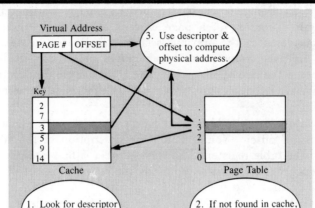

If the cache does not contain the descriptor, the page table is accessed normally. At the same time, the descriptor is now stored in a cache register, replacing an older one, on the assumption that it will be needed again. This assumption is generally correct; it is an illustration of the principle of locality, which we discuss in Section 11.7.

Although a paging cache is fairly small—typically a few hundred registers or less—it is likely that more than nine times out of ten, the desired descriptor will be found in the cache. We say that such a cache has a **hit rate** of over ninety percent, and the overall speed penalty associated with paging is reduced to less than ten percent, a much more acceptable figure.

The cache mechanism, implemented entirely in hardware, parallels the concept of virtual memory in many ways. Except for this it is of little direct concern to the OS. We will usually ignore the presence of the cache in our remaining discussions.

Using a Paging System

The procedures for managing process memories in a pure paging environment are similar to those discussed for mapping registers. It is possible to have a single page table for the entire system, as was done in OS/VS2 (Release 1). This is the easiest way to introduce some of the advantages of virtual memory to an OS originally designed without it. This characteristic is the basis for the more common name for this OS: Single Virtual Space (SVS). However, much greater benefits can be realized if a distinct virtual space and a distinct page table are maintained for each process. This strategy was provided through Release 2 of VS2, called MVS (for Multiple Virtual Space). Today, most large IBM systems use versions of MVS.

With a virtual space for each process, the corresponding page table is connected to the PCB and considered part of the context of the process. However, it is not necessary to copy the entire table when a new process is dispatched. All that is required is to load the page table register with a pointer to the start address of the correct table and the number of descriptors it contains.

An additional responsibility of the OS at the time a process is dispatched is to clear or invalidate the paging cache. A special instruction is usually provided for this purpose. If this step is not taken, invalid descriptors may be found in the cache, since they will be tagged with page numbers from a previous page table.

The OS assigns available physical memory to each new process as it is admitted or swapped in. The only requirement is that enough page frames be available for the number of pages in use by the process. All page frames are interchangeable.

With proper use, a paging system eliminates most of the problems of fragmentation discussed in the previous chapter. Because all allocation is in equal-sized units, all free pages are usable and no splitting will occur. Two types of storage overhead remain. One is the space wasted by allocating entire pages to each process; on the average this amounts to half a page. The other is the space required for the page tables themselves. These two forms of overhead are sometimes called internal fragmentation and external fragmentation, respectively.

The procedure described here, although reasonable, does not reflect the actual behavior of any real systems. In practice, paging is always combined with the additional mechanisms required to support full virtual memory, in which pages can be automatically swapped to and from secondary memory when there is not enough space in main memory. We consider the mechanisms required for this extension in the next section.

11.5 VIRTUAL MEMORY CONCEPTS

One-level Storage

In many OS environments, the main memory available is not sufficient to meet the full storage requirements of all active processes at once. Because of this problem, it may be necessary to systematically swap processes to and from a secondary storage device. While a few processes share the available memory, many other processes that are otherwise ready to run may be forced to wait.

In addition, the maximum virtual address spaces available in many newer architectures are extremely large, far larger than the physical memory that may actually be installed. It is possible to write programs that require more than the total physical memory available, even if they are the only programs being executed.

Both of these problems can be solved by a paging system that allows selected pages to be swapped to a secondary storage device when other pages are needed in main memory. With this approach it may be possible to keep more processes active, and even support processes whose needs exceed the total main memory, providing that each page can be made available in main memory as needed.

A mechanism that manages such swapping of pages automatically, without the awareness of user processes, is called a **virtual memory system.** As first introduced by ATLAS, such a system merges two levels of storage— main and secondary memory—into a unified whole, which is viewed by processes as a **one-level store.** This concept is depicted in Figure 11–9. The storage available to each process—a combination of main memory space and a much larger secondary memory space—is usually limited only by the maximum virtual address size of the computer.

Figure 11–9 One-Level Storage in a Virtual Memory System

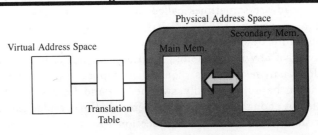

The secondary storage used in a virtual memory system may be a dedicated disk or drum, or a portion of a disk also used for file storage or other purposes. Effective management of a virtual memory system requires careful coordination of hardware and software mechanisms.

A virtual memory system makes use of page tables containing an extended form of page descriptor. The usual extensions consist of three new one-bit flags, as shown in Figure 11–10. Use of these descriptor flags, operated on by both hardware and software in a special way, is discussed in the following sections.

Figure 11–10 An Extended Page Descriptor for Virtual Memory

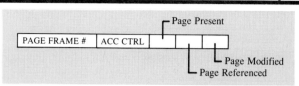

Address Translation

The process of address translation under a virtual memory system begins very much as in pure paging. If the page to be accessed is present in main memory, the pure paging procedure is followed. If the page is found to be missing, additional steps must be taken. Figure 11–11 illustrates the basic algorithm performed by the hardware.

The virtual address is first decoded into page number and offset. The page descriptor is initially sought in the paging cache. At the same time, the page table register is examined to locate the address of the current page table, and the descriptor address is computed. If the descriptor is not found in the cache, it is fetched from main memory.

Since not all pages are now resident in main memory, the hardware must determine if the desired page is resident. This is indicated by a flag bit in the page descriptor, called the **page present flag** (see Figure 11–10). The OS must arrange that this flag is set for all pages currently present in main memory, and cleared for all other pages.

If the page is present, translation is completed as described previously for pure paging. If the page is not present, however, it is necessary to locate its copy on the secondary memory and copy it into main memory so it can be used. This usually requires removing another page from main memory, since the memory is probably full. The total procedure in this case is too complex to be effectively implemented in hardware. Instead, when a missing page is detected, the hardware issues an interrupt, and the OS must take charge to supply the needed page.

Page Faults

The interrupt caused by the hardware when a missing page is detected is called a **page fault.** The page fault is a special kind of interrupt. The CPU can accept most interrupts only between instructions, although provisions

Figure 11–11   Address Translation in a Virtual Memory System

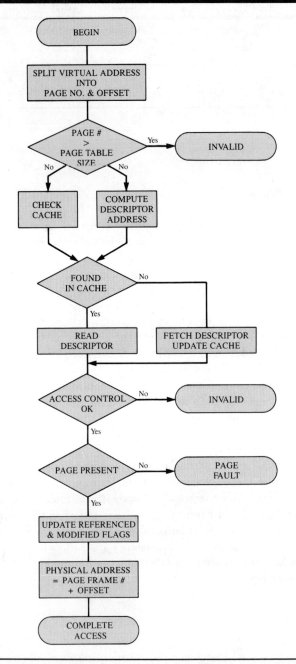

may be made for very long instructions, such as block moves. On the other hand, a page fault may need to be serviced *in the middle of an instruction.* What's more, a single instruction can cause more than one distinct page fault. Processing of a typical machine instruction involves several different memory accesses. The instruction must be fetched, data may be read into registers, and results may be stored. In addition, long data items and instructions may straddle page boundaries and be stored in part in two or more pages. Figure 11–12 shows a fairly extreme example of an instruction, the processing of which requires access to six distinct pages. Any or all of these steps could possibly cause page faults. In some architectures, single instructions can cause extensive data references, such as processing arrays or moving large blocks of memory. In this case, the number of faults could be even larger.

Figure 11–12 Six Page Faults in a Single Instruction

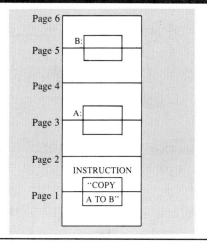

Because of the unique properties of page faults, it may be necessary for the hardware to provide special registers or other mechanisms to save the status of partially completed instructions when a fault occurs. A special return instruction may be used to resume processing from the exact point at which it occurred. Alternately, the CPU must analyze the instruction in some way before execution to determine if page faults will occur, or enable restarting by avoiding any irreversible changes until all memory accesses are complete.

When a page fault occurs, the OS must save the necessary status information and obtain the page from secondary storage. This involves locating the required page, making a page frame available (perhaps by swapping a page currently in memory), and loading the required page into main memory. The page table is then updated to reflect the new status of the affected pages, and processing is resumed from the point of interruption. This algorithm is illustrated in Figure 11-13.

Figure 11–13 Page Fault Processing

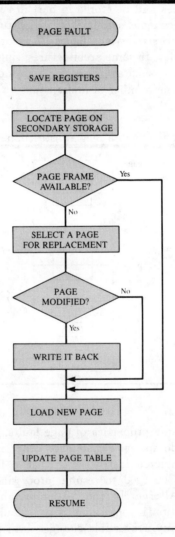

The OS must design its page fault processing carefully, recognizing the special properties of page faults and the extreme frequency with which they can occur. If faults are too frequent, or the time required to service them is too long, the performance of the OS can deteriorate rapidly. This condition is called **thrashing.** An OS in a thrashing state may spend the great majority of its time servicing page faults, leaving little time for useful work. This condition must be avoided in a practical system.

To prevent thrashing, it is necessary to design virtual memory algorithms and data structures with great care. The goals are both to limit the frequency of page faults and to ensure that, when faults do occur, the OS is prepared to respond by making the needed page available and resuming execution as soon as possible. Techniques to support this goal are considered in the next section.

11.6 VIRTUAL MEMORY MANAGEMENT

To develop a practical strategy for managing a virtual memory system, an OS is faced with three principal problems:

- The **fetch problem:** When should each page be loaded into the main memory?

- The **placement problem:** Where should pages be stored among the available page frames?

- The **replacement problem:** If pages must be removed from main memory, to make space for others, which pages should be removed?

We must choose effective strategies to address each of these problems. Other issues that we must consider include managing the storage of pages on secondary memory and scheduling processes in a multiprogramming environment to ensure that each active process has a reasonable amount of main memory.

In addressing these issues, the OS must work with the hardware structures that the computer makes available. It also must take care to minimize the amount of work that must be performed at the time each page fault occurs by scheduling preparatory work at convenient, idle times whenever possible.

Of the three problems cited, placement is the easiest to address. This is the problem of allocation, cast in a paging environment. Since all page frames are the same size, and the main memory is randomly accessed, all page frames are equivalent. There is no requirement that the pages of a process or segment retain a special ordering in physical memory. If page frames are available, any one will do.

The remaining problems, fetch and replacement, require more attention. The replacement problem, especially, is one that raises many difficulties, and the solutions chosen can have a profound effect on the performance of the total system.

11.7 THE PRINCIPLE OF LOCALITY

Most reasonable strategies for virtual memory management are based on certain expectations of the future pattern of page references to be exhibited by each process. The future behavior of a process is rarely known for certain; the best that can be hoped for is an educated guess. If we had no basis for such a guess, we would have to base our strategies on an arbitrary future; achieving good performance would be a matter of luck. In fetching pages, we might fetch many that were not needed; in removing pages, we might remove many that are just about to be referenced.

Fortunately, one principle of behavior, applicable to most processes, can provide, in the short term, the educated guess we seek. The rule is called the **principle of locality.** It can be stated as follows:

- Storage locations that have been recently referenced, and other locations near those recently referenced, are likely to be referenced again in the near future.

This principle tells us that the *recent* behavior of a process is a good indicator of its probable behavior in the *near* future. Note the emphasis on "recent" and "near." We do not claim to know anything from the behavior of a process five or ten minutes ago, or about its expected behavior five or ten minutes from now. Within a time span of a few milliseconds, however, the principle is quite useful.

Applied to a paging environment, locality tells us that pages recently referenced, and possibly others near them, are likely to be referenced again soon. This behavior was first demonstrated in studies by Belady [1966] at IBM. It has been observed repeatedly in many additional experiments.

Locality is also intuitively reasonable in most applications, especially if concepts of good program design have been followed. Instructions are fetched consecutively from memory locations in most cases. Software engineering principles, such as structured programming and modular design, help to ensure that programs spend time executing within procedures of limited size, and repeat compact loops. Finally, use of high-level data structures, such as arrays and records, leads to repeated systematic references to a limited region of data storage.

Locality does not perfectly describe the behavior of all processes at all times. Some programs have little locality; this is often true of those that manipulate very large data structures, such as artificial intelligence, database searching, very large matrix manipulation, or the like. Even well-behaved programs may have abrupt changes in locality, as discussed by Denning [1980]. Nevertheless, locality is a reasonable principle in most cases, and it serves as a cornerstone of most common strategies for virtual memory management.

11.8 FETCH STRATEGIES

The fetch problem addresses the question of *when* pages should be loaded into main memory. If a page fault occurs, a reference has been attempted to a page that is not in main memory. Clearly, it is then necessary to load the page immediately. If the reference to the page could be anticipated, it might also be possible to load pages in advance, having them ready when needed and preventing the occurrence of a fault when the page is actually referenced.

The practice of fetching pages only when needed is called **demand fetching.** Fetching pages in advance is referred to as **prepaging.** Any prepaging strategy is based on guesswork. If the right pages are loaded, page faults will be reduced. However, if pages are preloaded that will not actually be referenced for a long time, if ever, space will be taken up that is needed by other pages.

Many systems follow a pure demand fetch strategy. It is often observed that prepaging is about as likely to guess wrong as right, and does not significantly reduce the fault rate. There is one important exception: A process initially admitted to the system should be given an initial set of pages (typically about half its total requirements) in main memory. If this is not done, the new process will spend a great deal of time faulting on most references until a reasonable set of pages has been loaded.

In addition, if a process is returned to an active state after having been swapped out of memory, the pages it previously had loaded in main memory should normally be restored.

The principle of locality also suggests a form of prepaging known as **clustering,** in which several adjacent pages are loaded when a single page is referenced. Clustering is practiced, for example, by VMS. This strategy is chosen by VMS for two reasons. First, the page size is relatively small (512 bytes), so that nearby pages are likely to be included in the region of locality. Also, VMS uses shared storage devices for page swapping and file storage. Because of the great impact page transfers have on the performance of the file system, the reduction of disk traffic caused by transferring a full cluster at once is of high importance [Levy & Lipman 1982].

11.9 REPLACEMENT STRATEGIES

The choice of a strategy for page replacement is the central issue in most virtual memory management systems. The issue is to provide a method for choosing pages to remove from the main memory, which will try to avoid removing pages that will soon be needed again. The strategy chosen can have a profound effect on the performance of the entire system. The options for this strategy are driven to some degree by the available hardware mechanisms.

An Optimum Strategy

The best possible strategy for page replacement would be to remove pages that will never again be needed. If there are no unneeded pages, the next-best idea is to remove the page that will be unneeded for the longest time. These rules form an optimum replacement strategy, first proposed by Belady [1966].

The optimum strategy is of theoretical interest because other methods can be compared to it to evaluate their behavior. It is not a practical method itself, however, because the future sequence of page references is not known.

Least Recently Used Replacement

While we have no knowledge of the actual future behavior of our programs, we do have a rule that allows us to make an educated guess: the principle of locality. This principle suggests that pages in the neighborhood of recent references are *not* good choices for removal. Thus, we look for pages that have not had recent references. A straightforward strategy is the **least recently used**, or **LRU**, approach. This strategy tells us to remove the page that has been unused for the longest time.

The LRU strategy seems reasonable and has been shown to work well. To implement this approach, however, we must be able to maintain a record of the most recent reference for each page. This usually requires some help from the hardware. The OS cannot keep track of every page reference. Instead, the CPU must record each reference in the page descriptor.

One technique for doing this would be to reserve a field in each page descriptor, and require the hardware to record the current time of day (usually available to an accuracy of a few milliseconds) in the appropriate descriptor each time a page is referenced. The OS could then find the LRU page when needed by searching the page table for the lowest clock value.

But this method has disadvantages. The extra space required in each page descriptor is substantial, and the search time to find the lowest value is a high price to pay at every page fault. This overhead is not needed; experience has shown that a simpler mechanism works nearly as well. The simple mechanism is based on a single bit in each page descriptor, called the **page referenced bit** (see Figure 11–10). The hardware is required to set this bit only when a reference is made to the corresponding page.

The OS manages the page referenced bits to determine which pages are referenced during successive short time intervals. At the beginning of each interval, all of the reference bits are cleared. At the end of the interval, the bits are examined. Those pages whose bits are found to be set were referenced during that time interval. The scanning may be done at convenient times, perhaps every few hundred milliseconds. The reference information is used to order the pages in some way according to the number of time intervals since last reference. Although this approach provides only a coarse approximation to LRU replacement, it has been shown to work nearly as well in most situations. Because these methods do not always select the actual LRU page, they may be called **approximate LRU** methods. In the simplest case, we may distinguish only between pages that have been referenced in a single time interval and those that have not. The selection strategy then reduces to **not recently used (NRU)**.

Various techniques can be used by the OS to record the reference information. MVS maintains a counter for each page, which is incremented during each scan and cleared when the page is referenced. Pages that have not been referenced recently have high counter values. MULTICS uses the reference bits directly, distinguishing only pages that have been referenced in a single recent interval from those that have not.

A common technique is to maintain a small number of lists, ordered from "most recent" to "least recent," as shown in Figure 11–14. After each scan, all pages that were found to have been referenced are moved to the "most recent" list. All other pages are moved down one list, unless they are already in the "least recent" list. When a page frame is needed, one is selected from the "least recent" list.

Because pages are chosen from the "least recent" list for replacement, this list is often called the **available list.** In some systems, pages on the available list are considered no longer in use, and marked "not present" in the page table. This places them in a kind of limbo. A reference to such a page will cause a page fault, but if the page has not yet been replaced, it can be retrieved from the available list and returned to active duty. This technique is used to good advantage in VMS, as discussed in the next subsection.

Other Replacement Strategies

While some variation of LRU is the most common replacement strategy, other methods have been used. The first virtual memory system, ATLAS, employed

Figure 11–14 Page Lists to Manage Reference Information

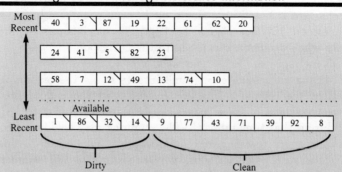

a more elaborate strategy. By keeping track of the last *two* references to each page, ATLAS watched for periodic references that might be caused by program loops. It then tried to keep pages in memory when the loop was about to repeat. In addition, the ATLAS strategy recognized when a page that was removed was needed again soon, and tried to protect this page from being removed too soon a second time. Because of this, the ATLAS strategy was called a "learning" program.

The ATLAS page replacement strategy worked quite well. However, later experiments showed that simpler LRU methods also work well. Because the ATLAS method was relatively complex, and not easily adapted to much larger memories (the ATLAS memory had only thirty-two page frames), it has not been repeated in other systems.

Observing only the most recent reference to each page does not take account of the frequency of page references. A page that has been heavily used may be a poor choice for removal, even if it has no very recent reference. Because of this, the **least frequently used (LFU)** strategy has been proposed; this would remove pages for which reference frequency has been lowest over an extended time interval. However, an efficient method for keeping track of the frequency of each page's use is not available, so this method has rarely been used.

A different approach must be used in computers that lack even a page referenced bit for recording recent references. The designers of the VAX, believing that its extremely large address space made it impractical to scan reference bits, did not include this bit. As a result, VMS can normally order its pages only by the one reference the OS knows about: the one at which it was first loaded into memory. This leads to a straight first-in, first-out (FIFO) strategy, in which pages that have been in memory the longest are chosen for replacement.

FIFO replacement alone cannot perform as well as LRU-based strategies.

Later references to resident pages are ignored, and pages that are used continuously will be periodically selected for removal. The FIFO technique is also subject to a curious anomaly which makes its behavior difficult to analyze: It is possible that, in some cases, increasing the size of main memory can lead to more, rather than fewer, page faults [Belady 1966].

VMS largely overcomes these problems by combining basic FIFO replacement with other techniques [Levy & Lipman 1982]. The most important technique is a large available list. Because pages in the available list are marked "not present" in the page table, references to these pages will cause a fault and be detected by the OS. Frequently used pages will often be detected in this manner and returned to the end of the list.

The designers of Berkeley UNIX on the VAX take this strategy a step further [Babaoglu & Joy 1982]. To obtain page reference information in the absence of a reference bit, *all* pages in the table are periodically marked "not present." The next reference to each page will cause a page fault. This technique is used by the OS to set a reference flag before allowing the reference to continue. Despite the seemingly great overhead of so many extra page faults, this technique has been shown to provide an effective simulation of hardware reference bits, allowing the OS to follow a standard LRU replacement strategy.

Handling Modified Pages

When a page is chosen for removal from main memory, the OS must ensure that an up-to-date copy is kept on secondary storage. This can be assured, of course, by writing each page to the storage device as it is removed. However, in many cases a copy of the page is already present on this device. Unless the page has been changed in some way in main memory, this writeback is unnecessary.

To determine the pages that have been changed in main memory, one final bit is required in the page descriptor (see Figure 11–10). This bit may be called the **page modified bit.** A page that has been modified is frequently referred to as *dirty,* so the page modified bit is also known as the **dirty bit.** The hardware sets the page modified bit whenever a store operation is performed on the associated page.

The OS initially clears the modified bit for each page when it is loaded into memory. If it is found to be set in the future, the page must be written back to the storage device. With this information the OS is able to write back only the pages that actually require it. Almost all virtual memory mechanisms (even the VAX) include a page modified bit.

When a modified page becomes a likely candidate for removal due to a lack of recent references, it may be a good idea to "clean" the page by writing it back at a convenient time, so this will not have to be done during page fault processing. Writeback may be managed by dividing the available list into two parts, dirty and clean. Modified pages reaching the available list are initially recorded as available-dirty. At this time they are scheduled for writeback. When the transfer completes, the modified bit is cleared and the page is moved to the available-clean list. Although this technique may occasionally write back a page that will be modified again, it ensures rapid page fault processing by maintaining a pool of clean available page frames.

The cost of replacing a modified page is greater than the cost of replacing an unmodified one. This fact can be used to influence the replacement strategy by trying to choose unmodified pages for removal whenever possible. Both recency of use and modification can be considered, with the best choice being an unmodified page that has not been referenced for a long time. Balancing these factors is handled in different ways by each OS. An example is provided by MULTICS, which makes use of a strategy called the **CLOCK algorithm** (a similar strategy is used by VM/370).

The MULTICS CLOCK algorithm is illustrated in Figure 11–15. All pages are organized in a single circular list that is scanned much like a clock hand moving around its dial. Each scan begins where the previous one stopped. Each page in the list may or may not be recently referenced, and may or may not be dirty. When a page frame is needed for replacement, a scan is made in search of a clean, not-referenced page. If any not-referenced but dirty pages are encountered, they are scheduled for cleaning so they will be available during future scans. If a full circle is made without finding a suitable page, then a less desirable page must be selected.

Figure 11–15 The MULTICS CLOCK Algorithm

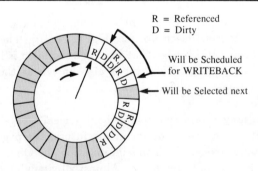

Dealing with Multiple Processes

The techniques for page replacement discussed so far would behave well in a single-process environment. However, most operating systems, especially those providing virtual memory, include multiple concurrent processes; these lead to significant new problems.

In a multiple-process OS that uses virtual memory most effectively, each process is provided with a private virtual address space, so each process has its own page table associated with its process control block. As each process is dispatched, the system page table register is set to point to the appropriate page table.

The principle of locality logically applies to each process separately. As each process obtains separate turns at using the CPU, its references can be predicted by its own behavior during the last turn, but not by the behavior of other processes that have run in the meantime.

A very serious problem arises if an LRU strategy is applied uniformly to all pages in a multiprogrammed system. When a process is not in the running state, all of its pages remain unreferenced while other processes run. A search for pages that have not been recently referenced will tend to choose pages from non-running processes. When a process is dispatched, it will often have few of its pages left in memory. An initial period of thrashing will occur until a reasonable number of pages is loaded.

By the time the process has recovered its active pages, it is likely that another process will be dispatched. Thus the cycle continues, and the page fault rate is unacceptably high. To prevent this raiding of pages from non-running processes, it is necessary to require that, in most cases, the needs of each process for new pages be met by removing pages belonging to the *same* process. By this technique, each process is confined to—and guaranteed—a limited portion of the space available in main memory.

A replacement strategy that considers all pages in the system equally for replacement is called a **global replacement strategy.** If pages are managed separately for each process, a **local replacement strategy** results. Some of the replacement techniques we have discussed so far can be adapted to local strategies. For example, VMS actually uses a separate FIFO queue for each process. In addition to this adaptation, some entirely different local strategies are possible.

Any local replacement strategy partitions the page frames in main memory among a number of competing processes, as illustrated by Figure 11–16. Frames not presently assigned to any process form a common available list. A local strategy is characterized by rules to determine how many page frames should be assigned to each process. This choice greatly affects the overall performance of the system. If it is too low, thrashing may occur as processes constantly require access to missing pages. If it is too high, the page fault rate will be low, but only a few processes can be simultaneously resident in main memory. Each process must be swapped frequently, and throughput and response times decrease. The set of pages that each process is permitted to have in main memory is called its **working set.**

Figure 11–16 Memory Partitioning for Local Replacement

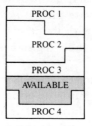

The appropriate working set for each process depends on the process characteristics. Clearly, large processes need more pages. A simple approach is to assign to each process a working set that is a fixed percentage of its total space allocation. A well-known rule of thumb states that the average process requires about half of its pages in main memory to avoid thrashing.

However, the actual needs of a process can vary with time even if the size of the process is unchanged. Often programs spend some time executing very limited sections of code and accessing only compact data structures. At other times their activity may cause them to reference many more pages. Because of this, the number of page frames allotted to each process should be individually adjustable. If a process has been observed to experience frequent page faults during a recent time interval, its page frame assignment should be increased. Conversely, if the fault rate has been low, this assignment can be reduced. As the number of frames assigned to each process continue to change, processes must also be swapped in and out of memory to suit the space available.

A more precise method to account for the variation in page needs for each process has been heavily studied by Denning [1980]. This method is called the **time-window working set.** In the time-window strategy, a record is kept of all pages referenced during a specific time interval of the immediate past. These pages form the instantaneous working set for the process. Whenever the time since a page reference exceeds the size of this time window, the page is removed from the set. The working set has a maximum size equal to the number of references in the chosen time interval, but its typical size is usually much smaller.

The time-window working set has attractive properties but is difficult to implement fully. Hardware mechanisms are required to keep track of the exact working set, much as special hardware is needed for exact LRU replacement. These mechanisms are becoming more cost-effective but have not yet appeared on widely-used architectures. However, approximations to this strategy are possible with traditional hardware and have been used in a few systems, including VMOS and CP-67.

11.10 MANAGING SECONDARY STORAGE

Pages not presently resident in main memory must be stored on a secondary storage device. The OS must maintain this database of non-resident pages so that page transfers between it and the main memory can proceed as rapidly as possible. This section discusses methods for maintaining pages on secondary storage.

The usual type of storage device used for paging is a high-speed disk. On large systems where the cost can be justified, head-per-track disks may be used for maximum performance. Small and medium-sized computers normally make use of the same moving-head devices on which their files are stored. Early virtual memory systems used dedicated paging drums. Such drums may still appear in a few mainframe environments, but most are being replaced with disks. (Characteristics of these storage device types are discussed in Appendix B.)

Page transfers place high demands on the devices used for storage. If these same devices are shared with other information, such as files, performance may be degraded. It is desirable to store pages on dedicated devices. In practice, however, devices often must be shared between paging and other applications. This situation requires care to reduce the volume of distinct I/O operations. This is an important reason why VMS makes use of clusters, because a full cluster can be transferred in a single operation.

MVS, although it operates in very large environments, also stores pages and files on the same device. However, MVS pages are distributed among multiple devices to limit the impact on each. Users are encouraged to reserve file space on paging devices for files that require only occasional access.

A straightforward way to assign page frames to a paging device would be to allocate a contiguous area for each virtual address space, having the maximum number of page frames required. This strategy is illustrated in Figure 11–17. Managing this space would be as simple as managing a contiguous file, and the proper location for any page could be determined by simple indexing. This method is not often used, however. One reason is that the potential maximum size of many virtual address spaces is very large, and the available secondary storage is limited.

A second reason has to do with the need to reduce the number of distinct transfers. At any time, a number of unrelated pages may be waiting for

Figure 11–17 Two Methods of Page Allocation on Secondary Storage

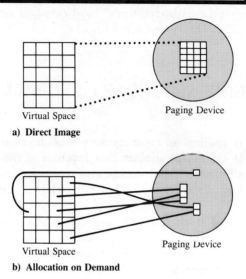

Virtual Space   Paging Device

a) Direct Image

Virtual Space   Paging Device

b) Allocation on Demand

transfer to the disk. If each page had to go to a distinct position depending on its identity, an individual transfer would be required for each. However, if space for each page is allocated as needed, a contiguous storage area could be chosen so that many waiting pages could be transferred at once.

This approach makes management of pages on disk more complex. You must keep a table of the current location of each page. Space must be allocated using a variable-space allocation strategy (except that groups of pages can be split, if necessary, at the cost of a slight performance reduction). In spite of the complexity, this is the method of choice for VMS, MVS, and many other systems. This method is also shown in Figure 11–17.

Another issue in page allocation has to do with the time at which pages are first loaded on the paging device. Again, a straightforward method would be to copy all pages for a process's program and data as soon as the process is created, but this may waste space and cause unneeded transfers. A more efficient approach is to load pages from the original program or data file into memory when first required. Pages are fetched from the original file as needed rather than all at once. Moreover, a page which is replaced but never modified may be fetched again from the original file. This method, used by VMS and MULTICS, requires that the original executable and data files contain exact copies of the information to be loaded in memory. If programs are stored in a modified form, as might be the case if software relocation is to be carried out upon loading, then this method cannot be used.

MULTICS carries the idea of paging from the original file to its logical extreme by writing modified pages back to the original file as well, so there is no separate paging storage. This practice is consistent with the MULTICS philosophy that both files and information in main memory are treated uniformly as segments, and all accesses to segments use the same copy.

Data pages that must be initialized are handled the same way as program pages, but uninitialized data pages do not have space reserved in the original file and need not be stored anywhere until they contain information. The OS can detect such pages when first loaded or referenced, and flag them in its page map. When an uninitialized page is referenced, a page frame in main memory is allocated and filled with zeroes. If such a page is removed after being modified, a new space must be allocated on the paging device.

11.11 SEGMENTED VIRTUAL MEMORY

Although a paged virtual memory can provide effective solutions to many of the problems associated with memory management, the logical partitioning of a program into segments may still have advantages. Segments representing individual procedures or data structures will tend to be referenced as a whole for a period of time. It may be desirable to swap their pages in and out as a single unit. Access restrictions, such as prohibition of writing or executing, logically apply to segments as a whole. If paging is applied to individual segments rather than complete programs, each page table will be smaller.

For such reasons, many memory management architectures provide a combination of segmentation and paging. A program may be first divided into segments, each with a distinct segment identifier, as seen previously in Figure 11–5 on page 342. Paging is then applied separately to each segment.

A hardware mechanism that supports both paging and segmentation must provide a two-level translation system. Each process is described as a whole in main memory by a **segment table,** which contains a **segment descriptor** for each distinct segment. A **segment table register** in the CPU is then used to identify the starting address and size of the current segment table. The form of a segment descriptor, shown in Figure 11–18, is similar to that used in a mapping register (see Figure 11–6). However, the physical start address for the segment is now interpreted as a page table address. The page table, in turn, contains page descriptors, as is also shown in Figure 11–18.

It is possible that entire segments as well as individual pages may be absent from main memory. For this reason, a **segment present flag** is provided in the segment descriptor. An access control field is also included; in this case, access control information is usually *not* present in the page descriptors. The page descriptors continue to include page referenced bits

Figure 11–18 Descriptors in a Segmented Virtual Memory System

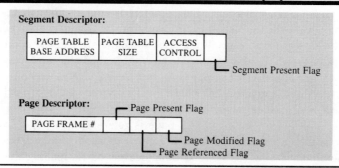

and page modified bits. This type of information is usually not recorded at the segment level.

A virtual address presented to this type of translation system is now considered to be composed of three fields: segment number, page number, and offset. The overall translation process is illustrated in Figure 11–19. The segment table register is first used to locate the segment table in memory. The segment number field from the virtual address is compared to the table size to ensure validity, and used as an index to fetch the segment descriptor.

The access control field in the segment descriptor is then checked to be sure that the operation being attempted is allowed. The segment present flag is checked; if it is not set, the hardware generates a **segment fault** similar to the page fault that occurs for a missing page. If a complete segment is missing, all of its pages are on the paging device and there is no page table. In response to a segment fault, the OS must reconstruct the page table and perhaps load one or more of the missing pages. The reference is then resumed or restarted. When the page table location and size have been found, access continues as we described previously for paging systems.

Although not shown in the figure, the paging cache continues to play an important role. At the beginning of the translation process, the cache is searched for the required page descriptor. If it is found, all accesses to segment and page tables can be bypassed. In some cases, segment descriptors may be stored in the cache as well.

Virtual storage management with segmentation and paging faces issues similar to those faced by simple paging systems, but will generally treat segments as a unit. Entire segments may be prepaged into memory when any part of them are needed, and complete segments may be chosen for replacement (for example, removed from the working set) rather than individual pages.

Although the mechanism described here is somewhat simplified, it is representative of structures found on such diverse architectures as the IBM

Figure 11–19 Translation in a Segmented Virtual Memory

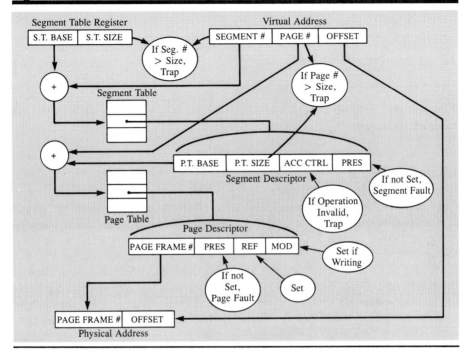

S/370, the GE645 used by MULTICS, and the INTEL 80386.

A segmentation mechanism can be a valuable addition to memory management systems, *provided that the segments can be large enough.* Unfortunately, providing a generous address space for each segment, plus an adequate number of segments, requires a huge address space overall. If segment size is limited so that some program units must be artificially divided into segments, the mechanism may be a burden rather than a help. Only a few architectures, such as the MULTICS machine, provide for very large segment sizes.

In some operating systems that support a segmented memory model, it is possible to defer initial loading of a segment until it is needed. It is possible that intersegment links can be recorded symbolically, and names can be resolved only when (and if!) the segment is actually required. This technique of **dynamic linking** was pioneered by MULTICS and is used to advantage in some later systems.

The MULTICS view of its segmented address space was quite extreme; in principle, all information structures known to the system, *including all files,* were considered to be segments. All such segments could be directly addressed by a two-level address including the segment name. There was no explicit reading or writing of files.

11.12 OTHER ISSUES

This section briefly examines some additional issues that may arise in virtual memory management in specific environments.

Input and Output

Care must be taken when a process requests direct memory input or output in a virtual memory system. In this type of I/O, an address for a memory buffer is passed to the I/O controller, which then transfers data to or from that buffer without intervention from the CPU. The address provided to the controller must be a physical, not a virtual, address. Memory translation is usually bound closely to the CPU, and the page table register and paging cache are not accessible to I/O devices. Even if they were accessible, they might contain the wrong information. While the I/O is in progress, the process that requested it is in a waiting state, and another process, with a different virtual space, may be in control of the CPU. Thus in processing I/O requests, the OS must translate the virtual addresses supplied by the process into physical addresses for the controller.

A second problem arises in ensuring that pages being accessed for input and output remain undisturbed while the I/O is going on. These pages are not being referenced by the CPU. They will be seen as not recently used, and may become candidates for replacement. To protect pages in use for I/O, the OS must lock them into memory. A table or other record is kept to indicate the pages that are locked. These pages cannot be candidates for replacement until the lock is removed.

Virtual Memory and Scheduling

Short-term scheduling may need to proceed somewhat differently in the presence of virtual memory. The problem comes from the high frequency of page faults. Each fault interrupts the running process, and may require one or two pages to be transferred to or from secondary storage. During these I/O transfers, the process must wait, and other processes may be scheduled. This leads to a very high frequency of context switching. Page faults are not voluntary I/O and should not be charged to a process in the usual way. A process interrupted by a page fault may be placed at the head, rather than the tail, of the same priority queue from which it was last taken. This ensures early resumption when the page transfers are complete. Such a process may also have the remainder of its CPU time quantum restored when it resumes, and be treated as though no interruption had taken place. Page faults do not signify an interactive process, and should not be considered in identifying processes that are CPU-bound.

Sharing Segments and Pages

A translation system that provides independent mappings for each process may include some of the same physical blocks in the virtual address space of more than one process. This is the basic implementation mechanism for shared memory.

The most logical unit of memory that may be shared among processes is the segment, since this represents a specific program or data unit that may be usefully shared as a whole. It is possible but less useful to share individual pages.

One important category of sharing that may be supported without explicit cooperation among processes is sharing of common program segments that are intended to be executed but not modified by any program. If the OS maintains a record of the program files that have been mapped to segments, the same segments may be reused when another process seeks to load the same program. This technique can save significant storage space when many processes may be executing the same programs, such as editors or compilers. Although many versions of UNIX provide no support for explicit memory sharing, they do make use of this hidden sharing of program segments.

The second category of sharing involves data segments that may be shared by the choice of certain processes for communication. Each process must identify the segment by a common name to advise the OS that it should be shared. Shared data segments form a valuable method of interprocess communication, but lead to problems of synchronization and management, as discussed in Chapter 7.

When pages or segments are to be shared, the OS must maintain records that identify the shared blocks and link together all of the virtual blocks that may be associated with each physical block. Problems arise similar to those associated with I/O, which is a type of shared use. If a block is swapped in or out of memory, all relevant page or segment tables must be updated. Use of the block by all sharers must be considered when the block is a candidate for replacement.

Swapping the Tables and the OS

In the majority of systems, page and segment tables are maintained in a data area controlled by the operating system. The OS and its data areas are not subject to paging. Instead, the memory translation system is switched off when the OS is active, and it operates directly in a region of the physical memory.

When the OS is very large, however, much of it may be stored in a virtual space and be subject to swapping. This practice is followed, for example, by VMS. The most critical portions of the OS, including those that control memory management, remain immune to the translation system. In such cases the page and segment tables themselves may be treated as segments subject to swapping. This fact can be helpful when virtual spaces are large, and much of the page tables may go unused for a long time. If these tables are kept in virtual, swappable space, then an attempt to reference a page table during page fault processing may itself cause a fault. The OS must be prepared to deal with nested faults, and handle the extra ones in the usual way.

Program Control of Paging

In some operating systems, system calls are provided to allow programs some explicit control of paging strategies. This provision can be useful when the program has knowledge of its intended behavior that the OS cannot deduce from basic locality. For example, the program may be about to begin a new phase of work that will cause an abrupt change of locality. In addition, it may wish to protect certain areas from paging even though they will not be referenced for a while.

As an example, VMS, which uses a simple working set strategy, includes system calls to

- adjust the size of the working set
- remove pages from the working set
- lock pages into the working set
- lock pages into physical memory

The second type of locking is stronger than the first; pages will remain in memory even if the process is suspended and swapped. Processes may require special privileges to use some of these services.

In some cases, services like these may be invoked directly by application programs. Alternately, compilers may be able to determine when a change of locality occurs or when, for any reason, a special strategy is called for.

Paging Without Hardware Support

A few operating systems have implemented a form of segmented or paged virtual memory purely by software. An example is T.H.E., in which each program is responsible for ensuring that the pages it requires are in memory, and swapping as required [McKeag et al. 1976, pp. 156-160]. This would be a severe burden for application programs. It is most feasible in operating systems that expect *all* programs to be processed by special compilers, allowing no direct assembly language programming. Such was the case with T.H.E., in which every application program was written in Algol.

11.13 SUMMARY

Memory management problems can be substantially reduced by the use of a mechanism for automatic memory translation, which separates the virtual address space of each process from the physical address space managed by the operating system. A memory translation mechanism is invisible to application programs, but requires hardware support and careful management by the OS.

Any memory translation system provides a means for translating blocks of locations in a virtual address space to corresponding blocks of addresses in physical memory. This translation takes place at each memory reference and must be performed by hardware. It is guided by a translation table, which specifies the corresponding addresses and may also include protection information to limit the access permitted to each block.

The unit of translation may be the total program and data storage of a process, or even the total system. In other cases, the total memory for a process is divided into logical units called segments. Each segment may represent a specific program or data module. It may be convenient for information to be managed in terms of segments, each translated independently to physical memory.

A simple translation mechanism implements the translation table as a set of mapping registers. The virtual memory space is divided into a small number of equally sized blocks, which could be used to represent a limited number of segments. This type of translation is fast and relatively simple, but deals with only a limited number of memory management problems.

A paging system addresses more needs by providing a large number of small, equal-sized blocks called pages. Much of the fragmentation problem is eliminated because all pages are of equal size. However, the translation table may be quite large, and must be stored in main memory rather than registers. Because of this, a paging cache is necessary to avoid serious performance problems.

A paging system can be extended to full virtual memory by providing a bit in the page descriptors that signals when pages are not present in main memory. The missing pages are stored instead on a storage device, such as a disk. When the CPU attempts to reference a missing page, it produces a page fault interrupt. The operating system must locate the missing page on the disk and copy it to the main memory.

Managing a virtual memory system raises problems of fetch, placement, and replacement. The placement problem is trivial, and the fetch problem is usually resolved by demand fetching, which loads new pages only when referenced.

The replacement problem is more difficult. The memory is usually full, so the OS must choose a page to remove to make room for a new one. The choice is usually based on the principle of locality, which states that pages recently referenced are likely to be referenced again soon. To take advantage of this, the hardware may record page references by a mechanism such as a page referenced bit. The OS collects this information and uses it to identify pages not recently referenced as good candidates for replacement.

To avoid excess overhead in copying referenced pages back to the disk, a page modified bit is also maintained in each descriptor. The hardware sets this bit when there is a store operation to the page. The OS need only rewrite modified pages, and may favor unmodified pages when choosing a page for replacement.

In a multiprogramming system, effective page replacement requires a local strategy that maintains a separate set of pages for each process, rather than a global strategy that treats all pages equally. Otherwise, each running process would tend to steal pages from processes that are not running. A local strategy establishes a working set for each process, based on some criteria such as a percentage of that processes total memory. The criteria can be tuned for each process to maintain reasonable fault rates. Performance is traded against the number of processes that can be maintained actively in memory. The time-window working set performs this tuning automatically by defining the working set to include all pages referenced in a fixed time interval, rather than a fixed number of pages. However, this method is hard to implement without specialized hardware support.

The secondary storage used for paging must be managed carefully for good performance. Since pages are most efficiently transferred in clusters, and not all pages need to be stored on the disk, page frames are usually allocated for groups of pages as needed.

Paging and virtual memory techniques may be applied to individual segments as well as to total process address spaces. The combination of segmentation and paging provides two levels of management. Logical segments are manipulated explicitly, while paging of each segment takes place with less awareness on the part of normal programs.

Consideration of a number of other issues may require additional features and adjustments to develop a practical virtual memory management system. Input and output can cause difficulties because transfers proceed independently of the running process and use physical rather than virtual addresses. Frequent page faults may have a significant impact on scheduling techniques. Memory management provides an effective method for implementing shared memory, but this feature must be carefully managed to avoid problems. Specialized applications may have unusual behavior which violates locality, requiring explicit communication between the program and the OS to maintain reasonable fault rates.

FOR FURTHER READING

Many operating system texts include good treatment of virtual memory issues. A reasonable introductory treatment can be found in Deitel [1984]. Additional description of implementation methods and selected replacement algorithms is given by Peterson and Silberschatz [1985], Tanenbaum [1987], Milenković [1987], and others. Some older and more theoretical analyses are provided by Brinch Hansen [1973] and Coffman and Denning [1973].

An early study by Belady [1966] at IBM developed a number of important ideas for virtual memory management and established the principle of locality. A review of memory management technology at IBM is given by Belady [1981]. Denning [1970] offers a readable early survey of virtual storage techniques. Denning [1980] provides a comprehensive study of the working set approach. An extensive survey of the operation of cache memories, including paging caches, is presented by Smith [1982].

The first virtual memory system on the ATLAS computer is described by Howarth et al. [1961] and by Lavington [1978]. The MULTICS segmented virtual memory is presented by Bensoussan and Clinger [1972] and extensively explored by Organick [1972]. Fogel [1974] describes a working set implementation for VMOS, and Levy and Lipman [1982] provide a thorough discussion of the strategies followed by VMS. The novel algorithm used in Berkeley UNIX to support an LRU strategy without reference bits is presented by Babaoglu and Joy [1982]. Other useful case studies include Bron [1972] for T.H.E., and Bobrow et al. [1972] for TENEX. The complex virtual memory support structures on a high-performance microprocessor, the Intel 80386, are described by Wells [1986].

≡ IMPORTANT TERMS ≡

access control field
approximate LRU
associative memory
available list
base address
block descriptor
CLOCK algorithm
clustering
content-addressable memory
demand fetching
dirty bit
dynamic linking
fetch problem
global replacement strategy
hit rate
least frequently used (LFU)
least recently used (LRU)
local replacement strategy
mapping registers
memory translation
not recently used (NRU)
one-level store
page
page descriptor
page fault
page frame number
page frame

page modified bit
page number
page present flag
page referenced bit
page table
page table register
paging
paging cache
physical address
placement problem
prepaging
principle of locality
replacement problem
segment
segment descriptor
segment fault
segment present flag
segment table
segment table register
segmentation
thrashing
time-window working set
translation table
virtual address
virtual memory
virtual memory system
working set

≡ REVIEW QUESTIONS ≡

1. Why is it reasonable to expect most programs to exhibit locality?

2. List and briefly explain the purpose of each field included in a typical page descriptor in a paged virtual memory system. Assume the system does not included segmentation.

3. Explain why page frames on a secondary storage device are usually allocated on demand, rather than preassigning a copy of the entire virtual space for each process.

4. In a system using mapping registers for memory mapping, each register specifies a block size, allowing the size of the blocks to vary. Explain why this is necessary, and explain one difficulty it causes.

5. Explain the difference between local and global page replacement algorithms in a virtual memory system.

6. Why must local page replacement algorithms be used in a multi-programmed OS?

7. Explain briefly each item of information required in a block descriptor in a translation system using mapping registers.

8. Compared to mapping registers, state one advantage and one disadvantage of paging.

9. List two ways in which the fetch strategy of a typical virtual memory system may differ from pure demand fetching.

10. In a virtual memory system, why is a least recently used replacement algorithm more common than least frequently used?

11. Describe briefly a unique characteristic of the virtual memory management strategy on each of the following:

   a. ATLAS
   b. Berkeley VAX/UNIX

12. Identify the three virtual memory control bits (other than access control) usually present in a page descriptor. State and distinguish how each bit is handled by (a) the hardware, and (b) the operating system.

13. State the principal difference between the MVS operating system and its predecessor, SVS.

ASSIGNMENTS

1. Describe the hardware structures that would be required to implement the memory translation model of Figure 11–1 as shown. What specific difficulties are encountered? Why is this model usually replaced by simpler but less powerful ones?

2. Describe the characteristics of the hardware structures that would be needed to support each of the following page replacement strategies:

   a. *exact* least recently used
   b. least frequently used
   c. time window working set

3. Comment on the following statement: "It is not necessary or useful to provide an independent translation for every distinct virtual address."

4. Explain why the most common types of memory access distinguished in an access control field are read, write, and execute. Describe a problem that could be resolved by this mechanism but not by a single bit indicating whether a page is writable. Can you think of other types of access that could usefully be distinguished?

5. In the IBM 370, a segment is treated as a higher-level page. The address space is divided into fixed-size segments, each of which is paged with a separate page descriptor. Why is this mechanism less useful than the logical segmentation described in the text?

6. In most memory-mapped systems, a request by a process for more memory is answered with a virtual address for a new block, which is not necessarily contiguous with other memory assigned to this process. In UNIX, however, all memory accessible to a process is at all times contiguous in the virtual space. More memory is obtained by moving the entire process to a new, larger location. Explain one possible advantage and one disadvantage of this approach.

7. Like the virtual memory system it supports, a paging cache operates on the principle of locality. Descriptors are loaded on demand. The cache is often treated as a circular buffer, with each new entry replacing the oldest one in a FIFO manner. Alternately, many caches use an exact LRU strategy, with a field associated with each entry used to keep descriptors ordered by time of last reference. If a change is made to a descriptor loaded in a cache, the descriptor is often updated immediately in main memory. The copy in the cache is either updated or removed.

   From the brief summary above and the descriptions in the text, list three similarities and three differences between cache management and virtual memory management. For each difference, explain why the method used in the cache is reasonable for the cache but would not be appropriate for virtual memory.

8. Consider the CPU instruction set of a computer architecture with which you are familiar. Give several examples of instructions that could be difficult to undo or restart if a page fault is caused at a late stage of instruction processing.

9. Some of the difficulties encountered in the interaction between virtual memory and input and output arise because I/O transfers use physical addresses. List several reasons why I/O transfers do not normally use virtual addresses.

≡ PROJECT ≡

This section describes a programming project to implement a page fault processing mechanism. Because the development environment in which you are working may not permit implementation of an actual virtual memory system, the project will take the form of a set of commands to be added to the command handler that simulate the required response to a series of page references. You should read the general description in this text in conjunction with the more specific descriptions given in your project manual.

a. Define a data structure to represent a page table with descriptors, as shown in Figure 11–10 (p. 351). For this project no use will be made of the page frame number or access control field. The page table will represent a virtual address space containing up to sixty-four pages, each 1K bytes in size.

Using this page table, implement procedures to simulate operation of the CLOCK algorithm, as illustrated in Figure 11–15 (p. 362). This algorithm uses the page referenced and modified bits of the page table to select pages for replacement. Your algorithm may scan the pages sequentially in the page table, ignoring pages that are not present. Assume that any page that is scheduled for rewriting may have its modified bit cleared immediately in preparation for the next pass.

b. Implement the following COMHAN commands to exercise your algorithm.

1. VMEM INIT: initialize the page table to indicate that no pages are currently present in main memory.

2. VMEM REFERENCE *addr*: simulate a non-modifying reference to location *addr* in the virtual address space. If this reference causes a page fault, a series of messages should be printed, indicating (a) if a fault occurred, (b) what page, if any, was replaced, and (c) if the replaced page was written to the disk.

3. VMEM MODIFY *addr*: simulate a modifying reference to location *addr* in the virtual address space. Page faults should be handled as in the preceding command.

4. VMEM STATS: display the total number of references (modifying or not), total number of page faults, and total number of simulated disk transfers since the last VMEM INIT command.

5. VMEM DUMP: display the complete contents of the page table, indicating the state of the page present, referenced, and modified bits for each page in the virtual address space.

File
Management

File Management

12.1 INTRODUCTION

A central responsibility of modern operating systems is to maintain convenient storage for collections of information on behalf of its users. Although some of the earliest OSs offered only temporary storage during each user's job, in most cases there is a need to store potentially large amounts of information that can remain available over long periods of time.

A collection of information maintained on long-term storage for a set of users is called a **file system.** Usually, the contents of a file system consist of a number of distinct sets of information called **files** (the term *data sets* is often preferred by users of IBM systems). At its simplest, a file can be viewed as a sequence of addressable storage units. Files are often considered to have a more complex internal structure, which divides them into parts called **records.** To allow identification of files, each file is assigned a **file name,** which is usually a string of characters.

The portion of an operating system responsible for managing a file system, the **file manager,** must provide users and programs with a suitable set of operations to maintain and use files. Many of the basic operations appear as services at the program interface. Programs must be able to read information from files, and modify or add to file contents. In most cases files may be created when needed and destroyed when no longer useful. Various attributes and characteristics may be associated with files; we require methods to examine and change these as needed.

Some operating systems provide much more elaborate services for managing special types of files. These may include support for indexed files, large text documents, database systems, and other categories. In other OSs only basic file support is available; other structures must be managed by application programs.

Files are stored on physical devices which allow reading, writing, and permanent storage. Usually these devices are magnetic disks or tapes.

Characteristics of such storage devices are described in Appendix B. A typical file system allows use of a number of physical storage units, each containing an independent collection of files. We discuss the overall structure of these collections in Section 12.2. The individual files that reside in a file system may have various organizations and internal structures that affect their suitability for certain uses. These issues are discussed in Section 12.3.

A file system must maintain descriptive information for each file, including its name, location, and various other attributes. This information is collected in a data structure called a **file descriptor.** These file descriptors, in turn, are organized into one or more special files or storage areas, called **directories.** Some of the information required in file descriptors under various conditions is discussed throughout the chapter. We consider the structure of descriptors and directories in Section 12.4.

In many operating systems, physical I/O devices may be accessed using the file system. Section 12.5 considers the interaction of device management and file management. The next section then examines basic operations that must be performed on files, and the data structures required to support these operations. The remaining sections of the chapter consider more advanced or unusual support mechanisms that may be found in some types of file systems.

12.2 VOLUME STRUCTURE

Typically, the total set of files for a computer system is stored on a number of distinct storage devices. Some of these devices are permanently attached to the system, but others may be physically removed and replaced with other similar devices. Most magnetic tapes and many types of disks fall into the removable category. Because such storage units may be installed and replaced as a whole, we need to consider the files on each unit as forming an independent collection. Such a collection is called a **volume.**

In most cases, a volume of files corresponds exactly to one physical unit. However, volumes may be constructed for other reasons, such as providing storage for distinct projects or users. In some cases a large (usually permanent) storage unit is partitioned into a number of volumes. Portions of a storage unit may also be reserved for uses outside of a file system, such as memory swapping or paging, or various kinds of temporary use. More rarely, a volume may span multiple storage devices if it is too large to be held on a single device. Where necessary, a distinction may be made between a **logical volume,** which is a single complete independent group of files, and a **physical volume,** which is a single storage device.

Because volumes may be replaced, a method is needed to identify each volume. In most cases, this is accomplished by storing a **volume name** in a standard location on the volume itself. The volume name identifies the volume just as a file name identifies a file.

The information contained in a file volume falls into three principal categories: files, directories, and a **volume descriptor.** A fourth area on some volumes may be set aside as a **system area.** This area is actually a special type of file storage containing copies of the operating system and certain system utilities. It is used to initialize the OS and to store components that will be loaded into transient areas as needed.

On selected physical disks additional space may be allocated for a **swap area,** for storing the information used by processes that are swapped out of memory. In virtual memory environments the swap area may be replaced or supplemented by a **paging area.** These areas may share a physical disk volume with a set of files. However, they are not considered part of the file system itself.

We discuss the content and organization of files and directories in later sections of this chapter. The volume descriptor contains the volume name and a small amount of essential information about the structure and status of the volume. It normally occupies the first one or two blocks on the volume. A simple volume descriptor is illustrated in Figure 12–1. This descriptor includes pointers to the directory, the file area, and an area reserved for allocation data, which is sometimes a part of the directory. A file system code is stored to identify the file system on which this organization is based; this code aids in detection of volumes with improper formats. The date the volume was created is also included in this descriptor.

Figure 12–1 A Simple Volume Descriptor

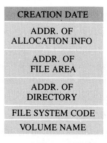

| CREATION DATE |
| ADDR. OF ALLOCATION INFO |
| ADDR. OF FILE AREA |
| ADDR. OF DIRECTORY |
| FILE SYSTEM CODE |
| VOLUME NAME |

The placement of information on a file volume is motivated by two considerations: The volume descriptor must be in a known place, and frequently used information should be positioned for rapid access. The most suitable known place for the descriptor is on the first block, which is always numbered zero. With this convention an OS can find the descriptor on an arbitrary, newly mounted volume, provided only that the volume is organized in an expected format.

The most frequently accessed information on most file systems is the main file directory. As much as possible, this directory should be kept in a consecutive set of blocks. The optimum position for these blocks on a disk file system is in the middle of the disk, since the middle is easiest to reach from a random starting position. This position becomes especially important with moving head and floppy disks, on which the seek time can be substantial. However, in practice, many file systems place the main directory near the lowest-numbered blocks on each volume.

The system area, if present, is placed immediately following the volume descriptor. The remaining blocks of the file system are available for file storage and, possibly, storage of additional directories.

Some examples of file volume layout are shown in Figure 12-2. These layouts are all fairly similar, but have subtle differences. The CP/M organization has no volume descriptor; CP/M volumes can be identified only by their content. All of the examples place the directory near the beginning of the disk. For UNIX, however, this directory contains only partial descriptors. Other information, including file names, is stored in special directory files in the regular file area. OS/MVT volumes have no system area; instead, entire volumes must be reserved to hold the operating system and its support programs.

12.3 FILE ORGANIZATION

The majority of the space on most file volumes is reserved for storage of the files themselves. The data for each file requires an appropriate set of blocks on the volume. The method for choosing these blocks may have an impact on the ease and speed with which desirable operations on files can be performed. The control information required to keep track of the blocks for each file is also determined by the organization method.

The discussion in this section is based on a low-level view of files, in which a file is viewed simply as a numbered sequence of storage blocks or of simple logical components called records. Many users and applications prefer higher-level views; for example, a file may be considered as a collection of information items, each associated with a key that can be used to access them. These files are also based on the simpler structures we discuss here. We consider the implications of such higher-level views in Section 12.8.

Figure 12–2   Examples of Volume Layout

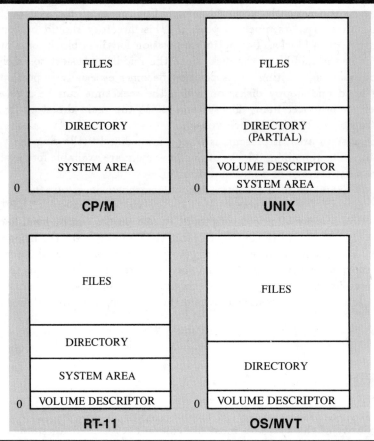

Some issues to be resolved in choosing a file organization strategy include how to obtain storage for a new or expanded file, how to recover storage no longer needed, how to keep track of the location of each file, and how to manage available space. There are four principal strategies that are commonly used to address these issues. Each strategy leads to a characteristic file organization; we will call these organizations **simple contiguous, contiguous with extents, blocked chained,** and **blocked indexed.** Most OSs support one or a variation of these strategies. A few support several methods. Each of these organizations will be discussed in the following subsections.

Simple Contiguous Organization

The simple contiguous method allocates space for each file in a continuous sequence of blocks. A typical example is the RT-11 file system shown in Figure 12–3. This type of allocation is very similar to the techniques used to allocate main memory in systems without mapping hardware.

Figure 12–3 Contiguous Organization: RT-11

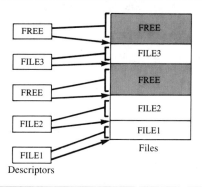

A principal advantage of contiguous organization is that it is simple to manage. The only information required to describe the location of a file is its starting block and its size. Thus, directory contents may be very simple. A second advantage is that random access to file contents is more efficient than with any other method. All parts of the file are grouped in a compact area. The location of any desired portion of the file can be computed and accessed directly.

A disadvantage to this method is that files cannot be expanded unless adjacent free space is available by sheer luck. Sufficient space must be allocated for a file's future needs when it is first created. The file may be made larger only by copying it entirely to a new region of the disk.

Fragmentation will develop gradually in a contiguous file system. Unlike the situation with main memory, though, disk fragmentation may be countered by occasionally reorganizing the disk. System programs with names like SQUEEZE (RT-11) or COMPACT (DOS-99) rearrange files so that all free space is in one place. This type of rearrangement is more feasible than main memory for disk storage, since the data does not have to be modified due to relocation and processes do not have to be stopped completely or restarted. However, no use can be made of the file system while such rearrangement is in progress.

In a variable space allocation strategy for main memory, free space is usually managed by including headers in each free area. These headers are linked together on a list. This technique is not used for disk allocation because traversing a linked list on disks is a slow and inefficient process. Instead, other methods must be found to keep track of free areas. A simple method, used by RT-11, records the free areas in the directory as if they were files. Each such "free file" is flagged in a special way to distinguish it from actual files. Often, the directory is maintained in order of disk location, to facilitate merging of free areas.

Contiguous organization is used by many simple file managers; One additional example is the business-oriented THEOS operating system [Stagner 1985]. This method may be an option on much more complex OSs. Contiguous organization is a desirable method for files that are not expected to grow, and must be accessed frequently in random order. This method is least effective for files that have unpredictable size requirements, or must expand and shrink frequently over their lifetime.

Contiguous Organization with Extents

The method of contiguous organization with extents is a modest extension to simple contiguous organization. In this approach, files are stored contiguously as far as possible. When contiguous storage is not possible, the file may be continued in one or more separate areas, called **extents.** Extents are required if an existing file must be expanded, or if there is not a large enough space to create a new file due to fragmentation. In addition, systems that use extents may place a limit on how large each extent, including the first one, can be.

An example of contiguous storage with extents is found in the CP/M structure, illustrated in Figure 12–4. With this structure, files and free space are managed by techniques similar to those discussed in the previous subsection. However, each extent is recorded in the directory as a separate entry, identified both by file name and extent number. A link also may be stored in each entry to locate the entry for the next extent, if any. This method is used by a variety of operating systems, including OS/360.

Blocked Organizations

As an alternative to maintaining a contiguous layout, file space may be allocated in individual blocks or groups of blocks with no requirement that the blocks be contiguous. This approach makes it much easier to allocate and release file space, but imposes the requirement of keeping track of each of the blocks of a file.

Fragmentation is not a concern with fixed-size block allocation, and there is no need for a special program to reorganize disk space. It should be noted, though, that even with this structure, access performance can be improved

Figure 12-4 Contiguous Organization with Extents: CP/M

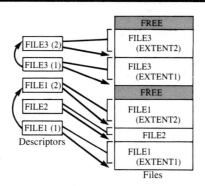

by occasional reorganization, so that the blocks for most files are clustered in a limited area of the disk.

There are two principal methods for organizing the blocks of a file in a blocked organization. The method we describe first is called blocked chained organization. In this method, all the blocks of a file are chained together sequentially in the form of a linked list. Often, the remaining free blocks are linked on a special list as well. The second method is called blocked indexed organization. In this technique, an index is maintained that directly records the location of every block.

Blocked Chained Organization

An example of blocked chained organization in the DOS-99 OS [Mooney 1979] is shown in Figure 12-5. In this system, a short header area is reserved in each data block. This header contains two-way links for the file chain, plus an identifier for the file as a whole. Free blocks are linked on a **free chain** with a similar structure.

The use of linked headers in the data blocks themselves is a natural approach to chaining. It also offers a reliability advantage: unlike other blocked methods, it is possible to recover most of a file system by analyzing the data blocks, even if the directory has been destroyed.

On the other hand, the many disk accesses required to follow such a chain make it difficult to access data in any order but sequential; general random access is out of the question. The information represented by the headers can also be encoded in a more compact way. These considerations led the MS-DOS designers to adopt a variation of blocked chained organization. In this variant, illustrated in Figure 12-6, the files are conceptually chained, but all

Figure 12–5 Blocked Chained Organization: DOS-99

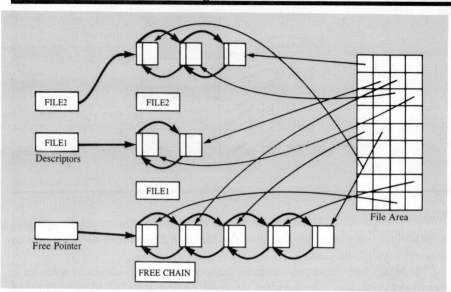

link information is stored in a special table stored on the disk called the **file allocation table (FAT)**. Each entry in this table corresponds to a data block in the file system. If a data block is part of a chained file, its corresponding FAT entry will contain a pointer to the next block in the chain. If the total number of blocks on the volume is moderate, the entire FAT can be retained in memory, making file access greatly more efficient. Because of the critical importance of the information in the FAT, MS-DOS maintains two copies of this table in separate areas of each disk.

Figure 12–6 Blocked Chained Organization: MS-DOS

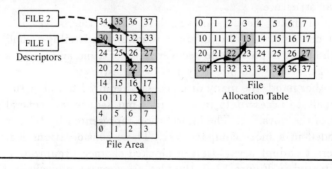

The blocked chained organization supports efficient and flexible allocation and release of file space. Entire groups of blocks, already linked, can be transferred between files and the free chain in a single operation. The directory information required is also simple; the address of the first block in the chain is all the description required.

Blocked chained organization fails greatly when effective random access is required. Even with the link information retained in memory, locating a random record requires work. With larger disk volumes, moreover, the required table could not fit in main memory all at once. Because of this limitation, designers of many larger systems prefer the more powerful blocked indexed organization.

Blocked Indexed Organization

To combine the benefits of blocked organization with efficient access in both sequential and random modes, it is necessary to maintain a record of the address of each block that makes up a file. This record forms an index to the file and is the basis of the blocked indexed method of organization.

A typical blocked indexed file system is illustrated in Figure 12–7. This figure shows the structure used by one version of UNIX. An index to the blocks of each file is maintained as part of the descriptor for that file in the directory. For very small files, all blocks are listed in the directory itself. However, to keep the descriptor size reasonable and uniform, a maximum of twelve block addresses can be stored in the directory itself. If additional blocks are included in the file, an entire block is set aside as an index block. This block may contain several hundred more addresses. For still larger files, indexes with two or three levels are possible.

The UNIX design has the interesting property that, regardless of the size of a file, the addresses of its first few blocks (which are often the most frequently accessed) are stored directly in the descriptor itself. Thus, access to these blocks is very fast. The next few hundred blocks can also be accessed reasonably fast, since only one level of indexing is required.

The blocked indexed organization combines the advantages of flexible allocation with a mechanism for reasonable direct access. The price paid for this flexibility is increased size and complexity of file directories, and some space consumed by index blocks.

Internal Structure of Files

Even with our low-level view of files, they are usually considered to have some internal structure. At the least, a file is a sequence of blocks, or other standard storage units, such as bytes or words. In addition, most systems consider a file

Figure 12–7 Blocked Indexed Organization: UNIX

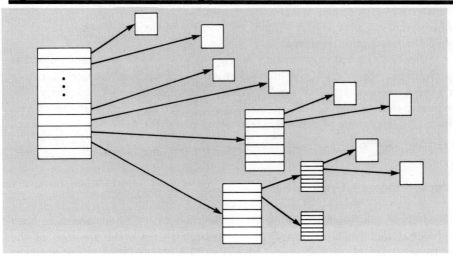

to be composed of a series of logical units, called records. The records within a single file all are considered to have the same format (though not necessarily the same length). A variety of record formats may be defined for the files in a complete file system. The file manager may keep track of the record structure associated with each file by storing its description in the directory.

Some common record formats are shown in Figure 12–8. Generally, record structures may be classified as of fixed or variable length. Fixed-length records allow efficient direct access, especially in a contiguous file organization. Variable-length records are used to contain data objects whose size may vary, in files that are expected to be accessed sequentially in most cases. A common example is a file containing lines of text, with each line stored in a single record. Variable-length records require some indicator of the record length to be stored in the record itself.

Records are often considered in turn to be divided into subparts, called **fields.** This substructure is usually managed by application programs, rarely by the OS itself. An exception is found in systems oriented to database applications, such as PICK [Cook & Brandon 1984]. The PICK file manager keeps track of up to five levels of hierarchical structure in each data file. (This OS is discussed further in Section 12.8.)

A further concern in the structure of a file is where the file's actual data is located within the allocated space. In most cases, the data starts in the first block and runs consecutively, filling all blocks. However, the data may end anywhere within a block, with additional unused blocks attached to the end of the file (see Figure 12–9). A few systems such as CP/M do not keep track

Figure 12-8 Common Record Formats

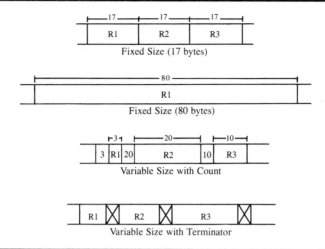

Figure 12-9 Data Space vs. Total File Space

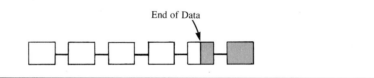

of the end-of-file point, treating all files as a whole number of blocks (CP/M does have a special convention for text files only). In most cases, though, the exact end location must be recorded as part of the directory information.

Some file managers allow individual records to be designated as "empty," especially in files designed for direct access. Such records are considered to contain no data, and will be skipped if the file is accessed sequentially.

In most files with record structure, each physical block contains one or more complete records. This organization is most suitable for efficient access, since blocks must be transferred as a whole. However, there may be space wasted in a block if the length of the records does not match the block length. At the cost of some complexity in record access, files may use a **spanning** technique, in which records are allowed to continue from one block to the next. This concept is illustrated in Figure 12-10.

In a few cases, the spanning concept can be extended to whole files, allowing a block to contain parts of more than one file. This procedure can

Figure 12–10 Spanned and Unspanned Records

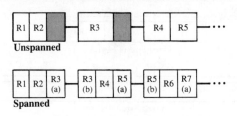

contribute to efficient storage if many small files are present. Support for spanning of files is often provided in the form of special library formats, as discussed in Section 12.8.

File Attributes

In addition to its name and organizational characteristics, a file may be assigned various **file attributes,** which influence how it can be used. These attributes are recorded in the file descriptor. Various file systems may support many kinds of file attributes, or almost none. Some of the types of information that may be recorded as file attributes include:

- *Owner.* This attribute specifies the name or identifier of the owner of the file. The owner, usually the one who created the file, may have special privileges for this file, and may be charged for the storage space it occupies.

- *Access restrictions.* This information specifies what basic operations may be performed on the file by various categories of users. For example, some files may be designated as read-only, not deletable, or readable only by their owner.

- *Access types.* This attribute specifies the methods or models that are suitable for accessing this file, such as sequential, or direct.

- *Type of contents.* Some file managers record extensive information on the type of data in each file to help ensure that it is used correctly. Other systems leave this to the application programs. The simplest type attribute might simply distinguish **text files** containing characters that can be printed or displayed from other file types. More elaborate attributes may distinguish executable programs, source files in various languages, and many other specialized categories of data.

- *Extension control.* This attribute can specify whether the file space is allowed to grow, and how much new space should be allocated at one time.

- *Deletion control.* This attribute may specify a date on which the file should be automatically deleted, or designate a file as "temporary," to be deleted immediately after use.

- *Visibility control.* This attribute may specify that in some cases a file should be omitted from directory listings or collective operations on groups of files.

- *Version number.* The file may represent a specific version of data that has gone through various revisions. A version number can distinguish the files containing different versions, whose names and other attributes may be identical.

- *File history.* Information about past use and history of the file may be retained. Often this takes the form of a set of dates, such as date of creation, last modification, or last use.

- *Current use.* In some cases the current status of the file is recorded in the directory, indicating if it is now in use, and by which users for what purpose.

12.4 DIRECTORY ORGANIZATION

To allow access to files and to maintain information about their characteristics, a file system must include directories in addition to the files themselves. Each file volume may have a single directory, or many directories, possibly organized into suitable relationships. Collectively, the directories contain the file descriptors for every file on the volume. Directories may be placed in various ways on the volume, and in some cases each file descriptor may be partitioned and stored in two or more distinct parts. In this section we consider issues that relate to these choices of directory organization.

File Naming

To allow external users and programs to identify files, every file is assigned a name. File names play a critical role in a file system. Given a name, the file manager must be able to rapidly locate the file, if it exists. File names are usually stored in each file descriptor, and they serve as a key by which the complete descriptor can be retrieved.

File names are usually defined as sequences of characters represented by a character code, such as ASCII. While users wish to define names as a convenient indicator of the contents of the file, each file system imposes different rules about how names may be constructed. The choice of rules can have an impact on both the usefulness of names and the efficiency with which they can be stored and manipulated. Some issues to be considered in selecting a structure for file names include types of components, length of names, and permissible characters.

File Name Components. Although some file systems employ names that are simple character strings with no meaningful structure, in most cases a name is made up of several distinct parts, separated by appropriate punctuation. Some examples of complete structured file names are:

```
CP/M:     B:FILEMGT.TXT
UNIX:     /usr/mooney/book/chapters/filemgt.t
VMS:      vaxa::dk1:[mooney.book.chapters]filemgt.txt;13
CMS:      filemgt text a
OS/MVT:   mooney.book.chapters.filemgt
```

In each of these examples, the main file name is the same: `filemgt`. Some components, usually written to the left of the name, identify groups of files to which the specified file belongs. Usually most or all of these components may be omitted if there is an understanding about what the "current" group is. The meaning of some of these components may include:

- *node name.* In a file system spanning a number of computers connected by a network, the node name identifies the network node where the file is located. In the VMS example, `vaxa` is a node name.

- *device name* or *volume name.* This component identifies the volume or storage device on which the file is found. Either a physical name, such as "disk1" or a logical volume name, such as "os-book" might be used. In the VMS example above, `dk1` is a device name. Other examples are B in the above CP/M example and a in the CMS example.

- *directory name.* If a file system supports multiple directories, this component identifies the directory in which the file resides. In some cases there are subdirectories within directories. In the VMS example, `mooney` is a directory name, and `book` and `chapters` are subdirectory names. UNIX has multiple directories but does not distinguish subdirectories. In the above UNIX example, all of the names `usr`, `mooney`, `book`, and `chapters` are considered directory names. Moreover, the first slash represents a special master directory with an empty name.

In the above OS/MVT example, the components mooney, book, and chapters do *not* represent distinct directories. Instead, the use of periods is a convenience available to the user for grouping files, which can be recognized by some elements of the operating system.

Note that most of the names shown explicitly distinguish each type of component by distinct punctuation. UNIX is an exception; each group is uniformly considered to be a directory. However, most directories are in fact confined to a single storage device.

Additional components of a file name, most often written to the right of the name, do not relate to the location of the file, but serve as a method of representing certain file attributes. The examples in this category are:

- *file type* or *file extension*. This component is by far the most common in this class. It is used to indicate the type of information contained in the file. In turn, this information is used by various application and system programs to identify suitable files. It is usually *not* used or required by the OS. File types text in CMS, TXT in CP/M, and txt in VMS are examples of such a component. In some environments, such as UNIX, this structure is often used by programs but is not even considered a distinct part of the file name by the OS itself.

- *version number.* The version number of the file is represented explicitly in VMS file names. In the example, 13 is a version number. This concept was first used by TENEX. By convention, if the version number is not specified, the highest existing version number is used for input, and the next higher number is used for output.

File Name Length. The choice of length restrictions on file names must balance several factors. On one hand, many users would prefer file names that are long and descriptive. Especially when one directory contains many files, names must be long enough to clearly distinguish each file and avoid conflicts.

On the other hand, searching of directories will be most efficient if file descriptors are of fixed length. To keep the size of each descriptor (which includes the name) reasonable, name length must be limited. Apart from this concern, it is difficult for programs to allocate space for file names if the names (perhaps including all components) may be arbitrarily long. This has been a difficulty with some versions of UNIX.

Most OSs impose a maximum length on file names. Typical values for this maximum include 6 (RT-11), 8 (CP/M), 9 (VMS), 14 (some versions of UNIX), 32 (DOS-99), 44(OS/MVT). A few, such as EXEC on UNIVAC, have required an exact number of characters in all names.

These limits apply to the main file name component only. In many cases, the file type component is limited to three characters. Directory names usually must adhere to the same rules as file names. Other components tend to have a very restricted structure.

Very short limits make it difficult to compose meaningful names. This problem is most serious if a large number of files must be maintained in a single directory. The use of hierarchical directories, discussed below, offers a way out of this dilemma: a file name may be formed from a series of directory names, providing a long complete name even though the individual parts are short. This has been a successful technique in MULTICS and UNIX.

Permissible Characters. The set of characters from which names may be constructed may be limited. One reason for this restriction may be storage economy; larger character sets require representation of more bits per character. For this reason RT-11 allows file names to be formed from a character set of only forty characters, including capital letters, digits, and a few special symbols. With this limitation, three characters can be packed into one 16-bit word of storage. Other systems may limit the character set to sixty-four characters, which allows a six-bit-per-character representation.

Character sets may also be limited to protect users from creating file names that are difficult to work with. In UNIX, which allows almost any characters in file names, names may be formed with embedded special characters of many types, including spaces and control characters. Care must be taken in using such freedom. Names that include certain control characters cannot be typed as command arguments. These control characters disrupt the organization of directory listings.

File Descriptors

A file descriptor collects the descriptive information about a file that the file system needs to retain. This information can vary over a vast range. Some simple operating systems maintain only a few words of information in addition to the file name. In OS/MVT, however, the shortest possible file descriptor contains 140 bytes.

In most file systems all descriptors are of fixed length, which simplifies descriptor storage and searching for desired files. In other environments, such as MVT, a limited number of descriptor formats is supported.

Information that may be stored in a file descriptor includes:

- *File name,* usually represented in a standard code, such as ASCII.
- *File location,* which can range from a single block address in a blocked chained organization to a large index in a blocked indexed organization.
- *File size,* which, for convenience, is often stored in the descriptor

Figure 12–11 File Descriptor Example: MS-DOS

```
1. File Name
2. File Type
3. File Attributes
        read only; hidden; system;
        directory; volume descriptor;
        changed since backup
4. Date and time last modified
5. Starting cluster (block group) number
6. File Size
```

even if it can be derived from other information.

- *File organization,* the organization technique used for this file, as discussed in Section 12.3.

- *Record organization,* the organization of the records into which the file is divided, if any.

- *File attributes,* the attributes maintained for files in this system, as discussed at the end of Section 12.3.

Examples of the information maintained in the file descriptors for several file systems are shown in Figures 12–11 through 12–13. We examine the physical organization of file descriptors and directories in the next subsection.

Figure 12–12 File Descriptor Example: UNIX (BSD 4.2)

```
struct  icommon
        u_short ic_mode;   /*  0: file mode and type */
        short   ic_nlink;  /*  2: number of links */
        short   ic_uid;    /*  4: owner's user id */
        short   ic_gid;    /*  6: owner's group id */
        quad    ic_size;   /*  8: file size in bytes */
        time_t  ic_atime;  /* 16: time last accessed */
        long    ic_atspare;
        time_t  ic_mtime;  /* 24: time last modified */
        long    ic_mtspare;
        time_t  ic_ctime;  /* 32: last time inode changed */
        long    ic_ctspare;
        daddr_t ic_db[NDADDR];/* 40: disk block addresses */
        daddr_t ic_ib[NIADDR];/* 88: indirect blocks */
        long    ic_flags;  /* 100: (not used) */
        long    ic_blocks; /* 104: blocks actually held */
        long    ic_spare[5]; /* 108: (not used) */
i_ic;
```

Figure 12–13   File Descriptor Example: VMS

```
Header area
    Identification area offset:          40
    Map area offset:                     100
    Access control area offset:          255
    Reserved area offset:                255
    Extension segment number:            0
    Structure level and version:         2, 1
    File identification:                 (10184,223,0)
    Extension file identification:       (0,0,0)
    VAX-11 RMS attributes
        Record type:                     Variable
        File organization:               Sequential
        Record attributes:               Implied carriage control
        Record size:                     47
        Highest block:                   2
        End of file block:               2
        End of file byte:                68
        Bucket size:                     0
        Fixed control area size:         0
        Maximum record size:             255
        Default extension size:          0
        Global buffer count:             0
        Directory version limit:         0
    File characteristics:                <none specified>
    Map area words in use:               2
    Access mode:                         0
    File owner UIC:                      [UN106007]
    File protection:                     S:, O:RWED, G:, W:
    Back link file identification:       (4665,2,0)
    Journal control flags:               <none specified>
    Active recovery units:               None
    Highest block written:               2


Identification area
    File name:                           CALC.ADA;1
    Revision number:                     2
    Creation date:                       15-SEP-1986 16:29:48.01
    Revision date:                       15-SEP-1986 16:29:48.57
    Expiration date:                     <none specified>
    Backup date:                         16-SEP-1986 00:01:31.58


Map area
    Retrieval pointers
        Count:          2      LBN:      11662

Checksum:                                48273
```

Directory Structures

The file descriptors for a file system must be stored in some fashion with the files. Usually the descriptors are gathered into one or more special files or storage areas, called directories. These directories may be placed and organized in various ways on the disk. Occasionally the information in a single descriptor may be split among two or more separate directories, or portions of this information may be stored with the file itself.

Directory Placement. In most applications, directories are accessed with very high frequency. On a disk the most efficient position for information that is constantly accessed is near the middle tracks on each surface because that location is most likely to be close to a random starting point. Therefore, if most of the directory information can be clustered in one place, the center tracks (or blocks) are the most desirable. The directory may be allocated space near the center of the disk, and its starting location recorded in the volume descriptor. This technique is illustrated in Figure 12–14.

Figure 12–14 Central Directory Placement

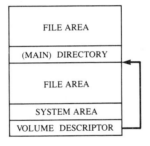

Some operating systems take advantage of this technique; however, a great many are content to position the directory (or main directory) at a fixed starting point among the low-numbered blocks of each volume, leading to a somewhat slower average access time. All of the volume layouts shown in Figure 12–2 cluster the main directory information in the low-numbered blocks.

Directories as Files. A directory, a collection of information that occupies storage, may be considered a type of file. Often the directory storage is managed in a special way. The directory may be assigned a contiguous storage area of fixed size, even if the remaining file area uses a more flexible allocation method.

Such directories may or may not be expandable by use of extents or similar techniques. If they are not, the choice of directory size becomes a critical variable to be decided when the volume is first created. If it is too large, space will be wasted; if too small, the directory may become full even though space remains in the file area.

File systems supporting multiple directories are more likely to treat directories by the same techniques used for files, and provide opportunities for directory space to be allocated as required. In a curious anomaly, UNIX stores part of its split descriptors in such flexible directories, but the remaining part is stored in a contiguous area that cannot be expanded.

Single Directories. A file system with a single directory per volume records descriptors for every file in that single directory. Directory management is simplified, since there is only one directory. However, the number of descriptors may grow quite large, increasing the search time required to locate files. In addition, it may be difficult for a user to conceptually segregate groups of related files, especially if there are severe restrictions on file name length.

Single directories are used by such systems as CP/M, RT-11, DOS-99, and OS/MVT. DOS-99 stores the directory as a chain of blocks like a file, while the others place it in a special contiguous area. In DOS-99 and MVT names can be fairly long; the use of periods in file names is encouraged as a grouping technique.

User Directories. If multiple users share files on a single volume, whether simultaneously or at different times, it is undesirable that all files should be equally accessible in a common directory. It is clear that files belonging to one user should be protected from reading and writing by others; this can be accomplished by suitable access-control mechanisms. More than this, a user should not need to be concerned with the files of other users when examining directories. Users would like to be able to create files without caring if someone else has used the same name.

A partial solution to this dilemma may be to "qualify" every file name by prefixing it with a code identifying the user. This technique can reduce the problem of name conflicts, and is frequently used with OS/MVT.

Another solution found in MVT is to create a special file for each user, which contains the names of only those files in which the user is interested, along with sufficient information to locate these files in the main directory. Such a file is usually called a **catalog.** Note, however, that a few systems use the term "catalog" as a synonym for "directory."

The most popular solution to this problem on recent multiuser systems is to provide a distinct directory for each user. When a user is identified during the start of a job or session, the appropriate directory is selected. All file operations requested by this user will then normally use this private **home directory** as a starting point. This technique—found in VMS, UNIX, and many other environments—is often combined with the hierarchical directory structure, which we describe next.

Hierarchical Directories. The flexibility of a private directory for each user can be extended greatly if it is possible to create distinct directories for each category of files that a user may wish to store. The ability to dynamically create and delete any number of directories has been a popular feature of newer file systems.

To organize a system with many directories, a hierarchical organization is almost always used. There is a single main directory, or perhaps a main directory on each volume or for each user. This directory contains descriptors for various named files; some of these files may themselves be directories. In this way a tree structure of any desired complexity can be created. Figure 12–15 illustrates this organization.

Figure 12–15 Hierarchical Directory Organization

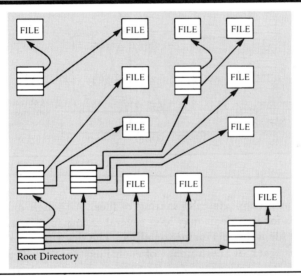

A file is identified in a hierarchical directory system by concatenating the names of all the directories that contain it, starting at the highest level, with the file name itself. This technique allows very long, descriptive names even if each individual directory and file name must be short. To avoid constant use of long names, the concept of a **current directory** can be used. If a user designates a certain directory as the current one, names can be used that start from that directory rather than the highest level.

Hierarchical directories lead to efficient searching of individual directories, since each directory will tend to contain few descriptors. However, a number of directories may need to be searched to locate a particular file.

Partitioned Descriptors. Some file systems divide descriptors into parts, distributing the parts to separate locations. One example of this approach is found in UNIX, which has both hierarchical and centralized directory structures. The UNIX structure is illustrated in Figure 12–16. The hierarchical directories are stored and managed like ordinary files. However, they contain partial descriptors that include only the file name and and index to the central directory. The central directory contains descriptors (called *i-nodes*) with all other file information.

Figure 12–16 Partitioned Directory: UNIX i-nodes

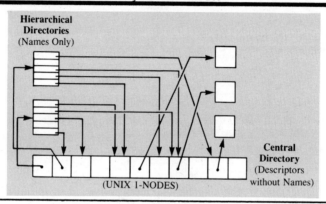

This approach supports easy sharing of files. Although only one central descriptor exists for any file, it may have several entries in different directories, each giving the file a distinct name, or **alias.** The descriptor itself records no name but keeps track of the number of such links that exist, so that it can determine when it is no longer needed. File aliases make sharing convenient but can cause problems in accounting if it is not clear which specific user "owns" each file.

Another type of partitioning maintains part of the file descriptor in a **file header** at the beginning of the file itself. A more centralized directory is still required to provide a starting point to locate the file. File headers provide a method for storing optional file descriptors that may be maintained separately from the OS itself.

Searching and Sorting. The most important operation performed on a directory is searching for a file descriptor matching a specified name. The directory must be organized to support rapid searching. This is the reason for the importance of fixed-length directories.

For optimum searching, an efficient technique such as binary search would be desirable. However, binary search requires a sorted directory. Since directories are accessed constantly, it would be necessary to maintain them in a constantly sorted order at all times. Each new addition would have to be put directly in the proper place, and the rest of the directory reorganized as necessary. Moreover, access to the directory by other users would not be possible during the rearrangement.

In addition, updating a directory is a very frequent operation. Rearrangement would consume a substantial amount of time. For these reasons, directories are rarely maintained in a sorted order.

Even rearrangement to reclaim space after deleting descriptors is seldom done. However, if all descriptors are the same length, vacated spaces may be reused in place and rearrangement is not necessary. The use of a blocked chained organization also supports effective space management, even with variable length entries. This approach is illustrated by DOS-99 (see Figure 12–17). Each block contains one or more complete descriptors (no spanning allowed). Thus, some space is available in many blocks. When a descriptor is deleted, the remaining descriptors in that block only are compacted. The block remains in the chain even if it becomes completely empty. When additions are made, a first-fit technique is used to store the new descriptor in the first block with sufficient space. If no space is found in any existing block, a new block is allocated.

Searching of unsorted directories must use a linear searching technique. For single directories with many files, this can be a serious bottleneck. The problem is clearly visible when locating files on large MVT volumes. When there are multiple directories, however, each directory contains fewer files and the cost of linear searching is much more bearable.

Preserving Deleted Files. A number of file systems attempt to provide the ability to recover recently deleted files. This ability can be of great value if a user has accidentally deleted files that are needed.

Deletion can be reversed as long as neither the data space nor the descriptor for a file have been reused. Preserving data space is most feasible in a blocked system that maintains available blocks on a free chain. If blocks are added to the chain at one end and removed at the other, the chain will tend to contain the most recently added information.

A similar strategy must be used with directory entries. As far as possible, new entries must be stored in new space or replace the oldest previous entries. Thus CP/M uses its available directory space in a circular fashion, and UNIX rarely reuses old directory entries. Even so, reverse deletion must proceed with care, as there may be no guarantee that all of the data blocks identified by deleted descriptors are still undisturbed.

12.5 DEVICES AND FILES

I/O devices may be accessible through the file system, although they generally lack the full capabilities of files for reading, writing, and storage. If this can be done, then devices can benefit as far as possible from the advanced operations and types of access the file system may make available.

Treating devices in a manner similar to files makes possible the important concept of **device independence**. If this concept is fully supported, it may be possible to select any of a variety of devices or files interchangeably as input and output sources for programs, and to change this selection each time a program is run.

There are three basic approaches to handling devices in a file system. The first approach is to treat files and devices in a completely separate way. The second is to consider devices as possible containers of files. The third and most flexible approach is to consider devices as a special kind of file. These approaches, illustrated in Figure 12–17, are discussed in the following subsections.

Devices as Separate Resource Types

In the approach most prevalent in earlier operating systems, access to I/O devices was considered entirely separate from file access. This distinction is still maintained at the program interface by many systems, such as CP/M and OS/MVT. System calls designed to access files must be given the names of true files only. Entirely different system calls must be used to access printers, terminals, complete disks, or other physical devices.

Even in these systems, however, some device independence is allowed at the command interface. CP/M provides for a few special device names to be used in place of file names in commands, while MVT allows both files and devices to be specified interchangeably in job control statements.

Devices as Containers of Files

A natural view of the relationship between devices and files places devices at the highest level. All data transfer is to or from physical devices, but some devices contain file systems. RT-11 is an example OS using this approach. Devices and files are both assigned names and managed by uniform techniques at both the program interface and the command interface. Each device has a permanent name, however, and device and file names are syntactically distinct. Under RT-11, the names TT:, DK0:, and DK0:MYFILE.DAT refer respectively to the terminal, disk unit 0, and a particular file stored on disk

Figure 12–17 Handling Devices in a File System

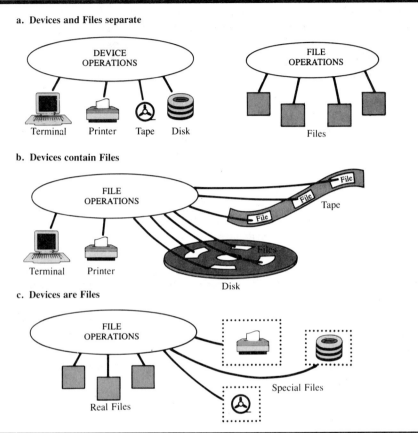

a. **Devices and Files separate**

b. **Devices contain Files**

c. **Devices are Files**

unit 0. (Note the required colon at the end of each device name.) The name MYFILE.DAT may also be used by itself to refer to a file on a designated default disk unit. A similar strategy is used by VAX/VMS.

Devices as Files

An alternate approach to merging devices with the file system is used by UNIX. Devices are viewed as special cases of files. When a device is installed in a UNIX system, it is assigned an ordinary name and given a descriptor in a suitable directory. However, the descriptor identifies it as a device and contains a suitable device description in place of an index to file blocks. There is no syntactic distinction between device and file names.

A UNIX file name contains no indication of the storage device on which the file is stored. Instead, the root directory and all files are normally assumed to be stored on a designated default device. If files on other storage devices are to be included in the hierarchy, entire subsystems can be attached to the existing file system by a special *mount* operation, which causes a directory entry on the original device to identify the device containing the new subsystem.

12.6 BASIC OPERATIONS ON FILES

The purpose of all the various organizations of files and related information is to enable users and programs to perform operations on file contents. Often the user views these operations at a very high level: accessing records by key, performing queries on a database, for example. However, the program interface must carry out these operations in terms of much simpler ones. The file management portion of the program interface provides a basic set of operations to manipulate file storage. All other access procedures must be constructed in terms of these.

This section examines these basic operations. Although their overall purpose is similar in most file systems, their precise form may vary greatly. Gradually, systems are evolving to a common view of the form many of these operations should take. This is the view we focus on in this brief study.

Data Structures to Support File Operations

File operations must make use of information stored in main memory while a sequence of operations is underway. The most important data structures required to support file operations are **buffers** and **file control blocks (FCBs).**

File buffers are storage areas reserved to contain copies of blocks or groups of blocks of data. These buffers are necessary because file information must be transferred in complete blocks. The file manager attempts to maintain copies of the most useful information in the available buffers, including both descriptors and file contents.

The file control block is a working data structure describing both the file and the operations currently being performed on it. An FCB often consists in large part of a copy of the permanent file descriptor. However, some information from the descriptor may not be needed, and additional data are generally required. These data may include the type of use currently permitted for the file, the current position in the file, and other information.

Some systems, such as CP/M and MVT, put much of the burden for managing FCBs on application or library programs. The programs must create and initialize the FCB and set it up properly before various operations occur. The file manager is then given a simple request and a pointer to the FCB, which provides the information needed to carry out the operation.

More commonly, FCBs are maintained privately by the OS itself. The user performs operations by specifying the file name directly. Usually these operations must start with an initialization step, such as OPEN, which notifies the OS to setup an FCB for future use. At the same time, the OS returns to the user a shorthand name, such as a small integer (often serving as an FCB index), which can be used to request further operations on this file.

System Calls for File Management

Operations for file manipulation and data transfer are performed by the file manager in response to requests submitted by processes. At the lowest level, these requests take the form of system calls through the program interface. On many larger OSs these system calls are rarely programmed directly, since extensive library procedures may be provided to support higher-level manipulation of files. The low-level system calls are always present, however, and form the fundamental building blocks on which more advanced procedures must be built. The rest of this section discusses these system calls.

To perform a file operation, a process must supply appropriate parameter values along with the system call, and result parameters may be returned when the operation is complete. In some OSs file control blocks are created and maintained by each process, and pointers to these blocks form a major parameter for each call. This is the approach chosen by MVT and CP/M. In other cases, the FCBs are maintained by the OS outside of the virtual space of the processes. The parameters required in this case specify operations and results in a simpler and more direct way. This is the method used by UNIX.

In general, explicit management of FCBs places more responsibility on programs and increases the likelihood of errors or security problems. In MVT, however, this manipulation is hidden from most programs by higher-level library procedures.

MS-DOS, in its versions 2.0 and above, provides two distinct sets of file manipulation system calls. One set, based on CP/M, requires FCBs to be managed by the application program; the other, based on UNIX, does not.

Unfortunately, there is little agreement among various operating systems on the precise set of file manipulation system calls that should be provided. This is a major barrier to portability of application programs, which may be overcome by more widely accepted standards. The following subsections describe typical system calls and file management operations.

File Access

The most universal file operations supported by most file managers are those that support reading and writing of file information. Processes must be able to request data transfers in either direction, specifying the location and size of the information to be transferred. This is accomplished by **read, write, and seek** operations. For various reasons, the OS needs to prepare a file for use, and to be notified when a sequence of use is completed—needs that are achieved by use of **open** and **close** operations.

A system call to open a file is required in all but a few systems. The process must identify the file by supplying either a name or an FCB, and specify the type of access intended for the file. The OS ensures that the request is valid and sets up the necessary data structures to enable access. Often, the OS also returns to the process a temporary identifier for the file, such as a small integer. This value is used by the process to identify the file during subsequent access operations.

The information provided about the intended access may include:

- whether the file will be read, written, or both.
- whether information will be accessed sequentially or randomly.
- the starting position in the file for sequential access.
- the units in which information should be transferred.
- the buffers that should be reserved for file transfers.
- whether the file may be opened simultaneously by other users.

When all intended reading or writing of a file has been completed, a *close* operation is normally used to advise the operating system that the file is no longer needed. This allows the OS to deallocate buffers and make any required adjustments to the file descriptor. A *close* operation is essential after writing because some data may not yet have been copied from buffers to the actual file. Occasionally the *close* operation has additional effects, such as deleting a file designated as temporary.

The system call structures for *read* and *write* operations are usually straightforward. Each request specifies a location in the process address space and the amount of data to be transferred. If access is sequential, each transfer starts from the position in the file where the last one ended. If access is random, the starting position (e.g., the record number) must be specified each time. This information may be included with the *write* call, but more often is provided by a separate *seek* operation.

Although the form of these calls is simple, the operating system may follow a complex strategy to form the best balance between performance, reliability, and convenient and natural behavior. Because storage devices must transfer data in full blocks, suitable buffers are normally maintained by the

OS. Data must be physically transferred between the buffers and the device, and separately copied between the buffers and the process's data structures.

If access is sequential, the file manager may perform **lookahead** by reading blocks, in advance, into additional buffers that are expected to be needed in the future. The OS may retain many blocks of a file in buffers, and search these buffers on each read request to see if the data is already in memory. When data are written by a process, the OS may retain the data in buffers, to be physically transferred at a more convenient time. This approach to file output is found in UNIX and can lead to unexpected data loss if the system fails or is shut down incorrectly.

This group of file access operations forms the basic model for the great majority of operating systems. In a few cases, a *read* or *write* request will automatically open a file, and an explicit *close* may be unnecessary. A significant variation is found in MULTICS, which treats both files and a process's program code and working data uniformly as **segments.** By one view, all segments are like files organized in a hierarchical file system. However, an operation roughly equivalent to *open* results in assigning a number to a selected segment and installing it directly in the virtual address space of the process. Thereafter, a two-level address (segment number, offset) is used directly in machine instructions to reference information in the file in the same manner as normal "main memory" information.

File Space Management

The fundamental system services required to manage file space in a dynamic file system are those that **create** and **delete** files. In addition, systems that provide for explicit management of file size may include operations to **extend** or **truncate** the size of an existing file.

A system call for file creation must specify a file name, information about its desired location and structure, and any attributes that should be assigned to the new file. Default values for much of this information may be provided so that little more than the file name is actually required as a parameter.

If a blocked file organization is used, you normally don't need to specify a size for the file when created. No blocks need be allocated initially; allocation may occur as information is actually written to the file. This is the case for UNIX. With contiguous organization, however, an initial size allocation must be specified so that contiguous space can be reserved. Both MVT and CP/M, for example, require explicit allocation. So does RT-11, but default parameters can be used to specify, for example, the largest available space.

Some program interfaces combine *create* and *open* in various ways. A newly created file may be automatically opened, or an *open* operation may automatically create the file if it doesn't already exist (this occasionally happens even when access for reading has been specified!). In RT-11 the *create* operation also opens the file, and is considered tentative until its first use is completed. No descriptor is stored for the file until it is closed. Upon closing, the file's size is normally reduced to that needed to hold the data actually written.

A straightforward *delete* operation removes a specified file. If a "contiguous with extents" file organization is used, an *extend* system call is provided to add extents to an existing file. The size of each extent may be specified by this call, or may have been specified when the file was created. Finally, a *truncate* operation is sometimes provided to remove space at the end of a file that is not currently occupied by data.

Support Operations

A variety of operations may be supported to access and change file attributes and related information, either in FCBs or in directory descriptors. While changes to structural information may not be possible, many logical characteristics of files may be subject to change at will.

The most common operation in this category is **rename,** which changes the name of a file. A general operation such as *get file information* may exist to get all useful information from the directory entry or FCB. Other operations may be available to change the file owner, type, access restrictions, or control information. Some of these changes may require suitable privileges. If files can be shared, the OS may support a *link* operation, as in UNIX, to provide an alias for an existing file.

Volume Control

In file systems where volumes may be physically removed and replaced, the OS needs to recognize when a change has taken place, and to adapt to use of the new volume. If the change can be detected by hardware, and each volume contains a suitable volume descriptor for identification, no explicit operations may be required. However, many systems provide *mount* and *unmount* operations to inform the system of a volume change and make necessary adjustments. In UNIX, these calls are used to attach the new volume to a selected position in the overall file hierarchy.

Asynchronous File Access

When operations requiring physical activity are performed on files, it may be some time before the operation can be completed. Example operations in this class are *create, open, read,* and *write.* Normally, it is assumed that a process requesting such operations does not wish to proceed until the operation is completed. The process is put into a blocked state, and other processes are scheduled. This mode of operation is called **synchronous file access.**

In some situations, processes do need to proceed while the operation is in progress. A good example may occur when reading from a file that is really a slow device, such as a terminal; it is not certain when or if input will be available. Similarly, a process performing output may prefer to proceed, assuming that the output will finish eventually and not waiting for it unless the buffer must be reused. To deal with these situations, some OSs allow **asynchronous file access.** In this mode the system calls may result in placing a request in a queue for later service. The process is resumed immediately, but with no guarantee that the operation is complete.

Asynchronous access may be supported by a parameter supplied with the system call or by a separate set of operations. The latter approach is more common (examples include non-waiting *read* and *write* on RT-11 and queued I/O on MVT.). If this type of access is permitted, the process needs a mechanism to check later to determine if the operation has completed, and to obtain its results, if any. The most flexible methods may allow the process either to simply check on the status of an operation, to sleep for a limited time period while waiting, or to abort the request. All of these are supported in the file operations proposed by the IEEE MOSI standard [IEEE 1985a].

12.7 ACCESS CONTROL

Files are an important sharable information resource that also can be important means of long-term storage and of communication. However, they can cause difficulties if misused. Although many files must be made accessible to users other than their original creator, it is necessary to have a system for controlling who may access a file and what type of access is permitted.

The usual solution to this problem is to include information in the file's directory entry, maintained by its owner (creator), which controls who can do what to the file. This information may consist of a list of user names and a code indicating what operations each may perform. Such a list is called an **access control list.** Operations that are often distinguished for this purpose include *read, write, execute, append,* and *delete.* More sophisticated access control systems may also control the ability to access and change file attributes, including the access control information itself. Access control lists were employed, for example, by MULTICS.

Access control lists can be quite lengthy and difficult to maintain. They are necessarily of variable length, consume a lot of space, and are slow to search unless sorted. For these reasons many systems simplify this mechanism by identifying a few classes of users. The privileges must be the same for all users in a class. Some classes commonly identified are:

- the owner of the file
- the system manager
- members of the owner's "group"
- everyone else (the "world")

This technique is easy to manage, but would not allow a file to be shared among, for example, just a few unrelated users. This strategy is used by UNIX and VMS.

Another possible way to distinguish authorized users of a file is to define a **password** for the file. The password is a secret part of the file's name. Any user may attempt operations on the file; however, the operation will be permitted only if the user supplies the password. Usually there is only one password, giving users either full access or no access to each file.

This discussion of access control is introductory. A full range of issues related to security and protection of files and other resources is closely examined in Chapter 16.

12.8 HIGH-LEVEL ACCESS METHODS

Many applications find it convenient to treat files as having more complex organizations than we have discussed, and to access these files with higher-level operations.   Software to support high-level views of files may be supplied by individual applications, may be provided by a library of standard procedures associated with the OS (such as the VMS Record Management System), or may be an integral part of the operating system itself.

A set of procedures included in an operating system or as an extension that supports a high-level file organization is known as an **access method.** These procedures are normally linked with the applications that make use of them, or loaded dynamically as needed.

One type of high-level organization commonly supported by access methods is the **library file,** also referred to as a *partitioned data set.* This type of file is illustrated in Figure 12–18. A library file collects a number of smaller sets of information and stores them as "subfiles" within the main file. A contiguous organization is used, with a directory included at the beginning of the main file. Space within the file is allocated in small units, such as bytes. Each subfile begins immediately after the previous one. If a number of small files are to be stored, the library file can save significant space because it does not require that each subfile begin in a new block.

Figure 12–18 Library File Organization

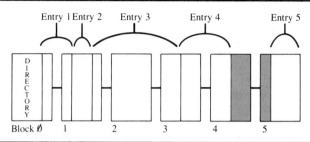

This type of file is suited for applications in which selected small subfiles must be accessed frequently; changes are not common. It is often used to store a set of procedures in source language form to be included in programs during compilation, or a set of procedures in object form to be combined with other programs during the linking process. Compilers and linkers are designed to search these libraries and extract the necessary information.

Another file organization frequently supported by access methods is the **indexed file.** As shown in Figure 12–19, this type of file consists of a collection of data records with associated keys, and one or more indexes that consist of a sequence of keys and pointers to associated records. Indexed files find extensive use in organizing large sets of information that must be searched frequently by various keys.

Figure 12–19 Structure of an Indexed File

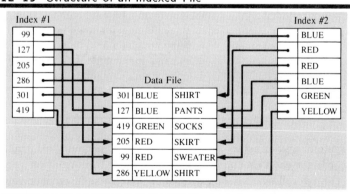

Indexed files may be implemented as a group of direct-access files and managed directly by applications using basic system calls. However, a standard access method that includes procedures to create files, enter data, search, and perform other common operations greatly simplifies their use by a wide variety of programs.

Other file organizations may be supported by access methods in selected cases, including various types of trees, lists, and graph structures. A few systems go further by integrating some of the features of a database management system into the OS. These features can allow users and applications to insert and retrieve information in databases, providing flexibility and logical consistency for the record organizations used by various files and the relationships established between different files and records.

A notable example is the PICK operating system. A PICK file system, as illustrated in Figure 12–20, consists primarily of two types of files: dictionary files and data files. The contents of all these files are in the form of ASCII characters. Dictionaries play a role somewhat like directories; there is a *system dictionary* for the entire system, a *master dictionary* for each user, and a *data dictionary* associated with each data file.

Figure 12–20   Files in the PICK Operating System

User 1 Files   User 2 Files

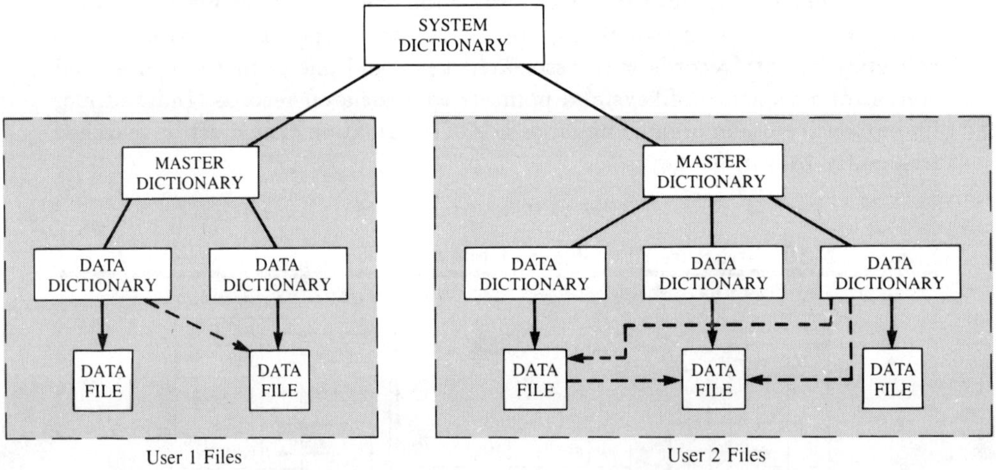

The system and master dictionaries contain account information and related records for each user and collect a variety of information required for managing the overall system or establishing each user's environment. Each data dictionary contains a description of the records in a data file and links to associated files. Each file can contain a hierarchy with up to four levels of information. The file itself is divided into "items" (records), which may be subdivided into attributes, values, and subvalues. The information in each component may be of variable length.

The PICK database may be manipulated by a query language built into the command interface, or by procedures invoked by application programs. It provides a small computer environment well tuned to various business applications.

12.9 SUMMARY

An important responsibility of operating systems is convenient long-term information storage. This need is met by a file system, which stores data in named collections, called files. File systems are maintained on physical storage devices such as disks. The OS component responsible for the file system is called the file manager.

A file system includes a number of volumes, or individual collections of files. Some of these may be removable. Each volume usually includes a volume descriptor, which identifies the volume and indicates its structure. Other important storage areas on a volume are file areas, directories, and system areas.

The time required to access information on a file storage device may depend on its location. Organization is an important consideration. Main directories are most efficiently accessed if stored at the middle of the storage area. Files may have several different fundamental organizations; for example, contiguous and contiguous with extents. These methods keep each file in one or a few continuous pieces. They are simple to manage and can provide fast access, but adding and extending files is difficult. Fragmentation can develop, which requires frequent reorganization.

Blocked organizations may be either chained or indexed. Chaining with a separate table of links is another option for small file systems. This type of organization is more flexible but can require more complex file descriptors and lead to somewhat slower access.

Files may be considered to have an internal structure. They are usually viewed as a sequence of records of fixed or variable length. Files may have various attributes associated with them, such as owner name, access restrictions, access methods, and content type. These attributes, together with information on where the file is located, are recorded in file descriptors, which are collected in directories.

Directories record information about each file, together with file names. These names may have many different forms and structures. Directories may be viewed as a special file or stored in independent areas. There may be a single directory for each volume, or multiple directories usually organized into a hierarchy. In some cases, directories containing file names may be separated from the remainder of the file descriptors, enabling files to be shared more easily.

Many file systems provide access to I/O devices through file operations. If devices are not considered entirely separate from files, they may be considered as higher-level elements that may contain files, or as special cases of files themselves.

The file system maintains file control blocks in memory to describe all files in current use. These data structures are set up by open operations, which inform the system that a particular file is going to be used. They are then used by various file operations until terminated by a close operation. Other basic operations supported for files include file access operations such as *read*, *write*, and *seek;* space management operations such as *create*, *delete*, *extend*, and *truncate;* and support operations such as *rename* or *get file information*. Asynchronous or nonblocking access is supported on some systems by separate system calls or special parameters.

Access control is usually enforced on files during all operations, to ensure that only permitted operations are performed on each file. The permitted operations may depend on the user, with maximum privileges usually belonging to the file's creator. This information is maintained in the descriptor by a mechanism, such as an access control list.

Higher-level file organizations are often needed by applications, and may be supported by procedures called access methods, which are provided as part of the OS or as associated procedures. Common organizations include library files and indexed files. A few systems provide support for an integrated database.

≡ FOR FURTHER READING ≡

Many practically-oriented operating system texts include a detailed treatment of file management. Some recommended examples include Peterson and Silberschatz [1985], Finkel [1986], Milenković [1987], and Tanenbaum [1987]. In addition, a number of texts have focused specifically on file management, especially higher-level structures. London [1973] provides a thorough if somewhat dated study with a detailed treatment of physical storage devices. Claybrook [1983] and Loomis [1983] provide full treatments of file organization, although the latter includes more extensive coverage of general data structures.

An early tutorial on file organization techniques was presented by Dodd [1969], and several techniques were compared by Chapin [1969]. A survey of file I/O control logic in several mainframe systems is given by Dependahl and Presser [1976]. Bailey et al. [1981] describe a method of supporting user-defined file formats.

The UNIX file system is summarized by Ritchie and Thompson [1974] and extensively described by Bach [1986]. MULTICS file management is covered by Organick [1972]. Other case studies include Zaks [1980] for CP/M, King [1983] for PC-DOS, Sisk and Van Arsdale [1985] for PICK, Powell [1977] for DEMOS, and Richards et al. [1979] for TRIPOS.

There is increasing interest in portable file systems, and in independent file systems for use as file servers in distributed environments. Hanson [1980] describes a portable "UNIX-like" file system. References for distributed file servers are given in Chapter 23.

IMPORTANT TERMS

access control list
access method
alias
asynchronous file access
blocked chained organization
blocked indexed organization
buffer
catalog
close
contiguous organization
contiguous organization
  with extents
create
current directory
delete
device independence
directory
extend
extent
field
file
file allocation table (FAT)
file attribute
file control block (FCB)
file descriptor
file header
file manager
file name

file system
free chain
home directory
indexed file
library file
logical volume
lookahead
open
paging area
password
physical volume
read
record
rename
seek
segment
simple contiguous organization
spanning
swap area
synchronous file access
system area
text file
truncate
volume
volume descriptor
volume name
write

≡ REVIEW QUESTIONS ≡

1. Explain why operating systems are usually stored on disk in a special system area rather than as regular files.

2. Besides the essential descriptive information (name, location and structure), some file directories record many types of file attributes. List and briefly explain five attributes that are likely to be included in file descriptors.

3. Explain the principal actions performed by an *open* operation.

4. List three types of information that may be present in a file volume descriptor.

5. List the minimum items of information required in a directory to describe the location of each file if files are stored using each of the following methods: (a) simple contiguous, (b) blocked chained, (c) blocked indexed.

6. The file allocation table method, used by MS-DOS to manage space on floppy disks, would be unsuitable for large systems with many large disk volumes. Explain why.

7. In a large file system, long descriptive file names are needed to distinguish each file. Why is it difficult to support this need?

8. Some OSs restrict the permitted character set for file names so that names can be stored more compactly. Give another advantage for a limited character set.

9. List four common primitive system calls concerned with the management of file space.

10. Which of the following system calls is NOT a primitive file operation:

   i. *read;* ii. *open;* iii. *rename;* iv. *copy;* v. *seek*

   Show how the system call you identified can be implemented in terms of other primitive calls.

≡ ASSIGNMENTS ≡

1. State a possible advantage and disadvantage of storing system programs, such as editors and compilers, in a system area rather than as regular files.

2. We have studied four types of file organizations. For each of the following applications, select a suitable organization and explain why it is suitable.

    a. a report that is being revised frequently

    b. an astronomical data base organized for random access

    c. a program source file

    d. a set of employee payroll records

3. Suppose you want to store multiple versions of a file, so that records that are identical in different versions are stored only once. Which file organization technique is best suited to this requirement? Explain why.

4. A file containing 500,000 bytes of data is to be stored on several file systems. Suppose that four bytes are required to specify a disk address. Give the total storage requirements for data blocks and overhead (but not counting the file descriptor itself) for each of the following organizational methods:

    a. simple contiguous

    b. blocked chained, as in DOS-99, with 512-byte blocks and two-way pointers in each block

    c. blocked indexed, as in UNIX, with 512-byte blocks and indexes for the first ten blocks maintained directly in the file descriptor

5. Two problems that arise in file system design are: (1) directory entries should allow efficient searching and contain little wasted space, and (2) files should be able to have clearly descriptive names. Explain how a hierarchical directory system can help resolve both of these problems.

6. Operating systems vary greatly in the amount of information stored in a file descriptor to describe the type of information it contains. Describe some problems that occur if a system does not distinguish text files from other types of data.

7. Explain one disadvantage (other than the space required) of storing detailed information about file types in file descriptors.

8. A certain operating system maintains no information in file descriptors except the name and location of the file. Suppose an application program needs to maintain more extensive attributes for a set of files in a header block in each file. Which of the attribute categories listed at the end of Section 12.3 could be managed in this way?

9. Almost all file systems with multiple directories use a hierarchical relationship between directories. Discuss some possible benefits and problems of allowing more general relationships, such as a network.

10. Describe some problems that could arise in a system that allows multiple names for the same file, such as UNIX.

11. Why do you think UNIX stores its i-nodes in a fixed contiguous area rather than in a more flexible structure, such as a regular file?

12. Why is it difficult to support direct access to a file with variable-length records? Suggest a method for managing such files if direct access is required.

13. A few operating systems automatically open a file on a *read* or *write* call, making a separate *open* operation unnecessary. Explain some weaknesses of this approach.

14. One proposal for a set of file manager system calls divides the IT "open" operation into two parts. The first step, *connect*, locates the file and sets up an FCB. The second step, *open*, enables access to the file with a specific access mode. When a file is *closed*, the FCB is not released until it is specifically *disconnected*. Comment on the merits of this approach.

15. State a possible advantage and disadvantage of combining each of the following operations in a single system call:

    a. open for output, automatically create if non-existent

    b. xreate file, automatically open for output

    c. delete file, automatically close if open

    d. combine *seek* with *read* and *write*

≡ PROJECT ≡

This section describes a four-part programming project to implement a simple blocked indexed file system. The project may make use of the disk driver implemented in Chapter 9. You should read the general description in this text in conjunction with the more specific descriptions given in your project manual. This mechanism is an important component of the multiprogramming executive (MPX) project described later in the text.

a. Using your disk driver or a preallocated direct access file as specified by your instructor, design a volume organization including a one-block volume descriptor, fixed-size directory area, and file area. Assume all space is allocated in 512-byte blocks. Characteristics of your file system should include the following.

- The volume descriptor includes a name of up to eight ASCII characters and a pointer to the directory.
- File names consist of up to eight ASCII characters. There are no special components.
- Files are organized in a blocked indexed form; the maximum file size is eight blocks.
- All files are accessed sequentially and viewed as a sequence of bytes. File attributes to be maintained consist of the name of the process that created the file and a flag indicating whether it is a text file.
- There is a single directory with fixed-size descriptors. Information in each descriptor consists of file name, attributes as listed above, and eight index pointers. Multilevel indexes are not needed.

b. Design a data structure for file control blocks to be maintained for open files. In addition to descriptor information, the FCB should record the type of access specified for the file (read or write), and the current position in the file. FCBs should be statically allocated with a maximum of two files open at the same time.

c. Implement a set of procedures to manipulate your file system. The operation of these procedures is as follows:

1. Init_Files: Initialize the entire file system.
2. E=Create_File(type): Create a new file of a type specified by type. A value of 1 indicates text, 0 indicates binary. No initial space needs to be allocated. A nonzero error code is returned in E if creation is not possible.

3. `id=Open_File(name, mode)`: Open the specified file for sequential reading or writing, as specified by `mode`. The value 0 means read, and the value 1 means write. The current location should be set to the beginning of the file for reading or to the end for writing. The procedure returns an identifier code (positive integer) for the file in the variable `id`. If the open fails, a negative error code is returned.

4. `E=Write_File(id,buffer)`: Write a single 512-byte block of data to the file specified by `id` at the current position. The variable `buffer` represents the starting address of the data in memory. This function should allocate new file space if required, as long as the maximum is not exceeded. A nonzero error code is returned if the write fails.

5. `E=Read_File(id, buffer)`: Read a single 512-byte block of data from the file specified by `id` into the location specified by `buffer`. A nonzero error code is returned if the read fails.

6. `E=Close_File(id)`: Close the specified file, deallocating its FCB. A nonzero error code is returned if the close fails.

d. Add a command FILE DUMP to the command handler, which displays the name and currently allocated sequence of blocks for each file in your system.

A Simple
Multiprogramming
Executive (MPX)

A Simple Multiprogramming Executive (MPX)

13.1 INTRODUCTION

This chapter presents a simple model of a MultiProgramming eXecutive called MPX. The purpose of this chapter is to bring together most of the ideas and projects presented in previous chapters in a simple project model that you can easily visualize and understand. The companion MPX project manual describes the project for a specific computer system environment; this chapter presents the more generic form of this MPX model.

13.2 OVERVIEW OF MPX

MPX provides a multiprogramming environment that allows the dynamic creation, suspension, destruction, and control of application processes via a command interface system process, COMHAN. There are a number of other components, most of which have been presented as projects in earlier chapters. Figure 13–1 presents an overview of the structure of the simple MPX model operating system.

The purpose of the specific components of MPX shown in the figure is as follows:

- MPX_INIT: MPX initialization procedure
- DISPATCH: process dispatcher
- SYS_CALL: system call handler
- IO_SCHED: I/O scheduler

Figure 13–1 The Structure of MPX

MPX_INIT
DISPATCH
SYS_CALL
IO_SCHED
IO_SUP
DISK_DRIVER
DISK_INT
PRINTER_DRIVER
PRINTER_INT
SERIAL_DRIVER
SERIAL_INT
CLOCK_DRIVER
CLOCK_INT
IO_COMPLETE
COMHAN Process
IDLE Process
System Data Structures and Process Load Areas

- IO_SUP: I/O supervisor, including I/O device drivers, clock driver, and their interrupt handlers
- IO_COMPLETE: I/O completion event handler
- COMHAN process: command interface (system) process
- IDLE process: system process that executes only when no other process is in the ReadyQ
- System data structures: working data area

13.3 OS RESPONSIBILITIES INCLUDED IN MPX

The MPX structure includes components to fulfill the OS responsibilities of device management, process management, memory management, and the user interface. Device management includes I/O scheduling and interrupt handling supported by various device drivers. Together these drivers comprise a resident I/O supervisor. Process management uses PCBs to represent processes. Process scheduling is priority-driven and a simple dispatcher is used to assign the CPU to the next process that is *ready*. Memory management is in the form of static allocation and memory partitioning, although there are options for using dynamic regions for process loading.

One system process fills the important role of user interface: the process COMHAN. This process and the process IDLE are created on system startup; all application processes are created using commands to COMHAN. IDLE is a low-priority system process that merely uses all CPU time when there is no other *ready* process in the ready queue. The system process COMHAN is central to the MPX project because all process creation, suspension, and destruction are controlled by COMHAN. Note that COMHAN has been implemented in stages to simplify the process. The final step in its operation in the MPX environment is to convert COMHAN's dispatching, which was in a test environment, to a true dispatcher DISPATCH. DISPATCH also dispatches COMHAN, which itself is represented by a PCB.

In reality, MPX includes the principal management responsibilities typically found in the kernel or resident portion of an operating system. Although some other common OS responsibilities are not included, the ones present provide an excellent model for understanding how the various components of a multiprogramming operating system interact.

The processes running under the control of MPX really are the data to the operating system. MPX, like any other operating system, does not "know" what problem is being solved, although it might "know" characteristics of processes (for example, whether a process is compute-bound or I/O-bound). MPX provides users with sufficient resources to accomplish their desired work on the computer. The ease with which a user can accomplish this work is a primary means of judging the operating system. For this reason, the process COMHAN is critical. The types of commands it provides, the responses it prints, and the help facility included will determine a user's impression of MPX.

13.4 PROCESS MANAGEMENT

The kernel of most operating systems is usually entered by some type of system call or interrupt. In MPX we treat a system call as a type of interrupt, so MPX will be entered by one of three types of interrupts: a system call interrupt, an I/O completion interrupt, or a timer interrupt. The initial interrupt processing by the MPX is done with interrupts disabled, as in many systems. The MPX project manual provides details on when and how interrupts are disabled when MPX has CPU control.

Distribution of CPU Control under MPX

The scheduling of CPU control by MPX is performed by the dispatcher. However, the distribution of this CPU control will be directly related to I/O demand placed on the system by processes under the control of MPX. The concept that will be used has sometimes been called *I/O demand multiprogramming*. Using this scheme, a process is dispatched for a variable time quantum, the length of which is determined by the time between successive I/O completion interrupts or by the process's next system call interrupt request. Hence, a process maintains control until some type of interrupt occurs. Context switching—and hence the entire operating system—become interrupt-driven. If interrupts were to be blocked permanently, control of the CPU would never be taken away from the *running* process. CPU control is thus distributed according to the I/O demand placed on the system by the processes being controlled by the MPX.

Event Control Blocks

Events such as I/O completion will be represented by event control blocks, or ECBs. ECBs for processes waiting for events can be associated with PCBs representing the processes. The dispatcher will be implemented in a manner such that processes waiting for I/O events (that is, those whose ECBs indicate the pending completion of an event) will not be dispatched.

It would be possible to allow processes to have an I/O event pending, yet not treat the processes as being blocked. In this case a process could remain in the *ready* state even though an I/O operation is waiting to be started or is in progress. In order to simplify the MPX design, this case is not allowed. Hence, any process that has an I/O request pending will always be placed in a *blocked* state.

Process States and Data Structures

Since a process that has an I/O event pending is non-dispatchable, a process requesting I/O will make a transition from a *ready* state to a *blocked* state. To avoid the need to search one long I/O queue, as discussed in Chapter 9, active I/O will be represented by a simple I/O control block (IOCB) and the MPX will recognize two distinct *blocked* waiting-for-I/O states rather than one:

- *IO_init* (waiting for the initiation of an I/O operation)
- *IO_active* (I/O is in progress and the process is waiting for the completion of an active I/O operation)

There will then be four *mutually exclusive* states for MPX processes: *ready, running, IO_init,* and *IO_active.* The MPX operating system will allow a variable number of current processes to run at any given instant in time up to some maximum limit, dependent upon how MPX is generated. There can be only one *running* process. There are a variable number of processes in the *ready* state and the *IO_init* state. However, there can never be more processes in the *IO_active* state than there are I/O devices supported by MPX, because only one I/O operation per device can be pending at any moment.

The following data structures will represent the above states:

- Running_Process: a pointer to the PCB of the *running* process

- ReadyQ: a linked list of PCBs of all processes in the *ready* state

- IO_initQ: a linked list of PCBs representing processes waiting for the initiation of some I/O operation

- IO_activeQ: a simple list of PCBs representing processes waiting for an I/O operation which is in progress

To simplify the implementation of MPX, the IO_activeQ has one double "word" entry (IOCB) per device, with each entry being assigned a *unique* device name. The first "word" of an IOCB is a pointer to the PCB for the process that requested the I/O operation in progress; the second "word" *is* the ECB for the pending I/O event. The ECB value for a device will be zero if the I/O event is in progress and nonzero if it is completed. A zero entry in a device's PCB pointer indicates no I/O operation is in progress for this device.

Figure 13-2 illustrates these data structures and some relationships that may exist among them. A process begins in the ReadyQ. When selected by the dispatcher, it will become the *running* process. Upon an I/O service request, the I/O scheduler IO_SCHED is called. If the device is ready and not busy, the process will enter the *IO_active* state, with its PCB address being placed in the appropriate IOCB. The I/O operation will be initiated by the appropriate device driver of the I/O supervisor. Note that only upon completion of this I/O request will this process once again become *ready.*

Had the I/O scheduler recognized that the requested device was busy (the first word of the IOCB for that device was nonzero, i.e., it pointed to a PCB of a process using the device), the process would have entered the *IO_init* state, with its PCB being linked into the IO_initQ in FIFO or priority order. The process remains in the *IO_init* state until the device completes its operation for another process, thus becoming available for another I/O operation, and the waiting process is selected to use the requested device. At that time, this *IO_init* process would move to the *IO_active* state. Figure 13-3 illustrates the state diagram and the events that move processes from state to state in MPX. Note that all state transitions result from an interrupt, thus reinforcing the idea that MPX is interrupt-driven. Figure 13-4 demonstrates how the queue structures change during these changes of states.

Figure 13–2   Running_Process, ReadyQ, IO_initQ, and IO_activeQ

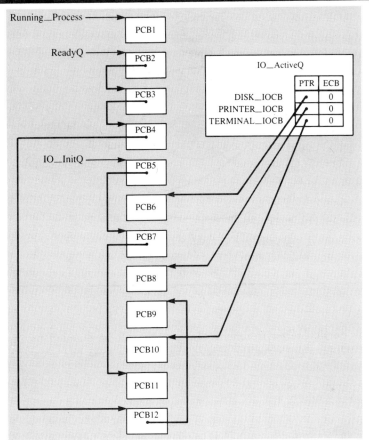

Critical Sections

In the simple MPX being considered, it is sufficient to block interrupts in order to guarantee permission to enter a critical section. This guarantees mutually exclusive update of shared system data areas within the MPX. The generic MPX user processes do *not* share any data areas and hence will not have critical section problems. However, the process COMHAN will access system information when controlling process states, loading processes, and so on. If an interrupt occurs while COMHAN is updating critical system information in a system data area like ReadyQ, the integrity of the system data could be destroyed. Thus, COMHAN will block interrupts prior to updating such critical system data using the appropriate function call (disable) as provided

Figure 13–3 State Diagram of Process State Transitions

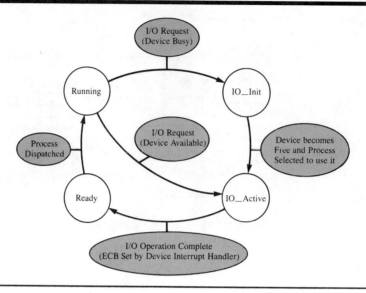

for in the particular environment. Interrupts will be enabled using another function call (enable) once the shared system data area has been changed.

Process Scheduling and PCBs

Processes scheduling in MPX is priority-driven. Each application process is assigned a priority that (initially) reflects its compute- or I/O-boundedness. Since the dispatcher controls the CPU resource, and I/O-bound processes use very little of this resource, I/O-bound processes are given higher priorities than compute-bound processes. The initial priority assigned to each test process has been chosen on this basis. The SETPRIORITY command of COMHAN allows one to observe the effects of changing dispatching priorities of processes. When this command is used, the PCBs in the appropriate queue (ReadyQ or IO_initQ) must be reordered to reflect the requested priority change.

Processes that are loaded by COMHAN in response to a LOAD or RUN command must be placed in the ReadyQ in priority order. The dispatcher will dispatch the first process found in the queue; *eventually* the loaded application process will be dispatched when higher priority processes are *blocked* waiting for I/O. Note that it is possible for a process to be loaded in a *suspended* substate. Although it will appear in the ReadyQ, it will not be dispatched

Figure 13-4 Process State Changes Represented by MPX Data Structures

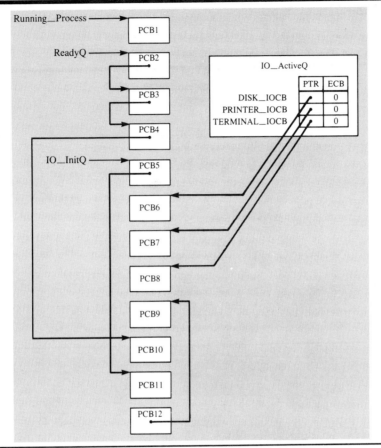

by the dispatcher until the operator removes it from the suspended state via a RESUME command.

All processes are represented by PCBs. There is always one "master" linked list of all PCBs, whether empty or in use (representing active processes). All active PCBs are in only one of the queues ReadyQ, IO_initQ, or IO_activeQ. The models presented show PCBs in appropriate linked lists for the ReadyQ and the IO_initQ, and PCB addresses in appropriate IOCBs of the IO_activeQ. An alternative to the use of linked lists to represent the *ready* and *IO_init* states would be the use of a "process state byte" in the PCB that contains different values for these two states. While the *IO_active* state would also be represented by a state byte value, the IOCB would still contain the address of the PCB of the process currently using the respective device. The PCB for a specific implementation of MPX is shown in the project manual. However, Figure 13–5 illustrates the type of information required in all implementations of MPX.

Figure 13–5   MPX PCB Contents

```
PCB_Ptr          Pointer to next PCB
PCB_Pname        Process name
PCB_Type         PCB type
                 = 0   free
                 = 1   system process
                 = 2   application process
PCB_Priority     Process Priority
                 = -128 to +127 for system processes
                 = -128 for free PCBs
                 = -126 to +126 for application processes
PCB_State        Process State
                 = 0   ready
                 = 1   running
                 = 2   blocked
PCB_Suspend      Process Suspended
                 = 0   not suspended
                 = 1   suspended
PCB_Save         Process Context Save Area
PCB_Memory       Pointer to memory for loading process
PCB_MemSize      Size of memory area
PCB_LoadA        Memory area for process loading
```

13.5 THE COMPONENTS OF MPX

MPX_INIT

As with any operating system, an initialization routine, MPX_INIT, prepares MPX for beginning operation. MPX_INIT sets appropriate interrupt vectors for all devices supported in the I/O supervisor. It also sets up the two initial system processes in the system: IDLE and COMHAN. IDLE will have the lowest (dispatching) priority in the system, while COMHAN will have the highest. MPX_INIT finally passes control to DISPATCH, which in turn will initially dispatch COMHAN, the highest-priority process in the ReadyQ. Figure 13–6 contains the logic for MPX_INIT.

Figure 13-6 MPX_INIT Logic

```
MPX_INIT:   set interrupt vectors
            set up IDLE process
            set up COMHAN process
            branch to DISPATCH
```

DISPATCH

The MPX dispatcher DISPATCH is very simple. It selects the first process in the ReadyQ, restores its context, and gives it control of the CPU using the appropriate instruction or support routine. The logic of DISPATCH is given in Figure 13-7.

Figure 13-7 DISPATCH Logic

```
DISPATCH:   set Running_Process to ReadyQ contents
            set ReadyQ to PCB pointer in Running_Process
            restore context of new Running_Process
            RETURN to Running_Process
```

The IDLE Process

The simplest process in the system is a process called IDLE. It is a one-line program that makes no system calls and never voluntarily releases control of the CPU:

```
IDLE:
        WHILE TRUE
        ENDWHILE
```

The purpose of IDLE is to provide a process that is always in the ready queue, thus eliminating the need for the dispatcher to deal with an exceptional condition if the queue is empty. IDLE's dispatch means that all other processes in the system are *blocked,* pending some interrupt; thus, the system has no other useful work to do. IDLE will remain in control of the CPU until some interrupt results in an ECB being set. The setting of an

ECB indicates the completion of a pending I/O event for a process in the IO_activeQ. The process waiting for this event will thus become *ready*. MPX will eventually invoke the dispatcher which simply selects the next process to receive control of the CPU. Since IDLE is the lowest-priority active process running under MPX, the process that just moved to the ReadyQ will be dispatched instead of IDLE.

Interleaved Execution of COMHAN and IDLE

After MPX is loaded and initialized, COMHAN and IDLE are the only active processes. They both begin in the ReadyQ. Each time COMHAN is dispatched, it will either print messages to the terminal screen or request input (of a command) from the user or operator. Each of these I/O requests will result in COMHAN entering the *IO_active* state since no other process will be using the terminal. While COMHAN is *blocked,* IDLE will be dispatched by DISPATCH. Whenever the I/O request for COMHAN completes, preemptive scheduling results in IDLE losing control of the CPU and COMHAN being dispatched. This interleaved dispatching of COMHAN and IDLE will continue until a new application process is created via a command to COMHAN. The intial state of MPX, with only the COMHAN and IDLE processes active, is shown in Figure 13–8.

COMHAN

The system process COMHAN has evolved over several chapters. By now, if all projects have been included, your command handler includes the following commands:

- process control: LOAD, RUN, SETPRIORITY, SUSPEND, RESUME, DISPATCH, TERMINATE
- help facilities: HELP
- information display: VERSION, SHOW, DIRECTORY, FILE
- time/date support: DATE, TIME
- memory management: MEMORY, VMEM
- termination of MPX: STOP

These commands provide an excellent user environment for observing dynamic operation of a multiprogramming OS. Figure 13–9 illustrates a typical sequence of commands for starting and controlling processes via COMHAN.

Figure 13–8 Context Switching with only COMHAN and IDLE Processes

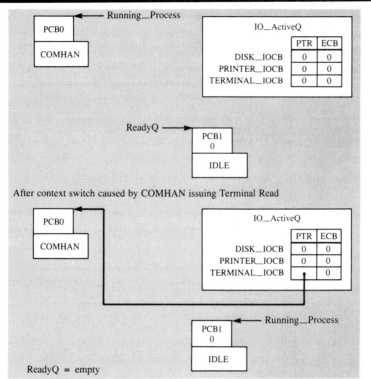

SYS_CALL

All MPX service requests are made via a system call to the SYS_CALL handler using the appropriate instruction or support routine of the MPX project environment. SYS_CALL interprets the type of request and determines whether or not it is an I/O request. If the request is an I/O request, the I/O scheduler IO_SCHED is called to process the request; otherwise, the appropriate SYS_CALL service routine is called. In either case, when service is complete, control passes to DISPATCH to dispatch the next process. Figure 13–10 presents this logic of SYS_CALL. Note that IO_SCHED and the other service routines can change the state of the process being serviced, and can even delete the process from the set of active processes (if the process is requesting termination).

Figure 13–9 Process Control Using COMHAN Commands

```
MPX Command Handler Version 1.4


Command? LOAD PRINT1
*** process PRINT1 loaded (suspended) at 36404, PCB address=1500


Command? SHOW ALL
================================================================
Process Priority    PCB      Load      State     Suspended
                  Address  Address
================================================================
COMHAN    127       1100     20200     IO_Active      No
PRINT1    098       1500     36404     Ready          Yes
IDLE     -128       1200     10100     Running        No




Command? LOAD CPUHOG1
*** process CPUHOG1 loaded (suspended) at 44222, PCB address=1600


Command? SHOW ALL
================================================================
Process Priority    PCB      Load      State     Suspended
                  Address  Address
================================================================
COMHAN    127       1100     20200     IO_Active      No
PRINT1    098       1500     36404     Ready          Yes
CPUHOG1   005       1600     44222     Ready          Yes
IDLE     -128       1200     10100     Running        No




Command? RUN PRINT2
*** process PRINT2 loaded at 66200, PCB address=1700


Command? SHOW ALL
================================================================
Process Priority    PCB      Load      State     Suspended
                  Address  Address
================================================================
COMHAN    127       1100     20200     IO_Active      No
PRINT1    098       1500     36404     Ready          Yes
PRINT2    097       1700     66200     IO_Active      No
CPUHOG1   005       1600     44222     Ready          Yes
IDLE     -128       1200     10100     Running        No
```

Figure 13-9 Process Control Using COMHAN Commands (Continued)

```
Command? RESUME ALL
*** PRINT1, PRINT2 Resumed

Command? SHOW ALL
================================================================
Process Priority    PCB      Load       State      Suspended
                  Address   Address
================================================================
COMHAN    127      1100     20200     IO_Active      No
PRINT1    098      1500     36404     IO_Active      No
PRINT2    097      1700     66200     IO_Init        No
CPUHOG1   005      1600     44222     Running        No
IDLE     -128      1200     10100     Ready          No



Command? SETPRIORITY CPUHOG1=100
*** Priority of CPUHOG1 set to 100

Command? SHOW ALL
================================================================
Process Priority    PCB      Load       State      Suspended
                  Address   Address
================================================================
COMHAN    127      1100     20200     IO_Active      No
CPUHOG1   100      1600     44222     Running        No
PRINT1    098      1500     36404     Ready          No
PRINT2    097      1700     66200     Ready          No
IDLE     -128      1200     10100     Ready          No
```

IO_SUP

The I/O supervisor of MPX consists of device drivers for all or some of the following devices:

- diskette
- printer
- serial interface (terminal)
- clock

The interrupt handlers for each device operate, more or less, as they did in the initial implementation described in earlier chapters, except for the case when the ECB is being set to indicate the requested I/O operation has been completed. Previously, the ECB was used by the calling program. In the MPX environment, the ECB is part of an IO_activeQ (IOCB) entry, and determines what device caused the current interrupt when control is passed

Figure 13-10 SYS_CALL Logic

```
SYS_CALL:
            /* switch calling process to ready */
            save context of Running_Process
            set Temp_Process to Running_Process
            set Running_Process to 0

            /* if I/O request, process I/O */
            IF system call is for I/O THEN
               CALL IO_SCHED

            /* if termination, free resources */
            ELSE IF system call is for process termination THEN
               call termination procedure to
                  free Temp_Process PCB and resources

            /* otherwise, service as required */
            ELSE
               move Temp_Process to ReadyQ
               call service routine
            ENDIF

            branch to DISPATCH
```

to the IO_COMPLETE routine. Note that the DISPATCH procedure will be invoked at the end of IO_COMPLETE in order to dispatch the first process found in the ReadyQ. This "modified" logic of the interrupt handlers in the MPX environment is shown in Figure 13-11.

Figure 13-11 Logic of Interrupt Handler after Setting an ECB

```
IO_Done:    set ECB to non-zero value
            reset device
            disable interrupts
            restore context of interrupted process
            branch to IO_COMPLETE
```

IO_SCHED

The I/O scheduler IO_SCHED services an I/O request. It first determines what device was requested and validates the calling parameters. Then IO_SCHED either starts the requested I/O operation or queues the request to be initiated later, placing the requesting process in the IO_activeQ or IO_initQ respectively. Note that any error detected in the I/O request (invalid device or invalid parameter) results in an error code being returned to the requesting process. In this case the process remains in the *ready* state. Figure 13–12 depicts the logic of IO_SCHED.

Figure 13–12 IO_SCHED Logic

```
IO_SCHED:
            get Requested_Device of Temp_Process

            /* if device busy, go to IO_init state */
            IF Requested_Device is busy or not ready THEN
                move Temp_Process to IO_InitQ
                RETURN

            /* otherwise call I/O supervisor */
            ELSE
                CALL IO_SUP
                set return code into Temp_Process's context
                IF return code indicates invalid request THEN
                    move Temp_Process to ReadyQ
                ELSE
                    move Temp_Process to IO_ActiveQ
                ENDIF
            ENDIF

            RETURN
```

IO_COMPLETE

IO_COMPLETE receives control from device interrupt handlers after an ECB is set by the handler. The state of the hardware must be as it was when the device interrupt occurred so that the appropriate context of the interrupted process may be saved. IO_COMPLETE must save the context of the interrupted process and change the previously *running* process to *ready*. The IO_activeQ is then searched for a nonzero ECB (there can be only one because nested interrupts are not allowed in this environment). The offset in the IO_activeQ (or the address of the IOCB that contains a nonzero ECB) determines the device that has just become available. The PCB address in this IOCB is used to put the PCB into the ready queue, thus changing the process's state from *IO_active* to *ready*.

IO_COMPLETE then searches the IO_initQ for another process waiting to use the now-available device. If such a process is found, IO_SCHED is called

to start the I/O and change this process's state to *IO_active*. IO_COMPLETE
then passes control to DISPATCH to dispatch the next process. Note that
the process to be dispatched will either be the one interrupted (the previous
running process) or the process that just moved to the ready queue, depending
on the priorities of the two processes. It is possible to bypass calling the
dispatcher if the priority of the interrupted process was somehow known to
be higher than the process that just became *ready*. However, for the sake of
simplicity, the dispatcher is always invoked, thus avoiding another exception
in the MPX logic. The logic of IO_COMPLETE is given in Figure 13–13.

Figure 13–13 IO_COMPLETE Logic

```
IO_COMPLETE:
                        /* switch running process to ready */
                        save context of Running_Process
                        move Running_Process to ReadyQ
                        set Running_Process to 0

                        /* identify event, activate waiting process */
                        get Done_Device from IOCB with
                            non-zero ECB in IO_ActiveQ
                        move PCB from Done_Device's IOCB to Temp_Process
                        set Done_Device's ECB value
                            into Temp_Process's context
                        move Temp_Process to ReadyQ
                        clear Done_Device's PCB address and ECB in IOCB
                        set Temp_Process to 0

                        /* initiate pending I/O request, if any */
                        IF IO_Process in IO_InitQ waiting for Device THEN
                            move IO_Process from IO_InitQ to Temp_Process
                            CALL IO_SCHED
                        ENDIF

                        branch to DISPATCH
```

Application Processes

Application processes are loaded in response to a LOAD or RUN command.
A library of such processes is provided for testing MPX, as is the support
software for loading these application processes. The set of application
processes includes all or some of these simple processes:

- NULL: a process that, upon receiving control, immediately
  requests termination

- CPUHOG1: a compute-bound process that occasionally prints a message and then "crunches" for many seconds
- CPUHOG2: a second compute-bound process
- DSK2LP1: a "utility" that reads a file from disk and prints to the printer (i.e., an I/O-bound process)
- DSK2LP2: a second disk-to-printer "utility"
- PRINT1: a process that prints many lines to the printer, with little CPU utilization (i.e., another I/O-bound process)
- PRINT2: a second "copy" of the I/O-bound PRINT1 process
- ERROR: a process that intentionally makes errors in system calls and checks return codes to be sure they are correct; used to validate MPX's error detection in processing system calls

The above processes and others are described more fully in the MPX project manual.

MPX Component Interaction

Figure 13–14 depicts the flow of control from processes to SYS_CALL and to the various components of MPX. Note that *every* entry into MPX is done via an I/O completion interrupt that sets an ECB or a system call interrupt. MPX does not get control on "intermediate" interrupts for devices that do not set ECBs (such as interrupts that simply result in another character being sent to a line printer).

13.6 MPX SERVICES

The specific MPX services supported depend on the MPX environment. Hence, details are presented in the project manual. Here we overview the types of services that normally are supported.

I/O Requests

MPX supports system calls for I/O requests for the devices supported. These services include *open, read, write* and *close.* In all cases, *read* and *write* requests that are valid will result in the requesting process being *blocked* in either the *IO_init* state or the *IO_active* state. *Open* and *close* generally will not result in a process leaving the *ready* state.

Figure 13–14 Overview of the Logic of MPX

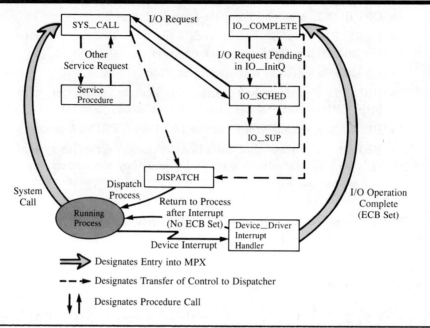

Process Termination Requests

A process can request termination using a *terminate* system call. The service routine for this system call merely removes the PCB from the active set of PCBs and frees the process's memory area (and other resources, if appropriate).

Time and Date Requests

Timer services are not really a part of the simplest MPX environment. However, a request for the system time and date can be made using the appropriate system calls (TIME and DATE respectively).

Other Services

Other system call services are possible, but they are optional. The MPX can be enhanced to provide other services: timer requests, sending and receiving messages, and allocating and freeing memory. Some of these services are specifically outlined as options in the project manual. Others can be added as "bells and whistles" if there is time to design and implement such features.

13.7 SUMMARY

This chapter serves two purposes. It can be used as a way of understanding the flow of control in a simple multiprogramming environment without requiring that the project be implemented. Or, it provides a "generic" overview of the MPX project described in detail in the MPX project manual. The "Keep It Simple, Stupid" (KISS) principle has been used whenever possible to simplify the implementation of MPX in a "hands-on" laboratory environment.

FOR FURTHER READING

The MPX project has evolved over many years of teaching a "hands-on" operating system course using a variety of hardware environments at West Virginia University. Early versions of the MPX project are described by Lane [1974, 1975, 1978], and Lane and Cooper [1976].

Error
Management

Error
Management

14.1 INTRODUCTION

The design and implementation of operating systems would be far more simple if one could assume that no errors would occur. This is true for the design and implementation of application programs as well. Error management encompasses all aspects of an operating system's management responsibilities. Included are the handling of errors in device drivers, of program fault errors (which the operating system should enable users to process) and of file system errors. The most important aspects of error management are attempting to recover from such errors and informing a user or process that an error has occurred.

This chapter concentrates primarily on errors that are recognized by software. Issues related to reliability are postponed until Chapter 15.

14.2 ERROR MESSAGE MANAGEMENT

The detection of errors within an operating system usually requires that the operator, user, and/or process be informed as soon as possible that an error has occurred. Errors may be detected in many places within the operating system, such as device drivers, file management routines, and system call service routines. Usually an error is made known to a process through some type of **return code,** that is a value returned by a program or procedure indicating that a problem has occurred, or perhaps through the execution of some asynchronously called procedure that, prior to the detection of the error, was designated as the error routine to control such errors. The designation of such an error routine also can be changed during execution so that a process can have complete control of handling errors.

If one assumes the necessity of displaying error messages on an operator console or a user terminal, then the formatting of those error messages is extremely important to error management. The timely reporting of such errors is critical to error recovery. Let us suppose that an error is detected by a device management routine, say a disk handler, and that the error was detected by hardware during a read I/O operation. The device driver will attempt to recover from that error. If the error persists, an error code will be passed back to the process that requested the I/O operation, indicating that the error has occurred. It is important to log such errors in a special file called a **system error log** so that, if an error is being caused by some type of hardware problem, it later can be recognized, diagnosed, and the cause eliminated. Hence, recognition of errors is not only provided to a process, but also must be provided to the operating system for logging.

In multiuser and multiprogramming systems, errors are usually displayed on an operator console so that the operator is aware of errors that have occurred within the system. Errors that are made known to a process also must be provided to an error management routine responsible for error message display on the operator console. A queue of error messages is required for eventual display on the operator console because many errors may be detected at the "same time," and hence must be queued before being displayed. Many large operating systems have error consoles separate from their operator command consoles. Other systems use one common terminal for both error message display and command input by an operator.

Error Message Processes

One method of providing for queued error message support is to have a system **error message process** solely responsible for the display of such messages. Such a technique operates like a print spooler. The operating system simply adds messages to the queue, and the error message process displays the messages on a FIFO basis. If the error message queue is empty, the error message process becomes *blocked* waiting for the posting of an error message to the queue. Figure 14–1 illustrates the operation of such an error message process responsible for printing messages from an error message queue.

In real-time systems, it is very important that critical messages have priority over "routine" messages. In other words, a priority structure must be supported in the error message queue. Also, it is likely that additional types of output, such as lighting emergency lights, sounding audible alarms, and the like might be required in addition to displaying error messages. These outputs also could be handled by the error message process, which would of course have a high priority in such an environment.

Figure 14–1 An Error Message Process

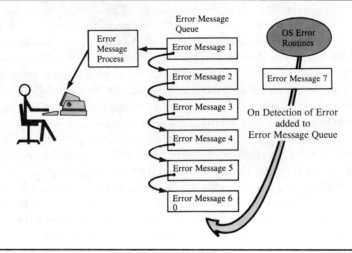

Error Message Format and Content

Error messages must include both the time and date of the error, the type of error, and the process affected by the error. Important information, such as a channel number, a device number, or a file name, is also critical for analysis of the error and identification of the error's cause. Figure 14–2 identifies some information normally required in various error messages.

Many systems simply use a coded scheme of error message reporting in which an eight- or ten-digit code and a terse message is provided to the operator or user. In such an environment, the detailed explanation of the error is found in a manual (which is often outdated or impossible to find when it is needed). In this situation, the operator often has difficulty deciding, in a timely manner, the proper procedure for recovering from the error.

On-line Error Message Support

The best environments are those that provide easily understood, complete error messages. These environments require an on-line facility for providing more detailed error and recovery information. Such a facility would help an operator or user recover more quickly from such errors.

In many batch multiprogramming operating systems, error messages that are displayed on an operator console are the same messages that appear on printed listings provided to the users. How many times have batch users

Figure 14–2 Information Required in Error Messages

Date
Time
Error Code
Channel ID
Controller ID
Device ID and sector/track or record
File name and record number
Process Name
Location at which error occurred
Description of Error

looked at such an error message, been confused by what it means, and simply resubmitted the job for execution, hoping the error would go away? The result, of course, is that they once again find the same cryptic error message displayed. Obviously, the failure of the operating system to describe the error in a way that the user can understand has wasted computer resources because resubmitted jobs fail once again.

There have even been cases of operating systems having the error message numbers mixed up in the error code manual. One such system once displayed the error message "error occurred on *output*" when the error actually occurred on *input*. Imagine the confusion that resulted for the programmer or user! Granted, such an error in a manual could also have occurred with on-line error message support; but the case of the manual requires correcting and reprinting the manual, while the on-line case simply requires correcting the on-line message, which *immediately* is used for all future error reporting. It could take weeks, months, years (or forever!) for all incorrect manuals in the hands of users to be replaced or updated.

Principles of Error Message Management

There are a number of important principles that should be kept in mind in error message management:

- Error messages must be displayed in a timely manner.

- Error messages should be accurate, complete, and easy to understand.
- An on-line error message facility should be available.
- There should be a system log of error messages.
- A facility should exist to suppress "routine" or warning messages to the operator console and/or system log if not desired in a system, and a facility to turn off error message logging.
- Error messages should be assigned priority in a real-time environment to allow for timely display of *critical* error messages about the environment being monitored.

Users and operators often judge the ease of use and user-friendliness of an operating system by the error management provided.

14.3 DEVICE ERROR MANAGEMENT

As we briefly observed in Chapter 9, a variety of errors can occur in the operation of I/O devices. Checksum errors on reads and writes for magnetic media (such as tape and disk), printer errors, and simple parity errors in terminal drivers all result in some type of error recovery in the device driver itself. The device driver's role is to read data from and write data to a device, as well as to provide certain control operations.

Error Recovery Processing

It is the responsibility of every device driver to complete an I/O operation successfully if at all possible. This means that error recovery should be totally transparent to a user if the error recovers. In disk read or write requests, the detection of errors is done automatically by the hardware using the appropriate checksum calculation. When the device interrupt handler detects such an error, a retry operation following some particular error recovery algorithm will be started. This retry procedure is controlled by the interrupt handler and results in many attempts to reread or rewrite data. If the retry operation is successful, and no error occurs on the read or write, the user or process is not informed of the error in any way.

If the error does not recover during retry operations performed under the control of the device interrupt handler, the requesting process, the system log routine or process, and the error message process must all be informed of the error via return codes and the posting of error messages to an error message queue.

In many cases, error recovery routines are transient because they are only required occasionally. Unless the environment requires "instantaneous" response for error recovery, the beginning of error recovery can wait until the **transient error routine** is loaded. Once error recovery begins, the error routine must remain resident until error recovery processing has completed.

Although devices differ in operational characteristics and in the types of errors that can occur, an operating system should support a uniform error reporting structure so that errors that are the same across devices are reported with the same error code. One obvious case of this would be the *not ready* condition that is not necessarily an error, but in some instances is processed like an error. The *not ready* condition should be designated by the same error code for every device in the system.

Device drivers may detect that a device is inoperable. In this case the error must be reported to the operating system so that the operating system will not attempt future I/O operations on that device. This is very important in providing reliability, if an alternate device could be used for all future I/O requests. If the resource was a critical resource for the operating system, the operating system may not be able to continue further execution, but might still be able to shut down in such a manner as to preserve the integrity of all directories and files in the system (unless they are on the device that just failed).

Some systems provide an environment in which a device controller can be accessed by two paths or channels. Device management generally will look at such alternate paths when the primary path is busy. More importantly, device error management must use the alternate path when the primary path is "down."

Permanent Device Errors

Magnetic media do develop areas in which there are "hard errors"—errors that cannot be corrected by reformatting the media or by rewriting the data. Device error management normally allows for locking out or mapping around such areas on the media, so that it can still be used.

There are two approaches for avoiding such bad areas:

- media mapping table
- bad file designation

Media mapping is provided by identifying bad sectors or blocks on the medium when it is initialized. Such blocks are written to a hidden table on the medium that is called a **bad block table,** a **bad track table,** or a **bad sector table.** (We use the term bad block table.) This table is used by the device driver to translate disk addresses so that they miss the "bad spots" on the medium. Errors in the beginning of the medium often make the medium unusable because certain system information (such as bad block tables or file directories) is kept in this area.

An OS utility must provide for formatting such media, identifying bad blocks, creating the bad block table, and writing this bad block table to the medium being formatted. Obviously, the device driver must "know" when absolute reads and writes, rather than reads and writes using the bad block table, are being done. Figure 14–3 illustrates the bad block table and the appropriate translation of disk addresses to miss the bad blocks.

Figure 14–3 The Use of Bad Block Tables

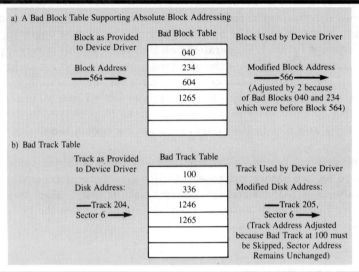

Some systems that allocate files in contiguous blocks (for example, RT-11) can lock out files from further use by identifying them as bad. RT-11 designates bad block areas as a file FILE.BAD (or any name with a .BAD extension). The .BAD files are not usable, and are not moved when the disk medium is "squeezed" to place all free space in one contiguous area at the end of the disk. The bad disk blocks remain in the .BAD files and hence are, in a sense, "mapped around." This scheme allows media with defective blocks to remain in use without forcing them to be reformatted. In such systems, there is no real need for a bad block table; .BAD files (blocks) are essentially avoided in all aspects of file system processing. In fact, formatting usually results in certain areas being simply designated as FILE.BAD files (many files can possess the name FILE.BAD). Figure 14–4 illustrates the use of files to identify and avoid bad blocks on a disk medium.

Figure 14–4 Use of File Entries for Locking Out Bad Blocks

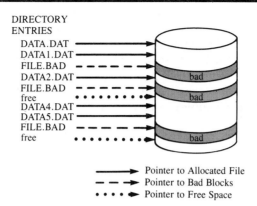

DIRECTORY
ENTRIES
DATA.DAT
DATA1.DAT
FILE.BAD
DATA2.DAT
FILE.BAD
free
DATA4.DAT
DATA5.DAT
FILE.BAD
free

⟶ Pointer to Allocated File
– – ⟶ Pointer to Bad Blocks
• • • ⟶ Pointer to Free Space

14.4 PROGRAM FAULT MANAGEMENT

Processes can experience **program fault interrupts**—errors in the executing programs caused by conditions such as divide by zero, reference to invalid memory addresses, or the use of invalid or privileged instructions. Even the operating system itself could be subject to such errors (also called "bugs"). There are two basic approaches to handling such errors:

- terminate (abort) the process
- execute an error routine provided by the process

Unless a process specifies otherwise, the default action in case of program fault errors is usually to terminate the process. The reason for process termination must be reported to the user and/or operator via an error message. In a batch environment, an error message would appear on a printed listing.

Process-Provided Error Routines

A process can provide the address of a completion or error handling routine that will execute on specific program fault errors. This allows a process to "catch" such errors and provide its own error recovery. The OS must provide services for activating such process-provided error routines.

Since program faults are usually interrupts, the interrupt handlers that service these faults must be able to recognize that such an error-handling routine is to be executed for a particular process. The process must be allowed to execute this error routine, with the possibility of continuing process execution at the location at which the program fault occurred.

Error handling routines might "catch" specific types of interrupts such as divide by zero. Or they may "catch" *all* such errors. Many programmers are familiar with ON ERROR statements of programming languages. The catching of program fault interrupts provides this capability in many such programming language environments. Figure 14–5 illustrates the use of process-provided error routines to handle program fault conditions.

Figure 14–5 A Process-provided Error Procedure for Program Faults

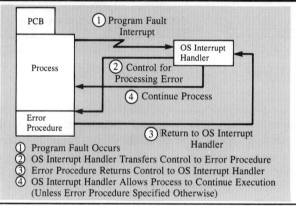

Program Faults in the OS

Incorrect behavior of an application program may result from software faults in places other than the program itself. One must recognize that system programs such as compilers or linkers, or even the OS itself, could contain bugs that result in program fault errors. Such conditions are especially severe because of their impact on a great many programs, and because it is difficult for an OS to recover from a program fault error in its own execution. If the error is in a support routine operating on behalf of a process, error recovery might be possible. If it occurred within a critical component like the process dispatcher, recovery would be unlikely. Because of the harmful effects that can be caused by OS errors, extra precautions must be taken to make such errors unlikely, and to recognize and deal with them if they do occur. This subject is discussed further in Section 15.6.

14.5 FILE SYSTEM ERROR MANAGEMENT

Errors detected in device drivers, such as disk drivers, could result in file system "contamination" in a file or directory. The file access routines must recognize such errors and avoid file or directory contamination whenever possible.

Maintaining the integrity of the file system is extremely important. One important aspect of protecting file system integrity is the use of backups to restore a file system to a valid system. Complex file systems need to validate the integrity of the file system. Even simple operating systems like MS-DOS provide a file system check program (CHKDSK) to do simple file system validation.

Some systems, such as UNIX, check the file system to see if the operating system was properly shut down. If it was not, there is a possibility that the file system was contaminated because file records were left in memory-resident cache buffers on system shutdown. In this case, the UNIX system does a file system check using a program called *fsck* and attempts to recover files and directories it determines are invalid. Sometimes orphaned files and directories (allocated but not referenced) are discovered by *fsck*. If the operator agrees, these orphaned files and directories are reconnected to the file system by placing them in a directory called *lost+found*. Note that in correcting invalid file system conditions, some data is usually lost. Checking the file system can also be done at any time via the command *fsck*.

In some simple operating systems, directory information is stored twice, with a backup entry being available for file system recovery when an error is detected by a file system check program. In such cases separate tracks would be used for storing the directory and backup directory information so this information will be separated on disk. This simplifies directory and file recovery if only the directory information has been contaminated and the backup copy is valid.

Maintaining the validity of a file system hence requires three facilities:

- **file system validation**
- **file system recovery**
- **file system backup and restoration**

File system validation is required so that an invalid file system can be recognized. File system recovery provides a means of attempted recovery of the file system to a valid state. However, it is clear that file system recovery can result in a loss of data. Hence, the backup and restoration facilities provide a means for restoring a file system to a valid (previous) state, and although data entered or changed since the backup will be lost, the integrity of the file system can be restored to a known state.

In some cases, the file system can be recovered with only a loss of specific known files or directories. In this case, it might be possible to restore these files or directories from a backup, thus bringing the file system to an *almost* current state.

14.6 SUMMARY

Error management is important for providing a user the integrity required in a computing environment. Furthermore, error message management will determine how a user or operator views the operating system. If such messages are accurate, complete, and easy to understand, the operating system will certainly be viewed more favorably than another with cryptic and inaccurate error messages.

If at all possible, the operating system should recover from errors, particularly device errors, in a manner that is transparent to a user. Programmers should be able to specify error routines for execution upon the detection of a program fault, and perhaps other errors detected by the hardware and the operating system.

File system integrity is critical to every operating system. Validation of the file system must be provided along with facilities to recover the file system if at all possible. The "fallback" protection of file system integrity must be provided via the file system backup system and procedures.

═══ FOR FURTHER READING ═══

There are few books and papers that devote substantial attention to error handling in an OS context. Brief discussions of specific error types are scattered throughout several texts. For example, Tanenbaum [1987] provides a reasonable discussion of handling disk errors on pp. 146-148.

Detailed examples of error processing algorithms for various situations can be found in extended case studies such as Bach [1986] for UNIX and Kenah and Bate [1984] for VMS.

The types of errors likely to be returned by various types of system calls are discussed in the IEEE MOSI and POSIX Trial-Use Standards [IEEE 1985a, 1986].

Other portions of this text discuss error handling in specific situations and provide additional references in many cases. See especially Chapter 4 for error messages, Chapter 9 for I/O errors, Chapter 15 for reliability issues, and Chapters 22 and 23 for error handling in the context of real-time systems and distributed systems, respectively.

IMPORTANT TERMS

bad block table
bad sector table
bad track table
error message process
file system backup and restoration
file system recovery

file system validation
program fault interrupt
return code
system error log
transient error routine

REVIEW QUESTIONS

1. Of what value is a system error log? How is it supported in an operating system?

2. In what instances can error routines be transient?

3. Explain the principles of error message management. How should *critical* messages be handled?

4. What techniques are used for avoiding bad areas (blocks, sectors, or tracks) on a disk?

5. List and explain the three facilities required to maintain the validity of a file system.

6. What are the various ways for an operating system to handle program faults?

ASSIGNMENTS

1. Compare the error message management of two different operating systems. What are the strengths and weaknesses of each?

2. Design an error message logging system. Your design should specify the format of message records in the log, and provide pseudocode for a system error message logging process.

Reliability

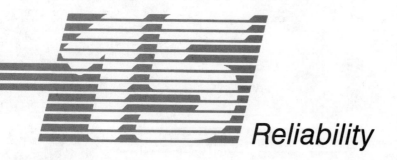 *Reliability*

15.1 INTRODUCTION

We rely more and more on today's computer systems to maintain sensitive data and control critical activities. Not long ago, some applications—such as storing tax and medical records, electronic funds transfer, and control of spacecraft or nuclear power plants—were unheard of. Increasing attention must be paid to techniques that ensure the continued correct operation of these systems.

Two closely related issues that we must address to meet this need are the **reliability** and **security** of computer systems. These concerns are related but distinct. In this text we will use them with the following meanings:

- A **reliable computer system** is one that can be expected to remain *available* and *correct* in spite of *hardware faults* and *software errors*.

- A **secure computer system** is one that can be expected to remain *available, correct,* and *private*, in spite of *hardware faults, software errors,* and *deliberate attacks*.

The terms are distinguished by their goals and by the threats that they must overcome. Note that the goals and threats for security expand on those for reliability alone: a secure computer system also must be reliable. The relationship between security and reliability is illustrated in Figure 15–1.

No techniques can guarantee perfect reliability or security under all conditions. Instead, we must be content with strategies that offer a high probability of success. These strategies can have significant costs in such forms as more expensive hardware and storage requirements or reduced performance. The costs rise dramatically as the required probability of success becomes higher and higher.

Figure 15-1 Security and Reliability: Goals and Threats

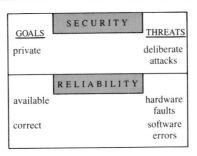

Because of these costs, most computer systems prior to the mid-1970s included few reliability or security mechanisms. Today, however, computers are much more widely used for sensitive and critical applications such as those mentioned above, in which failure could be catastrophic. For systems in these categories, the price for the necessary techniques, however high, must be paid.

Fortunately, new and less costly techniques are evolving to meet the growing need, placing reasonable reliability and security within the reach of systems that require it. The costs are still significant, though, so the level of reliability and security included in each system should be appropriate to the intended application. Critical applications must strive for extremely high levels. Most ordinary applications content themselves with more modest reliability and security goals, in which some possibility of failure can be tolerated.

In this chapter we examine some methods for addressing the fundamental problems of reliability. (We address security issues in Chapter 16.) In the following sections we outline in more detail the problems that may lead to failure (incorrect behavior by any component) in a computer system, and introduce strategies for dealing with such failures. These strategies fall into both hardware and software categories. We continue our discussion with a survey of hardware mechanisms that may improve reliability, and the operating system's role in managing these mechanisms.

We then consider software strategies for improving reliability, especially by minimizing the problems that can be caused by errors in application software. Finally, we consider techniques for constructing a highly reliable operating system.

15.2 THREATS AND PROBLEMS

The goals of reliability are **availability** and **correctness.** A computer system is available if its data and programs can be accessed by authorized users at all scheduled times. Availability fails if the system stops running for any reason, if files become inaccessible, or if needed terminals or I/O devices cannot be used. A computer system is correct if correct programs produce the expected results for any valid input data in a reasonable amount of time. (Note that the program itself is assumed to be correct.) The correctness goal fails if, due to malfunctions in the hardware or system software, wrong results are produced, incorrect data are read from files, or programs run indefinitely without completing.

Perfect correctness and availability cannot be achieved, and there is a tension between these goals. If some possibility of wrong results arises, a choice must be made. The system may refuse to complete the affected programs, violating availability; or it may continue to produce results, possibly violating correctness. Arguments can be made for both choices. In the extreme, a system that is never available is of little use, but it cannot be incorrect!

The threats to reliability come from problems that may exist in the hardware, including its physical environment, and the system software, including the operating system, language translators, and other utility programs. (Problems in the application program can also lead to incorrect results, of course, but are not within the scope of system reliability.)

We can consider the types of problems that may occur in three classes:

- **design errors,** by which elements of a system may have been designed so that incorrect behavior is possible;

- **construction errors,** by which a particular system may have been assembled in a way that does not correctly match its intended design; and

- **component faults,** by which system elements, although designed and constructed correctly, may sometimes behave incorrectly.

Hardware elements are subject to all three types of problems. In practice, the most important threat to reliability from the hardware is the inevitable deterioration of physical components, which leads to faults or total failure. Another serious problem is the periodic failure of electric power sources. Both hardware and operating system techniques must be combined to reduce the impact of these faults. A system that does a good job of continuing to be reliable in spite of such problems is called a **fault-tolerant system.**

Software elements are immune to deterioration. However, design and construction errors are quite possible in application programs, utility programs, and operating systems. Often these errors result in a failure to deal properly with certain input data, a failure to recognize invalid input, or a failure to handle valid but extreme values properly. If errors at any of these software levels produce incorrect results, a reliable OS must try to recognize the error and limit its damage to as small a portion of the system as possible. In particular, errors in one process must not be allowed to threaten the reliability of other processes. This is the problem of **error confinement.**

The OS can deal with errors in other software modules only by trying to detect and confine them as well as possible. To avoid errors in the design and construction of the OS itself, its developers should use a variety of careful strategies leading to the production of correct OS software. Some of these techniques, discussed in Chapter 3, are considered further in a later section of this chapter.

15.3 RECOVERING FROM FAILURES

A computer system that seeks high reliability must deal with failures in two principal ways: by design strategies that attempt to prevent failures from ever occurring, and by recovery procedures which try to detect and deal with problems when they do occur. Preventing failure is a laudable goal, but one that can never be achieved completely. A reliable computer system must expect periodic failures, and include the ability to survive and recover from them. As emphasized by Wulf [1975] after experiences with the Hydra OS, it is much more important to be able to recover from failures than to prevent them.

Siewiorek [1984] has identified ten distinct stages that may occur during a computing system's recovery from failure. Probably no system includes all these steps, but they illustrate a spectrum of possible responses.

- Fault confinement: Design the system to ensure that most classes of errors will be detected and handled before they can cause significant damage.
- Fault detection: Employ hardware and software techniques to detect incorrect data or behavior.
- Fault masking: Hide the effects of a failure and continue correct operation.
- Retry: Repeat a failed operation in case the failure was transient.
- Diagnosis: Identify the failed hardware or software component.

- Reconfiguration: Reorganize the system to remove the failed component from active use.
- Recovery: Try to undo the effects of a failure by correcting bad data or repeating failed operations.
- Restart: Reinitialize the system if complete recovery is not possible.
- Repair: Repair or replace the failed component.
- Reintegration: Return the repaired component to full operation within the system.

The first two of these steps are concerned with recognizing and identifying faults as well as responding to them. Although they sound deceptively simple on this list, they are likely to be the most difficult steps in most systems. Practical systems employ a selection of strategies from this list, implemented by both hardware and software means. A number of these strategies are discussed in the following sections.

15.4 HARDWARE SOLUTIONS

A variety of hardware mechanisms have been employed to assist in detecting and combating threats to reliability. Some of these mechanisms are of little cost and are very widely used. Others have high costs and are used only when reliability is an extremely important goal. Although the operating system cannot directly implement these techniques, it must be aware of many of them in order to manage them properly and cooperate in their common goals.

Confinement Mechanisms

A widely used set of hardware techniques contributes to reliability by limiting the ability of most processes to interfere with other processes or with the operating system. These techniques confine the effects of an error arising in any process to that single process in most cases. Three mechanisms are so widely used that they are considered essential requirements of a safe multiprogramming system:

- **privileged instructions,** which reserve the ability to perform actions with global impact to the OS only;
- **memory protection,** which confines the accessible address space of a process to memory it is permitted to use; and

- **timers,** which can interrupt a process after a predetermined amount of time, preventing it from keeping control of the CPU for too long.

The OS must utilize these mechanisms in its memory management and process scheduling strategies. Before a process is dispatched, the appropriate memory limits must be established and the timer must be set. Ordinary processes are always dispatched in a non-privileged mode so that privileged instructions cannot be used. If any of these protections are violated, an interrupt will occur, and the OS must take the necessary action to control the misbehaving process.

More extreme mechanisms are sometimes used to limit the types of actions available to a process. These mechanisms further support error confinement and reliability. A good example is the capability structure, to be discussed in Chapter 16. This mechanism is primarily seen as a solution for security problems, but it provides an effective solution for error confinement and other reliability problems as well [Denning 1976].

Consistency Checking

Several mechanisms can be introduced at modest cost to a typical computer system to ensure that values stored or results produced are consistent and reasonable. The most common use of these techniques is in main and secondary memory storage, where random failures of individual bits are fairly common.

In main memory units, an extra bit may be provided for each data word to be used for detecting errors. This bit, called a **parity bit,** is illustrated in Figure 15–2. Whenever data is stored into the other bits of the word, the parity bit is set to ensure that the total number of one-bits is odd (or even). When a word is read, the parity bit is checked for correctness. If any single bit has changed, an error will be detected. Such a scheme is used in the IBM-PC, which adds a ninth parity bit to each of its eight-bit bytes.

The parity bit provides no information about which bit failed, and may not help if many bits fail in the same word, which is frequently the case (see Figure 15–2). Additional bits can be used to improve the situation, but this technique is not common in memory systems.

Secondary storage devices may employ parity bits, but they usually also use a different technique for error detection. For each data block, a function is computed on all of the data and stored as part of the block. Often this function is a simple sum (with overflow bits discarded), called a **checksum.** When a block is read, the checksum is recomputed and compared with the stored value. If the values differ, an error has occurred. This technique is shown in Figure 15–3.

Figure 15–2 Use of a Parity Bit to detect Memory Errors

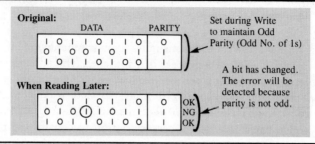

Figure 15–3 Use of Checksums for Disk Storage Blocks

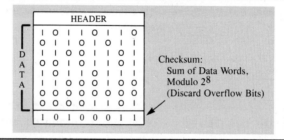

Simple consistency checks could be used in other parts of the hardware, such as arithmetic units and CPU registers, but they are far less common. Systems striving for effective checking throughout the CPU usually turn to the more elaborate methods based on redundancy, as discussed below.

Parity and checksum mechanisms are designed to produce interrupts if an error is detected. The role of the OS in dealing with memory parity and similar structures is to enable these interrupts and to respond to them when they occur. In most cases the only reasonable response is to suspend or abort the affected processes and report the problem to the user or operator.

Maintaining Power

A critical physical resource for any computer is electric power. If the power is interrupted, the system cannot operate. Often, even variations in the magnitude or quality of the power supply can be enough to introduce errors or damage components. Such variations are very common in standard public power sources.

A reasonable reliability goal for most systems is to ensure that, after a power failure, processing can resume with a minimum of lost work and no irreplaceable lost data. A more ambitious goal is to prevent power from failing at all.

The ambitious goal is simple to meet, but fairly expensive. A local generator or power source that can be switched in automatically if the normal source fails may be used. Such techniques are common in larger installations. One device fairly commonly used is the **uninterruptible power source (UPS)**, which can provide emergency power for a number of hours if needed. In addition, extra circuits are commonly used to "smooth out" power from public sources, preventing excessive variations and sudden surges caused by events such as lightning. Even the smallest computers can benefit from this technique.

Recovering after a failure is more difficult. A serious problem lies in the loss of data from the main memory. Years ago most main memories were made from magnetic cores. Such memories are **non-volatile;** that is, they retain their contents when the power is off. Minicomputers based on non-volatile memories often provided for power failure detection and recovery. When the power fell below certain limits, it would be detected by hardware and cause an interrupt. At this time several milliseconds would usually be left before the system failed completely. On detecting a powerfail interrupt, the OS would save all volatile CPU registers in the core memory. It would then set a status flag and halt.

When power resumed in such a system, processing would begin at a fixed location which contained a recovery routine. This routine would restore the registers, restart any I/O in progress, then resume processing where the interrupt occurred. If the I/O devices were also designed to tolerate power failures and restart properly, these methods could provide a complete recovery. Dramatic demonstrations were possible in some cases. In the middle of extensive multiprocessing, with lots of I/O going on, the main plug would be pulled. Everything came to a halt. When the plug was restored, all processing continued as though nothing had happened.

Today most memories are based on electronic storage, which is volatile. Because so much data can be lost, power failure is harder to tolerate. If this is a concern, battery systems are provided for backup power to main memory. Batteries can allow the memories to retain their information for several hours, overcoming short-term power failures.

Self-testing

Many failures in computer hardware can be detected by running **diagnostic programs** designed to test registers, CPU instructions, I/O devices, or other elements. The OS can improve reliability by running diagnostic programs automatically at reasonable points in time. Many small computers run simple diagnostic programs automatically when turned on. The short, sometimes frustrating delay allows failures to be detected before they lead to more serious problems.

More radical architectures have also been built in which periodic or continuous testing is carried out by hardware methods. These architectures also use techniques such as redundancy and dynamic reconfiguration, discussed briefly below.

Redundancy

The most powerful method for detecting failures in computer elements is to provide two or more elements that store the same data or carry out the same computation. This method is obviously quite expensive, but can be justified when reliability requirements are extremely high. This redundancy can be introduced at many levels, ranging from duplicate registers or arithmetic units to complete duplicate computers.

A number of architectures that employ redundancy have been described by Siewiorek [1984] and Serlin [1984]. The approach used as far back as SAGE used "standby redundancy"—a complete spare computer system kept on hand until needed. When the primary system failed, the standby system was substituted so work could continue. Both detecting the failure and substituting the backup system had to be performed manually.

Later systems designed for high reliability improved on this approach by duplicating individual components such as memories, CPUs, or I/O controllers. Automatic switching was employed; if failures were detected by hardware or software, replacement systems could be substituted quickly under program control.

A weakness in many systems with component redundancy was the continuing presence of critical elements that could not tolerate failure. Although the major subsystems were duplicated, certain communication paths, switches, or I/O ports often were not. In 1975 TANDEM introduced its NonStop architecture, which took a more systematic approach to redundancy. As shown in Figure 15–4, the Tandem architecture not only provides two (or more) CPUs, memories, and I/O devices, but all connecting buses are duplicated, and each device controller is connected to two distinct CPUs and memories. In addition, the design allows defective components to be removed and replaced without shutting down the entire system, a major problem in earlier redundant designs.

Redundant components in a computer system may be treated as spares, ready to be activated when and if failure is detected in the primary components. Alternately, they may be operated in a "hot backup" mode, duplicating the operation of the primary components at every step. This

Figure 15–4 The TANDEM NonStop Architecture

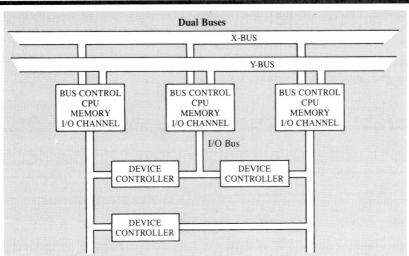

approach introduces further costs, but has some important advantages. The backup element can be ready to take over at a moment's notice, without any loss of information. Tandem provides a compromise approach. Each CPU and memory runs an independent copy of the Guardian operating system. For each active process there is a semi-active backup process, the purpose of which is to receive periodic **checkpoints** (copies of the current data) from the main process. If the backup process does not receive an expected checkpoint within a reasonable time, it assumes the main process has failed, and takes over its work. Full duplication of files is an optional (and costly) addition to the overall strategy.

If backup components fully duplicate all operations of the primary components, they may be used to *detect* failures as well as to assist with recovery. With this approach, the results of redundant computations, or redundant stored values, are compared by either hardware or software means each time they are changed. If they are the same, they can be assumed with high confidence to be correct. If they differ, an error has occurred.

If results are different, however, it may not be clear which one (if any) is correct. When elements such as memory also include independent consistency checks, a wrong result can be recognized. In the general case, however, it is necessary to include *three* of each element and use a "majority vote" strategy. In most cases, at least two elements will have the same value. That value is assumed to be correct.

This triple redundancy may seem extravagant, but it can be affordable for systems that place a high premium on reliability. At least one fault-tolerant architecture employs quadruple redundancy. The Stratus architecture (see Figure 15–5), known as "pair-and-spare," duplicates major elements to allow fault detection, and provides a second pair of elements, operating in hot backup mode, to serve as a spare. If a conflict is detected in one pair, the other pair automatically takes its place.

Figure 15–5 The Stratus Pair-and-Spare Architecture

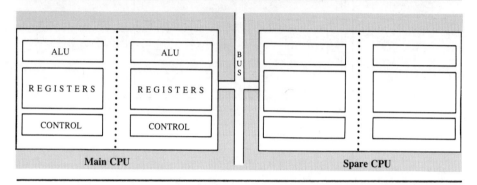

With a redundant system capable of determining the correct result, the system may mask the fault and continue working without any evidence that a problem has occurred. However, it is important that the failure be recorded in some way and brought to the attention of the operator. Otherwise, a failing component may continue unnoticed until its companions also fail.

Simple redundancy can combat component failures—and sometimes construction errors—but not design errors. If an element is designed incorrectly, no matter how many of them are provided, they will all fail in the same way. To combat this situation, some recent systems provide a more powerful type of redundancy, including different designs that should produce the same results. Elements with different designs are not likely to fail in exactly the same way.

Dynamic Reconfiguration

In most cases, when an element fails in a redundant system, the failed element must be removed manually, and replacements switched in as necessary. Meanwhile, the system must operate with fewer elements. A few experimental systems have been designed to allow **dynamic reconfiguration** of this type. In these computers, connection paths between components can be reprogrammed to deal with failures. Thus, the organization of the system can be changed automatically while the system is in full operation.

15.5 SOFTWARE SOLUTIONS

The unique fault-tolerant architectures discussed in the previous section require unique operating systems, which are outside the scope of this text. Simpler hardware mechanisms, such as consistency checks, call for a straightforward management by the OS, as already discussed. Most conventional operating systems may use a variety of additional techniques to improve reliability independent of special hardware mechanisms. This section, which discusses general OS strategies for detecting errors and coping with them when they do occur, expands on some of the error-handling concepts we considered in Chapter 14.

Defensive Programming

One important tool in the arsenal of fault-tolerant programming is **defensive programming.** This idea simply means that each procedure should generally mistrust all data it receives. Whether data appears in the form of procedure arguments or from a file or input device, and whether it is supplied by a user or another OS module, the program should check for and be prepared to handle illegal, even outrageous, values.

Repeated data checking by every procedure does reduce performance and increase complexity. Because of this, it is tempting to eliminate it when illegal data seems unlikely. However, the rule should be relaxed only if it is guaranteed that the data has already been checked by a (trusted) caller, and *could not have been modified since checking* (see the next subsection).

Recovery from data errors usually must be handled at a higher level, by the caller or supplier of the bad data. If the appropriate response has been well-defined, it may be handled (masked) by the low-level procedure. However, obvious solutions, such as aborting the process or sending a message to the user or a log, are very often inappropriate. Instead most procedures should return an error code if problems are detected; calling procedures should check this code and either respond to the error or propagate it to the next higher level. Alternately, the error may be handled as an exception or program-generated interrupt if appropriate exception handlers are provided.

Isolating Buffers and Control Blocks

In some operating systems, data structures that are relied on by the operating system over an extended period of time may be stored within the address space of its processes. Examples include file control blocks, process control blocks, buffers for temporary storage of file data, or parameter blocks containing information to be used by system calls. If this data is writable by the process, it must be considered suspect at all times. Accidentally or deliberately, the application or system process may change such data structures between or even during uses by the OS. This problem has been especially severe in versions of OS/360, such as MVT, and occurs also in small systems, such as CP/M, in which control blocks are visible to the user.

The best response to this problem is a design strategy in which all system data structures are isolated from the process address spaces. In addition, any data passed to the OS by a process, such as parameter blocks or output or message buffers, should be copied out of the process address space *before* the process may resume execution.

Failing this, the OS can ensure reliable operation only by checking the validity of these data in some satisfactory way before every use.

Software Redundancy

Just as redundancy in hardware can be used to help detect and recover from failures, redundant software can enhance reliability in many cases. The purpose of software redundancy is somewhat different, however, since software is immune to component failure. More accurately, if a software module will fail for a given set of input data, all copies of that module would fail in exactly the same way.

Redundant software can serve two principal purposes:

- provide duplicate software for redundant hardware, and
- provide alternate designs to guard against design errors.

When processors and memories are duplicated (as discussed in the previous section), each memory may contain a duplicate copy of the appropriate software to maintain independent operation and rapid recovery. However, this redundancy does not address the high likelihood of software design errors. In a well-known space flight failure some years ago, four computers were provided for redundancy, each running identical software. A fifth computer was also available for backup. But when one computer failed, the others could not continue because they each contained an identical software design error that prevented synchronization.

The idea of achieving reliability through duplicate software with independent designs is just beginning to be explored. If critical functions are performed by duplicate modules *designed by separate groups of people*, it is unlikely that design errors will cause both to fail in an identical manner. Experiments at UCLA have shown that design of multiple versions of functionally identical software may be feasible, but the development must start with good formal specifications, and the programs must be subjected to rigorous testing to ensure identical behavior. In addition, the designs for each version may need to be reviewed in some manner to ensure that they really are sufficiently different!

Note that redundant software, although provided to cope with design errors, normally must run on separate, redundant hardware. Otherwise each operation would have to be repeated on a single processor, leading to unacceptable performance delays.

15.6 RELIABLE OPERATING SYSTEMS

To support computer system reliability, the OS itself must be highly reliable. Many development techniques and software engineering principles may need to be combined to obtain the highest possible reliability.

We discussed a number of important principles in Chapter 3. The OS should be written in a high-level language with good type-checking and information-hiding capabilities. It should use a modular design, with all code affecting each specific resource or data structure confined to a small number of modules whenever possible.

The layered design strategy introduced by T.H.E. offers important help in maintaining confidence in system reliability. Because only a few functions need to be provided at the lowest level, the procedures and structures at this level can be thoroughly analyzed and tested to ensure correctness. Once each lower layer is considered reliable, additional layers can be constructed on top of it. The correctness and availability of the lower layers can be counted on during this process. As noted in Chapter 3, Dijkstra claimed an unusually high degree of confidence in the reliability of T.H.E. for this reason.

If each layer is sufficiently simple and can be treated in isolation, it may be possible to use formal proof techniques to ensure that the layer is correct. Such techniques provide arguments to show that, for all legitimate inputs, a program unit produces outputs that conform to its specifications. Although formal proofs of nontrivial programs are not common, several operating system kernels have been proved in this fashion. This offers the highest possible confidence that the kernel conforms to its specifications; thus the OS is reliable if the specifications themselves are correct.

15.7 SUMMARY

Reliability and security are increasingly important concerns for many computer systems called upon to control critical activities and sensitive data. Reliability is a prerequisite for security. A reliable computer system is one that remains available and correct in spite of hardware faults and software errors.

Threats to reliability are caused by design errors, construction errors, and component faults in both hardware and software. A reliable computing system must have a collection of hardware and software mechanisms for dealing with such threats. Perfect reliability is impossible; extremely high reliability may be achievable only with very high monetary costs and reduced performance.

Reliability strategies for a computing system may involve detecting errors, confining the damage they cause, correcting and reporting errors, and replacing faulty components. Hardware mechanisms can assist in error detection and confinement. Common mechanisms in this class include privileged instructions and memory protection as well as parity checks, backup power sources, self-testing components, and others. More radical architectures employ extensive redundancy of components and may provide for automatic reconfiguration of the system when components fail.

Software strategies for reliability include defensive programming, proper isolation of data structures, and many aspects of good software engineering. Software redundancy is an experimental concept that may be beneficial in some applications. The design and construction of the operating system itself, as well as other system software, must be as careful and well-validated as possible to ensure high reliability for these components.

FOR FURTHER READING

General issues of fault-tolerant or reliable systems (both hardware and software) are discussed by Siewiorek [1984]. Denning [1976] provides a survey of fault-tolerant operating systems that is focused especially on capabilities (which we consider in Chapter 16).

An article by Randell [1975] considers general OS structures to support software fault tolerance. Serlin [1984] describes the architecture of some systems specialized for high reliability, such as the Tandem and Stratus architectures. Wulf [1975] describes reliability experience with the Hydra OS for the C.mmp multiprocessor, and Lynch [1975] reviews reliability experience with a large data processing system, Chi/OS.

Issues concerning the design of dynamic, reconfigurable system architectures are explored by Kartashev and Kartashev [1978]. The UCLA experiments with software design redundancy are described by Avizienis and Kelly [1984]. Detailed treatments of formal verification of an OS kernel are provided by Kemmerer [1982] and Karp [1983].

IMPORTANT TERMS

availability
checkpoint
checksum
component fault
construction error
correctness
defensive programming
design error
diagnostic program
dynamic reconfiguration
error confinement

fault-tolerant system
memory protection
non-volatile
parity bit
privileged instruction
reliability
reliable computer system
secure computer system
security
timers
uninterruptible power source (UPS)

REVIEW QUESTIONS

1. List and briefly explain the goals of reliability and security, and the principal threats to these goals.

2. Explain why the two principal goals of reliability conflict.

3. Identify several hardware mechanisms that may be used in conventional computer systems to enhance reliability. Explain the role of the operating system in managing each of these mechanisms.

4. What is the possible danger of a good fault-masking mechanism?

5. Why is automatic recovery after power failures more difficult in newer computer systems than in older ones?

6. List and briefly explain five techniques that should be used in the design of an operating system to obtain maximum reliability.

7. Explain how redundant software modules can enhance reliability, even though software components are immune to deterioration.

ASSIGNMENTS

1. Suppose the average time between failures of a particular computing system may be increased five times if the initial cost and operating costs are doubled. Discuss the desirability of such an improvement in each of the following cases:

   a. a personal computer system

   b. a large timesharing system

   c. a patient-monitoring system in a hospital

   d. a transaction management system for a bank

2. Describe a computing system for which correctness may be more important than availability, and one for which availability may be more important than correctness.

3. The text suggests that design and construction errors are not nearly as serious a problem for hardware as they are for software. Do you think this is a fair conclusion? Why or why not?

4. The first two stages of response to failure listed in Section 15.3 are considered to be the most difficult. Explain why.

5. Investigate an operating system of your choice that tries to support reasonably high reliability. Explain which of the stages listed in Section 15.3 it provides, and what mechanisms exist for each.

6. As stated in the text, simple consistency checks, such as parity bits, are not common in CPU registers or arithmetic units. Suggest some possible reasons for this fact.

7. Suppose that a memory system with parity bits reports a failure of a location in main memory. What responses should the operating system make, if a virtual memory mechanism is in use? Why would the problem be more difficult if no memory translation mechanism existed?

8. Suppose a computing system uses volatile main memory and does not include a backup power source. A large amount of disk storage is available. Could complete automatic recovery after a power failure be achieved? What strategies might be employed, and what problems would be encountered?

9. Write a short procedure, which illustrates the use of defensive programming, to perform a typical operating system function.

10. Explain some potential problems in relying on hardware redundancy to greatly improve reliability.

11. Explain some possible difficulties in relying too greatly on software redundancy.

Security

 Security

16.1 INTRODUCTION

This chapter addresses the problem of maintaining **security** in a computer system. Security is a step beyond reliability; it requires not only a reliable system, but one in which both the integrity and the privacy of resources can be maintained even in the face of deliberate, intelligent attacks.

The importance of security in today's computer systems is no longer confined to a few environments handling classified military information. The amount and variety of information stored in present-day computer systems is incredibly large. Microcomputers of modest scale can store more data than many of the mainframes of the late 1960s and early 1970s. When you add to this the ability to transmit information throughout the world in seconds using simple communications and networking, the vulnerability of data stored in a computer system becomes obvious.

Computer systems are found everywhere—the home, small businesses, government installations, and large corporations. The large number of people who use computers and the heavy dependence on these computers by businesses, big and small, as well as by individuals, make the problem of security extremely important. Computers now are relied on for storage of a great deal of sensitive information, such as business records, census data, tax records, and bank accounts, as well as information considered important to "national security." Corruption or unauthorized access to this information not only may cause great harm or embarrassment, but is often forbidden by law. Whether this information concerns medical history, credit ratings, or bank balances, access to this information will violate the rights of individuals and can result in ruined careers or extortion by those who have obtained personal information. Even corporations are vulnerable. Access to corporate financial data, customer lists, or other classified data can severely damage a corporation. For example, illegal activities such as the recent insider securities trading can be exacerbated by outsiders accessing information stored in a computer and providing that information to other individuals and organizations.

The increasingly critical roles played by some computers in the control of physical systems—air traffic control systems, weapons control systems, electronic funds transfer (EFT) systems, life monitoring systems—make security even more important. In such cases, penetration can result in airplane crashes, disabling of weapons, launching of weapons, loss of life, and the transfer of large sums of money in just an instant's time. The scenario presented in the movie *War Games,* while filled with inaccuracies, might be closer to reality than we would like to admit.

Periodicals like the *Wall Street Journal, Time Magazine,* and daily national newspapers have frequently publicized computer crime. Teenage "hackers" have invaded supposedly secure systems to access private information, destroy data, and disrupt service. Often the computer is presented as an "attractive nuisance" that led these young people to their illegal capers. More serious (and often unreported) computer crime also continues to rise. This type of crime has two attractive characteristics: The take is high (more than $400,000 per reported crime) and the probability of being sent to jail is low (one in 20,000). Comparing that to bank robbery (an average take of $6,000, with the probability of going to jail being close to one in three), the smart criminal will trade in his guns for a computer terminal.

Solutions to the security problem include new laws to deal with computer crime, education of lay people and the professionals, and improved computer security. Often those looking for ways to deal with illegal computer activity believe that improved security mechanisms in the computer itself are all that is needed. Sometimes, indeed, that is true. However, security provided by operating systems and other software is always at risk because of the human element: managers and users who, by being careless or unscrupulous, make penetration into these systems relatively easy.

Even within the computer system, security is not cheap, and perfect security may be impossible. Mechanisms intended to ensure effective security may inconvenience users and reduce performance. The cost of hardware and software development to support security can be substantial, and the most sophisticated security systems can sometimes be thwarted by a single loophole. Because of this, many computer systems attempt to support only limited security, and those that seek higher levels of security must balance the protection to be gained against the costs.

Some specialized aspects of security have been discussed in previous chapters. Section 10.6 examined memory protection, and portions of Chapter 11 extended this discussion to virtual memory systems. Section 12.7 introduced the concept of access control for files. In Chapter 15 we introduced and defined the closely related concepts of reliability and security, and studied issues of system reliability. This chapter examines security issues and mechanisms in detail.

The next section considers the goals and objectives of security, the type of threats that must be overcome, and the costs that must be considered in developing a secure computer system. A truly secure system must consider all aspects of a total system strategy, since security, like a chain, is only as good as its weakest element. Everything from physical access to the computer itself to internal access to each resource must be subject to suitable controls. Although "external" security is outside the control of the OS, its importance in the total strategy should be understood; this is discussed in Section 16.3. Section 16.4 then overviews the principal issues in internal security, which must be supported by OS mechanisms.

The principal areas of concern for the OS in most cases are user authentication, access control for ongoing resource protection, and communication security. These subjects are examined in Section 16.5 through 16.7. Section 16.7 also discusses the important mechanism of encryption. Finally, the important subject of legal protection is discussed briefly in Section 16.8.

16.2 GOALS, THREATS, AND COSTS

Goals of Security

Computer security is intended to provide integrity and privacy for data and programs, in an environment of information sharing and access. The primary goals of security are to ensure that all resources remain

- correct (the integrity of information and programs is preserved)
- available (the system can be used at any time by authorized users)
- private (information cannot be accessed by unauthorized users)

Security is a measure of confidence in how well the above goals are met. This confidence is established by a combination of reasonable **security policies** and reliable **security mechanisms.** Security policies establish the rules governing the use of resources, considering the requirements of the environment for information sharing, performance, and user friendliness, as well as protection. Some policies are established by operating system design; however, a flexible OS should provide mechanisms that can support a variety of policies. The policies themselves must be established by the system management, and users also may play a role in establishing policies and determining their success or failure by the degree of user cooperation.

The overall goal of the security mechanisms implemented in a computer system can be summarized by the term **protection.** Security policies establish "what" is desired; protection mechanisms determine "how" it is accomplished. Thus the role of protection mechanisms, both in the OS and throughout the system, is to enforce security policies [Jones 1978].

Threats to Security

Security attacks on information stored in a computer system can be separated into the following categories:

- information theft
- information modification
- denial of use of information

Security policies and protection mechanisms must guard against all three types of attacks [Janson 1985].

Guaranteeing the privacy and integrity of resources in the face of deliberate, highly motivated attack, is an extremely difficult goal. While some system penetration attempts are carried out by average users "for fun," others are performed by highly trained professionals, using computers of their own and other equipment, and motivated by the hope of great financial or political gain.

Direct access to data is by no means the only way that private information can be revealed. Many more subtle means can be employed to violate security. Today's database systems, for example, can provide information by *inference.* If statistical summaries can be obtained from a body of data, such as census or tax records, a user may be able to reduce the summary to a set of one by restricting queries to characteristics that can only be satisfied by one individual. The addition of one other criterion—say, individuals treated for alcohol abuse—could then allow one to obtain information about an individual by inference.

Serious threats occur because some users and programs must be trusted; these trusted agents can be corrupted or fooled. In a common type of attack known as a **trojan horse**, a user may convince another user or manager to install a new and seemingly useful program such as an improved word processor or compiler. However, if the new program is given extensive access rights to system information, it may use these rights in hidden ways to violate security. In a particularly disturbing form of this attack that has recently developed, known as a **computer virus,** a single program gaining unauthorized access to a system may modify the OS or other system programs in such a way that an "infection" of modifications to suit the invaders purpose spreads throughout the system.

Many other types of subtle attacks on security are possible; these are just a few of the many examples.

Costs and Tradeoffs

Perfect security may be unattainable in most situations, and the cost of even moderately effective security mechanisms may be high. As the level of security increases, the cost will generally increase. To determine what degree of security is worthwhile, the cost must be evaluated in light of the value of the information being protected. Extremely critical systems must have the best security possible, while those storing information that is of minimal value might require only minimal security. Two general indicators of the need for effective security are:

- information and/or programs that require protection
- potential threats to people or information

If either of these conditions is not met, there may be no real need for a high degree of security. A system storing only public domain information that can be easily reconstructed is an example of such a case. Running a system in a locked environment, where only authorized users have access, would remove the need for protection provided by the operating system and other software [Janson 1985].

16.3 EXTERNAL SECURITY

A total strategy for security must consider all potential threats to a computer system. Necessary mechanisms certainly include **internal security** that must be supported by the operating system and computer hardware. The total security picture, however, must also consider **external security**, aspects of security outside the control of the computer itself. External security has two main aspects: physical security and operational security.

Physical Security

Physical security is concerned with protection against physical intrusion and against accidents and disasters, like flood, fire, tornados, or earthquakes. The key to providing such security is usually some type of detection equipment—heat and smoke detectors, motion detectors, burglar alarms, or water detectors. Automatic fire extinguishing systems and the proper fire extinguishers are also part of good physical security. Most installations have inadequate protection for disasters.

Protection against physical intrusion by outsiders can also be provided by other types of equipment, such as physical identification systems. Included in this category are identification cards with magnetic strips, photos, and signatures. More sophisticated systems include voiceprint and fingerprint identification.

Operational Security

Operational security is established by the policies and procedures that management implements and requires in a computer installation. These policies determine, for example, what individuals should be permitted to use the computer system, what restrictions should be placed on each user, and how strong the security mechanisms should be, even at the cost of reduced performance or user contentment. In some environments, such as military applications, **classification** policy may be appropriate. Such a policy provides a system of levels of access, with each level having certain access rights.

Some aspects of the selected security policy concern rules governing the sharing of information and access rights; these rules may be **discretionary** or **non-discretionary.** A non-discretionary policy establishes rules that all users must follow, and will be enforced by the system. Most classification policies, for example, are non-discretionary.

Operational security must be concerned with the division of responsibility so that no one person controls all aspects of the system. Also, no one individual should exclusively control a particular activity within a computer installation. This helps to provide some checks and balances of personnel so that security cannot be compromised without the cooperation of two or more employees.

Backup Procedures. One critical part of operational security that is often overlooked in creating a security plan consists of **backup procedures**—that is, strategies for preserving copies of critical information that can be used for restoration if the original data is corrupted. The operating system should provide easy backup facilities for total and selective backup in the shortest period of time possible. Backup procedures should include the following considerations:

- Data must be backed up according to a backup schedule.
- Backups must be easy to identify. They should be labeled with the date of backup and the information they contain.
- Rotating backups should be used to provide multiple generations of backup.
- Backups should be stored in safe locations, such as fireproof safes, and in locations away from the computer site.

- Programs and operating system must be backed up after changes.

The existence of sound backup procedures will determine whether a computer system can ever be restored after a disaster or intrusion, and if so, how long it will take to bring the system "back up." Storing backups off-site will help in recovery if total destruction of the computer site occurs. One key to the backup plan is a backup hardware site that could be used if the computer is down for a substantial amount of time, or if it is destroyed. The operating system's backup facilities often determine how closely the backup procedures are followed. If backup is too difficult or takes too long, operators and users will often bypass the backup with the assumption that it will never be needed. This is often a problem in microcomputer systems with high-capacity "hard disks," since it may take hours to backup all data onto floppy disks or magnetic tapes. Of course, backups usually *aren't* needed, but in the one case when they are, you'll find it worth all the time you spent making backups!

Protection of Materials. An important set of rules that must exist in operational security is that pertaining to the protection of output before it is picked up by the user requesting it, and to the disposal of materials or data produced by a computer system that are no longer needed. Included are printed reports, punched tapes, plotter output, and magnetic media (diskettes, magnetic tape, disks, and so on). Paper shredders are the most common method of destroying paper materials, but printer ribbons and single-use carbon ribbons, from which letters and reports can be deciphered by merely "reading" the ribbon, are often overlooked.

Magnetic media must be "wiped clean" of information that can be read by unauthorized parties. This improper reading could be done by requesting the mount of a scratch tape that can be read for valuable information. The operating system could help by not allowing such tapes to be read before they are written. However, because of the nature of magnetic tapes, it could be possible to write a file at the beginning of a tape and then read remaining files on the end of the tape, thus confusing the operating system of the true status of the scratch tape. The protection of such media should be through erasure. Because of the residual magnetization remaining, such media will require several erase procedures before being declared safe.

The radiation from electromagnetic devices is one possibility that is overlooked in all but the most secure environments (such as military installations). Protection against radiation can be achieved by iron nets functioning as a type of shield, called a Faraday cage, placed within the walls of the computer room [Janson 1985].

Auditing. Auditing of computer logs and other reports consists of periodic checks to verify that these records are consistent and reveal no improper activity. Auditing should be a regular activity in a computer installation. (Of course, auditing assumes the existence of appropriate logs and reports.) The role of the operating system here is the production of logon and logoff records, and records of attempted access with incorrect passwords or user identification. The problem in this area is not usually the production of such logs, but their actual regular auditing. Similar auditing procedures should be required for many types of sensitive applications, especially business applications like payroll, accounts payable, and so on.

16.4 INTERNAL SECURITY

The protection mechanisms that can be directly implemented and supported by the hardware or the operating system come under the heading of internal security. The principal internal security mechanisms to be considered for most systems include:

- **user authentication:** mechanisms such as passwords that verify the person trying to use the computer system is an authorized user.
- **access control:** the ongoing internal protection that controls access to each resource while allowing sharing information in a controlled manner.
- **communication security:** protection of information transmitted from one computer to another, often necessarily over physically vulnerable connections.

Goals of Protection Mechanisms

The technical protection mechanisms provided by computer hardware, the operating system, and application programs should follow certain principles if they are to be effective in supporting security policies. The most important of these principles are:

- Ease of use: Any mechanisms that are difficult to use will be avoided by users whenever possible. Defaults to files that make them private are transparent to the user and hence do not get in the way. Capabilities to change such files to make them available to other users should be provided.
- Keep it simple: Complex schemes are hard to prove foolproof.

- Open design: The protection mechanism may depend on the existence of secret codes, passwords, or keys, but it should not depend on the secrecy of the mechanism's design. Codes and keys can be changed; the design of the mechanism cannot.

- Flexibility: The flexibility to match the power of the protection mechanism to the value of the information that needs to be protected and to the potential for attack.

Again, we should point out that the security of a computer installation is not determined solely by the protection mechanisms provided by the computer hardware and operating system. The total security depends on many different measures. The primary goal of technical protection via the hardware, operating system, and application programs is to guarantee that the computer system itself is not the weakest link in the total security system.

16.5 USER AUTHENTICATION

A primary concern of internal security mechanisms is to authenticate users who wish to gain access to a computer system, usually by submitting a batch job or by logging on to an interactive terminal. Security policies establish which persons should be permitted to gain access, and what privileges should be assigned to each. Authentication mechanisms are intended to ensure that a person attempting to use the computer is really the user he or she claims to be.

How can a computer system know that a user's identity is authentic? Possible means for proving identity include:

- something a person has in his or her possession (an ID card or key)

- something that a person knows (a password, mother's birthdate, or combination of a lock)

- something that is a part of a person (a signature, fingerprint, or voiceprint).

Of all these mechanisms, the one most commonly used by far is the password. A number of special-purpose systems, however, now rely instead on a possession such as a magnetically-encoded credit card. Systems of the future may be able to rely more heavily on voiceprints, fingerprints, or other less transferrable characteristics in a cost-effective manner. However, they must be able to authenticate a user's identity in slightly abnormal cases. For example, what if the user has a cold (voiceprint problem) or a cut finger (fingerprint problem)?

Relying on a possession, such as a key or ID card, leaves a user vulnerable because the item may be lost. In such cases, losses must be reported immediately if the system is to minimize security risks.

Password Control

Since in many systems user authentication depends (perhaps unfortunately) on simple password facilities, the management of such passwords is extremely important. A number of common-sense rules should be employed both by the OS and by system users to make a password system more effective. Choosing easy-to-remember passwords (spouse's name, phone number, or social security number) makes the password system extremely weak; repeated trials using "obvious" passwords result in unauthorized access to the computer. The memorable quote from the movie *War Games,* "It can't be that simple" (uttered when the intruder found out that the author of the "game" had a son named Joshua) emphasizes this well—entering "Joshua" as a password allowed him access to all facilities of a supposedly secure military computer. It should not have been that simple, but due to the lack of procedures in password management, it usually *is* that simple!

Passwords should be long enough to make repeated trials futile. On the other hand, they should not be so long that they cannot be remembered by the user. In addition, one major aspect of password management is the requirement that passwords be periodically changed.

Because the OS must keep a record of each user's password, this record should be **encrypted**, or encoded, to avoid a security breach if the password file is penetrated. Encryption is discussed further below. One special consideration makes password encryption different from the encryption that may be applied to messages and other data. The trial password typed by users attempting to logon may also be encrypted, and the encrypted versions may be compared. Thus the encryption does not ever have to be reversed. Because of this, special codes may be used for which **decryption** is almost impossible.

Password management is one area that is directly affected by the operating system. Users are lazy when it comes to password security. They choose easy and obvious passwords, and do not like to change them. The operating system could force users to change passwords periodically by tracking when they were last changed, and requesting users who have not changed passwords in awhile to make a change when logging on. Users who do not comply would not be allowed to proceed. The problem of easy-to-guess passwords is more difficult to solve, unless the computer assigns the password. In this case, users are likely to select "randomly" generated passwords, which possibly results in constant requests to system managers to find out the current password or to assign a new password.

The operating system's role in password security can include limits on logon attempts with an incorrect password in a particular interval of time (per session, per hour, or per day). This limit could also be used to collect data to help detect attempted intrusion.

Monitoring usage via console listings and other reports is also an important means of detecting unauthorized intruders. Installation of call-back modems, encryption/decryption hardware and software, and other security support mechanisms are important considerations in system management.

16.6 ACCESS CONTROL

A very important responsibility of internal security is **access control**. This is the problem of ensuring, for every access attempted to a protected resource by any process, that the access is permitted by the established **access control policy**. The simplest and most common type of access control mechanism is simple file protection. More elaborate mechanisms are possible on highly secure systems. The most effective access control policies must be based on the **principle of least privilege:** each program unit, at each moment, should have access to *only* the resources it absolutely needs.

File Protection

As introduced briefly in Section 12.7, access control mechanisms that provide protection for files are an essential part of a secure computer system. As described in that section, operating systems such as UNIX provide users with the ability to allocate different types of protection to directories and files. The protection provision allows read (r), write (w), and/or execute (x) access to a file by three types of users—the owner, the owner's group, and "the world." The protection is implemented using nine bits—three bits for designating read, write, and execute for each of the three classes of users. Figure 16–1 illustrates a UNIX directory entry indicating that the file *temp* has read, write, execute access by the owner, read and execute access by a group of users, and no access for everyone else. Other popular operating systems provide file protection similar to that of UNIX.

An additional operating system feature that would be desirable—but is much less commonly found—is the capability to periodically inform users of files that are vulnerable due to the access rights assigned.

Figure 16–1 UNIX File Protection

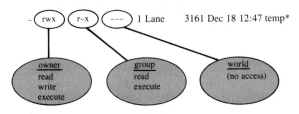

Isolation

Perhaps the simplest security policy is also the most drastic one—total isolation. In order to understand this and subsequent protection schemes, we will use the term **principal** to describe the authority, usually a person, who is accountable for the use or misuse of some entity within the computer system. The **policy of isolation** provides that a protected entity belongs to one and only one principal and cannot be accessed in any way by any other principal [Jones 1978]. This policy assumes that only one user at a time may use the computer system. Furthermore, there must be a "scrubbing" (that is, erasing all residual data) between users so that no information is left accessible in memory or on computer media. This "scrubbing" takes time. The alternative is for all principals to have their own computer system.

Providing each principal with a private *virtual machine* is an effective way to enforce a policy of isolation. If properly organized, the virtual machine can ensure that a user at some security level in no way can determine information about other security levels that are running concurrently [Jones 1978]. You must address a variety of problems if the virtual machine is to meet this requirement, but they are beyond the scope of this chapter. The reader is referred to Jones [1978] and to Chapter 21 for further discussion of the use of virtual machines for enforcing the policy of isolation.

It should be clear, however, that a policy of isolation as described is not cost-effective or even desirable in most situations. In today's computing environments including integrated databases, controlled sharing is usually mandatory.

The Access Matrix

In order to describe a more general access control policy, we define the following concepts:

- **Objects:** entities with unique names that can distinguish them from all other objects in the system. Hardware objects are such entities as the CPU, memory, and tape drives; software objects include programs and files.

- **Access rights:** permissions to execute an operation on an object; for instance, read, write, execute.

- **Subjects:** entities in a computer system that may be granted access rights. These include users, processes, and programs.

- **Domains** or **protection domains:** program units or time period during which the process's access rules and resources are constant. A domain defines a set of objects, and what operations are valid on each object.

Subjects must operate within a protection domain D, which essentially is a collection of ordered pairs: <object-name, access rights-set>, i.e., a collection of access rights. Consider a domain D having access right <file EMPLOYEES,READ,WRITE>. A process executing in domain D will be able to both read and write the file EMPLOYEES, but will not be able to perform any other operation (e.g., execute).

A simple view of this access control policy is to consider it as a two-dimensional matrix called an **access matrix,** with the domains listed in rows and the objects requiring or allowed access listed in columns. A user or process running in a particular domain D will have access to the objects as specified in each column according to the access rights found in that column for the row representing domain D.

Figure 16–2 illustrates an access matrix for domains D1, D2 and D3 with access to object files EMPLOYEES, TRANSACTIONS, TAPEDRIVE, and PRINTER. A process executing in domain D2 will be able to read the file EMPLOYEE and print to the printer. A process executing in domain D3 will be able to read or write files EMPLOYEE and TRANSACTIONS, and print to the PRINTER. The domains depicted in Figure 16–2 are not disjoint; for example, both D2 and D3 have access rights for the PRINTER.

Bear in mind that the access matrix does not represent a complete and permanent access control policy, but only a snapshot of the rules in force at a single instant of time. Under effective security policies this matrix is constantly changing, and effective implementations must support both use of and changes to the information it contains.

Implementing Access Matrices

As you can see, many domains and objects can make up the rows and columns of an access matrix. It should also be obvious that, if the principle of least

Figure 16–2 An Access Matrix

Domains / Objects	D1	D2	D3
EMPLOYEES		READ	READ WRITE
TRANSACTIONS	READ		READ WRITE
TAPE DRIVE	READ WRITE		
PRINTER		PRINT	PRINT

privilege is followed, many entries of this matrix will be empty, i.e., the matrix will be sparse. While techniques for representing such sparse matrices exist, they are not really applicable within this environment. Three possible approaches to implementing these matrices are:

- a global table: a set of ordered triples <Domain,Object,Access-Rights-Set>.
- an access list for each object: a list of ordered pairs <Domain,Access-Rights-Set>.
- capabilities for each domain: a list of objects and the operations allowed on those objects (capabilities).

Global Tables

The **global table** implementation of an access matrix is the simplest of the three outlined previously. Any operation X attempted on an object O within a domain D results in a search of the global table for an entry <D,O,R>, where R is an access rights set and X is in the set R (see Figure 16–3). If such an entry is found, the operation is allowed to continue; otherwise, an error or exception condition results.

It should be obvious that this table can be quite large and probably will not remain in primary storage, thus resulting in overhead of paging or other I/O in order to access the table. Thus, this large table, while simple to implement, is far from ideal. It lacks the ability to group objects that can be accessed by all or many domains and suffers from severe overhead.

Figure 16–3 Global Table Implementation of the Access Matrix

D1	TRANSACTIONS	READ
D1	TAPE DRIVE	READ
D1	TAPE DRIVE	WRITE
D2	EMPLOYEES	READ
D2	PRINTER	PRINT
D3	EMPLOYEES	READ
D3	EMPLOYEES	WRITE
D3	TRANSACTIONS	READ
D3	TRANSACTIONS	WRITE
D3	PRINTER	PRINT

Access Lists

An alternative to the global table approach is to set up an **access list** associated with each object, consisting of a list of <domain,access-rights-set> pairs that specifies exactly who may do what to that object. Using an access list, an operation X on an object O attempted in domain D results in a search of the access list of O for an entry <D,R> where X is in the access rights set R. If found, the operation continues; otherwise it results in an error or exception.

To prevent access lists from becoming extremely large and containing much redundant information, it is also possible to set up a **default access list** that can be searched either before or after the search of the access list for a specific object. If the operation X is in the default list, the operation will continue. Figure 16–4 illustrates the use of an access list along with a default list.

Figure 16–4 Use of Access Lists Plus Default Lists

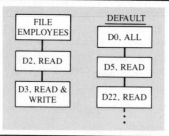

Capabilities

Yet another approach to representing the information contained in an access matrix is the use of data items called **capabilities** with special properties. Each capability is associated with a subject or domain, and specifies a set of access rights allowed for a specific object. A **capability list** is a list or set of capabilities usable in a specific domain. A capability acts like a token that, when possessed, permits a subject in a domain to access an object in certain ways. It is analogous to an airline ticket that allows an individual to board an airplane with restrictions (access rights), such as sitting in first class, business class, or economy class.

A capability is trusted by the system to prove that a subject is authorized to perform certain actions. For this reason, the operations permitted on capabilities must be restricted. If this were not the case, capabilities could be forged or modified by users to allow access beyond that to which they were entitled. The capabilities in a capability list must be viewed as protected objects, managed by the operating system or by special hardware mechanisms, and only indirectly accessible to a process. Because of conflicting requirements for frequent and efficient manipulation and effective protection, implementation of capabilities is a difficult problem usually solvable only with specialized hardware support.

Figure 16–5 depicts a capability as a protected pointer "possessed" by a process through which all accesses to an object are mediated. However it is implemented, a capability must specify an object identifier (pointer), the type of object, and the access rights the possessor of the capability has to the object.

A practical implementation technique for capabilities in some systems is to view all resources as memory segments, and protection as an extension of the memory management mechanisms. This approach extends the concept of an access control field in the segment descriptor to serve as a capability, controlling all access to that segment. The segment table assigned to each process becomes a capability list. During each attempt to reference a segment, the hardware ensures that the type of access being attempted is valid.

A subject that possesses a capability may pass a copy of that capability to other subjects. The copy may remain the same, or may have the access rights restricted or reduced. Note that as a capability propagates through the system, access rights can never increase. Furthermore, managing the copying and moving of capabilities can be quite complex. A balance between rapid access and protection of capabilities is required in a multiprogramming system in which there are often large numbers of capabilities that must be managed. The use of a directory strategy similar to that used for file management simplifies the management of large numbers of capabilities.

Figure 16–5 Capabilities as Protected Pointers

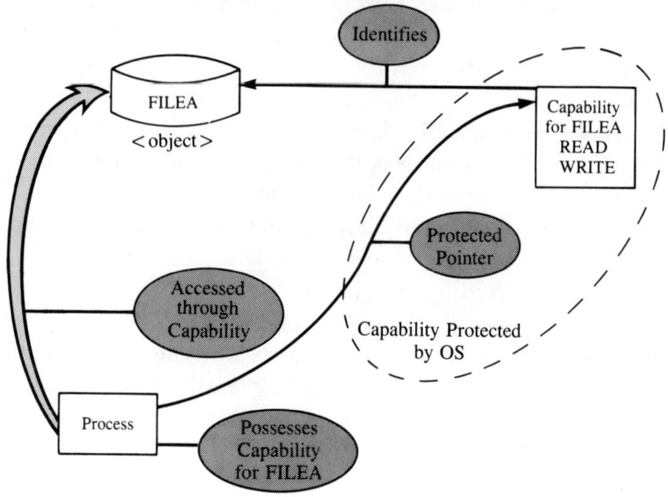

Revoking Access Rights

It is sometimes necessary to revoke a subject's access rights if circumstances change, or if the subject's behavior is not as expected. This revocation of rights could:

- be permanent or temporary.
- apply to all users or a subset of users.
- be delayed or immediate.
- revoke all access rights or a subset of them.

Hence, there are many considerations in such revocation [Peterson & Silberschatz 1985]. If simple access lists are being used, revocation simply involves the removal of one or more access rights from the list.

Capability-based systems present a more difficult problem. If many copies of a capability exist, and no central directory of capabilities exists, revoking capabilities will be quite complex. In such cases, the capability must first be found. Then there must be careful manipulation of the data structure representing the capability.

The most effective solution to this problem is the use of **indirect capabilities** to provide access rights that might need to be revoked. With this method, a subject is given a capability which points to another capability, which in turn identifies the resource itself. If the intermediate capability is later destroyed, the indirect capability is effectively revoked.

Flow Control

The requirements in some environments for non-discretionary access control policies and classification schemes must be met by rules that cannot be captured in the access matrix alone. Meeting these requirements is the problem of **flow control**. A flow control mechanism controls the ways in which subjects that possess rights or information may pass them on to others. This control prevents unauthorized users from acquiring information indirectly. Most systems that allow a user to copy a file from a directory (for example, a group member with read protection under UNIX), can then in turn pass a copy of this file to a user outside of the group, even though the original file had no access to users outside of the group. This is because the access rights of the file can now be set by the user without regard to previously allowed access rights.

Flow control requires the ability to know the history of an object, in this case a file, so that no additional capability can be added. With many copies of an object, managing flow control becomes quite complex. Capabilities must be protected so that subsequent copies of files cannot be passed on to unauthorized users. The weak link here, of course, is the person involved. If the person could be trusted not to pass on copies to unauthorized users, then there would be no real need for flow control. Even if flow control were implemented, there would be no way to prevent the passing of printed copies of protected information to unauthorized individuals.

Once again effective solutions to this problem may require hardware assistance, such as the novel "rings of protection" scheme found in MULTICS. This mechanism associates a ring number, or security level, with each file and with each process. Any attempt by a process to access files at a higher *or lower* security level than its own causes an interrupt, and the OS may determine if the access is permitted by the applicable security policy.

16.7 ENCRYPTION AND COMMUNICATION SECURITY

Security within the operating system does not address the problem of weaknesses in the data communications or networking environment. If data (messages, files, and the like) can be exchanged without encryption, then unauthorized individuals might be able to receive such data by other methods, such as physical wiretaps. While this is outside of the direct control of the operating system, the vulnerability of data being transmitted must be recognized by installation management so that users are aware of such "holes" in security.

Because of the inherent weakness in the physical security of communication, encryption of messages is a common strategy for providing protection. Besides its use for passwords, encryption can be used to protect information stored in the file system on magnetic media, such as disks and tapes, and transmitted over communication lines in a network environment. For encrypted information in the file system, the information must be decrypted prior to being read by an application program.

Encryption and decryption generally make use of some type of **encryption key** that determines the translation between unencrypted data and the encrypted, secret form to be stored or transmitted. Some encryption algorithms allow the use of a single secret key for both encryption and decryption. In this case, possession of the key along with access to the decryption algorithm allows access to the information. Obviously, management of the encryption key itself becomes a security issue: How are the keys to be securely stored and distributed to users?

Another promising approach to encryption, called **public key encryption**, [Rivest et al. 1978] is based on the use of two related keys: a **public key** for encryption and a different **private key** for decryption. With this method, each user has a distinct pair of keys. A user can send encrypted information securely to another user by encrypting it with the receiver's public key, without knowing the receiver's private key. The user receiving the information can decrypt it using the private key which no one else knows.

Encryption techniques could be applied in various situations that involve storing of sensitive OS-related data. Most users will agree that the systems they use today do not provide encryption and decryption as standard features. In every instance, the cost of security must be weighed against the value of the information being protected. Encryption and decryption require processing overhead and will affect system performance. This, along with the problems of key management, are certainly important issues in deciding whether to use encryption for storing and/or transmitting information.

16.8 LEGAL PROTECTION

Legal protection of information in computers is an important related concern for computer security. This type of protection is provided by federal, state, and local laws, and international treaties, relating to crimes involving computers. These include laws and rules that can be used to prosecute or sue corporations and individuals involved in security penetration attempts. Among these laws are patent laws, copyright laws, trade secret laws, and laws related to computer crime. This body of law helps to deter such attacks, but does not really prevent them from happening. It does at least help provide a means of recovering losses from guilty parties.

Legal protection is particularly important to vendors of operating systems because it provides a means of protecting the OS software. State trade secret laws and federal copyright laws are the most common ways to protect OS software. License agreements are also used to provide an operating system to users without actually selling the software to the user.

16.9 SUMMARY

A secure computer system is one that expands on reliability to preserve the integrity and privacy of data even in the face of deliberate threats. There are many problems to solve in meeting these requirements. Attacks on security can be sophisticated and subtle, and the costs of combating these attacks can be high. Thus, the importance of effective security must be balanced against the needs of a particular installation.

Security covers many aspects of computer system use. Not all of these are under the control of the operating system, but the OS must avoid being a weak link. External security includes physical security, or protection of systems against physical intrusion or damage; and operational security, which establishes the policies for effective and secure system use.

Internal security is the area of primary concern to the operating system. The principal issues are user authentication, access control, and communication security. User authentication most often is performed by a password system, which must take care to ensure proper selection and management of passwords. Access control may consist of simple file protection, total isolation, some implementation of an access matrix, or a more elaborate flow control mechanism. Popular access control mechanisms include access lists and capabilities. The flow control required for classified security systems may require hardware support like the MULTICS rings of protection.

Communication security is most effectively addressed by encryption mechanisms, including secret key or public key systems. The role of legal protection must also be considered in a total security strategy.

═══ FOR FURTHER READING ═══

Reasonably detailed discussion of various security issues is contained in some OS texts such as Deitel [1984], Peterson and Silberschatz [1985], Janson [1985], and Van Tessel [1972]. Deitel provides an extended list of possible threats to security, and some methods for dealing with those threats.

Morris and Thompson [1979] describe the evolution of techniques for password security on UNIX. Lamport [1981] describes a method to enhance password security by changing the password with each use.

Linden [1976] surveys operating system structures intended to support access control. Protection structures are reviewed by Popek [1974]. UNIX security issues are reviewed by Grampp and Morris [1984]. A special issue of ACM Computer Surveys [CSURV 1976] discusses structures to support security, including capabilities. A system for user-managed capabilities is presented by Mullender and Tanenbaum [1986]. Levy [1984] provides a comprehensive description of a number of capability-based computer systems. An issue of IEEE COMPUTER [COMPUTER 1983b] examines flow control mechanisms, and another issue [COMPUTER 1983a] contains several articles on communications security and public key encryption.

The MULTICS rings of protection are described in detail by Organick [1972]. Complete coverage of cryptography can be found in Meyer [1982]. Jones [1978] provides more detail on protection involving isolation via virtual machines. Legal protection of software, as well as other security issues, are discussed by Johnson [1985].

A number of articles have focused on attempts to penetrate the security of computer systems. These include Attanasio et al. [1976] (VM/370); Hebbard et al. [1980] (The Michigan Terminal System); McPhee [1974] (MVS); and Wilkinson et al. [1981] (Burroughs MCP). Other presentations describe projects to implement new operating systems designed for extremely high security. Examples include DeLashmutt [1979] (PSOS) and Popek et al. [1979] (Data Secure UNIX).

IMPORTANT TERMS

access control
access list
access matrix
access right
backup procedures
capability
capability list
classification
communication security
computer virus
decryption
default access list
discretionary security policy
domain

encryption
encryption key
external security
flow control
global table
indirect capability
internal security
non-discretionary security
   policy
object
operational security
physical security
policy of isolation
principal

principle of least privilege
private key
protection
protection domain
public key
public key encryption

security
security mechanism
security policy
subject
trojan horse
user authentication

≡ REVIEW QUESTIONS ≡

1. What are the common problems in password management? How can they be solved?

2. What is the difference between security and protection?

3. What are the goals of security?

4. What common fault in human beings resulted in easy penetration of the war game in the movie *War Games?*

5. What conditions mandate security? What is the impact of cost on security?

6. Contrast internal and external security. Which is most affected by the operating system?

7. What is the role of auditing in computer security? What data produced by an operating system can be audited?

8. Explain the file access control supported by UNIX systems.

9. Discuss the goals of internal security. Which are most difficult to attain? Why?

10. Explain ways that a computer system can authenticate who a user really is. Are they realistic?

11. What are the rings of protection provided by the MULTICS system?

≡ ASSIGNMENTS ≡

1. Discuss the differences between access lists and capabilities in implementing access control. Which is more complex? What are the advantages of this more complex approach? The disadvantages?

2. Do a literature search to find two systems that provide encryption and decryption facilities as a part of the operating system. How is key management supported? Is there a high cost associated with such systems?

3. If you were to implement an operating system that you wanted to market, how would you protect this software? Explain the steps that you would use to protect the software in every possible way.

System
Management
and Accounting

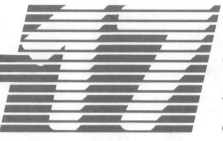

System Management and Accounting

17.1 INTRODUCTION

System management and accounting are two important aspects of multiuser operating systems and of some single-user operating systems. **System management** of an operating system includes:

- generation of an operating system for a specific hardware configuration
- installing the operating system in loadable form on auxiliary storage
- loading the operating system from auxiliary storage into primary storage and preparing it for execution
- shutting down the operating system
- tuning the operating system for the best performance in a particular environment

The activities of system management are performed by systems programmers and/or computer operators. Some, like the generation and loading of an operating system, are done only periodically. Others, such as loading and shutting down the operating system, are performed regularly.

Accounting includes tracking computer system resources used by jobs and/or users, and billing users for the use of these resources. This process is very important in larger multiuser systems because the users must pay for the computer system on a "pay as you go" basis. Accounting also requires that maximum resource allocations, such as disk space allocation, be enforced. Since much of the accounting function relates to session login and logout by a user in an interactive system, we also discuss session management in this chapter.

This chapter focuses on the requirements and design considerations for each of these operating system support services, with particular emphasis on the software necessary for these services. This software must be a part of an operating system. The software that provides these system management facilities—system generation, operating system loading, system shutdown, and tuning—and the accounting facilities should be included in the operating system design considerations rather than being implemented as an afterthought.

17.2 SYSTEM GENERATION

An important aspect of operating system support is **system generation,** which provides for the generation of a specific operating system matching the characteristics of the hardware on which it will run, and generation of the desired operating system features. An operating system design must take into consideration this requirement for tailoring the operating system; it should include the support software to produce particular configurations via this system generation process.

Requirements for the system generation facility of any operating system depend on which aspects of the operating system are variable from one generation to another. Hence, the first thing you must do to determine these requirements is to decide which features, aspects, or support are to be variable. Usually these will include:

- machine type
- number of CPUs
- CPU type(s) and options
- maximum number of simultaneous users and/or concurrent processes
- maximum number of devices (number of device table entries)
- specific "standard" devices to support and their addresses, logical names, and features
- special devices and identification of their device drivers
- maximum/minimum physical memory sizes
- operating system features to be included
- system console(s)
- character codes supported
- size of area for system control blocks (system queue area)

- access method services
- identification of swap/paging device
- default system device for system directory and/or files
- name of generated system image

How the above support features are made variable depends on the structure of the operating system and the tools provided for system generation. In some operating systems, system generation merely defines assembler or high-level language conditional values and constants, such as device addresses, which are used by the assembler or compiler to include the selected features in the operating system and to define device and other addresses. Each source module must be assembled or compiled using the defined values. The resulting object modules must be linked to create an executable operating system image with the desired features and configuration. This approach, perhaps the simplest, yields an operating system that can be more or less tailored to the exact desired configuration. However, it requires a complete assembly or compilation of the entire operating system, which could take much time if the operating system is large. Of course, it may be that only certain modules of the operating system must be assembled or compiled, with the others being provided in object code form for the linking of the operating system.

A structure that would eliminate the need for the assembly or compilation described above is one that uses tables to describe the operating system. Features selected would result in the inclusion of certain modules in object code form, which would later be linked to generate the desired operating system. There must be a means for specifying device addresses and other such constants; it might be that a small module must be assembled or compiled prior to the linking of the selected object modules from the operating system object library. This approach certainly minimizes the amount of time required to generate an operating system, while providing moderate flexibility. The problem with this approach is that it does not yield a generated operating system that is as tailored to the environment as does the source code assembly or compilation approach.

Many operating systems provide for a certain dynamic configuration at operating system load time. For example, the devices to be supported may be described in a device table, but the drivers themselves would be loaded only if the device was present (and perhaps powered up or ready) at load time. This implies that some of the operating system will not be in a generated single image, but rather will consist of the generated image plus a set of independently loadable modules (e.g., device drivers).

The use of tables to describe all features is an extension of the self-configuration for devices. You could then use these tables to dynamically select the parts of the operating system to load at the time of the initial loading of the operating system. Obviously, this process would impact the time it would take to load the operating system, but it would provide much flexibility in environments that are constantly changing (new devices, features, and so on).

The three approaches for system generation differ in the amount of tailoring provided and the time required for system generation or system loading. They are represented in Figures 17–1, 17–2, and 17–3.

Figure 17–1 System Generation Using Complete OS Source

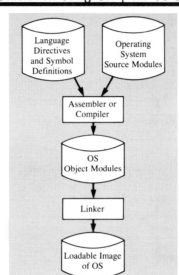

Facilities for System Generation

The operating system must provide support for system generation to avoid operating system images that are not correctly generated. Such generation-support programs should verify that the system generation parameters or features that have been selected are not conflicting prior to the generation of the operating system. All too often, the results of such conflicts are not known until after a long generation run produces an error message indicating this conflict.

Another consideration is the requirement for a method to initially load an executable operating system in order to do a system generation. In other words, a distribution media should be in some way loadable in order to provide this "startup operating system." Once this operating system is loaded, the appropriate system can be generated, using the distributed operating system libraries to generate the exact operating system.

Figure 17–2   Table-Driven System Generation using Object Modules

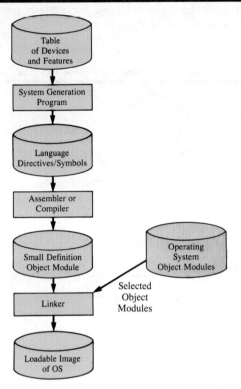

Sometimes one system must be used to generate an operating system for another hardware system. The operating system designer must take this possibility into account by allowing the generation of an operating system that does not necessarily match the configuration of the system being used for the generation. In particular, there should be a way of creating binary images that might be loaded on a different hardware unit (for example, a magnetic tape drive or disk drive requiring a different system device driver than the one being used to create the operating system).

Generally, you can use two approaches for defining system generation information: batch and interactive. However, as we will discuss, interactive facilities often produce a batch file, which can in turn be modified without answering all the interactive questions.

Figure 17–3 Tables Used at Load Time to Determine Configuration

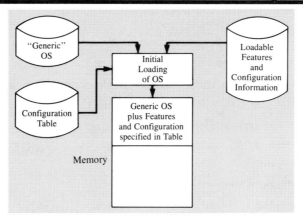

Batch-Oriented Methods

Many operating systems have some type of batch language that is used to generate an operating system. The most obvious example of such a system is IBM's MVS/XA. Another system that provides a far simpler method is the UNIX system. These two systems illustrate the batch language approach to operating system generation. Both require a second step to actually create the operating system.

IBM MVS/XA. IBM, which has always had some type of batch support in their mainframe operating systems, provides a classic example of a batch-oriented system generation process. For example, Figure 17–4 shows the process for IBM's MVS/XA operating system [IBM 1984]. There are two stages to this batch-oriented process:

- *Stage I* assembles the system generation macros and expands them into a typical IBM mainframe job stream consisting of job control statements, utility control statements, and documentation. This job stream is the input for the next stage.

- *Stage II* uses the job stream produced by Stage I to assemble, link-edit, and copy the appropriate modules from the distribution libraries to the new system files (datasets). The result of Stage II is the new (or perhaps updated) MVS/XA system libraries as well as a documentation listing.

The procedures listed in the *MVS/XA Installation: System Generation Manual* [IBM 1984] provide an idea of the complexity of a system generation for a large operating system on a mainframe computer:

- Verify the required environment exists for running SYSGEN
- Backup all previous distribution libraries
- Add the products being installed to the distribution libraries
- Initialize the disk volumes that contain the system files
- Define the system files
- Code the I/O configuration program and SYSGEN macro instructions
- Add required user-written routines
- Execute the I/O configuration program
- Execute SYSGEN
- Create a new system modification program control data set to reflect the new system libraries
- Install code not supported by the SYSGEN process
- Make backup copies of new system data sets
- After initial program load, test the generated system

The JCL and macro instructions used for system generation in MVS/XA are keyword-oriented. A command consists of a macro along with certain keyword information, as shown in Figure 17–5.

In the days of card-oriented systems, the commands given in Figure 17–5 would all have been on cards. The system generation deck was kept handy for modification or duplication. Today full screen editors allow a much better view of the system generation macros. This file of macros can be updated and changed with any desired editor. The keywords are critical, but once the macros have been set up, it is relatively simple to modify the file to add or delete devices and features. Of course, there must be a SYSGEN program to process these macros. In addition, an operating system design must include such a program if system generation is to be batch-oriented. Note that the last macro presented in Figure 17–5 specifies the type of system generation and where the output of the system generation is to be stored.

UNIX. The UNIX *config* program is used in the 4.2BSD UNIX system to configure and create bootable 4.2BSD system images. The configuration file contains at least the information shown in Figure 17–6. Statements in the configuration file follow a simple grammar used by *config* to parse the file. Note that the statements in a *config* file are far simpler than those shown in the MVS/XA SYSGEN file in Figure 17–4.

Figure 17-4 Overview of the IBM MVS/XA System Generation Process

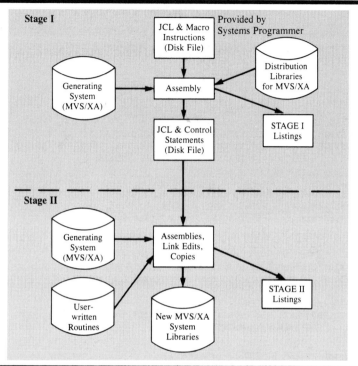

Figure 17-7 is an example of the contents of a configuration file used by *config* to create and build a UNIX system. This example is taken from Leffler and Joy [1983]. Note that it is considerably more straightforward than the MVS/XA example. As in the MVS/XA case, you can use an editor to modify and add statements to a configuration file.

These are the steps to build a UNIX system:

- Create a configuration file for the system
- Make a directory upon which the system will be built
- Run *config* using the configuration file to generate the files required to compile and load the system image
- Construct the source code interdependency rules for the configured system
- Compile and load the system

The *config* program produces output used to compile and create the desired UNIX system. One possibility in using *config* is to specify devices that

Figure 17–5 A Portion of Input for an MVS/XA SYSGEN

```
    TITLE     'PORTION OF MVS/XA SYSGEN'
    ID        'MSG1='I/O CONFIURATION USED WITH BASIC SYSTEM'
****
* CHANNEL 0 DEVICES
    IODEVICE   UNIT=3211,ADDRESS=(002,1)   HIGH SPEED PRT NO. 1
    IODEVICE   UNIT=3705,ADDRESS=OFF,                                    X
               ADAPTER=CA1
       .
       .
       .
****
* CHANNEL 3 DEVICES
    IODEVICE   UNIT=3330,ADDRESS=(310,8),FEATURE=SHARED DASD
    IODEVICE   UNIT=3420,ADDRESS=(380,5),MODEL=5,   800/1600 BPI TP  X
               FEATURE=(9-TRACK,DUALDENS),OFFLINE=YES
       .
       .
       .
*  REQUIRED ESOTERIC NAME-DEFINITION OF DASD UNITS
   UNITNAME NAME=SYSDA,VIO-YES,UNIT=(130,6),(230,8),(330,8),(340,8
),(420,8),(430,8),(440,8),(530,8),(540,8),(5A0,8),(5B0,8),(5E0,8)
,(630,8),(640,8),(6E0,8)
       .
       .
       .
*   THE MASTER CONSOLE IS A 3270 MODEL X AT ADDRESS 6F0
    CONSOLE    MCONS=6F0,ALTCONS=6F1,ROUTCDE=ALL
       .
*  CONTROL PROGRAM OPTIONS
CTRL   CTRLPROG OPTIONS=(DEVSTAT,RDE,RER,BLDL),SQA=1,REAL=4,           X
               TZ=(W,5),ASCII=INCLUDE

*   JOB AND MASTER SCHEDULER OPTIONS
SCH    SCHEDULR BCLMT=20,HARDCOPY=(SYSLOG,ALL,CMDS),                   X
               DEVPREF=(3330,2305-2,3330-1,3380,3400-5)

*   USER-WRITTEN COMPLETION CODES FOR AUTOMATIC RESTART
CHKPT  CHKPTREST ELIGBLE=(20,100,101,102,103,110,120,140,160,4092)     X

*   DATA MANAGEMENT OPTIONS
DATAMAN DATAMGT  ACSMETH=(BTAM,TCAM,ISAM),GRAPHICS=(PORRTNS,GSP)

TSO TSO   LOGTIME=200        TSO OPTIONS
EDIT EDIT  DSTYPE=SYSTEST,BLOCK=800,FORMAT=FIXED,   EDIT OPTIONS       X
               FIXED=(80-80),CONVERT=CAPSONLY

*  SYSTEM DATASET SPECIFICATIONS
BRODCAST  DATASET  BRODCAST,VOL=(SG2001,3330),SPACE=(CYL,(5))
CMDLIB    DATASET  CMDLIB,VOL=(SG2001,3330),SPACE=(CYL,(10,5,100))

*  THIS SYSGEN MACRO SPECIFIES A COMPLETE SYSGEN
    GENERATE  GENTYPE=ALL,OBJPDS=SYS1.OBJPDS,                          X
               RESVOL=(SG2001,3330),INDEX=SG2,JCLASS=K,OCLASS=K
    END
```

Figure 17-6 Information Required in a UNIX Configuration File

machine type

cpu type

system identification

timezone

maximum number of users

location of the root file system

available hardware

Figure 17-7 A Sample UNIX Configuration File

```
#
# A VAX
#
machine      vax
cpu          VAX/780
timezone     8 dst
maxusers     32

config       vmunix    root on hp0
config       hpvmunix root on hp0 swap on hp0 and hp2
config       genvmunix swap generic

controller   mba0    at nexus ?
disk         hp0     at mba? disk ?
disk         hp1     at mba? disk ?
controller   mba1    at nexus ?
disk         hp2     at mba? disk ?
disk         hp3     at mba? disk ?
controller   uba0    at nexus?
controller   tm0     at uba? csr 0172520   vector tmintr
tape         te0     at tm0 drive 0
tape         te1     at tm0 drive 1
device       dh0     at uba? csr 0160020 vector dhrint dhxint
device       dm0     at uba? csr 0170500 vector dmintr
device       dh1     at uba? csr 160040 vector dhrint dhxint
device       dh2     at uba? csr 0160060 vector dhrint thxint
```

are not currently on the system, but may be installed in the near future. Upon booting the UNIX system, an *autoconfiguration* phase is executed. This phase searches for the hardware devices that were specified in the *config* process and only enables (loads) the drivers for devices that are present at boot time.

Interactive Methods

Some operating systems provide an interactive system generation tool, which requires that displayed questions be answered with yes or no, the number of devices, addresses of devices, and so on. Some such facilities are menu-driven, allowing the user to select features and devices from a displayed menu. In most cases, the interactive program generates a batch file, which is compiled, assembled, or used by a specific system generation program. This batch file can usually be edited for minor changes using a full-screen editor, thus avoiding having to answer many interactive questions for subsequent system generations. The primary advantage of the interactive tool is that users who are unfamiliar with system generation, particularly when a new operating system is being installed, can generate a system without having to know the batch language to specify features.

Digital Equipment Corporation's RT-11 provides an interactive facility to generate the operating system. The output of this program is a file that is used during the assembly of the entire resident monitor of the operating system. The device drivers of RT-11 are loaded dynamically; hence, the system generation process must build a device table of the specified devices including their default device and interrupt vector addresses. Upon booting the system, devices such as the system disk driver and terminal driver must be present for the load to continue. Other devices are activated in the device table if they are present in the booted system. Device drivers are not loaded until required by a program or made resident by an RT-11 LOAD command. RT-11 also allows for dynamic installation of a device if there is room in the device table. A smart system manager will leave extra slots in this device table, an option provided in the interactive system generation program. Addresses for devices other than the system disk and terminal driver can be dynamically changed in this device table and made permanent for future booting of the operating system. Figure 17–8 illustrates a portion of the interactive RT-11 system generation program.

Installing the Operating System

Generating an operating system does not necessarily make it loadable. This may require an installation procedure, which includes copying the operating system and supporting programs (device drivers and the like) to a particular disk or directory, then writing a small loader program to a fixed location on disk (such as track 0, sector 0) that is automatically read upon system load

Figure 17–8 Interactive System Generation in RT-11

```
*********************************************************************
              RT-11 SYSTEM GENERATION PROGRAM   V05.00
*********************************************************************
Do you want and introduction to system generation (N)? N
Do you want to use a previously created answer file (N)? N
Do you want to create and answer file (N)? Y
What answer file do you want to create (SYSGEN.ANS)?
... checking for protected output files.
*********************************************************************
       MONITOR TYPE
*********************************************************************
Do you want the single-job (SJ) monitor (Y)? N
Do you want the foreground/background (FB) monitor (Y)? Y
Do you want the extended memory (XM) monitor (N)? N
Do you want device timeout support (N)? Y
Do you want an error message on system I/O errors (Y)? Y
Do you want system job support (N)? N
Do you want to use the .SPCPS request (N)? N
DO you want multiterminal support (N)? Y
...
Enter the size of the output buffers (40): 50
Enter the size of the input buffers (134): 160
...
Do you want all the keyboard monitor commands? Y
...
Do you want the start-up indirect file (Y)? Y
...
*********************************************************************
       DEVICE OPTIONS
*********************************************************************
Enter the device name you want support for (dd): DY
Do you want RX02 double-density only support (N)? N
Do you want support for a second DY controller (N)? N
What is the address of the 1st DY? 177170
What is the vector address the 1st DY?  264
...
Does your printer have a nonstandard vector or CSR (N)? N
...
How many extra device slots do you want (0)? 4
...
Do you want to change any of your responses (N)? N
*********************************************************************
       PHYSICAL DEVICE SELECTION AND SYSGEN CLEANUP
*********************************************************************
What is the physical name of the source input device? DL0
...
Do you want to retain the system OBJs (Y)? N
Do you want to retain the work files (Y)? N

END OF SYSGEN PROGRAM
```

(boot, reset, and so on, depending on the term used for a particular operating system).

17.3 LOADING THE OPERATING SYSTEM

As we have just described, some portion of a loader is usually written at a fixed location on a loadable media. In the early days, many computers required a small loader program (less than 100 bytes) to be keyed into memory using binary switches and the computer console, loading each word or byte separately. Once the program was loaded, the operator would set the start address to the beginning of the program just keyed in. This loader program would load a yet larger loader program from a fixed location on a particular media (record 0 of tape drive or track 0, sector 0 of a disk, perhaps), which would in turn load the operating system. With the core memory used then, the loader program would often stay in memory for weeks and months, even though the computer was periodically powered off. Today there is typically a hardware loader in ROM that loads the operating system or loads a software loader, which in turn loads the operating system image into memory.

Initialization

Once the operating system is loaded, certain initialization must be done. There could be a separate initialization program (for example, IBM mainframes use a Nucleus Initialization Program, or NIP) to run certain verifications of memory and devices before continuing the operating system load. Other responsibilities of such an initialization program might include:

- relocating all or parts of the operating system within memory, usually to high or low memory and setting appropriate interrupt vectors

- loading device handlers

- initializing hardware devices

- setting up the process control blocks of processes to be initially run

- passing control to the process scheduler (dispatcher)

Cold vs. Warm Start

Small computers with simple operating systems like MS-DOS always load in a **cold start** state. The OS does not "know" what was running before the reload occurred. Initialization is always the same, with only the configuration file determining certain minimal features or device support. More complex operating systems may be brought up with a **warm start,** in which certain information about the previous state of the system is preserved. For example, in a large batch-oriented operating system like IBM MVS/XA, jobs that were in the job queue and not yet executed are "known" to the system and will be scheduled for execution according to the priorities in the job queue. A cold start in this case would lose information; all previous jobs would be lost. On complex systems, a cold start should only occur after a catastrophic error causing the loss of the job queue itself.

A mechanism for preserving information which may be useful for a warm start is called **checkpointing.** This method preserves a collection of **checkpoint records,** which are written to track the progress of certain jobs in execution. Restart of these jobs is not from the beginning, but rather from the last checkpoint recorded by the system.

Self-Configuration

Certain operating systems have tables, such as I/O tables and configuration tables, which are used at load time to perform **self-configuration.** A device table like the one shown in Figure 17–9 will specify devices, device names, addresses, interrupt vectors, and so on. However, the device will be enabled only if it is present. This is a type of self-configuration.

Configuration of MS-DOS, for example, is performed dynamically at system load time. A file called CONFIG.SYS reads and executes the instructions found in this file. The CONFIG.SYS file allows a system to be "configured" in a limited way. Included in the configuration file can be instructions that determine:

- when to check for the BREAK condition (BREAK)
- what devices the system will recognize (DEVICE)
- how many disk buffers are to be used (BUFFERS)
- how many files can be open at any one time (FILES)
- which country and language should be used for prompts (COUNTRY)
- how many disk drives are to be recognized (LASTDRIVE)
- the file to be used as the command processor (SHELL)

Figure 17–9 Format of a Device Table

Device Physical Name
Status
Disk Address of Handler
Memory Address of Handler (If loaded)
Device Size (0 if non-file structured)
Device Handler Size
Device Logical Name(s)
Owner

Although the self-configuration of MS-DOS allows limited flexibility, it does provide the most important feature of adding device drivers to the system, which are loaded and made part of the Basic Input Output System module, or BIOS, when an MS-DOS system is generated. Figure 17–10 illustrates a sample CONFIG.SYS file.

Figure 17-10 An MS-DOS Configuration File

```
BREAK=OFF
BUFFERS=4
FILES=14
COUNTRY=044
DEVICE=C:VDISK.SYS 512/E
DEVICE=C:NEWDEV.SYS
LASTDRIVE=E
SHELL=C:SHELL1.COM
```

File Checking

Simple systems like MS-DOS suffer little in the event of an electrical power failure. A simple file checking program, "CHKDSK," can determine if clusters have been lost and reclaim them if necessary. Other similar systems provide for file header verification with backup header descriptors, which can be used to "fix" the files with damaged headers. Such redundancy is helpful in preventing the loss of data in a production environment.

In more complex systems, particularly multiuser systems, there is a much greater risk of loss upon unexpected or abnormal system shutdown. A file checking facility can help to restore a contaminated file system back to an acceptable state, although it cannot reclaim lost data that might have been "lost in computer memory" (e.g., in disk cache buffers) upon the shutdown.

Startup Diagnostics

Diagnostics for checking both the hardware and file structures are often a part of the operating system load. While often found in ROMs on microcomputers, similar mechanisms are very important in computers not having power-up diagnostics. Even for systems with such diagnostics, the start-up diagnostics can include checking of hardware and special features not included in the ROM diagnostics.

Another aspect of diagnostics is that of checking file structures to be sure they are valid. Other software-related checks could be added to such OS start-up diagnostics to help find any system problems *before* the operating system begins execution.

It is important that OS start-up diagnostics specifically identify any problems, isolate failing hardware components, and correct failing software or file system components before continuing. In some instances, the diagnostics will determine that the OS cannot be loaded and given control until corrective action is taken to remove detected failures, either in hardware or software, from the system environment.

17.4 SYSTEM SHUTDOWN

Users of simple single-user operating systems like MS-DOS have put up with the inconvenience of power failures, and perhaps a loss of some data that were in memory upon the power failure. Larger multiuser systems have more to keep track of than the data in memory during such a failure. The file system itself can be contaminated if the system is not shut down properly (e.g., a portion of cache not written to disk to properly close the file system). Other system shutdown considerations include warning users of imminent shutdown so that they might logoff with no loss of data, keeping track of the current batch or job queue (if a batch system), and other miscellaneous "housekeeping."

Upon operating system loading, the initialization program should be able to detect if the system is properly shutdown and proceed with "cleaning" the system (file system, queues, and so on) to an acceptable state. Xenix does this upon booting the system before loading the OS.

Normal Shutdown

In many systems, the shutdown procedure is very specific. Operators must follow the procedure, or the result will be a loss of data to users, corruption of the file system, or at the bare minimum a great inconvenience to users (for instance, if they are not warned of the imminent shutdown). Uninterruptible power supply systems minimize the problems of power failures, allowing the operator time for orderly system shutdown.

Abnormal Shutdown

At times the operating system itself might experience a failure. In most cases the system can recover enough to execute certain error procedures before system shutdown. The OS must preserve as much information about the system state as possible, usually through the form of system dumps written to disk files for later analysis. Of course, there is always a possibility of a failure so severe that the system dump facility cannot be invoked. In such cases a systems programmer should be on hand to determine the state of the system prior to reloading the operating system and losing the information about the system state. We will discuss such problem isolation in Chapter 19.

17.5 TUNING

Single-user operating systems such as those of the first microcomputers were never suspected of causing performance problems. In most cases, if users felt the system was slow, they eventually purchased a faster microcomputer with the same operating system. Large multiuser systems run on powerful computers; poor performance is often caused by or blamed on the operating system itself. In such cases it is necessary to identify what the system is doing and where the bottlenecks are in the operating system.

Performance Evaluation

Chapter 18 presents performance evaluation in more detail. For now, we'll look at a brief overview of evaluation techniques. The system programmer faced with **tuning** the operating system for better performance must know exactly what causes performance problems. Generally, the areas of concern are:

- **response time** for interactive users (the time between the entry of an operating system command on a terminal and the receipt of the response on the screen)
- **turnaround time** for batch users (the time from submission of a "job" to the time of receipt of its output)
- **device throughput** (the number of records, transactions, lines, and so on per second or minute)
- **CPU throughput** (measured in jobs per day, with some measure of the characteristics of the job)
- **CPU utilization** (how much of the CPU is used)
- **wait time** for a service, primarily for devices, which affects CPU throughput and utilization

The above measures will vary with the **workload**—the full set of work a system is doing at any given time. Hence, there must be some way of characterizing workloads in determining the types of tuning that might be necessary for improving system performance [Calingaert 1982]. This means, of course, that tuning is very dependent on a particular installation and the types of jobs typically run. In many installations, workload characteristics change periodically. For example, the workload of a large university computer center may be quite different in the summer than it is during a fall or spring semester, when many students are working on class projects using computers. Hence, the tuning for one period of time might differ from the tuning for another.

I/O-Related Tuning

The problems encountered in I/O within an operating system are more easily corrected or improved than many other performance problems because it is relatively easy to make changes to the I/O system. Problems within the I/O system may include:

- excessive I/O service wait time for a device by processes
- excessive idle time of a device
- excessive paging activity

Excessive I/O service wait time for a device by a process or processes can be caused by slow devices as well as contention by many devices for a channel, I/O controller, or I/O device. When device speed is slow, the most obvious solution is to acquire a faster device. However, this is often not the only solution. For example, a microcomputer's performance is often directly related to the speed of the floppy disk drives it uses. An easy method of greatly improving the performance of such a system is to set up and use a virtual disk. This is done by changing the CONFIG.SYS file in MS-DOS so that part of memory is used to emulate a disk device. Since no I/O is actually taking place, the speed of word processors, database programs, and the like is greatly enhanced when these programs are performing I/O. The only danger of such a device is that information is lost when the power is turned off, either intentionally or by power failure. The aware user can often set up word processors to automatically save files periodically to a floppy disk, or implement batch files to automatically copy the virtual disk files back to the floppy disk upon termination of the application program invoked by the batch file. Improvements in performance by the use of virtual disks are very noticeable, yet extremely simple to implement.

One other type of performance issue that arises in today's portable, battery-operated laptop computers is in the length of time the batteries stay charged. Although not directly an operating system problem, reduced activity on a floppy disk will increase the amount of usage of the computer before recharging batteries. The use of a virtual disk in word processing, for example, can eliminate most I/O to the physical disk during editing, with a copy to the diskette or hard disk being made only upon exiting the word processor.

Another improvement in microcomputer performance due to I/O wait time is by the use of print spoolers (software or hardware), which allow programs to direct output to a printer, and save and print the output while the user continues with other applications on the system. In the software case, the installation of a concurrent process that drives the printer (using spooled data as data to print) allows the computer to print at the printer's pace without interfering with the user's other work on the computer.

Performance measurement data, either real-time or long-term, can identify clear problems in **device contention, channel contention,** or **controller contention.** If there is heavy contention for a channel that has multiple controllers or for a controller that has multiple devices, an analysis of the numbers of requests for each controller or device, respectively, can help to identify when reconfiguration of the I/O system would help. Moving an I/O controller from one channel to another can greatly improve performance, when requests for two or more controllers on a channel are near the same. Moving an entire disk or set of files from a disk to a disk drive on another controller can likewise minimize controller contention. Obviously, the systems programmer must be able to identify files in the performance data if file movement is to be part of tuning the I/O system.

In systems that do swapping or paging, the operating system performance is greatly affected by the swapping or paging rate, but is also affected by contention involving the swapping or paging devices. Once again, this could be channel, control unit, or device contention that must be addressed. If the I/O system is causing excessive waits for the OS's I/O swapping or paging requests, then the tuning required will be a reconfiguration of the I/O system or the reassignment of swapping and/or paging devices to other devices on the same or other I/O controllers or channels.

Paging Problems

Other than the paging problems that are caused by I/O contention, high paging rates can be caused by problems with the paging algorithm or the size of the paging cache (VAX/VMS). Tuning can involve changing the paging cache size or values affecting working set sizes for processes. In MVS, an oversized page cache results in memory being taken away from processes, working sets, causing the working sets to become much smaller, so that pages must be borrowed from the page cache. If the paging cache is too small, primary paging comes from the disk (which is much faster than the cache) [Massie 1986, p432]. Hence, the systems programmer must be able to analyze long-term data to understand which condition, if any, is being caused by the sizing of the page cache.

Excessive paging under VMS can also be caused by working sets being too small due to system parameters related to paging. In this case, two critical parameters, the working set quotas and working set extents, can be examined and modified to improve paging performance [Massie 1986, p433].

Process Scheduling Problems

Systems that do not dynamically monitor process characteristics for compute-versus I/O-boundedness can be affected by a compute-bound process having a relatively high scheduling priority. Such performance problems could be recognized by an operator or systems programmer and remedied with brute force by lowering the scheduling priority of the compute-bound task. In systems that attempt to measure compute-boundedness and adjust scheduling priorities dynamically, it might be possible to change parameters of this algorithm to more accurately measure the compute- versus I/O-boundedness (e.g., changing a window of examination). Such problems could show up on both real-time and long-term monitoring data.

17.6 ACCOUNTING

Little if any accounting is required in simple single-user microcomputer operating systems. However, multiuser systems require a variety of accounting tasks. Management of accounting information is an important part of successfully utilizing these operating systems. The operating system must support the setup of user accounts, assignment of passwords, identification of resources accessible by a user, as well as the setting of resource quotas, such as disk space.

Managing User Accounts

Associated with almost every shared computer system in a multiuser environment is a pricing scheme that is used to bill users for the resources consumed during a given period. The first step in keeping track of usage is a means of identifying a user. This is done by setting up an account for each user, identified by an account ID. Although the format and tracking of account IDs differ from system to system, a majority of systems assign an alphanumeric account ID and associate an alphanumeric password with it, which should be changed periodically.

Systems like the IBM MVS/XA system use a system management facility that tracks information about jobs run by users. The account ID becomes the primary method of tracking resource utilization in a given period for each account. An operating system must provide the facility for recording resource utilization (CPU usage, I/O requests, and long-term disk storage) so that a billing program can use this information to charge users for time on a shared system. Most multiuser systems provide a means of limiting resource use for accounts. **Resource quotas** might be established for each user, specifying limits on the use of selected resources. The following resources might be limited in this way:

- maximum disk usage
- total CPU usage per session or job
- amount of memory per session or job
- total number of I/O operations per session or job
- total amount of CPU time per period (once zero, this time must be reallocated before use of the computer is allowed)
- operating system facilities or applications available (databases, interactive and batch capabilities, compilers, and so on)
- total number of sessions or jobs (often used in a college or university class)

Although the facilities for defining available resources and resource quotas are provided in a given operating system environment, the policies of how to assign resources, resource quotas, and pricing are management decisions that are installation-dependent. The operating system must provide the support environment and make it easy for authorized system managers to assign and modify such accounting data, based on the policies of an installation.

Interactive Session Management

Interactive and timesharing systems require users to log in using a CRT or hard copy terminal (or another computer emulating such a terminal). Session management involves the login, logout, and accounting functions.

Logins

A user usually must log in to a terminal after being prompted with the appropriate message. An account ID and password must be read and validated before the user is allowed access to any further resources of the computer. Figure 17–11 shows the logic of the login function.

The login procedure must guard against too many attempts by an unauthorized user to login. Note that there is no indication as to which was incorrect in the login attempt, the user ID or the password. This information is held back so as to deter an unauthorized user from trying to guess IDs or passwords.

The login procedure could involve some more complex security measures, such as a callback system in which a user is disconnected immediately and called back using a telephone number stored in the account file. Currently, such system features are rare in commercial systems.

Logouts

A logout command interpreted by the command interpreter will pass control to the logout procedure. Its logic is presented in Figure 17–12.

Billing

Programs for billing are important to large installations. They should provide a basic billing method that can be easily modified by each installation to meet the pricing policies of that installation. For example, some universities will bill for supplies but not for computer resource usage. Hence, the billing software should allow for easy modification to support such specific billing requirements.

Figure 17–11 Login Procedure Logic

```
Login:
        /* initialize flag and count */
        ValidLogin=False
        Attempt=Max

        /* process login attempts, if not too many */
        WHILE Attempt > 0 AND ValidLogin = False

          prompt for account or user ID
          read account
          prompt for password
          read password
          IF account not valid or password not valid THEN
            Attempt=Attempt-1
            print "Login Incorrect"
          ELSE
            ValidLogin = True
          ENDIF
        ENDWHILE

        /* if login failed, hang up */
        IF ValidLogin = False THEN
         call Hangup
        ENDIF

        /* accept valid user */
        print welcome message
        call Command Interpreter
```

Figure 17–12 Logout Procedure Logic

```
Logout:
        display "Are You Sure?"
        close open files
        post accounting information
        remove session control blocks
        call Login
```

17.7 BACKUP SUPPORT

Management of a multiuser system must provide a means for file backup. The simplest approach for the operating system designer would be to provide constantly available facilities for complete media backup and restore. While this approach can be used in many installations, the number of volumes and amount of data prevent it from being used as the daily approach to system backup. Hence, it is necessary to provide a means of backing up only files that have been created or modified since a particular date, usually the date of the last daily backup. To support this process the operating system must be able to track file creation and modification dates.

Backup procedures are an important part of system management. The power of the backup system provided with an OS greatly affects these procedures. Design considerations for the backup system include:

- ability to back up entire media
- time required for backup
- validation of backup
- alternatives for backup (disk, streamer tape, magnetic tape)
- automatic *required* backup facilities on system shutdown
- easy specification of criteria for selecting files to be backed up
- easy determination of files and directories on specific backup media, as well as the dates of the files and the date of the backup
- automatic backup log facilities with the ability to rapidly identify where a particular file/directory is backed up, in the order of most recent to oldest backups
- selective file/directory restoration

Users of microcomputers know that failure to back up files on a regular basis can be a disaster. Users of multiuser systems assume backups are being taken and expect them to be there when required. The backup policies and procedures, along with the backup facilities, determine whether or not this expectation is indeed met in a given computer installation.

17.8 SUMMARY

System management involves the procedures and policies of management as well as the software and hardware facilities of a computer system. Operating systems must provide the support software for system generation, system loading, system shutdown, tuning, accounting, and backup, if the installation is to be successful. Operating system designers must understand system management requirements in order to design and implement operating system support facilities such as those discussed in this chapter.

FOR FURTHER READING

Information about system management is most often found in system manuals for specific operating systems. These manuals describe system generation and installation of the operating system for production use. MVS/XA system generation is presented in IBM [1984]; Xenix installation is presented in SCO [1987]; RT-11 system generation is discussed in Digital [1985].

IMPORTANT TERMS

accounting
channel contention
checkpoint records
checkpointing
cold start
controller contention
CPU throughput
CPU utilization
device contention
device throughput

resource quota
response time
self-configuration
system generation
system management
tuning
turnaround time
wait time
warm start
workload

REVIEW QUESTIONS

1. What is the purpose of the CONFIG.SYS file of MS-DOS?

2. List and describe some important features of interactive system generation programs.

3. Why do startup diagnostics exist? How do they differ from "power-on" diagnostics of microcomputers?

4. What is the purpose of the UNIX *config* program?

5. How can a virtual disk improve system performance?

6. What is the difference between generating an operating system and installing an operating system?

7. Users of single-user operating systems often sustain sudden power failures with little loss of data. Why are multi-user systems more susceptible to data loss upon such a failure? What are the means of protecting against such power failures in a multi-user environment?

8. Discuss the aspects of an operating system that are typically subject to tuning operations by a systems programmer.

9. How can an operating system support dynamic installation of a device driver after the OS has been loaded?

10. How are users controlled in a multi-user environment? Why should they be controlled?

ASSIGNMENTS

1. Compare various approaches to system generation. Which one gives the most flexibility? Which is the easiest to implement?

2. Discuss the configuration capabilities in MS-DOS. What capabilities do you feel are missing?

3. What could be the result of an inadequate backup capability in an operating system? What is the *minimum* capability required in *any* operating system?

4. Discuss the accounting features of a multi-user operating system with which you are familiar. What are the weaknesses? Does the accounting system support billing of users? Is it adequate? Why or why not?

Performance Analysis

Performance Analysis

18.1 INTRODUCTION

In many previous chapters we examined design strategies and algorithms in a somewhat idealized way. We have addressed one problem at a time, paying limited attention to the interaction between components. We have sometimes not considered complications that may arise in a complete system. In this chapter we address the **performance** of an operating system.

Informally, performance can be described as the effectiveness with which a system carries out the tasks for which it was designed [Svoboda 1976]. Although an OS may include all necessary features and carry out its tasks correctly, it may be unusable if it has unsatisfactory performance. Thus, it is essential to be able to predict the performance that you can expect from a proposed system design, to measure the performance of actual systems, and to make adjustments to improve performance as well as possible.

The process of studying and improving system performance is called **performance analysis** or **performance evaluation**. This process is of continuing importance to those who design and work with operating systems. Performance analysis is necessary to guide the design of new systems and to aid in the selection of systems for new or modified installations. System managers and maintainers may continually engage in performance analysis to identify problems and to adjust systems for the best performance as changes occur in configuration or requirements. Moreover, the OS may be called upon to support performance analysis for the applications that run with it.

A thorough examination of performance analysis with all its related issues would require a textbook in itself. Here we will survey the issues of most importance to OS designers, and provide references for those desiring additional information.

The process of performance analysis involves two principal phases:

1. Evaluate the performance of one or more existing or proposed systems or system components, under suitable conditions.

2. Use this information to select systems or components, or to improve the performance of those selected.

Although simple in concept, this process raises some fairly difficult questions. How do we characterize "good" performance, so that systems may be compared? How can the performance of a system be measured and evaluated? And finally, how can we use performance information effectively to improve the performance of a given system? We will be concerned with answering such questions in the remainder of this chapter.

18.2 MEASURES OF SYSTEM PERFORMANCE

"Good performance" is obviously desirable, but the exact meaning of this phrase may be difficult to define. Performance is often equated to speed. A user will consider one system to have "higher performance" than another if it completes similar jobs quickly. Economical use of storage and other system resources may also be important, however, especially if resource use is translated into proportional costs for the user. In addition, inefficient resource use may limit the maximum size of problems that can be handled, and will reduce the rate at which multiple jobs can be serviced in a multiprogramming system.

The work that a computer system carries out is different, and is constantly changing, in each installation. The performance of a system can be evaluated only *with respect to a particular body of work*. As you'll recall from Chapter 18, the full set of work a system is doing while its performance is examined is called the **workload**. It may be difficult to provide a sample workload for evaluation that is truly representative of the work the system will be called upon to do.

Although good performance is difficult to capture in a single number, you can implement a variety of useful measures to characterize the performance of a system for a given workload, provided that their values can be determined. A few such measures were discussed in Section 6.4 for the evaluation of scheduling methods. Similar measures are used for all aspects of system operation. Most measures concern the *time* required for certain activities, or the *level of usage* of system resources. Measures of time may include:

- throughput, or number of jobs completed in a given time
- turnaround, or time required for completion of a single job

- response time experienced by interactive users or real-time events
- time spent by particular processes in various waiting states
- time during which particular resources are idle
- time and frequency of significant activities, such as page swapping

Other important measures quantify the use of resources other than time. Measures of resource usage may include:

- space used in main and secondary memory by processes for program and data storage
- space used by control blocks and other system data structures
- fragmentation or degree of unusable space in main or secondary memory
- size of queues on which processes wait for resources or events
- level of use of logical resources, such as system buffers
- level of use of physical devices, such as communication ports or tape drives

A variety of other measures are possible. Each of these values must be measured over a sufficient period of time. We may be interested in average values, extreme values, kth percentile values, or statistical distributions.

18.3 METHODS FOR PERFORMANCE EVALUATION

To evaluate the performance of a computer system, we must begin by selecting appropriate quantities to measure, as discussed above, and determining their values for the system under study. The techniques available to measure these values depend on the situation, the expense and effort we are willing to invest, and the type of results we want to obtain. In particular, the options we can use depend on whether the system itself, with a suitable workload, is actually available for observation. In many situations the system is not available; it may be a design that has not yet been built, or a candidate system that has not yet been acquired. The specific configuration or workload to be evaluated may not be available. Even if the system is on hand, it may not be possible to study it effectively due to continuing use by regular applications.

A variety of possible approaches to performance evaluation are discussed by Allen [1980]. We will briefly describe three techniques: analytic modeling, simulation, and direct measurement. These techniques are illustrated and contrasted in Figure 18–1.

Figure 18–1 Three Approaches to Performance Evaluation

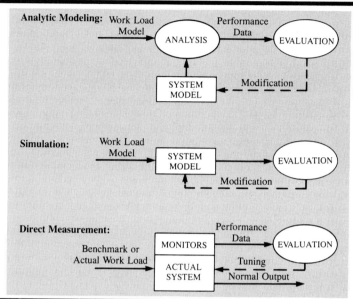

Analytic modeling and simulation are techniques for evaluating system performance when the system itself is not available. Each method relies on studying a suitable model of a system as a substitute for the real system. The system model is driven by a workload model, which is designed to represent the important statistical properties of the actual workload in a simplified form. Performance values observed or computed from these models are used to predict the behavior of real systems.

Analytic modeling is a mathematical analysis procedure that may be used to compute performance measures from a set of equations designed to model the system under study. Effective analytic models of computer systems are often structured as **queueing networks**, which treat resources as elements that provide services, and view processes or other active elements as waiting on queues to receive service. Units of work moving through such a network are assumed to have simple, well-defined statistical distributions. The well-developed mathematical field of **queueing theory** helps predict the behavior of such networks under various conditions. This technique is inexpensive and can provide useful results if the models are carefully designed. Many simplifications must be made, however, and the performance values obtained are likely to be less accurate than with other techniques.

Analytic modeling of computer systems using queueing theory has received a great deal of attention, and has been used effectively to evaluate scheduling algorithms, configuration changes, and other aspects of these systems. A detailed presentation of this technique is beyond the scope of this text; the interested student should refer to some of the books and articles discussed in "For Further Reading" at the end of this chapter.

Simulation, a computer-based technique for performance analysis, is based on construction of programs and databases that model the actual system under study. Simulation is more expensive than analytic modeling but is potentially capable of providing more detailed and accurate measurements. The simulated system is "run" by the program with simulated workloads. Enough detail must be included in the model to effectively represent the system parameters to be measured. Gathering information from a simulation study is usually a straightforward process. In contrast to analytic models, it may be possible to add more detail to selected portions of a simulation model if initial results are not satisfactory.

Simulation is also beyond the scope of our text, and the student is again referred to the references at the end of the chapter. However, we note that an especially good basis for simulation may be found in virtual machine monitors, described in Chapter 21.

When the system to be evaluated is available, there is another technique available for obtaining performance information: **direct measurement** of the system while it runs with the desired workload. Unfortunately, direct measurement may lead to problems, including reduced performance, and distortion of the very characteristics being measured. Thus there are still times when analytic modeling or simulation may be the more desirable choice. However, direct measurement is widely used for performance analysis, and the issues it raises are important to the OS designer. We will consider these issues in the next section. The characteristics of analytic modeling, simulation, and direct measurement are summarized and compared in Figure 18–2.

Figure 18–2 Characteristics of Performance Evaluation Techniques

	ANALYTIC MODELING	SIMULATION	DIRECT MEASUREMENT
cost	low	moderate	high
accuracy	low	moderate	high
work load	simulated	simulated	simulated or real
real system needed?	no	no	yes

18.4 PERFORMANCE MEASURING AND MONITORING

The most effective way to determine the performance of any system, in principle, is to observe the actual system in operation and measure the values of the system parameters that may be of interest. This strategy is called **performance measurement** (or **direct measurement**). Such measurement requires adding mechanisms called **instruments** or **monitors** to the system to observe and record the desired information. (The term *monitors* is more widely used; however, it must not be confused with other uses of the same term unrelated to performance analysis.) Performance monitors may be hardware or software mechanisms, or a combination. In order to obtain useful results, moreover, the measurement must be performed with an appropriate workload. Several problems must therefore be resolved if direct measurement is to be effective.

1. A suitable workload must be defined and made available at the time of the measurement.

2. The measurement instruments may themselves affect and change the system performance.

3. The instruments may add to the system cost in various ways.

A suitable workload must be one that is representative of the typical use anticipated for the system. In some cases, performance with a number of distinct workloads may be of interest. If the expected usage can be characterized adequately, an artificial set of jobs considered representative of the work to be done may be constructed. Such a workload is called a **benchmark**. It may be necessary to observe the actual work submitted to the system or a similar system over a period of time to determine what should go into a suitable benchmark. Some well-known benchmarks have been constructed to assess system performance in some individual application areas such as numerical processing. However, few benchmarks exist for measuring the overall performance of a multiple process operating system.

Benchmarking requires that the system be dedicated to performance analysis for a period of time. No other significant workload can be present at the same time, since this would affect the behavior to be measured in unpredictable ways. This is an acceptable restriction for testing new systems under development or evaluation. Such systems have not yet been put into production use, and no real workload may be available. However, benchmarking may be more difficult to arrange when a system is already in continuous use.

Serious difficulties may arise in constructing artificial workloads for a multiple process system, especially one to be used for interactive or real-time applications. Precise timing relations between events may have a significant effect on performance, and these timings may be impossible to reproduce accurately. Moreover, "submitting" a workload to such a system may require input at many terminals in a coordinated sequence, or special I/O devices that can generate input signals in a controlled way.

An alternative to benchmarking that may be possible on systems in operation is to measure their behavior as they perform normal work. To be sure that the results are representative, however, you may need to collect a large number of measurements over a long period of time. This approach is called **performance monitoring**. When monitoring is used, the measurement instruments must remain in the system continuously. It is important to be sure that the presence of these monitors does not degrade performance.

When performance monitoring is used, system parameters are sampled and recorded periodically. This sampling may occur either at regular, timed intervals or in response to certain events. The recorded information can be periodically processed to determine critical values, averages, or distributions.

18.5 PERFORMANCE MONITORS

The monitors used for measuring performance may be hardware mechanisms or software procedures. Each type of monitor has different capabilities and limitations. **Software monitors** are inexpensive and may take advantage of high-level knowledge about system activities. However, they necessarily consume CPU time, storage space, and possibly other resources. This can add overhead to the system, which is never desirable; what's worse, it can change the very performance values that we are trying to measure. **Hardware monitors** can be designed to have little impact on system performance, and can measure values that are inaccessible to software. However, they are expensive, more difficult to develop, and usually have only limited and specialized capabilities. Because of these differences, a combination of both types of monitors may be necessary to obtain satisfactory results.

Software Monitors

A software monitor is a sequence of instructions added to a program to collect information about the program's behavior. Examples of the type of information to be collected might include the size of a scheduling queue, frequency of certain types of disk transfers, and percentage of CPU time spent in context switching. The collected data are stored in a memory buffer or file until they can be analyzed or summarized at a convenient time.

Software monitors may be designed to measure parameters of the operating system, or characteristics of individual application programs. They may be added to the OS or program only for a short time during evaluation, or they may remain in place continuously for performance monitoring. Often monitors are installed only when a problem is suspected. However, at least one author [Svoboda 1981] recommends that they be included as an integral part of the original OS design.

Software monitors may be classified as **event-driven** or **periodic**. An event-driven monitor records information about every occurrence of a certain type of event. Typical operating system events that may be monitored in this way include interrupts, context switches, or invoking of selected system services. The monitor code is inserted among the instructions that are normally executed in response to each event. With the use of a system clock, the value of which can be read efficiently when desired, such monitors can determine the frequency of events or the average time spent in servicing each event. Various other system parameters may also be measured when each event occurs.

As an example, an event-driven software monitor to measure the average length of a queue is illustrated in Figure 18–3. This example is based on one presented by Ferrari [1983, p. 1364]. The monitor consists of a few machine instructions included in any procedures that may change the length of the queue to be monitored. The INSERT and REMOVE procedures for this queue are shown as examples. To minimize the execution time for the monitor, it is repeated in each procedure rather than organized as a procedure itself.

The length of the queue is maintained in the variable QLEN. The variable CLOCK is assumed to refer to a memory location or register that is updated directly by the system clock hardware. Each execution of the monitor determines the current queue length and the time since the monitor was last executed, and records the product of these values in a private variable called QLEN_PROD. Each new value for this product is added to the previous values of the variable. A second variable, LAST_EXEC, keeps track of the time the monitor was last executed, so that the time between executions can be determined. The mean queue length over a long period of time can be determined by dividing QLEN_PROD by the total elapsed time.

A periodic monitor is one that is invoked by a special type of regular event, such as an interrupt caused whenever the clock itself reaches certain values. This type of monitor samples system characteristics that may change frequently. The pattern observed in the sampled values is used as an approximation to the total behavior of the variable. A periodic monitor for the measurement of the mean length of a queue may not need to be executed as frequently as the event-driven monitor, but will provide less accurate results.

An effective software monitor must be limited to a few instructions that

Figure 18-3 A Software Monitor to Measure Average Queue Length

```
INSERT:
          add item to queue

          /* software monitor */
          QLEN_PROD:=QLEN_PROD + QLEN * (CLOCK - LAST_EXEC)
          LAST_EXEC:=CLOCK
          QLEN:=QLEN + 1

          RETURN

REMOVE:
          remove item from queue

          /* software monitor */
          QLEN_PROD:=QLEN_PROD + QLEN * (CLOCK - LAST_EXEC)
          LAST_EXEC:=CLOCK
          QLEN:=QLEN - 1

          RETURN
```

use negligible execution time compared to the rest of the program. Any other resources used by the monitor must also be severely limited. Our example assumes that reading the system clock is a simple register transfer, memory reference, or I/O instruction. It would be unacceptable if this step required the calling of a complex procedure.

Hardware Monitors

A hardware monitor is a physical device that may be attached to a computer system to detect the occurrence of certain measurable events and record information about those events. This type of monitor, illustrated in Figure 18-4, consists of a set of probes attached to selected measuring points within the CPU, and logic circuits that may analyze the signals detected by the probes. In some cases counters keep track of the number of occurrences of selected events. Significant data values are written to a magnetic tape or other output device as required.

Events that may be monitored by such a device include selected interrupts or data transfers and accessing of specified memory locations. Hardware monitors can access only low-level events that correspond directly to physical logic circuits. However, they can monitor some events, such as the storing of data in selected locations, that cannot easily be monitored by software.

Hardware monitors are physical devices and thus are considerably more

Figure 18-4 A Hardware Monitor

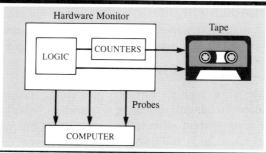

costly than software monitors. If properly designed, however, they can perform continuous monitoring without impairing performance, and without changing the characteristics of the system being measured.

18.6 PERFORMANCE TUNING

Performance analysis may have many objectives. It may be intended to aid in the design or selection of new systems, or to identify possible problems in existing systems. Even if a system initially had satisfactory performance, problems may emerge over time due to increased usage, changing workloads, and many other factors. When problems are identified, they may be addressed in several different ways. One response is to change the configuration of the system, such as by adding more memory or communication lines or substituting a more powerful CPU. Some problems may be addressed by changes in management strategy, such as limiting the times at which certain categories of jobs can be run. A final method for relieving problems identified through performance analysis is **performance tuning**. This strategy consists of adjusting a variety of changeable system parameters with the objective of improving overall performance.

This section considers the tuning process and the ways in which an operating system can be designed to be tuneable. Such an OS supports the philosophy of separating policy and mechanism in terms of performance; its flexible mechanisms may be adjusted to support a variety of possible policies selected by system managers in order to maintain satisfactory performance.

The process of tuning an OS consists of selecting values for various numerical or binary parameters associated with the algorithms performed by each component of the OS. Another aspect of tuning may involve selection of data or program units that may be given special treatment. If a widely used editor, for example, is kept permanently in main memory and all users are able to share the same copy, significant performance improvements may result. Tuning does not involve changes in the physical configuration, or redesign of algorithms. Some tuning parameters may be changed at any time by commands issued by a privileged user. Others may be changed only during system generation or initialization.

One example of a highly tuneable operating system is VAX/VMS. VMS includes about two hundred tuning parameters, which can be modified dynamically or during system initialization. A similar but usually smaller set may be found in most large multiprogramming systems. A small selection of VMS parameters is listed in Figure 18–5. The process of tuning VMS is described fully in a VMS manual called *Guide to VAX/VMS Performance Management* [Digital 1984c].

Figure 18–5   Some Tuning Parameters in VMS

default terminal characteristics

number of active (swapped in) jobs allowed
maximum number of batch jobs
maximum number of interactive jobs

base default priority for processes
default CPU time quantum
amount of idle time permitted before swapping
maximum number of swap files

threshold page fault rates
minimum sampling time for page fault rate
maximum working set size
minimum number of available pages to maintain

number of buffers to allocate for file transfers
time delay before checking for deadlock
default maximum message size for mailboxes
number of login break attempts tolerated

As outlined by the VMS guide, the process of tuning an operating system typically involves the following steps:

1. Using performance analysis techniques, determine that a problem exists.

2. Decide if tuning is an appropriate solution strategy for the problem.

3. Select a small set of tuning parameters to be adjusted.

4. Make trial adjustments and evaluate the resulting system behavior. Repeat as necessary.

5. Decide when to stop tuning.

6. Monitor the tuned system to ensure that its performance remains satisfactory.

None of these steps are straightforward. Even if an OS has many tuneable parameters, tuning may sometimes produce only limited benefits. If performance problems are based on improper operation or policies, inadequate system capacity, or unrealistic expectations, they cannot be solved by tuning. Although tuning may be appropriate in many cases, the choice of parameters to adjust and values to use is an art with few clear rules to guide it. As the VMS manual also points out, tuning can only improve overall, long-term performance, and may not improve performance in each specific situation.

In spite of these limitations, tuning is an important and often successful strategy for improving system performance. Most resource management algorithms may be designed with little difficulty to use tuneable parameters rather than fixed values. Attention to tuneability can be an important advantage for a well-engineered operating system design.

18.7 PERFORMANCE ANALYSIS OF APPLICATIONS

Performance analysis is an important procedure for many application programs as well as for the operating system. A complex program that is to be run frequently or continuously may contain design weaknesses that seriously reduce its performance. Evaluation strategies can help to identify these bottlenecks and correct them, resulting in improved performance.

It is a responsibility of the operating system to support performance evaluation for application programs and to provide mechanisms for tuning programs as necessary. This support can take the form of system calls for program analysis and tuneble parameters in the operating environment of each program. Elaborate analysis tools may also be available for use with some operating systems.

Some mechanisms that an OS may provide to support performance analysis of application programs include:

- reading the current real time or process time to measure the duration of program activities
- providing virtual timers that can be set and read by a program, or made to interrupt at predetermined times
- periodic monitors to interrupt a process at specified intervals and run a data collection procedure
- running a process under the control of another process that can monitor it as it executes

Among the tuning parameters that may be provided for individual processes are the following:

- memory management parameters, such as allocation unit size, working set size, or segments that should be locked into main memory
- scheduling priorities, time quanta, scheduling constraints among cooperating processes
- resource usage limits

Of course, some of these parameters may be tuneable only within limited bounds due to system-wide considerations. In addition, the OS may allow programs to advise it of changes in their behavior, such as a change in locality that may require adjustments to the working set.

18.8 SUMMARY

Performance analysis is the process of studying and improving system performance—that is, the effectiveness with which a system carries out its tasks. Performance analysis can aid in the design and selection of new systems and in the management of existing systems to maintain acceptable performance.

Performance analysis involves two principal steps: Study an actual system or system model using a suitable workload to collect performance data, and use this information to make improvements or decisions. In your analysis it is important to use a workload that adequately represents the real workload of the system. Many system parameters may be measured during performance analysis, including various measures of time and measures of resource usage.

Strategies for performance evaluation include analytic modeling, simulation, and direct measurement. The first two of these are useful when the system itself is not available for study. Analytic modeling represents the system as a mathematical model, such as a queueing network, and obtains results from computations based on the model. This technique has low cost, but careful modeling is necessary to obtain reasonable results.

Simulation involves development of a program to represent the significant aspects of a system's behavior. The program is then executed with a simulated workload, and its behavior is analyzed. Simulation can produce more accurate results than analytic modeling, but its cost is higher and care is still required to ensure an accurate model.

Direct measurement may produce the most accurate results if the actual system is available for study. Even so, care is needed to select a representative workload (or benchmark) for analysis. Direct measurement is performed by installing software or hardware monitors in the system to collect data. Software monitors are inexpensive and can analyze high-level activities, but they may reduce system performance and disturb the parameters being measured. Hardware monitors will have little impact on system behavior, but they are expensive and can measure only events represented by logic signals and electrical values.

An important strategy for improving the performance of an existing system is performance tuning. This process involves adjusting various system parameters for improved performance. Although tuning can sometimes be worthwhile, it may be difficult to select the appropriate adjustments to obtain the best results. However, operating systems designed for high performance should provide support for system tuning, as well as performance analysis and tuning of application programs.

≡ FOR FURTHER READING ≡

Comprehensive treatment of the principal issues in performance analysis is given by a number of texts. Some examples include Hellerman and Conroy [1975], Svoboda [1976], Ferrari [1978], and Borovits and Neumann [1979]. These issues are also well covered in an article by Muntz [1983].

The concepts of analytic modeling are introduced and placed in perspective in an article by Allen [1980]. Analytic modeling of computer systems using queueing theory receives a thorough mathematical treatment in the two-volume classic reference by Kleinrock [1975, 1976]. The mathematical background needed to understand many of these concepts may be obtained from a very readable text by Allen [1978]. These ideas are applied to particular problems of process scheduling by Brinch Hansen [1973]. Many of these treatments focus on single queues. A thorough treatment of queueing network models appears in a special issue of ACM Computing Surveys [CSURV 1978], which includes presentation of a new foundation for queueing analysis that does not depend on statistical assumptions [Denning and Buzen 1978], and specific extended examples of models for MVS [Buzen 1978] and VM/370 [Bard 1978].

Simulation methods are covered by a variety of texts such as Gordon [1978] and Lewis and Smith [1979]. A particularly readable treatment is provided by Payne [1982], and a good introduction is also given by Roth [1983]. See also the references related to simulation in Chapter 21.

Techniques for direct measurement and performance monitoring are surveyed by Plattner and Nievergelt [1981]. This survey focuses primarily on monitoring individual programs. Software monitors and hardware monitors are covered in articles by Ferrari [1983] and Noe [1983], respectively. Svoboda [1981] discusses software monitors and argues for their inclusion as an integral part of operating systems. Some issues in characterizing the workload of a multiprogramming computer system are discussed by Agrawala et al. [1976].

General treatments of system tuning are given in the performance analysis texts. Details of VAX/VMS tuning are contained in *Guide to VAX/VMS Performance Management* [Digital 1984c]. Another specific example, tuning the fair-share scheduler in VM/370, is presented by Agrawal [1984].

=== IMPORTANT TERMS ===

benchmark
direct measurement
event-driven monitor
hardware monitor
instrument
monitor
performance
performance analysis
performance evaluation

performance measurement
performance monitoring
performance tuning
periodic monitor
queueing network
queueing theory
software monitor
workload

REVIEW QUESTIONS

1. Identify four measures of time and four measures of other resource use that may be determined during performance analysis.

2. List and briefly explain the three main techniques presented in this chapter for performance evaluation.

3. Give two advantages and two disadvantages of analytic modeling compared to simulation.

4. Why is it necessary to monitor a system for a longer time if a real workload is used rather than a benchmark?

5. Contrast the strengths and weaknesses of software monitors and hardware monitors.

6. If a software monitor includes an identical sequence of instructions inserted at several points in the system, should this sequence be replaced by a procedure call? Why or why not?

7. Explain the process of tuning an operating system, and give two reasons why this process is difficult.

ASSIGNMENTS

1. For each of the following situations, suggest a strategy for performance evaluation. Justify your choice.

   a. Determining the number of interactive users an existing system can support with acceptable response time.

   b. Deciding which of two new computer systems should be acquired to process an existing workload more effectively.

   c. Deciding whether it would be cost-effective to add an additional printer to handle peak workloads.

   d. Selecting the size of a memory allocation unit that provides the most efficient usage of main memory.

2. For each of the following measurable values, state whether a software monitor or hardware monitor is most appropriate. Justify your answer.

   a. the average length of the ready queue

   b. the frequency of data transfers on a specific I/O channel

   c. the percentage of time spent by the CPU in an idle state

   d. the number of times a specific memory location is written

3. An OS may provide periodic software monitoring for use by application programs. Why is it more difficult to provide event-driven monitoring?

Implementation
and
Maintenance

Introduction • System Testing • Problem Isolation • Maintenance • Documentation

Implementation and Maintenance

19.1 INTRODUCTION

Whether testing a new operating system or solving problems in an existing operating system, the system programmer is often faced with a difficult task: to determine where a problem lies within the operating system. Unlike the user environment that usually consists of a single program with no subprocesses, the system programmer's environment often deals with all active and suspended system and user processes, the operating system itself, multiple virtual memory spaces, and/or virtual machines. Determining the exact state of the hardware and software upon the occurrence of a system failure is extremely difficult, particularly when testing a new operating system. As long as the debugging tools are able to run, the system programmer will be able to view and/or save the state of the system when the failure occurred. Those of us who have experienced system lockup, particularly on microcomputers, know how difficult it can be to isolate problems if one cannot access the state of the system.

19.2 SYSTEM TESTING

System testing of a new operating system or new releases of existing operating systems should be done in a very organized manner, as should testing of any software. The first step, of course, is ensuring that the operating system loads correctly. For a new operating system, this means that the operating system load and initialization programs must be tested. The following questions must be answered in this early stage of testing:

- Did the loader on disk load correctly?

- Did the loader find the operating system and the operating system initialization program?

- Did the operating system and operating system initialization program load correctly?

- Was the operating system relocated correctly in memory? Were the interrupt vectors set correctly?

- Were system initialization control blocks properly initialized, devices initialized, clocks started, and so on?

- Did the operating system receive control after the initialization program completed its task?

For new releases, the load and initialization is often tested by trying it. If no changes were made to the operating system that affected loading and initialization, then these steps should indeed work correctly. For new operating systems, and for new releases of operating systems that do affect loading and initialization, merely trying it is likely to fail; the operating system will not receive control, or when it does, it will not work.

There is, of course, a danger of just trying the load and initialization process without asking the above questions and verifying positive answers. It may be that the operating system *almost* loaded correctly, was *almost* initialized completely, or may *almost* work. The difficulty is that the problems during execution of the operating system may be assumed to be logic or design problems in the operating system itself, when in fact they were caused by faulty loading or initialization. Hence, the system programmer must keep this in mind in the early stages of testing and not hesitate to question the validity of both the load and initialization phases.

How one verifies that the answer to each of the above questions is *yes* varies from system to system. Debugging aids described below will certainly help, particularly those that relate to operating system loading, relocation, and initialization, because many of these facilities will allow easy analysis of the operating system image once in memory. The questions about the loader and initialization programs may have to be answered using interactive analysis programs called **debuggers.** Since the load process of the loader and the initialization program is more or less straightforward, a simple debugger should suffice.

Many times the load process fails because the loader on disk is configured for the wrong device type. When it receives control, it cannot read the disk from which it was loaded. This simple procedural problem in the system generation process has been known to cause hours of frustration for even experienced system programmers who forgot to consider this possibility. How many times do we (both applications and system programmers) forget to consider simple answers, only to be embarrassed and frustrated later when we realize the solution should have been obvious from the beginning!

Testing Facilities

Those of us who have been in the operating system development and testing area for years recall the early days of binary light displays. We flipped binary switches to examine locations, to correct values in memory, and to reset execution addresses in order to attempt to resolve an operating system problem. The advent of programs that could select devices for loading, display memory values in hexadecimal or octal, and provide display of register contents and machine states using a system hardcopy or CRT console recall how great these improvements were. Systems like the PDP-11 provide for this hardware debugging facility to be activated no matter what the state of the system. This advancement avoids the problem of a system hangup or lockup, in which the state of the system cannot be determined. Of course, the lights and switches of the early machines allowed us to determine system states, but the hardware-based debugging console is far superior. On microcomputers with no such hardware-based debugging facility, systems that lock up are destined to be reloaded along with debugging aids that might help determine the problem. Of course, it might be hours before the problem occurs again. To further complicate matters, it is possible that something will change in the state of the machine when a software debugger facility is loaded so that the problem does not occur.

Debuggers. Debuggers fall into a variety of classes. The simplest are machine language-oriented and usually have the following capabilities:

- dynamic loading of programs and data
- display of memory areas in octal or character form (ASCII or EBCDIC, depending on the character code of the system)
- display of memory contents in the form of machine instruction mnemonics
- the ability to trace program execution step by step
- the ability to execute instructions with or without tracing
- the ability to set breakpoints (i.e., locations that return control to the debugger when the program counter reaches them during execution)
- the ability to display registers and machine states
- the ability to change memory locations, registers, and machine states
- the ability to reset the program counter to begin or continue execution at a specific address
- the ability to save a program or data in memory to disk (useful for modifying a program and saving it for later use during debugging)

Such simple debuggers are of value in single user operating systems written in machine language, providing they can access all areas of memory and all machine registers, (in other words, change and display areas referenced or occupied by the operating system).

Another type of machine language-oriented debugger is a **symbolic debugger,** which is able to use symbol table information stored by a compiler and/or linker to display information about locations identified by symbols (names). The features described above would all be present, but references to memory could be symbolic as well as numeric. Again, for operating systems written in assembler language, this type of debugger would be very helpful, but the ability to use symbols related to the operating system would also help debug operating systems written in higher-level languages.

High-level language debuggers are language-specific and allow the types of display and changing capability described above, but are oriented to high-level structures, such as data structures or arrays. For operating systems implemented in specific high-level languages, such debuggers are extremely valuable.

Formatted Displays. An important type of debugging aid for system programmers is one that permits dynamic display of various system queues, and information about the state of the operating system and the computer itself in an easy-to-read display on a terminal. This capability could be provided as a utility or as part of the operating system commands. The problem with the former is that when a problem arises, the state of the operating system or hardware may be such that the required display utility may not be able to be loaded. The solution to this problem is to load the utility when the OS is loaded, so that it is always resident when needed. (This takes up a small amount of memory, but this should not be detrimental on most of today's computer systems).

Here is some information that is important to the system programmer during problem resolution and that should be displayable in an easy-to-read manner:

- hardware registers
- hardware stack contents
- process queue, with synopsis of each process's state *(Ready, Blocked* processes)
- PCB of a specific process, with easy display of a process's registers
- I/O queues
- device queue entry
- memory allocation queue, with specific memory control blocks
- paging queue

- queue of users logged on
- job queue (batch systems)

A facility that not only displays the above information on demand but also can automatically update the display on a particular interval could be very useful when you are trying to determine the cause of a particular problem. It can also be very useful for the displays to be automatically logged to disk for later analysis. Without the formatted display, a system programmer is forced to look at hexadecimal or octal representations of control blocks and mentally translate representations of system state. The displays of various states should be given in mnemonic form whenever possible so that the dynamic analysis of the state of the operating system is simplified. Figure 19–1 illustrates the types of dynamic terminal displays that are helpful in problem determination.

Figure 19–1 A Formatted Display Used in Problem Determination

```
            PC=046040          PSW= 000346         SP=020460


    R0=100476   R1=000005   R2=034060   R3=002010  R4=176170   R5=000120


                    Running Process=003504 (COMHAN)



    ReadyQ                 IO_INITQ              IO_ActiveQ
    =================      =================     ============================
    004406 (TEST1)         004506 (PRINT2)       DISK1      003602 (UTILITY)
    006404 (COMPILE)       006606 (TEST2)        DISK2      *idle*
    003406 (IDLE)          005004 (REPORT)       PRINTER1   004004 (RUN1)
                                                 COMM1      *idle*
                                                 TERMINAL1 *idle*
                                                 TERMINAL2 004204 (ENTRY)
                                                 CLOCK      004306 (TIME)



    OPTIONS:       1   Display Running Process PCB
                   2   Display PCB at location xxxxxx
                   3   Display device status
                   4   Display Memory Allocation Map
                   5   Display Terminal Status
                   6   Display TimerQ
                   7   Display Memory
                   8   Dump System Image
                   9   Debugger


    ENTER OPTION: __
```

System Dumps. In many cases, you will have no time to dynamically analyze a problem because it is so important to reload the operating system and minimize downtime for users. In these cases, a system dump facility is mandatory. This facility is a procedure that will write a system image, often called a **core dump** or **OS system image dump,** to tape or disk. Often an independent program that writes this memory image is resident at a fixed memory address. Should the operating system fail completely, you could start this program to obtain the dump.

In systems with virtual storage and virtual machines, a complete picture of the system requires not only the pages that are physically resident in memory but also those pages and programs that are paged out and swapped out, respectively. A system that dumps all these areas will write many megabytes of information to the dump file or media. It is best if such large dumps can be written quickly so that system restart can begin with little delay. Consideration should be given to labeling the images with the current time and date, although such information is usually in the memory image within the operating system.

In the days of one-megabyte mainframe memories, debugging operating systems was relatively simple. Today's virtual storage of sixteen to thirty-two megabytes per user or virtual machine, plus the operating system storage size, makes debugging and problem isolation quite complex. Facilities for analyzing memory dumps, such as formatters similar to the dynamic displays mentioned previously, are essential. Also, the ability to interactively scan a memory image that is stored on disk will greatly decrease the time it takes to solve system problems.

One facility used by one of the authors in the mid-1970s allowed him to reload a memory dump and restore the processor to the state it was in when the failure occurred. Thus, the system programmer could return to the problem at a more opportune time, and solve it when the system was "theoretically" in the same state it was in when the system failure occurred. This is probably impossible on large mainframe computers today, although the ability to load the system into a virtual machine and analyze the problem might prove to be a useful technique for problem solving.

System and Console Logs. The system console (a main terminal that types output on paper rather than displaying it on a video screen), and machine-readable system logs, can often be sources of valuable information in problem determination. Events leading up to the failure can be studied to determine if anything strange occurred just before it. Also, for repeated system failures, a search for a pattern indicating the cause of the failure is required. Random problems and failures are extremely difficult to diagnose. If the system programmer can succeed in recreating the problem, then it is likely the problem can be isolated and solved. The system and console logs can give many helpful hints to determine the exact cause of a system failure.

19.3 PROBLEM ISOLATION

As we have noted, isolating a problem can be quite difficult, particularly for random failures. The system programmer must search for a way to consistently reproduce the problem so that it can be studied and a solution found—and proved. An example from a simple multi-user microcomputer environment can help demonstrate the requirements for problem isolation.

A Case Study in a Microcomputer Environment

A problem on a multi-user microcomputer system was described by the user as "terminals in the system periodically lock up." The problem was being experienced by twenty out of approximately seventy installations. It was also stated that the problem only occurs when two or more terminals are running a particular data entry program. However, there appeared to be no other pattern in the problem, except that a particular application program always was running when terminals locked up. The first question asked by the system programmer was "What was the state of the system?" Because the microcomputer locked up in the particular situation, there was no way to determine the state of the system on previous system failures.

The approach to problem solution seemed obvious: Since the system supported four virtual consoles, load a system status utility via one virtual console and the dynamic debugging tool via another with the hope that they might remain enabled, even though terminals running application programs locked up. This was done, and the users attempted to get the system to fail. After three hours of application program utilization and data entry, the system did not fail. The user was delighted and wanted the system programmer to stay all day so the work could get done.

The next step was to make an exact copy of the users' disks in an attempt to create the failure on a test system. After many attempts, the system finally failed. As was hoped, the system status routines and dynamic debugging tool remained active. Initial analysis indicated the suspect program was "stuck" in a disk read queue. In fact, the applications terminals locked up because each application program eventually requested a disk read, after which each was placed in the disk read request queue behind one entry that was "stuck" in the disk device busy queue.

"A lost interrupt from the disk," was the first exclamation from the system programmer. But why *this* program? A study of the application revealed no obvious error. In addition, it failed only occasionally. During the next two hours, attempts to make the system fail again were in vain; the system staff was getting tired of keying. What next? How do we get the computer to fail when we want it to fail? It was thought that keying data had something to do with the problem, so why not let other *computers* do the keying? Three microcomputers running Microsoft DOS were set up running a terminal emulator. A file was built to key in a sequence of data that would make the program repeatedly read the disk and display data via the suspect application program.

The *first* use of the microcomputers as terminals caused them to lock up as they had in the user environment. The conclusion reached was that "rapid keying causes the problem." The state of the system again showed one execution of the suspect program "stuck" in a disk read queue. Reloading the system and trying the procedure again resulted in a second failure. "We can now make it fail consistently," we thought. But subsequent attempts did not cause a failure for more than an hour.

What was really going on here? A lost disk interrupt? Keying into a multiport device causes the disk to hang up? Why? How? Nothing but questions, not atypical of solving an operating system problem. In all cases where the terminals locked up, it was possible to print the status of the operating system using the system console. The status information included:

- user processes' load address and state
- device queues
- system processes' states
- console states

Furthermore, a random checking of the memory of the microcomputer allowed certain other raw information about the system state to be determined. What could be learned from these printouts? There seemed to be no pattern.

It was time to look for correlations and patterns in the printed status reports and memory dumps. After studying the results of various failures side by side, one thing "jumped off of the page" to the system programmer. Every failure had one copy of the suspect program loaded at a specific address (7000:0000, the 512K boundary within the system). Could this be the problem? With a little manipulation of loads and terminations of various programs, the suspect program was forced to load consistently at this address. Upon entry of the *first* record on the terminal running to this program, the terminal (computer) locked up. Repeated tests resulted in a consistent failure! No wonder the problem was random. In fact, it was quickly proved that only one terminal had to be running this program to cause the failure, as long as it loaded at the problem address. The users' observation that the failure only occurred when two or more terminals were running was correct; for the faulty program could not load at this memory location unless two terminals were active. Yet, the problem was isolated by running only one terminal once the pattern was established indicating a load address problem. With many terminals running, there was a certain probability, although somewhat small, that the load address of one of the copies of this program would be the address causing the difficulty. Once the system could be consistently made to fail, a solution to the problem was possible.

This particular multi-user operating system originally was designed for a 512K environment. Perhaps there was a bug in the operating system that caused certain programs to incorrectly load at this location, contaminating the disk read queue. By merely enlarging the program fifty bytes, the problem and the system failure disappeared. The users were satisfied—the problem no longer plagued the installations running the data entry application. In this case, the system programmer was able to isolate the problem and determine a **work-around,** a means of changing the application program to avoid an operating system problem. Although correcting the OS problem would seem to be the most logical approach, all too often an operating system "fix" is not possible because there is no documentation or system source listings to refer to in order to make such a correction.

This example demonstrates how tricky problem isolation can be. It is very easy to make the wrong diagnosis. In isolating system problems, the system programmer must explain *all* strange behavior, not just guess at a solution to the problem. In the above example, the dynamic displays were of great value, but *only a comparison of the results of many failures resulted in the isolation of the problem.* In this case, it was very important that the displays were able to be printed on the line printer for later use in such comparisons. Instead of going to the operating system vendor and saying, "the system fails," the system programmer was able to identify specifically the condition that caused the failure, and provide a program and situation to demonstrate that indeed it did fail. The vendor can take this information and determine the cause, fix it, and provide an update or subsequent release of the operating system that will correct the problem.

Thus, **problem isolation** is the first order of business in solving any operating system problem. The goal, of course, is to obtain a **reproducible failure** in order to solve the problem and prove the solution. In many instances, the system programmer is merely trying to identify when the failure occurs. The operating system vendor can then inform the system programmer about any known solutions, or can use the information for later problem resolution. In the meantime, the system programmer can proceed with possible work-around solutions so that the problem can be avoided.

In the previous example the following questions were asked and eventually answered:

- What was the state of the system (both process and device) upon the failure?
- What process, if any, caused the failure?
- How many processes must be loaded to cause the problem?
- How can the failure be recreated? What is the pattern causing it?

Using the operating system status displays and examining memory, the people in our example attempted to determine the true picture of the system when it failed. This is not unlike the process in any computer system, large or small, and illustrates specifically how a problem can be isolated.

A Case Study in a Mainframe Environment

Another example of problem determination occurred in the mid-1970s on an IBM 360/75 running OS/MVT. It is a good example because it demonstrates that bugs in operating systems do not always show up immediately.

The operating system and its HASP (Houston Automatic Spooling Program) subsystem had just been regenerated over the weekend. On Monday morning, after forty minutes of running, the message *"HASP Catastrophic Error"* appeared on the system console and the system crashed. A memory dump was taken, the system reloaded, and the operating system was once again in execution. It was not long before the same message appeared. In fact, all day long the system crashed within twenty minutes of loading, always with this same message. Imagine the panic of the system staff under such conditions.

After much examination of the memory dumps, it was discovered that the HASP internal job queue had been overlaid with twenty bytes of data, always the same pattern in the same place. The system staff started blaming the individual who had done the system generation. All he had done was expand some queue areas; he had made no logic changes! One of the authors suggested that one of the programmers write a program to quickly search all of memory (all 1.5 megabytes) for this fixed pattern that was overlaying the job queue area. After this was done, the specific pattern was indeed found in another area of the operating system that had not been changed for more than a year.

How could this operating system routine be causing the problem, if it had not been changed? The author had an idea. Perhaps this problem had been there for more than a year but had just never adversely affected the system. In this case, there had been some old system dumps stored in his office for use by students to learn debugging techniques. One was fetched. At *exactly* the same *physical memory address,* the same pattern of twenty bytes was found. The problem was there a year earlier, but what was getting destroyed then? A closer look demonstrated that an OS routine that directly dumped memory contents to a printer was located at that location in the memory dump prior to the expansion of the job queue, and the installation never used this facility. Hence, an existing problem had not been detected for over a year. Regenerating the operating system with larger queue areas resulted in location of a part of this most important job queue at exactly the fixed location that was being destroyed for over a year. The problem with the program module was the use of a register that was assumed to contain an address that it did *not* contain. A simple one-line fix solved the problem. Yet the hours that went into working on this problem were many.

This example demonstrates that operating system problems can show up after months or years with no explanation. The moral is that *recent changes do not always cause a problem, they merely uncover an existing problem.* Of course, with better designs in operating systems, such operating system modules are better protected from each other.

Other Debugging Techniques

The previous illustration demonstrated the use of the system display capabilities to isolate a problem. What does one do when an error occurs within the operating system itself, particularly when implementing a new operating system? The question "what is the state of the system?" is always pertinent. Using a hardware or software debugger, examination of the system's registers is critical. On a stack machine, the first place to look for a system failure is on the stack itself. Elements above the top of the stack reflect addresses of programs that may have recently been in control, and hence are suspect. Addresses on the stack give a trace of where the operating system might be in execution. Of course, there is always the possibility that the stack pointer has been destroyed; in fact, this might be the problem. The subproblem here would be *where* was it destroyed. Stack contamination and lost stack pointers can be a problem in debugging new operating systems written in assembly language. In such cases, activating a debugger to trace the operating system execution is recommended, if such tracing is possible.

Another common problem in early operating system development is lost or blocked interrupts. This is particularly true when implementing device drivers for new devices, where manuals about programming such devices are not always clear. In such cases, simple halts or breakpoints in the first location of the interrupt handler for the suspect device can provide a means to determine whether such an interrupt is being generated. One of the difficulties in isolating problems in the presence of interrupts is trying to trace dynamically the execution of the operating system in spite of interrupts from many different sources (clocks, devices, or operating system service requests).

19.4 MAINTENANCE

Maintenance of multi-user operating systems is an ongoing activity. How it is done is often dependent upon the vendor. No matter what the environment, the procedures for managing change are extremely important to maintaining a stable operating system environment for users.

Vendor-Supplied Fixes

Multi-user operating systems are updated with vendor-supplied fixes and new releases. Vendors can provide temporary fixes in either source or binary form. Such fixes can be supplied on magnetic media or simply on paper in the form of "release notes." Clearly, magnetic media fixes are superior to any type of printed corrections. Today few vendors supply operating system fixes in paper form.

The order in which temporary fixes are applied to a particular operating system release is critical. Temporary fixes are like "band-aids" that solve the problem; the permanent solution is provided in a subsequent release of the operating system. If fixes are applied to an operating system, all previous fixes are assumed to exist. If they do not, the new fixes may not work because the assumption is incorrect.

Configuration Management

Managing the application of system fixes to an operating system requires careful tracking of the fixes that have been applied earlier. It would be best if **automated maintenance logs** were supported for determining the fixes applied to particular operating system versions stored in the file system.

Management procedures must be established to control who authorizes changes to the operating system version in current use. Once the application of an operating system fix has been authorized, it should be applied, tested, and documented, and the modified operating system installed as the current, or production operating system. The change must also be logged in the appropriate configuration management log. This **configuration management** is as critical to operating system maintenance as it is to any application program maintenance.

Local Changes

Installations that have made local modifications to a vendor's operating system are faced with a far more difficult problem for applying temporary fixes to an OS release. The binary fixes are not applicable if a change to an OS source module caused the binary code to be different than the fix expects. In this case, source fixes must be applied. If the fix is in an area of a program that has been modified locally, it can be very difficult to determine what to do in applying the fix.

Although many local changes were made to large multiprogramming operating systems in the early days of computers, most installations today attempt to minimize such changes. The majority of local support is in the form of the addition or modification of device drivers to support particular hardware configurations not supported by the vendor.

19.5 DOCUMENTATION

OS documentation has improved dramatically since the 1960s. However, there is still room for improvement. Keeping the documentation accurate as new releases of an operating system become available is difficult. Updating documentation is also a part of configuration management by both the vendor and the installation management. The vendors and the installation management must be certain updated documentation is available when there is a move to a new release.

Most operating systems have very inadequate documentation. A good set of OS documentation may include many kinds of documents. The following list identifies some important types:

- **user introductory manual**: a simple overview of the OS for the benefit of new users
- **tutorial manuals**: instructional manuals which teach the use of various aspects of the system
- **command summary card**: a small card which summarizes the most frequently used commands
- **command reference manual**: a comprehensive description of all commands supported by the system
- **utilities manual**: a description of the principal utilities, or system programs, supplied with the OS
- **error message and recovery procedures manual**: an explanation of the types of error messages that might occur, and suggested procedures to recover from errors
- **programmers' guide**: a guide for programmers explaining how to write programs that interact with the OS and use its resources effectively
- **software support (logic) manuals**: explanations of the internal logic of various portions of the OS for the benefit of system programmers who may need to understand and possibly modify it

- **installation manual**: an explanation of the procedure for initially installing the operating system in a new environment

- **system generation manual**: an explanation of the procedure for generating a version of the OS with a specific set of options and parameters

- **release notes**: a description of changes made in the current release, or version, of the OS compared to the previous one

- **guide to documentation**: an overview of the types of OS documentation available

- **master index**: a comprehensive listing of all documentation and resources related to the operating system

For simple operating systems, much of this documentation may be included in on-line documentation facilities, available for display at a terminal on request. Even for larger systems, the on-line facilities can provide much of the documentation. However, complex systems will require carefully written OS software support manuals with many illustrations to help the system programmer maintain the operating system. If many manuals exist, a master cross-index is needed for easy identification of all manuals that provide information on a particular subject.

19.6 SUMMARY

Implementation and testing of operating systems requires much skill. The use of software development tools and modern debugging aids will greatly simplify this task. The system programmer must know what to do with information that is available in order to solve a problem. He or she must make a "diagnosis" of the problem in a manner very similar to that of a physician diagnosing an illness. The more experience the system programmer has, the easier the diagnosis will be.

Configuration management is extremely important for multi-user operating systems. Software engineering principles of configuration management must be rigidly applied in an installation if the operating system is to run reliably.

Documentation must be complete. All too often the technical manuals are not kept up to date; hence, they give erroneous information for the current release of the operating system.

☰ FOR FURTHER READING ☰

Specific OS maintenance techniques are often described in vendor's manuals. Configuration management is addressed in general terms in Martin [1983], Bersoff [1980], and Vallabhaneni [1987]. Documentation is an issue that goes beyond just operating systems. Pressman [1987], Aron [1974], and Gilbert [1983] provide discussions of documentation issues.

☰ IMPORTANT TERMS ☰

automated maintenance log
command reference manual
command summary card
configuration management
core dump
debugger
error message and recovery
   procedures manual
guide to documentation
high-level language debugger
installation manual
master index
OS documentation

OS system image dump
problem isolation
programmers' guide
release notes
reproducible failure
software support (logic) manuals
symbolic debugger
system generation manual
tutorial manuals
user introductory manual
utilities manual
work-around

☰ REVIEW QUESTIONS ☰

1. List and discuss the type of information that is needed for problem resolution within an operating system.

2. What are the important questions to ask in the initial stages of testing a new operating system?

3. What is a debugger and how can it be used in the implementation and maintenance of an operating system?

4. Why are printed listings of different system images after a failure valuable for solving OS problems?

5. Of what value are console logs in system maintenance?

6. What is the impact of local changes to an operating system or to configuration management of an operating system?

7. What types of OS documentation are needed and why?

8. What are two of the most important steps to solving an operating system problem? What tools and resources can be used to accomplish these steps?

ASSIGNMENTS

1. For an operating system that you are using currently, analyze the types of documentation available. What are the strong points of the documentation? What are its weak points?

2. Determine the types of fixes that are available from the vendor that supplied one of the operating systems you are using currently. Are temporary fixes available? How often are new releases available? Discuss whether or not the vendor is providing timely updates and releases of the operating system.

Portability
and
Standards

Portability
and
Standards

20.1 INTRODUCTION

The last decade or two has seen an explosion of computer types, ranging from the smallest microcomputers to highly parallel supercomputers. Many of these computers are intended to run a broad range of general-purpose applications. However, often the structure of these systems has little in common. They may use differing CPU architectures and instruction sets; their I/O port usage and memory allocation may differ markedly (even with identical CPU's); and a variety of operating systems may appear even on the same computer hardware.

This proliferation of computer systems presents a serious dilemma to the developer of general-purpose applications such as word processors, spreadsheets, business systems, or graphics systems. Because a large investment of time and money goes into the development of these programs, their designers would like to make them available on as many computer systems as possible. If a program must be redesigned and rewritten for each type of computer environment, the effort required is vast, perhaps unmanageable.

The problem is increasing, not only because the number of system types is growing, but also because of the high costs of software development. To combat this problem, software designers are seeking ways to reduce or eliminate the effort required to design a program for a wide variety of systems, or adapt an existing program to new systems. The goal of this effort is to greatly improve the **portability** of programs—that is, their ability to be easily transported and adapted to new environments. The problem can be addressed in many ways, and in some cases the operating system can play an important role in supporting—or obstructing—portability.

20.2 PORTABILITY ISSUES

The process of creating a typical, possibly large, application program, as we saw in Chapter 3, involves at least the following steps:

1. Design the program to run in certain types of user environments.

2. Prepare source files for each module of the program in a suitable programming language.

3. Translate the source files to intermediate "object" files using a compiler.

4. Combine the object files and certain system library files using a "link" program.

The result of this sequence is an executable program file that can be loaded into memory and run in a specific computer system. Various data files may also be required to support the program.

In the development stages, of course, the actual process may involve numerous repetitions. At each stage errors may be detected, and earlier stages must be repeated. Figure 20–1 shows the basic development process.

The objective of portability is to minimize the effort required to repeat this sequence for a different computer system by allowing the existing components to be reused, as much as possible, with few (if any) changes. This objective can be met if the various computer systems can be made to "look the same" to the program in certain ways. This apparent similarity is achieved by establishing similar or identical **interfaces** between a program and the services it uses on various computing systems.

In the extreme case of perfect portability, no effort at all would be required to adapt a program to a different system. *Identical* executable files could be loaded and run in different systems. This type of portability is called **binary portability.** Transporting a program with binary portability to a new system is illustrated in Figure 20–2.

Although it is an attractive ideal, binary portability can be achieved in practice only for a very limited range of systems. Binary portability requires at least the following elements of each environment to be identical:

- the CPU architecture
- the OS system calls used by the program
- the program's view of any I/O devices used, including terminals and graphic devices
- the memory organization as viewed by a user process

Figure 20–1   The Application Program Development Process

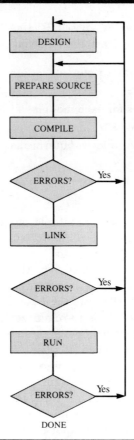

Figure 20–2   Transporting a Program with Binary Portability

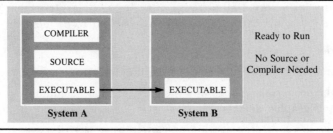

In addition, the file formats required by each system must be similar, so copies of the executable file can be moved among systems in a straightforward way, and accepted by each system's loader.

Reasonable binary portability is achievable today among some significant groups of extremely similar systems. Examples include the IBM PC and its "clones"; some large systems like the IBM S/370 and their imitators; and some of the computers running CP/M or UNIX.

By its nature, binary portability is limited to systems with extremely similar structure. A broader portability goal is to make programs easily adaptable to systems that differ in significant ways. The target systems may have different CPU architectures, or fail to match in some of the other ways listed above. Binary portability is impossible across such dissimilar systems. A reasonable alternative goal is **source portability**, illustrated in Figure 20–3. The goal of this process is to reduce or eliminate the repetition of the design and source file editing stages, as well as the problems of maintaining system-specific versions of each source program file. The need to repeat the compilation and linking phases for each system is accepted, since these phases are usually straightforward and automatic.

Figure 20–3 Transporting a Program with Source Portability

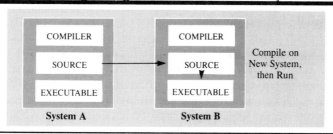

A possible disadvantage of source portability is the need to have the source files available to users who want to transport them to new systems. To protect their proprietary nature, many suppliers of commercial software do not make source files available, or they offer them only at extremely high prices.

Source portability can be achieved if the source files required for each target system are identical or at least differ only in limited and predictable ways. The remainder of this chapter will consider some methods for achieving source portability.

If different computing systems are to accept identical source files, at least the following conditions must be met:

1. Each system must have a compiler that accepts the language used by the program.

2. Each system must support all library procedures invoked by the program, and produce identical effects.

3. Each system must provide appropriate file system interfaces, I/O device interfaces, and system service interfaces to perform the operations expected by the program.

Systems may fail to meet these conditions in many subtle ways. Compilers may handle obscure constructs differently, may accept different character sets, and may use different directive formats to control listings, optimization, and the like. Library procedures may differ slightly in numerical accuracy or in the maximum values that can be handled. File names may vary widely in form. System timing services may differ in resolution. The list of possibilities could be extended greatly.

Because of the wide range of target systems, source portability usually requires compromises. Portability can introduce overhead, and the performance of a portable program may be somewhat lower than that of a program optimized for one specific environment. In addition, a portable program may have to be designed for the lowest common denominator of the characteristics of I/O devices, user interfaces, and other system elements within its target range. For example, a program designed to use the full features of the MacIntosh user interface, or the color graphics of a specific microcomputer or terminal, would be unusable in environments not supporting these features.

In spite of the problems, there are a variety of ways to limit the differences between systems, as observed by application programs, and thus improve their source portability. Each method addresses the establishment of a **standard interface** between a program and a portion of its environment. Some possible techniques will be discussed in the remaining sections of this chapter.

20.3 COMPUTER STANDARDS

To enable elements of different computing systems (or any other type of system) to provide a common interface at which the elements can be interchanged, **standards** have evolved to determine the form each interface should take. A standard is a commonly accepted definition for an interface between certain kinds of elements, which can be used by any designers of these elements to ensure that the elements will match properly. For example, early standards ensured that nuts and bolts could be freely interchanged, making mass production and assembly lines possible. In the same way, computer standards enable various components of a computing system, both hardware and software, to fit together properly, even though they are developed by many different sources.

Some important computer standards are **de facto standards.** In this case an interface designed by a single supplier becomes so widely used that other suppliers decide to follow the same structure. Although there is no formal agreement, most suppliers see a market advantage in following the rules of the dominant producer. On the other hand, the dominant supplier may see no advantage in maintaining the standard, and is free to change it at will. An important example of de facto standards is found in the various hardware and software interfaces of the IBM PC, all of which are carefully copied by many other suppliers.

To define standards that are more stable and meet the needs of a wide group, interested parties may form committees to define **formal standards.** A formal standard is a document that carefully defines aspects of the structure of various objects or interfaces. Formal standards may also be used to define procedures, terminology, or performance criteria. The documents are publicly available. Although no one is obliged to use them, they may be used freely by any interested parties.

To organize the process of developing and maintaining formal standards, a number of **standards organizations** have been formed. These organizations sponsor and encourage the development of standards, try to ensure that reasonable procedures are followed, and distribute and maintain the resulting standards.

The principal standards organizations that maintain computer-related standards in the United States are:

- The **American National Standards Institute (ANSI)**

- The **Institute for Electrical and Electronic Engineers (IEEE)**

Other organizations maintain and distribute standards in specific subject areas like electrical parts or communication systems, and standards for specific audiences such as the Federal Government.

In addition, several groups are concerned with the development of international standards. ANSI represents the United States in the **International Organization for Standardization (ISO)**. This cooperation helps to ensure that national and international standards remain consistent.

Note that these standards organizations do not initiate and develop standards on their own. Instead, they accept proposals from interested persons or organizations, who then may form committees to develop particular standards under the sponsorship of the standards organization.

In recent years there has been a proliferation of computer-related standards. The majority of these have been sponsored by ANSI or IEEE, and many address software interfaces that are significant for program portability. Some of these standards will be discussed in the remaining sections.

20.4 STANDARD PROGRAMMING LANGUAGES

To have any hope of transporting a source program among different computing systems, a first requirement is that each system understand the language in which the program is written. A common language must be chosen for communication, and a language translator (a compiler or interpreter) that understands that language must be available on each target system. A language that fills this role is called a **standard programming language**.

Although there is no single universal programming language, a number of languages have become sufficiently popular that their compilers can be found on a wide variety of systems. Two such early languages are FORTRAN and COBOL. More recently, the languages Pascal and C have achieved widespread use, and the Ada language is likely to be widely used in the near future.

Unfortunately, the existence of a Pascal compiler (for example) on two systems does not guarantee that they will accept the same set of programs, nor produce the same results for all programs. While there may be general agreement on the definition of a language, often supported by a de facto standard in the form of a reference manual, the definition breaks down on many details for which the manual may be silent or ambiguous. In such cases the compiler writer must decide how the question is to be resolved; different compilers may resolve it in different ways.

To reduce these ambiguities, formal standards have been developed for many popular languages. These standards take care to resolve problems and ambiguities that are known to exist in a language definition. Currently there are ANSI standards for FORTRAN [ANSI 1978], COBOL [ANSI 1974], Pascal [ANSI 1983a], Ada [ANSI 1983b], and C [ANSI 1988], as well as other more specialized languages.

These formal standards increase the similarity of compilers and enhance portability, but they do not solve the entire problem. Compilers based on the same standard may still differ for a variety of reasons:

- Many features required by some programs are not covered by some languages. Standard methods for I/O or operating system services are often not part of the language. Pascal provides no standard method of specifying a reference to a procedure in an external module, resulting in variations such as those shown in Figure 20–4.

- Some languages define optional features that are supported by some compilers but not by others.

- Compilers accept directives as well as language statements. Such directives may affect listing formats, code optimization, and so on. There is no standard form for these directives.

Figure 20–4 Referencing an External Procedure in Pascal

```
1. EXTERN P1;            2. EXTERNAL P1;
        .                       .
        .                       .
   PROCEDURE P1();          PROCEDURE P1();

3.      .                4.      .
        .                       .
   <EXTERNAL>               @EXT
   PROCEDURE P1();          PROCEDURE P1();

5. (external procedures not permitted)
```

20.5 STANDARD PROCEDURE LIBRARIES

Since no language contains statements to directly perform all of the possible operations desired, every nontrivial application program makes use of procedures. Many of these procedures are an integral part of the application program, and are supplied by its developer along with the main program itself. For these procedures, portability must be achieved by the same techniques used for the main program. However, additional procedures are often relied on for functions and operations so widely used that they are expected to be available as part of the computer system, rather than supplied with each application. Procedures to meet this need are normally supplied in **procedure libraries.** They are combined with the application program by system programs, such as compilers or linkers. Some procedure categories often supplied in such libraries include character and string processing, file manipulation, and a wide variety of numerical operations.

If a distinct procedure library is supplied by each computing system, these procedures will be an obstacle to portability unless each includes all of the procedures required by an application, and each operates in the same way. The probability of this similarity existing can be enhanced by the definition of **standard procedure libraries.**

Since the definition of a procedure, from an application's point of view, depends on the language used, standard procedure libraries are usually associated with specific languages. Occasionally they are included in a formal standard for the language itself; for example, a number of "standard packages" are defined as part of the Ada language. A number of de facto standard procedure libraries associated with the C language are available on most installations. In the area of numerical methods, a procedure library supported by an independent group forms an important de facto standard for the FORTRAN language. Other languages, such as Pascal, have few standard procedures associated with them, to the detriment of portability.

The behavior of "standard" procedures is rarely perfectly identical across systems. Results in some cases are unavoidably influenced by differences in data formats, word sizes, or accuracy of floating point hardware. (A new IEEE standard offers relief for this last problem.) However, standard procedures can go a long way to improving source portability of many applications, especially for operations that do not depend on the properties of the computer or operating system.

20.6 PORTABLE COMPILERS

As we have observed, the compilers that process applications on each system can be a source of portability problems because of subtle differences in the input they will accept or the results they will produce, even if a standard exists for the language itself. One way to avoid this problem is to use the *same* compiler on every system. Since a compiler is a program like many others, we may be able to achieve reasonable source portability for a specific compiler and transport it to a wide variety of environments. This has been achieved to some degree for many compilers, which can be called **portable compilers**. Examples include the Portable C Compiler used on UNIX systems, and a number of Pascal compilers ranging from those of Pascal's creator, Niklaus Wirth, to Borland's Turbo Pascal, now widely used in microcomputer systems.

It is important to note that, even though a compiler on two different computers may be derived from the same source code, each must be translated to fit the architecture of the computer system on which it will run. Thus, the compilers are not truly identical. Although they may accept virtually the same input, there can still be subtle differences in the results they produce.

20.7 PORTABLE OPERATING SYSTEMS

Although many of the techniques discussed above can do much to attain portability for applications that do not interact in detail with system resources, difficulties remain when programs perform complex file manipulation, timing, process communication, or other activities requiring explicit interaction with the program interface. These interfaces, and the views of system resources they support, vary widely among operating systems.

A possible solution to the problem of differences in program interfaces is to use the same operating system on different computers. In some cases the OS may be transported in the same way as portable compilers, becoming a **portable operating system**. Because of the close association of an operating system with the physical resources of the computer, however, providing the same OS on very different computers may be difficult or impossible. A unique example of an operating system that has been transported with some success across truly different CPU architectures is UNIX. Other OSs such as CP/M, MS-DOS, RT-11, MVT, etc., have been implemented on different computers, but only occasionally on dissimilar architectures.

Even if a portable OS can be achieved, there are many reasons why users would not want to use the same OS in every situation. Some of these reasons may include compatibility with existing applications or files, a preferred user interface, or good performance for particular application categories. Thus portable operating systems are not likely to be a sufficient solution for the program interface problem.

20.8 STANDARD OPERATING SYSTEM INTERFACES

Both operating systems and the application programs they support interact with various hardware and software components of a total system through numerous interfaces. The interfaces present in a typical system are illustrated in Figure 20–5 [Mooney 1986]. This figure illustrates both direct interfaces (heavy arrows) and indirect interfaces (dashed arrows). For example, the operating system communicates directly with the application program through the program interface, but indirectly with an interactive user through the command interface, which is mediated by the terminal.

Standardization of any of these interfaces, as already noted, may lead to increased portability. This section focuses on the interface between the operating system and the application programs. The goal of standardization in this area is to produce a **standard operating system interface** by making the program interface supported by each operating system, or a sufficient subset of it, identical as viewed by the application program. This may provide programs with a consistent view of both logical and physical system resources, even though the structure of the resource itself may differ. It is not necessary to standardize *all* of the system calls in a program interface; only those normally used by application programs.

Two IEEE standards being finalized at this writing address the program interface. These standards are known by the names POSIX and MOSI. POSIX [IEEE 1986] is the product of long effort to produce a highly detailed specification for a "UNIX-like" interface. It defines a full range of system

Figure 20–5 Operating System and Program Interfaces

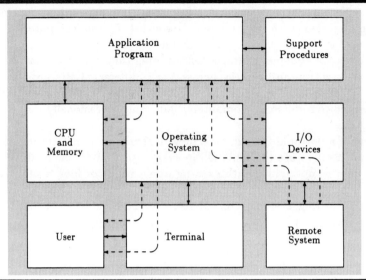

calls and data structures based on various versions of UNIX, and is intended to support both source and binary portability of applications designed to run on UNIX systems. The widespread implementation of UNIX versions for many different computers makes this a very important standard.

The MOSI goal is broader and complementary to POSIX [IEEE 1985]. MOSI defines a limited set of system calls for functions commonly required by applications, which can be supported by a variety of dissimilar operating systems. These definitions are intended to support source portability across many different environments, of which UNIX is one possibility. No existing operating system has a program interface identical to MOSI, but its functions may be implemented for most environments in the form of a procedure library. Many of the program interface examples presented throughout this text have been based on the MOSI model.

A more elaborate standard OS interface, partly based on MOSI, is specified by the CTRON system [Ohkubo et al. 1987]. CTRON is a component of Japan's TRON project, designed to develop both a standard CPU architecture and a family of standard operating systems. However, CTRON is intended to work with a variety of existing computers, supporting applications through a common OS interface. Because it is intended for use in networks of communicating processors, CTRON includes extensive facilities to support communication.

An important de facto operating system interface standard is likely to develop for IBM personal computers. A special subset of the system calls

available from OS/2 is designed to ensure application portability over a range
of IBM computer models.

20.9 OTHER ISSUES

A number of other standard models have been developed for aspects of the
translation and execution support of programs. All of these contribute to
increased portability.

A serious limitation to the reuse of program units, even within the same
system, has been the lack of a standard format for linkable object modules.
Often this format is unique to each linker, and compilers frequently supply
their own linkers rather than making use of a common linker in the computing
system environment. As a result it may be impossible to combine program
units processed by different compilers. A recent IEEE standard attempts to
remedy this problem by defining a common object code format, suitable at
least for small computers.

Binary portability is limited by the lack of a standard CPU architecture.
For good reasons, no single architecture can be suitable for all uses. However,
certain architectures are becoming more widespread and less tied to a single
manufacturer. The development of the microprocessor has led to inclusion
of a few common CPU chips, such as Intel's 8088 and Motorola's 68000,
in many different microcomputers. The TRON project seeks to further
promote a standard microprocessor architecture by encouraging development
of chips embodying this architecture by many different manufacturers. The
disturbing variations in floating-point processing architectures are addressed
by the new IEEE standard, which resolves such questions as how each possible
value should be represented, how much accuracy must be preserved by each
operation, and what should be done in response to various errors.

Another mechanism for preserving architectural similarity among families
of computers has been the use of microprogramming. This strategy is used
by a great variety of models of the IBM S/370, the VAX, and others to
support binary portability despite widely different internal structures. A few
computers provide adaptable microprogramming, by which one computer may
be made to emulate another.

A somewhat similar strategy adopted by several portable compilers and
operating systems is the definition of a standard **virtual CPU architecture,**
together with interpreters or translators to make programs written for such an
architecture usable on various real machines. This approach requires that all
application programs be processed by compilers that produce programs for
the virtual architecture. This method is used by several Pascal compilers,
including UCSD Pascal, and by the PICK operating system. With this

strategy the portable compilers and operating systems are also written to be translated for the virtual architecture. Ideally, a relatively simple translator or interpreter is then all that is required to transport the entire software system to a new machine.

20.10 SUMMARY

The wide variety of computer types and system and application programs leads to serious problems in the attempt to provide similar capabilities in many different environments. This problem can be greatly relieved if a single program can be made to run in many different environments with little change. Portability is the characteristic of certain programs which makes it easy to move them to new environments.

Portability takes two principal forms. Binary portability is achieved if an executable program can be copied directly to a new environment and run without change. This is only possible for highly similar systems. Source portability implies that source programs can be copied to new environments and translated and run with only limited changes. Source portability may be achievable over a greater variety of systems.

Portability is aided by the use of standard components and standard interfaces. If a program encounters the same mechanisms in different environments, it will be able to adapt with fewer changes. Many standards exist for various components and interfaces. De facto standards are mechanisms developed by one system but widely adopted by others. Formal standards are developed by committees of interested parties specifically to ensure similarity of system elements. Many formal computer standards in the U.S. are sponsored and supported by ANSI and IEEE.

An essential step to enable transporting of a program to various environments is use of a programming language that is supported in each environment. Standard languages assist in meeting this requirement. An additional important interface for most programs can be addressed with standard procedure libraries. In some cases the compiler itself may be portable, ensuring similar translation in each environment.

A missing element in the standard environment of many programs may be operating system services. The OS program interface can be standardized either by portable operating systems or by use of a standard OS interface. The latter approach may allow programs to view the services of a variety of operating systems in a consistent manner.

Other approaches to enhancing portability through standardization include a standard object code format, common CPU architectures, a floating point standard, and use of a virtual architecture with associated translators.

FOR FURTHER READING

A good overview of the issues involved in software portability is given by Brown [1976]. These issues are further addressed in a more recent text by Lecarme & Pellissier Gart [1986]. Wallis [1982] provides a textbook on portable programming. Tanenbaum et al. [1978] present guidelines for portable software based on a family of portable compilers.

Snow [1978] describes an exercise in transporting an operating system. A number of accounts of the portability of specific operating systems have been published. Systems covered by these accounts include UNIX [Miller 1978], MS-DOS [Myers 1983], SOLO [Powell 1979], THOTH [Cheriton 1977, 1982], TRIPOS [Richards et al. 1979], MUSS [Theaker & Frank 1979], FADOS [Tuynman & Hertzberger 1986], and others. An interesting account of the problems of transporting a large application program (Donald Knuth's TeX text formatter) is given by Zabala [1981].

The process of formal standards development is described by Card et al. [1983]. IEEE computer-related standards in particular are considered by Buckley [1986]. The process of developing the MOSI standard is discussed and reviewed by Mooney [1986].

Formal standards for programming languages include ANSI standards X3.23 for COBOL [ANSI 1974], X3.9 for FORTRAN [ANSI 1978], X3.97 for Pascal [ANSI 1983a], X3.159 for C [ANSI 1988], and the joint ANSI and Department of Defense standard ANSI/MIL 1815A for Ada [ANSI 1983b]. The MOSI and POSIX standards for operating system interfaces are described by IEEE Trial-Use standards 855 [IEEE 1985a] and 1003.1 [IEEE 1986], respectively. ANSI/IEEE Standard 754 [IEEE 1985b] provides specifications for binary floating-point arithmetic, while Trial-Use standard 695 [IEEE 1985c] defines a common object code format.

The TRON project and its associated CPU chip are described by Sakamura [1987a, 1987b], and the concepts of the CTRON operating system interface are presented by Ohkubo et al. [1987].

IMPORTANT TERMS

American National Standards
    Institute (ANSI)
binary portability
de facto standard
formal standard
Institute for Electrical and
    Electronic Engineers (IEEE)

interface
International Organization for
    Standardization (ISO)
portability
portable compiler
portable operating system
procedure library

source portability
standard
standard interface
standard operating system inteface

standard procedure library
standard programming language
standards organization
virtual CPU architecture

REVIEW QUESTIONS

1. Explain the meaning and objectives of portability.

2. Identify several obstacles to perfect portability.

3. Explain the difference between source portability and binary portability. State one advantage of each.

4. Explain the difference between de facto standards and formal standards.

5. Give two reasons why use of a standard programming language is not sufficient to guarantee complete source portability.

6. Explain the meaning of a virtual CPU architecture. Give an advantage and a disadvantage of this approach to portability.

7. Explain the potential benefits of each of the following:

   a. standard procedure libraries

   b. a standard floating-point mechanism

   c. a standard object code format

ASSIGNMENTS

1. The text lists several elements of computing environments that must be identical to enable binary portability. Explain why each of these elements must be identical. Is this list complete, or can you think of others?

2. Examine the manuals for two different compilers for a programming language of your choice. List several examples of differences between the compilers that could lead to different behavior when processing identical programs.

3. Formal computer standards often take years to develop. Discuss some of the problems that could arise if standardization was too quick and easy.

4. Identify each of the direct and indirect interfaces shown in Figure 20–5. Select three of these interfaces and discuss the portability problems associated with each one, and how they could be resolved.

5. As mentioned in the text, a standard for an OS program interface need not standardize all system calls, only those that are useful for portable application programs. List at least five common system calls that you believe should not be standardized, and explain why.

Virtual
Machines

Introduction • VM/370 and CMS • Virtual CPUs • Virtual I/O Devices • Recursive Virtual
Memory • Performance Considerations • Isolation and Communication • Simulation Applications

Virtual Machines

21.1 INTRODUCTION

Two fundamental operating system concepts that have been evolving since the 1960s can be combined to produce an unusual type of software system, called a **virtual machine system,** which is extremely useful in addressing certain kinds of problems.

The primary concept on which virtual machine systems are based is the *abstract machine* concept pioneered by T.H.E. In an abstract machine, the OS is viewed as a series of layers, each extending and refining the mechanisms available from the previous layer. The second concept, the virtual memory mechanism introduced by ATLAS, makes possible an effective abstraction of one of the most intensely used resources in a computing system. If the abstract machine concept is developed in a specific way on a suitable architecture, using virtual memory as an important building block, the result is a virtual machine system. The specific program interface presented to each process running on a virtual machine system is called a **virtual machine,** and the software that implements this interface is known as a **virtual machine monitor,** or **VMM.**

The terms *virtual machine* and *abstract machine* have sometimes been used interchangeably. In the meanings now generally recognized for these terms, a virtual machine is *an abstract machine which appears identical to, or very similar to, the actual physical hardware.* Rather than hiding some features of the machine (like privileged instructions or I/O devices) while adding new features (files, processes, or storage management), the virtual machine monitor offers an almost transparent view of the original hardware. Such abstract machine systems as T.H.E. or TENEX would not qualify as virtual machines by this definition.

The view presented to a process by a virtual machine includes all of the processor features normally available to programs at the level of machine language, including features normally available only to privileged software such as an operating system. A program running on a virtual machine may apparently place itself in privileged mode, and may use the complete instruction set for the machine, including privileged instructions that manipulate I/O devices and sensitive CPU registers. The VMM, however, does not allow programs to enter a true privileged mode at all, but simulates the effect of all attempts to execute such privileged instructions.

The virtual address space provided to a program by a virtual machine is viewed as a complete copy of the physical memory space, including special memory locations, such as interrupt vectors. Except for the CPU instruction set, a pure VMM offers no visible services. There is no "system call" to the monitor; an attempt by a program to execute a system call instruction simply would result in a transfer to a trap location in the program's own virtual address space.

In a sense, then, a virtual machine monitor is a software system that behaves like no software at all. If this structure provided a single virtual machine for a single user, its usefulness would be limited to providing possible improvements on the real machine architecture. However, the VMM timeshares the real hardware among multiple users, allowing *each* user the illusion of a private, bare machine. But the program running on each such machine must fill the role of a normal operating system on its own. Application programs may then be run on each operating system. This model is distinguished from a conventional OS in Figure 21-1. The first diagram in this figure shows a conventional OS, which directly controls the hardware. All applications communicate with the OS through the program interface. The second diagram shows a VMM in control of the hardware. Several operating systems communicate with the VMM through its "program interface." All applications in turn must communicate with the system through one of these OSs.

Figure 21-1 Virtual Machine Monitors vs. Conventional Operating Systems

Conventional Operating System	APPL 1	APPL 2	APPL 3
	OS		
	HARDWARE		

Virtual Machine System	AP	AP	APPL	AP	AP
	OS		OS		OS
	VMM				
	HARDWARE				

Since a virtual machine monitor is not an operating system in the usual sense, but reproduces copies of the existing physical architecture, it may be difficult to envision uses for this mechanism. The original motivation for the VMM concept was to support the work of IBM engineers in software

Figure 21–2 A Recursive Virtual Machine Monitor

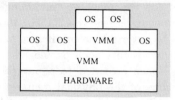

development, including development of operating systems. Goldberg [1973] has listed the following potential uses of a virtual machine system:

1. testing of new OS versions concurrent with production use
2. running hardware diagnostics during normal operation
3. running different operating systems or versions of the same OS on the same physical machine
4. running a virtual configuration of storage devices, memory units, CPU options, etc. which is different from that actually present
5. collecting statistics and measuring OS performance
6. isolating existing software from changes and improvements made to the hardware
7. providing a high degree of isolation for processes and data to ensure privacy

Some of these applications will be discussed in some detail in this chapter.

In most virtual machine systems, the VMM directly controls the physical hardware. It is possible, however, to implement a VMM as a user process, possibly with special privileges, running on a standard host operating system. An example of this approach is found in the VOS VMM, which implemented a virtual S/360 on the Michigan Terminal System [Srodowa & Bates 1973].

Perhaps the ultimate test of a VMM is the ability to run the monitor itself on one of its own virtual machines, as illustrated in Figure 21–2. This figure is similar to the second diagram in Figure 21–1, except that a second VMM is now included among the OSs that communicate with the primary VMM. This feat requires a faithful reproduction of all of the features of the original hardware, including those features required to support virtual machines. Quite a few VMMs fall short of this objective by failing to reproduce some features of the target architecture, such as virtual memory. A VMM that can run a copy of itself is called a **recursive VMM.**

The recursive property is desirable in many applications to ensure that the reproduction of the original hardware is truly correct and complete. In addition, it makes possible the development and testing of the VMM itself in a production environment.

As outlined in Chapter 2, the story of virtual machines to the present day is very much the story of IBM's VM/370. Although a number of other virtual machine monitors have been developed, none has been widely used. Most other VMMs have required special adaptations to a standard machine architecture.

This situation is slowly changing. The desire in many environments to support software designed for more than one OS, especially UNIX together with non-UNIX systems, is leading to new interest in virtual machines as a possible solution. As an example, the Intel 80386 microprocessor is capable of supporting multiple virtual 8086 machines, allowing copies of XENIX, MS-DOS, or other 8086 operating systems to run at the same time [Shiell 1986]. This approach is sure to be exploited more fully as microprocessor architectures continue to evolve.

21.2 VM/370 AND CMS

The dominant example of a successful virtual machine system is IBM's VM/370. This section introduces the characteristics of that system, which will be used as the primary example for the rest of the chapter.

VM/370 evolved gradually from a number of earlier IBM experiments with the virtual machine concept. This work arose because of the practical need of developers to carry on both production and experimental work at the same time with limited hardware. The earlier systems in the series included M44/44X, which ran on a modified 7044, and CP-40 and CP-67, which ran on special models of the S/360.

Newer versions of this system have been given the name VM/SP, which stands for Virtual Machine/System Product, since IBM's newer computers no longer use the 370 designation (although they retain a similar architecture). The fundamental concepts of the VMM have not changed greatly. We will continue to use the name VM/370 by which this system is widely known.

VM/370 consists of a VMM called the **Control Program (CP)** plus several additional programs designed to operate in one of CP's virtual machines. The principal program in this set is a single-user interactive operating system named the **Conversational Monitor System, or CMS.** Other programs supplied with VM/370 support communication and data transfer between virtual machines, and detection and reporting of system problems.

The Control Program

The VM/370 Control Program is a virtual machine monitor that runs on, and emulates, the S/370 architecture. As a VMM, its principal role is to provide each of a set of users with a set of virtual resources derived from the real resources of a single system. Its primary responsibilities include process management, virtual memory management, and support for virtual CPUs and I/O devices. Normally, no file system or file management is visible to users.

The process manager maintains a process for each virtual machine. Round-robin scheduling is employed for both storage and CPU time, with interactive processes favored strongly over CPU-bound ones. Because a goal of the system is isolation of virtual machines from one another, there are few facilities for interprocess communication.

Virtual memory management uses a basic demand fetch strategy and a variation of the CLOCK algorithm for page replacement. Each virtual machine has an individual virtual space, designed to be an identical copy of a real memory. In principle each virtual space can be as large as sixteen megabytes—the S/370 architectural limit—but usually a much smaller limit is imposed.

Methods for implementing virtual CPUs and I/O devices are at the heart of the VMM concept. We describe these in Sections 21.3 and 21.4. Some further issues concerning virtual memory in this type of environment are discussed in Sections 21.5 and 21.6.

Although not strictly part of the VMM model, CP does include a user interface. A command interface for system operators is clearly necessary to initialize and adjust the system, control users, and cope with errors. In addition, a CP command interface is made available to users when no OS is active in their virtual machine, or when certain events cause the OS to terminate. Records for each user are maintained by CP and used to authenticate users and control resource limits, assigned disk storage space, and so on. The user's command interface handles login and session control, allows users to control the configuration of their virtual machine, assists in error handling, and controls initial loading of operating systems.

A program interface is also supported by CP. This interface is not accessed by a normal system call instruction, but by a special machine instruction normally reserved for hardware error checking. CP system calls are invoked only by operating systems that *know they are running on a virtual machine* and wish to "cheat" by taking advantage of that fact. This type of interface is discussed in greater detail in Section 21.6.

CMS

CMS is designed as a straightforward, single-user, interactive operating system. Although the earliest versions of CMS at IBM's Cambridge Laboratories were independent operating systems, today CMS is designed specifically to run with VM/370. Because it relies on the special program interface of CP, it cannot run on a bare physical machine.

Because CMS runs in a virtual machine environment, it does not duplicate features provided by CP. Since CP provides timesharing and virtual memory, CMS does not attempt to support multiple users and provides little memory management. Like many single-user OSs we have already seen, its principal facilities are an interactive command interface, a simple program interface, a file system, and I/O device handling.

Other System Components

A few other specialized programs are provided with VM/370 to run in virtual machines for special purposes. The principal ones include the Remote Spooling Communication System (RSCS), which supports remote communication and file transfer between a virtual machine and the "outside world" (including other virtual machines), and the Interactive Problem Control System (IPSC), used for performance monitoring and error handling.

21.3 VIRTUAL CPUS

A virtual machine monitor implements a **virtual CPU** for each of its processes. This CPU must appear to have all of the properties of a real CPU, except for time-dependent behavior. In the discussion that follows, we assume the CPU being simulated has a traditional architecture, including a distinction between privileged and non-privileged mode. When the CPU is not in its privileged mode, certain privileged instructions cannot be executed.

Privileged Resources

The most prominent component of a CPU is a set of executable instructions. Execution of an instruction may produce some effect in the form of changes to memory, changes to CPU registers, or I/O operations. Because changes to some CPU registers can affect the correct operation of other processes or the OS, these registers are divided into privileged and non-privileged groups. Privileged registers can be accessed and modified only by privileged instructions. These instructions, in turn, can be executed only when the

CPU is in privileged mode. A one-bit flag indicating whether the CPU is in privileged mode is among the registers in the privileged set.

Examples of registers that are usually privileged include memory management or page table registers, interrupt control registers, and certain status flags, including the privilege mode flag. A typical register set is illustrated in Figure 21–3. Any instructions that directly access I/O devices are also privileged. Instructions that access main memory are usually not privileged; however, the region of memory that can be accessed is controlled by the privileged memory management registers.

Figure 21–3 Privileged and Non-privileged CPU Registers

Non-Privileged | Privileged

PROGRAM COUNTER | STATUS FLAGS

INDEX REGISTERS | INTERRUPT CONTROL

DATA REGISTERS | MEMORY MAPPING REGISTERS

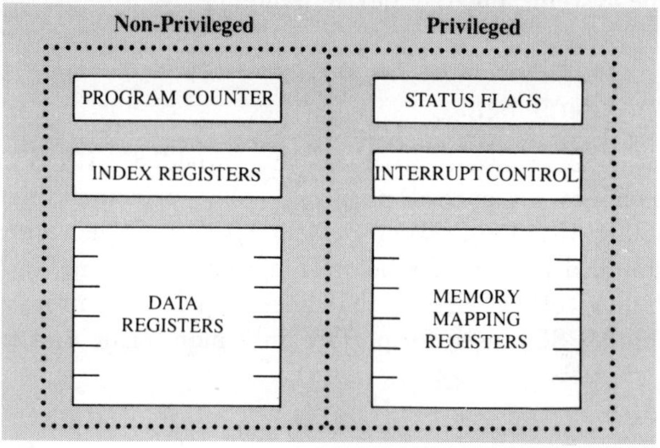

Simulation of Privileged Instructions

The VMM must ensure that, when any instruction is attempted by a process running on a virtual machine, including privileged instructions, the apparent effect must be as though the instruction worked correctly. This illusion must be maintained even though the process actually runs in non-privileged mode, and privileged resources cannot be accessed. Instead, the expected effect of all attempts to access privileged resources, which would occur on a real machine, must be simulated by the VMM.

When a process runs in a virtual machine, accesses to (virtual) memory and non-privileged registers proceed normally. I/O operations and accesses to privileged CPU registers must be simulated. In most cases, attempts to execute privileged instructions in a non-privileged mode cause an interrupt. A traditional OS responds to such an interrupt by terminating the offending process. A VMM must respond instead by simulating the effect of the instruction and allowing the process to continue execution.

Simulation of I/O operations is considered in the next section. Simulation of privileged registers is achieved by maintaining private copies of these registers in the PCB of each process. These registers co-exist with the rest of the saved CPU state, as shown in Figure 21–4. Unlike copies of other registers, however, these copies are *never* loaded into the real CPU registers. Instead, all attempted accesses to privileged registers are translated by the VMM into accesses to these private copies.

Figure 21–4 A Saved CPU State for Virtual Machine Processes

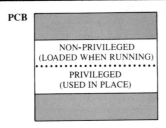

The basic algorithm carried out by a VMM is shown in Figure 21–5. At any moment the virtual machine may or may not be in **virtual privileged mode.** This mode occurs if the private copy of the privileged mode flag is set. During virtual privileged mode, instructions accessing privileged CPU registers are allowed to read or modify the private copies and continue normally. If the virtual mode is non-privileged, however, such instructions must cause a **virtual interrupt,** which is achieved by restarting the process at the location in its virtual address space that represents the interrupt vector for illegal instructions.

Clearly, the simulation of a large proportion of the instructions executed by an OS can lead to serious problems of performance. Great care must be taken in the design of the VMM to complete the simulation of most common cases in as few instructions as possible. Performance may be greatly improved by hardware assistance for the simulation. This issue is discussed further in Section 21.6.

Simulation of Unimplemented Instructions

An additional capability that may be provided by a VMM is the simulation of instructions which, although not privileged, do not work as desired in the real hardware. Many instruction sets include instructions that are defined to cause an interrupt rather than perform a useful action. These may include instructions to make use of an option not present on the

Figure 21–5 An Algorithm for Simulating Privileged Instructions

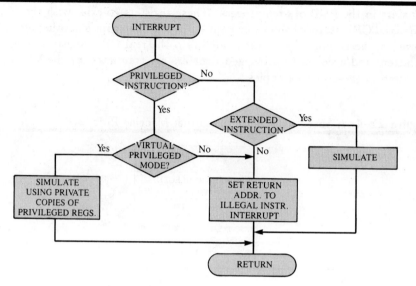

machine, such as floating-point arithmetic hardware. They may also include instructions reserved for use in future extensions of the architecture. As long as these instructions cause an interrupt when executed, they may be used to perform any desired function in the virtual machine, effectively extending its instruction set.

Hardware Requirements

To allow a VMM to consistently intercept and simulate accesses to privileged registers, *all* instructions that access these registers must be privileged, and *all* privileged instructions, when attempted in non-privileged mode, must cause an interrupt. This is an essential requirement for a **virtualizable CPU architecture.** Perhaps surprisingly, this requirement is not met by many computers. Some machines ignore all privileged instructions when privilege mode is not set. Others ignore a few instructions they consider harmless, such as switching into non-privileged mode when the program is already in that mode, or allow non-privileged programs to read some privileged registers although they cannot modify them. The IBM S/370 is still the only widely-used architecture that is fully virtualizable. This is a major reason why VM/370 is the dominant virtual machine system.

21.4 VIRTUAL I/O DEVICES

Simulation of I/O devices can be achieved by a variety of techniques, ranging from using a real device as is, to simulating the required behavior without any real device at all. The appropriate strategy depends on the nature of the device and the goals to be achieved. Generally, the goal of virtual I/O devices is to share the available real devices as effectively as possible among the virtual machines while maintaining the required form of interaction with the outside world.

The VMM must simulate all I/O instructions, which consist either of distinct privileged instructions designed for I/O operations, or memory references to a portion of the address space reserved for memory-mapped I/O. In the latter case, the translation tables can be set to cause an interrupt, such as a page fault, whenever these I/O locations are accessed.

The method for simulation depends on the model chosen for the I/O device being accessed. Common models include:

- virtual device equals real device
- real device is timeshared among multiple virtual devices
- real device is space-shared among multiple virtual devices
- virtual device has no corresponding real device

Virtual Device Equals Real Device

Some devices cannot be usefully shared in any way because of their nature and the ways in which users directly interact with them. The most prominent example is an interactive terminal. Each terminal can serve exactly one user for the duration of an interactive session. The I/O software of a VMM could virtualize the terminal to improve its properties. For example, it could intercept and expand data passing between the terminal and a process to provide editing and screen control operations, assign meanings to keys, and so on. However, a distinct real terminal is needed for each virtual terminal connected to the virtual machine. This situation is illustrated in Figure 21–6. Another viewpoint of a virtual terminal might connect many such terminals to distinct "windows" on a screen. Even with this approach, however, no single real terminal can be shared by multiple users at the same time.

Another category of device that cannot usually be shared is a storage device with removable media such as a tape drive or a floppy disk drive. Here the user presents a physical storage unit to be mounted as a whole, and removes the entire unit when the work is finished. The user expects a physical drive to be dedicated to this use as long as each disk or tape is mounted. Usually, no strategy for sharing the device is possible.

Figure 21–6 Virtual Terminals and Real Terminals

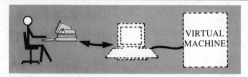

Timeshared Real Device

For an important class of I/O devices, the user presents input data and receives output data as a stream of data items or groups of items. Continuous control or possession of the device is not required. Devices in this category include card readers, punches, and printers. In a conventional multiuser OS, such devices are usually managed by a spooling technique. Input data is read into disk files in distinct jobs, and made available to the OS as needed. Output data is initially written to files, and then copied to the slower output devices one job at a time as the opportunity arises. This spooling buffers the speed difference between processes, which may produce output in bursts, and output devices, which can process information slowly but steadily. As a result, both waiting by processes and idle time for output devices are minimized.

A virtual machine system may also make use of a spooling mechanism. However, it can hide this mechanism from its users, creating the illusion of direct control of a private device, as shown in Figure 21–7. Although a virtual machine sends direct data to its virtual printer, this data is actually saved in a spool file and printed at a later time. The illusion breaks down only if the user must be concerned with the immediate physical behavior of the devices while the program is running.

A tighter form of timesharing is possible with communication devices. These devices are often multiplexed, intermixing individual characters belonging to various processes. Each character is marked in some way to identify the process that owns it. A multiplexed communication channel can be presented as a virtual dedicated channel to each process.

Space-shared Real Device

Some devices cannot be shared over time, because they are used over an extended period of time. This is true of most storage devices, which must retain files and data for long periods. If the data is removable and will be directly controlled by users, dedicated real devices must be used. If the storage is permanently attached to the computing system, however, users may interact with it only by writing and reading information. In this case a different type

Figure 21–7   Virtual Printers sharing a Real Printer

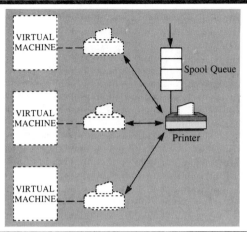

of sharing is possible.

Although the amount of total storage space available is fixed, the space required by each user may not correspond to the size of actual physical units. A single physical disk, for example, can be partitioned into several virtual disks, called **minidisks** in VM/370 terminology. This partitioning is illustrated in Figure 21–8. A minidisk is assigned to a user on a long-term basis. Each minidisk appears to be a whole storage unit; its tracks, sectors, or other address components are numbered sequentially from zero. All use of this space is at the discretion of the virtual machine. Note that a minidisk is not a file system. The file system, if any, is created by the OS running in the virtual machine, not by the monitor.

It is also possible, but less common, to define a virtual disk that covers two or more physical disks, or that has a structure different from the physical disk on which it is based.

No Real Device

For the final category—devices for which effects can be simulated without any physical device—the principal example is a virtual communication device, which is used to communicate with another virtual machine on the same system. As shown in Figure 21–9, this simulation creates an illusion of normal communication paths going outside the system. In fact, however, the only path needed is a logical connection using buffers within the VMM itself.

Figure 21–8 Minidisks sharing a Single Physical Disk

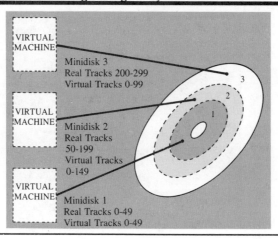

Figure 21–9 A Virtual Device with No Corresponding Real Device

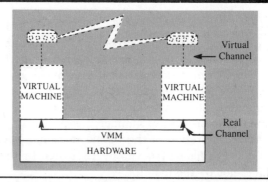

Block Transfers and I/O Programs

A complication can arise in a virtual I/O device that accesses memory directly after an operation is started while the CPU proceeds with other work. Such is the case in systems performing block transfers between memory and disk, which proceed independently after a start instruction is executed. As discussed in Chapter 11, care must be taken to avoid disturbing the physical memory participating in the transfer, even though the process that started the I/O is no longer running.

In the IBM S/370, I/O is handled by channel programs constructed by the operating system. These programs contain addresses for data buffers.

The channel hardware which reads the programs expects the addresses to be physical, not virtual. Because of this need, VM/370 must translate the original channel program to a different form before it is actually used. In fact, it constructs a substitute program in its own storage area. Thus the channel program that remains visible to the virtual machine after I/O has been started is not the one actually being executed. Because of this, programs that access or modify a channel program while it is in use may not behave the same way under VM/370 as on a real machine.

21.5 RECURSIVE VIRTUAL MEMORY

An essential component of an effective virtual machine system is a paged virtual memory. If the system is to be recursive, it must also be possible to operate a virtual memory operating system within a virtual machine. Processes running within a virtual machine may set up their own page tables and use them to construct virtual address spaces for their own use.

For such a structure to work as intended, the VMM and its associated hardware would have to support two levels of page translation. The page descriptors used in the virtual machine would point to pages that are still virtual from the point of view of the VMM. Another translation step would be needed to convert these to physical page frame numbers. The problem is illustrated in Figure 21–10.

Figure 21–10 Multiple Levels of Paging

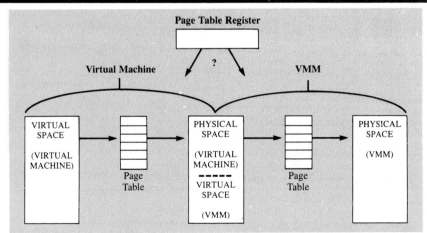

For reasons of performance and reliability, paged memory translation is always performed by hardware. Translation mechanisms able to support two levels of paging are not provided by current computers. Moreover, two levels may not be enough. The generality of a recursive system allows the VMM to run copies of itself. These in turn may run other systems employing virtual memory, including other VMMs, leading to a potentially unlimited level of nesting.

The solution provided by VM/370 is similar to the translation of channel programs described in the previous section. When an attempt to establish new page tables is detected in the virtual machine (by a privileged instruction, which modifies the page table register), CP constructs a private new page table that combines the translation defined in both of the existing page tables. The new tables, which become the ones actually used, are called **shadow page tables.**

As shown in Figure 21–11, the VMM uses page tables to map the virtual space of individual virtual machines into the available physical memory. The process running in the virtual machine creates page tables that map its own virtual spaces into those of the VMM. The shadow page tables substitute a map directly from the virtual spaces defined by the process to the real physical memory.

Figure 21–11 Use of Shadow Page Tables

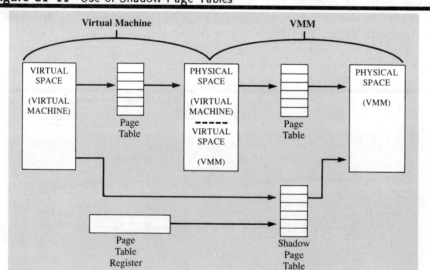

This method can work even with multiple levels of recursion. Each VMM, starting at the highest levels, constructs shadow tables, which map into what they consider to be physical memory. They then load the page table register. If the VMM is a higher-level one, this action will attract the attention of the lower-level VMM which supports it. This VMM will then construct its own shadow page tables, continuing the process until the real hardware is reached.

Just as problems can arise with channel programs if they are accessed or modified while in use, similar problems can arise with page tables. An operating system which modifies a page table that is currently in use may get unexpected results. Fortunately, the need for this type of behavior is rare.

21.6 PERFORMANCE CONSIDERATIONS

Although the virtual machine concept is sound and attractive in principle, and reasonably effective implementations are possible for a moderate number of virtual machines, performance of each OS will clearly be much lower than if it had sole use of the physical machine Sometimes such great penalties are unacceptable, at least for more critical applications. VM/370 provides a number of mechanisms to improve performance for the entire system or for a selected virtual machine.

A valuable performance enhancement may be provided by hardware options, such as VM-assist. This option provides hardware and microcode to perform the actual simulation of many privileged instructions. With VM-assist, even when a non-privileged program attempts a privileged instruction, software intervention will usually not be necessary.

A second key mechanism for performance improvement is the CP system call interface, which allows an OS running in a virtual machine to communicate with the VMM. Such communication may be used by an OS, for example, to request CP to set up page tables and manage virtual memory, rather than attempting to handle this task itself. This removes the need for shadow page tables and enhances overall performance. Modified versions of MVS and other IBM operating systems are available to run with CP in this way.

When still greater performance is needed, selected virtual machines may be set up to run in a "virtual-equals-real" mode, with minimum translation. Such a process may be given a region of real memory that is protected from paging. It may also receive special scheduling priority, real I/O devices, and other considerations.

Finally, the VM environment may provide assistance in the performance monitoring and evaluation of programs and systems running in a virtual machine. This analysis may allow adjustments that considerably improve overall performance in some cases.

21.7 ISOLATION AND COMMUNICATION

In some applications, an important benefit of the virtual machine concept is the total isolation between machines. A pure virtual machine system provides extremely high security. Each virtual machine is in a private world, and cannot access any type of shared resource, whether memory, storage devices, or system data structures. Processes cannot communicate in any way, except possibly through influencing and observing the timing behavior of the system.

On the other hand, processes in distinct virtual machines that want to communicate will have a difficult time. Communication can be performed only as though it were between two physically separate systems using (virtual) communication devices. Of course, the VMM may optimize this communication as described above, when the sender and receiver are actually on the same physical machine. The presence of "violations" of the virtual machine model, such as the CP system call interface, reduces the security level and increases the potential for communication.

21.8 SIMULATION APPLICATIONS

An important potential use of a virtual machine monitor is to simulate and study hardware configurations that may differ somewhat from those physically available. For example, you may study the effects of adding a CPU option or a new type of disk drive.

A system running in a virtual machine may be provided with software performance monitors to study its behavior. The greatest difficulty lies in proper measurement of time. Since it is obvious that the timing of events in a virtual machine does not correspond to real time, a consistent **virtual time** must be maintained.

Standard VM/370 systems do not provide full support for virtual time. However, experimental systems have developed this concept successfully. In one such study [Canon et al. 1980], the behavior of I/O devices, such as disks and channels, was studied closely by modeling details such as the continuous rotational position of the disk. The model matched closely with a corresponding real system, except that the performance of one real I/O channel was lower than observed in the simulation model. Investigation revealed a wiring error in this channel, causing reduced though correct performance, which had gone undetected for several years.

21.9 SUMMARY

A virtual machine system provides sharing of a single real computer among multiple users, each of whom have the illusion of operating on a private, bare machine. A virtual machine system can support multiple operating systems simultaneously. The concept of structuring an OS as an abstract machine, together with the development of successful virtual memory mechanisms, led to the development of this mechanism.

A specialized "operating system" designed to implement virtual machines is called a virtual machine monitor. Some possible applications for a VMM include testing new OS versions, running different operating systems on the same machine, or isolating processes to ensure privacy. If a VMM can support a copy of itself, it is called a recursive VMM.

The dominant example of a virtual machine system in common use is IBM's VM/370. VMMs are unusual on other architectures because few computers provide all of the necessary features to support them. VM/370 consists of a virtual machine monitor (CP), a conversational single-user OS (CMS), and several other support programs. CP provides the basic capabilities expected of a VMM, plus a command interface for direct communication with users, and a program interface through which programs may gain assistance from the VMM. CMS is a simple OS designed to run under CP and does not include features that CP can provide.

A VMM must support virtual memory, virtual CPUs, and virtual I/O devices. Virtual CPUs are implemented by simulating the effects of privileged instructions when executed by non-privileged software. Virtual I/O devices are simulated by one of several techniques depending on the nature of the device to be represented. Possible problems caused by I/O include block transfers that do not operate on virtual addresses, and channel programs that must be modified by the VMM prior to execution.

Virtual memory is provided by conventional techniques. However, a problem arises when the OS running in a virtual machine includes a virtual memory mechanism of its own. To avoid multiple levels of virtual memory, which the hardware cannot support, a recursive VMM may make use of shadow page tables, which substitute for the multiple page tables otherwise required.

To ensure reasonable performance, a VMM may benefit from hardware assistance for simulating privileged instructions and for other necessary activities. Other strategies for improving performance include "virtual-equals-real" mode and support for performance evaluation and tuning. Some additional applications for a virtual machine system include separation of processes for high security, and effective simulation of modified system configurations.

≡ FOR FURTHER READING ≡

The history and evolution of virtual machines is described in articles by Buzen & Gagliardi [1973] and Goldberg [1974]. Goldberg [1974] proposes an architecture for a formally virtualizable system, and Belpaire & Hsu [1975] present some formal properties required for an architecture to be virtualizable.

CP-67, predecessor to VM/370, is described in articles by Meyer & Seawright [1970] and Parmelee et al. [1972]. The latter also includes an annotated bibliography on virtual machine systems. VM/370 is explored in a special issue of the IBM System Journal [IBMSJ 1979], and its history is described by Hendricks & Hartmann [1979] and Creasy [1981]. The various uses of VM/370 are examined by Seawright & MacKinnon [1979]. A particularly good case study of VM/370 is included in the text by Madnick & Donovan [1974, pp. 549-563]. Canon et al. [1980] discuss the use of VM/370 for performance evaluation, and explore the concept of virtual time.

Only a few descriptions exist of virtual machines on non-IBM hardware. Popek & Kline [1975] discuss the PDP-11 "virtual machine architecture." Srodowa & Bates [1973] describe VOS, which is implemented on the Michigan Terminal System. Shiell [1986] discusses the virtual machine architecture of the Intel 80386, which can support multiple virtual 8086s.

≡ IMPORTANT TERMS ≡

Control Program (CP)
Conversational Monitor System
　(CMS)
minidisk
recursive VMM
shadow page table
virtual CPU

virtual interrupt
virtual machine
virtual machine monitor (VMM)
virtual machine system
virtual privileged mode
virtual time
virtualizable CPU architecture

≡ REVIEW QUESTIONS ≡

1. List five possible purposes for a virtual machine monitor. Illustrate each with a specific example.

2. Explain why the Control Program in VM/370 includes a command interface, and why it includes a program interface.

3. Explain carefully how a virtual machine monitor implements the concept of a virtual CPU.

4. Name two categories of I/O devices that cannot be simulated or shared using a virtual machine system. Explain why.

5. In a virtual machine system, some I/O devices can be shared either by sharing time or by sharing space. Give one example of each type of sharing and explain how it works.

6. A virtual memory mechanism can provide a process with a virtual memory larger than the real physical memory. In a virtual machine, can we construct a virtual disk larger than the physical disks available? Why or why not?

7. In a virtual machine system, a problem arises when a process running within a virtual machine attempts to set up its own virtual memory system. Explain carefully what the problem is, and how it can be solved.

8. Describe three ways to improve the performance of a virtual machine system.

ASSIGNMENTS

1. Describe the operation of three system calls which a VMM might usefully provide for the OSs which use it.

2. Identify at least five OS activities that an OS could omit or perform differently if it is known to be operating with a virtual machine monitor. Which of these could be aided by a direct program interface to the VMM?

3. Identify the architectural features that would be necessary to support a recursive VMM. Why do you believe this capability is not commonly supported, even on newer computers?

4. Design an assembly language program and associated data structures for a computer of your choice, which implements the flowchart of Figure 21-5. Describe any difficulties you encounter.

5. Modifying I/O channel programs or page tables are two activities that could lead to incorrect behavior in a virtual machine, because the VMM does not perfectly simulate, and hide, the real situation. Can you describe additional examples of "holes" that may be likely to occur in the complete virtual environment?

6. Following chapter 11, give a detailed example of a set of contents for the page tables shown in Figure 21-10. Then construct a corresponding shadow page table that could be used as shown in Figure 21-11.

7. Explain the meaning of virtual time. Why is this a difficult mechanism to implement?

Real-Time
Systems

Introduction • Real-Time Processes • Real-Time Executives • Process Management
• Memory Management • Events and Interrupts • Device Management • Interprocess
Communication • Real-Time Processes in Standard Systems • Distributed Real-Time Systems

Real-Time Systems

22.1 INTRODUCTION

Operating systems designed to support batch or interactive styles of operation are systems in control of the environment with which they interact. Although users may insist on satisfactory job turnaround or response to commands, each processing step proceeds at the convenience of the OS. The I/O devices that must be handled in such environments (terminals, printers, card readers, modems, tapes, and disks) are all willing to accept output as the OS supplies it and, within reason, to hold input until the OS is ready.

This situation changes radically when the computer is asked to interact with real-time activities. To monitor or control external events with their own inherent timing requirements, the computer system must respond according to the dictates of the I/O device. The external activities, rather than the operating system, are in true control. Because the presence of even limited real-time activities in a computer system has a major impact on its structure and behavior, we refer to all systems that support real-time processing as **real-time systems.**

Computer interaction with real-time events began with the use of SAGE to monitor the status of air defense systems. Early minicomputers found an important application in laboratories, where real-time events were used to both monitor and control the progress of a great variety of experiments. This technology soon moved into factories to help automate industrial processes, and into military and space environments, where it was necessary to control increasingly sophisticated forms of aircraft and spacecraft.

Today applications such as these continue, while the microprocessor has found a role in controlling many more widely used systems and devices. Automobiles, sewing machines, kitchen appliances, entertainment systems, and environmental control systems are just a few of the many items that may rely on computers for proper operation. Many real-time applications are in critical areas, such as vehicle control, patient monitoring, or nuclear systems.

Failure of systems like these could lead to loss of life or major destruction of property.

In many of these applications, the computer is a **dedicated system,** spending most or all of its time on a single job. Work such as laboratory experiment monitoring or environmental control within buildings requires continuous processing, with little opportunity to use the computer for unrelated purposes. Often a dedicated computer system is "embedded" in a larger system, such as an automobile or industrial facility. An **embedded system** is viewed as a single component of a larger system, with no interface of its own to the outside world.

In other environments, a single computer may be required to handle a mixture of applications in which real-time control is combined with standard batch or interactive processing. Because of the radically different nature of these applications, the design of operating system software is especially difficult in these environments. Embedded, dedicated, and general-purpose real-time systems are contrasted in Figure 22–1.

22.2 REAL-TIME PROCESSES

Most **real-time applications** need to monitor or control a number of external activities that are taking place at the same time. As in other environments, multiple concurrent activities can be effectively modeled as processes. The great majority of real-time applications are organized as systems of multiple interacting processes (**real-time processes**). In some **real-time environments**, however, the term "task" (**real-time task**) is used, and systems supporting multiple processes are known as **multitasking systems.** For consistency within this text, we will continue to favor the term "process."

We note here that the term "task" in real-time environments is becoming frequently associated with the Ada language concurrency mechanism. Since Ada is supported and required by the U.S. Department of Defense (DOD), and much of the software implemented in Ada for DOD relates to real-time environments, Ada is extremely important to future real-time operating systems. Although Ada supports tasks, or programming units that execute in parallel, it does not specify how such tasks are to be implemented, or how many processors are to be used. However, Ada does interpret tasks as behaving as though they were running in parallel on *different* computers [Vasilescu 1987]. This will be discussed further in Section 22.10.

Earlier we distinguished real-time processes as a category separate from the other major process categories of batch and interactive. An operating system that supports real-time processes may or may not support other types

Figure 22–1   Types of Real-Time Systems

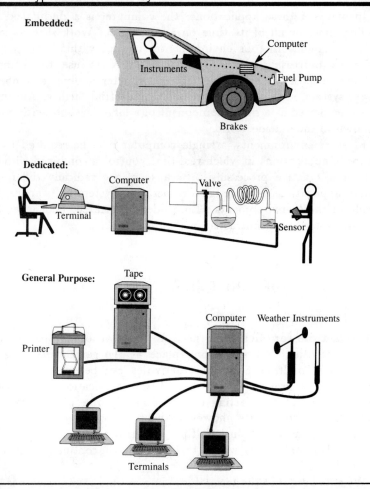

Embedded:

Dedicated:

General Purpose:

that have a major impact on the system. The essential requirement that a real-time process imposes on a computer system may be simply stated:

> A computer system that supports real-time processes *must* produce an appropriate response to certain events and conditions within a specified time constraint.

Usually the time constraint takes the form of a maximum time limit; less often it may specify a minimum time or an exact time as well. If a valve must be shut off within ten seconds to prevent an overflow, this requirement must be honored. If a compact disk player generates 20,000 sample values per second, each must be processed when it is available, and before the next one arrives. If an aircraft can sustain only thirty seconds of instability before recovery is impossible, a correction must be made within that period.

A real-time process places requirements on the *worst-case* behavior of a system, not its probable behavior. The time permitted for response is not always extremely short, but response within that time must be guaranteed. A real-time multitasking system must consider not only the time required to respond to events when idle, but also the time to complete or suspend other activities that may themselves have timing constraints. The time requirements must be met no matter what else is occurring in the system. It is no good to correct a potential airplane stall within seconds *most* of the time. A single failure is too many.

In some cases, a distinction is made between **hard real-time requirements** and **soft real-time requirements**. Hard real-time requirements are timing requirements that absolutely must be met, while soft real-time requirements are expectations that should be met as closely as possible, but for which an occasional delay can be tolerated. A similar distinction may be made between systems or processes based on the type of requirements they have. Most of the discussion in this chapter is focused on meeting hard real-time requirements.

To make timing guarantees possible, there must be an upper bound on the time required for each activity that may delay a running process, including interrupt handling and responding to each type of system service request. Any request that could normally block a process, such as allocating a resource or obtaining input data, must be able instead to return and notify the process if the request cannot be quickly met. The worst sequence of such delays can then be computed to find a bound on various processing activities. Note that guaranteed response time is not required by all processes at all times, but only when specific events occur.

To gain the necessary level of control and efficiency, real-time processes usually must be trusted. It may be necessary for them to directly interact with I/O devices, control other processes, or influence the system scheduling algorithm. These needs are made more palatable because the general behavior and resource needs of a real-time process are often known when the process is initialized. Trusting real-time processes is usually acceptable in dedicated environments, although it may lead to problems in a general-purpose system.

The absoluteness of the timing requirements also places a great burden of reliability on systems supporting real-time processes. It is clearly unacceptable to respond to errors by shutting down the system. In practice, various types of backup and safety systems, including manual override, may be necessary in specific cases.

22.3 REAL-TIME EXECUTIVES

As we have observed, real-time processes may coexist with other process categories in a general-purpose environment, or they may appear in systems that are only or primarily real-time oriented and that often are dedicated to a single application. This section, and several that follow, will discuss the characteristics of operating systems for dedicated or embedded real-time environments. A later section will consider real-time processing in a general-purpose system.

In a computer system dedicated to a single application (real-time or not) it is reasonable to ask whether an operating system is necessary at all. This question is especially appropriate in a real-time context. OS features designed for more general purposes can easily get in the way, consuming valuable time and storage space. It may seem that the best performance could be achieved by software designed from scratch for the specific application. Indeed, this argument is often compelling, and many embedded real-time systems have no distinguishable operating system.

Most real-time applications, however, do require certain types of resource management, and some requirements are similar across a wide range of applications. Two usual necessities are multitasking and efficient sharing of limited storage, leading to common requirements for process scheduling and memory management. Other very common needs may include device handling, error handling, and interprocess communication.

These needs can often be met by a suitably designed operating system. Although software designed from scratch might, in theory, achieve better performance, it is attractive to start with an OS that already exists, *if* the limited system overhead can be tolerated. This overhead is in fact acceptable in many applications. It is also doubtful that most designers could produce special-purpose operating software for a complex application that performs better than established real-time executives and is also highly reliable.

A number of limited operating systems have been designed to meet the general needs of real-time applications. Such systems are known as **real-time executives (RTEs).** RTEs are usually modular and highly adaptable, so they can be customized to specific applications. One widely-known real-time executive is RSX-11 from Digital Equipment Corporation. This OS was designed for the PDP-11, based on an earlier version for the PDP-15. Other RTEs in common use include VRTX from Hunter and Ready, iRMX-86 from Intel, and RTE-1, RTE-2, RTE-3, and so on, from Hewlett-Packard. We'll look at examples from some of these executives in the following sections.

Several typical OS components, such as file systems or a command interface, may be absent or optional in real-time executives. Dedicated real-time applications may run wholly contained in main memory, perhaps with programs installed permanently in ROM. If these applications perform the same set of tasks continuously, no commands may be needed. If file systems and a command interface are present, they may be used only for occasional purposes, such as modifying the system or responding to serious errors.

A real-time executive is frequently viewed as a layered system, in which functions are organized into components that interface with others in controlled ways. Many of the components may be optional, or may be replaceable with user-supplied alternatives. Most of the layers have breaks, permitting direct access from outer to inner layers where necessary for acceptable response. Examples of this layer structure for two RTEs, iRMX-86 and VRTX, are shown respectively in Figures 22–2 and 22–3. The iRMX-86 example is based on Tucker [1983]. The VRTX example, illustrating the VRTX version for the Motorola 68000 (VRTX/68000), is taken from Hunter and Ready [1986].

Figure 22–2   Structure of the iRMX-86 Real-Time Executive

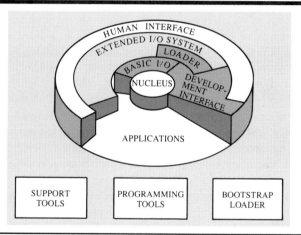

The principal responsibilities of a real-time executive can be identified as process management, memory management, event and interrupt handling, device management, and interprocess communication. Each of these will be considered in the following sections.

22.4 PROCESS MANAGEMENT

Processes (tasks) are the basic unit of activity in a real-time executive. The OS is responsible for creating, deleting, controlling and scheduling processes,

Figure 22–3 Structure of the VRTX/68000 Real-Time Executive

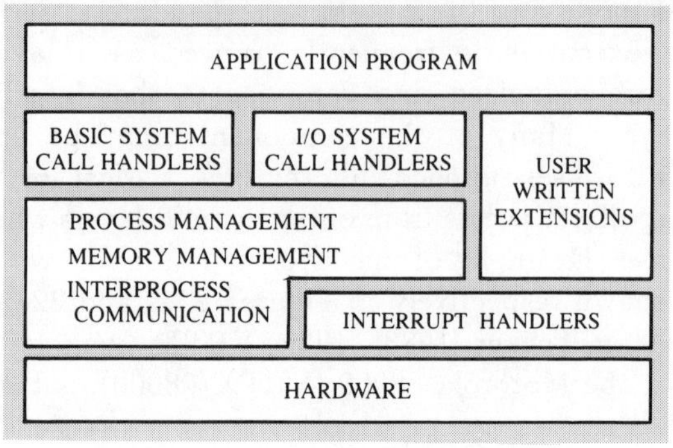

switching context when necessary, and enabling communication between processes. (Interprocess communication is discussed in a later section.)

Because most real-time processes carry out a continuous activity, a fixed set of processes is adequate for many applications. Thus the RTE may make no provision for dynamic process creation. In other applications, processes may be created to perform activities that are occasionally necessary, such as data compression or error handling. These processes rarely create additional processes, and are destroyed when their work is done. This behavior precludes the creation of an excessive number of processes, and ensures that a process creation request will always succeed. Memory may be permanently allocated for the maximum number of PCBs that will ever be required.

To make process creation and management as inexpensive as possible, the amount of information maintained in PCBs is kept to a minimum. A typical PCB for VRTX/68000 is shown in Figure 22–4. This PCB contains eighty bytes, of which more than half are needed for saving CPU registers. If an OS needs to maintain extensive information for some processes, it may provide a separate category of "lightweight" processes that can be more easily created.

Process creation is normally separated from program loading. The initial program for a new process to execute is expected to be already found in memory.

Real-time processes are normally active at all times and subject only to short-term scheduling. This scheduling usually follows a strict priority algorithm with immediate preemption. Priorities for real-time processes are normally static; they are assigned initially based on the intrinsic importance of the activity controlled by each process. In some cases a process may be permitted to change its own priority explicitly, or that of other processes. Aging strategies are not used.

Many real-time processes are subject to **deadline scheduling.** This

Figure 22–4 A Process Control Block in VRTX/68000

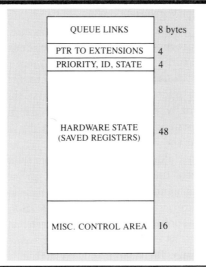

QUEUE LINKS	8 bytes
PTR TO EXTENSIONS	4
PRIORITY, ID, STATE	4
HARDWARE STATE (SAVED REGISTERS)	48
MISC. CONTROL AREA	16

means that the process must *complete* its activity by a specific time. Clearly this means that the execution time for the process must be known. The essential requirement for processes subject to deadline scheduling is that they must not finish late. It may not be necessary or even desirable to allow them to finish early.

Processes are entered into the ready queue or queues in order of priority. When the CPU is available, the process at the head of the highest priority queue is always dispatched. As long as no higher-priority process is ready, the running process may continue running until it requests service or voluntarily suspends itself. This is essentially similar to the priority-based strategy for batch processes, which was illustrated in Figure 6–9.

If an event signaled by an interrupt, or the process itself, results in a higher-priority process becoming ready, the current process is preempted and the new highest-priority process is dispatched immediately. The stopped process is returned to its normal position in the queue according to priority.

Because a real-time process knows best when its activities are critical, and is trusted not to abuse its privileges, a running process may be permitted to lock out preemption by an appropriate system call. While this locking is active, the process will continue running *even if a higher priority process becomes ready*. Of course, a process is expected to use this mechanism for short periods only, and to cancel the lock as soon as it is no longer needed.

Scheduling of processes with the same priority may be handled in several ways. Often real-time priorities are carefully assigned so that no processes share the same priority. Otherwise round-robin scheduling is available but often optional. Individual processes may enable or disable round-robin scheduling within priority groups.

As an alternative to standard timesharing, some RTEs permit a process to create its own subprocesses, called **microprocesses** or **threads**. These subprocesses may take turns running within the main process's scheduled time period. Although not primarily a real-time executive, IBM's OS/2 operating system for the PS/2 microcomputers supports this type of mechanism. Microprocesses are usually dispatched on a simple round-robin basis. Their creation and management is handled principally by the parent process, with limited assistance from the operating system.

Medium-term scheduling that rotates processes among the available memory is rare in a real-time executive. Most processes could not tolerate being involuntarily suspended.   However, processes may often suspend voluntarily or under direction of other processes. Some processes are needed only occasionally, in response to unusual occurrences. Others are needed on a regular schedule, such as once an hour. These suspended processes may be swapped to disk if storage for swapping is available.

In the approach taken by RSX-11, each compiled program, to be recognized and run by the OS, must be converted to an "installed task." As shown in Figure 22–5, these tasks are essentially load modules that remain stored as files on the disk. However, their PCB information is set up in advance in a file header, and their names and locations are listed in a task directory maintained by the executive. All such programs are treated as existing but suspended processes, ready to be loaded and run very rapidly when needed.

Figure 22–5 Installed Tasks in an RSX-11 System

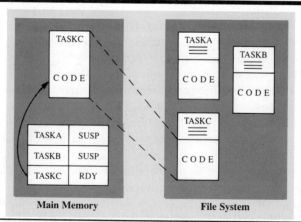

Scheduling for Ada Real-Time Environments

A primary goal of the Ada language was to be useful in real-time environments, especially embedded systems. Recently, much attention has been focused upon the requirements of practical Ada real-time environments. Strategies for process scheduling within such environments have differed, and there is disagreement as to whether preemptive or nonpreemptive scheduling should be used. Supporters of the preemptive approach argue that a higher-priority ready process should not have to wait for any lower-priority process to complete before getting control. The argument against preemptive scheduling seems to focus on the overhead and complexity associated with context switches; the context switch itself may adversely affect a system's response time [Forinash 1987].

The alternative given by those opposed to preemptive scheduling for Ada environments is the use of cyclic executives. This is actually close to a "bare machine" approach, using "non preemptive, voluntary context switching mechanisms" [Laird]. In other words, the programmer controls context switching, eliminating (it is claimed) unnecessary context switches. The obvious question is: "What burden does this place on the programmer?" since there is no scheduling help in critical situations from the executive.

The point of this discussion is that the Ada requirements for real-time environments are giving rise to new debates and approaches to real-time systems. Much research remains to be done in this area.

22.5 MEMORY MANAGEMENT

Like most computer systems, a real-time executive may be required to provide memory management services if available main memory is not large enough to meet all needs at the same time, although this is not common. In such cases, there must be a means of assigning memory priority to lock critical processes in memory so that they cannot be swapped.

Real-time environments require that memory management be simple and straightforward. A process requesting memory, or any other system resource, cannot afford to wait long for the request to be met, and cannot risk being blocked because the resource is unavailable.

If hardware support is available, simple memory mapping may be used in real-time systems. This mapping does not introduce performance penalties while data is in main memory, and its advantages for allocation, relocation, and protection, described in Chapter 13, are beneficial for all types of environments.

Virtual memory, however, can seldom be tolerated by a real-time process.

The time required to process page faults, coming at unpredictable moments, would be unacceptable, and the page replacement algorithm cannot be relied on to always remove the right pages and leave those that are needed. If real-time processes coexist with other processes in a virtual memory environment, most pages used by the real-time processes must be locked into memory so they are not subject to normal swapping.

A dedicated real-time system with sufficient physical memory available will use static allocation, avoiding memory allocation problems altogether under normal conditions. In general, however, RTEs must support dynamic allocation, accepting requests to allocate and release blocks of various sizes, which may arrive in random order.

Many of the allocation strategies discussed in Chapter 10 can be used. However, fast worst-case response is necessary, and it is essential to avoid fragmentation. So allocation may be restricted to fixed-size blocks, because allocation from a pool of fixed-size blocks (whatever the size) is extremely rapid, and fragmentation is not possible.

If fixed-size allocation is used without paging hardware, the OS must tolerate the space wasted when an assigned block is larger than requested. Each process, for its part, must accept the inconvenience of dividing a large space request into smaller-sized units. Both of these may be acceptable to obtain real-time support.

To reduce these inconveniences, it is possible to maintain several pools of fixed-size blocks, each with a different block size. If a pool is currently free, moreover, its block size may be changed. Finally, in a strategy reminiscent of the buddy system, a single large block taken from a pool might be treated as a pool in itself, to be divided into smaller blocks. All of these strategies are supported by VRTX (see Figure 22–6).

Figure 22–6 Memory Allocation in VRTX

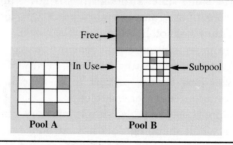

22.6 EVENTS AND INTERRUPTS

A real-time system is **event-driven.** External events occur on an unpredictable schedule; other events are caused by running processes. In many cases these events require extremely fast response. They must be detected and processed immediately. A process may signal an event by a message to another process, by a system call, or by generating an interrupt. External events are always signaled by interrupts.

In a non-real-time environment, all interrupts are processed initially by interrupt handlers supplied by the operating system. This may involve multiple levels of handling to identify the cause of the interrupt and decide what response is required in the present context. Eventually a suitable procedure is executed, which may be a default procedure or one supplied by the application. Since interrupt handlers cannot be allowed to run for a long time, the complete response to an event may be assigned to a separate process that must be run. A number of context switches may be required before handling is entirely complete. This type of interrupt processing is shown in Figure 22–7.

Figure 22–7 Interrupt Handling in a Conventional Environment

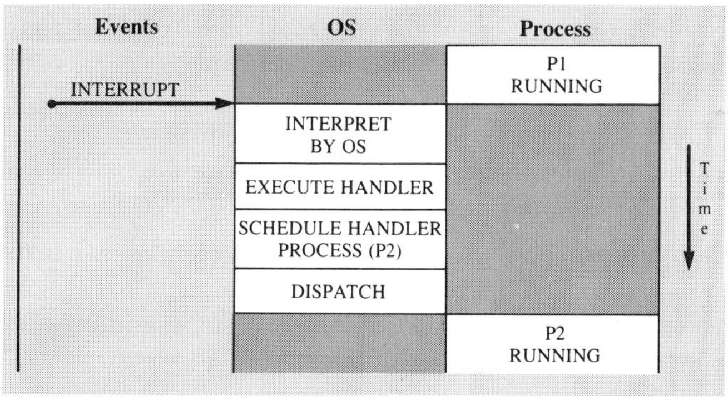

In a real-time environment, unnecessary delays in responding properly to interrupts, as well as unnecessary context switching, must be avoided. To provide the most efficient handling, the appropriate process may be given direct control of the interrupt vector location, so that an interrupt for suitable events causes an immediate transfer to a procedure within a real-time process. No context switch is necessary. In many cases such a procedure can establish the appropriate response and resume the interrupted process without any formal rescheduling. Interrupt handling in a real-time system is shown in

Figure 22–8.

Figure 22–8 Interrupt Handling in a Real-Time Environment

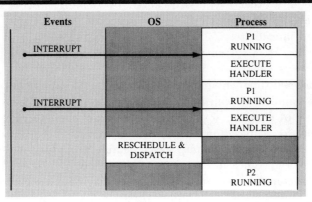

Some real-time executives have stringent requirements for implementing device driver interrupt handlers in order to maintain the "fast, real-time response of the overall system" that is normally required [Digital 1981]. RSX-11 is an excellent example of such a system. There are three conventions that must be followed when processing device interrupts:

- No registers can be used unless a system service routine is first called to save them, or unless the process explicitly performs save and restore operations.

- Non-interruptible processing cannot exceed twenty instructions (approximately 100 microseconds). If interrupt servicing can be completed in this number of instructions, the interrupt handler simply returns from the interrupt.

- If the driver requires additional processing beyond the limit above, it must call a service routine, specifying the interrupting (hardware) priority of the interrupt being serviced. Processing time at this priority cannot exceed 500 microseconds.

- If more processing time is required for the interrupt, a new process called a **fork process** is created. This process becomes a member of a special group that uses a secondary interrupt stack, whose members are processed in first-in, first-out order [Digital 1981].

Figure 22–9 illustrates interrupt processing following the RSX-11 conventions.

Figure 22–9 Interrupt Handling in RSX-11

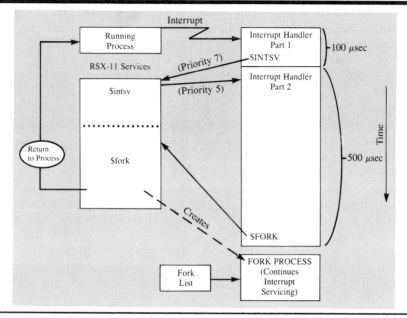

The obvious concern of the RSX-11 conventions is maintaining fast real-time response for critical events being monitored. A device driver that does not follow these conventions could cause unacceptable delay in the servicing of such events, leading to disastrous results in a real-time system.

22.7 DEVICE MANAGEMENT

A real-time system may include standard I/O devices, such as terminals, printers, or disks, that are managed in the usual way by the operating system. Requests for service from these devices are presented as system calls, and the details of data transfer, including responding to I/O completion interrupts, may be handled by the OS.

However, I/O devices that exist in a real-time environment, play a more vital role; they are the connection between the system and the external events that they must monitor or control. As seen from the outside world, these devices are diverse and unique. They may include sensors and measuring instruments, switches and motors of all types. They may be parts of a vehicle, such as carburetors, brakes or propellers. They may be all or part of mechanical, electrical, chemical, or biological systems.

Most such devices accept or produce information as some type of physical value that is normally translated to electrical current. This data may vary in discrete steps or take on a continuously changing value that is measured at periodic intervals. This "analog data" is converted to or from digital form by circuits known as analog-to-digital converters and digital-to-analog converters.

As seen from the computer, most of these devices produce or accept streams of data words, much as a terminal does. However, data may appear at an unpredictable and sometimes high rate, and immediate response may sometimes be required.

Usually a specific real-time process is dedicated to controlling and responding to each device that requires real-time handling. These devices are controlled *directly* by the process. As far as possible the process uses input and output machine instructions, or the equivalent memory-mapped device references, to direct the flow of data to or from the device. If interrupts are required from the device, they are handled directly by the same process. Although this approach requires the process to be trusted with appropriate privileges, it leads to the most efficient interaction.

22.8 INTERPROCESS COMMUNICATION

Because most real-time applications are viewed as systems of cooperating processes, extensive facilities for interprocess communication are frequently provided by a real-time executive. Shared memory is usually supported, since it provides the most efficient communication as long as it is properly used.

Interprocess communication in a real-time executive must proceed without blocking. **Mailboxes,** as discussed in Chapter 7, are commonly provided for this purpose. Mailboxes with capacity for one or more messages provide a necessary buffering that avoids the synchronization problem of direct message passing. For efficient message exchange, addresses alone may be actually passed, with the message itself remaining in shared memory.

Other message passing and synchronization mechanisms are supported by selected RTEs. For example, iRMX provides semaphores, while RSX-11 offers communication by event flags.

22.9 REAL-TIME PROCESSES IN STANDARD SYSTEMS

Most of the discussions of this chapter have assumed real-time processes are running under real-time operating systems. Is it possible that such real-time processes could run successfully under general-purpose operating systems? The answer to this question, of course, depends on the specific system. If a real-time process is to run in a preemptive scheduling environment and can be given a high enough priority to guarantee the response time required and prevent its being swapped to disk, then the answer is probably yes. Otherwise the answer is no.

The problem with most systems is that "normal" application or user processes cannot get such high priority, or avoid being swapped to disk. In such cases, local modifications might be required to allow special real-time processes to get the required scheduling priorities and remain resident in memory. If such processes are to be permanent and should always be resident and active, they might even be made a part of the operating system kernel.

22.10 DISTRIBUTED REAL-TIME SYSTEMS

Increasingly, real-time applications controlled by computers are including more than one processor in the total environment. Whether the application is a large industrial facility which includes several types of control computers, or an embedded system using multiple microprocessors, computers are working together to meet the requirements of real-time monitoring and control. A real-time system that includes multiple computers cooperating on common tasks is called a **distributed real-time system.** Distributed systems in general will be examined in Chapter 23. Here we consider some issues connected with their use in real-time environments. Our discussion will focus on distributed real-time systems programmed in Ada. We have mentioned that Ada tasks behave as though they were running in parallel on *different* computers [Vasilescu 1987]. Future implementations of real-time systems will often assume use of both multiple processors and the Ada language, particularly for U.S. government-sponsored projects. The implementation of real-time executives for multiple processor Ada environments using shared memory could utilize one of three approaches:

- Master-slave, in which a processor is dedicated to the executive; a failure in this processor results in the entire system failing.

- Separate executives, in which each processor is responsible for es managing its own resources. This eliminates the disastrous effect of the failure of the dedicated processor in the master/slave approach. The association of specific processes to a particular processor could result in one or more processors being idle while others have multiple processes ready for execution.

- Symmetric processors, in which the processors are viewed as having identical capabilities. The executive may execute on any processor at any time, thus providing more balanced workloads and improved system reliability. This approach is more complex to implement because of the need for exclusive access to system resources. This approach also does not lead to total system failure when one processor fails [Forinash 1987].

The addition of multiple processors to the real-time environment does complicate the implementation of real-time executives. Problems in timer management arise. Ada requires global clocks, yet does not prevent the use of local clocks on each processor. Critical section problems of the single processor environment will exist also in multiprocessor environments. While many of the principles of implementing batch and interactive operating systems for uniprocessor environments have been well-proven and used successfully in many systems, there are many complex issues in Ada real-time environments that are yet to be resolved. The student interested in operating systems research may find rewarding and important work in these environments.

22.11 SUMMARY

Implementing real-time executives and real-time processes requires guaranteed maximum response times to critical events. More and more real-time embedded systems are being developed. New issues for implementation of real-time systems in Ada are raising new questions and providing new challenges. Issues of process scheduling and interaction, memory management, interrupt handling, and timer management all take on a different perspective in a real-time system.

⟨ FOR FURTHER READING ⟩

Conferences on real-time systems have been and will continue to be a primary means of information exchange on the problems and solutions of real-time implementations. Wirth [1977] attempts to define a discipline of real-time programming. Most publications deal with specific real-time operating systems; for example, Schwann et al. [1985] provides information about the GEM operating system used on multiprocessors with robotic applications. A real-time operating system for a distributed environment is presented by Taynman [1986]. Scheduling issues are discussed in Abbott [1984].

Design principles for a minicomputer RTE are discussed by Purser and Jennings [1975] and Purser [1976]. Whittaker [1971] describes necessary architectural attributes of a real-time executive. Van der Linden and Wilson [1980] review principles of real-time executives for microcomputers, and compare three 8080-based systems: RMX/80, RTM8, and REX80.

Weiler et al. [1970] describe a real-time OS for manned spaceflight. The evolution of small real-time computers at IBM is reviewed by Harrison et al. [1981]. Case studies are presented by many authors; among them are Cheriton [1977, 1982] (THOTH), Day and Krejci [1968] (Sigma 7), Frailey [1975] (DSOS), Funck [1984] and Ready [1986] (VRTX), Hememway [1983] (MSP), Lindgard [1979] (MERT), Pruitt and Case [1975] (MOSS), Raimondi [1976] (LABS/7), Tucker [1983] (iRMX), and Tuynman and Hertzberger [1986] (FADOS).

As has been indicated, research for real-time systems has begun to focus on Ada environments. Forinash [1987] provides an excellent literature search of such Ada-related research as well as issues relating to the design of a scheduler to support real-time Ada programs. Fisher [1986] is concerned with issues related to distributed operating systems for Ada. Greeley, Laird, Lane [1983], Lee [1985], Maule, Pratt [1985], and Roark [1987] deal with the issues of implementing Ada real-time executives.

See also Chapter 23 for additional references related to distributed real-time systems.

IMPORTANT TERMS

deadline scheduling
dedicated system
distributed real-time system
embedded system
event-driven
fork process
hard real-time requirements
mailboxes
microprocess

multitasking system
real-time application
real-time environment
real-time executive (RTE)
real-time process
real-time system
real-time task
soft real-time requirements
thread

REVIEW QUESTIONS

1. What makes real-time operating systems different from batch and interactive operating systems?

2. What are the primary goals of a real-time executive?

3. What is meant by the term embedded system? Give some examples of embedded systems that you have used.

4. Using RSX-11 as an example, discuss some restrictions in the implementation of device interrupt handlers. Explain why each of these restrictions exist.

5. Why should real-time processes be able to be locked in memory (i.e., not swapped to disk)?

ASSIGNMENTS

1. What are the issues in scheduling in a real-time system? Will preemptive scheduling work effectively? Why or why not? When can round-robin scheduling be used in a real-time system?

2. What is the significance of Ada to real-time system environments? Why is Ada becoming more and more important in these environments? Using references provided under the For Further Reading section, discuss any known restrictions or problems of Ada for implementing real-time processes and/or operating systems.

Distributed
Operating
Systems

Introduction • Objectives of Distributed Computing • Multiprocessors • Networks • Design Issues
• Some Example Systems • Organizing the Operating System • Distributed File Systems
• Distributed Processes • Synchronization Issues • Increasing Reliability • Other Issues

Distributed Operating Systems

23.1 INTRODUCTION

As you know, the fundamental physical components of a conventional computing system consist of a CPU, a memory, various input, output, and storage devices, and an interconnection structure. The organization of a typical computer of this type is shown in Figure 23–1.

Figure 23–1 Organization of a Conventional Computing System

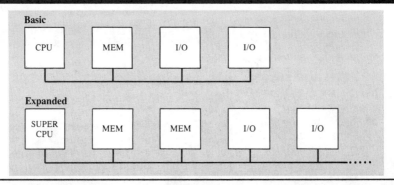

The performance or capacity of such a computing system can be increased by expanding the individual components or by adding additional ones. For example, additional memory units may be added, or the CPU may be replaced with a more powerful one, producing an expanded system as also shown in Figure 23–1.

A more radical technique for increasing computing power has become practical with current technology: inclusion of more than one CPU. In principle, a two-CPU computer could complete its work twice as fast as a system with a single CPU. In a system organized around the process concept, the use of such a system is straightforward: Each CPU may be assigned to execute a distinct process, so that more than one process may be in the *running* state at the same time. Until recently, the cost of CPU hardware has made multiple CPUs prohibitive for all but the largest and most expensive systems. Today entire CPUs can be implemented on a single VLSI chip, and multiple CPUs are possible in systems of modest scope.

In reality, the use of multiple CPUs presents many problems, but the potential performance gains offered by this approach are so attractive that solutions to these problems are being rapidly developed. A single computing system having two or more CPUs is called a **multiprocessor** (as opposed to single-CPU systems, which we may call **uniprocessors**. Some multiprocessors, with as few as two CPUs, have been in use for many years. They include high-end models of IBM mainframes, VAXes, and the like. The OS essentially views the additional CPU as an extra resource to which work can be assigned.

Other multiprocessors have been built with dozens of CPUs. Recently, examples have appeared in which the number of CPUs is in the tens of thousands. These multiprocessors have typically been unique systems used primarily for research; however, a number of them are now being put to use in production environments. Typical multiprocessor organizations are shown in Figure 23–2.

Figure 23–2 Typical Multiprocessor Organizations

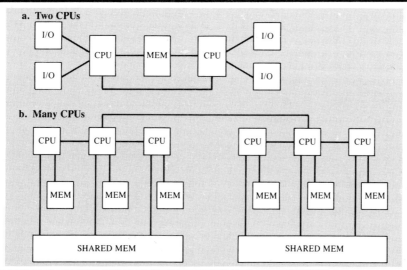

With increasing frequency, independent computers, although usually uniprocessors themselves, are being joined through communication systems, which may include either permanently wired connections or temporary connections established through a telephone system.   These connections allow computers to share information; however, the time required to transfer information may be substantial. The reliability of the transfer may also be a problem, especially if the distance is great. A collection of computers and related devices, with the ability to communicate in this fashion, is called a **network.**

It is useful to further divide networks according to the physical distance between computers.   If this distance is limited to about a mile or less, the network may be considered a **local area network (LAN).** LANs are often confined to a single building or adjoining group of buildings such as a university campus. Because the distance is small, they can be connected permanently with expensive, high-performance communication lines. These networks feature very high-speed communication.

A network that covers a wider geographic area is called a **wide area network (WAN).** The name **long-haul network** is also used.   These networks may use ordinary phone lines for communication and may literally span the entire world. Because of the distance, communication is more costly and less reliable, and must be considered a limiting factor in system cooperation. Each of these network types is illustrated in Figure 23–3.

Each processor (CPU) in a multiprocessor or network is responsible for a specific process or set of processes. The processes being executed by a group of processors may be related. They may form a common workload submitted on behalf of a single collection of users.   In some cases they may share common resources or need to communicate directly. If a group of processors is used to carry out related activities in this way, it is reasonable to view it as a unified computing system. Because the workload is distributed among multiple processors, we call it a **distributed computing system (DCS).**

Each of the system organizations outlined above—multiprocessor, local area network, and wide area network—may be treated as a distributed computing system. However, their differing characteristics lead to different goals and different problems.   The computers forming a network do not necessarily all share a common workload.   In practice, a *subset* of these computers may form a DCS, and this subset may change from time to time.

Since a distributed computing system handles a common workload, it requires a unified control mechanism to manage its work. Individual operating systems for each CPU do not meet this need. A more powerful resource manager is required to tie together the complete DCS. This need must be met by a **distributed operating system.** The distributed OS can be either a special layer of software added to a conventional OS, or a complete operating system for each processor. The purpose of a distributed OS, and the principal issues in its design, are the subject of this chapter.

Figure 23–3 Computer Networks

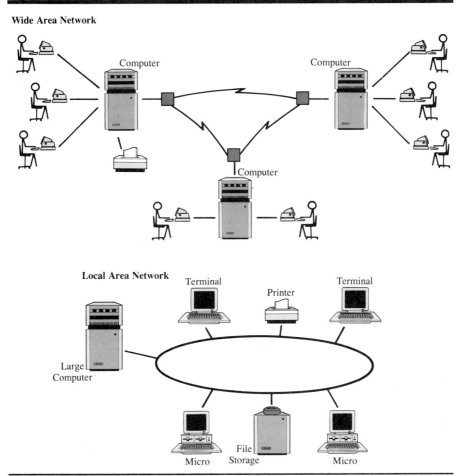

Wide Area Network

Local Area Network

23.2 OBJECTIVES OF DISTRIBUTED COMPUTING

A DCS offers a number of potential benefits not available in a conventional isolated uniprocessor. Among the principal benefits are:

- HUMAN COMMUNICATION: Users at different sites may conveniently exchange messages through electronic mail systems and similar techniques.
- RESOURCE SHARING: Resources located at one site may be used by other sites. These resources may include unique files or

databases; computers with specific power, instruction sets, or system software; or available space for file storage.

- RELIABILITY: The presence of multiple CPUs and other hardware units can improve reliability by ensuring that, if one unit fails, another is available to take its place.
- LOAD BALANCING: If a number of CPUs are available, work may be assigned to those that are least busy, reducing the likelihood of overload of individual processors.

Each of these objectives can be achieved on suitable types of distributed systems, but each carries costs and introduces difficult problems of implementation. For example, the potential performance gain from shifting processes to other sites to balance the load must be compared to the cost of communicating the necessary information. Such a strategy may play an important role in a multiprocessor OS, but is usually not feasible over a wide area network.

Because the characteristics of a multiprocessor environment and a network environment have substantial differences that impact the structure of a distributed computing system, these environments will be considered in further detail in the next two sections.

23.3 MULTIPROCESSORS

A multiprocessor is a single computing system including two or more CPUs. Other elements in such a system include various memory units, I/O devices, and communication buses. Each physical memory unit may be associated with only one CPU, or shared by more than one. If physical memory is shared, it may be mapped to the address space of different processes executing on different CPUs.

Thus processes on a multiprocessor may communicate by shared memory, message passing, or a combination of the two. In either case, communication is considered to have relatively low cost. In the Cm* multiprocessor, processes effectively are provided with shared memory in their virtual address space, even though in some cases reading and writing requires the OS to access a remote memory using messages.

A multiprocessor operating system is concerned with providing a unified view of the complete system to users, in which all resources, including CPUs, are effectively shared. Usually load balancing is an important objective of such a system. Multiprocessor operating systems tend to be unique just as the architectures on which they run are unique, and they are largely outside the scope of this text. Some well-known multiprocessor OSs include Hydra for C.mmp, and MEDUSA and StarOS, both for Cm*.

23.4 NETWORKS

A computer network can exist whenever two or more physically separate computers are connected to one another by a communication path over which messages, or sets of data, can be sent. The connection paths may be permanent, or they may be established as needed, such as by a telephone system. In addition to computers, terminals, printers, storage units, and other devices may be connected to the network at various locations. A single computer with remote terminals, though, is not considered a network.

A specific location on a network is generally referred to as a network **site.** A computer located at a site is termed a network **host.** A distributed operating system in a network environment may be called a **network operating system (NOS).** However, some authors use the name "network OS" only to describe a system that forms a layer above a conventional OS. This distinction is shown in Figure 23–4. The Newcastle Connection [Brownbridge et al 1982], for example, is a network operating system used with a standard version of UNIX to connect UNIX-based systems in a common network. The designers of this system consider it a significant advantage that the UNIX OS does not have to be modified. We will try to use the term "network operating system" only as described above, to avoid confusion.

Figure 23–4   Network vs. Distributed Operating Systems

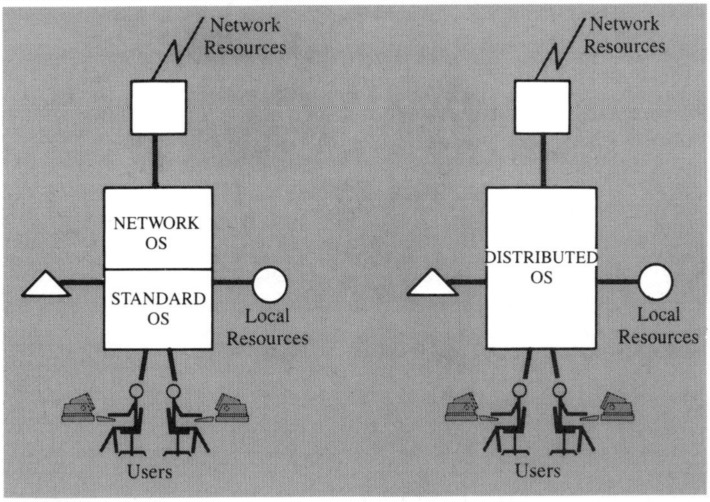

The structure and characteristics of computer networks can be very complex, and are the subject of many specialized texts such as those by

McNamara [1981] and Lane [1985]. Further examples are given in the For Further Reading section at the end of this chapter. In this section we will only outline briefly some basic characteristics of networks that will aid in the understanding of network-based distributed operating systems.

The central responsibility of any computer network is to provide *reliable message transfer* between communicating sites. Simple physical connection of computers does not create a network. Rather, the network requires a combination of hardware and software mechanisms to achieve its goals. The message transfer must be satisfactory even though the physical connections are imperfect and messages may be garbled or delayed. All pairs of sites are not directly connected. Messages may need to be accepted and forwarded by many intermediate sites to reach their final destination. Long messages are usually divided into a sequence of discrete units, called **packets.** Each packet is handled by the network as an individual item. A series of packets may not arrive at their destination in the same order in which they are sent.

Some networks, such as the venerable Arpanet or the Ethernet LAN, address these problems in part with dedicated high-speed physical connections and relatively expensive hardware interfaces at each site. A typical LAN using these techniques may be able to sustain an information transfer rate of several million bytes per second. Other networks use only basic communication hardware, relying on software techniques to maintain the message system. Transfer rates in these networks may be limited to a few hundred bytes per second or less.

Some other network design issues have an important impact on system performance. A key issue is the **network topology,** the pattern by which sites are physically connected to one another. This topology is a tradeoff between the need for fast communication among all sites and tolerance of failures in sites or communication paths, versus the cost of many long communication lines and the difficulty of connecting a single site to a very large number of others.

Another important issue is the philosophy by which connections are established between sites. In the **virtual circuit** strategy, a path is first identified between the sites, after which a sequence of packets is routed along this path. This method usually includes various types of error checking. In the alternative **datagram** strategy, each packet is individually routed to its destination. Processing may be more efficient, but more error checking is left to the higher-level software.

Every network must solve a series of increasingly higher-level problems to provide effective communications. Recent international standards have organized these issues into a seven-layer model of communications, the **Open Systems Interconnection Model (OSI)** [ISO 1983]. The lowest four layers in this model are:

- PHYSICAL LAYER: Establishes electrical and physical connection mechanisms for transmission and recognition of individual bits

- DATA LINK LAYER: Organizes groups of bits into "packets" of data, usually with additional bits for error detection
- NETWORK LAYER: Establishes routes for packets to travel to their destination sites
- TRANSPORT LAYER: Organizes outgoing messages into packets, and assembles incoming packets into messages. Detects errors in packets, requests retransmission, and ensures proper sequencing

A typical distributed operating system assumes the presence of an underlying network that includes these four layers.

The higher-level layers of the OSI model address issues oriented toward the users and the specific application for which the network is being used. These issues may be addressed by a distributed operating system. They include:

- SESSION LAYER: Establishes a logical connection between "users" (or processes) at communicating sites
- PRESENTATION LAYER: Maintains the semantics of data between sites, providing for changes of representation when necessary; provides for compression and decompression of data.
- APPLICATION LAYER: Establishes the appropriate interface to the network for users running specific applications

A distributed OS has at its disposal a large range of useful resources. However, its ability to provide effective sharing of these resources is constrained by several factors:

- NO SHARED MEMORY: All communication between sites must take place through message passing.
- COMMUNICATION LIMITS: The time required to transmit messages is significant, and the volume of messages that can be handled in a given time may be limited.
- DIFFERENT RESOURCE TYPES: The host computers attached to a network may be of different types, and other resource types may differ as well. It can be difficult to make resources equally usable in these diverse environments.
- EXPECTATION OF FAILURES: Because of the large number of hardware and software components included in a complete

computer network, periodic failure of some parts of the network is inevitable.

23.5 DESIGN ISSUES

It has been rightly pointed out by Lamport [1985] that the problems of managing a distributed system are not as radically different from conventional system issues as they may first appear. In each case, the central objective is to execute a body of processes and share a collection of resources. We simply have more than one physical processor to which a process can be assigned.

In a multiprocessor OS, this view may be close to the truth. However, problems arise in areas such as synchronization, since one processor cannot force another to suspend activities. Methods that are adequate to solve such problems in a uniprocessor environment may no longer be satisfactory.

In a network-based OS, additional problems arise due to the costs of communication, and issues over the view of the network presented to the user.

A significant design issue is the basic communication method. Just as in a uniprocessor, processes on a distributed system may communicate either through **shared memory** or by **message passing.** Multiprocessor operating systems may use either method. In a network, shared memory is not feasible, and message passing is the only available mechanism. The two methods lead to markedly different system designs. We will focus primarily on message passing systems in the remainder of this chapter.

Consideration of the user's view of the network leads to the concept of **network transparency.** Ordinarily, each user of a computer connected to a network is fully aware of the network's role in accessing remote resources, and must explicitly work through the network to make use of these resources. A separate login procedure may be required for each remote site, and transfer of information between sites may be cumbersome and subject to errors.

A distributed operating system can alleviate some of the problems by providing a common login procedure and user information file for a group of computers. However, access to remote files and programs may still require explicit communication with the remote site.

The concept of transparency establishes an objective of hiding the network from the user to the greatest extent possible. In a perfectly transparent system the user is unaware of where each file is stored, or which site may be executing each program. Resources may be assigned to sites, and moved between sites, at the discretion of the operating system, but the user is unaware of this activity.

Transparency may not be desirable in all cases, and it was not an objective of the earliest DCSs. Full transparency leads to a high volume of message traffic initiated by the operating system, which may cause substantial reductions in performance. Moreover, at times explicit control over resource location is wanted. A user may want to run a specific processor or to store files at a specific location (or set of locations). Local sites may want to keep some resources under their own control and not yield them to the system.

Transparency is also generally not possible in an added-layer or network operating system. Since each user accesses resources through an unmodified OS designed for a uniprocessor, more visible mechanisms must be used to extend this access to remote resources.

In an increasing number of contexts, however, a high degree of transparency is seen as both feasible and desirable. In a local area network comprised largely of similar computers and under the control of a single organization, all the ingredients are present to support the transparency goal. A high volume of communication can be supported, and the system is best viewed as a unified pool of resources.

23.6 SOME EXAMPLE SYSTEMS

An early example of a non-transparent distributed operating system is the National Software Works (NSW) [Forsdick 78] developed on the Arpanet. The object of the NSW, shown in Figure 23–5, was to make a body of "tools," including specialized processors, databases, and files, easily available to researchers distributed throughout the network. Its features included a common user file and login procedure for the entire network, stored at a single master site. A common file-naming system is also supported, using a central catalog that translates network file names to the names used by the host system storing the file. The site location is an explicit part of the network file names.

A typical network operating system was RSEXEC, also operating on the Arpanet [Thomas 1973]. This system attempted to unify a set of PDP-10s, each operating under the TENEX operating system. Another example already cited is the Newcastle Connection.

A recent example of a fully transparent operating system for a local area network is LOCUS [Popek & Walker 85], an extensive redesign of UNIX to provide distributed processing capabilities. LOCUS, originally developed at UCLA, is now available as a commercial product. This system will be used as an example throughout this chapter.

Figure 23–5 The National Software Works

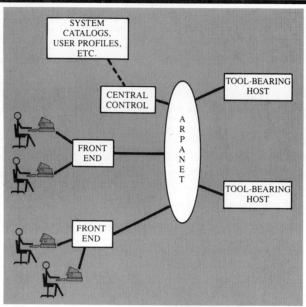

23.7 ORGANIZING THE OPERATING SYSTEM

Two fundamental requirements of any running process or program are memory space to hold instructions and data and a CPU to execute the program. These requirements apply to an operating system as well. In a uniprocessor with a single CPU and a single physical memory, the appropriate memory and CPU for the OS or other programs is obvious. In a distributed computing system, these issues raise two important questions about the operating system: "Where is it stored?" and "Who runs it?" The first question arises if there is more than one memory; the second because there is more than one CPU.

In a system using shared memory, the single shared memory may be the obvious place to store the OS. If there is no central memory, there are three choices, contrasted in Figure 23–6:

1. CENTRALIZED: Store the entire operating system in one memory

2. PARTITIONED: Divide the OS into parts and store different parts at different sites

3. REPLICATED: Store multiple copies of the OS (or partitions of the OS) at several different sites

Figure 23-6 Placement Strategies for a Distributed Operating System

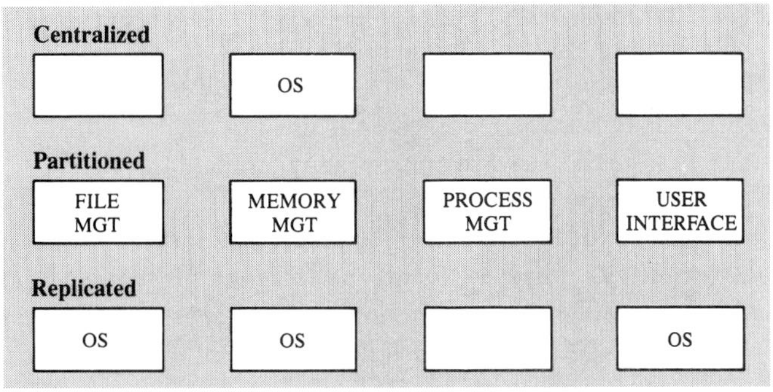

Centralized			
	OS		

Partitioned			
FILE MGT	MEMORY MGT	PROCESS MGT	USER INTERFACE

Replicated			
OS	OS		OS

In a multiprocessor, the question of "who runs" the OS is often resolved by a **master-slave** approach. One CPU executes the OS, while the rest are seen only as processing resources which can be scheduled. In a network environment, a more autonomous approach must be taken. Each of several CPUs may participate in running the OS, and there may be no distinct master CPU.

23.8 DISTRIBUTED FILE SYSTEMS

Many of the important issues in the design of a transparent distributed OS revolve around the design of a **distributed file system (DFS).** The objective of a DFS is to present the user with a virtual, unified file system in which files may be accessed without concern for their actual location, local or remote. In addition, a DFS may support multiple copies of files to improve storage reliability, or to provide copies close to their users to improve performance.

There are thus two unique requirements imposed on a DFS:

- LOCATION-INDEPENDENT NAMES: No part of the name of a file may relate to its physical location, since that location may change, or copies may exist at various locations.
- MULTIPLE COPIES: The system should allow multiple copies of selected files possibly at different sites.

When a file is opened in a DFS, a nearby copy may be chosen for access. If there is no nearby copy, a new copy may be made at a close location.

Alternately, data may be transferred as needed to or from the closest copy available. This approach may be more efficient if only small amounts of data are to be transferred.

When a file having multiple copies is updated, all copies must be kept consistent. If the update is made initially to one copy and then propagated to others, the OS must avoid using copies that are not up to date. The problem becomes serious if some copies are temporarily unavailable.

LOCUS solves many of these problems in a UNIX-like file system by extending the concept of "mounting" a filegroup contained on a physical volume, to allow multiple physical locations for each filegroup. Each location may store any subset of the files in the group. Updates are always made to a specific "primary" storage site, which holds a copy of every file in the group, and then propagated to other sites. A system of "version numbers" is used to detect file copies that are not up to date.

23.9 DISTRIBUTED PROCESSES

A distributed operating system must support moving processes between sites, often without explicit control of the user. This activity is called **process migration.** It may occur when processes are created, or at later points in their lifetime. Process migration may be desired for several reasons:

- EFFICIENT RESOURCE ACCESS: As an alternative to moving required resources to the vicinity of a process (which is not always feasible), the process may move closer to the resources.

- LOAD BALANCING: When some CPUs are excessively busy and others are idle, processes may relocate to balance the load.

- TASK FORCES: A process may be part of a group of cooperating processes, sometimes called a **task force.** It may be desirable to have processes in such a group executing at the same time on different CPUs. At other times, it might be preferable to locate them on the same CPU.

LOCUS supports an explicit form of process migration, allowing programs to specify the moving of processes to a remote site when they are created or at a later time. A predetermined list of suitable sites is used to determine where the process will be moved.

23.10 SYNCHRONIZATION ISSUES

The presence of true concurrency in a distributed system, and possibly a very large set of concurrent processes, greatly complicates issues of synchronization. Mutual exclusion must be enforced on files and other resources that are much more likely to be requested by multiple users. Standard methods such as semaphores may not be sufficient. A "test-and-set" instruction located at one CPU will not guarantee mutual exclusion; instead, a lock is required at the resource itself.

LOCUS provides some measure of synchronization on files by assigning a single "current synchronization site" (CSS) to each filegroup. This approach is illustrated in Figure 23–7. All file openings must be mediated by the CSS. This site becomes a weakness in case of failure, but other sites can assume the role of CSS as necessary.

Figure 23–7   File Access Synchronization in LOCUS

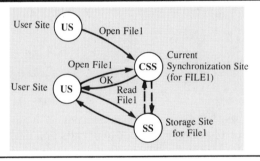

Deadlock is much more likely in a distributed system, and is difficult to detect because there is no central up-to-date knowledge of the complete system state. A possible solution is based on special messages, which move throughout the system gathering the necessary information. LOCUS avoids dealing with this problem due to the centralized CSS and the generally relaxed attitude of UNIX toward deadlock problems.

Other types of synchronization are necessary for explicit communication between processes. One interesting requirement for processes in a task force may be to ensure that several processes are active at the same period of real time.

23.11 INCREASING RELIABILITY

A distributed OS can improve reliability; however it begins with serious reliability problems. With so many physical resources of various types, some are bound to fail periodically. This problem cannot be ignored.

One method of improving reliability is to maintain multiple copies of selected files, as we discussed under the topic of distributed file systems. Another, more general solution seeks to improve the reliability of processes by partitioning their activity into **atomic transactions.** An atomic transaction is a sequence of activities which, once started, should be completed in its entirety. This technique minimizes the risk of failure while the changes caused by such a transaction are in a partial state. If the transaction can almost always be viewed by other processes as either not yet begun or already complete, then it can be restarted in case of failure, and no process will observe an inconsistent state.

In LOCUS, file updates are made into atomic transactions by delaying the visible installation of the updates until a COMMIT operation is performed. This is accomplished simply under UNIX by reflecting all changes only in a private copy of the file's i-node kept in memory, which can be used to rapidly update the disk copy when changes are complete.

23.12 OTHER ISSUES

Several additional issues raise further difficulties in a distributed OS. For example, the concept of **remote procedure calls** is a desirable feature that would allow any procedure to be called at a remote site as easily as a local site. Problems of maintaining efficiency while keeping the procedure call atomic need to be overcome to provide this capability.

The benefits of atomic transactions are increased if transactions can be nested. This flexibility, which would allow their use more generally as a program construction tool, is quite difficult to support in current systems.

To take advantage of the potential for concurrent cooperating processes, a distributed OS should support concurrent programming languages—that is, languages that include built-in mechanisms to specify concurrency within a program. Tools for the construction of concurrent programs are also important. Facilities in these categories are only beginning to be developed.

Another serious problem that must be dealt with in many systems is **network partitioning.** Partitioning may occur when elements of the network fail or are removed. The result can be the temporary separation of isolated sites or subnetworks; these may continue functioning but be unable to communicate with the main network. If copies of a replicated file exist in separate partitions, they may be separately updated, and then need to be recognized and reconciled when the partitions rejoin. Only partial solutions exist to this problem.

Transparency becomes difficult to maintain when the network includes different types of host computers. Executable programs must be adapted to the proper computer. Data formats may need to be translated when files or processes are moved. This is also a difficult problem, for which only limited solutions have been developed.

23.13 SUMMARY

The capabilities of a computing system may be increased by including two or more CPUs in a single system. A multiprocessor is a single computing system that includes multiple CPUs. A network is a collection of distinct computing systems that are able to communicate reliably by message passing. If the elements of a network are confined to a relatively small area and connected by high-performance communication links, the network is a local area network; otherwise it is a wide area network. Both multiprocessors and networks have become increasing common with declining hardware costs and improving communication mechanisms.

If a set of processors in a multiprocessor or network can cooperate on a common workload, they are said to form a distributed computing system. Some possible objectives of a distributed computing system include human communication, resource sharing, increased reliability, and load balancing. To meet such objectives, a distributed computing system generally requires a distributed operating system as a common control mechanism.

Multiprocessor operating systems tend to be unique and are not considered by this text. Distributed operating systems for networks may be called network operating systems, but this term is often reserved for control software that forms a layer above a conventional OS.

Although a few distributed operating systems have appeared on WANs like the Arpanet, most are designed to control systems on a LAN. In this environment computers tend to be similar and under common jurisdiction, so communication is less costly and more reliable.

Distributed operating systems on a LAN often strive for a high degree of transparency so that the network is hidden from its users, making all resources appear the same whether they are actually local or remote. An important consideration in such a system, which has no shared memory, is the location of the OS. A centralized location would limit the benefits of the distributed system. More often, the functions of the OS are partitioned or replicated, and assigned to many different sites.

One important objective of a distributed OS in such an environment may be to support a distributed file system. Such a DFS makes files throughout the network seem equally accessible to all sites. It may include mechanisms to move files around as needed, and to maintain multiple copies of files for improved performance and increased reliability. A somewhat more ambitious goal is support for process migration.

Synchronization problems, such as mutual exclusion and deadlock, must be reexamined in a distributed environment. Solutions are very important but may be more difficult to provide than in a non-distributed system. New mechanisms are required to address these problems. A number of other problems unique to distributed environments must also be considered.

FOR FURTHER READING

A very large body of literature on distributed operating systems has been produced; indeed, the majority of OS research in the 1980s has focused on distributed environments. Much of the literature, however, is fairly advanced, and intended for readers experienced in OS design.

An introduction to many issues of distributed OS design is given by Tanenbaum & van Renesse [1985]. This article includes a survey of issues and a comparative description of four systems. Selected issues are discussed in the texts by Deitel [1984, Chapters 11 & 16], Peterson and Silberschatz [1985, Chapter 13], and Maekawa et al. [1987, Chapters 6 & 7]. An excellent but sophisticated presentation of a wide range of issues is found in the course notes edited by Lampson et al. [1981]. The extended case study of LOCUS [Popek & Walker 1985] provides a lucid discussion of many important issues as well as a set of solutions designed for a UNIX environment.

Many other books and papers treat specific issues. Raynal [1986] gives a thorough and readable survey of solutions to mutual exclusion in both centralized and distributed situations. Ho & Ramamoorthy [1982] consider distributed deadlock detection. Lamport [1978] discusses methods of establishing the order of events in a distributed system. Birrell & Nelson [1984] study remote procedure calls, and Brereton [1983] considers issues of network partitioning. Lamport [1984] offers an interesting perspective on a number of issues.

Descriptions of operating systems for multiprocessors and other types of parallel processors include those of Hydra [Wulf et al. 1980] for C.mmp, StarOS [Jones et al. 1979] and MEDUSA [Ousterhout 1980] for Cm*, DEMOS [Powell 1977] for the CRAY-1, and the HEP OS [Schmidt 1980] for the HEP parallel processor. The network OSs NSW and RSEXEC are described by Millstein [1977] and Thomas [1973], respectively, and compared by Forsdick et al. [1978].

Besides LOCUS, descriptions of a very large number of specific distributed OSs for LAN environments have been published.   A selection of examples includes the Newcastle Connection [Brownbridge et al. 1982], the V Kernel [Cheriton 1984], Eden [Lazowska et al. 1981], Accent [Rashid & Robinson 1981], Amoeba [Tanenbaum & Mullender 1981], and the Cambridge Model Distributed System [Wittie & van Tilborg 1980]. Further examples are listed in Appendix C.

IMPORTANT TERMS

atomic transaction
datagram
distributed computing system (DCS)
distributed file system (DFS)
distributed operating system
host
local area network (LAN)
long-haul network
master-slave
message passing
multiprocessor
network
network operating system (NOS)
network partitioning

network topology
network transparency
Open Systems Interconnection
   Model (OSI)
packet
process migration
remote procedure call
shared memory
site
task force
uniprocessor
virtual circuit
wide area network (WAN)

REVIEW QUESTIONS

1. Explain the difference between a network and a distributed computing system.

2. Give three reasons why distributed operating systems are more common on local area networks than on wide area networks.

3. Explain briefly four possible objectives of a distributed operating system on a local area network.

4. Describe the potential benefits of transparency.

5. Describe three resource management problems that may be especially difficult to solve in a transparent distributed operating system. Explain why.

6. Explain three strategies for deciding where to locate the operating system in a distributed OS without shared memory. State a possible advantage of each strategy.

7. In a distributed file system, it may be necessary to support multiple copies of a single file.

    a. Give two reasons why multiple copies are desirable.

    b. Explain two problems that may arise in implementing this feature.

8. Why is deadlock detection more difficult in a distributed system than in a non-distributed system?

9. A distributed LAN OS is more likely to experience failures than an OS on a single computer, yet it can be made more reliable than any single OS. Explain why this is possible, and describe two mechanisms to achieve it.

⟰ ASSIGNMENTS ⟰

1. Give some examples of situations in which complete transparency in a distributed OS might not be desirable.

2. In a single computing system, timing information is derived from a master clock provided by the hardware. On a network, however, no single clock can be directly accessible by all systems. Suggest a way in which two processes located at different sites could agree on "what time" a certain event occurred.

3. Describe an application for which each of the following mechanisms would be useful:

    a. replicated files

    b. task forces

    c. remote procedure calls

    d. nested atomic transactions

4. Describe some problems that may need to be overcome in implementing a transparent distributed OS on a network including several different types of computers.

Hardware and Software

A.1 INTRODUCTION

This appendix provides an overview of basic concepts of computer hardware and software discussed throughout the text. The first several sections deal with computer hardware organization. An understanding of some basic hardware concepts is of great importance to the student or designer of operating systems. The resources that an OS must control are either hardware elements or logical resources created within hardware storage. The tools that the OS has available to carry out its management responsibilities are based on computer instructions and physical resources manipulated by those instructions.

The abilities and limitations of each OS are profoundly influenced by the structure of the specific computer or computers on which it must execute. Functions that may be performed by hardware on one computer may need to be carried out by operating system software on another. Algorithms, which are highly effective when special hardware resources are available, may be impractical without those resources. Some OS objectives, especially in the areas of memory management and security, cannot be achieved without appropriate hardware structures.

The complexity of an architecture can also affect the implementation. Managing complex architectures can be a difficult and time-consuming problem in the design of an operating system. Differences in hardware organization greatly limit the ability to adapt operating systems to work on more than one type of computer. For all of these reasons, an operating system designer must thoroughly understand the structure of the computer on which the operating system is to be implemented.

In its role of providing effective support for programs submitted by users, an operating system must also work together with a variety of other software components in a total computing system. Chief among these programs are compilers and other software used to translate programs from the languages in which they were originally written to the form required for execution. Programs of this type, together with the operating system itself, are called **system programs** to distinguish them from **application programs** which perform the normal work of most computer users. The organization of system programs, and their implications for the operating system, are considered in additional sections of this appendix.

A number of general software concepts of program and data structures are of particular importance in designing operating systems. These concepts are reviewed briefly in the final sections of the appendix.

Much of the material of this appendix will be familiar to students who have completed basic courses in programming, data structures, and assembly language. However, because the ideas and terms presented here are used throughout this text, all students should read through them for review and to establish some consistent terminology. The presentation of many concepts in this appendix is necessarily brief. References that provide additional detail on these concepts are cited at the end of the appendix.

A.2 ARCHITECTURE AND IMPLEMENTATION

The structure and organization of a computing system may be studied from many different viewpoints. The student of operating systems is concerned with the elements that the OS can use in some way and the operations available for manipulating these elements. These elements may be studied individually or grouped into subsystems within the total computer system. Elements accessible in this way to a particular user or program are said to be **visible** to that user or program. Those elements and operations that are visible to application or system programs (including the operating system), together with their interconnections and relationships, will be considered to be part of the **architecture** of a computer system.

The elements and operations of a computer architecture are in turn constructed from low-level parts, such as electronic circuits. These lower-level components are considered part of the **implementation** of a computer architecture. Thus, architecture refers to all of the features of a computer that affect the types of programs it can run or the outcome of those programs; implementation refers to internal components and methods, mainly hardware, that may be used to produce these features. This distinction is important in computer series, such as the IBM S/370 or Digital Equipment PDP/11 or VAX, in which a family of computers can run the same programs, although some are larger or faster than others and differ in other limited ways. Computers in the same family have the same architecture but may differ radically in their implementation.

The exact boundary between architecture and implementation is not easily agreed upon. We use the working definitions given above. In this text we are concerned primarily with the architecture of computer systems.

A.3 COMPUTER SYSTEM ORGANIZATION

This section begins our examination of the hardware architecture of computer systems. We will focus particular attention on structures that are of greater importance to the operating system than to most other programs.

A very high-level view of a typical computer architecture includes four principal components, as shown in Figure A-1. The heart of the computer, the **central processing unit (CPU)**, is responsible for interpreting and executing the individual instructions of any computer program. The CPU works closely with the **main memory**, which is the component having principal responsibility for information storage. All instructions to be executed, and most data to be accessed, must be stored in the main memory in order to be used.

Figure A-1 A Typical Computer System Organization

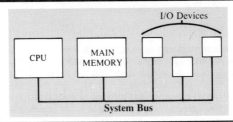

A third major component is a collection of **input and output (I/O) devices**. ("Input and output" is usually abbreviated as I/O, and this convention will be followed throughout the text.) These devices provide the means by which the computer communicates with the outside world. They include such familiar elements as video terminals, printers, punched-card readers, and communication modems. Also in this category are **storage devices**, which supplement the main memory by providing additional forms of information storage. Magnetic disks and tapes are the most common examples of storage devices.

The components described so far must be connected to one another in some way. This interconnection structure is the final component in our high-level view. Its form can vary among different computers and has an important impact on the architecture. For example, it may or may not be possible for data to be transferred directly from main memory to output devices without passing through the CPU.

A common interconnection structure now found in most small and medium computers is the **system bus**. This is the structure shown in Figure A-1. All elements are connected to a common communication path which includes control circuits with the ability to direct each message to its proper destination. This structure is very flexible; its major disadvantage is that communication can be somewhat slow.

A.4 INSTRUCTIONS AND DATA

A computer operates by executing programs that manipulate data. Both programs and data, when in actual use, are stored in the main memory of the computer.

A main memory stores all information as sequences of binary (or base 2) values called **bits**. This name is a contraction for "binary digit"; in the binary number system, each digit may be either a one or a zero. Information of all types may be encoded as sequences of bits using this method.

Bits are grouped for convenience into various types of units. The term **byte** is used for a set of bits large enough to represent the code value assigned to one **character** (a printable symbol such as a digit or letter). In most computers, the size of a byte is eight bits. The term **word** is applied to the number of bits required to hold the most common data item such as an integer. The most common word sizes on current computers are 16 or 32 bits.

The main memory is divided into distinct locations identified by a number called an **address**. Usually the addresses available form a consecutive sequence of integers starting from zero. Each location usually holds the same number of bits; most often there is a distinct location for each byte. The distinction between memory locations and the values they contain is a fundamental concept that must be understood by all computer programmers.

Quantities of memory are often referred to in units of approximately (but not exactly) one thousand or one million bytes. A **kilobyte** is 1,024 bytes, or 1K bytes. The exact number is useful because it represents 2 to the 10th power. A memory of 16K bytes is one that contains 16 x 1,0234, or 16,384 bytes. Similarly, the term **megabyte**, or 1M bytes, describes the quantity 2 to the 20th power, or 1,048,576 bytes.

Programs are encoded and stored as sequences of **machine instructions**, each specifying a simple action, as discussed below. Each machine instruction occupies one or more words.

A.5 CPU ORGANIZATION

The CPU is responsible for executing the machine instructions that comprise a computer program. The CPU must read each instruction from memory, examine it, and execute it. Execution may involve reading data from memory, performing basic arithmetic or logical operations on data, and storing results in memory. In addition to data in main memory, a limited local storage for individual items is provided within the CPU itself.

The CPU can be partitioned logically into three sections, as shown in Figure A-2. The **storage section** includes the local storage for the CPU, which consists of devices called **registers** Each register is usually the size of a memory word and is designed to hold one data item. The collection of registers provided varies greatly between architectures. The majority are usually used as **data registers**, which hold data as needed for CPU operations. Additional register types that may be present include:

- **index registers** and **base registers**, used for computing data and instruction addresses
- **stack pointers**, which manage one or more pushdown stacks used automatically by certain machine instructions
- a **program counter (PC)**, which keeps track of the location of the current instruction
- a **program status word (PSW)**, which records the value of assorted CPU conditions, modes, and status values

Another section of the CPU is the **processing section**, which is responsible for carrying out most of the data manipulations required by each instruction. The principal component of the processing section is the **arithmetic and logic unit (ALU),** which contains circuits to perform basic arithmetic computations such as addition, subtraction, multiplication and division and basic logical operations such as "and," "or," and complement.

The final section of the CPU is the **control section**, which is responsible for directing the activities of the CPU in processing its various instructions.

The set of instructions available in a machine instruction set varies widely among computer architectures. Section A.7 discusses the general properties of instruction sets and identifies some specific instructions of importance to operating systems.

Figure A–2 Sections of a CPU

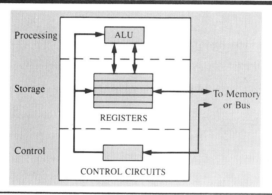

Under normal conditions, the CPU continues indefinitely fetching and executing instructions in a prescribed order. Each new instruction is taken from the memory location immediately following the previous instruction. This sequence changes only when certain instructions specify a different location for fetching the next one. Occasionally, special program conditions or external events can cause the CPU to suspend normal execution of a program and begin executing instructions from a different part of memory. Such an occurrence is called an **interrupt**.

An important concept of CPU control, present in all but the smallest computers, is the designation of certain instructions as **privileged instructions.** These instructions may be executed only when the CPU is set to **privileged mode**, which is accomplished by setting a specific bit in the PSW. As a general rule, the operating system runs in privileged mode; most other programs do not. If a program attempts a privileged instruction in the wrong mode, the CPU will refuse to execute it. Instead, it will perform an interrupt so that suitable action can be taken by the operating system. Privileged instructions allow certain sensitive resources, such as I/O devices, to be controlled exclusively by the operating system. They are essential in multiprogramming operating systems to allow safe management of more than one process at the same time.

Another important element of the control section of most CPUs is an **interval timer**. This device maintains an accurate count of time in units of some small fraction of a second. Timer values can be set and examined by machine instructions (usually privileged). A timer can also be set to cause an interrupt when a certain value is reached. This mechanism can determine the time between various events or force an activity to stop after a certain time period. An important additional role of a timer is to allow an OS to keep track of the actual time of day.

A.6 MEMORY STRUCTURES

The second major component of a computer system is the collection of elements that are capable of storing information. The terms **memory** and **storage** are both widely used to describe such elements; we will use these terms interchangeably in this text. (The alternate name **store** is also preferred by some writers). We will call the memory unit that works directly with the

CPU and holds the bulk of programs and data in current use **main memory**; this unit is also frequently referred to as **primary storage**.

The main memory and the other storage elements present in a computer system form a memory system that must provide both working storage and long-term storage for all the information that needs to be retained. This section examines some concepts associated with memory systems.

Memory Hierarchy

The main memory is perhaps the most important component of a memory system. However, a number of other components play an important role as well. These various memories form a **memory hierarchy**, as shown in Figure A-3. Each level in this hierarchy has different characteristics and is used for a somewhat different purpose. Memories at the highest level tend to be fast, small, and expensive; those at the lowest levels are slow but inexpensive and have a much higher capacity. Not all systems include exactly the same set of levels, but a roughly similar hierarchy is almost always present.

The main memory is the most visible level in this hierarchy. The registers of the CPU form another level, which we have already introduced. The remaining levels in our example are:

- **cache memory:** a small fast memory often present within the CPU. It is used to hold selected data from the main memory, providing faster access than would be possible if the cache were not present.
- **secondary memory:** a storage level, usually provided by magnetic disks, that contains large amounts of data not currently required in main memory but likely to be needed at a future time. Much of this memory is usually organized into a file system.
- **archival memory:** a storage level, provided by magnetic tapes or certain kinds of disks, for information that can be removed from the computer and stored on a shelf until needed. Because the storage devices are removable, the capacity of this level is unlimited. However, time is required to make this data available for use. Archival memory is used for large collections of data that will be needed only rarely, and for backup copies of important data to be preserved in case the original data is destroyed.

Figure A-3 A Typical Memory Hierarchy

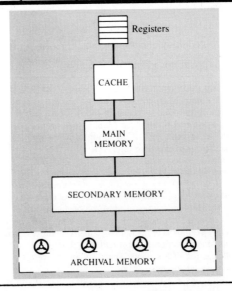

Cache memories are automatically managed by hardware, and are of minor concern to the operating system. However, they have important similarities to virtual memory systems. This level is absent on some smaller computers.

Management of secondary storage is an important OS responsibility. File systems are implemented on secondary storage devices. These devices are also important for various types of temporary storage required by the operating system itself.

The OS is also responsible for the management of archival storage devices. An important factor in the reliability of a computer system is a systematic use of this level of the storage hierarchy for backup storage.

Management of secondary and archival memory depends greatly on the properties of the physical devices used. Typical storage devices are described in Appendix B.

Address Spaces

Machine instructions reference data which is stored, or appears to be stored, in main memory. The instructions themselves are stored in a similar fashion. Each location in memory is identified by an address. Many data items and structures actually occupy a series of consecutive locations.

The collection of addresses that can be specified by machine instructions forms an **address space**. Here, the word "space" is used in the mathematical sense as a collection of locations. An address space is usually characterized by a consecutive sequence of address values ranging from zero to some fixed maximum. The maximum value for an address space is determined by the computer architecture and is an important concern in the management of larger programs.

Often, a single address space corresponds directly to locations in the main memory. In other cases, a computer may use two or more address spaces, such as separate spaces for instructions and data. Yet another address space may be reserved for input/output devices, which must be assigned some type of address, as discussed below.

Important advantages can be gained by separating the address space visible to a program from the memory locations physically present in the computer. This separation can be achieved by hardware mechanisms that translate addresses expressed in instructions to different addresses in the physical memory system. This type of memory translation is the basis of virtual memory techniques.

Memory translation separates the address space seen by a program, called its **virtual address space** (also called the **logical address space**), from the **physical address space** (also known as the **real address space**) provided by the main memory (see Figure A-4). In many cases, each process is provided with its own virtual address space. An address in a virtual address space is called a **virtual address**. This distinction between various types of address spaces is used as needed throughout the text.

Addressing Techniques

An important characteristic of the architecture of a computer system is the collection of methods available for expressing addresses within machine instructions. These **addressing techniques** are very important to an operating system for several reasons. First, addressability of programs and data areas within the operating system must be managed. Second, requirements for loading programs and controlling processes can be greatly affected by how addressing is done on a given computer. Several common methods are described below. Each method begins with an address value contained in a portion of the machine instruction. The result address value produced by each addressing technique is called the **effective address** specified by the instruction. This effective address is a virtual address. A separate translation mechanism, not visible to most programs, may also be used to convert this virtual address to a physical address.

Figure A–4 Virtual and Physical Address Spaces

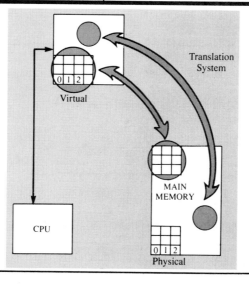

- **direct addressing,** also called **absolute addressing:** In this method, addresses in the machine instructions are precisely the effective addresses. This is the simplest and most straightforward technique.
- **indirect addressing:** In this method, the address contained in the machine instruction identifies a memory location at which the actual address is stored. Indirect addressing is useful when the space available for address values in each instruction is not large enough to cover the entire virtual address space.
- **indexed addressing:** This technique constructs an address from two parts. The first part is the address contained in the instruction; the second is a value contained in a specified index register. These two values are added to form the virtual address. Indexed addressing is often used explicitly by programs to separate the starting address of a table or array from relative locations within it.
- **based addressing:** This technique is identical to indexed addressing, except that the value added is taken from a base register rather than an index register. Based addressing is usually used to systematically modify addresses throughout an entire program section, rather than to aid in accessing specific data structures.

    IBM's S/370 and its successors provide prominent examples of this technique. A limited area of memory is addressable by each instruction. A base register points to the beginning of this area and the address contained in the instruction (called an "offset") determines the specific location within this area to be addressed. The addressability is managed by loading and maintaining base registers to point to the desired data and program areas.
- **PC-relative addressing:** In this method, the program counter is used as a "floating" base register. Addressing memory is done by adding the value contained in the PC to the address contained in the instruction. If the address to be referenced is within a program, its offset from the current instruction (which the PC points to) will remain the same, no matter where the program loads. Using PC relative addressing can simplify writing what is called position independent code—code that executes the same way without adjusting addresses, no matter where it loads. This technique is used, for example, on the PDP-11.

Some of these methods may be combined in a single instruction. In particular, indexed addressing is often combined with based or PC-relative. If a computer supports multiple types of addressing, each instruction must specify in some way what type is to be used.

Examples of each addressing technique are shown in Figure A-5. Each example starts with an instruction located at virtual address 672 and contains the value 500 in an address field. This value, together with the contents of other locations and registers, determines the effective addresses shown in the right-hand column.

The type of addressing available can have an important impact on the procedure required for loading programs and the ability of the OS to move programs and data as required. If direct addressing is used, programs must contain the actual addresses to be used for data references and branching. This can be a problem for larger operating systems that run multiple processes simultaneously. The location available for a particular program may not be known in advance. Moreover, it may be desirable to move a program that has partially completed.

Figure A–5 Examples of Addressing Techniques

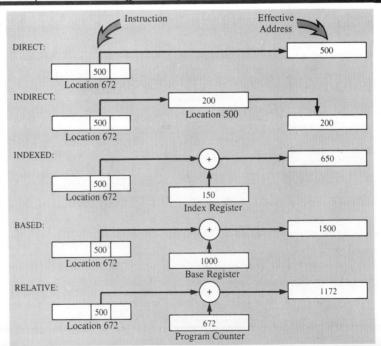

Therefore, if you must use direct addressing, it may be necessary to systematically modify programs during the loading process to adapt them to the particular location in which they are loaded. Usually, it is impossible to move programs once they have been loaded into memory.

Base addressing and PC-relative addressing provide two possible solutions to this problem. Using these techniques, programs can be made insensitive to locations, provided that certain disciplines are followed carefully by the compiler or assembly language programmer.

A more comprehensive solution is available on architectures providing separation of address spaces. In this case, the virtual address space visible to each process can be constant and predictable, even though its relation to the physical address space is unpredictable and changing.

A.7 INSTRUCTION TYPES

The types of machine instructions provided by various computer architectures can vary greatly. Some systems offer very rich and complex instruction sets, featuring operations on a large assortment of data types. Other architectures provide a much simpler set of operations from which more complex ones can be built. The detailed structure of each instruction will be vastly different from one architecture to another.

Examining the full range of possibilities for computer instruction sets is a subject for a computer architecture text and is well outside the scope of this book. Here we will summarize some general categories of machine instructions and discuss one instruction of particular interest to operating systems.

The instructions recognized by most conventional CPUs can be grouped into four main categories:

1. **data manipulation instructions** operate on data values (input) and produce new data values (results). The input data values are obtained from main memory or from registers, and results are stored in similar places. The operations include simple copying, integer arithmetic, logical transformations, and a variety of more complex operations that support a selection of data types.
2. **branch instructions** specify a possible location for the next instruction other than the usual one (the location following the current instruction in memory). Usually the branch is conditional—that is, it will only be taken if certain conditions are true in registers or status flags. This category includes "call" instructions that are branches to subprograms. A call instruction must save the value of the PC in some way before branching so that a proper return can be made to the instruction following the call.
3. **I/O instructions** specify data transfers and control operations involving I/O devices. This category can be empty in some computers that handle I/O transfers in a different way, called **memory-mapped I/O.**
4. **control instructions** include miscellaneous categories such as halting the computer or modifying certain system flags and control registers. Most control instructions are usually privileged.

A number of specific instructions present in many architectures are of particular interest to the operating system. Prominent in this category is the **system call instruction**, used by application programs, similar to a procedure call. However, its exclusive purpose is to request services from the operating system. This instruction performs two important actions simultaneously:

1. It transfers control to a location within the operating system, saving the return address like a normal call.
2. It switches the CPU into privileged mode.

Unlike normal call instructions, the destination for a system call is not specified by the instruction. Instead, the destination address is either fixed by the hardware or is fetched indirectly from a location that is fixed by the hardware. Thus it can be guaranteed that the system call always gives control to the operating system, providing a safe solution to the problem of how to switch into privileged mode without violating the integrity of the privilege system.

Because the destination is not specified by the instruction, the system call instruction itself can be shorter. Shorter length helps reduce the storage requirements of many programs. Moreover, the system call provides a link between application programs and the OS that will not change if the OS is modified. The impact upon programs caused by changes to the OS is limited. The system call instruction is sometimes considered to be a special type of interrupt, as discussed in the next section.

Other instructions of particular importance to the OS are needed to fulfill specific responsibilities in memory management, process management, and other areas. Some newer architectures are offering extensive support for operating system requirements as these requirements become better understood.

A.8 SYSTEM SOFTWARE

An operating system must interact with a variety of other system programs in a computing environment to provide effective support for users and application programs. This section surveys some of the more important system program issues related to their function.

Programming Languages

All programs, including the operating system itself, must be written in some type of programming language. Each program is then converted into a sequence of machine instructions through a translation process.

Machine language is the binary language that the computer understands. While used in the early days directly for programming, its value is now limited to debugging and problem solving within an operating system.

Assembly language provides a series of readable codes or "mnemonics," which correspond to machine language, roughly on a one-to-one basis. Use of assembly language is a first step toward expressing programs in a form more convenient to the programmer. Assembly language is usually combined with abbreviation mechanisms called **macros**. These provide a means of generating many assembler language instructions with one higher-level statement. Many operating systems are written in or supported in assembly language.

Most application programs today are written in **high-level languages**. Well-known examples include FORTRAN, COBOL, PL/I, Pascal, C, and Ada. These languages are much better suited to specific application problems but require complex translators to convert them to machine instructions.

Traditionally, operating systems have not been written in high-level languages because of the need for optimum performance and direct access to hardware resources. As discussed in Chapter 4, this situation is changing. Languages like C and PL/I have been used as implementation languages for well-known operating systems, proving that operating systems do not have to be written in assembly language. The advantage to high-level languages in implementing operating systems is twofold:

1. It is more efficient to write in these languages, and the cost of implementing an operating system should be lower than when using assembly language.
2. The resulting operating system should be more portable.

In many cases the majority of the operating system is written in a high-level language, with only a very small machine-dependent portion written in the assembler language of the computer on which the OS will run.

System Programs

This subsection reviews some important system programs and their relation to the operating system. These programs are often also called **software tools**.

Editors.   Programs that provide convenient, interactive manipulation of text support the creation and modification of document files and programs. Early editors were line-oriented and provided few features. Today's editors are **full-screen editors**, which allow a user to display a screen at a time and easily modify screen text as well as perform complex searches and replacements on text in an entire document or file. All computer science students are familiar with one or more editor programs.

An editor can form an important part of the user interface, at least in the eyes of many users. It is the most commonly used interactive program besides the command interpreter itself. Consistency and cooperation between editors and the overall user interface is very desirable in the design of a complete computing environment.

Assemblers.   Programs that translate assembly language into machine instructions are called **assemblers**. Because the required translation is one-to-one, assemblers can be relatively simple programs. They accept **source programs** in assembly language as input and produce an **object program** as output. In simple cases, this object program may be ready to load and run. More often, it must be processed by a linker, as explained below.

Compilers.   Programs that translate high-level languages to machine instructions are called **compilers**. The work of a compiler is much more complex than that of an assembler. It must examine statements and expressions in a language very different from machine language and determine the correct instruction it should produce for many different cases. Often the compiler produces an assembly language program, which must then be processed by an assembler in a separate step.

Compilers can combine many distinct source program files into a single output file. In addition, they may read input from special files called **libraries**. Libraries are designed to store large numbers of relatively small units of information in a compact, easily accessible way. Efficient management of these libraries can be an important responsibility for the operating system.

Linkers and Loaders. **Linkers**, originally called "linkage editors," are very important in creating loadable images of programs, including their dynamically loadable parts. Linkers accept object programs as input and produce output files known as **load modules**. Linkers have two principal responsibilities:

1. to **relocate** programs by adjusting absolute addresses as needed, if this problem is not solved by hardware techniques
2. to resolve cross-references between distinct object files by determining addresses of global symbols and by loading external subroutines from libraries, inserting their addresses in the appropriate locations in the load module

Another important job performed by many linkers is the management of **overlays**. If the virtual memory space available to a process is not sufficient to hold all needed program modules at once, an overlay system allows selected modules to be loaded as they are required.

A final task that must be carried out is to load an executable program or load module into memory for actual use. This job is sometimes carried out by a distinct system program called the **loader**. Often the loader is a part of the linker. If both are present, their responsibilities may be divided in various ways. Most often, however, the loader **is** considered a part of the operating system itself.

Debuggers. A debugger is a program used during software development or maintenance to examine, analyze, and possibly modify a program that has been suspended after partial execution. Usually, the program may then be allowed to continue. In a few cases, by use of communication techniques between processes, a debugger may analyze a program while it continues to run. Similar tools are available to analyze programs that have completed execution. For effectiveness, an operating system that will support software development applications may need special mechanisms to allow debuggers the type of close control of other processes required for effective use.

Software Development Tools. There are many **software development tools** available to today's OS designer to improve source code control and production of source code. These should be used in operating system development whenever possible, no matter what language is used to implement an operating system.

A.9 PROGRAM AND DATA STRUCTURES

The final section of this appendix surveys a few program and data structuring techniques of particular importance in the design of operating system software.

Events

When a device completes an I/O operation, this is a physical **event**. Events may also be caused by software, such as the completion by a process of some specific activity. Often, processes will wait for the occurrence of specific events. An important job of an operating system is to manage events. Their occurrence is usually recorded in a data structure called an event control block or event flag. Processes waiting for an event will not be given control of the CPU until that event has occurred.

Lists and Queues

As a resource manager, an important responsibility of an operating system is to receive requests from processes for service and to record the requests until the service can be provided. A critical data structure for this purpose is the **queue**. A queue allows information records to be stored in some order as they arrive and to be removed in some order, possibly by a different process, as they are needed. The order of removal is often, but not always, the same as the order of arrival.

To support the types of operations required, queues are usually implemented as **linked lists** on conventional architectures. A few computers, such as the VAX, include machine instructions for queue management, which can contribute to efficient implementation of operating systems.

Reentrant Programs and Subroutines

In a multiprogrammed operating system, often many processes need to execute the same programs or subroutines at the same time. If a program will change in memory during execution, only one process can use it at a time. In this case, each process must have a separate copy. This can lead to inefficient use of storage if many users are running the same editor or command handler or many programs are using the same subroutines to access files.

If programs are designed so they will not change during use (i.e., if all data that is changed resides outside of the executable code and is pointed to by hardware registers), many processes can execute the same program using a single copy of the machine instructions. Of course, each process still requires separate storage for its data pointed to by appropriate hardware registers. Programs and subroutines that are sharable in this way are called **reentrant**. An important use of reentrant programs is in supporting multiple devices of the same type. In this case, control blocks representing each device will be pointed to by registers, and shared instructions will execute using these control blocks as data to determine the device that needs service. Hence, supporting four printers of the same type requires four different control blocks representing the devices, but only one copy of the program (called a **device driver**). An important job of many operating systems is to support automatic sharing of reentrant programs by recognizing when a program or subroutine requested by one process has already been loaded into memory.

IMPORTANT TERMS

absolute addressing	full-screen editor	physical address space
address	high-level language	primary storage
address space	I/O device	privileged instruction
addressing technique	I/O instruction	privileged mode
application program	implementation	processing section
architecture	index register	program counter (PC)
archival memory	indexed addressing	program status word (PSW)
arithmetic and logic unit (ALU)	indirect addressing	queue
assembler	interrupt	real address space
assembly language	interval timer	reentrant
base register	kilobyte	register
based addressing	library	relocate
bit	linked list	secondary memory
branch instruction	linker	software development tool
byte	load module	software tool
cache memory	loader	source program
central processing unit (CPU)	logical address space	stack pointer
character	machine instruction	storage
compiler	machine language	storage device
control instruction	macro	storage section
control section	main memory	store
data manipulation instruction	megabyte	system bus
data register	memory	system call instruction
device driver	memory hierarchy	system program
direct addressing	memory-mapped I/O	virtual address
editor	object program	virtual address space
effective address	overlay	visible
event	PC-relative addressing	word

REVIEW QUESTIONS

1. What type of addressing will best support the implementation of reentrant programs?
2. What is the disadvantage of polling a device to determine when it has completed an I/O operation? How do interrupts solve this problem?
3. How does an architecture that supports a separate I/O space differ from an architecture that supports memory-mapped I/O?
4. List two important differences between a system call instruction and a procedure call instruction, and explain why they are important.
5. Some resource management responsibilities can only be performed effectively with hardware assistance. Describe three examples.

6. Which type of hardware support is *not* required for a safe multiprogramming system?
   a. privileged instructions
   b. timer
   c. mapping registers
   d. interrupts
   e. storage protection

≡ ASSIGNMENTS ≡

1. The following list includes various hardware elements present in a typical computing system. Using the distinctions of this chapter, which would you consider part of the architecture and which part of the implementation?
   a. number of general-purpose registers
   b. size of the address space
   c. microcode implementation of arithmetic instructions
   d. choice of logic circuit types
   e. memory access speed
   f. index registers
   g. memory mapping registers

2. Some typical values for the number of bits provided to represent addresses in various computers include 12 bits (PDP-8), 16 bits (PDP-11,Z-80), 24 bits (S/360), 32 bits (VAX), 48 bits (Intel 80386). Determine the number of distinct locations that can be addressed for each of these cases.

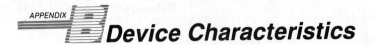

Device Characteristics

B.1 INTRODUCTION

Operating systems must support a wide variety of I/O devices. This appendix describes the characteristics of a number of typical devices. You must understand thoroughly such characteristics before implementing device drivers for a device. Students making use of the projects in this text should pay special attention to the characteristics of devices for which they will be implementing device drivers.

B.2 STORAGE DEVICES

Most file systems are maintained on magnetic storage devices. Implementation of device drivers to control such devices can be quite complex. Chapter 12 concentrates on file systems. The concern in this section is to understand the operation and control of magnetic storage devices. For practical working storage on present-day file systems, these devices are almost always magnetic disks of some type. Magnetic tape was used for early and very simple file systems, but its usefulness is limited by its strictly serial nature. However, tape is still widely used for backup and long-term archiving of file systems, and for transporting files between computers. One non-magnetic technology that promises to gain importance is optical storage. Although writable optical devices are still in the future, read-only disks that combine rapid access and extremely high capacity are currently appearing on the market.

Properties of Magnetic Devices

Magnetic tapes and disks of all types store information by a similar technology. Each device consists of a base of plastic material, on which a thin magnetic surface is deposited. This forms the basic **storage medium**. Information is recorded on this magnetic surface along a set of long, thin regions, called **tracks**. At various points on each track, a bit of information can be written by establishing a certain pattern of magnetic polarization. This is accomplished by maintaining a suitable electric current in an element called a **write head** as the desired spot is moved past it. This magnetization is permanent until disturbed, and it can be sensed by observing the current generated in a similar **read head** as the spot once again moves past. Physical movement of the storage medium is an essential requirement for this type of storage, which is illustrated in Figure B-1.

Figure B–1 Magnetic Storage of Information

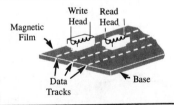

On most disks and some tapes, control information must be recorded initially in certain places to aid in locating the current positions to read and write data. The process of writing this initial information, called **formatting**, must be carried out once before the device can be properly used.

Also on most magnetic devices, some space is set aside for check information to ensure the correctness of the stored data. This is necessary because storage devices sometimes develop flaws that can result in the loss of data. The interface hardware or device driver software must maintain this information and use it to verify the correctness of data that is read from the device. Also, device drivers must often provide the function of formatting these magnetic media.

Magnetic tapes and disks share some common properties that affect their use in file systems. The most important of these properties are:

- NONRANDOM ACCESS. To some degree, all devices fail to provide random access to any part of their contents at equal cost. The time required to reach a desired location depends on the starting location. The extreme serial nature of tapes is obvious. Nonrandom behavior in disks is less severe and varies widely with the type of disk. In most cases, however, the physical placement of information can have a significant effect on performance.

• BLOCKING. Information on tapes and disks is organized into physical blocks, each containing a large number (typically hundreds) of bytes of data. In most cases blocks must be transferred to or from primary memory as a whole. It is not possible to access or modify a partial block.

Magnetic Tapes

Magnetic tapes consist of a continuous strip of a thin storage medium, which can contain a number of parallel tracks. A typical tape for a large computer system is shown in Figure B-2. This tape is one-half inch wide and 2,400 feet long, with nine tracks. It is stored on a large plastic reel, similar to a high-quality audio tape. Tapes are mounted on drives as needed, and may readily be changed.

Figure B–2 Magnetic Tape Structure

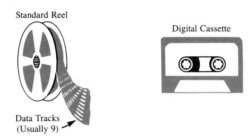

Eight-bit bytes of data are written in parallel on eight tracks; the ninth track receives a parity bit for error checking. Information may be written as densely as several thousand bytes per inch within a block; however, an inch or more may be required between blocks for control information, or simply as an erase gap to separate records. The size of each block may be chosen by the program that writes the data, and could vary from a few bytes to an entire tape.

The appearance of the first microcomputers led to the development of low-cost tape storage on cassettes. This type of storage is also shown in Figure B-2. These tapes are similar to audio cassettes but may be manufactured under more stringent requirements. They have a single track on which data is stored serially. Such cassettes are slow and of limited capacity, but form the only file storage available for some low-cost systems.

In most magnetic tape systems, data can be located and read only when the tape is moving forward. To access data behind the present point, it may be necessary to rewind the tape to the beginning and then search forward. On a large tape this could take several minutes. It is often impossible to write data to a tape without destroying all existing data following that point. Although some tape systems have been devised to overcome some of these problems, as a whole they form a serious limitation.

Because of these limitations, practical use of tapes is confined to applications in which an entire tape will be read or written in sequence. Copying of entire file systems for backup or other purposes is a good example. Within its limits, tape offers a means of inexpensive and compact storage for unlimited amounts of data.

Magnetic Disks

A magnetic disk is a circular base of support material on which a magnetic film is deposited. The base may be heavy and rigid, or more similar to magnetic tape material—thin and flexible. The diameter can range from a few inches to more than a foot. Tracks, formed on this base in a series of concentric circles, may be placed on both surfaces of a disk, or on one surface only. A disk operates by rotating at high speed, usually thousands of times per minute. If a suitable head is positioned over a track, it can read and write data at any position as the track passes under it. On rigid disks, such disk heads ride on a cushion of air created by the rapid rotation of the disk platter. In this case, springs push the head(s) toward the disk, but the air cushion prevents the heads from touching the surface, the clearance being only a few thousandths of an inch.

Any particle, scratch, or other foreign body can break this cushion of air and result in a **head crash** if the surface of the disk and the head are damaged by this contact. On a flexible disk, a head often rides on the surface of the disk because the disk does not spin fast enough to provide this cushion of air. Hence, constant use results in wear of the disk surface and oxide collecting on the disk read/write head. Periodically, such disks should be replaced and the disk head(s) should be cleaned. Device drivers that can recognize and record the occurrence of intermittent, recoverable errors on such disks can warn of impending problems with these media.

Each track may contain one or more blocks of data. Often each track is permanently divided into parts, either by mechanical marks or by formatting. Each part is called a **sector**. Generally, a sector holds a block of data and is the smallest addressable unit for reading and writing from a disk.

Some larger disk units include multiple disk platters mounted on a common spindle. All disks on such a unit rotate together. The IBM 3330, for example, includes ten disk platters, each of which provide two surfaces for data storage. On a unit with multiple surfaces, the set of tracks which are at corresponding positions on each surface is called a **cylinder**.

A number of types of disks are illustrated in Figures B-3 through B-5. Early disks were large and rigid, and could not be removed. These disks, equipped with a separate head for every track, are called **head-per-track disks**. Gradually a new type of disk became more common, the **moving-head disk**, in which a single head is provided for each surface. The heads are mounted on a moving arm, which can be positioned over any desired track. More recently, versions of the moving-head disk that use a small, thin, flexible base mounted in a paper envelope have been developed. These **floppy disks**, which are removable and inexpensive, form an important storage method for small computer systems. Each of these types is discussed below.

Many disk units, like tapes, can be physically removed and replaced. These disks may be used for long-term data storage. However, except for floppy disks, the units are bulky and very expensive.

Head-per-track Devices.   Figure B-3 shows the similarities in structure of a head-per-track disk, and a magnetic drum unit. Instead of a set of concentric tracks, the drum has a set of tracks that form a single cylinder.

Figure B–3 Example of a Head-per-Track Disk and Drum

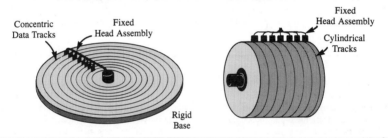

A read and write head is permanently positioned over each track. This type of disk is very expensive, due to the large number of heads. Moreover, its storage capacity is limited. The spacing between tracks must be much larger than on moving-head devices to provide sufficient room for the heads.

On the positive side, head-per-track devices offer very fast data access, and access that comes closest to being truly random. For these reasons such devices are still used in larger systems, especially in applications demanding very high performance, such as virtual memory.

Moving-head Disks.   The structure of a typical moving-head disk is shown in Figure B-4. A single head for each surface is mounted on a moving arm. The arms for each surface are tied together and move as a unit, so that at any time, all heads are positioned on the same cylinder.

Figure B–4 Example of a Moving-Head Disk (IBM 3330)

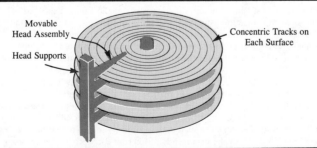

To access data on a moving-head disk, it is first necessary to move the heads to the proper cylinder. This introduces a delay, called **seek delay**, which is roughly proportional to the distance moved. This seek delay is a major factor limiting the speed of access.

Thus, moving-head disks have much slower average access speeds than head-per-track devices, and the actual access time is strongly dependent on the position. However, these devices are much less expensive, physically compact, and can have a high data capacity. Many moving-head disks are removable.

A new type of moving-head disk that has recently become popular includes both storage media and read/write mechanism within a compact sealed unit. This type of construction is known as a **Winchester disk**. Because it is precision-made and sealed, this type of disk can have a high data density, low cost, and good reliability even when subject to physical shocks. Winchester disks can store tens of megabytes of data on a unit about six inches in diameter. This technology is the basis of low-cost, high-capacity "hard" disks on small computer systems.

Floppy Disks.   The final type of magnetic disk is the floppy disk, also called a "flexible disk" or "diskette." The structure of a floppy disk is shown in Figure B-5.

Floppy disks are a special type of moving-head disk, always removable, with a thin, flexible base. The disk is mounted inside a paper jacket, with a coating that allows it to rotate freely. A slot in the jacket allows data to be accessed as it passes by the slot.

The first floppy disks were eight inches in diameter. Newer types use smaller sizes, such as 5 1/4 inches or 3 1/2 inches. Various formatting techniques are used to obtain high data density. Early disks could store only a few hundred kilobytes. Newer disks, even the smallest, can often store over a megabyte of data.

Figure B-5   Example of a Floppy Disk

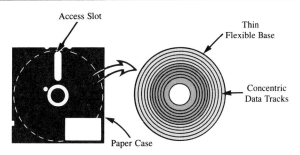

Floppy disks are often mounted in inexpensive drive mechanisms that rotate only when needed. On such devices, there is a start-up delay for each new block transfer. As a consequence, it may not be possible to read all the sectors of a track in their physical order during a single rotation of the disk. This leads to the practice of **sector interleaving**. The sectors on each track are numbered in such an order that one or more sectors are skipped between consecutively numbered positions. This technique defines an order by which sectors can be accessed in the fewest possible revolutions.

Floppy disks are very slow to access, and highly nonrandom. Because of this they are not suitable for general-purpose working storage, which must be randomly accessed with high frequency. They perform quite well for occasional use. Because floppies are removable and very inexpensive, they form a low-cost alternative to tape for archival storage of moderate quantities of data.

Optical Storage

A very new technology that is emerging as a possible competitor to magnetic storage is that of optical disks. These disks have a structure similar to audio compact disks. They consist of a base of glass or similar transparent medium coated by a thin film of material, the optical properties of which can be changed by a laser beam's heat. As the disk is scanned with a laser, the surface is melted in a prescribed way, forming patterns of bubbles and pits. These features reflect light in a different way than the original surface.

Unlike the concentric tracks on magnetic disks, data on optical disks are written on one long spiral track as on audio disks. Each block occupies the same length on the track. This allows the highest data density, but complicates block location; in addition, the rotation speed must be varied as the access position changes between inner and outer tracks.

To read information another laser beam scans the surface, and the reflected pattern is detected by suitable sensors. The beam is reflected at a different angle where data marks have been formed on the surface. The structure of an optical disk is illustrated in Figure B-6.

Figure B–6 An Optical Storage Disk

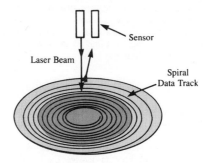

Optical storage offers the advantage of very high density. A disk the size of an audio CD can store hundreds of megabytes. Once properly recorded, information on an optical disk cannot deteriorate.

However, optical disks under present technology are generally read-only devices. These CD-ROM disks are most suitable for distribution of permanent databases of information. A slightly different type of disk can be written once only by the user with a suitable drive mechanism; thereafter the data is permanent. This type of disk has been dubbed with the name **Write Once**, **Read Mostly (WORM)**.

Although data on an optical disk cannot deteriorate, the initial writing process has a high failure rate. Thus, you may need to include extensive error checking data to ensure reliability.

Because of the difficulty of rewriting, optical devices are not currently suitable for general-purpose file storage. However, they are being used to distribute large databases of permanent information, such as law libraries or encyclopedias.

Abstract Block Storage Devices

Many of the storage devices we have discussed have a similar basic structure, despite their many differences. It is possible to treat most devices uniformly by defining a model for an **abstract block storage device**, the properties of which are assumed to be simple and consistent, even if the physical device is more complex. Such a device is considered to contain an address space consisting of an ordered sequence of blocks, all the same size. The size is chosen to be reasonably consistent with the physical devices to be used; typical choices are 512 or 1024 bytes.

The sequence of blocks is assigned to the physical device in such a way that accessing a consecutive sequence of blocks in order will be efficient. It is understood that random access may be more costly and that the exact cost varies with the device.

This approach, used by UNIX and other OSs, allows software that works with storage devices to assume a common set of characteristics, even if the actual devices vary widely. A possible reduction in performance in some cases is accepted as the price of such independence from the structure of the physical device.

B.3 TERMINAL AND PRINT DEVICES

A large variety of devices help users display and enter data into a computer. Compared to the storage devices described earlier, these devices are relatively slow in data transfer to and from computer memory. Control of these devices, quite often driven in direct program control mode, requires many device-specific character sequences.

Terminals have both keyboards for entering data and some type of screen for displaying information. Such terminals are usually one of the following types:

- hardcopy display (e.g., matrix or thermal paper display)
- cathode ray tube (CRT)
- liquid crystal display (LCD)
- plasma display

How terminals interface to computers varies. The most common technique is via the use of an **RS-232 serial interface**. Another common technique uses a **memory-mapped display**.

RS-232 Terminals

The code RS-232 is a designation assigned to a serial interface standard developed by the Electronic Industries Association. Characters, originally presented as eight-bit codes, must be converted to a stream of single bits (serialized) by the interface over some type of medium (twisted wire pair, or telephone lines, for example). Sometimes modems (modulator/demodulators) are required to electronically change the digital signal to one that can transmit information on such media. Common transmit and receive rates for such terminals are 300, 1200, 2400, 9600, and 19,200 bits per second (bps).

The simplest transmit operation by the computer to a terminal is to send characters one at a time for display. The simplest receive operation of data entered by a keyboard is for characters entered on the keyboard to be automatically **echoed** by the terminal as they are sent to the computer. A slightly more complex, common technique is for the entered character to be sent to the computer and for the computer to echo the character onto the display. In this case the "echo" must be performed by the terminal device driver. Terminals that operate in such simple modes are often called **dumb terminals**. The earliest terminal was the Teletype, a very slow hardcopy unit referred to as a **tty**. Today the term tty is used by many operating systems, particularly UNIX, to refer to any interactive terminal.

Modern terminals have many features controlled by control or **escape sequences**. These control sequences vary from terminal to terminal; many terminals can emulate a variety of different terminals. Such terminals contain microprocessors and programs in EPROM and ROM, which provide this emulation. Hence, a terminal device driver for one terminal can be used for a variety of different terminals if all of the terminals are emulating one common terminal type.

Buffered Terminals.   Unlike our earlier examples of terminals, buffered terminals have internal memory for storing one or more screens (pages) of information at a time. This information can be sent in a continuous stream to the computer using a **protocol** on a **serial interface**. A full screen of display information is sent at one time from the computer to the terminal. This information often contains control sequences specifying protected and unprotected fields of a screen. Data can only be entered in an unprotected field, without intervention from the computer. Entries on a screen can also be corrected in the terminal before they are sent to the computer. A SEND or TRANSMIT key sends the data on the current screen to the computer. A delay is required after this key is struck because the entire screen is sent as a stream of characters.

Support of buffered terminals requires control of display screens to be sent to the terminal and pages of data sent to the computer. More complex error detection procedures for sending and receiving such blocks of data on these terminals add complexity to device drivers for such buffered terminals.

Memory-Mapped Terminals

Another class of terminals, **memory-mapped terminals**, are interfaced via what is known as **video RAM**, whereby a portion of addressable memory corresponds to display locations on the screen. The IBM PC's console is a **character-mapped display** with two character locations in the video RAM that correspond to each character position on the display. The first position specifies the character to be displayed (in ASCII) while the second position specifies display attributes, such as reverse video, or blinking. Characters placed in the corresponding positions in the video RAM determine what appears on the display with no intervention from the computer.

Another type of mapped display is **bit-mapped display**. Instead of character locations corresponding to character positions on the display, each bit in the video RAM corresponds to a **pixel** on the display, which can be turned on or off. A device driver for a bit-mapped display can become very complex.

Keyboards for memory-mapped displays are generally not coupled to the screen in any way. They are usually interfaced with either a parallel or serial interface. Striking keys causes interrupts, which can be processed by the keyboard input handler. In many memory-mapped terminals, character values are not sent to the keyboard input handler. In such cases, the key position or number is sent to the computer, rather than a particular character value. The IBM PC contains an even more complex environment for the implementation of the console driver because it provides interrupts both when a key is struck and when it is released. Hence, the device driver must keep track of when the control key is held down by tracking both the striking and the releasing of the key. The device driver then can determine whether the key number representing the letter C is C or CTRL-C. This technique must also be used for other keys, like the shift key. The driver can also distinguish between numbers on an auxiliary keypad and numbers on the top row of the standard typewriter keyboard. While complex, such a memory-mapped terminal does provide great flexibility. However, implementing device drivers for such terminals becomes much more difficult.

Printers

Today's **printers** are of many different types. Impact printers rely on hammers or print heads, which strike a character onto paper using a ribbon. Some commonly used types of impact printers include dot-matrix printers with a single movable printhead, matrix shuttle printers with multiple printheads, daisy wheel printers, thimble printers, rotating drum printers, chain printers, and band printers. Nonimpact printers, which do not have hammers, include ink jet printers, thermal printers, and laser printers.

Drum, chain, ban, and matrix shuttle printers have control characters for carriage control and line spacing, but the size of print cannot be changed without changing a drum, or cnain. Single head matrix printers allow the changing of character pitch and size, provide for automatic underlining, and offer a variety of other special effects. Support for such capabilities can be provided within the driver or by application program, which merely send characters to the printer. Thus device drivers for printers can be complex or simple depending on the level of support for special features within the driver itself.

Like terminals, printers may be attached to the computer using a serial interface. However, many printers make use of a **parallel interface**, in which all of the bits of a character code are transmitted to the printer at once.

═══ IMPORTANT TERMS ═══

abstract block storage device
bit-mapped display
character-mapped display
cylinder
dumb terminal
echoing
escape sequence
floppy disk
formatting
head crash
head-per-track disk
memory-mapped display
memory-mapped terminal
moving-head disk
parallel interface
pixel

printer
protocol
read head
RS-232 serial interface
sector
sector interleaving
seek delay
serial interface
storage medium
terminal
track
tty
video RAM
Winchester disk
write head
Write Once Read Mostly (WORM)

APPENDIX

A Catalog of Operating Systems

C.1 INTRODUCTION

This appendix contains an alphabetic listing of most operating systems, past and present, that have been distributed commercially or reported in English-language literature. We include this extensive catalog because we believe that, for the serious student who wishes to understand OS implementation, there is no substitute for studying a variety of actual systems. Most of the systems in this catalog have something to teach, and in many cases the best explanations are given by designers or users in published literature.

The listing attempts to be as comprehensive as possible. However, it does not always distinguish closely related versions or releases of the same OS or reimplementations of substantially the same OS on different computers. Many systems developed primarily for educational use are not listed. Our catalog is limited to those systems that have actually been implemented (although perhaps only once), directly control the CPU hardware, and are general purpose, at least within broad application areas (including business and real-time control).

The operating systems are classified roughly into fourteen categories. Each category is explained briefly at the beginning of the section. The classification is somewhat arbitrary; many OSs could reasonably be placed in several classes. Those we found difficult to classify are placed in the miscellaneous section at the end.

Each listing includes, where possible, a short characterization of the OS; the CPUs or computer types on which the OS runs; the approximate time it was first released or reported; the company or place where it was developed; and, if possible, at least one reference to a published description.

A catalog such as this is bound to have errors or omissions. The authors regret any that may be found here. We welcome comments, additions or corrections that could lead to an improved catalog in future editions of this text.

Some of the material in this listing was gathered from a number of published surveys, including Computerworld [1984], Datapro [1974], Goldberg [1974], Hindin [1984], Mini-Micro [1985], Mini-Micro [1986], Rosen [1969], Rosen [1972], Rosin [1969], Weizer [1981], Zarella [1981], and Zarella [1982]. Useful information was also obtained from ongoing discussions on several computer conference systems, including USENET, BIX, and COMPUSERVE.

Many of the system names listed in this catalog are trademarks of the companies named in each listing.

C.2 SYSTEMS OF HISTORICAL INTEREST

This section lists operating systems of the 1950s and 1960s that are primarily of historical interest. Most of these systems were batch systems or single-job monitors for large computers. Early examples of other categories, such as timesharing, minicomputer, or real-time systems are listed with their respective sections.

ADMIRAL Operating system for the Honeywell 800/1800. Early 1960s [Bouvard 1964].

Atlas I Supervisor Supervisor program for the first computer designed to use an operating system. Introduced system calls and virtual storage. U. of Manchester, mid-1960s [Kilburn 1961, Howarth et al. 1961].

B1, B2, B3, B4 Operating systems for NCR Century series computers. Early 1960s [Datapro 1974].

Basic Executive System Memory-based real-time executive for the IBM 1710. Early 1960s [Harrison et al. 1981].

FMS FORTRAN Monitor system. Operating system developed by North American Aviation for the IBM 709. Late 1950s [Weizer 1981, Bashe et al. 1986].

GM OS A very early operating system developed by General Motors for the IBM 701. Unnamed. About 1955 [Steel 1964].

HES Honeywell Executive System. Operating system for the Honeywell 800. Early 1960s [Bouvard 1964].

IBM 1410/1710 OS OS for the IBM 1410/1710. Early 1960s [Barnett & Fitzgerald 1964].

IBSYS Predecessor to IBM OS/360 for 709x architectures. Early 1960s [IBM 1963].

Input Output Selector An IO control system for the DDP-116 minicomputer. One of the earliest OSs for minis. Mid-1960s [Koudela 1973].

Input Output System A very early operating system developed by General Motors and North America Aviation for the IBM-704. About 1956 [Steel 1964, Bashe et al. 1986].

IOCS Input Output Control System. An early I/O executive for the IBM 7090. About 1960.

SABRE Semi-Automatic Business Related Environment. The first major transaction processing system, developed by IBM and American Airlines for the IBM 7090. Early 1960s [Jarema & Sussenguth 1981].

SAGE Semi-Automatic Ground Environment system. Control program for IBM AN/FSQ7 to monitor weapons systems. First real-time control system. Late 1950s [Everett et al. 1957].

SOS Operating system developed by the IBM SHARE Users Group for the 709. Late 1950s [Shell et al. 1959].

C.3 BATCH SYSTEMS FOR LARGE COMPUTERS

This section includes OSs for large "mainframe" computers that are primarily batch-oriented. Very early systems of this type are listed in the previous section. Timesharing systems are listed in the next section.

BKY A batch-oriented OS for the CDC 6600 at Lawrence Berkeley Laboratories. Early 1970s [Tanenbaum & Benson 1973].

BOS/360 Basic Operating System for the IBM/360. Early 1960s [Weizer 1981].

BPS/360 Business-oriented OS for the IBM/360. Late 1960s [Weizer 1981].

CAL Research OS for the CDC 6400. Late 1960s. [Lampson & Sturgis 1976].

Chios OS for the UNIVAC 1108 in a service bureau environment. Case Western Reserve, early 1970s [Lynch 1972, Lynch1975].

CHIPPEWA Original name for CDC SCOPE Operating System. Developed at CDC Chippewa Labs.

DOS Disk operating system for RCA Spectra 70 series. Late 1960s [Weizer 1981].

DOS/360 Operating system for IBM S/360. IBM Corp. Mid-1960s [Bender et al. 1967].

DOS/VS Operating system for the IBM S/370. Virtual Storage version of DOS/360. IBM Corp., early 1970s [Birch 1973].

DOS/VSE Operating system for the IBM 43XX. Extended version of DOS/VS. Early 1980s.

EMAS, EMAS 2900 Edinburgh Multi-Access System for ICL 4-75. Late 1970s [Whitfield & Whight 1983, Stephens et al. 1980].

EXEC I, EXEC II Single-user OSs for UNIVAC 1107 computers. Early 1960s [Borgerson et al. 1978].

EXEC 3, EXEC 4 Improved versions of EXEC II for UNIVAC 1108. Late 1960s [Lynch 1972].

EXEC 8 Multiprogrammed OS for UNIVAC 1108. Late 1960s [Sayers 1971, Borgerson et al. 1978].

GCOS General Comprehensive OS. Honeywell Series 60 and 6000 systems. Based on GECOS. Early 1970s.

GECOS III Multiprogrammed OS for GE 600 series computers. Late 1960s [Sayers 1971].

George 1,2,3, and 4 OS for various models of ICL 1900 series computers. Late 1960s [Cuttle & Robinson 1970, Goodman 1972, Oestreicher 1971].

IDA, IDASYS OS for the CDC 6600 developed at the Institute for Defense Analyses, based on the concept of a supervisory computer. Late 1960s [Gaines 1972].

MASTER OS for Control Data 3300/3500. Late 1960s [Sayers 1971].

MCP Master Control Program. Generic name used for Burroughs operating systems, including 1700 and 5500, 6600, and 7700 series. Early 1960s through mid-1970s [McKeag et al. 1976, Sayers 1971].

MFT Operating system for the IBM S/360. See OS/MFT.

MVS Virtual storage OS for IBM S/370. See OS/MVS.

MVT Popular OS for IBM S/360 and S/370. See OS/MVT.

OS/360 Generic name for operating systems for the IBM S/360, and later S/370. First version released 1966 [Mealy et al. 1966]. See also OS/PCP, OS/MFT, OS/MVT, OS/VS1, OS/SVS, and OS/MVS.

OS/1100 Operating system for UNIVAC 1106 and 1110.

OS/MFT, OS/MFT-II Mulitprogramming with a fixed number of tasks. Simple version of OS/MVT suitable for processors with limited memory. First release 1967, substantial revision 1968. [Mealy et al. 1966, Auslander et al. 1981].

OS/MVS Multiple Virtual Space. Virtual storage OS for IBM 370, derived from MVT. Originally called VS2, Release 2. First release 1974 [Scherr 1973, Auslander et al. 1981].

OS/MVT Multiprogramming with a variable number of tasks. Popular OS for IBM 360/370. First release 1967 [Flores 1973, Auslander et al. 1981].

OS/PCP Primary Control Program. Early batch-serial version of IBM OS/360. First release 1966 [Mealy et al. 1966, Auslander et al. 1981].

OS/SVS Single Virtual Space. Initial release of OS/VS2. Virtual storage OS for IBM S/370, based closely on OS/MVT. First release 1972 [Auslander et al. 1981].

OS/VS1 Virtual System 1. Virtual storage OS for the IBM 370, based on OS/MFT. First release 1972 [Wheeler 1974, Auslander et al. 1981].

OS/VS2 Virtual System 2. Virtual storage OS for the IBM 370, based on OS/MVT. Release 1 became known as OS/SVS. Release 2 became known as OS/MVS.

PCP Early version of IBM OS/360. See OS/PCP.

POS Primary OS for RCA Spectra 70. Late 1960s.

SCOPE Supervisory Control of Program Execution. Early OS for CDC 6000 Computers. Late 1960s [McKeag et al. 1976].

SIPROS Experimental advanced OS developed for CDC 6600 computers.

SUE Experimental OS for the IBM S/360. Late 1960s [Sevcik et al. 1972, Tsichritzis & Bernstein 1974].

SVS Virtual Storage OS for IBM S/370. See OS/SVS.

Tape Scope 2 Tape based OS derived from SCOPE for the CDC System 17. Early 1970s [Datapro 1974].

TDOS Tape and Disk operating system for the RCA Spectra 70. Late 1960s [Sayers 1971].

TITAN Operating system for the Titan (Atlas II) Computer, successor to Atlas I at the University of Manchester (England). Mid-1960s [Hartley 1972, McKeag et al. 1976].

TOS Tape Operating System. Early operating system for the RCA Spectra 70 [Weizer 1981].

TOS/360   Early operating system for the IBM S/360. Mid-1960s [Bender et al. 1967].
VS-1   IBM Virtual Storage OS. See OS/VS1.
VS-2   IBM Virtual Storage OS. See OS/VS2.

C.4 TIMESHARING SYSTEMS

This section lists operating systems for large and medium computers primarily oriented to interactive timesharing use. Although some of these systems also support batch processing and, occasionally, real-time activities, these are considered secondary uses. Very early timesharing systems are included here. Multiuser small computer systems, supporting only a few users, are not included; these are listed in the sections on minicomputer and microcomputer OSs.

2000E & 2000F   Timesharing operating systems for the HP 2100. Early 1970s [Datapro 1974].
Adept-50   An early experimental timesharing system for the IBM S/360. Late 1960s [Linde et al. 1969].
BTM   A Batch Timesharing Monitor for XDS Sigma 5/7. Late 1960s [Sayers 1971].
CMAS   Cambridge Multiple Access System.   University of Cambridge (England). Late 1960s [Wilkes 1973].
CTSS   The Compatible Timesharing System.   Early timesharing OS developed at MIT for a modified IBM 7090. Early 1960s [Crisman et al. 1964].
DTSS   Dartmouth Timesharing System.   Timesharing with the BASIC language for liberal arts students, on a novel 2-computer system (GE-235 + Datanet 30). Mid-1960s [Kemeny & Kurtz 1968].
JOSS   JOHNNIAC Open Shop System.   An early on-line computing system for the JOHNNIAC computer. Early 1960s [Shaw 1964].
KOS   Kent On-Line System, Kent University (England), Late 1960s [Brown 1971].
KRONOS   Timesharing OS for CDC 6000 and CYBER computers. Successor to SCOPE. Control Data Corp., early 1970s [Atwood 1976].
LTSS   Lawrence Timesharing System.   Early timesharing OS at Lawrence Livermore Laboratories. [Sutherland et al. 1971].
MACE   Original name for CDC KRONOS OS.
MCTS   Multiple Console Timesharing System developed to support CAD applications at General Motors. Early 1970s [Brown et al. 1975, Elshoff & Ward 1976].
MDOS   Operating System for the Data General MV4000. Early 1980s [Computerworld 1984].
MINIMOP   Multi-Access OS. Late 1960s [Rees 1971].
MTS   Michigan Terminal System.   Late 1960s [Boettner & Alexander 1975].
MULTICS   the MULTiplexed Information and Computing Service. A timesharing system featuring novel techniques for memory management and resource protection. Developed by MIT, Bell Labs, & General Electric for the GE645. Later developed by Honeywell. Late 1960s [Corbato & Vyssotsky 1965, Organick 1972].
NOS   OS for CDC Cyber Computers. Based on KRONOS.
OS-3   Oregon State Open Shop OS. A timesharing system for the CDC 3300. Late 1960s [Meeker et al. 1969].
Pitt Time Sharing System   An early timesharing system developed at the University of Pittsburgh for the IBM S/360. Late 1960s [Badger & Johnson 1968].
PTSS   People's Timesharing System.   A timesharing system for the CDC 6600 at Lawrence Berkeley Laboratories, based on BKY. Early 1970s [Tanenbaum & Benson 1973].
Tenex   A timesharing system for a modified PDP-10. Based partially on abstract machine concepts. Early 1970s [Bobrow et al. 1972].
TOPS-10   Total Operating System.   Timesharing OS for DEC PDP-10. Digital Equipment Corporation. Late 1960s [Bell et al. 1978].
TOPS-20   Improved version of TOPS-10 for the DEC System 20, also using concepts from TENEX. Early 1970s [Bell et al. 1978].
TSM   Timesharing Monitor.   Early timesharing OS developed by IBM for the 7090. Early 1960s [Kinslow 1964].
TSOS   Early name for UNIVAC VMOS.
TSOS   Timesharing OS for RCA Spectra 70/46. Mid-1960s [Weizer 1981].
TS8/E   Timesharing OS for the DEC PDP-8. Late 1970s [Datapro 1974].
TSS   An early timesharing system for the AN/FSQ-32. Early 1960s [Schwartz et al. 1964].
TSS   Timesharing OS for General Automation System 18/30. Early 1970s [Datapro 1974].
TSS/8   Experimental timesharing OS for a modified PDP-8, developed at Carnegie-Mellon University. Late 1960s [van de Goor et al. 1969, Sayers 1971].
TSS/360   Timesharing OS developed by IBM for the S/360. Mid-1960s [Lett & Konigsford 1968, Katzan 1986].
UTS   Timesharing OS for Xerox Data System SIGMA computers. Early 1970s.
VAX/VMS   Standard operating system for DEC VAX. Based on RSX-11. Late 1970s [Kenah & Bate 1984].
VMOS   Timesharing OS for the RCA Spectra 70. Late 1960s [Fogel 1974, Weizer 1981].
VMS   Standard OS for DEC VAX. See VAX/VMS.
VS/9   Operating System for the UNIVAC Series 90. Derived from VMOS. Early 1970s.

C.5 MINICOMPUTER OPERATING SYSTEMS

This category includes single-user and small multiuser operating systems for minicomputers. Real-time OSs are listed in a later section.

AMIGO/300   Small, user-friendly OS for the Hewlett-Packard 300. Late 1970s [Carpenter 1979].

AMS Advanced Monitor System.   A single-user interactive disk or tape OS for the PDP-9 & PDP-15. Digital Equipment Corp., late 1960s.

AOS   Advanced Operating System for Data General Eclipse and MV series. Late 1970s.

BCM   Basic Control Monitor for Xerox 530. Early 1970s [Datapro 1974].

BCS   Basic Control System for HP 2100. Early 1970s [Datapro 1974].

BEST   Business System for Timesharing.   OS for Qantel Minicomputers [Datapro 1974].

BEST   Basic Executive & Timekeeper.   OS for Varian minicomputers. Early 1970s [Datapro 1974].

BMS   Basic Monitor System for the DEC PDP-9 and PDP-15. Early 1970s [Datapro 1974].

BOS   Basic OS for Interdata (later Perkin-Elmer) Minicomputers. Early 1970s [Datapro 1974].

BOS   Batch operating system for Honeywell System 700.

BOS   OS for Billings computers. Late 1970s(?) [Computerworld 1984].

BOS/5 Business Operating Software.   Business-oriented OS for Z80, PDP-11, 8086, and 68000. BOS National, Inc. Early 1980s [Mini-Micro 1986].

BOSS   Basic OS Software for Basic/Four 350/400/500. Includes monitor, real-time executive, BASIC. Early 1970s [Datapro 1974].

BOSS-2   OS for the RC-4000 Computer.

BOSS-15   Batch OS for the DEC PDP-15. Late 1970s [Datapro 1974].

BPS-99   Business oriented operating system for the GRI-99. Mid-1970s.

CAPS-8   Cassette Monitor system for the DEC PDP-8. Early 1970s [Datapro 1974].

CAPS-11   Cassette Monitor system for the DEC PDP-11. Early 1970s [Datapro 1974].

CiMOS   Batch oriented disk operating system for the Cincinnati Milacron CIP/2200. Early 1970s [Datapro 1974].

COS   Cassette OS for Computer Automation Alpha LSI and Naked Mini LSI. Early 1970s [Datapro 1974].

COS Commercial Operating System.   Early OS for PDP-11.

COS Concurrent Operating System.   Provided limited multiprogramming for UNIVAC 9200, 9300. Early 1970s [Datapro 1974].

COS   Operating System for GEC Computers. Early 1970s [Datapro 1974].

COS300   Commercial data management system for the PDP-8. Late 1970s [Datapro 1974].

CP-6   Operating System for the Honeywell DPS 8C/L66. Early 1980s(?) [Computerworld 1984].

CPF Control Program Facility.   Operating System for the IBM System 38. Early 1980s [Taylor 1981].

CPPS   Card/Paper Tape Programming System for the IBM 1130. Early 1970s [Datapro 1974].

CPS   An early OS for DEC minicomputers. Late 1960s [Cederquist 1970].

CTOS   Cassette Tape OS for Datapoint 1100, 2200, 5500. Late 1970s [Datapro 1974].

CTS-300   Commercial single or multiuser OS for small PDP-11 systems. Digital Equipment Corp. [Digital 1984a].

DBLDOS   OS for the Tandy TRS-80. Simple updates to TRSDOS to support the Percom double-density board. Percom Data Co. Early 1980s [Kelly 1981].

DBOS   Disk/Drum Based OS for General Automation SPC-16 & System 18/30. Late 1970s [Datapro 1974].

DMS   Disk Monitor System for IBM 1130. Early 1970s [Datapro 1974].

DMS   Disk Monitor System for General Automation System 18/30. Early 1970s [Datapro 1974].

DNOS   OS for NCR computers. Early 1980s? [Computerworld 1984].

DOS   OS for Datapoint minicomputers. Late 1970s [Computerworld 1984].

DOS   Disk OS for Interdata computers; Lockheed computers; HP 2100; Datapoint 1100, 2200, 5500; DEC PDP-11; Prime 100,200,300; Four-Phase System IV; GEC Computers; Computer Automation computers. Early 1970s [Datapro 1974].

DOS-15   Disk OS for DEC PDP-15. Early 1970s [Datapro 1974].

DOS-99   Single-user operating system for the GRI-99 Minicomputer. GRI Corp. Late 1970s [Mooney 1979].

DX-10   Operating System for the TI-990. Late 1970s(?) [Computerworld 1984].

EDOS   Operating System for the Hitachi 8400. Early 1970s.

EGDON   Serial batch OS for the English Electric KDF9, designed to support program development. Mid-1960s [Burns et al. 1966].

EGDON 3   OS for the British KDF9. Based on EGDON. Late 1960s [Poole 1968].

ELDON 2   Operating System for the British KDF9. Late 1960s [Wells 1971].

ELF   A multiprogrammed OS for the PDP-11.

Foreground/Background/8   Experimental Foreground/Background OS for the PDP-8. Late 1960s [Alderman 1969].

FSOS   Free Standing Operating System. Basic memory-resident OS for General Automation SPC-16 mini. Early 1970s [Datapro 1974].

IMOS   OS for NCR 8200 series. Early 1980s(?) [Computerworld 1984].

IRX   OS for NCR 8200 series. Early 1980s(?) [Computerworld 1984].

ITS   Operating System for the PDP-10.

MAX   Principal OS for ModComp Computers. Early 1970s [Datapro 1974].

Min I   Basic Operating System for the ModComp Computers. Early 1970s [Datapro 1974].

MOD4   OS for the Honeywell Series 200. Late 1960s [Sayers 1971].

MOD-400   OS for the Honeywell VPS 6. Early 1980s(?) [Computerworld 1984].

MODUS4   OS for Computer Technology minicomputers. Late 1970s [Datapro 1974].

MOS   Master OS for Varian minicomputers. Tape or disk based batch system.

MOS   Minimum Operating System.   Card-based batch monitor for UNIVAC 9200, 9300. Early 1970s [Datapro 1974].

MOS   Multiprogramming OS for NCR Century 300 computer. Late 1960s.

MPE-3000   OS for HP 3000. Early 1970s.

MTDS   Magnetic Tape OS for Computer Automation Alpha LSI & Naked Mini LSI. Early 1970s [Datapro 1974].

MTOS   Magnetic Tape OS for Datapoint 1100, 2200, 5500. Early 1970s [Datapro 1974].

MTS   Magnetic Tape System for HP 2100. Early 1970s [Datapro 1974].

MU5   OS for the MU5 computer at the University of Manchester (England). Early 1970s [Morris et al. 1972].

MUMPS   Multiuser multiprogramming, database oriented OS for DEC computers. Early 1970s [Datapro 1974].

NCOS   nonconcurrent OS. Tape- or disk-based OS for UNIVAC 9200 & 9300. Early 1970s [Datapro 1974].

NUCLEUS   Operating System for GEC Computers. Early 1970s [Datapro 1974].

OS/4 and OS/7   Operating Systems for UNIVAC 9700. Late 1960s(?).

OS6   Experimental OS for a small computer. Early 1970s [Stoy & Strachey 1972].

OS7   Operating System for HITAC 8700/8800. About 1975.

OS/8   Operating System for the PDP-8. Ancestor of RT-11. Digital Equipment Corp. Mid-1970s [Datapro 1974].

OS/200   OS for Honeywell Series 200 family. Late 1960s.

OS2000   OS for Honeywell 200/2000. Early 1970s(?).

PDP-6 Monitor   Monitor System for the DEC PDP-6. Mid-1960s [Bell et al. 1978].

PDP-10/50 Swapping Monitor   An early OS for the DEC PDP-10. Late 1960s [Thomas 1972].

P/OS   Professional Operating System, standard OS for the PRO-350 and PRO-380. Derived from RSX-11. Digital Equipment Corp. Early 1980s.

PrimOS   OS for the PRIME minicomputers. Early 1980s [Computerworld 1984].

PRO/TSX-PLUS   Version of TSX-PLUS for the PRO-350.

PTOS   Paper Tape OS for the Cincinnati Milacron CIP/2200.

RC-4000   Research OS for RC-4000 Computer. [Brinch Hansen 1973].

RDOS   Single-user OS for the Data General NOVA. Mid-1970s [Datapro 1974].

RMS   OS for Datapoint computers. Early 1980s(?) [Datapoint 1984].

RSTS   Multiuser OS for DEC PDP-11. Digital Equipment Corp. [Digital 1984a].

RT-11   Single-user OS for DEC PDP-11. Digital Equipment Corp. About 1975 [Digital 1984a].

SCP   System Control Program.   Basic OS for the Burroughs B700 series. Early 1970s [Datapro 1974].

SCP   System Control Program.   Mulitprogramming OS for the IBM System/3. Early 1970s [Taylor 1981].

SEL 810A/810B OS   Batch Serial Operating System for the SEL 810A/810B minicomputer. Late 1960s [Sayers 1971].

SOS   Stand-alone OS for Data General Nova & Supernova. Early 1970s [Datapro 1974].

SSP   System Support Program.   Multitasking OS for the IBM System/34. Mid-1970s [Taylor 1981].

SUN   General Purpose OS kernel for the HP 9000 Series 500. Early 1980s [Georg et al. 1984].

SYSEX   System Executive.   A timesharing monitor for SIGMA/2 and small IBM S/360 computers. Early 1970s [Reiter 1972].

TOS   Teletype Operating System for the Microdata 1600 & 3200 minicomputers. Early 1970s [Datapro 1974].

TRIPOS   A portable OS for Minicomputers. PDP-11, 68000 series, 32000 series. Late 1970s [Richards et al. 1979].

VENUS   Experimental OS for a modified Interdata minicomputer, based on matching the computer architecture to the operating system. Early 1970s [Liskov 1972, Tschiritzis & Bernstein 1974].

VOS   Operating System for Harris 600, 700, 800 computers. Early 1980s(?) [Computerworld 1984].

VULCAN   Operating System for Harris computers. Early 1980s(?) [Computerworld 1984].

XOS   Batch Processing OS for the Xerox Data Systems SIGMA Computers. Early 1970s(?).

C.6 MICROCOMPUTER OPERATING SYSTEMS

AmigaDOS   Basic operating system for Amiga computers. Derived from TRIPOS. Mid-1980s [Pountain 1986].

AMOS   Multiuser, multiprocessing OS for the 68000 family of microprocessors. Alpha Microsystems. Early 1980s.

AppleDOS   Basic Operating System for Apple II Computers. Late 1970s.

AtariDOS   Operating System for the Atari 400/800. Late 1970s.

BTRON   Business-oriented version of TRON.

CDOS   OS based on CP/M for Cromemco Computers (8080 series). Late 1970s.

Concurrent 68K, Concurrent 286   Real-time multiuser OS for the 68000 and 80x86 family. Combines features of PC-DOS and UNIX. Digital Research, mid-1980s.

Concurrent CP/M-86 A version of CP/M-86 supporting limited multitasking. Digital Research, early 1980s [Kornstein 1983]

Concurrent DOS, Concurrent PC-DOS Multitasking OS combining capabilities of PC-DOS and CPM. For 8086 & 68000 families. Digital Research, early 1980s.

Concurrent DOS 8-16 Combined version of Concurrent DOS and CP/M 2.2 CompuPro, early 1980s.

CP/M Control Program for Microcomputers. For Intel 8080 and Z-80. Digital Research Inc. Widely used version is CP/M 2.2. First OS for Microcomputers. About 1975 [Kildall 1981, Zaks 1980].

CP/M-86 Extended CP/M based OS for 8086 family. Digital Research, early 1980s [Kildall 1981].

CP/M 8-16 Combined version of CP/M 2.2 and CP/M-86. CompuPro, mid-1980s.

CP/M Plus Extended version of CP/M supporting segmented addressing, etc. Digital Research, mid-1980s [Dahmke 1983].

DOS 3.3 Standard OS for Apple II Computers.

DOSPLUS OS for the Tandy TRS-80. Substantial extension of TRSDOS, including support for double-density disks. Micro Systems Software, early 1980s [Kolya 1981].

86-DOS Early version of MS-DOS. Seattle Computer Products, late 1970s [Paterson 1983].

EUMEL Multitasking OS for Z80, 8086, 68000, Z8000. Developed by GMD in Germany. Mid-1980s.

FLEX A small OS for the 6809 and others. Technical Systems Consultants [Mini-Micro 1985].

GEM Graphics OS environment for IBM-PC. Digital Research, early 1980s.

GEOS Graphics Operating System for Commodore 64, based on GEM. Commodore Business Machines, Inc. mid-1980s.

HDOS Heath Disk OS. Operating System for H-89 and other Heath Computers. Early 1980s [Jorgenson 1981, Pechura 1983].

K-DOS An alternative OS for the Atari 400/800. Early 1980s [Leemon 1982].

LDOS Extended version of TRSDOS for the TRS-80 (Z80). Logical Systems, Inc., early 1980s [Daneliuk 1982].

MBOS/5 Multitasking version of BOS/5.

Microdisk Op Sys OS for MS2000 using 1805. RCA Microsystems. [Mini-Micro 1985].

Micropower/Pascal A small Pascal Operating Environment for the LSI-11. Digital Equipment Corp. [Digital 1984a].

MicroVMS Version of VMS for the MicroVAX. Digital Equipment Corp., mid-1980s.

MOS p-code system for Z80, 8080, 8086, 68000. Volition Systems [Mini-Micro 1985].

M/OS-80 Small OS for Z80. UTC/Mostek [Mini-Micro Systems 1985].

MP/M Multiuser version of CP/M. Digital Research, late 1970s [Kildall 1981].

MP/M-86 Version of MP/M for 8086 family CPU. Digital Research, early 1980s [Kildall 1981].

MP/OS Version of AOS for the Data General Micro-Nova. Late 1970s [Zarella 1981].

MPX-32 OS for Gould Concept-32 computers. Early 1980s.

MS-DOS Improved OS for 8086 family, based partly on CP/M. Newer versions somewhat similar to UNIX. MicroSoft Corp. Adapted as PC-DOS for IBM-PC. Late 1970s [Paterson 1983, King 1983].

MSX Small ROM-based version of MS-DOS for Z80 home computers. MicroSoft Corp., early 1980s.

MSX-DOS Limited version of MS-DOS for the Z80. MicroSoft Corp., early 1980s [Mini-Micro 1985].

MTOS Multitasking, Multiprocessing OS for 8086 and 68000 families. Industrial Programming, Inc., early 1980s [Mini-Micro 1986].

MULTIDOS Disk Operating System for the Tandy TRS-80. Features ability to read and write various file formats. Cosmopolitan Electronics Corp., early 1980s [Archer 1982].

MULTI-FORTH A FORTH operating environment for the 68000. Creative Solutions [Mini-Micro 1985].

NEWDOS An extended version of TRSDOS for the TRS-80. Apparat, Inc., early 1980s [Kelly 1982].

OASIS Original name for THEOS.

O/S OS for 8086, 68000. Applied Systems [Mini-Micro 1985].

OS/2 Operating system for IBM Personal System 2. IBM Corporation, late 1980s [White & Grehan 1987, Letwin 1988].

OS-9 Small computer OS similar to UNIX, stripped down and with real-time capabilities. M68000 and 6809 systems, including TI Color Computer, Tandy, Dragon, others. MicroWare Corp. Mid-1980s [Bidmead 1984].

p-System Support environment for UCSD Pascal, based on an abstract "p-machine." Developed at University of California at San Diego, now distributed by SofTech Microsystems. Late 1970s [Campbell 1983].

PC-DOS For IBM-PC. Version of MS-DOS. Early 1980s [King 1983].

PCVMS Small, inexpensive VMS lookalike. Wenden Corp. Mid-1980s.

Personal CP/M ROM-based version of CP/M 2.2 for small home computers. Digital Research Inc., early 1980s.

polyFORTH FORTH environment for Z80, 8080, 8086, 6809, 68000, and PDP-11 families. FORTH Inc., early 1980s [Mini-Micro 1986].

ProDOS Advanced operating system for APPLE computers. M6502 CPU [Campbell 1984, Moore 1984].

QDOS Quick and Dirty Operating System. First version of 86-DOS, later MS-DOS. Early 1980s [Paterson 1983].

QDOS OS for the British Sinclair QL. Power of UNIX, SuperBASIC command language, up to twenty concurrent tasks with windows. Early 1980s [WMSR 1984].

REX-80/80, REX-80/86 OS for 8080 and 8086. Systems & Software, late 1970s [van der Linden & Wilson 1980, Mini-Micro 1985].

SCP-DOS Early version of MS-DOS. Seattle Computer Products, late 1970s.

SDOS Operating System for 6809. Software Dynamics [Mini-Micro 1985].

SOS Sophisticated OS for the Apple III. Late 1970s.

THEOS Business oriented operating system for small computers. Versions for Z80, 8086, and 68000. Originally named OASIS and distributed by Phase One Systems. Now distributed by THEOS Corporation. Early 1980s [Stagner 1985].

TOS Operating system for the Atari 520ST and 1040ST. Derived from Concurrent 68K.

TP/M Version of CP/M for the Epson QX-10.

TRSDOS Standard operating system for TRS-80 computers. Z80 CPU.

TurboDos Enhanced multitasking version of CP/M for Z80 and 8086. Software 2000, early 1980s [Fowler 1984, Bierman 1984].

ULTRADOS OS for the Tandy TRS-80. Level IV Products. Early 1980s [Archer 1982].

UMD OS for 8080, 6800, 68000, Z8000 series, and others. Boston Systems Office. [Mini-Micro 1985].

VERSAdos MS-DOS compatible system for 68000. Motorola Corp., late 1970s [Glaser 1981].

VTOS OS for the Tandy TRS-80. Virtual Technology, early 1980s [Archer 1982].

Waterloo Port PC-DOS version. Waterloo Microsystems Inc., early 1980s [Mini-Micro 1986].

WIZRD Small OS for the 6800. Wintek [Mini-Micro 1985].

ZRTS Operating System for the Z8000. Zilog Corp., late 1970s [Savitzky 1981, Zarella 1981].

C.7 WORKSTATION OPERATING SYSTEMS

This category includes operating systems for personal workstations, usually with extensive graphic capabilities and designed for professional use.

BTRON Business-oriented version of the TRON OS for office workstations with bit-mapped displays. Late 1980s [Sakamura 1987c].

Macintosh OS Operating system for the Macintosh series. Apple Computer Corp., early 1980s.

MeDos Operating System for the Lilith Computer, developed by Niklaus Wirth for Modula-2 programming. Early 1980s [Sand 1984].

PERQ OS Original Operating system for the PERQ Computer. Three Rivers Computer Systems. Early 1980s.

PILOT Research workstation OS written in the MESA Language. Xerox Corp., late 1970s [Redell et al. 1980].

C.8 HIGHLY RELIABLE AND SECURE SYSTEMS

This section lists operating systems designed with very high reliability or security as a principal goal. Some of these systems are designed to control specialized architectures that include features to support this goal.

AUROS Reliable Operating System for the fault-tolerant minicomputer AURAGEN System 4000. Early 1980s [Glazer 1984].

DSU Data Secure UNIX. A security kernel for UNIX developed at UCLA. Late 1970s [Popek et al. 1979].

GUARDIAN Operating System for Tandem NonStop Computers, featuring high reliability. Early 1980s [Serlin 1984].

KeyKOS Capability based OS for the IBM/370. Early 1980s [Hardy 1985].

KSOS Kernelized Secure Operating system. UNIX-like OS with a secure kernel. Late 1970s. [McCauley & Drongoski 1979].

NonStop An OS for Tandem Computers featuring high reliability through redundant components. Late 1970s [Bartlett 1981].

Perpos Perpetual Processing OS for Computer Consoles Power 55/5. 68000-based multiple CPUs. UNIX-based system featuring high reliability. Early 1980s [Serlin 1984].

PSOS An Experimental Provably Secure Operating System. Late 1970s [DeLashmutt 1979].

STRATUS OS for Stratus-32 Computers. Early 1980s [Computerworld 1984].

Synthesis Fault tolerant OS for Synapse N + 1 system. Early 1980s [Serlin 1984].

VOS Virtual OS. Operating System for STRATUS computers featuring high reliability. Early 1980s [Serlin 1984].

C.9 UNIX AND ITS DERIVATIVES

This section lists variants of the UNIX operating system, including the standard versions from AT&T and The University of California at Berkeley, and various commercial implementations that bear different names but are substantially similar. Fully identical implementations are not listed. Systems that are based on UNIX but include substantial differences, such as distributed processing, real-time facilities, or simplified versions for microcomputers, are listed in other sections as appropriate.

Berkeley UNIX Version of UNIX for VAX, developed at the University of California at Berkeley. Late 1970s [Quarterman et al. 1985].

BSD UNIX Berkeley Standard Distribution. Official name for Berkeley UNIX.

COHERENT Version of UNIX. Mark Williams Corp. Early 1980s.

CROMIX UNIX System V port for Cromemco (68000 CPU). Cromemco Corp., Late 1970s.

DRM System UNIX-Compatible system for 68000. NV Philips. [Mini-Micro 1985].

GENIX UNIX version for the NSC 32016. National Semiconductor [Mini-Micro 1985].

GNU A public domain OS under development by Richard Stallman and the Free Software Foundation. Expected to be fully compatible with UNIX. The name stands for "Gnu is Not UNIX."

IDRIS Version of UNIX. 68000, 8086, PDP-11, VAX. Whitesmiths, Ltd. Late 1970s [Plauger & Krieger 1980].

INOS UNIX lookalike for the Artisan DP-09 (6809 CPU). Based partly on Uniflex. Introl Corp., mid-1980s.

IS/3 Version of UNIX (System 3) for PDP-11 and VAX. Interactive Systems [Digital 1984a].

ONIX Version of UNIX. Onyx Corp.

OSx Operating System for Pyramid Computers. Supports UNIX System V and BSD 4.2 concurrently. Early 1980s.

PC/IX Version of UNIX for 8086. IBM. [Mini-Micro 1985].

PCUNIX Small, inexpensive UNIX lookalike. Wendin Corp. Mid-1980s.

QNX UNIX lookalike for 80286 and others. Quantum Software Systems. Early 1980s (?).

REGULUS Version of UNIX. Alcyon Corp. 68000 family.

RT/EMT UNIX compatible OS for the PDP-11. Human Computing Resources.

SUNIX Version of UNIX for Z8002. SGS-Ates. [Mini-Micro 1985].

System V Standard version of UNIX licensed and distributed by AT&T. Early 1980s.

ULTRIX Version of UNIX for DEC PDP-11 and VAX. Digital Equipment Corp. Early 1980s. [Digital 1984a].

UniPlus Version of UNIX for the 68000 family. Unisoft Systems Corp.

Uniq Version of UNIX for PDP-11. Uniq Digital Technologies. [Digital 1984a].

Unity Version of UNIX for the DEC PDP-11 and VAX. Human Computing Resources. [Digital 1984a].

UNIX Widely used OS developed by Ken Thompson and Dennis Ritchie at Bell Laboratories around 1970. Based somewhat on MULTICS. Name probably derived from MULTICS, with "uni" signifying a single-user system. Many versions and imitators. Originally on DEC PDP-7 and PDP-11. Ported to VAX, M68000, and various other processors. Early 1970s [Ritchie & Thompson 1974, Thompson 1978, Bach 1986].

UNOS UNIX-compatible real-time OS. Charles River Data Systems [Mini-Micro 1985].

VENIX Version of UNIX (System V) for 8086 family, LSI-11. Venturcom [Mini-Micro 1985].

XENIX Version of UNIX for various CPUs. Microsoft Corp.

ZEUS Version of UNIX. Zilog Corp. Late 1970s [Zarella 1982].

C.10 VIRTUAL MACHINE SYSTEMS

This section includes virtual machine systems and monitors, and other OSs designed to be used in virtual machine environments.

CMS Cambridge Monitor System or Conversational Monitor System. Single-user interactive OS developed in conjunction with the Virtual Machine Control Program CP-40 at IBM Cambridge Laboratories. Later adapted for CP-67 and VM/370. Late 1960s [Meyer & Seawright 1970].

CP Control Program. A component of VM/370 for the IBM/370. CP is the kernel that implements the virtual machine. Early 1970s.

CP-40 Virtual machine control program for a modified IBM 360/40. See also CMS. Mid-1960s [Goldberg 1974].

CP-67 Virtual machine control program for the IBM 360/67. Successor to CP-40. See also CMS. Late 1960s. [Meyer & Seawright 1970].

HITAC 8400 OS A Virtual machine system for the Hitac 8400 (RCA Spectra 70/45). Late 1960s [Goldberg 1974].

IBM 360/30 OS Virtual machine for the IBM 360/30. Late 1960s [Goldberg 1974].

M44/44X Virtual machine system for modified IBM 7044. An early exploration of virtual machine ideas. Mid-1960s [Goldberg 1974, Belady et al. 1981].

Newcastle Recursive VM Virtual Machine system developed on a Burroughs 1700. Early 1970s [Goldberg 1974].

PDP-10 Virtual machine system for the PDP-10. Early 1970s [Goldberg 1974].

UCLA VM Virtual machine system developed at UCLA for modified PDP-11/45 for data security studies. Early 1970s [Goldberg 1974].

UMMPS Virtual machine system for the IBM 360/67. Early 1970s [Goldberg 1974].

VM/370 Virtual machine system for IBM 370. Successor to CP-67. See also CMS. First Release 1972 [IBMSJ 1979, Creasy 1981].

VM/PC A version of VM/370 for the PC/370. Early 1980s [Daney & Foth 1984].

VOS Virtual machine OS running on the Michigan Terminal System. Early 1970s [Srodowa & Bates 1973].

C.11 REAL-TIME EXECUTIVES

This category includes operating systems designed substantially for the purpose of controlling and monitoring external activities with timing constraints. Because effective real-time support dominates the design of such systems, most OSs with real-time capabilities are listed here even if they could logically be placed in other categories as well. This includes large and small systems, and distributed real-time systems.

Basic Real-Time Monitor   Real-time OS for the Phillips P-855 and P860. Early 1970s.

BLMX   Board-level multitasking executive for National Semiconductor 8080 and Z-80 based CPU boards. Late 1970s [Zarella 1981, Rhodes 1981].

BSO/RTOS   Small real-time OS for Z80, 6809, 8086, 68000. Boston Systems Office. Early 1980s [Mini-Micro 1986].

C Executive   Memory-based real-time UNIX-like executive for the PDP-11 or VAX. Runs multiple C or Pascal tasks. JMI Software Consultants. [Digital 1984a].

CCP   Communications Control Program. Limited OS for the IBM System/3. Early 1970s [Taylor 1981].

CTOS   Real-time, multitasking, multiprocessing OS for 8086 family. Convergent Technologies Inc., early 1980s [Mini-Micro 1986].

CTRON   Specification for a version of TRON for communication and network control. Late 1980s [Ohkubo et al. 1978].

DES RT   Real-time, UNIX-like OS for 16-bit microprocessor families and Micro-Vax, DGC MV series. Destek Group [Mini-Micro 1985].

DMERT   The Duplex Multiple Environment real-time operating system. An extension of MERT providing both real-time telecommunications support and general timesharing. Predecessor to RTR. Early 1980s [Grzelakowski et al. 1983].

DSOS   A skeleton for a real-time minicomputer OS on the TI-980A, using a structure of multiple layers. Early 1970s [Frailey 1975].

E4   Real-time OS for the Modular One. Early 1970s.

EDX   Event-Driven Executive. Interactive real-time operating system for the IBM System/7 and Series/1. Mid-1970s [Harrison et al. 1981].

EIS-110   Real-time executive for 8086. Electronic Information Systems. [Mini-Micro 1985].

Executive II   Real-time disk operating system for the IBM 1710. early 1960s [Harrison et al. 1981].

FADOS   Operating System for the Fast Amsterdam Multiprocessor (FAMP). A distributed, real-time OS based on a network of M68000s with a UNIX host. Mid-1980s [Tuynman & Hertzberger 1986].

GEM   Generalized Executive for real-time multiprocessor applications. An experimental OS for robotics systems at Ohio State University. Mid-1980s [Schwann et al. 1985].

iRMX   Real-time multitasking executive for Intel 8086 family CPUs. Intel Corp., late 1970s [Zarella 1981, Tucker 1973].

ITRON   Specification for an industrial version of TRON for embedded applications. Late 1980s [Monden 1987].

LABS/7   A distributed real-time OS for laboratory control. [Raimondi 1976].

MERT   Multiple Environment, real-time OS based partly on UNIX. Late 1970s [Lycklama & Bayer 1978].

MINI-EXEC   A portable executive for 8-bit microcomputers. Early 1980s [Wicklund 1982].

MIRAGE   Multitasking real-time OS for 68000 series.

MOSS   Modular OS for the RCA SUMC Computer (Space Ultrareliable Modular Computer). A real-time OS designed to be modifiable. S&H Computing, mid-1970s [Pruitt & Case 1975].

MROS-68K   Small memory-resident OS for the Motorola 68000. Late 1970s [Pohjanpalo 1981].

MSP/7   Modular System Program 7. Real-time OS for the IBM System/7. Early 1970s [Harrison et al. 1981].

MSP   Multitasking system program. Real-time executive for 68000 and Z8000. Uses a "split onion" structure with access to all layers. Hemenway Corp., Early 1980s [Hemenway 1983].

MTK-11   Small real-time kernel for Z80, 6502, 6800, 8086, 68000. United States Software Corp., early 1980s [Mini-Micro 1986].

OS/32-ST and OS/32-MT   Real-time serial and multitasking operating systems for Interdata (later Perkin-Elmer) 7/16 and 7/32 minicomputers. Mid-1970s [Interdata 1974].

OS/700   Real-time multiprogramming OS for Honeywell System 700. Early 1970s [Datapro 1974].

OS/RT   Real-time OS kernel for a variety of CPUs. Destek Group. [Mini-Micro 1985].

p   Timesharing OS for laboratory automation. Late 1970s [Lindgard 1979].

PDOS   Multi-user, multitasking, real-time OS for the 68000, and TI-9900 and 9905. Eyring Research [Roper 1984].

PORTX   ROM-based real-time OS. Destek Group [Mini-Micro 1985].

pSOS   Real-time Memory-Based Kernel for 68000. Software Components [Mini-Micro 1985].

Reduced Core Monitor   Minimum real-time executive for the CDC System 17. Early 1970s [Datapro 1974].

RMS09, RMS68K   Real-time operating system for 6809 and 68000 family. Motorola. Early 1980s [Mini-Micro 1985, 1986].

RMX-80, RMX-86   Real-time OS for the 8080 & 8086. Intel Corp., late 1970s [van der Linden & Wilson 1980].

RPS   Real-time Programming System. Real-time interactive operating system for the IBM Series/1, based on MSP/7 and MPX/1800. Late 1970s [Harrison et al. 1981].

RSX-11   Real-time multitasking executive for DEC PDP-11. Based on RSX-15. Digital Equipment Corp. [Digital 1984a, Cutler et al. 1976].

RSX-15   Real-time multitasking executive for DEC PDP-15. Digital Equipment Corp. [Krejci 1971].

RTE-I, RTE-II, RTE-III, RTE-IV   Real-time Operating Systems for Hewlett-Packard HP 2000 series. Mid-1970s [Anzinger 1975, Averett 1975, Wong 1978].

RTE-6/VM   Real-time virtual memory OS for dual HP1000s, featuring high reliability. Early 1980s [Serlin 1984].

RTE-A   Real-time Executive for HP 1000 A-series. Early 1980s [Hartman et al. 1984].

RTEX   Real-time executive for Interdata minicomputers. Ealry 1970s [Datapro 1974].

RTMOS   Real-time multiprogramming OS for GE computers.

RTM8   Real-time executive for the AMC 95/4000. Late 1970s [van der Linden & Wilson 1980].

RTMS   Real-time multiprogramming OS for General Automation System 18/30. Early 1970s [Datapro 1974].

RTOS   A real-time disk OS for Interdata Minicomputers. Early 1970s [Datapro 1974].

RTOS   Real-time OS for Data General Nova. Early 1970s [Datapro 1974].

RTOS   A real-time executive with foreground/background processing for General Automation SPC-16. Early 1970s [Datapro 1974].

RTOS   A real-time multiprogramming OS for Prime 100, 200, 300. Early 1970s [Datapro 1974].

RTOS-16   A real-time OS for the Digico Micro-16V. Early 1970s [Purser & Jennings 1975].

RTOS/360   A real-time OS for the IBM S/360, designed to support manned spacecraft. Late 1960s [Weiler et al. 1970].

RTR   Successor to DMERT for the AT&T 3B20 Duplex computer, featuring high reliability. Mid-1980s [Wallace & Barnes 1984].

RTTS   Real-time Task Scheduler. OS for August Systems Can't Fail 300 with triple 8086s, featuring high reliability. Mid-1980s [Serlin 1984].

RTUX   Real-time OS based on UNIX for 68000 based systems. Multiprocessing, multitasking, message driven. Emerge Systems, Early 1980s.

RTX   Real-time executive for General Automation System 18/30. Early 1970s [Datapro 1974].

RTX-16   Real-time executive for General Automation SPC-16. Early 1970s [Datapro 1974].

RTX-16   A real-time OS for the Honeywell Series 16. Early 1970s.

Rx   Real-time executive for the Texas Instruments TMS9900. Late 1970s [Zarella 1981].

SAX   Real-time OS for Mod Comp Computers. Early 1970s [Datapro 1974].

SIGMA 7 OS   OS for the SDS Sigma 7 real-time data processing computer. Mid-1960s [Day & Krejci 1968].

SPHERE   Real-time, ROM-based development system. Infosphere. [Mini-Micro 1985].

STARPLEX II   Real-time OS for the Z80A. National Semiconductor [Mini-Micro 1985].

TRON   The real-time Operating System Nucleus. Specification for a family of real-time operating systems and an associated CPU architecture. Developed at University of Tokyo. Mid-1980s [Sakamura 1987a, 1987b].

USX   Real-time development system for 8086, 68000. United States Software Corp., early 1980s [Mini-Micro 1986].

VAXELN   A real-time object-oriented OS for the MicroVAX. Early 1980s [Heinen 1984].

VORTEX   Omnitasking real-time executive for Varian minicomputers. Early 1970s [Datapro 1974].

VRTX   Versatile real-time executive. Modular real-time OS, portable to various micro CPUs. Hunter & Ready. Early 1980s [Funck 1984, Foard 1986, Ready 1986].

C.12 DISTRIBUTED OPERATING SYSTEMS

This section lists distributed operating systems, designed to provide common control for a set of computers communicating through a network. Distributed operating systems intended primarily for real-time applications are listed in the previous section.

ACCENT   Network OS kernel developed at Carnegie-Mellon University for the PERQ workstation. Early 1980s [Rashid & Robertson 1981].

AEGIS   OS for the Apollo DOMAIN distributed system. Early 1980s.

AMOEBA   A distributed OS based partly on UNIX. Early 1980s [Tanenbaum & Mullender 1981, Mullender & Tanenbaum 1986].

Arachne   A distributed operating system developed at the University of Wisconsin. Late 1970s [Finkel 1980].

BOS/NET   Multitasking, multiprocessing version of BOS/5.

Charlotte   Distributed OS for the Crystal Multicomputer project at the University of Wisconsin. Mid-1980s [Artsy et al. 1986].

CMDS   The Cambridge Model Distributed System. University of Cambridge (England). Late 1970s [Wilkes & Needham 1980].

COCONET   A local network operating system based on UNIX. Early 1980s [Rowe & Birman 1982].

CP/NET   Networking version of CP/M. Digital Research, early 1980s [Kildall 1981, Rolander 1981].

CP/NOS   A memory-resident, diskless version of CP/NET. Digital Research, early 1980s [Kildall 1981].

DISTOS   A Distributed OS for a network of 68000s.

DISTRIX   Message-based distributed version of UNIX. Early 1980s.

DPPX   An IBM Operating System for distributed processing. Late 1970s [Kiely 1981].

EDEN A distributed OS at the University of Washington, based on an integrated distributed network of bit-mapped workstations. Early 1980s [Lazowska et al. 1981].

LOCUS Distributed OS based on UNIX. Mid-1980s. [Popek & Walker 1985].

MICROS Distributed OS for MICRONET, a reconfigurable network computer. Late 1970s [Wittie & van Tilborg 1980].

MOS A Multicomputer distributed OS at the Hebrew University of Jerusalem. Controls four linked PDP-11s. Mid-1980s [Barak & Litman 1985].

MP/NET Version of MP/M with networking facilities. Digital Research, early 1980s [Kildall 1981].

MP/NOS Memory-resident, diskless version fo MP/NET. Digital Research, early 1980s [Kildall 1981].

Newcastle Connection A network OS layer for UNIX systems providing transparent distributed access. Early 1980s [Brownbridge et al. 1982].

NSW National Software Works. Late 1970s [Millstein 1977].

PC/NOS Network OS for MS-DOS or CP/M. Applied Intelligence [Row & Daugherty 1984].

REPOS Operating System for small PDP-11s attached to a host computer. Late 1970s [Maegaard & Andreasan 1979].

RIG Rochester Intelligent Gateway. Network OS developed at the University of Rochester. Early 1970s [Ball et al. 1976].

RIO/CP Network operating system for the ZNET. Late 1970s [Zarella 1981].

Roscoe Distributed OS for multiple identical processors (LSI-11s). University of Wisconsin, Late 1970s [Solomon & Finkel 1979].

RSEXEC .OD Network OS for the ARPANET, based principally on TENEX. Early 1970s [Thomas 1973].

Saguaro Distributed OS at the University of Arizona, supporting varying degrees of transparency. Mid-1980s [Andrews et al. 1987].

SODA A Simplified OS for Distributed Applications. Mid-1980s [Kepecs & Solomon 1985].

SODS/OS OS for a Distributed System developed on the IBM Series/1 at the University of Delaware. Late 1970s [Sincoskie & Farber 1980].

Sprite Distributed OS based on UNIX featuring remote procedure call, network file system, and process migration, developed at the University of California at Berkeley. Mid 1980s [Ousterhout et al. 1988].

TRIX A network-oriented OS. Late 1970s [Ward 1980].

uNETix Network OS for the 8086, 68000, and 16032 families. Multitasking with transparent remote file access, load balancing, and multiple windows. UNIX and PC-DOS compatible. Lantech Systems, mid-1980s [Foster 1984].

Uniflex Multitasking, multiprocessing OS for the 68000 family. Technical Systems Consultants, early 1980s [Mini-Micro 1986].

V Experimental Distributed OS linking powerful bit-mapped workstations at Stanford University. Early 1980s [Cheriton 1984, Berglund 1985].

C.13 SYSTEMS FOR UNUSUAL ARCHITECTURES

This section lists operating systems designed to control multiprocessors and other parallel and unconventional computer architectures. OSs for architectures designed for high reliability were listed in a previous section.

AMOK A Modular Operating Kernel for the CRAY-1 at the Institute for Defense Analysis. A modular timesharing system providing files, directories, processes, and pipes. Early 1980s [Huskamp 1985].

COS Cray Operating System. OS for the Cray-1 Pipelined Supercomputer. Late 1970s [Larson 1984].

CTSS Cray Timesharing System at Lawrence Livermore Labs. Early 1980s. Based on LTSS. [Fong 1985].

DEMOS Message-based OS for the CRAY-1, developed at Los Alamos. Late 1970s [Baskett & Montague 1977, Powell 1977].

EMBOS Message-based OS for the ELXSI multiprocessor. Mid-1980s [Olson 1985].

HEP Parallel OS for the HEP MIMD Computer. Late 1970s [Schmidt 1980].

HYDRA OS for C.mmp Research Multiprocessor. Carnegie-Mellon University, early 1970s [Wulf et al. 1974, 1975, 1980].

iMAX Multiprocessor OS for the Intel iAPX 432 object-based computer. Intel Corp., early 1980s [Kahn et al. 1981].

Mach Multiprocessor version of UNIX developed at Carnegie-Mellon University. Late 1980s.

Medusa OS for Cm* Research Multiprocessor. Carnegie-Mellon University, late 1970s [Ousterhout et al. 1980].

Meglos OS for a multiprocessor supercomputer, built from multiple 68000s and a VAX. Provides virtual circuits for two-way and broadcast messages. Mid-1980s [Gaglianello & Katseff 1985].

StarOS One of two major operating systems developed for the Cm* multiprocessor. Based on concept of task forces. Carnegie-Mellon University, late 1970s [Jones et al. 1979].

TWOS Time Warp Operating System. An OS developed at the Caltech Jet Propulsion Laboratory for the Mark III Hypercube multiprocessor, primarily to support asynchronous discrete event simulation. Synchronizes events by unlimited process rollback. Late 1980s [Jefferson et al. 1987].

VSOS Operating system for the Cyber 205 pipelined processor. Mid-1970s.

XOS Operating System for the experimental X-Tree computer architecture at the University of California at Berkeley. Early 1980s [Miller & Presotto 1981].

XYLEM   OS for the Cedar Multiprocessor, a high-speed, floating-point, shared memory, UNIX-like system at the University of Illinois. Mid-1980s [Emrath 1985].

C.14 EDUCATIONAL OPERATING SYSTEMS

KMOS   Kernel of a Multiprocess Operating System, designed for educational use in conjunction with a textbook by Milenkovic [1987]. Mid-1980s.

MINIX   Educational OS designed to be highly compatible with UNIX, for use with a text by Tanenbaum [1987]. Mid-1980s.

MPX   Multiprogramming Executive. Multitasking executive for small computers, designed for educational use at West Virginia University. Student project for this text (see Chapter 13).

TUNIS   Toronto University System. UNIX lookalike written in the EUCLID language. Early 1980s [Holt 1983].

XINU   Limited UNIX lookalike developed for educational purposes, for use with a text by Comer [1984]. "XINU Is Not UNIX." Early 1980s.

C.15 MISCELLANEOUS OPERATING SYSTEMS

This section is reserved for operating systems that could not readily be assigned to any other category.

DJS200/XT1   An OS for the Chinese DJS210 & DJS220 computers. Late 1970s [Zhongxiu et al. 1980].

DOS   Disk Operating System. Generic name used for many operating systems. Well-known ones include DOS/360, DOS/VS, and DOS/3.3.

DSM-11   Database oriented operating system for MUMPS applications on the PDP-11 and VAX. Digital Equipment Corp. [Digital 1984a].

IAS   Operating system for larger PDP-11 systems. Real-time, multiuser, or both. Digital Equipment Corp. [Digital 1984a].

MODULAR ONE   A portable, modular OS at the University of Warwick. Late 1970s [Footit & Whitby-Strevens 1974].

MPX   Multiprogramming Executive. Real-time multitasking plus batch OS for the IBM 1800. Late 1960s [Harrison et al. 1981, Sayers 1971].

MSOS   Mass storage OS supporting real-time plus batch processing for the CDC System 17.

MUSS   OS designed to emphasize portability. Late 1970s [Frank & Theaker 1979a, 1979b, Theaker & Frank 1979].

NIDOS   OS for the Nixdorf 8890. Early 1980s(?) [Computerworld 1984].

OS   Generic name for many operating systems. Most often applied to OS/360.

OS/2 and OS/10.   Operating Systems for the MDS Series 21. Early 1980s(?) [Computerworld 1984].

PICK   Business-oriented OS featuring an integral relational database. Pick Systems. IBM PC-XT and others. Early 1970s [Cook & Brandon 1984a, 1984b, Sisk & Van Arsdale 1985].

RBM   Real-time Batch Monitor for Xerox Data Systems minicomputers. Early 1970s [Sayers 1971].

REALITY   Early version of PICK.

RM/COS   Multiuser, multiprocessing OS for 68000. Cobol-based business environment for an abstract C-machine. Ryan-McFarland Corp., early 1980s [Hindin 1984].

ROS   OS with Ada Support for 8086, 68000. Telesoft [Mini-Micro 1985].

S1   Modular building block OS adaptable to various configurations. 8080, 8086 and 68000 families. Multi-Solutions, Inc. Mid-1980s [Little 1984].

S5   OS for the ALTOS computer (?).

SOLO   Single-user research OS written in Concurrent Pascal to demonstrate its concurrency mechanisms. Developed by Per Brinch Hansen. Mid-1970s [Brinch Hansen 1976a, 1976b, 1976c].

T.H.E.   Research OS developed by Edsgar Dijkstra. Named for the Technische Hoogeschool (University) at Eindhoven (Holland), where it was developed. Early exploration of program verification techniques. Early layered system design. First implementation of semaphores. Late 1960s [Dijkstra 1968, McKeag et al. 1976].

THOTH   Experimental real-time portable OS. Late 1970s [Cheriton et al. 1979, Cheriton 1982].

Trio   Operating system for three users, written in Concurrent Pascal, based on SOLO. Late 1970s [Brinch Hansen & Fellows 1980].

TSX   Timesharing Executive. Real-time plus batch OS for the IBM 1800. Mid-1960s [Harrison et al. 1981].

TSX-PLUS   RT-11 compatible multitasking, multiprocessing OS for PDP-11 family. S&H Computer Systems. Early 1980s [Sherrod & Brenner 1984, Yardley 1985].

Ultimate   Version of PICK. The Ultimate Corp.

VRX   Operating System for NCR 8455. Early 1980s(?) [Computerworld 1984].

VS   OS for Wang VS series systems. Early 1980s(?) [Computerworld 1984].

XT1   Operating system for the Chinese DJS210 and DJS220, developed at Nanking University. Multiprogrammed and deadlock-free. Late 1970s [Zhongxiu et al. 1980].

Dictionary

Absolute address An address that directly and completely identifies a location in the current address space; *compare with* relative address.

Absolute addressing An addressing mode in which the value contained in the address field of an instruction is an absolute address.

Abstract block storage device A model that uniformly represents various storage devices, which store and transfer information in blocks.

Abstract machine A formal definition of a processor architecture, including both the instruction set and specifications for memory access; often simulated by software or firmware on computers having a different architecture, so that programs translated to abstract machine instructions can run on many different computers.

Access control A computer system protection mechanism that controls the types of operations permitted on each resource by each process, allowing sharing of information in a controlled manner.

Access control field A portion of a page or segment descriptor, or of a capability, that specifies the set of access rights permitted for the object represented by the descriptor.

Access control list *See* access list.

Access control policy A security policy, established by system management, that specifies how access to stored data is controlled.

Access list An access control mechanism that associates a list of subjects or domains *(q.v.)* and corresponding access rights with each object or resource.

Access matrix A two-dimensional matrix, representing an access control policy, in which the domains or subjects are listed in rows and the objects or resources ae listed in columns.

Access method A procedure or collection of procedures implementing operations that support a particular type of access to a file; usually used for high-level file structures, such as indexed files.

Access right A permission to execute an operation (e.g., read or write) on an object.

Accounting An OS activity dealing with the tracking of user sessions, jobs, and resources used; required for proper billing of users for computer service.

Active set The set of processes that may compete at any given time for use of the CPU; usually corresponds to those processes currently swapped into the main memory.

Ada language A standard computer language, defined and developed primarily for the U.S. Department of Defense; designed especially for real-time applications.

Ada tasks Separate program units in an Ada program that execute concurrently.

Address A numerical value identifying the location of an object in physical memory or a particular address space.

Address field A portion of a machine instruction that specifies an address or a component of an address.

Address space A collection of addresses that can be specified by the machine instructions of a particular computer architecture; usually forms a sequence of values beginning with zero; used to identify locations in memory, I/O devices, and possibly other resources. A specific architecture may provide a single address space for both memory and I/O devices, or a separate address space for each. *See also* I/O space.

Addressing techniques The collection of methods available for expressing addresses within machine instructions.

Aging Increasing scheduling priorities for processes or I/O requests that have waited a long time for service; used to prevent a process from waiting forever or for an unreasonable amount of time.

Alert interrupt An unexpected interrupt from a source outside of the computer; for example, a request signal from another computer system.

Alias One of a set of alternative names that designate the same file or other object.

Allocate A system call that requests the assignment of a block of memory or other resource for use by the calling process.

Allocated memory control block A control block *(q.v.)* representing a block of memory allocated to a process; *abbreviated* AMCB.

Allocation The assignment of memory or resources to a user or process.

ALU *See* arithmetic and logic unit.

AMCB *See* allocated memory control block.

American National Standards Institute An organization devoted to developing and maintaining formal technical standards in the United States; *abbreviated* ANSI.

Analytic modeling The representation of a computing system by a mathematical model, especially a queueing model, and the analysis of this model in order to predict its performance under various conditions.

ANSI *See* American National Standards Institute.

Application process A process that runs an application program, and is not part of the operating system; *compare with* system process.

Application program In a computer system, a program that runs to perform the work required by users, rather than the work of the operating system and its associated programs; *compare with* system program.

Approximate LRU A virtual memory page replacement algorithm that approximates "least recently used" *(q.v.)* by grouping pages into a few groups according to recency of use.

Architecture The set of elements and operations of a computer system that are normally visible to application or system programs (including the operating system), together with their interconnections and relationships; *compare with* implementation.

Archival memory A type of memory or storage device used for storing large quantities of data for long periods of time and that is not normally on-line. Archival memory usually is on sequential media, such as magnetic tape, and must be mounted by an operator when read.

Arithmetic and logic unit The principal component of the processing section of a CPU that contains the circuits to perform basic arithmetic computations like addition, subtraction, multiplication, and division, and basic logical operations like "and," "or," and complement; *abbreviated* ALU.

Assembler   A program that translates simple instruction statements, called mnemonics, written in assembly language *(q.v.)*, to binary machine language or object code. Each statement generally translates into one machine instruction, although "macro" facilities are sometimes included to represent multiple instructions with a single statement; *compare with* compiler.

Assembly language   A language, representing the instructions for a particular computer as mnemonic instructions, that can be translated by an assembler *(q.v.)*; *compare with* high-level language.

Associative memory   A type of memory in which data items can be accessed directly by specifying a portion of their contents rather than an address; *also called* content-addressable memory.

Astonishment factor   A measure of the surprise experience by a user when an interactive command interface provides an unexpected response to an action performed.

Asymmetric message passing   A mechanism for message passing between process in which only the sender must name the other process; the receiver accepts any available message without specifying the sender; *compare with* symmetric message passing.

Asynchronous file access   A method for accessing files in which, after a process requests a read or write operation, control may return to the process before the transfer is complete; the process may perform other actions during the transfer but must check explicitly before assuming that the operation has completed; *compare with* synchronous file access.

Asynchronous I/O   I/O operations like read and write that return control to the caller as soon as the operation has been set up, even though the actual transfer has not completed, or perhaps has not even begun.

Asynchronous interrupt   A pending interrupt whose exact time of occurrence is unknown.

Atlas   An early computer system developed at the University of Manchester in the early 1960s. *See* Section C.2.

Atomic transaction   A sequence of activities performed by a process which, when viewed by any other process, must always appear either as if it was not yet started or entirely complete.

Auditing   1) Checking the use of computing facilities using OS accounting records; 2) validating financial information or other sensitive data stored in a computer system, and the software that processes this information.

Authentication   A procedure implementing passwords or other measures to verify that a user trying to access a computer system or a specific set of resources is properly authorized; *also called* user authentication.

Authorization of access   A security policy specifying who may access certain entities in a computer system.

Automated maintenance log   A log stored in a disk file that tracks changes to the operating system; produced by software tools that force systems programmers to enter required information, such as date of change, identification of systems programmer, the problem solved, and change mode.

Availability   The degree to which a computing system or set of resources is available for use when required.

Available list   A list of pages or memory blocks in a memory allocation system that are available for allocation when required.

Backup procedures   The set of activities that provide for the regular or on-demand copying of data from disk to back up media, such as another disk or magnetic tape; these procedures include the operating system's programs for making such backups, including the ability to selectively backup data.

Bad block table   A table stored on a disk medium at a fixed, known location that lists blocks on disk found to be bad during formatting or by a file-check facility.

Bad sector table   A table stored on a disk medium at a fixed, known location that lists the addresses of sectors on disk found to be bad during formatting.

Bad track table   A table stored on a disk medium at a fixed, known location that lists the addresses of tracks on disk found to be bad during formatting.

Banker's algorithm   An algorithm for dynamically avoiding deadlock *(q.v.)* by ensuring that resource allocation requests are honored only if the resulting state of the system contains no immediate risk of deadlock.

Base address   The first address in a physical block that is stored in a translation table and used for translating a virtual address to real address.

Base addressing   A common addressing technique in which the value contained in the address field of an instruction is added to the contents of a special register, called a base register, to form the actual address. Often used to systematically modify all addresses with a program by the same value to perform relocation *(q.v.)*; *compare with* indexed addressing.

Base-plus-displacement addressing   *See* base addressing.

Base register   A register normally used to address value for base addressing *(q.v.)*.

Basic Input/Output System   The portion of CP/M, MS-DOS, and other microcomputer operating systems that provides a standard program interface for control of I/O devices; *abbreviated* BIOS.

Batch multiprogramming system   A batch processing system *(q.v.)* that interleaves the execution of several batch processes *(q.v.)* concurrently, enabling some processes to execute while others are waiting for I/O operations; *compare with* batch serial system.

Batch process   In a batch multiprogramming system, a process that executes a series of batch jobs.

Batch processing system   An operating system in which units of work, called jobs *(q.v.)*, are submitted as a batch rather than interactively, and results are returned later when the work is complete. *See also* batch multiprogramming system, batch serial system.

Batch serial system   A batch processing system *(q.v.)* that executes only a single batch job at a time.

Benchmark   An artificial work load, or set of jobs, representative of the work normally done by a computer system; used to measure and evaluate performance.

Best-fit   An algorithm for memory allocation that considers all free blocks and selects the one that results in the smallest "hole," or remainder, after allocation.

Binary portability   A type of portability in which executable programs, which have been compiled and linked on one computer system, can be transported to another system and run without change; *compare with* source portability.

Binary semaphore   A semaphore *(q.v.)* that can take on only the values 0 and 1; normally used to control access to resources that can be used by only one process at a time; *compare with* general semaphore.

BIOS   *See* Basic Input/Output System.

Bit   An acronym for BInary digiT; a single binary value that may be either 1 or 0; also, a storage element that represents a single bit.

Bit map   A representation of a set of binary information as a series of bits; especially, a technique for managing fixed-sized blocks of memory or disk space in which each bit represents the state (allocated or free) of a specific block.

Bit-mapped display   A video display unit connected to a computer system in which a bit or group of bits in main memory or a separate programmable memory represents the attributes of each pixel *(q.v.)* on the screen. Changing these bits in memory automatically changes the corresponding pixels on the display screen; *compare with* character-mapped display.

Block descriptor   A data item that describes the translation of a particular block of memory in a memory translation system. In general, a block descriptor must specify the starting address of the block in the virtual and physical address spaces, the size of the block, and possibly a set of access rights. *See also* page descriptor, segment descriptor.

Block transfer   Transfer of a block of data that consists of a number of bytes or words between main memory and an I/O device in a single operation; generally associated with direct memory access device *(q.v.)*.

Blocked chained organization   A file system organization in which all files consist of a sequence of fixed-size blocks that may be located independently on the storage device. Each block contains a pointer to the following block, forming a chain or linked list; *compare with* blocked indexed organization, contiguous organization, contiguous organization with extends.

Blocked indexed organization   A file system organization in which all files consist of a sequence of fixed-size blocks that may be located independently on the storage device. A tree-structured index is used to keep track of the location of each block; *compare with* blocked chained organization, contiguous organization, contiguous organization with extends.

Blocked state   A process state *(q.v.)* assigned to a process that is unable to proceed because it is waiting for a resource or event. A process in the blocked state must be moved to the ready state *(q.v.)* before it can be scheduled for execution; *also called* waiting state; *compare with* IO_active state, IO_init state.

Booting   The process of loading a computer system's operating system from disk and preparing it for initial execution; short for "bootstrap loading," so named because it resembles lifting oneself by one's own bootstraps (starting something from nothing). *See also* cold start.

Boot time   The time in which an operating system is loaded and initialized; *also called* initial program load time.

Boundary   A specific physical memory address used to check the validity of a program's address reference for both instruction execution and data.

Boundary register   A register that keeps track of a low or high boundary to validate a program or process's address reference.

Boundary tag   A technique used in memory allocation, in which a "tag" and length value are maintained at the beginning and end of each allocated or free block so that free blocks may be easily collapsed from multiple free contiguous blocks to a single, larger free block.

Bounds register   One of a pair of registers used to provide both an upper and a lower bound on memory that is accessible to an application program.

Branch instruction   A machine instruction *(q.v.)* that may modify the flow of control within a program by changing the value in the program counter, causing the next instruction to be fetched from a location other than that sequentially following the current instruction.

Break character   1) a special character input to an interactive command interface that will be immediately recognized and may cause some action such as aborting the current program, even if normal input is being buffered for later processing; 2) a condition on an asynchronous communications line that is forced by holding the line in a zero (space) condition for longer than the duration of the START (space) condition, the data character, and the STOP (mark) condition; break "characters" result in a framing error condition in the receiving hardware that is often used as an attention signal in interactive environments.

Brief mode   A mode that may be selected for a command interface in which prompts and messages from the system are displayed in an abbreviated form.

Buddy system   A memory allocation strategy for variable-sized blocks in which blocks are restricted to a limited set of sizes, each half as large as the next. A block may only be divided into two equal-sized halves; if a block is divided, the two halves are considered "buddies" and eventually will be rejoined when they are both free.

Buffer   A data area used for storing data that must be buffered during transmission between processes or between a process and an I/O device; may be located within the address space of a process, or within a device drive or the operating system's I/O routines.

Buffering   A technique for storing data to be sent from one process to another or transmitted between a process and an I/O device, if the data is produced by the sender before the receiver is ready to accept it; buffering often involves blocking and deblocking of data from large physical records to smaller logical records.

Busy waiting   A method by which a program or process waits for an event or condition by repeatedly testing whether the event has occurred or the condition is true, rather than by entering a blocked state or relying on an interrupt.

Byte   A unit of storage in a computer used to store a set of bits, usually eight bits, large enough to represent the code assigned to one character; often the smallest unit that is separately addressable.

Cache memory   A small, fast memory located in the memory hierarchy between the main memory and the CPU registers used to hold selected data from main memory, providing faster access than would otherwise be possible.

Capability   A data item that specifies a set of access rights for a particular object or resource, and controls access to that object. *See also* capability list, object, access control.

Capability list   A set of capabilities associated with a specific process or domain *(q.v.)*.

Catalog   A file directory *(q.v.)* that identifies a selected set of files for use by a particular user or application; also, a synonym for directory.

CCB   *See* channel control block.

CCW   *See* channel command word.

Central processing unit   The hardware unit within a computer system that fetches and executes instructions; *also called* processor; *abbreviated* CPU.

Channel   A type of I/O processor *(q.v.)* used on IBM mainframe computers.

Channel command word   An instruction within a channel program *(q.v.)* used to direct an I/O operation for a device, or to force a branch to fetch the next channel command word at an address other than the next sequential address; usually produced by the CPU, but fetched and executed by a channel *(q.v.)* that controls devices; *abbreviated* CCW.

Channel contention   The attempted use of the same channel *(q.v.)* by two or more processes at the same time; heavy channel contention results in excessive wait time for processes. *See also* waiting time.

Channel control block   A control block *(q.v.)* that represents channel activity to the operating system; *abbreviated* CCB.

Channel number   The identifying number assigned to a channel.

Channel program   A series of channel command words *(q.v.)* forming a program that is "executed" by a channel to direct I/O for devices attached to that channel.

Character   A binary representation for a printable symbol or associated control code; usually eight bits or less, and able to be stored in one byte; the most common character codes are ASCII and EBCDIC.

Character conversion   The process of translating a character from one representation to another (e.g., ASCII to EBCDIC.)

Character-mapped display   A display that is driven by characters stored in a series of bytes; *compare with* a bit-mapped display.

Checkpoint   A point in the execution of a program at which all data necessary to represent the current status of the program is recorded in a checkpoint record *(q.v.)*, so that execution may be restarted from this point in case the program is normally or abnormally interrupted later; particularly useful in a program or series of programs that take a long time to complete.

Checkpoint records   Records written periodically to external storage devices in order to track the progress of certain jobs or programs in execution; typically used to restart the job at the last checkpoint *(q.v.)* without requiring the job to be rerun from the beginning.

Checksum   A binary value computed from all values in a block of data, often by adding all values and ignoring overflow; often used to detect errors in reading data from a storage device or communication line. The checksum is computed for the data read or transmitted, and compared with the original checksum that was also transmitted or stored; if the checksums match, the data is assumed to be correct.

Child process   A process that is created by another process (the parent process) and is subordinate to that parent process in a hierarchy of processes.

Circular list   A linked list of data items in which every item contains a pointer to another; a program following the pointers from any item would reach all other items and return to the original one.

Circular requests   A condition that may occur during resource allocation, in which two or more processes may request resources held by another in such a way that a circle is formed in the request for resource, with each process in the set holding a resource being requested by another; each process is thus blocked with no means of receiving the resource, resulting in deadlock.

Classification   A policy that provides a system of levels of access, with each level having certain access rights.

Clock   A hardware device or software data structure used to measure time. *See also* hardware clock, software clock.

CLOCK algorithm   A page replacement algorithm in a virtual memory system, in which all pages are organized in a circular list and scanned in a manner resembling the moving hand of a clock. Pages not recently used are selected for replacement when reached if they are unmodified; if modified (dirty), they are scheduled for rewriting (cleaning).

Clock resolution   The time interval between two clock ticks *(q.v.)*; thus, the smallest time interval the clock is able to measure.

Clock tick   A discrete signal generated by a hardware clock, at time intervals that may be fixed (e.g., every sixtieth of a second) or variable; may cause an interrupt or increment, or may decrement a counter. The time interval between successive ticks determines the clock resolution *(q.v.)*.

Close   A system call used to advise the operating system that the file is no longer needed for I/O; results in the operating system's deallocating buffers and making adjustments to the file descriptor; essential after writing because some data may not yet have been copied from buffers in memory to the actual file; *compare with* open.

Clustering   A strategy for fetching pages in a virtual memory system, by which a cluster of adjacent pages is fetched into main memory when any page in the cluster is referenced.

CMS   *See* Conversational Monitor System.

Cold start   The action of loading an operating system "from scratch" without retaining any of the information in main memory representing work in progress when the previous OS execution was terminated; *compare with* warm start.

Command   A statement in a command language *(q.v.)* that specifies an action to be performed by the operating system, such as running a program, together with a set of file names or other parameters to be used for that action; generally typed by users during an interactive session.

Command abbreviation   1) A short form for a command that may be recognized by a command interface; 2) a feature of some command interface that allows the use of such short forms.

Command arguments   The additional parameters supplied in a command, along with the command name, specifying options or entities, such as files, to be used when executing the command.

Command completion   A facility provided by some command interfaces, in which the system may automatically supply the remainder of a command name after a sufficient initial portion has been typed.

Command file   A file that contains commands that the command interface can interpret as if they had been entered by a user via a terminal.

Command handler   A program unit that interprets and executes commands; a principal component of a command interface *(q.v.)*.

Command herald   A special character that a user may enter to a command interface or terminal handler, indicating that the next sequence of characters represents a command; normally recognized in a wide variety of contexts, during interaction with both command interfaces and application programs.

Command interface   One of the two major components of the user interface *(q.v.)* in an operating system, responsible for receiving and interpreting instructions from users to carry out actions such as executing programs, and for returning associated messages to users; most often associated with interactive sessions.

Command language   A language that specifies a set of commands and a form for commands and arguments.

Command line   A synonym for command *(q.v.)*; especially, one or more commands typed on a single line.

Command log   A file that records all of the commands executed by a system over a period of time, and possibly other interactive communication.

Command name   The portion of a command that specifies the action to be performed or program to be executed, distinct from the command arguments *(q.v.)*.

Command reference manual   An operating system manual that is organized like a command-specific encyclopedia.

Command summary card   A card that summarizes an operating system's commands and their syntax.

Communication   1) The exchange of information between two processes, especially in the form of messages *(q.v.)*; 2) transmission of data between two computing systems, or between a computing system and a remote terminal or I/O device.

Communication deadlock   A form of deadlock *(q.v.)* in which a process waits indefinitely for a message from another process that has already been sent and lost, or that will never be sent.

Communication security   Protection of information that is transmitted from one computer to another, often necessarily over physically vulnerable connections.

Compaction   The technique of moving programs and data in a computer's memory, or on a storage device such as a disk, so that all free space is in one block; used to solve fragmentation problems in systems that allow dynamic relocation of programs.

Compatible Time Sharing System   An early timesharing OS developed at M.I.T.: *abbreviated* CTSS. *See* Section C.4.

Compiler   A program that translates source programs written in a high-level language *(q.v.)* into object programs or executable programs. One statement in such a language generally is translated into many machine language instructions; *compare with* assembler.

Completeness   A property of a command language by which all commands and structures that logically "should" be included are included.

Component fault   A failure of a computing system component, which previously functioned properly, that may result in incorrect operation.

Compute-bound   A characteristic of a process by which it uses relatively large amounts of CPU time without making an I/O request; *also called* CPU-bound; *compare with* I/O-bound.

Computer network   A collection of computers and related devices with the ability to communicate via communications media controlled by a communications protocol. *See also* wide area network and local area network.

Computer virus   A single program that gains unauthorized access to a system and modifies the operating system or other system programs in such a way that an "infection" of modifications to suit the invader's purpose spreads throughout the system.

Computing system   A system made up of one or more central processing units, memory, and a variety of I/O devices, together with an operating system and associated system programs.

Concurrent execution   Execution of a collection of processes or other activities in such a way that they appear to proceed at the same time; may be achieved by a collection of distinct processors, but more often by interleaved execution *(q.v.)* by a single processor or CPU.

Concurrent processes   A set of processes undergoing concurrent execution.

Concurrent sequential processes   A synonym for concurrent processes that emphasizes the sequential nature of the activity performed by each individual process.

CONFIG.SYS   A file that specifies configuration information used by MS-DOS when it is loaded; allows limited configuration, e.g., specifying additional devices to be recognized.

Configuration management   Managing changes and variations in an operating system or other program by maintaining suitable records and controlling the procedures by which changes may occur.

Consistency   A characteristic of a command interface by which the meaning and behavior of similar structures is consistent and predictable in a variety of different contexts.

Construction errors   Errors in the construction of hardware or software components of a computing system or application program, in which the components fail in some way to conform to their intended design.

Consumable resource   A resource, such as a message, which is consumed or "used up" when it is implemented; *compare with* reusable resource.

Content-addressable memory   *See* associative memory.

Context   The environment of a process during execution, including registers, program counter, stack pointer, and hardware status.

Context switching   Switching CPU control from one process, saving its context, selecting another process, restoring its context, and transferring CPU control to this new process.

Contiguous organization   A type of file organization in which all the information for a file is stored in sequential locations on a storage device; *compare with* blocked chained organization, blocked indexed organization, contiguous organization with extents.

Contiguous organization with extents   A type of file organization in which all the information for a file is stored in a single sequential block or a small number of sequential blocks; *compare with* blocked chained organization, blocked indexed organization, contiguous organization.

Control block   A data structure used by the operating system to represent the current status of a process, resource, or activity.

Control instructions   Machine instructions *(q.v.)* that include miscellaneous categories, such as halting the computer or modifying certain system flags and control registers; usually these are privileged instruction.

Control Program   The name of the virtual machine monitor in VM/370. *See* Section C.10.

Control section   The section of a CPU responsible for directing its activities in processing various instructions.

Controlled sharing   A principal goal of most operating systems; supporting the sharing of information or resources among users or processes while controlling access to that information or those resources to ensure that they are used in a correct and secure manner.

Controller contention The attempted use of the same device controller by two or more processes at the same time. Heavy controller contention results in excessive wait time for processes. *See also* wait time.

Convenient use A principal goal of most operating systems; making the resources of a computing system easier to use than if the operating system were not present.

Conversational Monitor System A single-user interactive operating system that is a principal component of VM/370; *abbreviated* CMS. *See* Section C.10.

Copyright law A law that deals with the protection of the expression of ideas, but not the idea itself; typically used to protect literary works but can be used to protect software; *compare with* patent law.

Core An early type of main memory, each bit of which consisted of a magnetic core that was magnetized by wires passing through the core, with current flowing in one direction to represent 0 and another to represent 1; often used as a generic synonym for any main memory, particularly by "old-timers" in the computer field.

Core dump An exact image of the memory of a computer written to some storage medium or printed on a printer; used for analyzing operating system problems; *also called* OS system image dump.

Correctness A property of a computer system by which the correct outputs are produced in a reasonable amount of time for a given set of inputs; one of the principal goals of reliability.

Counting semaphore *See* general semaphore.

CP *See* Control Program.

CP/CMS A predecessor to VM/370. *See* Section C.10.

CP/M An early microcomputer operating system. *See* Section C.6.

CPU *See* central processing unit.

CPU-bound *See* compute-bound.

CPU register A hardware storage unit within a CPU, usually the size of a memory word, that is capable of storing a single data item; *compare with* register.

CPU throughput A measure of the amount of work done by a CPU per unit of time, often measured in jobs or sessions per day along with some measure of the characteristics of the jobs or sessions.

CPU time quantum A time quantum *(q.v.)*, or time interval allocated to a process, specifying how long it may run when placed in the running stage; if the time quantum expires, the process is returned to the ready state and another process may be selected for execution.

CPU utilization A measure of the level of use of the CPU; typically, a measure of the time the CPU is not idle, but is executing the operating system, system processes, or application processes.

Create process A system call requesting the creation of a new child process.

Critical section A portion of a program during which a serially reusable resource is used in such a manner that mutual exclusion is required. Correct operation requires that entry into the critical section be controlled by an entry protocol *(q.v.)*, which ensures that a process may not enter a critical section while the required resource is in use by another process.

CTSS *See* Compatible Time Sharing System.

Current directory The directory that is used by default when no directory is explicitly specified, in file systems supporting multiple directories.

Cylinder A set of tracks on a disk, including multiple surfaces or platters, consisting of one track from each surface, all in the same relative position.

Dartmouth Timesharing System An early timesharing operating system; *abbreviated* DTSS. *See* Section C.4.

Data manipulation instructions Machine instructions *(q.v.)* that operate on data (input) and produce new data values (results).

Data registers Registers in the storage section of a CPU that holds data as needed for CPU operations.

Datagram A strategy in a communications network for routing each packet individually to its destination; *compare with* virtual circuit.

DCB *See* device control block.

DCS *See* distributed computing system.

De facto standards Standards *(q.v.)* that arise through widespread use rather than from a formal standard *(q.v.)*, such as the "IBM-compatible" standard for microcomputers.

Deadlock A condition in which each of a group of processes is waiting for an event, such as the release of a resource, which can be caused only by another process in the set; therefore, none of the processes can make further progress.

Deadlock avoidance A technique for dynamically avoiding deadlock by granting requests for resource allocation only when these requests will not place the system in immediate risk of deadlock. *See also* banker's algorithm.

Deadlock detection A technique that may be used to discover deadlock if it exists among a set of processes.

Deadlock prevention A strategy for preventing deadlock by designing the system in such a way that at least one of the necessary conditions for deadlock cannot occur; these conditions include mutual exclusion, resource holding, no preemption, and circular waiting *(q.v.)*.

Deadlock recovery The process of restoring a system to normal operation after deadlock has been discovered, while limiting the consequences of the deadlock.

Debugger A system program used during software development or maintenance to examine, analyze, trace the execution of, and possibly modify a program that is being executed. Early debuggers were hardware-oriented, using commands that allowed registers to be examined and physical memory addresses to be specified without regard to the fact that programs being executed were high-level language programs. *See also* high-level language debugger, symbolic debugger.

Decryption Translation of a message or data item from an encoder form, which effectively hides its meaning, to an unencoded form, in which its meaning is clear; used to enhance the security of messages and data. *See also* encryption.

Dedicated system A (computer) system normally used exclusively for processing a particular program or set of programs, such as an airline reservation system or a navigation system.

Default access list A list consisting of <domain,access-rights-set> entries that can be searched either before or after the search of an access list, thus eliminating entries in access lists for certain standard default access rights.

Defensive programming Programming techniques that assume errors will be made by other modules or portion of the program, and that verify that data provided is indeed correct before using the data.

Delete An OS system call (file operation) used to remove a specified file from a file system.

Demand fetching A strategy for fetching pages or segments into main memory in a virtual memory system, which fetches a page or segment only when it is actually referenced. This strategy avoids loading pages or segments that may never be needed.

Design error An error in a hardware or software component of a computer system resulting from incorrect design—that is, a design that fails in some way to meet the requirements of the component.

Destroy process A system call that may be used by one process to request the termination of another.

Detection equipment Equipment installed in the vicinity of a computer system to detect physical threats to security such as intrusion, fire, or electronic signals.

Determinism A property normally expected of a system of concurrent processes, whereby the outputs of each process are determined only by its inputs and not by the behavior of other processes.

Device contention The attempted use of the same device by two or more processes at the same time. Heavy device contention results in excessive wait time for processes. *See also* waiting time.

Device control block A control block that represents the status of a specific I/O device.

Device driver A software module that controls an I/O device, including the handling of interrupts.

Device idle time Time during which a given device performs no useful work.

Device independence The ability of an operating system to provide an I/O environment that supports uniform reading from and writing to devices independent of the device type; usually allows the selection of input and output devices to be made or changed without modifying the programs that access them.

Device interrupt handler The portion of a device driver that is responsible for handling or servicing interrupts produced by the device.

Device management The portion of an operating system that deals with scheduling and control of I/O devices.

Device name A name used by an OS to refer to an I/O device.

Device polling A technique for managing I/O devices that uses repeated checking of a device's status, rather than interrupts, in order to determine when an I/O operation has finished.

Device read overrun An error condition occurring during a device read operation on a programmed-I/O device caused by the next input character arriving before the previous character has been processed by the program (interrupt handler); the result is the loss of one data character and the device read overrun error bit for the device being turned on.

Device registers Registers that control or transfer data to and from an I/O device.

Device simultaneity Simultaneous operation of two or more devices.

Device throughput The number of records, transactions, lines, and so on that a device can transfer in a given unit of time.

DGS *See* distributed file system.

Diagnostic program A program executed to validate hardware operation. Portions of diagnostic programs are typically executed upon the loading of the operating system, or on demand when a hardware problem is suspected.

Direct addressing 1) A synonym for absolute addressing; 2) an addressing technique in which the address computed from the address field, plus a possible base register or index register, is the address of the actual operand to be used; *compare with* indirect addressing.

Direct measurement *See* performance measurement.

Direct memory access An input/output mechanism by which a device or its associated interface has a direct physical connection to the main memory, and is capable of transferring data to or from the main memory without intervention by the CPU; *abbreviated* DMA.

Directory A storage area within a file volume that contains descriptive information specifying the location and attributes of the file, together with a name for the file; used to access files and their descriptive information by specifying their names.

Directory name An identifying name assigned to a directory, usually in a file system that supports multiple directories.

Dirty bit A one-bit field in a page or segment descriptor that indicates whether the corresponding page or segment has been modified since it was loaded into main memory; *also called* page modified flag.

Discretionary security policy Rules in a security policy that allow users some discretion in applying the rules under certain conditions; *compare with* nondiscretionary security policy.

Disk operating system An operating system for which a disk is the principal storage medium for files, usually including both application and system files and copies of the operating system itself; *compare with* tape operating system.

Disk scheduling The selection of the next request from one or more I/O queues that is to be processed by a disk; the request selected depends on the scheduling techniques being used. *See also* shortest seek time first.

Dispatcher The module in the operating system that is responsible for immediate assignment of the CPU to processes in the ready state—that is, for context switching.

Distributed computing system A computing system consisting of a group of computers or processors used to process a common work load submitted on behalf of a single collection of users and viewed as a unified computing system; *abbreviated* DCS.

Distributed file system A file system in a distributed computing system in which file storage is distributed among a number of different locations; its objective is to present each user with a virtual, unified file system in which files may be accessed without concern for their actual location, remote or local; *abbreviated* DFS.

Distributed operating system An operating system that provides control for a distributed computing system, allowing its resources to be accessed in a unified way.

DLIB An acronym for OS distribution libraries in an IBM mainframe operating system environment.

DMA *See* direct memory access.

Domain *See* protection domain.

DOS *See* disk operating system.

Double buffering A buffering technique in which two or more buffers are used for the same stream of data, allowing data to be simultaneously stored into one buffer and read from another.

DTSS　*See* Dartmouth Timesharing System.

Dumb terminals　Terminals that are not programmable; includes terminals that provide emulation of a variety of terminals and hence have some configuration capability, but are yet not programmable in the traditional sense.

Dynamic allocation　Allocation of resources to a process during its execution, as opposed to allocation only upon initial loading or prior to execution; *compare with* static allocation.

Dynamic linking　Resolution of references by a program unit to another program unit or data structure during program execution, rather than by a linking process prior to execution; allows components of a program to be loaded only when and if they are actually referenced. MULTICS is the classic example of a system that provides dynamic linking via symbolic segmentation support.

Dynamic memory area definition　A strategy for defining memory blocks that can be assigned to a process when it is loaded; blocks are defined and assigned dynamically by the OS based on the state of memory allocation at the time of a request for loading a process; *compare with* static memory area definition.

Dynamic priority　A process scheduling priority that may change based on the current characteristics or past behavior of the process; *compare with* static priorities.

Dynamic process management　Process management *(q.v.)* in which processes may be created or destroyed during the operation of the system; *compare with* static process management.

Dynamic reconfiguration　The action of changing the effective physical interconnections and configuration of a computing system under program control while the system is in operation, in order to maintain reliability.

Dynamic regions　Areas of main memory assigned to a process whose size can change while the process is in operation.

Dynamic relocation　The ability to move or relocate a program to a different region of main memory after it has begun execution.

ECB　*See* event control block.

Echoing　Displaying each character typed on a keyboard on the corresponding display screen or hardcopy printer as soon as it is typed; normally performed by the terminal interface.

Editor　A system program provided with most operating systems that supports convenient interactive manipulation of text. Two important types of editors are line-oriented editors and full-screen editors *(q.v.)*.

Effective address　The final address value computed from the address field of a machine instruction after application of addressing techniques, such as base, indexed, or indirect addressing, but before translation by a memory mapping or virtual memory system.

Embedded system　A dedicated computer system that is a part of a larger total physical system, such as an automobile or industrial facility. An embedded system frequently has no command interface of its own.

Encryption　Translation of a message or data item from its normal, unencoded form to an encoded (encrypted) form, which effectively hides its meaning; used to enhance the security of messages and data. Techniques that deal with the secret coding of information stored on computer media and transmitted over communications media. *See also* decryption.

Encryption key　A code used to determine the translation between unencrypted data and the encrypted, secret form to be stored or transmitted.

Encryption key management　Managing the storage and distribution of keys used for encryption and decryption of information.

Entry protocol　A sequence of actions to be performed by a program before entering a critical section *(q.v.)*, which manipulates a shared data structure such as a semaphore *(q.v.)*, causing the process to wait as long as other processes are in conflicting critical sections, and to inform other processes before entering its own critical section. *See also* exit protocol.

Error confinement　Reducing and limiting the results of various errors in a computing system.

Error handling　The operating system activity that deals with the detection of and recovery from errors.

Error interrupt　An interrupt caused by some type of error; the error can be due to an I/O device, program error, or operating system malfunction (e.g., memory parity error).

Error message process　A system process that manages the display and logging of error messages for an operating system.

Error message/recovery procedure manual　An operating system manual that summarizes all error messages of the operating system and the appropriate recovery action for each error.

Escape sequence　A series of control characters following an escape character (ASCII decimal 27, octal 33) that control special features of serial devices, such as printers and terminals. *See also* break character.

Event　A significant occurrence within a computer system that may cause some action or for which processes may wait; examples include completion of an I/O transfer, release of a resource, a message sent by one process to another, or an external occurrence such as pressing a key on a keyboard.

Event control block　A control block representing pending events within an operating system; a type of event flag *(q.v.)* maintained by the operating system.

Event-driven　A characteristic of a system or process by which actions, such as process scheduling, are caused by events, typically indicated by an interrupt.

Event-driven software monitor　A software monitor *(q.v.)* activated by the occurrence of specific events; *compare with* periodic software monitor.

Event flag　A data structure, usually shared and normally consisting of a single bit, which may be used to represent the occurrence of events.

Exit protocol　A sequence of actions performed by a program after leaving a critical section *(q.v.)*, which notifies other processes that the associated resource is now available. *See also* entry protocol.

Extend　An OS system call used to add extents to an existing file when contiguous with extents file *(q.v.)* organization is used.

Extents　Portions of a file stored in a region of the storage device separate from the initial portion, often because they were added at a later time. *See* contiguous organization with extents.

External security　Security measures that fall outside the domain of an operating system, such as physical security and fire protection.

Extracode   A mechanism in the Atlas computer used to invoke special procedures, such as operating system services; the earliest type of system call mechanism.

Fair share scheduling   A type of short-term of medium-term process scheduling in which processes are organized into groups, and each group as a whole is guaranteed a specific fraction of the available processing time.

FAT   *See* file allocation table.

Fault-tolerant system   A computing system that is able to sustain hardware faults by having the software detect such faults and isolate and/or replace the faulty component so that the system can continue operating.

FCB   *See* file control block.

Feedback queues   A short-term scheduling mechanism in which the priority of a process is represented by residence on one of a series of queues, and a process that completes its CPU time quantum at a given priority is placed on a lower-priority queue with a fresh (longer) time quantum for rescheduling.

Fence address   The highest address a process is permitted to reference. Attempts to reference higher addresses result in an interrupt. Used as a type of memory protection. *See also* fence register.

Fence register   A register containing a fence address *(q.v.)* used in memory protection.

Fetch problem   The problem in a virtual memory system of when to fetch particular pages from secondary storage into main memory.

Field   A subdivision of a data structure, especially one containing characters; often, a subdivision of a record *(q.v.)* in a file.

FIFO   *See* first-in-first-out.

File   A named collection of information maintained on a disk or other storage device.

File allocation table   A data structure used by MS-DOS and other operating systems to manage the allocation of blocks in a blocked chained file organization *(q.v.)* by recording the status of each block, and its successor, if any, in a central table within each file volume.

File attributes   Information maintained in a directory describing the characteristics of each file in a file system.

File control blocks   Control blocks used to represent the status and characteristics of files currently in use.

File descriptor   Within a directory, a data structure that records the name, location and attributes of a single file or file extent.

File extension   The act of increasing the size of a file after the file has been initially allocated.

File header   A block of information stored at the beginning of a file that contains information describing the file.

File management   The operating system responsibility that concerns management of storage space for files, and providing access to files as required.

File manager   The component of an operating system that deals with file management.

File name   An identifying name assigned to a file so it can be accessed by users and programs.

File system   A collection of files, together with directories and file management information.

File system backup   The process of copying the contents of a file system, or those portions that have changed since the last backup, to a separate, removable storage medium to enable recovery if the file system suffers future damage.

File system recovery   The process of correcting errors in a damaged file system to the greatest extent possible, and preparing it for normal use.

File system restoration   The process of replacing a file system or portions of a file system with information from a backup copy.

File system validation   The process of systematically examining a file system to ensure that the file structures are consistent—for example, that all storage areas are in use for exactly one purpose.

File type   A file attribute indicating the kind of information a file contains, often represented by a short extension to the end of the file name.

Filter   A program designed to process one continuous stream of input, and produce a continuous stream of output; in UNIX, filters may be combined using pipes *(q.v.)* to cause a stream of data to be processed (filtered) by several concurrent programs, one after another.

Firmware   1) A microprogram *(q.v.)*; 2) any programs or data permanently stored in a read-only memory (ROM).

First-fit   A memory allocation strategy for variable sized blocks, which starts searching from the top of the free block list and selects the first block that is large enough to fulfill the request.

First-fit-with-roving-pointer   A memory allocation strategy for variable-sized blocks; selects the first block large enough to meet the request. All available free memory is treated as a circular list, and each search begins at the place where the last block was allocated; *also called* next-fit.

First-in-first-out   An ordering of insertions and removals in a queue or set such that the next item removed is always the item that has been present for the longest time. A common strategy used in an operating system for scheduling processes and resource and I/O requests; *abbreviated* FIFO.

First-level interrupt handler   An interrupt handler in a hierarchy of interrupt handling that first gets control, determines the cause (channel, device, etc.), and passes control to the appropriate second-level interrupt handler *(q.v.)*; *abbreviated* FLIH.

Fixed partition   A memory allocation strategy in which available memory is divided into a set of partitions, each of a fixed size; each process is assigned one complete partition, and the size of the partitions may be changed only by reinitializing the operating system.

FLIH   *See* first-level interrupt handler.

Floppy disk   A magnetic medium consisting of a small flexible plastic disk with a magnetic coating, onto which data are written or from which data are read by magnetic heads.

Flow control   A type of access control that prevents users from acquiring information indirectly; i.e., by having authorized users of information pass the information on to unauthorized users.

FMCB   *See* free memory control block.

FMS   *See* FORTRAN Monitor System.

Fixed-head disk   *See* head-per-track disk.

Force   In a command interface, the amount of effort required by a user to carry out a specific action; the force required for potentially destructive actions, such as deleting all files, should be greater than that required for more routine actions.

Foreground-background   1) A multiprogramming environment with two processes, one in the foreground (high priority) and one in the background (low priority); 2) a term used to describe processes started by another process that can continue running while the original process receives control; for example, a UNIX process may start several background processes.

Fork   A UNIX system call that creates a new (child) process and makes it ready; the child process initially runs the same program (from the same location) as its parent.

Fort process   A process created in RSX-11 when more than 500 microseconds of processing time is required for servicing an interrupt; this process becomes a member of a special group that uses a secondary interrupt stack, whose members are processed in first-in-first-out *(q.v.)* order.

Formal standards   Standards *(q.v.)* defined and adopted by a group or organization, such as ANSI, through a formalized procedure; *compare with* de facto standards.

Formatting   The process of initially writing the appropriate patterns on magnetic media prior to their use by the operating system; e.g., soft sectors on disks.

FORTRAN Monitor System   An early operating system for IBM computers; *abbreviated* MFS. *See* Section C.2.

Fragmentation   A condition that arises in allocation of variable-size blocks in main memory or on disks, in which most available memory becomes divided into isolated small blocks of little use.

Free   A system call requesting that a specific resource, such as a memory block, currently allocated to the calling process, be returned to the operating system and made available for other processes.

Free chain   A linked list of free blocks of memory or of control blocks representing free memory.

Free memory control block   A control block *(q.v.)* that represents a free block of main memory, available for allocation when needed.

Full screen editor   An editor *(q.v.)* that allows users to display as much information as possible from one or more files on a video display screen, and to modify the information by moving the cursor to appropriate locations for insertion, deletion, and overtyping of characters.

Fully vectored   A term used to describe a hardware architecture in which every device and source of interrupts has a unique interrupt vector.

General semaphore   A semaphore *(q.v.)* that may assume any integer value; often used to represent the number of available units of a resource having multiple interchangeable units, such as a set of memory buffers; *compare with* binary semaphore.

Global replacement strategy   A page replacement strategy in a virtual memory system that allows pages to be selected for page-out from all pages resident in physical memory, not necessarily from pages belonging to the current process; *compare with* local replacement strategy.

Global table   An implementation strategy for access control that consists of entries $<D,O,R>$, where D is a domain, O is an object, and R is an access-rights-set; an operation X attempted with a domain D on an object O is allowed only if X is in the set R.

Guide to documentation   An operating system manual that summarizes all documentation available for the operating system.

Hard disk   A disk constructed from a rigid base medium, often sealed and nonremovable; hard disks generally have a higher storage capacity than floppy disks *(q.v.)* but are substantially more expensive.

Hard real-time requirement   Timing requirements in a real-time system that must be met absolutely.

Hardcopy terminal   A terminal *(q.v.)*, used for interactive communication between a user and a computing system, which displays information by typing or printing on paper; the paper copy forms a permanent record of the information; *compare with* video terminal.

Hardware   The physical components of a computer system; *compare with* software, firmware.

Hardware buffer   A storage unit contained in the hardware of an I/O device or associated control unit, used for temporary storage of data to be transferred between the device and the CPU or memory. *See also* printer buffer.

Hardware clock   A clock *(q.v.)* implemented as a physical device, which produces a continuous sequence of clock ticks at a known, accurate rate.

Hardware environment   The set of physical elements of a computer system with which a program interacts; normally, the physical elements of the architecture of a computing system, including its instruction set, registers, memory, and I/O devices.

Hardware interrupt   A signal generated by the hardware of a computer that causes the current program's execution to be temporarily stopped, its execution address and certain hardware status saved, and transfer of control to another program called an interrupt handler *(q.v.)*. *See also* interrupt.

Hardware monitor   A physical device that may be attached to a computer system to detect the occurrence of certain measurable events, and to record information about those events to determine system performance; *compare with* software monitor.

Hardware stack   A stack whose pointer is a hardware register called the stack pointer; elements are automatically pushed onto the stack on the occurrence of hardware interrupts and the execution of subroutine call instructions, with the stack pointer register being appropriately adjusted; elements are popped from the stack by return instructions (e.g., return from subroutine and return from interrupt).

Head crash   A failure in disk hardware that results in a disk head coming in contact with a rigid disk. The head normally rides on a cushion of air and the head does not physically touch these rigid disks. A crash results in damage to head and disk media; data are permanently lost from the medium.

Head-per-track disk   A disk that has multiple heads, one per track, as opposed to moveable head disks mounted on an arm that must seek to a particular track; arm seek time is eliminated in head-per-track disks; *also called* fixed-head disk.

Heap management   A memory management strategy in which variable sized blocks of memory are allocated and freed in random order from an overall memory region, called a heap.

Help facility   A feature of a command interface that provides users with information about the use of commands and other system facilities.

Help message   A message displayed when a user requests help from a help facility.

Hierarchical ordering A strategy for deadlock prevention *(q.v.)*, in which all resources are assigned a level number in a hierarchy, and processes are premitted to request resources at a given level only when they are holding no resources at the same level or at higher levels.

High-level language A programming language designed for convenient expression of the algorithms or requirements of applications, and not necessarily matching the instruction set of a specific computer. Programs in a high-level language are translated by compilers *(q.v.)*, and each statement normally generates many machine language instructions; well-known examples include COBOL, FORTRAN, Ada, PL/I, Pascal, and C.

High-level language debugger A debugger *(q.v.)* in which examination, analysis, and modification of a program in execution is performed in terms of the source program and the high-level language in which it was written; for example, variable contents can be examined using variable names, and procedure names are used for program tracing. *See also* debugger, symbolic debugger.

Hit rate The frequency with which data, or page or segment descriptors that must be accessed in main memory, are successfully located in a cache, so that main memory access is not necessary. Most practical cache memories have hit rates of over 90 percent.

Home directory A directory *(q.v.)* assigned to a specific user in a file system supporting multiple directories; the home directory is the initial current directory *(q.v.)* when the user logs on, and is considered the default directory.

Host A computer located at a specific network site whose services and resources can be used from remote locations.

I/O *See* input/output.

I/O block *See* I/O control block; *abbreviated* IOB.

I/O-bound A characteristic of a process such that it uses very little CPU time between I/O requests; *compare with* CPU-bound.

I/O completion event An event that results from the completion of an I/O operation.

I/O completion interrupt An interrupt caused by the completion of an I/O operation.

I/O control block A control block *(q.v.)* that represents a requested or pending I/O activity; *abbreviated* IOCB; *also called* I/O block, *abbreviated* IOB.

I/O control unit A hardware unit that controls the operation of a specific I/O device, typically a device requiring relatively complex control such as magnetic tape, disk units, and other DMA devices; *also called* I/O controller. *See also* I/O interface.

I/O controller *See* I/O control unit.

I/O device *See* input/output device.

I/O driver A software module controlling a particular device or type of device.

I/O instructions Machine instructions that specify data transfers and control operations involving I/O devices.

I/O interface A hardware unit used to control an I/O device and connect it to a computer system; allows the computer to handle a wide variety of I/O devices in a consistent manner. *See also* I/O controller.

I/O processor Used primarily on large mainframe computers, a processor dedicated to performing I/O operations. The I/O processor performs a series of I/O transfers for a device or set of devices, as specified by a special program. *See also* channel.

I/O scheduling The selection of the next request from one or more I/O queues that is to be processed by an I/O device; the pending request selected depends on the scheduling techniques being used.

I/O space An address space used specifically to identify I/O devices; a computer architecture providing an I/O space separate from the memory address space includes a distinct set of instructions for performing I/O.

I/O subsystem *See* I/O supervisor.

I/O supervisor A collection of modules within the operating system that controls all I/O requests; *also called* I/O subsystem.

I-node A type of file descriptor used in UNIX directories, which contains information specifying the location and attributes of a file but does not contain a file name; each file is also identified by one or more descriptors in directory files in the regular file hierarchy, which contain only a file name and an identifier for the corresponding i-node.

Icons Symbols displayed on a terminal screen in a type of command interface which represent objects, such as files, and operations, such as programs or commands; actions and data are selected in such systems by pointing to the appropriate icons with a mouse or other pointing device.

Idle process A system process, the sole function of which is to use up CPU time in a multiprogramming operating system when no other process is ready to run (dispatchable). Eliminates the use of or need for a hardware wait instruction; loses control whenever another process becomes dispatchable.

Idle time Time during which a CPU is performing no useful work; often, time when there are no processes in the ready or running state, other than, possibly, an idle process *(q.v.)*.

IEEE *See* Institute for Electrical and Electronic Engineers.

Image 1) An exact copy of the machine instructions and data in use by a program during its execution in memory; if a program's image is stored in a file, it may be used to reload and start or resume that program at any time; 2) the information displayed on a video terminal or graphic display device.

Immediate commands Commands that have an immediate effect when they are entered at an interactive terminal, even if the system is engaged in unrelated activities.

Implementation 1) The physical elements and mechanisms by which a computer system is constructed *(compare with* architecture); 2) the phase in the software life cycle that involves actual programming as opposed to design or testing.

Indefinite blocking A condition in a computer system in which a process is blocked for a possibly unlimited period of time; *also called* livelock. *See also* deadlock.

Index register A register in a CPU used for indexed addressing *(q.v.)*.

Indexed addressing An addressing technique that constructs an effective address by adding the value contained in the address field to the value contained in an index register *(q.v.)*; typically used for accessing elements in tables and arrays, and characters in buffers; one component of the address specifies the starting location of the data structure, while the other specifies a relative position within it.

Indexed file   A file consisting of a set of data records together with one or more indexes; each index associates records with data items, called keys, which often form a part of the record; the structure is designed so that records can be accessed rapidly by specifying their keys.

Indirect addressing   An addressing technique in which the effective address initially determined from the address field, after possible use of based or indexed addressing, is considered to be the address of a location containing another address, rather than the data itself; usually this address then identifies the location of the data. In a few architectures, multiple levels of indirect addressing may be possible; *compare with* direct addressing.

Indirect capability   A capability *(q.v.)* that is provided indirectly by the use of a pointer that points to a capability that points to the resource itself; helps to solve the problem of revoking capabilities.

Initial state   A process state *(q.v.)* assigned to a process when it is first created, before it has ever been admitted to the active set *(q.v.)*; *compare with* blocked state, ready state, running state, terminal state.

Input   The process of transferring data from a storage device or external source into a computing system. *See also* input/output.

Input device   An input/output device *(q.v.)* used to transfer data from an external source to the CPU, the memory, or another system component; examples include keyboards, punched card readers, and magnetic badge readers.

Input/output   A generic term for input, output, or both *(q.v.)*; the process of transferring data between a computing system and a storage device *(q.v.)* or an external source or destination; *abbreviated* I/O.

Input/output device   Any physical component of a computing system used to perform input, output, or both; also often describes a storage device *(q.v.)*; *abbreviated* I/O device.

Input/Output System   1) The first operating system, developed by General Motors for the IBM 701. *See* Section C.2; 2) a synonym for input/output control system *(q.v.)*.

Input/Output control system   An operating system, or a portion of an operating system, responsible for managing the use of I/O devices; *abbreviated* IOCS.

Installation manual   An operating system manual that describes how to install an operating system for a particular computer; often combined with a system generation manual.

Institute for Electrical and Electronic Engineers   A professional organization of electrical and electronic engineers that is active in establishing standards for the computer industry; *abbreviated* IEEE.

Instrument   *See* monitor (def. 3).

Interactive computing environment   A computing environment in which users interact with the computer using hardcopy or video terminals; most activities in such a system are performed in response to commands entered by these users, rather than from a batch stream such as that of a batch operating system *(q.v.)*.

Interactive process   A process in an interactive computing environment that communicates with a user via a terminal; especially, one which communicates frequently.

Interface   1) A mechanism for communicating information between two or more components of a computing system, or between a computing system and a user or external object. (*See also* user interface, I/O interface); 2) a set of procedures or protocols that one process may use to access resources or services controlled by another process or by the operating system.

Interleaved execution   The technique of executing processes in a multiprogramming environment so that each process gets a certain amount of CPU time between execution of other processes. Each process gradually moves toward completion by execution in small intervals; the system creates an illusion of concurrent execution, although only one process is executing at any moment.

Interleaving   1) A synonym for interleaved execution; 2) a technique to improve the speed of sequential access by writing sequential data to a magnetic disk so that data is not on contiguous sectors; 3) a technique for allocating sequential data in memory among separate physical memory units to improve speed by permitting concurrent access.

Internal memory   A synonym for main memory *(q.v.)*.

Internal security   Security that includes the many controls and facilities provided by both the hardware and the operating system that help to guarantee that the computer system remains available, private, and correct.

International Organization for Standardization   An international organization devoted to developing and maintaining formal technical standards; *abbreviated* ISO.

Interprocess communication   The activity of sending information from one process to another, often in the form of messages *(q.v.)*.

Interrupt   A hardware signal that causes the automatic suspension of the currently executing program in order to execute a special program, called an interrupt handler *(q.v.)*.

Interrupt-driven   A characteristic of an operating system in which all process state transitions are caused by a hardware interrupt.

Interrupt key   A key on a terminal's keyboard that generates a hardware interrupt.

Interrrupt level   A value assigned to a specific type of interrupt, which is interpreted as a priority relative to other interrupts; interrupts at a high level may be serviced before those at a low level, and interrupt masking *(q.v.)* may be used to disable all interrupts below a specified level.

Interrupt mask register   A CPU register that is used to block certain interrupts; a specific bit in the register corresponds to a particular interrupt to be blocked; setting the bit to 1 usually allows the interrupt to occur, while setting it to 0 blocks the interrupt.

Interrupt masking   Disabling certain types of interrupts, so that the CPU will not respond to them if they occur, while allowing other types to remain enabled; normally performed either by setting bits in a register to identify the interrupt types to be disabled (masked); or by storing a value in a register representing the lowest interrupt level *(q.v.)* that should remain enabled.

Interrupt vector   A location in a physical main memory, usually at a low address, that is associated by hardware with a specific type of interrupt; when the interrupt, if enabled, occurs, the CPU will either branch directly to this location, or read an address from this location that specifies where to branch. Usually an associated location or locations automatically store the program counter and other necessary status information.

Interval timer   A hardware clock that allows loading of a particular value into the timer for automatic decrementing at a fixed resolution (small fraction of a second); expiration of the interval (contents of interval timer equals zero) results in timer interrupt.

IO_active state   A subdivision of the blocked state *(q.v.)* to represent processes waiting for an I/O operation that is currently in progress.

IO_activeQ   A queue containing PCBs or IOCBs for processes in the IO_active state *(q.v.)*.

IO_init state   A subdivision of the blocked state *(q.v.)* to represent processes waiting for an I/O operation that has not yet begun.

IO_initQ   A queue containing PCBs or IOCBs for processes in the IO_init state *(q.v.)*.

IOB   *See* I/O block, I/O control block.

IOCB   *See* I/O control block.

IOCS   *See* Input/Output Control System.

IP   *See* instruction pointer.

IPC   *See* interprocess communication.

iRTX   A real-time executive produced by Intel Corp. *See* Section C.11.

ISO   *See* International Organization for Standardization.

JCL   *See* job control language.

Job   1) A unit of work submitted by a user to a batch operating system; 2) a collection of input data and associated statements in a job control language which specify a unit of work for a batch operating system.

Job control language   1) A command language used with a batch operating system; 2) the name of a specific batch command language used with large IBM systems; *abbreviated* JCL.

Job scheduling   The selection of the next batch job to run in a batch operating system; a type of long-term scheduling *(q.v.)*.

Kernel   1) Synonym for nucleus; 2) a small portion of an operating system permanently resident in main memory or read-only memory, and which is responsible for the most critical activities of the system.

Key   1) A protection key *(q.v.)* used for memory protection; 2) a value associated with a record in an indexed file *(q.v.)*, often recorded in a field of the record, which may identify and access that record; 3) a code for encrypting and decrypting *(q.v.)* information.

Keyword argument   A command argument *(q.v.)* identified by specifying a descriptive name, called a keyword, along with the argument; *compare with* positional argument.

Kilobyte   A measure of storage equalling 1,024 bytes; this value is equal to two to the 10th power, and is the closest power of two to the value 1,000; often inaccurately equated to 1,000 bytes.

Kth percentile value   A value of a computing system parameter that can be measured or computed, such that the actual value will be less than (or greater than) the kth percentile value in k percent of the cases. For example, a process scheduling queue in which 90 percent of the processes are served within one minute of arrival has a ninetieth percentile waiting time of one minute.

LAN   *See* local area network.

Laptop computer   A small portable computer light enough to be used on a person's lap; RAM disks *(q.v.)* are important to laptop computers because they preserve batteries by avoiding constant floppy disk or hard disk use.

Least frequently used   In a virtual memory system, a replacement strategy *(q.v.)* that attempts to select pages for removal that have been accessed least frequently over a recent time interval; not usually implemented because of the need for special hardware to maintain records of the frequency of use of each page or segment; *abbreviated* LFU.

Least recently used   In a virtual memory system, a replacement strategy *(q.v.)* that attempts to select pages for removal that have not been accessed for the longest time in the recent past; difficult to implement exactly, but approximate versions are often used; *abbreviated* LRU.

LFU   *See* least frequently used.

Library   *See* library file.

Library file   A file designed to store large numbers of relatively small units of information in a compact, easily accessible way. Because files must usually occupy a whole number of blocks or other storage units, the space required for storage of many small units in a library may be much less than required if they are stored in individual files. Library files are often used to store a set of commonly used program sequences for use by compilers, or commonly used procedures in object form for use by linkers; *also called* library.

Lightweight process   A process having a limited context, which can be easily executed without a normal context switch; usually intended to perform system or real-time activities that must be performed frequently and quickly.

Limit register   A register designed to implement a form of memory protection; the address contained by a limit register is the highest address that can be referenced by the current process.

Line buffering   A feature in a terminal interface by which it is able to store a line of characters being typed in a buffer until an end-of-line character is typed, indicating that the line is complete; limited editing of the current line, such as deleting characters or canceling the entire line, is usually allowed.

Line clock   A hardware clock *(q.v.)* that has a clock rate based on the electric power line frequency (usually 50 or 60 ticks per second).

Line-oriented editor   An editor *(q.v.)* able to display and modify a single line of text at a time; *compare with* full-screen editor.

Linkage editor   *See* linker.

Linked list   A data structure consisting of a set of elements in which each element contains a pointer to the next.

Linker   A system program that reads object modules from independently translated programs and builds an executable image, selecting modules for inclusion based on external references or specific linker commands; two primary responsibilities of linkers are relocation *(q.v.)* and the resolution of cross-references between distinct object files; *also called* linkage editor.

Livelock   *See* indefinite blocking.

Load module Produced by a linker, a file that contains a program in a form suitable for loading and execution by the computing system.

Loader A program or module within the operating system that loads programs for execution, and may provide relocation of programs if required.

Local area network A network *(q.v.)* that connects computers and other resources within a limited geographic area, and makes use of dedicated, reliable, high-performance communications media; often all computers on such a network are of the same, or a small number of, types and are subject to a common administration; *abbreviated* LAN.

Local replacement strategy A page replacement strategy *(q.v.)* that selects pages for use by a process only from the pages allocated to that process; *compare with* global replacement strategy.

Locality A property observed in the behavior of many programs during execution, wherein locations recently referenced, and others near them, are likely to be referenced in the near future; this assumption is basic to the design of virtual memory systems and cache memories.

Log off To terminate an interactive session by presenting an appropriate command to the command interface. *See also* log on.

Log on To begin an interactive session in a multiuser computing system by entering a user name and probably a password at a terminal; if the user name and password are recognized and accepted, the interactive session is begun. *See also* log off.

Logical address space *See* virtual address space.

Logical name An alternative name for a file that can be defined in VMS *(q.v.)*, that can be reassigned at will to real file names or portions of file names.

Logical resource A resource *(q.v.)* consisting of information rather than physical objects; examples include data structures or files; *compare with* physical resource.

Logical volume A collection of files that is logically complete, but does not necessarily occupy exactly one physical storage device; *compare with* physical volume.

Long-haul network *See* wide area network.

Long-term scheduling A process scheduling level that controls the initial admission of units of work into the system. *See also* job scheduling.

Lookahead A feature of a file manager by which file blocks may be read into buffers before they are needed when the file is being accessed in a sequential manner.

LRU *See* least recently used.

Machine fault interrupt An interrupt *(q.v.)* generated when a fault is detected in the hardware; for example, a memory parity error.

Machine instruction A data word specifying a single operation in the instruction set of a CPU architecture, along with an appropriate set of operands.

Machine language 1) A language that contains all machine instructions recognized by a particular architecture; 2) the form taken by a program when it is loaded in main memory, ready for execution.

Macro A representation of a sequence of text, especially statements in a programming language, by a name and possibly a set of parameters; specifying a macro causes the corresponding complete text string to be generated with a form that may depend on the parameters.

Macro facility A feature in a programming language that permits the definition and use of macros *(q.v.)*; most commonly found in assembly languages.

Mailbox A named, shareable message buffer for interprocess communication; when mailboxes are used, messages are sent to and received from mailboxes rather than directly between processes.

Main memory The memory unit that works directly with the CPU and holds the bulk of programs and data in current use; main memory is used for fetching and executing instructions; *also called* primary storage, internal memory.

Mainframe A large computer system characterized by high cost and high performance.

Mapping register A register used to translate the location of a block of data in a virtual address space to its corresponding location in a physical address space.

Master Control Program The name given to a series of operating systems for computers produced by Burroughs Corporation. *See* Section C.2.

Master-slave A type of organization for a multiprocessor or distributed operating system in which one CPU executes the OS, while the rest of the CPUs are considered to be resources that can be scheduled.

MCB *See* memory control block.

MCP *See* Master Control Program.

Mean The expected or average value of a system parameter, which varies over time.

Mechanism A structure provided by a computing system to implement a desired algorithm or policy, or to meet a specific set of requirements; *compare with* policy.

Medium-term scheduling A process scheduling level that controls the admission of processes to the active set *(q.v.)*; often coincides with the scheduling of process residence in main storage; *also called* storage scheduling.

Megabyte A measure of storage equalling 1,048,576 bytes. This value is equal to two to the 20th power, and is the closest power of the two to the value one million; often inaccurately equated to one million bytes exactly.

Memory Any portion of a computing system that is used or can be used to store information; often, a synonym for main memory *(q.v.)*.

Memory control block A type of control block used in memory management to represent allocated and free blocks of memory. *See also* allocated memory control block, free memory control block.

Memory hierarchy A collection of memory types in a computing system organized as a series of levels such that the highest level is the smallest and fastest, and contains data most actively in use by the CPU. Each lower level is generally larger, slower and less expensive, and serves as a backup or bulk storage for the previous one. Typical levels, from highest to lowest, include registers, cache memory, main memory, secondary memory, and archival memory *(q.v.)*.

Memory management The operating system responsibility concerned with controlling the use of main memory *(q.v.)* and the possibly secondary memory *(q.v.)*.

Memory map   A table containing a set of block descriptors *(q.v.)* and respresenting a mapping from a virtual address space to a physical address space. *See also* page table.

Memory-mapped display   A graphic display whose image is controlled by the contents of a particular area of memory; storing a character or a bit pattern in this area immediately changes the corresponding portion of the display.

Memory-mapped I/O   An architecture for input and output control in which device registers are assigned to particular fixed (or predefined) addresses in the same address space that is used for main memory; I/O is performed by reading and writing to these locations using memory reference instructions, rather than by a separate set of instructions.

Memory-mapped terminal   *See* memory-mapped display.

Memory partitioning   A strategy for allocating main memory by which each process is assigned a contiguous region, called a partition, at the time it is initiated; the size of the partition will not be changed while the process is active.

Memory protection   A mechanism that protects memory assigned to one process or the operating system from unauthorized access by other processes. Memory protection requires hardware structures that either detect and reject accesses to illegal addresses, or ensure that only allowable physical addresses are included in the memory map assigned to each process.

Memory translation   1) The process of translating virtual addresses to physical addresses using a memory map; 2) an OS mechanism that supports such translation.

Menu system   For a video terminal, an interactive command interface in which users are presented with a display listing a set of possible choices, and enter commands by selecting one of the choices indicated.

Message   1) Information provided to users through a command interface, often in the form of text displayed on a terminal; 2) a unit of information sent to or received from a remote computing system using a communication device, or sent from one process to another through an interprocess communication mechanism *(q.v.)*.

Message passing   A form of interprocess communication *(q.v.)* using messages that are sent from one process to another.

Microcomputer   A small computing system using a microprocessor as its CPU.

Microprocess   A subprocess of a real-time process running under a real-time executive. Microprocesses are scheduled privately by the parent process, and normally take turns running during the main process's scheduled time period; they are usually dispatched on a simple round-robin basis.

Microprocessor   A CPU that is substantially contained on a single integrated circuit chip.

Microprogram   A program stored in a special fast memory within a CPU and which specifies the execution of each instruction in the CPU instruction set in terms of a series of simpler steps. Each step consists essentially of a set of control signals to be generated simultaneously.

Minicomputer   A small- to medium-scale computing system, generally larger than a microcomputer but substantially less powerful and less expensive than a mainframe.

Minidisks   A portion of a disk used as a virtual disk in a virtual machine system *(q.v.)*.

Monitor   1) A simple single-user operating system allowing a user to execute programs one at a time by entering commands at a terminal for a simple command interface; an example is the IBM 1130 Disk Monitor System (DMS); 2) a synchronization mechanism that combines a shared data structure and all operations on that data structure in a single package, and ensures use of the data structure by only one process at a time; 3) a mechanism added to a system to observe and record aspects of its behavior for use in performance evaluation; *also called* instrument. *See also* hardware monitor, software monitor.

Mouse   An input device consisting of a small hand-held unit with a roller, which can be rolled in any direction about a flat surface, and with one or more buttons. Rolling the mouse causes a cursor to move about a display screen, selecting a position. Actions may be performed at the selected position by pressing a button.

Moving-head disk   A disk that has a single read/write head per surface mounted on a movable arm that must move (seek) to a particular track for a read/write operation. Access time for such a disk is dominated by the time required to move the arm; *compare with* fixed-head disk.

MPX   1) the MultiProgramming eXecutive project described in this text. *See* Chapter 13; 2) an early multiprogramming executive for the IBM 1800. *See* Section C.15.

MS-DOS   A widely used microcomputer operating system developed by Microsoft Corporation. *See* Section C.6. *See also* PC-DOS.

MULTICS   An innovative timesharing system developed by M.I.T., General Electric, and Bell Laboratories. *See* Section C.4.

Multiprocessor   A single computing system having two or more CPUs.

Multiprogramming   A technique for interleaved execution *(q.v.)* of independent programs or processes by a single CPU.

Multitasking   A synonym for multiprogramming *(q.v.)*; 2) an operating system mechanism that supports interleaved execution of multiple tasks or processes, often cooperating on a common objective, or acting on behalf of a single user; used especially in real-time environments.

Mutual exclusion   A requirement, imposed on the use of some shared resources to ensure correct operation, that specifies that only one process may use the resource at any time; for example, mutual exclusion is required for main memory assigned to a process, or else information stored by one process could destroy that stored by another.

MVS   IBM mainframe operating system that supports multiple virtual spaces; *See* Section C.2.

Name space   The set of all possible names or identifiers that may be given to objects of a certain type. An address space *(q.v.)* is a name space in which the names are normally restricted to a range of integers, and correspond to physical locations.

National Software Works   An early example of a nontransparent distributed operating system developed on the Arpanet. *See* Section C.12.

Naturalness   A quality of a command language by which commands and related elements are expressed in a form that seems "natural" to the users.

Network   A collection of independent computing systems, together with a mechanism that allows them to reliably exchange information with one another. *See also* local area network, wide area network.

Network operating system   A distributed operating system in a network environment; especially an OS that coexists with a local OS in a single computing system connected to a network, and provides access to remote resources.

Network partitioning A problem that occurs when elements of the network fail or are removed; the remaining elements may form two or more groups that continue to function but cannot communicate with each other.

Network site *See* site.

Network topology The pattern by which sites in a network are physically connected to one another.

Network transparency A characteristic of a network, under control of a distributed operating system, that allows users to be unaware of where each file is stored or which site is executing each program; resources may be assigned to sites and moved between sites, at the discretion of the operating system without knowledge by the users of these resources.

Newcastle Connection A network operating system used with standard versions of UNIX. *See* Section C.12.

Next-fit For variable sized blocks, a memory allocation strategy that selects the first block large enough to meet the request. All available free memory is treated as a circular list, and each search begins at the place where the last block was allocated; *also called* first-fit with roving pointer; *compare with* best-fit, first-fit, worst-fit.

No preemption In the strategy for managing a particular resource, a condition required to make deadlock possible on that resource. It provides that the operating system will not take resources away from a process while it is waiting for others. Deadlock prevention *(q.v.)* may be achieved by removing this condition.

Node name A name assigned to a computer system connected to a network to identify it to other computers in the network.

Nondiscretionary security policy A security policy with rules governing the sharing of information and access rights that all users must follow and are enforced by the system.

Nonvolatile A characteristic of certain types of memory by which stored information is not lost when electric power is removed.

NOS *See* network operating system.

Not recently used An approximation of the least recently used page replacement strategy *(q.v.)*, which divides all pages or segments into two classes: those that have been recently used, and those that have not; *abbreviated* NRU.

NRU *See* not recently used.

Nucleus The portion of an operating system that remains resident in main memory at all times during normal operation. *See also* kernel.

Object 1) An entity with a unique name that can be used to distinguish it from all other objects in the system, used in particular in describing an access control policy; 2) a synonym for object program *(q.v.)*.

Object deck A set of punched cards representing an object program module *(q.v.)* used in card-based systems.

Object program A representation of a program or program unit that is in binary form, but that may contain external references to other object modules; produced by many compilers and assemblers. In general, object programs may require processing by a linker to produce executable programs (load modules), ready for loading and execution.

One-level store A name used by the Atlas Computer for a memory system that seems to be all of one level or type, although it is actually composed of different types; especially, a uniform virtual address space constructed from both main and secondary physical memory. *See* Section C.2.

On-line documentation A computing system's documentation that is displayed and read at a terminal as needed, rather than being printed on paper.

Open An OS system call (file operation) used to prepare a file for use by a process.

Open environment A computing system or environment in which the resources of the operating system and computer are fully accessible to users without any type of protection; operating system services, in particular, are viewed as ordinary procedures that may be used, bypassed, or replaced, as desired.

Open shop Prevalent in the early days of computing, a computer system environment in which users and programmers had direct access to computer hardware facilities, and the computer was assigned to only one user at a time.

Open operating system *See* open environment.

Open system An operating system model used in a single-user computer system that treats the operating system, literally, as a collection of procedures and nothing more.

Open Systems Interconnection model A reference model, consisting of seven layers, developed by the International Organization for Standardization (ISO) *(q.v.)* for describing networks; *abbreviated* OSI model.

Operating system The software that manages the resources of a computer system; *abbreviated* OS.

Operating System Command and Response Language A language that serves as both an operating system command language and an operating system response language *(q.v.)*; *abbreviated* OSCRL.

Operating System Command Language A language used by a command interface to express messages provided for a user by programs or by the operating system; *abbreviated* OSRL.

Operating System Response Language A language used by a command interface to express messages provided for a user by programs or by the operating system; *abbreviated* OSRL.

Operational security Aspects of security that concern the policies and procedures that system managers implement and require in a computer installation, including backup procedures.

OS *See* operating system.

OS documentation A set of documents, guides, or manuals that describe the structure or operation of an operating system.

OS Master Index A document that contains an index to all other documents forming the OS documentation for a particular operating system; this index is especially valuable when the number of documents is large.

OS Release Notes A document containing a description of changes and features of the current release of an operating system, compared to a previous release; can be distributed on paper or on magnetic media.

OS Software Support (Logic) Manual An operating system manual that provides information about the operating system logic, data structures, tuning parameters, and other information required to support the operating system.

OS system image dump *See* core dump.

OSCL *See* Operating System Command Language.

OSCRL *See* Operating System Command and Response Language.

OSRL *See* Operating System Response Language.

OS/360 The generic name for a family of well-known operating systems for IBM S/360 and S/370 computers. *See* Section C.3.

OSI *See* Open Systems Interconnection model.

OS/MFT   An operating system for IBM S/360 computers. *See* Section C.3.

OS/MVS   *See* MVS.

OS/MVT   An operating system for IBM S/360 computers. *See* Section C.3.

Output   The process of transferring data from a computing system to a storage device or external destination. *See also* input/output.

Output device   An input/output device *(q.v.)* used to transfer data from the CPU, the memory, or another system component to an external destination; examples include printers, display screens, and card punches.

Overhead   The time spent during computer system operation in which no useful work is being performed, due to necessary OS activities such as accounting, context switching, or page fault processing.

Overlapped control operations   Operations issued by a single control unit to different devices attached to it, that are executed simultaneously by the devices; such operations do not involve data transfer and simply provide device control like backspacing a record on a tape drive and seeking to a particular track on a disk drive.

Overlay   *See* overlay segment.

Overlay segment   A program unit within a program that uses overlaying *(q.v.)*; overlay segments are loaded independently by the overlay supervisor *(q.v.)*.

Overlay supervisor   A system module that is invoked during execution by a program that uses overlaying *(q.v.)*; used to load overlay segments *(q.v.)* not currently resident, replacing others as needed.

Overlaying   A technique used primarily in systems without paging or segmentation to execute programs that have storage requirements exceeding the available memory. Programs using the technique must be divided by the programmer or compiler into independent units called overlay segments *(q.v.)* which have limited communication. Each overlay segment is designed to occupy a specific region of the available memory, and segments that do not interact may share the same region. A control program called an overlay supervisor *(q.v.)* loads the appropriate overlay segments as necessary.

Packet   A discrete unit into which longer messages are divided for transmission over a communication medium controlled by a communication protocol.

Page   In memory, a unit of information of a small, fixed size, typically several hundred bytes, used as the basic unit of storage in paging systems and virtual memory systems *(q.v.)*; *compare with* page frame, segment.

Page descriptor   A block descriptor describing the translation of a single page to a corresponding page frame *(q.v.)*. Because page locations are fixed and page sizes are uniform, only the page frame number and access control field are normally required. Additional information may be included to support virtual memory management. A collection of page descriptors forms a page table *(q.v.)*.

Page fault   A type of hardware interrupt *(q.v.)* in a paging system caused by a reference to a page not currently resident in main memory. The response to a page fault requires a page *(q.v.)* operation from secondary storage.

Page frame   A block of physical main or secondary memory into which a single page can be loaded.

Page frame number   A sequence number or address that identifies a page frame.

Page-in   In a virtual memory system, the process of transferring a page from the secondary memory to the main memory.

Page modified flag   A bit in a page descriptor *(q.v.)* that specifies if a page in memory has been changed in any way; used to determine if a page-out *(q.v.)* operation is required during page replacement; *also called* dirty bit.

Page number   A sequence number or address that identifies a page.

Page-out   In a virtual memory system, the process of transferring a page from the main memory to the secondary memory.

Page present flag   A bit in a page descriptor *(q.v.)* that indicates whether the corresponding page is currently resident in main memory.

Page referenced flag   A bit in a page table that indicates whether a particular page has been referenced since the page reference flag was last cleared; used to implement page replacement algorithms that must "know" when a page was last referenced.

Page table   A table containing a set of page descriptors, normally stored in main memory and organized sequentially by page number.

Page table register   A CPU register that identifies the location and size of the current page table.

Paging   A memory mapping technique that provides automatic translation by hardware of all references to a page in a virtual address space into a corresponding page frame that may be independently located in a physical address space. Normally used in conjunction with a virtual memory system *(q.v.)*; may be combined with segmentation *(q.v.)*.

Paging cache   A cache memory *(q.v.)* incorporated in a paging system and used to contain recently accessed page and segment descriptors.

Parallel interface   An I/O interface *(q.v.)* that allows transfer of all bits in a byte simultaneously; *compare with* serial interface.

Parent process   In a process hierarchy *(q.v.)*, a process that has a superior relationship to another process, its child process *(q.v.)*. A parent process often is the creator of a child process, and is usually able to communicate with it and control it using operations such as suspend, wake up, and terminate, as long as both processes exist.

Parity bit   A bit in a character or other data unit used for error checking; set to 0 or 1 so that the sum of the one bits in the data, including the parity bit, is always even (even parity) or always odd (odd parity).

Partition   *See* fixed partition.

Password   A word or character string that a user is required to specify in addition to a user name (in order to be permitted to log on to a computer system) or along with a file name or resource name (in order to access a specific file or other resource).

Patent law   A body of law protecting an invention, process, or the like, by granting exclusive right to produce, use, sell, or get profit from such an invention or process; a patent protects an idea, which can be embodied in a physical object; *compare with* copyright law.

PC   1) *See* program counter; 2) abbreviation for personal computer—that is, a microcomputer, especially, a type of microcomputer developed by IBM.

PCB   *See* process control block.

PC-relative addressing   An addressing technique in which the program counter is used as a "floating" base register. In effect, the value in the address field is interpreted as a relative address, or an offset from the address of the instruction itself. This addressing facilitates coding of "position-independent" programs that can be relocated anywhere in memory without adjusting addresses within the program.

Performance   A measure of the effectiveness with which a system carries out the tasks for which it was designed.

Performance analysis   The process of studying and improving computer system performance; *also called* performance evaluation.

Performance evaluation   *See* performance analysis.

Performance measurement   A technique for performance analysis, which consists of measuring parameters related to the performance of a computer system while the system is running with the desired workload. Requires adding mechanisms such as software or hardware monitors *(q.v.)* to the system to observe and record the desired information; *also called* direct measurement; *compare with* analytic modeling, simulation. *See also* benchmarking, performance monitoring.

Performance monitoring   A type of performance measurement *(q.v.)* by which characteristics of a computer system are observed and measured over an extended period of time during normal operation. *See also* hardware monitor, software monitor.

Performance tuning   Adjusting changeable system parameters in a computer system with the objective of improving overall system performance.

Periodic software monitor   A software monitor that is invoked at regular time intervals by an interrupt caused whenever a clock reaches a certain value; *compare with* event-driven software monitor.

Physical address   An address in a physical address space.

Physical address space   An address space consisting of a set of locations in a physical memory; often, the address space identifying the memory locations actually available in the system, as compared to those apparently available to each process; *also called* real address space; *compare with* virtual address space.

Physical memory   A tangible memory unit or set of units forming a collection of actual locations for storing information; *compare with* virtual memory.

Physical resources   Resources that consist of tangible objects rather than information; examples include CPUs, physical memory, and I/O devices, *compare with* logical resources.

Physical security   A type of security that provides protection against accidents and disasters such as floods, fire, and physical intrusion; safeguarding of physical media such as disks and tapes by storing them in a safe location; safeguarding the computer system itself.

Physical volume   A single complete storage device or unit such as a disk or magnetic tape; *compare with* logical volume.

Pipe   An interprocess communication mechanism *(q.v.)*, made popular by UNIX, that allows output from one process to be used directly as input to another process executing concurrently.

Pixel   In a video display, a single dot or picture element that may be turned on or off and may possess a color, intensity, or other attributes.

Placement problem   The problem in virtual memory systems that deals with where to place pages that must be loaded into main memory, if more than one page frame is available.

Policy   A strategy or set of rules for the management or operation of a computing system; a flexible system will provide mechanisms *(q.v.)* that allow the use of a wide range of policies to be chosen by the users and managers of each specific installation.

Policy of isolation   A security policy that states that a protected entity in a computer system belongs to one and only one principal, and cannot be accessed in any way by any other principal. *See also* principal.

Polling   A technique for programming I/O devices whereby the device is constantly checked by instructions in a programmed loop to determine when the device is ready or has completed a previous I/O operation; used primarily in single-user operating systems such as MS-DOS.

Port number   A number assigned to an I/O device on a microcomputer; for example, the number of a serial port on a multi-line serial interface; thus, an address in an I/O space *(q.v.)*.

Portability   A characteristic of a program that allows it to be transferred from one computer system to another of a different type, and be executed with minimal changes to the source code [source portability *(q.v.)*] or with no changes to the executable or object code [binary portability *(q.v.)*].

Portable compiler   A compiler that is portable among a variety of different computing systems; use of the same compiler in different environments helps ensure that programs having the same source code produce the same results.

Portable operating system   An operating system that is portable among a variety of computer architectures, and can be implemented in similar form on additional architectures with limited effort.

Positional argument   A command argument *(q.v.)* identified by its position in a command line *(q.v.)* in relation to other arguments; *compare with* keyword argument.

Preemption   A characteristic of some scheduling techniques whereby resources held by a process may be taken away by the OS before the process releases them; especially, taking away the CPU and removing a process from the running state when a time limit has elapsed or a higher-priority process is waiting.

Preemptive scheduling   *See* preemption.

Prepaging   In a virtual memory system, a fetch strategy that may load into main memory pages that are considered likely to be needed before they are actually referenced.

Primary storage   *See* main memory.

Principal   An authority, usually a person, who is accountable for the use or misuse of some entity within a computer system.

Principle of least privilege   A principle of access control that specifies that each program unit, at each moment, should have access to only the resources it absolutely needs.

Principle of locality   *See* locality.

Printer   An output device that displays information in a form readable by users, by printing or typing characters and images on paper.

Printer buffer A hardware unit, used to store data destined for a slow device such as a printer, that controls the data flow into the device by the computer and sends data to the device as the device becomes ready; *also called* hardware spooler. *See also* hardware buffer.

Priority A number assigned to a job or process and used to determine the relative importance of that job or process compared to others; for example, high-priority processes will be scheduled for use of the CPU ahead of low-priority processes, and high-priority jobs will be admitted to the system before low-priority jobs. *See also* dynamic priority, static priority.

Priority-driven A process scheduling algorithm that uses priorities stored in PCBs to determine where processes are placed in the ready queue upon transition to the ready state; the dispatcher *(q.v.)* always schedules the highest priority ready process in the ready queue.

Private key An encryption key *(q.v.)* that must be kept secret to ensure a secure encryption of messages; *compare with* public key.

Privileged instruction A machine instruction, usually one performing input or output or having an effect on certain privileged registers *(q.v.)*, that can only be executed when the CPU is in a privileged mode *(q.v.)*; an attempt to execute a privileged instruction in a nonprivileged state fails, and usually causes an interrupt that must be dealt with by the operating system.

Privileged mode A mode of operation for a CPU, indicated by one or more bits in a status register, that permits the execution of privileged instructions *(q.v.)*; usually intended for use by the operating system only, and entered only by instructions, such as system call instructions that simultaneously transfer control to the OS.

Problem isolation An activity performed by programmers to isolate failures to particular modules or conditions; in most cases, problem isolation is accomplished when a particular failure can be consistently reproduced. *See* reproducible failure.

Procedure library 1) A library file containing a collection of procedures in object code form to be linked to programs by a linker as needed; 2) a library file containing a collection of procedures that are sequences of statements in a job control language *(q.v.)*. *See also* command file.

Process 1) A program in execution in an operating system, especially one that supports interleaved execution of multiple programs; 2) a formal representation of a program in execution, often by a process control block *(q.v.)*; *also called* task.

Process complete interrupt A software interrupt *(q.v.)* that specifies that a process has finished execution.

Process control block A control block that represents the characteristics, status, and associated information for a process *(q.v.)*.

Process hierarchy A set of relationships among processes, such that each process except one—the root process *(q.v.)*—is considered a child process of another, called the parent process. The resulting set of relationships forms a tree structure. Often, parent processes are the creators of child processes and exercise control over them throughout their existence.

Process management The operating system responsibility concerned with creating processes and managing their operation, including allocation and scheduling of the CPU, memory, and other resources.

Process migration Movement of processes between sites in a distributed operating system.

Process scheduling Determining the order in which resources, especially CPUs and memory, will be assigned to processes when multiple processes are waiting.

Process state A name or value identifying a possible status of a process, which identifies in part the scheduling operations appropriate for that process or the resources or events for which it may be waiting. *See also* blocked state, initial state, IO_active state, IO_init state, ready state, running state, suspended state, terminal state.

Process state byte A byte within a PCB that represents the state of a process. *See* process state.

Processing section The section of a CPU responsible for carrying out most of the data manipulations required by each instruction. *See also* control section, storage section.

Processor 1) Synonym for CPU *(q.v.)*; 2) any component of a computing system responsible for performing a sequence of activities.

Profile A file that is executed when a session or job is started and defines the characteristics of the environment for an interactive session or job.

Program counter A CPU register that contains the address of the next instruction to be executed by the CPU; *abbreviated* PC.

Program fault interrupt An interrupt caused by an error in a program's execution, such as divide-by-zero or illegal memory reference.

Program interface The facility provided by an operating system for providing access to its resources for application programs; normally viewed as a collection of procedures of a special type, called system calls, which can be invoked by an appropriate machine instruction such as a system call instruction or trap.

Program status word A CPU register that represents the status of the CPU, including information such as condition codes, processor priority, and interrupt masks.

Programmable clock A clock *(q.v.)* whose value or rate can be changed under program control.

Programmed I/O *See* simple I/O.

Programmers Guide An operating system manual that contains information required for accessing operating system services from programs.

Progress message A type of message, provided by a command interface, that indicates that an activity is in progress, and possibly how much of that activity has been completed.

Prompt message A type of message displayed by most interactive command interfaces to indicate readiness to accept a command or an item of information.

Protection The process of controlling and limiting access to the resources of a computer system. *See also* access control.

Protection domain A program unit, or a portion of a program unit, such as a procedure, for which the access rights to be associated with a process while executing that unit are constant; the rights for a domain are described by a set of objects and the operations that are valid on each object; *also called* domain.

Protection key A bit pattern set in hardware for a given process that only allows storage references to memory blocks whose storage key matches this protection key; used in IBM mainframe computers.

Protection mechanism   A technique that provides protection of data and programs from unauthorized or accidental use or modification.

Protocol   A set of rules for establishing agreement and cooperation between two processes or other entities; especially, rules for sending data between computers or between a computer and a communication device. *See also* entry protocol, exit protocol.

PSW   *See* program status word.

Public key   An encryption key *(q.v.)* that is used in secure encryption of messages, but is intended to be publicly known rather than kept secret; *compare with* private key.

Public key encryption   Encryption *(q.v.)* that uses a key that is publicly known rather than kept secret. *See also* public key.

Punched cards   A medium for storing and representing information; consisting of stiff paper cards with holes punched in selected positions; especially used in older mainframe computers.

Queue   1) A data structure consisting of a collection of elements, together with insert and remove operations, which are performed in a first-in-first-out manner; 2) a collection of control blocks in an operating system, with rules for insertion and removal in a definite order, but not necessarily first-in-first-out.

Queue length   The number of elements present in a queue at a specific time.

Queueing network   A representation of a computing system or portions of a computing system as a set of interconnected queues, providing a system model for analytic modeling *(q.v.)*.

Queueing theory   A body of mathematical theory used to predict the behavior of queues and queueing networks under various conditions; used in analytic modeling *(q.v.)*.

RAM disk   A simulated disk constructed from high-speed, random-access storage units similar to main memory. Accessed like a disk, it may contain file volumes, but requires no actual input or output; used to improve the performance of systems with slow disk drives, particularly on microcomputers.

Read   An OS system call (file operation) used to read a record from a file in the file system.

Read head   A mechanism in a magnetic storage device such as a disk or tape drive, which detects information stored in the magnetic field of a moving magnetic media, and converts it to a digital form useable in computing systems.

Read-PCB   A system call that obtains the information contained in a specified process control block *(q.v.)*.

Ready state   A process state *(q.v.)* assigned to a process ready to begin or continue execution but waiting for the CPU; *compare with* blocked state, initial state, running state, suspended state, terminal state.

ReadyQ   A queue containing PCBs for processes in the ready state *(q.v.)*.

Real address space   *See* physical address space.

Real time   Time that corresponds to actual "wall clock" or elapsed time.

Real-time application   An application that must monitor or control one or more external activities that have timing characteristics and requirements not controllable by the program, but that must be met for correct operation.

Real-time control system   A real-time system *(q.v.)* involving control of one or more physical devices or processes with essential timing requirements; examples include navigation systems, rapid transit systems, industrial control systems.

Real-time environment   A computer system environment that includes real-time applications.

Real-time executive   An operating system designed to support real-time applications.

Real-time process   A process that interacts with a physical device or process having essential timing requirements, and that must respond to external events within a fixed maximum amount of time; *also called* real-time task.

Real-time system   A computer system used for real-time applications *(q.v.)* involving monitoring or control of one or more physical devices or processes with essential timing requirements. *See also* real-time control system.

Real-time task   *See* real-time process.

Reasonableness   1) A quality of a command language that provides reasonable responses to most normal or abnormal inputs and situations; 2) a consideration in programming that provides for inspection and examination of data, and tests them against some condition or set of conditions that indicates that the data are not reasonable, and hence are probably in error.

Receive   A system call used in interprocess communication to request or accept a message sent by another process to the calling process.

Record   A unit of storage or information within a file, usually having a consistent format for any specific file; sometimes further divided into fields *(q.v.)*.

Recursive virtual machine monitor   A virtual machine monitor that can run a copy of itself.

Reentrant program   A program that can be in use by two or more processes at the same time, each sharing the same copy of the executable code but having separate data areas; such a program must not modify its machine instructions in any way during normal execution, and must use no absolute physical addresses in its data references.

Region   A unit of storage assigned to a job or process, the size of which may be changed while the program is executing; used especially by OS/MVT; *compare with* partition.

Register   A hardware storage unit, often within a CPU, capable of storing a single data item.

Relative addressing   A variation on based addressing *(q.v.)*, exemplified by the PDP-11, in which the program counter is used as a base register.

Release notes   Documentation provided in hardcopy and/or electronic form as part of a new operating system release that informs users or systems programmers of changes and features in that release.

Reliability   A characteristic of a computer system by which it tends to remain correct and available in spite of hardware faults and software errors.

Reliable computer system   A computer system that possesses a high degree of reliability *(q.v.)*.

Relocatable object code   A representation of a program in the form of object code, which includes information about the locations in the program that should be modified, and in what way, to perform relocation.

Relocate   To move or load a program or process and adjust location-dependent addresses to allow the program to execute correctly. *See* relocation.

Relocating linker   A linker *(q.v.)* that processes relocatable object code and performs relocation as well as linking. Relocation is performed by modifying addresses contained in the program as it is processed. The output of such a linker may be again relocatable object code, or it may be an executable load module.

Relocating loader   A loader that accepts relocatable object code and performs relocation by modifying addresses contained in the program as it is loaded, to provide proper operation at the locations chosen for loading.

Relocation   Modification by software or hardware of the addresses specified by a program for branches or data references, to allow the program to execute correctly when loaded into a specific area of memory, the location of which was not known when the program was created.

Relocation dictionary   Information within a program in relocatable object code form that specifies locations that should be adjusted, and in what manner, during relocation; this information is used by a relocating linker or relocating loader to perform relocation.

Relocation register   A CPU register whose contents are added to every address used to reference data or instructions during program execution; this provides dynamic relocation and eliminates the need for software adjustment by a relocating linker or loader.

Remote procedure call   A procedure call made by a process operating in a distributed operating system to a procedure located at a remote site; this mechanism is supported by some operating systems but is difficult to provide in an effective way.

Rendezvous   A message-passing mechanism without buffering, supported by the Ada programming language; in using this mechanism, two processes exchanging a message must both be ready before the message can be exchanged; the process that is ready first must wait.

Replacement problem   In a virtual memory system, the problem of deciding which page or segment to remove from main memory when a page frame is needed and the memory is full.

Reproducible failure   A failure in an operating system that can be forced to occur again, and hence be more easily isolated.

Resident component   An operating system component that remains in main memory at all times during normal operation; *compare with* transient component.

Resident loader   A loader, often a relocating loader, that is a resident component of an operating system.

Resource   Any physical object, information, service, or other entity existing within a computing system that may be used by the system or application programs.

Resource deadlock   A type of deadlock *(q.v.)* that arises when a group of processes is blocked, with each one waiting for some resource currently held by another in the group; *compare with* communication deadlock.

Resource holding   A characteristic of a resource allocation strategy by which processes that must wait for resources do not release others that may have been allocated to them; one of the necessary conditions to make deadlock possible.

Resource sharing   The use of a resource by two or more processes, either concurrently or one at a time.

Response ratio   A measure of the waiting time experienced by a process waiting for service, compared to its expected service time; consists of waiting time divided by the sum of waiting time plus service time; in theory, a fair criteria for use in process scheduling, but difficult to compute in practice.

Response time   The time required for a computing system to produce the expected response to any input; in particular, the time between the entry of a command on an interactive terminal and the display of the response to that command.

Return code   A value returned as a parameter by a procedure or program to the program that invoked it or to the operating system, indicating the outcome of execution and the type of error that occurred, if any.

Reusable resource   A resource that may be used repeatedly, such as physical objects or information stored in files; *compare with* consumable resource.

Revocation of a capability   A mechanism in a capability system for canceling or revoking access rights that have been given to another subject by supplying that subject with a suitable capability; possible only by use of indirect capabilities.

Ring buffer   A buffer consisting of a set of storage locations organized as a circular list *(q.v.)*.

Root process   The initial process that is executed upon the starting of a session or job in an operating system supporting a hierarchical process structure.

Round-robin   *See* round-robin scheduling.

Round-robin scheduling   A scheduling strategy for a set of processes that provides for first-in, first-out scheduling, with all processes organized in a circular list.

RS-232 serial interface   A type of serial interface *(q.v.)* that uses a standard designated RS-232, developed by the Electronics Industry Association (EIA) for signal and control voltages and pin layout; widely used to connect terminals, printers, and similar devices to computer systems.

RSX-11   A real-time executive for the PDP-11 developed and supported by Digital Equipment Corporation. *See* Section C.5.

RT-11   A single-user operating system for the PDP-11, developed and supported by Digital Equipment Corporation. *See* Section C.5.

RTE   *See* real-time executive.

Running state   A process state *(q.v.)* assigned to a process currently running—that is, has control of a CPU; *compare with* blocked state, initial state, ready state, suspended state, terminal state.

Running_Process   The process that is currently assigned the CPU and executing instructions.

SABRE   An early transaction-processing system, developed by IBM and American Airlines. *See* Section C.2.

SAGE   An early real-time system, developed by IBM. *See* Section C.2.

Scheduler   An operating system component responsible for scheduling *(q.v.)*. *See also* dispatcher.

Scheduling   1) Determining the order in which resources, especially CPUs and memory, will be assigned to processes and jobs. *See* job scheduling, process scheduling; 2) determining the order in which pending activities, such as I/O operations, will be carried out. *See also* I/O scheduling.

Second-level interrupt handler   An interrupt handler *(q.v.)* that receives control after a first-level interrupt handler *(q.v.)* has determined that the cause of the interrupt was a device or condition for which the second-level interrupt handler is responsible.

Secondary memory   A type of storage used to contain large amounts of data not currently required in main memory, but likely to be needed at a future time; commonly takes the form of a magnetic disk or drum; usually much of this memory is organized into a file system.

Sector   The smallest unit that can be written to a disk; a division of a track.

Sector interleaving   A technique for numbering sectors on a disk whereby sectors in a track are not allocated one after another, but rather interleaved in another order; used to increase sequential access time, especially for slower disks.

Secure computer system   A computer system that possesses a high degree of security *(q.v.)*.

Security   A characteristic of a computer system by which its resources are able to remain available, correct, and private, despite hardware faults, software errors, or deliberate, intelligent attacks.

Security mechanism   A facility or feature of an operating system that is used to support the enforcement of security policies.

Security policy   A policy that determines who may obtain or change information stored in a computer system; the security policy of a computer installation specifying how security is "guaranteed" in the installation.

Seek delay   A delay experienced during use of a moving-head disk drive while its arm is moving from one track or cylinder to another.

Seek operation   1) An OS system call (file operation) used to select the position of the next read or write in random access files; 2) a control operation on a moving-head disk *(q.v.)* that moves the head to the requested track.

Segment   A division of a program's information, usually a logically complete unit such as a procedure or data structure, that is managed independently by a memory translation system. *See also* segmentation.

Segment descriptor   In a segmented virtual memory system, a block descriptor describing the translation of a segment *(q.v.)* to a corresponding region of physical or virtual memory *(q.v.)*; its fields normally include the location and size of the segment, or of a page table representing it; a segment present flag, and an access control field; a collection of page descriptors forms a segment table *(q.v.)*. *See also* page descriptor.

Segment fault   A hardware interrupt in a segmented virtual memory system caused by a reference to a segment not currently resident in main memory; the response to a segment fault requires that the segment be loaded from secondary storage, and that a page table be constructed for it if paging is used.

Segment number   An address or sequence number assigned to a segment that identifies it while in use by a program.

Segment present flag   A bit in a segment descriptor *(q.v.)* that indicates whether the corresponding segment, or a page table describing it, is currently resident in main memory.

Segment table   A table containing a set of segment descriptors *(q.v.)*, normally stored in main memory and organized sequentially by segment number.

Segment table register   A CPU register that identifies the location and size of the current segment table.

Segmentation   A characteristic of a memory management system in which the storage required by a program or process is divided into segments *(q.v.)*; each segment is independently translated to a region of physical memory. If virtual memory is used, each segment may be loaded or removed as a unit; if paging *(q.v.)* is also used, each segment may be represented by an independent page table..

Self-configuration   OS configuration that is performed at OS load time using I/O tables, configuration tables, and/or configuration files.

Selfish scheduling   A type of process scheduling *(q.v.)* in which processes newly admitted to the ready state must wait for a period of time before their priority may equal that of other processes already present.

Semaphore   A type of shared data item that may assume only binary or integer values and that, after initialization, may be accessed by only two operations; the P, or wait, operation attempts to reduce the value of the semaphore and may cause the calling process to wait; the V, or signal, operation increases the value of the semaphore or causes a waiting process to proceed; used to provide mutual exclusion and other types of synchronization. *See also* binary semaphore, general semaphore.

Send   A system call used in interprocess communication to send a message to another process.

Sequential process   A process consisting of a sequence of actions to be carried out one at a time.

Serial interface   An I/O interface *(q.v.)* that transfers data items, usually eight-bit bytes, between a computer and an I/O device, in the form of a sequence of single bits preceded and followed by certain control bits; *compare with* parallel interface. *See also* RS-232 serial interface.

Serially reusable resource   A reusable resource that can be used by only one process at a time.

Service request interrupt   An interrupt generated by a type of machine instruction that passes control to the program interface; *also called* system call interrupt.

Session   The collection of activities performed by and on behalf of a user of an interactive computing system, beginning with a log on by that user, and ending with a log off by the same user.

Shadow page table   A mechanism used by a virtual machine monitor *(q.v.)* to avoid the multiple-level paging translation required when an operating system supporting virtual memory is running on a virtual machine. The shadow page table provides a single mapping that replaces the multiple levels of mapping that would otherwise be required.

SHARE   An IBM users' group.

SHARE Operating System   An early operating system developed by SHARE *(q.v.)*.

Shared memory   A region of main memory accessible by two or more processes, or by two or more CPUs.

Shell   A type of command interface introduced by MULTICS and made popular by UNIX, having the form of an application process that supports all necessary communication for interactive users, but that may be modified or replaced by individual users.

Shortest job next   A long-term process scheduling strategy that always selects the waiting job having the shortest expected total execution time; *abbreviated* SJN.

Shortest remaining time next   Used with preemption, a process scheduling strategy that selects the waiting job or process having the shortest expected remaining execution time.

Shortest seek time first   A disk scheduling strategy that select the pending I/O request that results in the least arm movement during a seek operation.

Short-term scheduling   A level of process scheduling concerned with determining the order in which processes will be selected for immediate use of the CPU; *compare with* medium-term scheduling, long-term scheduling.

SIL   *See* system implementation language.

Simple contiguous   A technique for file space allocation in which each file is allocated one contiguous sequence of blocks; *also called* contiguous organization.

Simple I/O   An input/output strategy used on small and medium computers to manage character-by-character devices that can produce or accept one byte (or word) at a time, at the convenience of the CPU; a distinct I/O instruction is used to transfer every word of data to or from the device; *also called* programmed I/O.

Simulation   A performance analysis *(q.v.)* technique based on the construction of programs and databases that model the actual system under study; the simulated system is "run" by the program with simulated work loads; *compare with* analytic modeling, performance measurement.

Site   A specific location on a network containing one or more computer systems; *also called* network site.

SJN   *See* shortest job next.

Sleep   A system call requesting that the calling process or another process be "put to sleep," that is, placed in a suspended state *(q.v.)* until "awakened" by a specified event.

SLIH   *See* second-level interrupt handler.

Soft real-time requirement   A timing requirement in a real-time environment that should be met as closely as possible, but for which an occasional delay can be tolerated; *compare with* hard real-time requirement.

Software   Any programs or data used in a computer system, normally stored in main memory while in use; *compare with* hardware, firmware.

Software caching   A technique of maintaining buffers *(q.v.)* of recently-read records, or records to be written, in order to minimize the number of physical device I/O operations; the assumption here is that recently accessed records will tend to be accessed again, and thus should be kept in the software cache.

Software clock   A clock implemented by software using one or more hardware clocks.

Software development tool   A program or software facility for improving programmer productivity or control software development.

Software device   A device that is simulated in software, using internal memory (RAM disk *(q.v.)*) or a portion of a physical device (virtual disk *(q.v.)*) as the storage "medium."

Software interrupt   The execution of a hardware instruction by a program (e.g., a trap or supervisor call instruction) that causes a hardware interrupt.

Software monitor   A sequence of instructions added to a program to collect information about the program's behavior; a mechanism for performance measurement *(q.v.)*; *compare with* hardware monitor.

Software tool   *See* software development tool.

SOS   *See* Share Operating System.

Soundness   A quality of a command language whereby any command that can reasonably be formulated and accepted has a reasonably expected effect.

Source code   A representation of a program in the form in which it was originally written or expressed, usually using a high-level language or assembly language.

Source deck   A set of punched cards containing the source code for a program.

Source portability   A type of portability of programs that permits them to be implemented in new environments by installing a copy of their source code in the new environment, with only limited changes required to that source code. When processed by compilers, linkers and loaders available in the target system, the program executes correctly and satisfactorily.

Source program   A representation of a program in the form of source code *(q.v.)*.

Spanning   A technique for storing files on a block storage device, such as disk or tape, whereby a single physical block may contain portions of more than one record.

Spool device   *See* spooler (def. 2).

Spooler   1) A component of an operating system that performs spooling *(q.v.)*; 2) a hardware unit installed between a computer system and selected I/O devices, especially printers, to perform spooling. *See* hardware buffer.

Spooling   The activity of buffering, in memory or a disk file, input received from certain I/O devices such as card readers or output destined for certain I/O devices such as printers to minimize the waiting that must be done by either the devices or the processes performing the I/O; originally an acronym for Simultaneous Peripheral Operation On-Line.

Stack pointer   1) A CPU register that identifies the location of a hardware stack *(q.v.)* or of information within such a stack; 2) a pointer to a process's stack that is saved and restored on a context switch.

Standard   A definition for aspects of an object, procedure, or interface that enables objects produced or developed by different persons or groups, or activities performed by different persons or groups, to work together in some consistent and useful way; for example a standard for threads cut into nuts and bolts ensures that various types of nuts and bolts will fit together. *See also* de facto standard, formal standard.

Standard interface   An interface between two objects, especially hardware or software components of a computing system, defined by and conforming to a standard *(q.v.)* to ensure proper interaction.

Standard operating system interface   A standard interface between an operating system and another element of a computing system; especially, the software interface between operating systems and application programs.

Standard procedure library   A library of procedures used in a particular programming language that is provided by most implementations and may be freely used by programmers; this effectively extends the facilities of the language itself, assisting the source portability of many applications; the C programming library is a well-known example.

Standard programming language   A programming language defined by a recognized standard *(q.v.)*.

Standards organization   An organization whose purpose is to establish and maintain formal standards that can be used to increase portability and reduce problems of incompatibility in hardware and software and other areas; examples include ANSI, IEEE, and ISO.

Starvation   A possible occurrence in some scheduling strategies in which a process or activity may be required to wait indefinitely due to the constant presence of processes or activities having a higher priority.

Static allocation   Allocation of resources to a process only when the process is initiated, and not during execution; *compare with* dynamic allocation.

Static memory area definition A strategy for defining memory blocks that can be assigned to processes, in which free memory is mapped into fixed size blocks when the operating system is loaded; once defined, the blocks to be allocated remain the same throughout the execution of the operating system; *compare with* dynamic memory definition.

Static priorities A system for assigning priorities to processes or activities such that the priorities do not change during execution or while the process or activity is waiting for service; *compare with* dynamic priorities.

Static process management A type of process management in which processes are permanent, and are not created or destroyed during normal operation; *compare with* dynamic process management.

Static relocation Relocation that is or can be performed only at or before the time a program is loaded, not after execution has begun; *compare with* dynamic relocation.

Storage 1) A synonym for memory *(q.v.)*; 2) the act of storing information on a storage device for later retrieval.

Storage device An I/O device that allows data to be written and later read, usually used to hold information that will be used at a later time, rather than to communicate with users; common examples include magnetic disks and tapes.

Storage management *See* memory management.

Storage medium An object or material capable of recording information and used for that purpose by a storage device; examples include magnetic tapes or disks and optical disks.

Storage scheduling *See* medium-term scheduling.

Storage section A section of a CPU that includes the local storage for the CPU, especially CPU registers.

Storage time quantum A time quantum *(q.v.)* that defines the time during which a process is permitted to remain loaded in main memory.

Store *See* memory.

Subject An entity in a computer system that may be granted access rights to objects in implementing access control policy; subjects include users, processes, and programs.

Subprocess A process created and controlled by another process, or that is a component of another process, such as a microprocess *(q.v.)*.

Suspend A system call that requests that a process other than the calling process be placed in a suspended state. *See also* sleep.

Suspended state A process state *(q.v.)* assigned to a process that is or has been waiting for an event that occurs only after a long or indefinite time; such a process is not a member of the active set, and may have its information swapped out of memory; it is considered suspended-blocked if the event has not occurred, or suspended-ready if the event has occurred and it is waiting for medium-term scheduling; *compare with* blocked state, initial state, ready state, running state, suspended state, terminal state.

Swap area A region of a storage device used to hold images of processes that have been swapped.

Swapping A technique for moving entire programs from memory to auxiliary storage in order to execute another program; programs often must be swapped back in at the same address if the architecture does not provide for dynamic relocation.

Symbolic debugger A debugger *(q.v.)* that uses symbols from a source program to assist in the examination, analysis, tracing, and modification of a program in execution. *See also* high-level language debugger.

Symmetric message passing Message passing *(q.v.)* in which both the sender and the receiver must identify each other in order to exchange messages; *compare with* asymmetric message passing.

Synchronization The activity of ensuring that events in a computing system occur in a proper order and with suitable timing relationships, even though carried out by multiple processes.

Synchronous file access A strategy for file access by which system calls requesting the transfer of information to or from files do not return to the caller until the transfer has been completed; *compare with* asynchronous file access.

System area A portion of a file volume reserved for storing system programs, usually including a copy of the operating system.

System bus A common hardware interconnection structure found in most small and medium computers used to connect hardware elements; the system bus enables a uniform means of communication among all devices connected to it.

System call A request made to the operating system by a process to obtain a service or access to a resource; usually performed by use of a system call instruction *(q.v.)*.

System call instruction A machine instruction used by a process to request service from the operating system; the system call instruction performs two important actions simultaneously: 1) it transfers control to a location within the operating system, saving the return address; and 2) it switches the CPU into privileged mode.

System-controlled resource A resource for which all access is under the direct control of the operating system; such a resource cannot be accessed by any process without OS permission; *compare with* user-controlled resource.

System error log A file maintained by an operating system to record information about errors that have been detected.

System generation The production, usually by system managers through an automated process, of a specific operating system matching the characteristics of the hardware on which it will run and the desired operating system features.

System generation manual An operating system manual that describes the procedures for system generation *(q.v.)*; often combined with the installation manual *(q.v.)*.

System implementation language A programming language intended especially for writing system programs such as operating systems; *abbreviated* SIL.

System management Activities required to install, operate, and maintain an operating system, such as installation, adjusting characteristics for each particular environment, beginning normal operation after a shutdown or serious error, maintaining user information, and billing users for services.

System process A process that is an integral part of the operating system, or that performs activities on behalf of the operating system; *compare with* application process.

System program A program that is a required part of a total computing environment, but generally is loaded and executed as an application process; examples include editors, assemblers, compilers, linkers, loaders, software development tools, and debuggers *(q.v.)*.

System request interrupt A machine instruction that causes an interrupt and is intended to function as a system call instruction *(q.v.)*.

System utilities manual An operating system manual that describes OS utilities like linkers, compilers, and editors.

Tape operating system An operating system that uses tape as the system storage device for storing the operating system, programs, and data; common in the early and mid-sixties and briefly reintroduced on early micros using cassette tapes; *compare with* disk operating system.

Target system 1) A system to which software in binary or source form is being converted or moved. *See also* binary portability, source portability; 2) the system for which a program is being prepared for execution using a cross-compiler.

Task 1) A synonym for process; 2) a unit of activity within a process, especially in real-time systems.

Task force A group of cooperating processes.

Technical protection Protection provided by the hardware, operating system, and application programs.

TENEX A timesharing operating system for the PDP-10. *See* Section C.4.

Terminal An I/O device that can input and output information in the form of characters that can be typed and read by users during an interactive session, or in other forms that users can produce or understand; common forms include hardcopy terminals, video terminals *(q.v.)*.

Terminal handler A device driver that supports input and output to a hardcopy or CRT terminal; often plays a special role in a command interface *(q.v.)*.

Terminal handling The activity performed by a terminal handler.

Terminal state A specific condition or status of a terminal, together with its handler, which causes certain behavior in response to the input or output of specific data; for example, enabling or disabling of line buffering, or display of characters in a specific color or form.

Termination message A message produced by a command interface to indicate that an activity has terminated.

Text file A file containing text characters, normally directly readable by a user.

T.H.E. Developed by Dijkstra, an operating system that introduced significant concepts in structure and synchronization. *See* Section C.15.

Thrashing A condition in a virtual memory system in which an excessive amount of page or segment faults occurs, causing a high proportion of overhead and little useful work.

Thread A subprocess created by a process in a real-time executive, that may take turns running within the main process's scheduled time period.

Time-of-day The current time or a specific time in a normal twenty-four-hour day.

Time-out interval An interval of time used to check on a device I/O completion or other event that should occur prior to the expiration of the time-out interval.

Time quantum A time limit assigned to a process for execution or residence in main memory; after the process has used its time quantum, the resource is preempted, and a new time quantum is assigned for later use; plural time quanta; *also called* time slice.

Time slice *See* time quantum.

Time-window working set A working set *(q.v.)* whose contents consist of all pages referenced during a specific number of previous references by the current process; this time interval is called the time window.

Timer *See* clock.

Timer interrupt An interrupt generated by a hardware clock.

Timer management The aspect of the operating system that deals with the management of hardware and software clocks and process timing services.

Timer queue A data structure that represents times at which a timer event must be signalled to the operating system or a process.

Timer queue element A single element in a timer queue.

Timesharing system A type of operating system that provides interactive access to the computer for multiple users at the same time.

Timeslicing A technique used in process scheduling that permits a process to remain in control for no more than a specific interval of time called a time quantum *(q.v.)*.

Track A long, thin region on a storage device on which information can be stored; especially, one of a few regions running the length of a magnetic tape on which data may be stored by magnetic means, or one of a number of circular regions on a disk on which data may be stored by magnetic or optical means.

Trade secret law A law that protects any formula, pattern, device, or compilation of information developed or possessed by a company, which gives a company or individual an opportunity to obtain an advantage over competitors who do not have access to the information, provided that the company takes reasonable steps to keep it secret.

Transaction processing system A type of operating system designed to support a large number of users, especially inter-active users, normally performing simple, well-defined activities called transactions; for example, an airline reservation system.

Transient component A component of an operating system that is loaded into main memory from secondary storage when needed; often used for error recovery routines, file access routines, and other purposes; *compare with* resident component.

Transient error routine A transient component *(q.v.)* of an OS that deals with error recovery.

Translation table 1) A table that specifies the translation of information from one representation to another, e.g., from EBCDIC to ASCII character codes; 2) a table that specifies the physical address associated with the virtual address in a system supporting virtual memory.

TTY Acronym for teletype, often used to describe any terminal.

Tuning *See* performance tuning.

Turnaround time The time from the submission of a batch job to the time of receipt of its output.

Tutorial manual An operating system manual that has a tutorial orientation for learning how to use the operating system; could be provided using tutorial programs that are self-explanatory.

Typeahead The ability of the terminal interface of an operating system to save information entered by a user in a buffer if necessary until the operating system or program is ready to accept it.

UCB *See* unit control block.

Uninterruptible power source An electric power source that ensures that power remains available in case of failure by the normal electric utility; *abbreviated* UPS.

Uniprocessor A computing system with a single CPU.

Unit control block A control block that represents the status of a specific I/O unit or device; *See also* device control block.

UNIX A popular interactive operating system developed by researchers at AT&T Bell Laboratories. *See* Section C.9.

UPS *See* uninterruptible power source.

User A person who interacts with a computer system, or who submits work for processing by a computer system.

User authentication *See* authentication.

User-controlled resource A resource that can be accessed directly by certain processes, and is controlled only be agreement among processes that use it; for example, a data structure within a shared file or shared memory.

User environment A set of conditions established for a specific user at a particular time during operating, especially in an interactive system; may include a collection of usable commands, defined object names and abbreviations, or terminal characteristics.

User interface The component of an operating system that interacts with users, normally consisting of the command interface and the program interface.

User introductory manual An operating system manual that introduces the concepts of the operating system to a novice user.

User name A name that uniquely identifies a user when logging into or using a computer system that is used for authentication and accounting purposes.

Utilities manual An operating system manual that contains information about various system utilities like sort, index, edit, and file support utilities.

Variance A statistical property of a measurable value that represents the degree to which individual values tend to deviate from the mean.

VAX/VMS An operating system for VAX computers developed by Digital Equipment Corporation. *See* Section C.4.

Verbose mode A mode in a command interpreter in which all information is displayed in detail rather than in abbreviated form; typically used by inexperienced users.

Version number 1) A number associated with a file that may distinguish different versions of the same file; 2) a number that indicates the release of a particular system program or the operating system itself.

Video RAM An area of main memory *(q.v.)*, that is used to control the display on a video terminal; each location or set of locations in this video RAM corresponds to a position on the display and determine(s) the character to be displayed at this location.

Video terminal A terminal consisting of a keyboard and a video display screen similar to a television screen.

Virtual address An address in a virtual address space.

Virtual address space An address space consisting of a set of locations in a virtual memory—that is, the memory apparently available to a specific process; *compare with* physical address space.

Virtual circuit A fixed path, established in a network environment, that is used for subsequent routing of all packets transmitted.

Virtual clock A clock that may be allocated to and used by a process, not necessarily corresponding to a real hardware clock *(q.v.)*.

Virtual CPU A CPU implemented for each of its processes by a virtual machine monitor; the CPU appears to have all the properties of a real CPU, except for time-dependent behavior.

Virtual CPU architecture An architecture that defines a CPU that can be emulated or simulated in order to provide portability.

Virtual device *See* virtual I/O device.

Virtual disk A disk simulated by the use of a physical disk being partitioned into smaller blocks, each of which provides the apparent properties of the physical disk except for size; used by virtual machine systems *(q.v.)*.

Virtual interrupt An interrupt simulated by a virtual machine operating system in response to a real interrupt that maps to an interrupt in the virtual machine.

Virtual I/O device An I/O device simulated by the operating system that provides the behavior expected from a physical device, but does not necessarily correspond directly to a physical device; used by virtual machine systems *(q.v.)*.

Virtual machine 1) the specific environment presented to each process running on a virtual machine system; 2) an abstract machine that appears identical to, or very similar to, the actual physical hardware of a computer.

Virtual machine monitor A type of operating system that supports multiple concurrent processes and implements a virtual machine environment for each process it runs. Each process has the illusion of access to a complete set of hardware resources, usually a copy of the real physical resources, but no operating system or other system software. Typically, each process running in a virtual machine executes an operating system, allowing multiple operating systems to execute on a single physical machine; *abbreviated* VMM.

Virtual machine system A computer system controlled by a virtual machine monitor.

Virtual memory Memory apparently useable by a process in a virtual memory system, which does not necessarily correspond to physical main memory and may be larger than the main memory actually available; generally implemented by a combination of hardware and software mechanisms that allow for some of the information in the virtual address space to be stored on a secondary storage device; an attempt to reference this information causes a special type of interrupt, called a page fault or segment fault *(q.v.)*, and the operating system then moves the required data into main memory.

Virtual memory system An operating system mechanism that supports the use of virtual memory.

Virtual privileged mode The mode of a virtual machine in which it is allowed to execute privileged instructions.

Virtual time Consistent time maintained for a virtual machine that does not necessarily correspond to real time.

Virtualizable CPU architecture A CPU architecture that allows the implementation of a virtual CPU; requires that all instructions that access privileged registers be privileged and that *all* privileged instructions, when attempted in non-privileged mode, generate an interrupt.

Visible A term describing elements of a computing system that are accessible to a user or program.

VMM   *See* virtual machine monitor.

VRTX   A general purpose real-time executive produced by Hunter and Ready. *See* Section C.11.

Volume   *See* file volume.

Volume descriptor   An information area within a file volume that provides descriptive information for the volume itself.

Volume name   A name assigned to a file volume.

Waiting state   *See* blocked state.

Waiting time   The time spend by a process waiting for service, primarily for I/O device operations, that affects CPU throughput and utilization.

Wake up   A system call that requests the activation of a process which is currently in a suspended state *(q.v.)*. *See also* sleep, suspend.

WAN   *See* wide area network.

Warm start   The starting of a computer operating system in which certain information about the previous state of the system, usually stored on disk when the system was last shut down, is used to determine the state of the system when restarted; commonly used to preserve jobs in a job queue in a large mainframe operating system environment; *compare with* cold start.

Wide area network   A network *(q.v.)* that connects computers and other resources within an extended geographic area; connection is carried out via common carrier communications facilities, such as satellite and telephone lines, in which data transfer is controlled by protocols; systems on such a network can be miles or hundreds of miles apart, and often are of many different types and under no common administration; *compare with* local area network.

Warm start   A process of initiating an operating system after a shutdown or failure, while retaining portions of the previous state of the system; used especially in large multiprogramming operating systems to preserve job queues, checkpoints, and other ongoing work; *compare with* cold start.

Winchester disk   A type of hard disk that is sealed and uses a special aerodynamically designed head to minimize the probability of a head crash.

Word   An addressable unit of memory, usually consisting of one or more bytes.

Work around   A means of changing an application program to avoid incorrect behavior caused by an operating system problem.

Working set   1) A collection of pages to be retained in main memory for each process in a virtual memory system; 2) description of a strategy for virtual memory management based on working sets.

Work load   1) The full set of work that a system is assumed to be doing while its performance is being measured; 2) the mix of jobs or processes currently executing under the control of an operating system.

Workstation   A small single-user computer intended for professional use, usually possessing high performance and including a high quality graphic display.

WORM   *See* write-once read-mostly.

Worst-fit   A memory allocation algorithm that allocates the free block in memory that results in the largest remaining block after allocation; *compare with* first-fit, next-fit, best-fit.

Write   An OS system call (file operation) used to write a record to a file in the file system.

Write head   A mechanism in a magnetic storage device, such as a disk or tape drive, that stores information on a moving magnetic medium by use of an electric field.

Write-once read-mostly   A term used to describe a property of some optical storage devices, by which information may be stored on them once by a programming technique; thereafter, the information cannot be erased or modified.

 *Bibliography*

ABBREVIATIONS

ACM	*Proceedings of ACM Annual Conference*, annual
BLTJ	*Bell Labs Technical Journal* (continues *BSTJ*), monthly
BSTJ	*Bell Systems Technical Journal*, monthly
CACM	*Communications of the ACM*, monthly
CJ	*Computer Journal*, quarterly
COMPCON	*Proceedings of the Conference of the IEEE Computer Society*, semiannual (Spring and Fall)
COMPUTER	*IEEE Computer Magazine*, monthly
CSURV	*ACM Computing Surveys*, monthly
DECUS	*Proceedings of meetings of the Digital Equipment Users Group*, semiannual (Spring and Fall)
EJCC	*Proceedings of the Eastern Joint Computer Conference*, AFIPS press, annual (predecessor to *FJCC* and *SJCC*; see also *WJCC*)
FJCC	*Proceedings of the Fall Joint Computer Conference*, AFIPS press, annual (predecessor to *NCC*; see also *SJCC*)
HPJ	*Hewlett-Packard Journal*
IBMJRD	*IBM Journal of Research and Development*, bimonthly
IBMSJ	*IBM Systems Journal*, monthly
IFIP	*Proceedings of the Congress of the International Federation of Information Processing*, North Holland, triennial
JACM	*Journal of the ACM*, quarterly
MICRO	*IEEE Micro Magazine*, bimonthly
MIDCON	*Proceedings of Midcon, annual Midwestern Electronic Conference*; see also *WESCON*
MMS	*Mini-Micro Systems*, monthly
MP&MS	*Microprocessors and Microsystems*, 10 per year
NCC	*Proceedings of the National Computer Conference*, AFIPS press, annual
OSR	*Operating Systems Review, Newsletter of the ACM Special Interest Group on Operation Systems*, monthly
PROC IEEE	*Proceedings of the IEEE*, monthly
SASPLOS	*Proceedings of the Symposium on Architectural Support for Programming Languages and Operating Systems*, ACM publication, occasional
SIGPLAN	*SIGPLAN Notices, Newsletter of ACM Special Interest Group on Programming Languages*, monthly
SJCC	*Proceedings of the Spring Joint Computer Conference*, AFIPS press, annual (predecessor to *NCC*; see also *FJCC*)
SOFTWARE	*IEEE Software Magazine*, bimonthly
SOSP	*Proceedings of the Symposium on Operating Systems Principles*, ACM publication, biennial
TC	*IEEE Transactions on Computers*, monthly
TOPLAS	*ACM Transactions on Programming Languages and Systems*, quarterly
TSE	*IEEE Transactions on Software Engineering*, monthly
WESCON	*Proceedings of Wescon, annual western electronic conference* (see also *MIDCON*)
WJCC	*Proceedings of the Western Joint Computer Conference*. AFIPS press, annual (predecessor to *FJC* and *SJCC*; see also *EJCC*)

REFERENCES

[Abbott 1984] Abbot, C. Intervention Schedules for Real-Time Programming. *TSE*, Vol. SE-10, No. 3, May 1984, pp. 268-274.

[Abernathy et al. 1973] Abernathy, D.H., et al. Survey of Design Goals for Operating Systems. In three parts. *OSR*, Vol. 7, No. 2, April 1973, pp. 29-48; *OSR*, Vol. 7, No. 3, July 1973, pp. 19-34; *OSR*, Vol. 8, No. 1, Jan 1974, pp. 25-35.

[Agrawal et al. 1984] Agrawal, S.C., et al. On Tuning the Fair-share Scheduler in Virtual Machine Operating Systems. *Proc. CMG XV, Int. Conf. on the Management and Performance Evaluation of Computer Systems*, Dec. 1984.

[Agrawala et al. 1976] Agrawala, A.K., et al. An Approach to the Work load Characterization Problem. *COMPUTER*, Vol. 9, No. 6, June 1976, pp. 18-32.

[Akkoyunlu et al. 1974] Akkoyunlu, E., et al. Interprocess Communication Facilities for Network Operating Systems. *COMPUTER*, Vol. 7, No. 6, June 1974, pp 46-55.

[Alderman 1969] Alderman, J.C. Foreground/Background/8 now. *DECUS*, Fall 1969, pp. 269-272.

[Allen 1978] Allen, A.O. *Probability, Statistics, and Queueing Theory with Computer Science Applications*. Academic Press, New York, 1978.

[Allen 1980] Allen, A.O. Queueing Models of Computer Systems. *COMPUTER*, Vol. 13, No. 4, April 1980, pp. 13-24.

[Anderson 1981] Anderson, D.A. Operating Systems. *COMPUTER*, Vol. 14, No. 6, June 1981, pp. 69-82.

[Andrews & Schneider 1983] Andrews, G., and Schneider, F. Concepts and Notations for Concurrent Programming. *SCURV*, Vol. 5, No. 1, March 1983, pp. 3-44.

[Andrews et al. 1987] Andrews, G.R., et al. The Design of the Saguaro Distributed Operating System. *TSE*, Vol. SE-13, No. 1, Jan. 1987, pp. 104-118.

[ANSI 1978] *Programming Language Fortran. ANSI X3.9-1978*, ANSI, New York, 1978.

[ANSI 1983a] *American National Standard Pascal Computer Programming Language. ANSI/IEEE770X3.97-1983*, ANSI, New York, 1983.

[ANSI 1983b] *Military Standard: Ada Programming Language. ANSI/MIL-STD-1815A*, ANSI, New York, 1983.

[ANSI 1985] *Programming Language COBOL. ANSI X3.23-1985*, ANSI, New York, 1985.

[ANSI 1988] *Programming Language C. ANSI X3.159-1988*, ANSI, New York, 1988.

[Anzinger 1975] Anzinger, G.A. A Real-Time Operating System with Multiterminal and Batch/Spool Capabilities. *HPJ*, Vol. 27, No. 4, Dec. 1975, pp. 21-24.

[Archer 1982] Archer, R. Multidos: A New TRS-80 Disk Operating System. (Review) *BYTE*, Vol. 7, No. 12, Dec. 1982, pp. 392-397.

[Arnold et al. 1974] Arnold, J.S., et al. Design of Tightly-coupled Multiprocessing Programming. *IBMSJ*, Vol. 13, No. 1, 1974, pp. 61-87.

[Aron 1974] Aron, J.D. *The Program Development Process: The Individual Programmer*. Addison-Wesley, Reading, MA, 1974.

[Artsy et al. 1986] Artsy, Y., et al. *Interprocess Communication in Charlotte*. University of Wisconsin at Madison, Technical Report, 1986.

[Attanasio et al. 1976] Attanasio, C.R., et al. Penetrating an Operating System: A Study of VM/370 Integrity. *IBMSJ*, Vol. 15, No. 1, 1976, pp. 102-116.

[Atwood 1976] Atwood, J.W. Concurrency in Operating Systems. *COMPUTER*, Vol. 9, No. 10, Oct. 1976, pp. 18-26.

[Augenstein & Tenenbaum 1979] Augenstein, M. and Tenenbaum, A.M. *Data Structures and PL/I Programming*. Prentice-Hall, Englewood Cliffs, NJ, 1979.

[Auslander et al. 1981] Auslander, M.A., et al. The Evolution of the MVS Operating System. *IBMJRD*, Vol. 25, No. 5, Sept. 1981, pp. 471-482.

[Averett 1975] Real-time executive system manages Large Memories. *HPJ*, Vol. 27, No. 4, Dec. 1975.

[Avizienis & Kelly 1984] Avizienis, A., and Kelly, J.P. Fault Tolerance by Design Diversity: Concepts and Experiments. *COMPUTER*, Vol. 17, No. 8, Aug. 1984, pp. 67-80.

[Babaoglu & Joy 1981] Babaoglu, O., and Joy, W. Converting a Swap-Based System to do Paging in an Architecture Lacking Page-Referenced Bits, *SOSP-8*, 1981, pp. 87-95.

[Bach 1986] Bach, M.J. *The Design of the UNIX System*. Prentice-Hall, Englewood Cliffs, NJ, 1986.

[Badger & Johnson 1968] Badger, G.F., Jr., and Johnson, E.A. The Pitt Time-Sharing System for the IBM System 360: Two Years' Experience. *FJCC*, Vol. 33, Part 1, 1968, pp 1-7.

[Bailey et al. 1981] Bailey, K.A., et al. User Defined Files. *OSR*, Vol. 15, No. 4, Oct. 1981, pp. 75-81.

[Ball et al. 1976] Ball, J.F., et al. RIG, Rochester's Intelligent Gateway: System Overview. *TSE*, Vol. SE-2, No. 4, Dec. 1976, pp. 321-328.

[Barak & Litman 1985] Barak, A. & Litman, A. MOS: A Multicomputer Distributed Operating System. *SPE*, Vol. 15, No. 8, Aug. 1985, pp. 725-737.

[Bard 1978] Bard, Y. The VM/370 Performance Predictor. *CSURV*, Vol. 10, No. 3, Sept. 1978, pp. 333-342.

[Barnett & Fitzgerald 1964] Barnett, N.L., and Fitzgerald, A.K., Operating System for the 1410/7010. *Datamation*, May 1964, pp. 40-43.

[Barron & Jackson 1972] Barron, D.W., and Jackson, I.R. The Evolution of Job Control Languages. *SPE*, Vol. 2, No. 2, 1972, pp. 143-164.

[Barron 1984] Barron, D.W. *Computer Operating Systems for Micros, Minis, and Mainframes, Second Edition*. Chapman & Hall, New York, 1984.

[Bartlett 1981] Bartlett, J., A NonStop Kernel. *SOSP-8*, 1981, pp. 22-29.

[Bashe et al. 1986] Bashe, C.J., et al. *IBM's Early Computers*. MIT Press, Cambridge, MA, 1986.

[Baskett & Montague 1975] Baskett, J.H., and Montague, J.T. Task Communication in DEMOS. *SOSP-6*, 1975, pp. 23-32.

[Bayer et al. 1978] Bayer, R., et al., eds. *Operating Systems: An Advanced Course*. Springer-Verlag, Berlin, 1978.

[Beck 1982] Beck, L. A Dynamic Storage Allocation Technique based on Memory Residence Time. *CACM*, Vol. 25, No. 10, Oct. 1982, pp. 714-724.

[Beech 1980] Beech, D., ed. Command Language Directions. *Proceedings of an IFIP Conference*. North-Holland, Amsterdam. 1980.

[Beech 1982] Beech, D. Criteria for a Standard Command Language based on data abstraction. *NCC*, Vol. 51, 1982, pp. 493-500.

[Beidler 1982] Beidler, J. *An Introduction to Data Structures*. Allyn and Bacon, Boston, MA, 1982.

[Belady 1966] Belady, L. A Study of Replacement Algorithms for a Virtual Storage Computer. *IBMSJ*, Vol. 5, No. 2, 1966, pp. 78-101.

[Belady et al. 1981] Belady, L., et al. The IBM History of Memory Management Technology. *IBMJRD*, Vol. 25, No. 5, Sept. 1981, pp. 491-503.

[Bell et al. 1978] Bell, C.G., et al. The Evolution of the DECsystem 10. *CACM*, Vol. 21, No. 1, Jan. 1978, pp 44-63.

[Belpaire & Hsu 1975] Belpaire, G. and Hsu, N.T. Formal Properties of Recursive Virtual Machine Architectures. *SOSP-5*, 1975, pp. 89-96.

[Ben-Ari 1982] Ben-Ari, M. *Principles of Concurrent Programming*. Prentice-Hall, Englewood Cliffs, NJ, 1982.

[Bender et al. 1967] Bender, G., et al. Function and Design of DOS/360 and TOS/360. *IBMSJ*, Vol. 6, No. 1, 1967, pp. 2-21.

[Bensoussan & Clinger 1972] Bensoussan, A., and Clinger, C.T. The Multic Virtual Memory: Concepts and Design. *CACM*, Vol. 15, No. 2, May 1972, pp. 308-318.

[Berenbaum 1982] Berenbaum, A., et al. The Operating System and Language Support Features of the BELLMAC-32, *SASPLOS*, 1982, pp. 30-38.

[Berglund 1986] Berglund, E.J. An Introduction to the V System. *MICRO*, Vol. 6, No. 4, Aug. 1984, pp. 35-52.

[Bernstein & Knobe 1977] Bernstein, N., and Knobe, B. A Non-general-purpose Operating System. *SPE*, Vol. 7, No. 2, 1977, pp. 223-226.

[Bersoff 1980] Bersoff, E.H., et al. *Software Configuration Management*. Prentice-Hall, Englewood Cliffs, NJ, 1980.

[Bic & Shaw 1988]   Bic, L., and Shaw, A. *The Logical Design of Operating Systems* (*second edition*). Prentice-Hall, Englewood Cliffs, NJ, 1988.

[Bidmead 1984]   Bidmead, C. OS-9. (Review). *Practical Computing*, Vol. 7, No. 9, Sept. 1984, pp. 80-83.

[Bierman 1984]   Bierman, K.H. The TurboDOS Operating System. *ACM SIGSMALL Newsletter*, Vol. 10, No. 3, Aug. 1984, pp. 24-34.

[Biggerstaff 1986]   Biggerstaff, T.J. *Systems Software Tools*. Prentice-Hall, Englewood Cliffs, NJ, 1986.

[Birch 1973]   Birch, J.P. Functional Structure of IBM Virtual Storage Operating Systems. Part III: Architecture and Design of DOS/VS. *IBMSJ*, Vol. 12, No. 4, 1973. pp. 401-411.

[Birrell & Nelson 1984]   Birrell, A.D., and Nelson, B.J. Implementing Remote Procedure Calls. *TOCS*, Vol. 2, No. 1, Feb. 1984, pp. 39-59.

[Bobrow et al. 1972]   Bobrow, D.G., et al. TENEX, a Paged Time Sharing System for the PDP-10. *CACM*, Vol. 15, No. 3, March 1972, pp. 135-143.

[Bodenstab et al. 1984]   Bodenstab, D.E., et al. UNIX Operating System Porting Experiences. *BLTJ*, Vol. 63, No. 8, Part 2, Oct. 84, pp. 1769-1790.

[Boettner & Alexander 1975]   Boettner, D.W., and Alexander, M.T. The Michigan Terminal System. *PROC IEEE*, Vol, 63, No. 6, June 1975, pp. 912-918.

[Borgerson et al. 1978]   Borgerson, B.R., et al. The Evolution of the Sperry Univac 1100 Series: A History, Analysis, and Projection. *CACM*, Vol. 21, No. 1, Jan. 1978, pp. 25-43.

[Borovits & Neumann 1979]   Borovits, I., and Neumann, S. *Computer Systems Performance Evaluation*. Lexington Books, D.C. Heath, Lexington, MA, 1979.

[Bott 1984]   Bott, R.A. Dual Port Solves Compatibility Problem. *Computer Design*, Vol. 23, No. 9, Aug. 1984, pp. 205-214.

[Bouvard 1964]   Bouvard, J. Operating System for the 800/1800. *Datamation*, Vol. 10, No. 5, May 1964, pp. 29-34.

[Boyd 1978]   Boyd. Implementing Mass Storage Facilities in Operating Systems. *COMPUTER*, Vol. 11, No. 2, Feb. 1978, pp. 40-45.

[Bratman & Boldt 1959]   Bratman, H., and Boldt, I.V. The SHARE 709 System: Supervisory Control. *JACM*, Vol. 6, No. 2, April 1959, pp. 152-155.

[Brereton 1983]   Brereton, P., Detection and Resolution of Inconsistencies Among Distributed Replicates of Files. *OSR*, Vol. 17, No. 1, Jan. 1983, pp. 10-15.

[Brinch Hansen 1970]   Brinch Hansen, P. The Nucleus of a Multiprogramming System. *CACM*, Vol. 13, No. 4, April 1970, pp. 238-241.

[Brinch Hansen 1973]   Brinch Hansen, P. *Operating System Principles*. Prentice-Hall, Englewood Cliffs, NJ, 1973.

[Brinch Hansen 1976a]   Brinch Hansen, P. The Solo Operating System: A Concurrent Pascal Program. *SPE*, Vol. 6, No. 2, 1976, pp. 141-150.

[Brinch Hansen 1976b]   Brinch Hansen, P. The Solo Operating System: Job Interface. *SPE*, Vol. 6, No. 2, 1976, pp. 151-164.

[Brinch Hansen 1976c]   Brinch Hansen, P. The Solo Operating System: Processes, Monitors, and Classes. *SPE*, Vol. 6, No. 2, 1976, pp. 165-200.

[Brinch Hansen 1977]   Brinch Hansen, P. *The Architecture of Concurrent Programs*. Prentice-Hall, Englewood Cliffs, NJ, 1977.

[Brinch Hansen & Fellows 1980]   Brinch Hansen, P., and Fellows, J. The Trio Operating System. *SPE*, Vol. 10, No. 11, Nov. 1980, pp. 943-948.

[Bron 1972]   Allocation of Virtual Store in the T.H.E. Multiprogramming System. In [Hoare & Perrot 1972], pp. 168-193.

[Brooks 1975]   Brooks, F.P. *The Mythical Man Month*. Addison-Wesley, Reading, MA, 1975.

[Brown 1971]   Brown, P.J. The Kent On-Line System. *SPE*, Vol. 1, No. 3, 1971, pp. 269-277.

[Brown 1976]   Brown, P.J. (Ed). *Software Portability*. Cambridge University Press, Cambridge, England, 1976.

[Brown et al. 1975]   Brown, R.R., et al. The GM Multiple Console Time Sharing System. *OSR*, Vol. 9, No. 4, Oct. 1975, pp. 7-17.

[Brown et al. 1984]   Brown, R.L., et al. Advanced Operating Systems. *COMPUTER*, Vol. 17, No. 10, Oct. 1984, pp. 173-190.

[Brownbridge et al. 1982]   Brownbridge, D.R., et al. The Newcastle Connection. *SPE*, Vol. 12, No. 12, Dec. 1982, pp. 1147-1162.

[Buckley 1986]   Buckley, F.J. An Overview of the IEEE Computer Society Standards Process. *Proceedings of the IEEE Computer Standards Conference*, 1986, pp. 2-8.

[Budzinski 1981]   Budzinski, R.L. A Comparison of Dynamic and Static Virtual Memory Allocation Algorithms. *TSE*, Vol. SE-7, No. 1, Jan. 1981, pp. 122-131.

[Bunt 1976]   Bunt, R.B. Scheduling Techniques for Operating Systems. *COMPUTER*, Vol. 9, No. 10, Oct. 1976, pp. 10-17.

[Burns et al. 1966]   Burns, D., et al. The Egdon System for the KDF9. *CJ*, Vol. 8, No. 4, Jan. 1966, pp. 297-302.

[Buxton et al. 1976]   Buxton, J.M., et al. Software Engineering: Concepts & Techniques. *Proceedings of the NATO Conferences*, 1968 and 1969. Petrocelli/Charter, New York, 1976.

[Buzen 1978]   Buzen, J.P. A Queueing Network Model of MVS. *CSURV*, Vol. 10, No. 3, Sept. 1978, pp. 319-333.

[Buzen & Gagliardi 1973]   Buzen, J.P., and Gagliardi, U.O. The Evolution of Virtual Machine Architecture. *NCC*, Vol. 42, 1973, pp. 291-300.

[Calingaert 1982]   Calingaert, P. *Operating System Elements: A User Perspective*. Prentice-Hall, Englewood Cliffs, NJ, 1982.

[Campbell 1983]   Campbell, F. The Portable UCSD p-System. *MP&MS*, Vol. 7, No. 8, Oct. 1983, pp. 394-398.

[Campbell 1984]   Campbell, J. *Inside Apple's ProDOS*. Brady Communications Co., Bowie, MD, 1984.

[Canon et al. 1980]   Canon, M.D. et al. A Virtual Machine Emulator for Performance Evaluation. *CACM*, Vol. 23, No. 2, Feb. 1980, pp. 71-80.

[Card et al. 1983]   Card, C., et al. The World of Standards. *BYTE*, Vol. 8, No. 2, Feb. 1983, pp. 130-142.

[Carpenter 1979]   Carpenter, R.L. Amigo/300: a Friendly Operating System. *HPJ*, Vol. 30, No. 7, July 1979, pp. 17-24.

[Carr & Hennessy 1981]   Carr, R. and Hennessy, J. WSClock — A Simple and Effective Algorithm for Virtual Memory Management. *SOSP-8*, 1981, pp. 96-108.

[Carroll 1974]   Carroll, H. *OS Data Processing with Review of OS/VS*. John Wiley & Sons, New York, 1974.

[Cederquist 1970]   Cederquist, G.N. CPS — an Operating System for DEC minicomputers. *DECUS*, Spring 1970, pp. 153-163.

[Chapin 1969]   Chapin, N. Common File Organization Techniques Compared. *FJCC*, Vol. 35, 1969, pp. 413-422.

[Cheriton et al. 1977]   Cheriton, D.R., et al. THOTH: A Portable Real-Time Operating System. *CACM*, Vol. 22, No. 2, Feb. 1979, pp. 105-115.

[Cheriton 1982]   Cheriton, D.R. *The Thoth System: Multiprocess Structuring and Portability*. North Holland, Amsterdam, 1982.

[Cheriton 1984]   Cheriton, D.R. The V Kernel: A Software Base for a Distributed System. *SOFTWARE*, Vol. 1, No. 2, April 1984, pp. 19-42.

[Chesson 1975]   Chesson, G.L. The Network UNIX System. *SOSP-5*, 1975, pp. 60-66.

[Claybrook 1983]   Claybrook, B.G. *File Management Techniques*. John Wiley & Sons, New York, 1983.

[Coffman et al. 1971]   Coffman, E.G., et al. System Deadlocks. *CSURV*, Vol. 2, No. 3, June 1971, pp. 67-78.

[Coffman & Denning 1973]   Coffman, E.G., and Denning, P.J. *Operating Systems Theory*. Prentice-Hall, Englewood Cliffs, NJ, 1973.

[Coffman & Kleinrock 1968]   Coffman, E.G., and Kleinrock, L. Computer Scheduling Methods and their Counter-measures. *SJCC*, 1968, Vol. 32, pp. 11-21.

[Colijn 1976]   Colijn, A.W. Experiments with the Kronos Control Language. *SPE*, Vol. 6, No. 1, 1976, pp. 133-135.

[Colijn 1981]   Colijn, A.W. A Note on the Multics Command Language. *SPE*, Vol. 11, No. 7, July 1981, pp. 741-744.

[Comer 1984]   Comer, D. *Operating System Design: The XINU Approach*. Prentice-Hall, 1984.

[COMPUTER 1980]   *COMPUTER*. Special issue: Analytical Queueing Models, Vol. 13, No. 4, April 1980.

[COMPUTER 1983a]   *COMPUTER*. Special issue: Data Security in Computer Networks, Vol. 16, No. 2, Feb. 1983.

[COMPUTER 1983b]   *COMPUTER*. Special issue: Computer Security Technology, Vol. 16, No. 7, July 1983.

[CSURV 1976]   *CSURV*. Special issue: Reliable Software II: Fault-Tolerant SOFTWARE, Vol. 8, No. 4, Dec. 1976.

[CSURV 1978]   *CSURV*. Special issue: Queueing Network Models of Computer System Performance, Vol. 10, No. 3, Sept. 1978.

[Computerworld 1984]   Computerworld. Buyer's Guide: Large Systems Software. *Computerworld*, Vol. 18, No. 26a, June 27, 1984.

[Cook & Brandon 1984a]   Cook, R. & Brandon, J. The Pick Operating System. Part 1: Information Management. *BYTE*, Vol. 9, No. 11, Oct. 1984, pp. 177-198.

[Cook & Brandon 1984b]   Cook, R. & Brandon, J. The Pick Operating System. Part 2: System Control. *BYTE*, Vol. 9, No. 12, Nov. 1984, pp. 132-133, 474-483.

[Corbato & Vyssotsky 1965]   Corbato, F.J., and Vyssotsky, V.A. Introduction and overview of the MULTICS system. *FJCC*, 1965, Vol. 27 Part I, pp. 1985-196.

[Creasy 1981]   Creasy, R.J. The Origin of the VM/370 Time-Sharing System. *IBMJRD*, Vol. 25, No. 5, pp. 483-490.

[Crisman et al. 1964]   Crisman, P.A., et al. (Eds). *The Compatible Time Sharing System*. MIT Press, Cambridge, MA, 1964.

[Curry 1984]   Curry, B.J. OCCAM Solves classical OS problems. *MP&MS*, Vol. 8, No. 6, 1984, pp. 280-283.

[Cutler et al. 1976]   Cutler, D.N., et al. The Nucleus of a Real-Time Operating System. *ACM*, 1976, pp. 241-246.

[Dahmke 1982]   Dahmke, M. *Microcomputer Operating Systems*. BYTE Books, Peterborough, N.H., 1982.

[Dahmke 1983]   Dahmke, M. CP/M Plus (Review). *BYTE*, Vol. 8, No. 7, July 1983, pp. 360-384.

[Daney & Foth 1984]   Daney, C., and Foth, T. A Tale of Two Operating Systems. *BYTE*, Vol. 9, No. 9, 1984, pp. 42-56.

[Danieliuk 1982]   Danieliuk, T. LDOS — Disk Operating System for the TRS-80. *BYTE*, Vol. 7, No. 3, March 1982, pp. 372-382.

[Datapro 1974]   *Datapro*. Reports on Minicomputers. Datapro Research Corp., Delran, NJ, 1974.

[Davis 1977]   Davis, W.S. *Operating Systems: a Systematic View*. Addison-Wesley, Reading, MA, 1977.

[Day & Krejci 1968]   Day, P., and Krejci, H. An Operating System for a Central Real-Time Data Processing Computer. *FJCC*, 1968, Vol. 33, Part 1, pp. 1187-1196.

[Deitel 1984]   Deitel, H.M. *An Introduction to Operating Systems* (revised first edition). Addison-Wesley, Reading, MA, 1984.

[DeLashmutt 1979]   DeLashmutt, L.F., Jr. Steps Toward a Provably Secure Operating System. *COMPCON*, Spring 1979, pp. 40-43.

[Denning 1970]   Denning, P.J. Virtual Memory. *CSURV*, Vol. 8, No. 3, Sept. 1970, pp. 153-189.

[Denning 1976]   Denning, P.J. Fault-Tolerant Operating Systems. *CSURV*, Vol. 8, No. 4, Dec. 1976, pp. 359-389.

[Denning 1978]   Denning, P.J. Operating System Principles for Data Flow Networks, *COMPUTER*, Vol. 11, No. 7, July 1978, pp. 86-96.

[Denning 1980]   Denning, P.J. Working Sets, Past and Present. *TSE*, Vol. SE-6, No. 1, Jan. 1980, pp. 64-84.

[Denning & Brown 1984]   Denning, P.J., and Brown, R.L. Operating Systems. *Scientific American*, Vol. 251, No. 3, Sept. 1984, pp. 80-90.

[Denning & Buzen 1978]   Denning, P.J., and Buzen, J.P. The Operational Analysis of Queueing Network Models. *CSURV*, Vol. 10, No. 3, Sept. 1978, pp. 225-261.

[Denning & Stone 1980]   Denning, P.J., and Stone, H.S. An Exchange of Views on Operating System Courses. *OSR*, Vol. 14, No. 4, Oct. 1980, pp. 71-82.

[Dependahl & Presser 1976]   Dependahl, R.H., and Presser, L. File Input/Output Control Logic. *COMPUTER*, Vol. 9, No. 10, Oct. 1976, pp. 38-42.

[Digital 1981a]   *RT-11 Software Support Manual*. AA-H379A-TC, Digital Equipment Corp., Maynard, MA, 1981.

[Digital 1981b] *RSX-11M Guide to Writing an I/O Driver*. Digital Equipment Corp., Maynard, MA, 1981.

[Digital 1984a] *PDP-11 Software Source Book (third edition)*. Vol. 2: Systems Software. Order Code EB-26030-41. Digital Equipment Corp., Maynard, MA, 1984.

[Digital 1984b] *Guide to Writing a Device Driver for VAX/VMS*. AA-Y511A-TE, Digital Equipment Corp., Maynard, MA, 1984.

[Digital 1984c] *Guide to VAX/VMS Performance Management*. AA-Y515A-TE, Digital Equipment Corp., Maynard, MA, 1984.

[Digital 1985] *RT-11 System Generation Guide*. Digital Equipment Corp., Maynard, MA, 1985.

[Dijkstra 1965] Dijkstra, E.W. *Cooperating Sequential Processes*. Technical Report EWD-123, Technological University, Eindhoven, the Netherlands, 1965. Reprinted in [Genuys 1968], pp. 43-112.

[Dijkstra 1968] Dijkstra, E.W. The Structure of the T.H.E. Multiprogramming System. *CACM*, Vol. 11, No. 5, May 1968, pp. 341-346.

[Dion 1980] Dion, J. The Cambridge File Server. *OSR*, Vol. 14, No. 4, Oct. 1980, pp. 26-35.

[Dodd 1969] Dodd, G.G. Elements of Data Management Systems. *CSURV*, Vol. 1, No. 2, June 1969, pp. 117-133.

[Dolotta & Mashey 1980] Dolotta, T.A., and Mashey, J.R. Using a Command Language as the Primary Programming Tool. In [Beech 1980], pp. 35 ff.

[Dubner & Abate 1970] Dubner, H., and Abate, J. TICKETRON — a Successfully Operating System without an Operating System. *SJCC*, 1970, pp. 143-151.

[Efe et al. 1983] Efe, K., et al. The Kiwinet-Nicola Approach: Response Generation in a User-Friendly Interface. *COMPUTER*, Vol. 16, No. 9, Sept. 1983, pp. 66-78.

[Elshoff & Ward 1976] Elshoff, J.L., and Ward, M.R. The MCTS Operating System. *OSR*, Vol. 10, No. 1, Jan. 1976, pp. 18-38.

[Emrath 1985] Emrath, P. Xylem: An Operating System for the Cedar Multiprocessor. *SOFTWARE*, Vol. 2, No. 4, July 1985, pp. 30-37.

[Everett el al. 1957] Everett, R.R., et al. SAGE — A Data-Processing System for Air Defense. *EJCC*, 1957, pp. 148-155.

[Feder 1984] Feder, J. The Evolution of UNIX System Performance. *BLTJ*, Vol. 63, No. 8, Part 2, Oct. 1984, pp. 1791-1814.

[Ferrari 1978] Ferrari, D. *Computer System Performance Evaluation*. Prentice-Hall, Englewood Cliffs, NJ, 1978.

[Ferrari 1983] Ferrari, D. Software Monitors. In [Ralston & Reilly 1983], pp. 1362-1364.

[Finkel 1980] Finkel, R. *The Arachne Kernel*. University of Wisconsin Technical Report TR-380, April 1980.

[Finkel 1986] Finkel, R.A. *An Operating Systems Vade Mecum*. Prentice-Hall, Englewood Cliffs, NJ, 1986.

[Fisher 1986] Fisher, D.A., and Weatherly, R.M. Issues in the Design of a Distributed Operating System for Ada. *COMPUTER*, Vol. 19, No. 5, May 1986, pp. 38-47.

[Forinash 1987] Forinash, D.E. *An Investigation of Ada Run-times Supportive of Real-Time Multiprocessor Systems*. M.S. Thesis, Department of Statistics & Computer Science, West Virginia University, Morgantown, WV, 1987.

[Forsdick et al. 1978] Forsdick, H.C., et al. Operating Systems for Computer Networks. *COMPUTER*, Vol. 11, No. 1, Jan. 1978, pp. 48-57.

[Flores 1978] Flores, I. *OS/MVT*. Allyn and Bacon, Boston, 1973.

[Foard 1986] Foard, R.M. The Portable Approach. *PC Tech Journal*, May 1986, pp. 75-89.

[Fogel 1974] Fogel, M.H. The VMOS Paging Algorithm: A Practical implementation of the Working Set model. *OSR*, Vol. 8, No. 1, Jan. 1974, pp. 8-17.

[Fong 1985] Fong, K.W. CTSS — Cray Timesharing System. *SPE*, Vol. 15, No. 1, Jan. 1985, pp. 87-104.

[Footit & Whitby-Strevens 1974] Footit, R.M., and Whitby-Strevens, C. The University of Warwick Modular One Operating System. *SPE*, Vol. 4, No. 4, 1974, pp. 309-340.

[Fosdick 1979] Fosdick, H. High-Level Languages for Operating Systems Development — A Historical Overview. *SIGPLAN*, Vol. 14, No. 7, July 1979, pp. 31-37.

[Foster 1984] Foster, D. UNIX-Compatible Networking OS Provides Virtual File Access. *MMS*, Vol. 17, No. 3, March 1984, pp. 211-214.

[Fowler 1984] Fowler, R. For Networks and Multiuser Systems — TurboDOS. *Microsystems*, Vol. 5, No. 8, Aug. 1984, pp. 58-76.

[Frailey 1975] Frailey, D.J. DSOS — A Skeletal, Real-Time Minicomputer Operating System. *SPE*, Vol. 5, No. 1, 1975, pp. 5-18.

[Frank & Theaker 1979a] Frank, G.R., and Theaker, C.J. The Design of the MUSS Operating System. *SPE*, Vol. 9, No. 8, Aug. 1979, pp. 599-620.

[Frank & Theaker 1979b] Frank, G.R., and Theaker, C.J. MUSS — The User Interface. *SPE*, Vol. 9, No. 8, Aug. 1979, pp. 621-631.

[Freiberger & Swaine 1984] Freiberger, P., and Swaine, M. *Fire in the Valley*. Osborne/McGraw-Hill, Berkeley, CA, 1984.

[Funck 1984] Funck, G. Component-Based Operating System Works in Real Time. *Computer Design*, Vol. 23, No. 8, July 1984, pp. 203-211.

[Gaglianello & Katseff 1985] Gaglianello, R.D., and Katseff, H.P. Meglos: an Operating System for a Multiprocessor Environment. *Proceedings of the 5th International Conference on Distributed Computing Systems*, Denver, CO, May 1985, pp. 35-42.

[Gaines 1972] Gaines, R.S. An Operating System Based on the Concept of a Supervisory Computer. *CACM*, Vol. 15, No. 3, March 1972, pp. 150-156.

[Gallacher 1983] Gallacher, J. 16-bit Operating Systems. *MP&MS*, Vol. 7, No. 8, Oct. 1983, pp. 364-368.

[Gelenbe & Kaiser 1974] Gelenbe, E., and Kaiser, C. (Eds). Operating Systems. *Proc. of an International Symposium. Lecture Notes in Comp. Sci.*, Vol. 16. Springer-Verlag, New York, 1974.

[Genuys 1968] Genuys, F., ed. *Programming Languages*. Academic Press, London, 1968.

[Georg et al. 1984] Georg, D.D., et al. A General-Purpose Operating System Kernel for a 32-bit Computer System. *HPJ*, Vol. 35, No. 3, March 1984, pp. 28-34.

[Gilbert 1983] Gilbert, P. *Software Design and Development*. Science Research Associates, Chicago, 1983.

[Gillett & Pollack 1982] Gillett, W.D., and Pollack, S.V. *An Introduction to Engineered Software*. CBS College Publishing, New York, 1982.

[Glaser 1981] Glaser, J.G. VERSAdos. *MIDCON/81*, Nov. 1981, pp. 7/4/1-6.

[Glazer 1984] Glazer, S.D. Fault-tolerant mini needs enhanced OS. *Computer Design*, Vol. 23, No. 9, Aug. 1984, pp. 189-198.

[Goldberg 1973] Goldberg, R.P. Architecture of Virtual Machines. *NCC*, 1973, pp. 309-318.

[Goldberg 1974] Goldberg, R.P. A Survey of Virtual Machine Research. *COMPUTER*, Vol. 7, No. 6, June 1974, pp. 34-45.

[Gordon 1978] Gordon, G. *System Simulation (second edition)*. Prentice-Hall, Englewood Cliffs, NJ, 1978.

[Goullon et al. 1978] Goullon, H., et al. Dynamic Restructuring in an Experimental Operating System. *TSE*, Vol. SE-4, No. 4, July 1978, pp. 298-307.

[Grampp & Morris 1984] Grampp, F.T., and Morris, R.H. UNIX Operating System Security. *BLTJ*, Vol. 63, No. 8, Part 2, Oct. 84, pp. 1649-1672.

[Grzelakowski et al. 1983] Grzelakowski, M.E., et al. DMERT Operating System. *BSTJ*, Vol. 62, 1983, p. 315 ff.

[Habermann 1969] Habermann, A.N. Prevention of System Deadlocks. *CACM*, Vol. 12, No. 7, July 1969, pp. 373-385.

[Habermann 1976] Habermann, A.N. *Introduction to Operating System Design*. Science Research Associates, Chicago, 1976.

[Hanson 1980] Hanson, D.R. A Portable File Directory System. *SPE*, Vol. 10, No. 8, Aug. 1980, pp. 623-634.

[Hardy 1985] Hardy, N. KeyKOS Architecture. *OSR*, Vol. 19, No. 4, Oct. 1985, pp. 8-25.

[Harrison et al. 1981] Harrison, T.J., et al. Evolution of Small Real-Time IBM Computer Systems. *IBMJRD*, Vol. 25, No. 5, Sept. 1981, pp. 441-451.

[Hartley 1972] Hartley, D.F. Techniques in the Titan Operating System. In [Hoare & Perrott 1972], pp. 271-276.

[Hartman et al. 1984] Hartman, D.O., et al. New Real-Time Executive Supports Large Programs and Multiple Users. *HPJ*, 1984.

[Havendar 1968] Havendar, J.W. Avoiding Deadlock in Multitasking Systems. *IBMSJ*, Vol. 7, pp. 74-84, 1968.

[Hebbard et al. 1980] Hebbard, B., et al. A Penetration Analysis of the Michigan Terminal System. *OSR*, Vol. 14, No. 1, Jan 1980, pp. 7-20.

[Heinen 1984] Heinen, R., Jr. VAX Executive develops realtime applications. *Computer Design*, Vol. 23, No. 3, March 1984, pp. 79-91.

[Hellerman & Conroy 1975] Hellerman, H. and Conroy, T.E. *Computer System Performance*. McGraw-Hill, New York, 1975.

[Hemenway 1983] Hemenway, J.E. Advanced 16-bit Operating System Handles Multiple Tasks in Real Time. *MP&MS*, Vol. 7, No. 8, Oct. 1983, pp. 375-379.

[Hendricks & Hartmann 1979] Hendricks, E.C., and Hartmann, T.C. Evolution of a Virtual Machine Subsystem. *IBMSJ*, Vol. 18, No. 1, 1979, pp. 111-142.

[Henry 1984] Henry, G.J. The Fair Share Scheduler. *BLTJ*, Vol. 63, No. 8, Part 2, Oct. 1984, pp. 1845-1857.

[Hindin 1984] Hindin, H.J. Micro Operating Systems Yield Mixed Blessings. *Computer Design*, Vol. 23, No. 8, July 1984, pp. 155-165.

[Ho & Ramamoorthy 1982] Ho, G.S., and Ramamoorthy, C.V. Protocols for Deadlock Detection in Distributed Database Systems. *TSE*, Vol. SE-8, No. 6, Nov. 1982, pp. 554-557.

[Hoare 1985] Hoare, C.A.R. *Communicating Sequential Processes*. Prentice-Hall International, Englewood Cliffs, NJ, 1985.

[Hoare & Perrott 1972] Hoare, C.A.R., and Perrott, R.J. (Eds). *Operating Systems Techniques*. Academic Press, New York, 1972.

[Hofri 1980] Hofri, M. Disk Scheduling: FCFS vs. SSTF Revisited. *CACM*, Vol. 23, No. 11, Nov. 1980, pp. 645-653.

[Holt 1983] Holt, R.C. *EUCLID, the UNIX System, and TUNIS*. Addison-Wesley, Reading, MA, 1983.

[Hopper & Newman 1986] Hopper, K., and Newman, I.A. (Eds). Foundation for Human-Computer Communication. *Proceedings of the IFIP WG 2.6 Working Conference on the Future of Command Languages* (Rome, Sept. 1985). North-Holland, Amsterdam, 1986.

[Howarth et al. 1961] Howarth, D.J., et al. The Manchester University Atlas Operating System. Part II: User's Description. *CJ*, Vol. 4, Oct. 1961, pp. 226-229.

[Hunter & Ready 1986] *VRTX/68000 User's Guide*. Document No. 591313002, Hunter & Ready, Palo Alto, CA, 1986.

[Huskamp 1986] Huskamp, J.C. A Modular Operating System for the CRAY-1. *SPE*, Vol. 16, No. 2, Dec. 1986, pp. 1059-1076.

[IBM 1963] *IBSYS Operating System*. C28-6248, IBM Corp., 1963.

[IBM 1971] *HASP System Manual*. IBM Corp., Hawthorne, N.Y., 1971.

[IBM 1984] *MVS/Extended Architecture Installation: System Generation*. GC26-4009-2, IBM Corp., San Jose, CA, 1984.

[IBMSJ 1979] IBM Systems Journal. Special Issue on VM/370. *IBMSJ*, Vol. 18, No. 1, 1979.

[IEEE 1985a] *Trial-Use Standard Specifications for Microprocessor Operating Systems Interfaces*. IEEE Std 855. IEEE, New York, 1985.

[IEEE 1985b] *IEEE Standard for Binary Floating-Point Arithmetic*. ANSI/IEEE Std 754-1985. IEEE, New York, 1985.

[IEEE 1985c] *Trial-Use Standard for Microprocessor Universal Format for Object Modules*. IEEE Std 695. IEEE, New York, 1985.

[IEEE 1986] *Trial-Use Standard: Portable Operating System for Computer Environments* (IEEE Std 1003.1). IEEE, New York, 1985.

[Interdata 1974] Interdata Corp. Interdata Announces 32-bit MultiTasking OS (product announcement). *COMPUTER*, Vol. 7, N7, July 1974, p. 57.

[ISO 1984]   *Open Systems Interconnection — Basic Reference Model.* ISO 7498-1984. International Organization for Standardization, Geneva, Switzerland, 1984.

[Janson 1985]   Janson, P.A. *Operating Systems: Structures & Mechanisms.* Academic Press, New York, 1985.

[Jarema & Sussenguth 1981]   Jarema, D.R., and Sussenguth, E.H. IBM Data Communications: A Quarter Century of Evolution and Progress. *IBMJRD*, Vol. 25, No. 5, Sept. 1981, pp. 391-404.

[Jarvis 1975]   Jarvis, J.E. The Many Faces of Multics. *CJ*, Vol. 18, No. 1, Feb. 1975, pp. 2-6.

[Jennings 1984]   Jennings, M.S. Evaluating the Macintosh Finder (review). *BYTE*, Vol. 9, No. 13, Dec. 1984, pp. A94-A101.

[Johnson 1985]   Johnson, D.G. *Computer Ethics.* Prentice-Hall, Englewood Cliffs, NJ, 1985.

[Jones 1978]   Jones, A.K. Protection Mechanisms and the Enforcement of Security Policies. In [Bayer 1978], pp. 228-250.

[Jones et al. 1979]   Jones, A.K., et al. StarOS, a Multiprocessor Operating System for the Support of Task Forces. *SOSP-7*, 1979, pp. 117-127.

[Jorgenson 1981]   Jorgenson, E.T. Dissecting the HDOS Diskette. *Microcomputing*, July 1981, pp. 66-70.

[Joseph et al. 1984]   Joseph, M., et al. *A Multiprocessor Operating System.* Prentice-Hall International, 1984.

[Kahn et al. 1981]   Kahn, K.C., et al. iMAX: A Multiprocessor Operating System for an Object-Based Computer. *SOSP-8*, 1981, pp. 127-136.

[Kaisler 1983]   Kaisler, S.H. *The Design of Operating Systems for Small Computer Systems.* John Wiley & Sons, New York, 1983.

[Kane 1986]   Kane, G. *Guide to Popular Operating Systems.* Scott Foresman, Glenview, IL, 1986.

[Karp 1983]   Karp, R.A. *Proving Operating Systems Correct.* UMI Research Press, Ann Arbor, MI, 1983.

[Kartashev & Kartashev 1982]   Kartashev, S.I. and Kartashev, S.P. A Distributed Operating System for a Powerful System with Dynamic Architecture. *NCC*, 1982, Vol. 51, pp. 103-116.

[Katzan 1986]   Katzan, H., Jr. *Operating Systems, A Pragmatic Approach* (*second edition*). Van Nostrand Rheinhold, New York, 1986.

[Kelly 1981]   Kelly, M.G. Percom's Doubler (Review). *BYTE*, Vol. 6, No. 7, July 1981, pp. 344-352.

[Kelly 1982]   Kelly, M.G. NEWDOS/80 Version 2.0 (Review). *BYTE*, Vol. 7, No. 6, June 1982, pp. 376-400.

[Kemeny & Kurtz 1968]   Kemeny, J.G., and Kurtz, J.G. Dartmouth Time Sharing. *Science*, Vol. 162, No. 3850, Oct. 11, 1968, pp. 223-228.

[Kemeny & Kurtz 1985]   Kemeny, J.G., and Kurtz, T.E. *Back to Basic: the History, Corruption, and Future of the Language.* Addison-Wesley, Reading, MA, 1985.

[Kemmerer 1982]   Kemmerer, R.A. *Formal Verification of an Operating System Kernel.* UMI Research Press, Ann Arbor, MI, 1982.

[Kenah & Bate 1984]   Kenah, L.J., and Bate, S.F. *VAX/VMS Internals and Data Structures.* Digital Press, Maynard, MA, 1984.

[Kepecs & Solomon 1985]   Kepecs, J., and Solomon, M. SODA: a Simplified Operating System for Distributed Applications. *OSR*, Vol. 19, No. 4, Oct. 1985, pp. 45-56.

[Kernighan & Pike 1984]   Kernighan, B., and Pike, R. *The UNIX Programming Environment.* Prentice-Hall, Englewood Cliffs, NJ, 1984.

[Kernighan & Ritchie 1978]   Kernighan, B., and Ritchie, D. *The C Programming Language.* Prentice-Hall, Englewood Cliffs, NJ, 1978.

[Kiely 1981]   Kiely, S.C. An Operating System for Distributed Processing — DPPX. *IMBSJ*, Vol. 18, No. 4, 1979, pp. 507-525.

[Kilburn 1961]   Kilburn, T. The Manchester University Atlas Operating System. Part I: Internal Organization. *CJ*, Vol. 4, Oct. 1961, pp. 222-225.

[Kildall 1981]   Kildall, G. CP/M: A Family of 8- and 16-bit Operating Systems. *BYTE*, Vol. 6, No. 6, June 1981, pp. 216-232.

[King 1983]   King, R.A. *The IBM PC-DOS Handbook.* SYBEX Inc., Berkeley, CA, 1983.

[Kinslow 1964]   Kinslow, H.A. The Time Sharing Monitor System. *FJCC*, Vol. 26, 1964, pp. 443-454.

[Kleinrock 1965]   Kleinrock, L. A Conservation Law for a Wide Class of Queueing Disciplines. *Naval Research Logistics Quarterly*, Vol. 12, No. 2, June 1965, pp. 181-192.

[Kleinrock 1970]   Kleinrock, L. A Continuum of Time-Sharing Scheduling Algorithms. *SJCC*, 1970, Vol. 36, pp. 453-458.

[Kleinrock 1975]   Kleinrock, L. *Queuing Systems. Volume I: Theory.* John Wiley & Sons, New York, 1976.

[Kleinrock 1976]   Kleinrock, L. *Queuing Systems. Volumn II: Computer Applications.* John Wiley & Sons, New York, 1976.

[Knuth 1973]   Knuth, D.K. *The Art of Computer Programming, Vol. 1: Fundamental Algorithms* (*second edition*). Addison-Wesley, Reading, MA, 1973.

[Kolya 1981]   Kolya, Y. DOSPlus: Double-Density Operating System for the TRS-80 (Review). *BYTE*, Vol. 6, No. 7, July 1981, pp. 334-343.

[Kornstein 1983]   Kornstein, H. Concurrent CP/M-86 and Recent Advances in Operating Systems. *MP&MS*, Vol. 7, No. 8, Oct. 1983, pp. 391-393.

[Koudela 1973]   Koudela, J., Jr. The Past, Present, and Future of Minicomputers: A Scenario. *PROC IEEE*, Vol. 61, No. 11, Nov. 1973, pp. 1526-1534.

[Krejci 1971]   Krejci, H. RSX-15 Real-Time Executive. *DECUS*, Spring 1971, pp. 67-72.

[Kurzban et al. 1975]   Kurzban, S.A., Heines, T.S., and Sayers, A.P. *Operating Systems Principles.* Petrocelli-Charter, New York, 1975.

[Laird et al.]   Laird, J.D., et al. *Implementation of an Ada Real-Time Executive — A Case Study.* Technical Report, Aerospace Systems Group, Intermetrics, Inc.

[Lamport 1974]   Lamport, L. A New Solution of Dijkstra's Concurrent Programming Problem. *CACM*, Vol. 17, No. 8, Aug. 1974, pp. 453-455.

[Lamport 1978]   Lamport, L. Time, Clocks, and the Ordering of Events in a Distributed System. *CACM*, Vol. 21, No. 7, July 1978, pp. 558-564.

[Lamport 1981]   Lamport, L. Password Authentication with Insecure Communication. *CACM*, Vol. 24, No. 11, Nov. 1981, pp. 770-772.

[Lamport 1985]   Lamport, L. Solved Problems, Unsolved Problems and Non-Problems in Concurrency. *OSR*, Vol. 19, No. 4, Oct. 1985, pp. 34-44. Reprinted from Proceedings of the Third Conference On Principles of Distributed Computing, 1984.

[Lampson 1974]   Lampson, B.W. An Open Operating System for a Single User Machine. In [Gelenbe & Kaiser 1974], pp. 208-217.

[Lampson et al. 1981]   Lampson, B.W., Paul, M., and Siegert, H.J. (Eds). *Distributed Systems: Architecture and Implementation*. Springer-Verlag, New York, 1981.

[Lampson & Sturgis 1976]   Lampson, B.W., and Sturgis, H.E. Reflections on an Operating System Design. *CACM*, Vol. 19, No. 5, May 1976, pp 251-265.

[Lane 1974]   Lane, M.G. *The Teaching of Systems Programming Using Small Computers: Three Years' Experience*. Computers at the University, Zagreb, Yugoslavia, Nov. 1974.

[Lane 1975]   Lane, M.G. A Hands-On Approach to Teaching Systems Programming. *ACM*, SIGCSE Bulletin, Vol. 7, No. 1, Feb. 1975.

[Lane 1978]   Lane, M.G. The Subsystem Approach to Enhancing Small Processor Operating Systems. Proc. *First ACM SIGSMALL Symposium on Small Systems*, New York, 1978.

[Lane 1985]   Lane, M.G. *Data Communications Software Design*. Boyd & Fraser, Boston, MA, 1985.

[Lane et al. 1983]   Lane, D., et al. Implementation of a Real-Time Distributed Computer System in Ada. *AIAA Proc. of the Fourth Conference on Computers in Aerospace*, 1983, pp. 325-330.

[Lane & Cooper 1976]   Lane, M.G., and Cooper, R.T. An Improved Hands-On Approach to Teaching Systems Programming. *Proc. Sixth ACM SIGCSE Symposium*, Williamsburg, VA, July 1978.

[Larson 1984]   Larson, J.L. Multitasking on the Cray X-MP-2 multiprocessor. *COMPUTER*, Vol. 17, No. 2, July 1984, pp. 62-69.

[Lavington 1978]   Lavington, S.H. The Manchester Mark I and Atlas: A Historical Perspective. *CACM*, Vol. 21, No. 1, Jan. 1978, pp. 4-12.

[Lazowska et al. 1981]   Lazowska, E., et al. The Architecture of the Eden System. *SOSP-8*, 1981, pp. 148-159.

[LeCarme & Pellissier Gart 1986]   LeCarme, O., and Pellisier Gart, M. *Software Portability*. McGraw Hill, New York, 1986.

[Lee 1985]   Lee, I., and Gehlot, V. Language Constructs for Distributed Real-Time Programming. *Proceedings of the IEEE Real-Time Systems Symposium*, 1985, pp. 57-66.

[Leemon 1982]   Leemon, S. An Alternative to Atari DOS. *Creative Computing*, Vol. 8, No. 11, Nov. 1982, pp. 148-151.

[Leffler & Joy 1983]   Leffler, S.J., and Joy, W.M. *Installing and Operating 4.2BSD on the VAX*. Department of Electrical Engineering and Computer Science, University of California at Berkeley, 1983.

[Leitch 1982]   Leitch, D. Handling Realtime Applications with the RMS68K OS. *MIDCON/82*, Dec. 1982, pp. 15/2/1-8.

[Lett & Konigsford 1968]   Lett, A.S., and Konigsford, W.L. TSS/360: A Time-Shared OS. *FJCC*, Vol. 33, pt. 1, 1968, pp. 15-28.

[Letwin 1988]   Letwin, G. *Inside OS/2*. Microsoft Press, Redmond, WA, 1988.

[Levy 1984]   Levy, H.M. *Capability-Based Computer Systems*. Digital Press, Bedford, MA, 1984.

[Levy & Lipman 1982]   Levy, H.M., and Lipman, P.H. Virtual Memory Management in the VAX/VMS Operating System. *COMPUTER*, Vol. 15, No. 3, March 1982, pp. 35-41.

[Lewis & Smith 1979]   Lewis and Smith. *Computer Principles of Modeling and Simulation*. Houghton Mifflin, New York, 1979.

[Lin & Gannon 1985]   Lin, K-j., and Gannon, J.D. Atomic Remote Procedure Call. *TSE*, Vol. SE-11, No. 10, Oct. 1985, pp. 1126-1135.

[Linde et al. 1969]   Linde, R.R., et al. The Adept-50 Time-Sharing System. *FJCC*, 1969, Vol. 35, pp. 39-50.

[Linden 1976]   Linden, T.A. Operating System Structures to Support Security and Reliable Software. *CSURV*, Vol. 8, No. 4, Dec. 1976, pp. 409-445.

[Lindgard 1979]   Lindgard, A. p — A Timesharing Operating System for Laboratory Automation. *SPE*, Vol. 9, No. 12, Dec. 1979, pp. 971-986.

[Lindsey 1978]   Lindsey, C.H. ALGOL 68 and your Friendly Neighborhood Operating System. *ALGOL Bulletin*, No. 42, May 1978, pp. 22-35.

[Liskov 1972]   Liskov, B.H. The Design of the Venus Operating System. *CACM*, Vol. 15, No. 3, March 1972, pp. 144-149.

[Little 1984]   Little, J. A Module Approach to Microcomputer Operating Systems. *Computer Design*, Vol. 23, No. 8, July 1978, pp. 217-224.

[London 1973]   London, K.R. *Techniques for Direct Access*. Auerbach Publishers, Philadelphia, 1973.

[Loomis 1983]   Loomis, M.E. *Data Management and File Processing*. Prentice-Hall, Englewood Cliffs, NJ, 1983.

[Lu & Carey 1986]   Lu, H., and Carey, M.J. *Load-Balanced Task Allocation in Locally Distributed Computer Systems*. University of Wisconsin at Madison Technical Report, 1986.

[Lycklama & Bayer 1978]   Lycklama, H., and Bayer, D.L. The MERT Operating System. *BSTJ*, Vol. 57, No. 6, Jul-Aug. 1978, pp. 2049-2086.

[Lynch 1972]   Lynch, W.C. An Operating System Designed for the Computer Utility Environment. In [Hoare & Perrott 1972], pp. 341-350.

[Lynch 1975]   Lynch, W.C. Reliability Experience with Chi/OS. *TSE*, Vol. SE-1, No. 2, June 1975, pp. 253-257.

[Madnick & Donovan 1974]   Madnick, S.E., and Donovan, J.J. *Operating Systems*. McGraw-Hill, New York, 1974.

[Maegaard & Andreasan 1979]   Maegaard, H., and Andreasan, A. REPOS — An Operating System for the PDP-11. *OSR*, Vol. 13, No. 3, July 1979, pp. 6-11.

[Maekawa & Belady 1982]   Maekawa, M., and Belady, L.A. (Eds). Operating Systems Engineering. *Proc. of an IBM symposium. Lecture Notes in Comp. Sci.*, Vol. 143, Springer Verlag, New York, 1982.

[Maekawa et al. 1987]   Maekawa, M., et al. *Operating Systems: Advanced Concepts*. Benjamin/Cummings, Menlo Park, CA, 1987.

[Martin 1973]   Martin, J. *Design of Man-Computer Dialogues*. Prentice-Hall, Englewood Cliffs, NJ, 1973.

[Martin & McClure 1983]   Martin, J., and McClure, C. *Software Maintenance*. Prentice-Hall, Englewood Cliffs, NJ, 1983.

[Massie 1986]   Massie, P. *Operating Systems Theory & Practice*. Burgess Communications, Santa Rosa, CA, 1986.

[Maule 1985]   Maule, R.A. *Run-Time Implementation Issues for Real-Time Embedded Ada*. Technical Report, Software Technology, Boeing Aerospace Co., 1985.

[McCauley & Drongowski 1979]   McCauley, E.J., and Drongowski, P.J. *NCC*, Vol. 48, 1979, pp. 345-353.

[McGowan & Kelly 1975]   McGowan, C.L., and Kelly, J.R. *Top-Down Structured Programming Techniques*. Petrocelli/Charter, New York, 1975.

[McKeag et al. 1976]   McKeag, R.M., Wilson, R., and Huxtable, D.H.R. *Studies in Operating Systems*. Academic Press, New York, 1976.

[McKinney 1969]   McKinney, J.M. A Survey of Analytical Time Sharing Models. *CSURV*, Vol. 1, No. 2, June 1969, pp. 105-116.

[McNamara 1982]   McNamara, J.E. *Technical Aspects of Data Communication (second edition)*. Digital Press, Bedford, MA, 1982.

[McPhee 1974]   McPhee, W.S. Operating System Integrity in OS/VS2. *IBMSJ*, Vol. 13, No. 3, 1974, pp. 230-252.

[Mealy et al. 1966]   Mealy, G.H., et al. The functional structure of OS/360. *IBMSJ*, Vol. 5, No. 1, 1966, pp. 3-51.

[Meeker et al. 1969]   Meeker, N.R., et al. OS-3: The Oregon State Open Shop Operating System. *SJCC*, 1969, Vol. 34, pp. 241-248.

[Meyer & Matyas 1982]   Meyer, C.H., and Matyas, S.M. *Cryptography*. John Wiley & Sons, New York, 1982.

[Meyer & Seawright 1970]   Meyer, R.A., and Seawright, L.H. A Virtual Machine Time Sharing System. *IBMSJ*, Vol. 9, No. 3, 1970, pp. 199-218.

[Milenkovic 1987]   Milenkovic, M. *Operating Systems: Concepts and Design*. McGraw-Hill, New York, 1987.

[Miller 1978]   Miller, R. Unix — a Portable Operating System? *OSR*, Vol. 12, No. 3, July 1978, pp. 32-37.

[Miller & Presotto 1981]   Miller, B., and Presotto, D. XOS: An Operating System for the X-Tree Architecture. *OSR*, Vol. 15, No. 2, April 1981, pp. 21-32.

[Mills 1973]   Mills, D.L. Executive Systems and Software Development for Minicomputers. *PROC IEEE*, Vol. 61, No. 11, Nov. 1973, pp. 1556-1562.

[Millstein 1977]   Millstein, R.E. The National Software Works: A Distributed Processing System. *ACM*, 1977, pp. 42-52.

[Mini-Micro 1985]   Mini-Micro Systems annual survey. Operating Systems Directory. *MMS*, Vol. 18, No. 2, Feb. 1985, pp. 164-175.

[Mini-Micro 1986]   Mini-Micro Systems annual survey. Operating Systems. *MMS*, Vol. 19, No. 8, June 1986, pp. 183-187.

[Monden 1987]   Monden, H. Introduction to ITRON, the Industry-oriented Operating System. *MICRO*, Vol. 7, No. 2, April 1987, pp. 45-52.

[Mooney 1979]   Mooney, J. *DOS Level 5 Reference Manual*. Itek Composition Systems, Wilmington, MA, 1979 (available from the author).

[Mooney 1982]   Mooney, J. USIM: A User Interface Manager. *OSR*, Vol. 15, No. 1, Jan. 1982, pp. 32-39.

[Mooney 1986]   Mooney, J. Lessons from the MOSI Project. *Computer Standards & Interfaces*, Vol. 5, No. 3, 1986, pp. 201-210.

[Moore 1984]   Moore, R. ProDOS (review). *BYTE*, Vol. 9, No. 2, Feb. 1984, pp. 252-262.

[Morland 1983]   Morland, D.V. Human Factors Guidelines for Terminal Interface Design. *CACM*, Vol. 26, No. 7, July 1983, pp. 484-494.

[Morris et al. 1972]   Morris, D., et al. The Structure of the MU5 OS. *CJ*, Vol. 15, No. 2, 1972, pp. 113-116.

[Morris & Thompson 1979]   Morris, R., and Thompson, K. Password Security: A Case History. *CACM*, Vol. 22, No. 11, Nov. 1979, pp. 594-597.

[Mullender & Tanenbaum 1986]   Mullender, S.J., and Tanenbaum, A.S. The Design of a Capability-Based Distributed Operating System. *CJ*, Vol. 29, No. 4, 1986, pp. 289-299.

[Muntz 1983]   Muntz, R.R. Performance Measurement and Evaluation. In [Ralston & Reilly 1983], pp. 1121-1126.

[Myers 1983]   Myers, D. Porting a new Microcomputer Operating System. *MP&MS*, Vol. 7, No. 3, Oct. 1983, pp. 380-385.

[Myers 1975]   Myers, G.J. *Reliable Software Through Composite Design*. Van Nostrand, New York, 1975.

[Noe 1983]   Noe, J.D. Hardware Monitor. In [Ralston & Reilly 1983], pp. 679-681.

[Norton 1985]   Norton, P. *Programmer's Guide to the IBM PC*. Microsoft Press, Bellevue, WA, 1985.

[Noyce & Hoff 1981]   Noyce, R.N., and Hoff, M.E. A History of Microprocessor Development at Intel. *MICRO*, Vol. 1, No. 1, Feb. 1981, pp. 8-21.

[Nutt 1977]   Nutt, G.J. A Parallel Processor Operating System Comparison. *TSE*, Vol. SE-3, No. 6, Nov. 1977, pp. 467-475.

[Oestreicher 1971]   Oestreicher, M.D. The design of the internal structure of the ICL George 3 Operating System. *SPE*, Vol. 1, No. 2, 1971, pp. 189-200.

[Ohkubo et al. 1987]   Ohkubo, T., et al. Configuration of the CTRON Kernel. *MICRO*, Vol. 7, No. 2, April 1987, pp. 33-44.

[Oldehoeft & Allan 1985]   Oldehoeft, R.R., and Allan, S.J. Adaptive Exact-fit Storage Management. *CACM*, Vol. 28, No. 5, May 1985, pp. 506-511.

[Oliphint 1964]   Oliphint, C. Operating System for the B5000. *Datamation*, May 1964, pp. 42-45.

[Olson 1985] Olson, R. Parallel Processing in a Message based Operating System. *SOFTWARE*, Vol. 2, No. 4, July 1985, pp. 39-49.

[Organick 1972] Organick, E.I. *The Multics System: An Examination of its Structure*. M.I.T. Press, Cambridge, MA, 1972.

[Ousterhout et al. 1980] Ousterhout, J.K., et al. Medusa: An Experiment in Distributed Operating System Structure. *CACM*, Vol. 23, No. 2, Feb. 1980, pp. 92-105.

[Ousterhout et al. 1988] Ousterhout, J.K., et al. An Overview of the Sprite Project. *COMPUTER*, Vol. 21, No. 2, Feb. 1988.

[Parker et al. 1983] Parker, D.S., et al. Detection of Mutual Inconsistency in Distributed Systems. *TSE, Vol. SE-9, No. 3, May 1983, pp. 240-246.*

[Parmelee et al. 1972] Parmelee, R.P., et al. Virtual Storage and Virtual Machine Concepts. *IBMSJ*, Vol. 11, 1972, pp. 99-130.

[Patterson 1983] Patterson, T. An Inside Look at MS-DOS. *BYTE*, Vol. 8, No. 6, June 1983, pp. 230-252.

[Payne 1982] Payne, J. *Introduction to Simulation*. McGraw-Hill, New York, 1982.

[Pechura 1983] Pechura, M.A. Comparing Two Microcomputer Operating Systems: CP/M and HDOS. *CACM*, Vol. 26, No. 3, Mar. 1983, pp. 188-195.

[Peterson 1981] Peterson, G.L. Myths about the Mutual Exclusion Problem. *Information Processing Letters*, Vol. 12, No. 3, June 1981, pp. 115-116.

[Peterson 1983] Peterson, G.L. A New Solution to Lamport's Concurrent Programming Problem Using Small Shared Variables. *TOPLAS*, Vol. 5, No. 1, Jan. 1983, pp. 56-65.

[Peterson & Silberschatz 1985] Peterson, J., and Silberschatz, A. *Operating System Concepts* (second edition). Addison-Wesley, Reading, MA, 1985.

[Plattner & Nievergelt 1981] Plattner, B., and Nievergelt, J. Monitoring Program Execution: A Survey. *COMPUTER*, Vol. 14, No. 11, pp. 76-92.

[Plauger & Krieger 1980] Plauger, P.J., and Krieger, M.S. The IDRIS Operating System. *MIDCON/80*, Nov. 1980, pp. 15/1/1-4.

[Pohjanpalo 1981] Pohjanpalo, H. MROS-68K, a Memory-Resident OS for MC68000. *SPE*, Vol. 11, No. 8, Aug. 1981, pp. 845-852.

[Poole 1968] Poole, P.C. Some Aspects of the EGDON 3 Operating System for the KDF9. *IFIP*, 1968, pp. 43-47.

[Popek 1974] Popek, G.J. Protection Structures. *COMPUTER*, Vol. 7, No. 6, June 1974, pp. 23-33.

[Popek et al. 1979] Popek, G.J., et al. UCLA data secure UNIX. *NCC*, 1979, Vol. 48, pp. 355-364.

[Popek & Kline 1975] Popek, G.J., and Kline, C.S. The PDP-11 Virtual Machine Architecture: A Case Study. *SOSP-5*, 1975, pp. 97-105.

[Popek & Kline 1978] Popek, G.J., and Kline, C.S. Issues in Kernel Design. *NCC*, 1978, pp. 1079-1086.

[Popek & Walker 1985] Popek, G.J., and Walker, B.J. *The LOCUS Distributed System Architecture*. M.I.T. Press, Cambridge, MA, 1985.

[Pountain 1986] Pountain, D. Tripos — The Roots of AmigaDOS. *BYTE*, Vol. 11, No. 2, Feb. 1986, pp. 321-328.

[Powell 1977] Powell, M.L. The DEMOS File System. *SOSP-6*, 1977, pp. 33-42.

[Powell 1979] Powell, M.S. Experience of Transporting and Using the SOLO Operating System. *SPE*, Vol. 9, No. 7, July 1979, pp. 561-569.

[Pratt & Sherrill 1985] Pratt, K.D., and Sherrill, R.L. Experiences with the Development of a Real-Time Multiprocessor Executive in Ada. *Proceedings of the IEEE Real-Time Systems Symposium*, 1985, pp. 672-678.

[Pressman 1987] Pressman, R. *Software Engineering: A Practitioner's Approach* (second edition). McGraw-Hill, New York, 1987.

[Prieve & Fabry 1976] Prieve, B.G., and Fabry, R.S. VMIN — An Optimal Variable-Space Page Replacement Algorithm. *CACM*, Vol. 19, No. 5, May 1976, pp. 295-297.

[Pruitt & Case 1975] Pruitt, J.L., and Case, W.W. Architecture of a Real Time Operating System. *SOSP-5*, 1975, pp. 51-59.

[Purser & Jennings 1975] Purser, W.F.C., and Jennings, D.M. The Design of a Real-Time OS for a Minicomputer. Part I. *SPE*, Vol. 5, No. 2, 1975, pp. 147-167.

[Purser 1976] Purser, W.F.C. The Design of a Real-Time OS for a Minicomputer. Part II. *SPE*, Vol. 6, No. 3, 1976, pp. 327-340.

[Quarterman et al. 1985] Quarterman, J.S., et al. 4.2 BSD and 4.3 BSD as Examples of the UNIX System. *CSURV*, Vol. 17, No. 4, Dec. 1985, pp. 419-470.

[Raimondi 1976] Raimondi, D.L. A Distributed Real-Time Operating System. *IBMSJ*, Vol. 15, No. 1, 1976, pp. 81-101.

[Ralston & Reilly 1983] Ralston, A., and Reilly, E.D., eds. *Encyclopedia of Computer Science and Engineering*. Van Nostrand Reinhold, New York, 1983.

[Randell 1975] Randell, B. System Structure for Software Fault Tolerance. *TSE*, Vol. SE-1, No. 2, June 1975, pp. 220-232.

[Rashid & Robinson 1981] Rashid, R.F., and Robertson, G.G. Accent: A Communication Oriented Network Operating System Kernel. *SOSP-8*, 1981, pp. 64-75.

[Raynal 1986] Raynal, M. *Algorithms for Mutual Exclusion*. MIT Press, Cambridge, MA, 1986.

[Rayner 1980] Rayner, D. Designing User Interfaces for Friendliness. In [Beech 1980], pp. 233-241.

[Ready 1986] Ready, J.F. VRTX: A Real-Time Operating System for Embedded Microprocessor Applications. *MICRO*, Vol. 6, No. 4, Aug. 1986, pp. 8-17.

[Redell et al. 1980] Redell, D.D., et al. Pilot: An Operating System for a Personal Computer. *CACM*, Vol. 23, No. 2, Feb. 1980, pp. 81-92.

[Rees 1971] Rees, M.J. Some improvements to the MINIMOP Multi-Access OS. *SPE*, Vol. 1, No. 2, 1971, pp. 175-188.

[Reiter 1972] Reiter, A. A Resource-Oriented Time-Sharing Monitor. *SPE*, Vol. 2, No. 1, 1972, pp. 55-71.

[Rhodes 1981] Rhodes, N.C. BLMX-80 — A Realtime Multitasking OS. *MIDCON/81*, pp. 7/2/1-4.

[Ricart & Agrawala 1981] Ricart, G., and Agrawala, A.K. An Optimal Algorithm for Mutual Exclusion in Computer Networks. *CACM*, Vol. 24, No. 1, Jan. 1981, pp. 9-17.

[Richards et al. 1979] Richards, M., et al. TRIPOS — A Portable Operating System for Minicomputers. *SPE*, Vol. 9, No. 7, July 1979, pp. 513-526.

[Ritchie & Thompson 1974] Ritchie, D.M., and Thompson, K. The Unix Timesharing System. *CACM*, Vol. 17, No. 5, May 1974, p. 365.

[Ritchie 1980] Ritchie, D.M. The Evolution of the UNIX Time-sharing System. *In Language Design & Programming Methodology*. Springer-Verlag, 1980. Reprinted by BLTJ, Vol. 63, No. 8, Part 2, Oct. 1984, pp. 1577-1594.

[Rivest et al. 1978] Rivest, R.L., et al. On Digital Signatures and Public Key Cryptosystems. *CACM*, Vol. 21, No. 2, Feb. 1978, pp. 120-126.

[Roark et al. 1987] Roark, C., et al. Supporting Ada Applications in a Distributed Real-Time Environment. *Proceedings of the IEEE 1987 Aerospace and Electronics Conference*, Vol. 3, 1987, pp. 831-838.

[Rolander 1981] Rolander, T. CP/NET: Control Program for a Microcomputer Network. *MP&MS*, Vol. 5, No. 2, March 1981, pp. 69-71.

[Roper 1984] Roper, P.R. 68000 PDOS — An Overview. *MP&MS*, Vol. 8, No. 9, Nov. 1984, pp. 458-469.

[Rosen 1967] Rosen, S. *Programming Systems & Languages*. McGraw Hill, New York, 1967.

[Rosen 1969] Rosen, S. Electronic Computers: A Historical Survey. *CSURV*, Vol. 1, No. 1, March 1969, pp. 7-36.

[Rosen 1972] Rosen, S. Programming Systems & Languages 1965-1975. *CACM*, Vol. 15, No. 7, July 1972, pp. 591-600.

[Rosin 1969] Rosin, R.F. Supervisory and Monitor Systems. *CSURV*, Vol. 1, No. 1, March 1969, pp. 37-54.

[Roth 1983] Roth, P.F. Simulation. In [Ralston & Reilly 1983], pp. 1327-1341.

[Row & Daugherty 1984] Row, J., and Daugherty, D. Operating System Extensions Link Disparate Systems. *Computer Design*, Vol. 23, No. 8, July 1984, pp. 171-182.

[Rowe & Birman 1982] Rowe, L.A., and Birman, K.P. A Local Network Based on the UNIX Operating System. *TSE*, Vol. SE-8, No. 2, 1982, pp. 137-146.

[Ryckman 1983] Ryckman, G.F. The IBM 701 Computer at the General Motors Research Laboratories. *Annals of the History of Computing*, Vol. 5, 1983, pp. 210-212.

[Ryder 1970] Ryder, K.D. A Heuristic Approach to Task Dispatching. *IBMSJ*, Vol. 9, No. 3, 1970, pp. 189-198.

[Sakamura 1987a] Sakamura, K. The TRON Project. *MICRO*, Vol. 7, No. 2, April 1987, pp. 8-14.

[Sakamura 1987b] Sakamura, K. Architecture of the TRON VLSI CPU. *MICRO*, Vol. 7, No. 2, April 1987, pp. 17-31.

[Sakamura 1987c] Sakamura, K. BTRON: The Business-oriented Operating System. *MICRO*, Vol. 7, No. 2, April 1987, pp. 53-65.

[Sand 1984] Sand, P.A. The Lilith Personal Computer. (review) *BYTE*, Vol. 9, No. 10, Sept. 1984, pp. 300-311.

[Savitzky 1981] Savitzky, S. ZRTS: Zilog Real-time Software. *WESCON/81*, Sept. 1981, pp. 26/3/1-6.

[Sayers 1971] Sayers, A.P. (Ed). *Operating Systems Survey*. The Comtre Corp. Auerbach, Princeton NJ, 1971.

[Scherr 1973] Scherr, A.L. Functional structure of IBM virtual storage operating systems. Part II: OS/VS2-2 concepts and philosophies. *IBMSJ*, Vol. 12, No. 4, 1973, pp. 383-401.

[Schmidt 1980] Schmidt, R.A. A parallel Operating System for an MIMD Computer. *Proceedings of the Conference on Parallel Processing*, Aug. 1980, pp. 3-4.

[Schneider et al. 1980] Schneider, M.L., et al. Designing Control Languages from the User's Perspective In [Beech 1980], pp. 181-198.

[Schroeder et al. 1984] Schroeder, M.D., Birrell, A.D., and Needham, R.M. Experience with Grapevine: The Growth of a Distributed System. *TOCS*, Vol. 2, No. 1, Feb. 1984, pp. 3-23.

[Schwann et al. 1985] Schwann, K., et al. *GEM: Operating System Primitives for Robotics and Real-Time Control Systems*. Ohio State University, Technical Report, OSU-CISRC-TR-85-4, 1985.

[Schwartz et al. 1964] Schwartz J.I., et al. A General Purpose Time Sharing System. *SJCC*, 1964, Vol. 25, pp. 397-411.

[SCO 1987] *Xenix System V Operating System Installation Guide*. The Santa Cruz Operation, Santa Cruz, CA, 1987.

[Seawright & MacKinnon 1979] Seawright, L.H., and MacKinnon, R.A. VM/370 — a Study of Multiplicity & Usefulness. *IBMSJ*, Vol. 18, No. 1, 1979, pp. 4-17.

[Serlin 1984] Serline, O. Fault-Tolerant Systems in Commercial Applications. *COMPUTER*, Vol. 17, No. 8, Aug. 1984, pp. 19-30.

[Sevcik et al. 1972] Sevcik, K.C., et al. Project SUE as a Learning Experience. *FJCC*, 1972, Vol. 41, Part I, pp. 331-338.

[Shaw 1964] Shaw, J.C. JOSS: A Designer's View of an Experimental On-Line Computing System. *FJCC*, 1964, Vol. 26, pp. 455-464.

[Shaw 1974] Shaw, A. *The Logical Design of Operating Systems*. Prentice-Hall, Englewood Cliffs, NJ, 1974.

[Shell et al. 1959] Shell, D.L., et al. The Share 709 System. (Six Papers). *JACM*, Vol. 6, No. 2, 1959, pp. 123-155.

[Sherrod & Brenner 1984] Sherrod, P., and Brenner, S. Minicomputer System offers timesharing and realtime tasks. *Computer Design*, Vol. 23, No. 9, Aug. 1984, pp. 223-228.

[Shiell 1986] Shiell, J. Virtual Memory, Virtual Machines. *BYTE*, Vol. 11, No. 11, 1986, pp. 110-121.

[Shneiderman 1987] Shneiderman, B. *Designing the User Interface: Strategies for Effective Human-Computer Interaction*. Addison-Wesley, Reading, MA, 1987.

[Siewiorek 1984] Siewiorek, D.P. Architecture of Fault-Tolerant Computers. *COMPUTER*, Vol. 17, No. 8, Aug. 1984, pp. 9-18.

[Sincoskie & Farber 1980] Sincoskie, W.D., and Farber, D.J. SODS/OS: A Distributed OS for the IBM Series/1. *OSR*, Vol. 14, No. 3, July 1980, pp. 46-54.

[Sisk & Van Arsdale 1985] Sisk, J.E., and Van Arsdale, S. *Exploring the PICK Operating System*. Hayden Book Co., Hasbrouck Heights, NJ, 1985.

[Sites 1980] Sites, R.L. Operating Systems and Computer Architecture. *An Introduction to Computer Architecture*, H.S. Stone, ed., Science Research Associates, Chicago, 1980, pp. 591-643.

[Smith 1982] Smith, A.J. Cache Memories. *CSURV*, Vol. 14, No. 3, Sept. 1982, pp. 473-530.

[Smith et al. 1982] Smith, D.C., et al. The Star user interface: an overview. *NCC*, 1982, Vol. 51, pp. 515-528.

[Snow 1978]   Snow, C.R. An Exercise in the Transportation of an Operating System. *SPE*, Vol. 8, No. 1, 1978, pp. 41-50.

[Solomon & Finkel 1979]   Solomon, M.H., and Finkel, R.A. The Roscoe Distributed Operating System. *SOSP-7*, 1969, pp. 108-114.

[Sommerville 1986]   Sommerville, I. *Software Engineering (second edition)*. Addison-Wesley, Reading, MA, 1986.

[Spector & Schwartz 1983]   Spector, A.Z., and Schwarz, P.M., Transactions: A Construct for Reliable Distributed Computing. *OSR*, Vol. 17, No. 2, April 1983, pp. 18-31.

[Srodowa & Bates 1973]   Srodowa, R.J., and Bates, L.A. An Efficient Virtual Machine Implementation. *NCC*. 1973, Vol. 42, pp. 301-308.

[Stagner 1986]   Stagner, W. *THEOS/OASIS User's Handbook*. Weber Systems, Chesterland, OH, 1986.

[Steel 1964]   Steel, T.B., Jr. Operating Systems. *Datamation*, Vol. 10, No. 5, May 1964, pp. 26-28.

[Stephens et al. 1980]   Stephens, P.D., et al. The Evolution of the OS EMAS 2900. *SPE*, Vol. 10, No. 12, Dec. 1980, pp. 993-1008.

[Stephenson 1983]   Stephenson, C.J. Fast Fits: New Method for Dynamic Storage Allocation. *SOSP-9*, Oct. 1983, pp. 30-32.

[Stoy & Strachey 1972]   Stoy, J.E., and Strachey, C. OS6 — An Experimental Operating System for a Small Computer. *CJ*, Vol. 15, Nos. 2 & 3.

[Sutherland et al. 1971]   Sutherland, G.G., et al. Livermore time-sharing system for the CDC 7600. *OSR*, Vol. 5, No. 2, 1971, pp. 6-26.

[Svoboda 1976]   *Computer Performance Measurement & Evaluation Methods: Analysis and Applications*. Elsevier, New York, 1976.

[Svoboda 1981]   Svoboda, L. Performance Monitoring in Computer Systems: A Structured Approach. *OSR*, Vol. 15, No. 3, July 1981, pp. 39-50.

[Tanenbaum 1987]   Tanenbaum, A.S. *Operating Systems: Design and Implementation*. Prentice-Hall, Englewood Cliffs, NJ, 1987.

[Tanenbaum et al. 1978]   Tanenbaum, A.S., et al. Guidelines for Software Portability. *SPE*, Vol. 8, No. 6, 1978, pp. 681-698.

[Tanenbaum & Benson 1973]   Tanenbaum, A.S., and Benson, W.H. The People's Time Sharing System. *SPE*, Vol. 3, No. 2, 1973, pp. 109-119.

[Tanenbaum & Mullender 1981]   Tanenbaum, A., and Mullender, S. An Overview of the Amoeba Distributed Operating System. *OSR*, Vol. 15, No. 3, July 1981, pp. 51-64.

[Tanenbaum & van Renesse 1985]   Tanenbaum, A.S., and van Renesse, R. Distributed Operating Systems. *CSURV*, Vol. 17, No. 4, Dec. 1985, pp. 419-470.

[Taylor 1981]   Taylor, R.L. Low-End General Purpose Systems. *IBMJRD*, Vol. 25, No. 5, Sept. 1981, pp. 429-440.

[Theaker & Frank 1979]   Theaker, C.J., and Frank, G.R. MUSS — A Portable Operating System. *SPE*, Vol. 9, No. 8, Aug. 1979, pp. 633-643.

[Thomas 1972]   Thomas. The Structure of a Time-Sharing System. In [Hoare & Perrot 1972], pp. 351-361.

[Thomas 1973]   Thomas, R.H. A Resource Sharing Executive for the ARPANET. *NCC*, Vol. 42, 1973, pp. 155-163.

[Thompson 1978]   Thompson, K. Unix Implementation. *BSTJ*, Vol. 57, No. 6, July-Aug. 1978, pp. 1931-1946.

[Tsichritzis & Bernstein 1974]   Tsichritzis, D.C., and Bernstein, P.A. *Operating Systems*. Academic Press, New York, 1974.

[Tucker 1983]   Tucker, S. iRMX 86 — A Realtime Operating System for advanced 16-bit microcomputers. *MP&MS*, Vol. 7, No. 8, Oct. 1983, pp. 387-390.

[Turner 1986]   Turner, R.W. *Operating Systems: Design and Implementation*. Macmillan Publishing Co., New York, 1986.

[Tuynman & Hertzberger 1986]   Tuynman, F., and Hertzberger, L.O. A Distributed Real-time Operating System. *SPE*, Vol. 16, No. 5, May 1986, pp. 425-442.

[Unger 1975]   Unger, C. (Ed). Command Languages. *Proceedings of an IFIP Conference* (Lund, Sweden, 1974). North-Holland, Amsterdam, 1975.

[Vallabhaneni 1987]   Vallabhaneni, S.R. *Auditing the Maintenance of Software*. Prentice-Hall, Englewood Cliffs, NJ, 1987.

[van de Goor et al. 1969]   van de Goor, A., et al. Design and behavior of TSS/8: a PDP-8 based Time Sharing System. *TC*, Vol. C-18, No. 11, Nov. 1969, pp. 1038-1043.

[van der Linden & Wilson 1980]   van der Linden, F., and Wilson, I. Real-time Executives for Microprocessors. *MP&MS*, Vol. 4, No. 6, Jul/Aug. 1980, pp. 211-218.

[Van Tassel 1972]   Van Tassel, D. *Computer Security Management*. Prentice-Hall, Englewood Cliffs, NJ, 1972.

[Vasilescu 1987]   Vasilescu, E.N. *Ada Programming with Applications*. Ally and Bacon, Boston, MA, 1987.

[Walker et al. 1983]   Walker, B., et al. The LOCUS Distributed Operating System. *SOSP-9*, Oct. 1983, pp. 49-70.

[Wallace & Barnes 1984]   Wallace, J.J., and Barnes, W.W. Designing for Ultrahigh Availability: The Unix RTR Operating System. *COMPUTER*, Vol. 17, No. 8, Aug. 1984, pp. 31-39.

[Wallis 1982]   Wallis, P.J.L. *Portable Programming*. John Wiley & Sons, New York, 1982.

[Ward 1976]   Ward, M.R. A Simple Approach to Operating System Generation and Initialization. *OSR*, Vol. 10, No. 1, Jan. 1976, pp. 61-71.

[Ward 1980]   Ward, S.A. TRIX: A Network-oriented Operating System. *COMPCON*, Spring 1980, pp. 344-349.

[Webster 1981]   *Webster's New Collegiate Dictionary*. Merriam-Webster, Springfield, IL, 1981.

[Weiler et al. 1970]   Weiler, P.W., et al. A Real-Time Operating System for Manned Spaceflight. *TC*, Vol. C-19, No. 5, May 1970, pp. 388-398.

[Weizer 1981]   Weizer, N. A History of Operating Systems. *Datamation*, Jan. 1981, pp. 119-126.

[Wells 1971]   Wells, M. The Eldon 2 Operating System for KDF9. *CJ*, Vol. 14, No. 1, Feb 1971, pp. 21-24.

[Wells 1986]   Wells, P. Intel's 80386 Architecture. *BYTE*, Vol. 11, No. 11, 1986, pp. 89-106.

[Welsh & McKeag 1980]   Welsh, J., and McKeag, R.M. *Structured System Programming*. Prentice-Hall International, Englewood Cliffs, NJ, 1980.

[Wheeler 1974]   Wheeler, T.F. OS/VS1 concepts and philosophies. *IBMSJ*, Vol. 13, No. 3, 1974, pp. 213-229.

[White & Grehan 1987]   White, E., and Grehan, R. Microsoft's New DOS. *BYTE*, Vol. 12, No. 6, June 1987, pp. 116-126.

[Whitfield & Whight 1973]   Whitfield, H., and Whight, A.S. EMAS — The Edinburgh Multi-Access System. *CJ*, Vol. 16, No. 4, 1973, pp. 331-346.

[Whittaker 1971]   Whittaker, G.A. Architecture of a Real-Time Executive. *Instrument Soc. of America, Transactions*, Vol. 10, No. 2, 1971, pp. 183-188.

[Wichman 1968]   Wichman, B.A. A Modular Operating System. *IFIP*, 1968, pp. C48-C54.

[Wicklund 1982]   Wicklund, T.L. MINI-EXEC: a Portable Executive for 8-bit Microcomputers. *CACM*, Vol. 25, No. 11, Nov. 1982, pp. 772-780.

[Wilkes 1973]   Wilkes, M.V. The Cambridge Multiple-Access System in Retrospect. *SPE*, Vol. 3, No. 4, 1973, pp. 323-332.

[Wilkes 1982]   Wilkes, M. Hardware Support for Memory Protection, *SASPLOS*, 1982, pp. 107-116.

[Wilkes & Needham 1979]   Wilkes, M.V., and Needham, R.M. *The Cambridge CAP Computer and its Operating System.* North Holland, New York, 1979.

[Wilkes & Needham 1980]   Wilkes, M.V., and Needham, R.M. The Cambridge Model Distributed System. *OSR*, Vol. 14, No. 1, Jan. 1980, pp. 21-29.

[Wilkinson et al. 1981]   Wilkinson, A.L., et al. A Penetration Analysis of a Burroughs Large System. *OSR*, Vol. 15, No. 1, Jan, 1981, pp. 14-25.

[Wirth 1976]   Wirth, N.K. *Algorithms + Data Structures = Programs.* Prentice-Hall, Englewood Cliffs, NJ, 1976.

[Wirth 1977]   Wirth, N. Toward a Discipline of Real-Time Programming. *CACM*, Vol. 20, No. 8, Aug. 1977, pp. 577-583.

[Wittie & Van Tilborg 1980]   Wittie, L.D. & Van Tilborg, A.M. MICROS, A Distributed Operating System for MICRONET, a Reconfigurable Network Computer. *TC*, Vol. C-29, No. 12, Dec. 1980, pp. 1133-1144.

[WMSR 1984]   *Which Micro & Software Review.* Getting 2500 pounds into 400 pounds. March 1984, pp. 13 ff.

[Wong 1978]   Wong, E.J. RTE-IV: the Megaword-array Operating System. *HPJ*, Vol. 29, No. 14, Oct. 1978, pp. 6-11.

[Wong 1986]   Wong, W.G. Program Interfacing To MS-DOS, Part VI: Device Drivers — Why and How. *Micro/Systems Journal*, Vol. 2, No. 2, March/April 1986, pp. 50-53.

[Wulf et al. 1971]   Wulf, W., et al. BLISS: A Language for Systems Programming. *CACM*, Vol. 14, No. 12, Dec. 1971, pp. 780-790.

[Wulf et al. 1974]   Wulf, W., et al. Hydra: The Kernel of a Multiprocessor Operating System. *CACM*, Vol. 17, No. 6, June 1974, pp. 337-345.

[Wulf et al. 1975]   Wulf, W., et al. Overview of the Hydra Operating System Development. *SOSP-5*, 1975, pp. 122-131.

[Wulf et al. 1980]   Wulf, W., et al. *Hydra: An Experimental Operating System.* McGraw Hill, New York, 1980.

[Yardley 1985]   Yardley, J. TSX-Plus: A Multiuser Operating System for the LSI-11 and PDP-11. *MP&MS*, Vol. 9, No. 5, June 1985, pp. 253-257.

[Yourdon 1979]   Yourdon, E.N. (Ed). *Classics in Software Engineering.* YOURDON Press., New York, 1979.

[Zabala 1981]   Zabala, I. Some Feedback from PTEX Installations. *TUGBoat, the TeX Users Group Newsletter*, Vol. 2, No. 2, July 1981, pp. 16-19.

[Zaks 1980]   Zaks, R. *The CP/M Handbook with MP/M.* SYBEX Inc. Berkeley, CA, 1980.

[Zarella 1979]   Zarella, J. *Operating Systems: Concepts and Principles.* Microcomputer Applications, Suisun City, CA, 1979.

[Zarella 1981]   Zarella, J. (Ed). *Microprocessor Operating Systems, Vol. I.* Microcomputer Applications, Suisun City, CA, 1981.

[Zarella 1982]   Zarella, J. (Ed). *Microprocessor Operating Systems, Vol. II.* Microcomputer Applications, Suisun City, CA, 1982.

[Zarella 1984]   Zarella, J. (Ed). *Microprocessor Operating Systems, Vol. III.* Microcomputer Applications, Suisun City, CA, 1984.

[Zhongxiu et al. 1980]   Zhongxiu, S., et al. An Introduction to DJS200/XT1. *OSR*, Vol. 14, No. 3, July 1980, pp. 70-74.

[Zobel 1983]   Zobel, D. The Deadlock Problem: A Classifying Bibliography. *OSR*, Vol. 17, No. 4, Oct. 1983, pp. 6-15.

Index